Selected Serbian Plays

Selected Serbian Plays

Edited by
Branko Mikasinovich
and Dejan Stojanović

Afterword by Dennis Barnett

New Avenue Books

Copyright © 2016 New Avenue Books

All rights reserved.
No part of this book may be reproduced in any form without written permission from the publisher.

New Avenue Books

First Edition

Cover design by Dejan Stojanović,
based on a photograph of the Elgin Theatre, Toronto, Canada,
by Anton Belousov

Library of Congress Control Number: 2016909039

ISBN: 0692730559
ISBN-13: 978-0692730553

CONTENTS

Acknowledgments	i
Guide to Pronounciation	ii
Introduction, Branko Mikasinovich	iii
Branislav Nušić, *The Deceased*	9
Đorđe Lebović, *Hallelujah*	115
Aleksandar Obrenović, *The Bird*	197
Aleksandar Popović, *Hats Off!*	215
Ljubomir Simović, *The Traveling Troupe Šopalović*	271
Dušan Kovačević, *Balkan Spy*	357
Siniša Kovačević, *Times Have Changed*	439
Nebojša Romčević, *Caroline Neuber*	529
Biljana Srbljanović, *Barbelo, on Dogs and Children*	581
Milena Marković, *A Boat for Dolls*	651
Afterword, Dennis Barnett	701
About Editors	709

ACKNOWLEDGMENTS

We would like to thank Professor Dennis Barnett for his expert advice, translation and editing of five plays, writing of the Afterword, as well as for his unselfish support in helping us edit and complete this anthology. We would also like to express our gratitude to Miroslav Miki Radonjić, director of Sterijino Pozorje in Novi Sad, for his great help and cooperation and to authors and translators who offered their assistance during our work on this demanding book.

GUIDE TO PRONOUNCIATION

c	*ts* as in ha*ts*
ć and č	pronounced like *ch* as in *ch*urch; ć is softer than č.
đ and dž	pronounced like the *j* in *j*udge; đ is softer than dž.
j	pronounced like *y* in *y*ellow.
š	pronounced like *sh* as in *sh*arp.
ž	pronounced like the s in mea*s*ure.

INTRODUCTION

Modern Serbia's theatrical drama began in 1804, when Serb leader Đorđe Petrović, also known as Karađorđe (1762–1817), liberated Serbia from the Ottoman Empire. This volume follows the culmination of a long and progressively successful tradition of the dramatic arts in the country, leading to the zenith of Serbian dramaturgy in the twentieth century. The theatre's limited achievements in the eighteenth century were the result of the Serbian people's negative and sarcastic perception of theatre as an institution. Yet this attitude changed in the subsequent two centuries, when plays based on the concept of realism—both political and social—became popular, contributing to the development of the country's dramaturgy and theatre. Selected writers from this modern period include Branislav Nušić, Dušan Kovačević, Biljana Srbljanović, and Milena Marković—names readily recognized by today's Serbian theatre-goers. The choice of authors for inclusion in this anthology is based on their acknowledged reputations and individual excellence in areas of topical significance, theatrical innovation, continuous performance and acclaim, and enduring truth and message.

It is also important to mention two notable authors of Serbian dramaturgy who are not included in this anthology: Joakim Vujić and Jovan Sterija Popović. Vujić (1772–1847), known as the initiator of Serbian theatre, was also one of the most accomplished dramatists in nineteenth-century Serbia. He was director of the first Royal Serbian Theatre established in 1825 in Kragujevac, the capital of the Principality of Serbia at the time. Vujić wrote nearly thirty plays and translated and adopted a number of foreign plays, mainly from German and Hungarian. His personal contribution to Serbian dramaturgy was immense; beyond the many plays he wrote, he was also an actor, producer, director, and a man of great refinement and influence. As a Serbian patriot, he encouraged the performance of plays in

Serbian, with an emphasis on history and tradition. He also cooperated with the Flying Dilettante Theatre theatrical group, which conducted plays in various towns in Serbia and Vojvodina, especially in Novi Sad, Serbs' cultural center in Austro-Hungary. Prince Miloš Obrenović (1780–1860) also supported Vujić's ideas and efforts to create a national theatre.

In 1841, the capital of Serbia was moved from Kragujevac to Belgrade, and the first plays in the new capital were performed in Theatre Đumruk, a customs' house converted into an improvised theatre. This marked the first attempt at forming a professional playhouse in Serbia. The increasing number of theatres encouraged playwrights to dedicate themselves more to the writing of plays.

Although Vujić is the initiator of Serbian theatre, Popović (1806–1856), regarded as the leading Serbian intellectual of his time and a prolific playwright, is considered the father of modern Serbian drama. His historical plays include *The Death of Stefan Dečanski*, *Fall of the Serbian Empire*, and *Miloš Obilić*, eulogizing Serbia's past and the great personalities of medieval Serbia. Meanwhile, in his comedies *Liar and Super-liar*, *Miser*, *Evil Woman*, *A Talkative Husband*, and others, Popović presented a picture of the social life of his time; he stigmatized the members of the young Serbian bourgeoisie and their craving for wealth and lack of patriotism. The theatre festival Sterijino Pozorje, established in 1956 in Novi Sad and named after Popović, is held yearly and presents the most outstanding works of Serbian authors.

One of the most productive playwrights who remains widely performed and extremely popular to this day was Branislav Nušić (1864–1938), who also served as the head of the Serbian National Theatre and Secretary of the Ministry of Education. His works include a number of admired comedies, such as *Mrs. Minister*, *The Bereaved Family*, *The Deceased*, *The Suspicious Character*, and others. Nušić's comedies depicted the private and public life of the middle class with all of its deficiencies. In one of his best plays, *The Deceased*, the author presents in a masterly way distorted family and marital relations, corruption and unfounded professional ambitions.

Roughly speaking, the period since the World War II has been characterized by gradual and eventually full artistic freedom, leaving behind social realism—a type of theatre that glorified Communist values. Plays were now being created with different and even more original forms of expression and topics, as in the works of the outstanding playwrights included in this anthology. During this era, under the rule of Yugoslav Communist leader Josip Broz Tito, Serb writers discovered their own form of expression, despite state censorship and oppression. Their originality and courage played a great role in gaining artistic freedom for themselves as well as for future generations of writers.

Three of the most prominent playwrights during this era were Đorđe Lebović, Aleksandar Obrenović, and Aleksandar Popović. Lebović's (1928–2004) earliest play, *The Heavenly Squadron* (co-authored with Aleksandar Obrenović), won first prize at Sterijino Pozorje, the famed Novi Sad theatre festival, in 1957. He received the same prize for *Hallelujah* in 1965 and for *Victoria* in 1968. *Hallelujah* takes place in a hospital for former World War II German camp prisoners and in private homes. The characters are patients who barely survived life in the hellish concentration camp. The most important aspect of this play is the dynamic dialogue, which provides a stark contrast to the monotony of the actions and setting.

Obrenović (1928–2005) worked as a dramatist for Radio-Television Belgrade, where he wrote and directed the acclaimed play *The Return of Don Juan*. Obrenović's plays present a happening, an event, or a moment in the life of his characters. His work focuses on the lives of ordinary people, often with a sardonic quality, as in his play *Variations*, of which *The Bird* is one part. In this segment, the author dwells on the intimate and personal feelings of the "little man" and his human situation.

A. Popović's (1929–1996) plays attracted great attention in the early part of the 1960s and continuing into the 1990s. They were performed in theatres, on radio, and on television, and Popović was applauded as a man who set new standards in drama and comedy, introducing a new circle of ideas and a fresh scenic language, as in *Hats Off*. Popović was radical in his efforts to call Aristotelian dramaturgy into question by giving primacy to linguistic qualities and philosophical aspects of his heroes in their socialist reality. He was also the creator of some of the most unusual characters in Serbian dramatic and satirical literature.

In presenting and promoting the contemporary plays, Serbia's four theatres and the Belgrade International Theatre Festival (BITEF) played a major role. The four theaters included the Serbian National Theatre, founded in 1861 in Novi Sad; the National Theatre in Belgrade, built in 1869; the Yugoslav Drama Theatre, set up in Belgrade in 1947 to gather the best actors from across Yugoslavia and eventually becoming an outstanding European theatre; and Atelje 212, established in 1956 to introduce the avant-garde to Belgrade, often producing challenging and provocative plays. Indeed, Atelje 212 was the first in Eastern Europe to perform Samuel Beckett's *Waiting for Godot,* a play banned in all other Communist states. Meanwhile, BITEF, instituted in 1967, supported and performed the latest theatre trends and became one of the most important cultural festivals in Serbia as well as Europe, staging both significant classics and more experimental forms. BITEF was the first international festival to be awarded a special prize, Premio Europa Per Il Teatro, in 1999 for its input and crucial relevance in the theatre arts.

After the breakup of Yugoslavia in 1991, the spirit and character of Serbian plays shifted to a basis on altered values and culture as a result of the wars and existential hardships. The most prominent Serbian playwrights following Lebović, Obrenović, and Popović were Ljubomir Simović and Dušan Kovačević. Although primarily a poet, Simović's (1935) plays are readily described as poetic dramas. His *The Traveling Troupe Šopalović* depicts actors travelling together and sharing their destiny. The play centers on two characters, Vasilije and Jelisaveta, whose best years are behind them. The plot and characters oscillate between reality and self-delusion, from "extreme realism to a poetic vision and we hardly notice the moment when the author of the drama has been joined by a poet", as drama critic Jovan Hristić pointed out.

Kovačević (1948) is a prolific writer best known for his more than a dozen plays and movie scripts. Two of his best known plays are *Balkan Spy* and *The Professional*, which reflect the political and—as some attest—conspiratorial minds of Serbs, with all the ensuing collusions. Kovačević's plays remain very popular in Serbia and have been translated into more than twenty languages and performed abroad.

Similar in ideology and artistry to the majority of post-World War II authors, who continued along the path of more original and innovative directions, were Siniša Kovačević, Nebojša Romčević, Biljana Srbljanović, and Milena Marković. Kovačević (1954) is an author and professor at the Belgrade Academy of Arts and a triple Sterijino Pozorje theatre festival award winner for his plays *The Times Have Changed*, *General Milan Nedić,* and *Janez*. *The Times Have Changed*, one of his finest play, relates the fate of Ilija Pevac, a rich farmer who endures forced labor in Germany during World War II, returns to his village, where he faces a new social order and human relations during the "changed times".

Romčević (1962), a professor, playwright, and screenwriter, has written seventeen plays, some of which have been performed in twenty countries. Romčević's drama *Caroline Neuber* is a tragic telling of the true story of a German actress who strived to create a reputable theatre, something different from the silly entertainment popular in eighteenth-century Germany and Europe. After her tragic death, although she failed to build such a theatre, her tireless efforts toward this goal were celebrated as a success.

Srbljanović (1970) is a playwright and controversial political activist whose plays have been staged in fifty countries, making her one of the most significant living Serb playwrights. She has received a number of Serbian awards, including the Joakim Vujić and Sterijino Pozorje prizes. In 1999 she became the only foreign writer to receive Germany's Ernst–Toller Award. Her play *Barbelo* presents a view of the history of Christianity, marking the first appearance of God, his origin and background, and the metaphysical space from which everything is created. The play shares lofty and sentient work about love, life, death, and human alienation.

Finally, Marković (1974) is a playwright and screenwriter as well as a poet. Her plays have been performed in Serbia and abroad, in Poland, Germany, and the USA. For her play *A Boat For Dolls*, perhaps the most provocative play in the collection, she won the Serbian Borislav Mihailović Mihiz Prize for Drama and the Sterijino Pozorje prize. Marković's main character, an artist who achieves some notoriety, lives a sexually abusive and promiscuous life, shared in the play through a series of popular fairy tales. The contrast between the traditional innocence of these narratives and the brutality of the life she lives is haunting.

All of the authors in this anthology have made important contributions to the advancement of the theatre arts in modern Serbia. Others could also have been included if not for space limitations. Each of these authors has enjoyed great recognition and popularity in Serbia itself, where their plays have been performed in numerous theatres throughout the country, side by side with the best dramatic literature from around the world. Many of them have also been recognized abroad.

This international acknowledgement is a clear sign that Serbian drama has emerged on the world theatrical stage with potency and commendation. It is our sincere hope that this anthology will introduce modern Serbian plays to a wider audience of English language readers and perhaps even to a new theatre audience.

Branko Mikasinovich

BRANISLAV NUŠIĆ
(1864—1938)

Nušić was born in Belgrade, Serbia, where he graduated from the University of Belgrade. He fought in the Serbo-Bulgarian war in 1885, and in 1889 started his career in the Ministry of Foreign Affairs, and then moved to the Ministry of Education. Afterwards, he worked as a journalist and writer in Belgrade and as a dramaturgist in the National Theatre.

Nušić was not only a playwright but an analyst of Serbian society and its mentality at a specific historic period. One of his best plays is the *The Deceased* (1937), which represents a lasting and caustic satire of human greed, reminiscent of today's society and human relations. Comically powerful, it is at once vaudevillian and modernist characterized by clever plotting and biting dialogue and as such embodies a darkly comic play, which rightly belongs to the world classics.

THE DECEASED

CHARACTERS:

Pavle Marić
Milan Novaković
Spasoje Blagojević
Mr. Đurić
Ljubomir Protić
Anta
Mladen Đoković
Mile
Aljoša
Adolph Schwartz
Rina
Agnija
Vukica
First Police Agent
Second Police Agent
Marija – a maid
Ana – a maid
Sofija – a maid

Three years pass between the prelude and the first act.
(Written and set in Belgrade in the 1930s.)

THE PRELUDE

A tastefully arranged room in Marić's house.

1. PAVLE, MARIJA
MARIJA *(an elderly maid, enters)*: Sir, there's a gentleman . . . he says he's been called.
PAVLE *(sitting at a small table, engrossed in a book)*: Oh, yes, let him in!
MARIJA *(goes to the door and lets the Agent in)*.
PAVLE *(to Marija)*: Please send the lady in.
MARIJA *(goes left)*.

2. PAVLE, AGENT
PAVLE: If I'm not mistaken, you are from the Police.
AGENT: Yes, sir.
PAVLE *(nonchalantly)*: The matter is not that tragic at all, you see. However, my wife was so upset that she called the police immediately. *(He notices Rina at the door.)* Anyway, she is here now, so she can explain.

3. RINA, PAVLE, AGENT
RINA *(wearing an elegant dressing gown)*: The gentleman is from the Police?
AGENT: Yes, madam.
RINA: There isn't much to explain: we had a robbery last night.
AGENT: Can you be a bit more precise?
PAVLE: I'll explain. My wife and I went to the theatre last night. When we came back at about 11 o'clock, we came through this room . . . our bedroom is just over there . . . and, as far as I remember, everything was in perfect order. This morning, however, I found this desk . . . which is normally locked . . . broken into and everything in it turned upside down, as you can see.

AGENT *(approaches a ladies' writing desk with one open drawer and all contents in disarray):* Anything else apart from this?

RINA: Just that.

AGENT: Could you tell me who was the first to notice, please?

PAVLE: I always get up first, my work is such that I have to leave early . . . so, I came through here and this is what I found. I woke my wife straightaway and she phoned the police.

AGENT *(inspecting the desk):* The drawer has obviously been opened by force. Can you tell me what is missing?

PAVLE: That's my wife's desk, she'll know.

RINA: I keep small pieces of jewellery and some trinkets in here . . . just insignificant toiletries. I always have two or three hundred dinars of my spending money in here, and none of that is missing . . . even the money is still here. Only this safe-box has been broken . . . it is normally locked and I keep my letters in here. Some letters have been stolen.

AGENT: It means that the theft was not motivated by material gain. Consequently, I do not think that the thief came from the outside. Have you got anyone else in the house?

RINA: We have a maid, but I don't think it was her. She is an honest and honourable old lady who has served us faithfully for many years.

AGENT *(thinking):* Could you tell me whether any particular letters have been stolen . . . or is it . . .

RINA *(confused):* Oh dear . . . I don't know . . . they are all equally important to me: some of them are intimate, from my youth.

AGENT *(after a bit of thought observing both of them):* If you wish, I can start an official enquiry, however, with your permission, I'd rather not give the matter more significance than it really has.

PAVLE and RINA *(keep quiet).*

AGENT: All I can conclude is that the theft was not motivated by self-interest, the thief did not come from the outside; he is in the house. I do not think there is any need to go any further than that. I ask for your permission to leave. Madam, Sir. *(He leaves.)*

4. PAVLE, RINA

PAVLE *(again engrossed in the book)*.
RINA *(having glanced scornfully at him, goes to her room. Stops at the door, turns around and with an emphasis):* The police agent concluded that the thief is in the house.
PAVLE: Yes, I heard.
RINA *(goes to her room)*.

5. PAVLE, MARIJA

PAVLE *(lifts his head and glances at Rina leaving; after she closes the door, he goes to the telephone, takes the telephone book and looks for a particular number)*.
MARIJA *(enters):* The building site supervisor.
PAVLE: Aljoša? Let him in.
MARIJA *(lets Aljoša in, exits)*.

6. ALJOŠA, PAVLE

PAVLE: What is it, Aljoša? Is everything all right out there?
ALJOŠA *(speaks with a Russian accent):* Yes, mister engineer!
PAVLE: Have you increased the numbers on the site?
ALJOŠA: Yes, mister engineer.
PAVLE: Any problems with the transport of materials?
ALJOŠA: No, mister engineer.
PAVLE: Why have you left work?
ALJOŠA: I was waiting for you there, thinking you will come, like every morning, but you didn't come –
PAVLE: Do you need me?
ALJOŠA *(confused):* I think you will come, but you didn't come.
PAVLE: Tell me then, what is it; why were you waiting for me?

ALJOŠA: Mister engineer! I am grateful to you, very grateful. You were like my father; good, generous father. Three years ago you gave me job –

PAVLE: But why all this gratitude! You are a good worker, I am very pleased with you, and that's all.

ALJOŠA: That's why I am sad, I am very sad, and I am afraid to hurt you. I wouldn't like to, I wouldn't like to hurt you.

PAVLE: You look very strange, Aljoša. You look as though you'd like to tell me something and you don't know how? Maybe you are not happy with your salary?

ALJOŠA: Oh, no, sir!

PAVLE: Is your work getting too hard?

ALJOŠA: No, no, no!

PAVLE: So what is it?

ALJOŠA: I came to thank you for everything you did for me, and to ask you to accept my resignation.

PAVLE: Resignation? You've found a better job?

ALJOŠA: No. I would never leave you for another job, for a better salary, but, but –

PAVLE: Are you ill?

ALJOŠA *(shakes his head looking at the floor)*: Nyet.

PAVLE: Well, what is it then, tell me?

ALJOŠA: I have to, I have to tell you, I cannot hide from you. *(Pause, he fights himself, and finally raises his head.)* You know my Lidočka?

PAVLE: Your wife?

ALJOŠA: Yes!

PAVLE: I think I caught a glimpse of her once when she came to see you at work. A kind and pretty lady, if I remember well.

ALJOŠA: She leaves me.

PAVLE: She left you?

ALJOŠA: Yes. There was a singer, an opera singer here, Pierkovski . . .

PAVLE: A Russian?

ALJOŠA: Not Russian, Polish. He was on tour here –
PAVLE: Your wife left with him?
ALJOŠA: She tells me she loves him very much, she cannot live without him. She says goodbye to me; I cry; she leaves.
PAVLE: Did it happen recently?
ALJOŠA: Three months ago!
PAVLE: Three months ago! That's a long time, you must've gotten used to it by now?
ALJOŠA: No, mister engineer, I love Lidočka, I love her very much.
PAVLE: But she doesn't love you?
ALJOŠA *(sighs)*.
PAVLE: I don't understand why you'd want to leave your job because of that; do you want to go after her?
ALJOŠA: Not that. I do not want to spoil her happiness; she is happy there with him. Why should I spoil her happiness?
PAVLE: You think she is happy?
ALJOŠA: Yes, she writes to me, she writes she is happy, but still I have to help.
PAVLE: Financially?
ALJOŠA: Oh, no, she has, she has money. But will you allow me to read a letter I received yesterday?
PAVLE: Where is she writing from?
ALJOŠA: From Berlin. He is there on business.
PAVLE: So what does she say?
ALJOŠA *(unfolds the letter):* She writes in Russian.
PAVLE: I think I might not understand that much.
ALJOŠA *(reads):* "Milyenki moy" *(He's embarrassed)* "My dearest". Sorry, that's just tenderness –
PAVLE: Yes, go on.
ALJOŠA *(Reads):* "Mnye zdyes ocheny harasho, ya sosvyem schastlyiva."
(Speaks) She says she is very happy there.

(Reads) "Dorogoy moy Andryusha kazhdim dnyem balyshey menya lyubit"
(Speaks) He loves her more and more every day.
(Reads) "On ocheny laskoviy ko mnye; smotrit na menya kak na obraz."
(Speaks) He looks after her like a relic.
(Reads) "Ya schastlyiva, ya schastlyiveyshaya zhenshchina na svyetye."
(Speaks) She is the happiest woman in the world.
(Reads) "Maya schastiye adno obsoyatelystvo trevozhit."
PAVLE: I don't understand that one at all.
ALJOŠA: She says only one thing spoils her happiness.
(Reads) "Ya znayu chto ti svyo vremya dumayesh oba mnye."
(Speaks) She knows that I think about her all the time.
(Reads) "Yesli by i ty nye dumal oba mnye, maya schastiye bylo by v dvoyne balyshey."
PAVLE: If you didn't think of her, she would be twice as happy.
ALJOŠA: Da! *(Reads)* "Zdelay odalzheniye, perestany dumat oba mnye, tym zdelayesh menya schastivlyeyshey zhenshchinoy na svyetye".
PAVLE: If you stopped thinking about her, you would make her the happiest woman in the world.
ALJOŠA *(reads):* "Do groba lyubyashchaya tebya, Lidočka"
PAVLE: So this woman that "loves you to death" . . . what does she actually want?
ALJOŠA: She wants that I don't think about her.
PAVLE: Well, you can do that for her. Write to her that you won't think about her anymore.
ALJOŠA: I cannot. I cannot! I cannot not think about her; I want to make her the happiest woman in the world. Why can't she be happy? If we can't both be happy, let her be happy at least, let her be happy.
PAVLE: How do you mean to make her happy?

ALJOŠA: I must think about her. I love her. I cannot not think about her . . . If I am dead I won't think about her.
PAVLE: What do you mean?
ALJOŠA: I wrote to her.
PAVLE: What did you write?
ALJOŠA: I wrote: When you get this letter, the water of the Danube will cover me and I will not think about you anymore.
PAVLE: What are you talking about; what water, what Danube?
ALJOŠA: I wrote like that.
PAVLE: You wrote such a letter to her?
ALJOŠA: Yes, and I come to apologize to you, to say goodbye and thank you.
PAVLE: What are you talking about Aljoša?
ALJOŠA *(taking some papers out of his pocket):* These are receipts for materials; this is a copy of a contract with the brick manufacturer, it is signed; these are tax returns; this is your ID that you gave me when I went to the auction on your behalf –
PAVLE *(interrupting):* Please, Aljoša, you keep all those papers with you; you can't die like that. How do you imagine you can just die like that? Does an unfaithful woman deserve that you die because of her? On the contrary, that's precisely why you should continue to live, continue to be here. If you give her the peace of mind, she will ridicule your death; no, my dear Aljoša, one doesn't die for the love of an unfaithful woman.
ALJOŠA: I cannot!
PAVLE: You mustn't be so weak.
ALJOŠA *(wants to protest).*
PAVLE *(interrupts him):* It can't be just that, just the letter. Aljoša, you are embroiled in a lot of negative feelings, and the four months of hard work have weakened you mentally. You must be a bit homesick as well. While Lidočka was around, your heart was full of feelings towards her; and now you are lonely, your heart is empty and the nostalgia has set in. All of that is only natural, and believe you me, you can get over it.

ALJOŠA *(shakes his head)*: Nyet!

PAVLE: Listen to me, Aljoša, a man is susceptible to women's charms; it's always been that way. We all have our weaknesses towards them, but not to the extent that we should sacrifice our life for them. We mustn't be despondent. Would a shipwrecked person simply give in to the sea? No, they'd look for a way to save themselves and reach the shore! Believe me, it is only mental tiredness, as I said before, you are disappointed and nostalgic. Listen to me Aljoša, I'm giving you a day off today and tomorrow; please rest!

ALJOŠA *(refusing)*: Ah!

PAVLE: Just you listen to me, go out, have a bit of fun, and you'll feel better. I know, you might not be able to afford it. *(He takes some money from his wallet.)* Here is 500 dinars.

ALJOŠA *(protesting)*: But mister engineer –

PAVLE: You may consider it as a bonus for overtime work; you must accept it! *(He pushes the money into Aljoša's pocket.)* Go out, go to "The Russian Lyre" or to "Casbeck" or . . . I don't know the names of your bars. Go there, and you'll find your friends, you'll listen to the balalaikas, you'll hear the songs from your homeland and, maybe you'll cry a little, but those are healing tears, please believe me. Just do that, and you'll feel much better.

ALJOŠA: Nyet, sir.

PAVLE: You northern people, although you don't get much heat from the sun, you are a bit softer than us, your heart is more vulnerable, you are dreamers. We are not, we are a little more rational and more resilient. So please accept my advice and you'll see the difference.

ALJOŠA *(fighting himself)*: I cannot, I cannot!

PAVLE: Please, Aljoša!

ALJOŠA: I wrote to her.

PAVLE: Just accept my advice today, and if tomorrow you feel the same, if you are still determined, then that's your destiny, I

can't stop you. Will you try to do as I ask you, just for today? *(He stretches out his hand.)*
ALJOŠA *(looks him in the eye and stretches out his hand without enthusiasm.)*
PAVLE: That's it! Go out and meet people, cheer up! *(Looks at him.)* Wait, you can't go out like that. Have you got another coat? This one is too worn out and dirty, you can't go like that. *(He starts to go towards his room.)*
ALJOŠA: No, mister engineer, no, no, no! I'm too embarrassed; all of this is from you anyway, the coat, the shirt, the shoes, I can't take anymore, no!
PAVLE: Please, don't mention it! *(He goes to his room and comes back carrying a nice coat.)* That's it, take that off!
ALJOŠA: Please, sir, in God's good name.
PAVLE: Please take it off, please!
ALJOŠA *(takes off his coat.)*
PAVLE *(helping him to put the new coat on)*: That's it! Transfer all those papers here, that's it! And the old coat? Well, you can still wear it at the building site. Now, you look decent, ready to go out on the town. Now, just do as I ask you. Tomorrow when we meet, you'll see, everything will be different.
ALJOŠA *(folding his old coat, after transferring all the papers)*: Only, you know I wrote to her – *(Exits.)*

7. PAVLE, RINA

PAVLE *(first he goes to Rina's door listening in, and having heard something he returns quickly to the table where he was reading, sits down and pretends to be engrossed in the book again.)*
RINA *(comes out of her room, dressed to go out, and goes to the main door, without looking at Pavle.)*
PAVLE *(after she's gone, raises his head, and after a pause, gets up and rings the bell.)*

8. MARIJA, PAVLE

PAVLE: The lady has left?
MARIJA: Yes!
PAVLE: Listen, whoever asks for me, I am not at home. Do you understand?
MARIJA: I understand!

9. Add LJUBOMIR

LJUBOMIR *(at that moment he appears at the door carrying a big book)*: May I come in?
PAVLE *(a little confused, unconvincingly)*: Yes, yes . . . please! Come in!
LJUBOMIR *(feeling a bit uncomfortable)*: I don't want to impose; I just wanted to return this book to the maid, but I didn't find her. I do apologize, it seems I came by at the wrong time. *(He puts the book down on the table.)*
PAVLE: It's not the most suitable moment, but it doesn't matter; I always have enough time for my young friends. *(To Marija)* You may go!
MARIJA *(exits)*.

10. LJUBOMIR, PAVLE

LJUBOMIR: I am so sorry. *(He wants to go)* May I?
PAVLE: Please stay, I insist. I am a bit perturbed . . . In fact, maybe it's good that you came, I . . . I need a friend at the moment; I need someone to talk to. Please, sit down.
LJUBOMIR: I'd be delighted if I could be of any help to you at all.
PAVLE: For the one who is in pain, genuine understanding is sufficient.
LJUBOMIR *(surprised)*: What . . . You're in pain?
PAVLE *(startled)*: No, no I'm not in pain . . . Although, why deny it, it's a kind of pain! *(Upset)* Dear young man, my wife is unfaithful to me! *(He is startled again, it seems too rash to him*

to have confided in a young man, keeps quiet, walks around in an agitated manner.)
LJUBOMIR *(surprised, follows him with his eyes.)*
PAVLE *(finally feels the need to justify himself and stands in front of Ljubomir):* I do not know why I have just confided in you, but . . . there you are, you came by, you were the first to come by, and I had the need to say it out loud ever since this morning.
LJUBOMIR: Have no regrets that you've confided in me, you've confided in a friend. I am very much indebted to you, Mr. Marić; you know how much respect and admiration I have for you. I would be very happy if I could in any way offer some consolation.
PAVLE: In this case any consolation would be illusory; it would seem like a statement of commiserations offered to the bereaved.
LJUBOMIR: Well . . . who knows. Maybe it's not that bad, maybe it's just petty gossip of the malcontents!
PAVLE: Yes, gossip . . . I tried to ignore the gossip, but . . . *(He takes a pack of letters from his pocket.)* These are the letters from her lover; I committed robbery and got hold of them. The gossip was only a speculation which never gave me the name, but the name is here now, in my hands . . . his name is here! *(He crumples the letters in his hand with excitement.)* Here it is!
LJUBOMIR *(feeling embarrassed, shrugs).*
PAVLE *(still excited):* Here it is, but I can't, I don't have the courage to look! I'm afraid that my suspicions will be confirmed, and that would be terrible. That would be a defeat. I'm afraid of the truth; wouldn't it be easier to run away from it? It is bad enough that I know of her infidelity! *(He fights himself.)* However, it vexes me, it will vex me, it would vex me all my life. I've made my bed, now I must lie in it. *(He opens one of the letters and looks at the signature. Another upsurge of emotion.)* It is him! I thought so, I thought so –

LJUBOMIR *(approaching him):* Please, calm down! Please! Those things always look worse at the first glance.

PAVLE: My childhood friend, my school friend, my business partner, my best friend –

LJUBOMIR: Mr. Novaković!?

PAVLE: Yes, he, he! Ah, that's so mean, so vile!

LJUBOMIR *(pause, still uncertain):* So what are you going to do?

PAVLE: What? That's what I ask myself. I ask myself . . . and I cannot decide.

LJUBOMIR: Surely, you don't mean to –

PAVLE: Leave her, take a revenge on him? Oh, no! But what? In order to make a decision I need to get over it, for I loved that woman, I need to get over the pain!

LJUBOMIR: I fully understand, but I am not able, nor is it right for me to give you advice.

PAVLE: I am afraid that in this moment of agitation I might make a wrong decision. If I could only be on my own for a while, so I can think it over.

LJUBOMIR: Maybe you can go somewhere for a couple of days.

PAVLE: Yes, that would be best. *(Short thinking pause.)* That's what I'll do, I'll go somewhere.

LJUBOMIR: For a couple of days.

PAVLE: I don't know for how long, I don't know where; unknown destination for an undetermined period. I do not have any plans, but I have a need to isolate myself for a while so I can get over it and think it over in peace. To prevent a rash decision, the best thing to do is run away from myself. Thank you, my friend, you gave me good advice.

LJUBOMIR: Can I do anything for you?

PAVLE *(remembers):* Yes, thanks for your offer, you could do me a little favor.

LJUBOMIR: With pleasure!

PAVLE *(takes his passport out)*: If you could get me a visa . . . *(Leafing through his passport).* Oh, look, what a lucky coincidence! I got a visa six weeks ago when I was planning to go to an international fair. It is still valid. That's good, that's very good! *(He puts the passport away.)*
LJUBOMIR *(starting to go)*: I shall be on my way then.
PAVLE *(stretching his hand out)*: I rely on your discretion. *(He remembers something and withdraws his hand.)* Just a moment, I've just thought of a great favor you could do for me.
LJUBOMIR: Certainly.
PAVLE *(goes to another room and comes back with a big file of manuscripts)*: This, my young friend, is my most precious possession. I have worked for seven years on this thesis in hydrography, and I have worked on it with great conviction that it will make an impressive contribution to the pool of knowledge.
LJUBOMIR: You work in this area as well?
PAVLE: Yes, though I am an architect and a civil engineer first and foremost, hydrography is my great passion, and I've spent all my free time on it. The hydrographical problem is a general problem; three quarters of the globe's most fertile land is covered in swamps, marshes and aquatic sediments, and overpopulation causes great crises and problems in the world! I have even tried to establish new hydrographic methods. I am telling you all this to point out to you the significance of this work and what it means to me. I normally keep this manuscript locked in the drawer of my desk; however, I have just had a terrible thought that in my absence my wife might resort to the same act that I used against her and break into my desk. She would not find anything interesting, but she might, just out of spite, knowing how important this manuscript is to me, she might decide to take her revenge on me and pull out a few pages.
LJUBOMIR: Ah!

PAVLE: Oh, when they are angry, women are capable of most horrible things. I would like to entrust this manuscript with you for safekeeping.

LJUBOMIR *(surprised at this demonstration of trust)*: Oh, Mr. Marić!

PAVLE *(handing out the manuscript)*: Here, I entrust you with it; you know its value and I'm sure you'll know how to look after it.

LJUBOMIR: Rest assured, Mr. Marić, I'll take good care of it.

PAVLE: Thank you, and now: goodbye!

LJUBOMIR: Goodbye! *(Exits.)*

11. PAVLE *(alone)*

PAVLE *(on the telephone)*: Hello . . . hello! Radić and Todorović? Who is speaking, please? That's you, Peter? This is engineer Marić. I wanted to inform you that I am going to be away for a while; however, your deadline is in two days time. Please, could you deal with my partner Mr. Novaković instead; he is fully authorized to deal with you on my behalf, and our bank account is in the name of the company . . . yes, yes, please, contact him.

12. MARIJA, PAVLE

MARIJA *(enters)*: Mr. Novaković.

PAVLE *(startled with agitation)*: He?

MARIJA: I said you were –

PAVLE: No, no, let him in!

MARIJA *(withdraws)*.

13. NOVAKOVIĆ, PAVLE

NOVAKOVIĆ *(approaches with a pleasant expression)*: Good afternoon! I was at the site, but as you never turned up, I thought I'd come round to see whether you are all right.

PAVLE *(controlling his feelings with difficulty):* You were not at the site, nor have you come round to see whether I'm all right; my wife has sent you here. She visited you not long ago with great alarm; she told you that I broke into her desk and that your secret is out. She has clearly sent you to probe me.

NOVAKOVIĆ: What secrets are you talking about!? I don't understand you.

PAVLE *(approaches him and talks into his face):* You scoundrel!

NOVAKOVIĆ *(insulted):* What does this mean?

PAVLE: It means that you are a worthless scoundrel!

NOVAKOVIĆ: I do not approve of your talking to me like that!

PAVLE: You are right, I can see that one should talk to you in a different way too, but . . . I am controlling myself for the moment; we shall talk later! I promise you, we shall have it out!

NOVAKOVIĆ: All right, Pavle, we'll talk openly about the matter.

PAVLE: If you think that your confession constitutes an open conversation . . . you are mistaken. I do not need your confession.

NOVAKOVIĆ: Not a confession, but maybe a justification.

PAVLE: Can immorality be justified!?

NOVAKOVIĆ: You are undoubtedly right, you feel offended, your pride is injured.

PAVLE: My honour!

NOVAKOVIĆ: Pride!

PAVLE: Even if it is pride, who gives you the right over it.

NOVAKOVIĆ: For God's sake, Pavle, are you not able to see life for what it is? That's life, that's how it is. It's always been like that. You are busy all the time, you go to the site at the break of dawn, you have a quick lunch, in the evening you come back tired, and even then you spend all your time with your books, and some kind of scientific theses. You never have any time for your wife. She, however, is a young woman, she loves life, she needs attention and affection.

PAVLE: And she will achieve that by ruining her marriage, she will achieve it through the shameful assistance of my friend and my business partner.

NOVAKOVIĆ: Me or anyone else, it doesn't make any difference. I happened to have enough time, and maybe I even had the ability to give her attention.

PAVLE: And enough baseness to lose all consideration.

NOVAKOVIĆ: I don't see why you are so upset? There are some things in life that one just has to accept. Any opposition in this case is true barbarity.

PAVLE *(gets angry at this cynicism, opens the door, gets hold of a chair and swinging it at Novaković)*: Out! Out!

NOVAKOVIĆ *(getting up)*: True barbarity, is it not?

PAVLE: Out!

NOVAKOVIĆ *(exits)*.

14. PAVLE, MARIJA

PAVLE *(having calmed down a little, rings the bell)*.

MARIJA *(arrives)*.

PAVLE: Marija, can you please pack my luggage, prepare the blue suit and everything else.

MARIJA: You are going on a journey, sir?

PAVLE: Yes!

MARIJA: A long journey?

PAVLE *(irritated)*: How would I know!

MARIJA: I ask because of the suitcase, shall I use the bigger one, or –

PAVLE: Don't use any, I don't need any luggage! I won't take a single handkerchief out of this house . . . I don't need anything!

MARIJA: As you wish, sir.

PAVLE: I don't need anything. You may go now, I'll call you later!

MARIJA *(exits)*.

15. PAVLE, RINA

PAVLE *(thinks for a moment, then takes all the stolen letters out of his pocket, crumples them up and throws them on the floor with disgust)*.

RINA *(entering she goes straight to him; stands in front of him, without the courage and pride she'd had before)*: I would like to explain some things to you, Pavle.

PAVLE: Sorry, I have no time for that at the moment, I am about to go away.

RINA: Where?

PAVLE: Unknown destination.

RINA: For how long?

PAVLE: I don't know, but it is likely to be for a while, for a very long while.

RINA: Does it mean –

PAVLE *(leaving)*: That means that I am going away. *(He leaves suddenly, slamming the door after himself and without turning back.)*

RINA *(realising the truth of the situation, scared)*: Pavle! *(Falls into a armchair next to the door and starts sobbing.)*

CURTAIN

ACT 1

Tastefully arranged room at Milan Novaković's.

1. NOVAKOVIĆ, RINA

NOVAKOVIĆ *(after the morning tea, he is sitting at the table somewhat ruffled, holding a silver teaspoon in his hand and looking at it).*

RINA *(sitting opposite him in a luxurious morning dress):* Tired again, what? Under a little cloud? *(She gets up, goes behind him and embraces him.)* No clouds, please, I want everything to be bright and cheerful.

NOVAKOVIĆ: A happy marriage is always bright and cheerful.

RINA: Well, isn't our marriage happy!? Do you have anything to tell me?

NOVAKOVIĆ *(decisively):* Oh, no!

RINA *(kissing him):* Then cheer up.

NOVAKOVIĆ: Oh, it's nothing, just a trifle, nothing worth mentioning.

RINA: So there is something?

NOVAKOVIĆ: It's insignificant, really.

RINA: Go on . . . what is it?

NOVAKOVIĆ *(pointing at the teaspoon):* You see this monograph. Your old name. It's two and a half years since we got married, and these things are still around.

RINA: For goodness' sake, Milan!

NOVAKOVIĆ: Well, yes, it's totally insignificant, but I'm not comfortable having to be reminded of your ex-husband every morning.

RINA *(embracing him, she is laughing):* For goodness' sake, Milan! It never occurred to me, and it's so easy . . . *(She rings a bell.)* Honestly, it never occurred to me.

2. Add ANA

ANA *(young pretty girl, enters)*.

RINA *(pointing at the table):* You can clear up now, thanks. In the future, Ana, you will not lay these silver teaspoons. You can bring the other ones from the small cupboard.

ANA: Yes, I understand!

RINA *(picking up one of the spoons):* And afterwards, after the gentleman's gone to work, you will take these teaspoons . . . you know the little jeweller's shop opposite the Kasina? That jeweller used to do some work for me. Please pay him a visit and ask him if he can re-melt these 12 spoons and make me another set.

ANA: Certainly. *(By then she has collected everything onto a tray; exits.)*

3. NOVAKOVIĆ, RINA

RINA: There you are!

NOVAKOVIĆ *(kissing her):* You are so attentive and so decisive!

RINA: Well, should I allow some trifles to spoil my happiness?

NOVAKOVIĆ *(getting up, embraces her):* Thank you, you almost smother me with your love.

RINA: I don't just do it to please you, I really feel that way.

NOVAKOVIĆ *(kissing her hand):* Goodbye for now, my treasure!

RINA: Oh, I might be being silly, but wouldn't it be nice if you hadn't gone into the civil service, so you could stay at home the whole day, and be with me all the time. *(She is laughing.)* Silly, isn't it?

NOVAKOVIĆ: Still, I like it. Bye, my love!

RINA *(embracing him, follows him to the door):* One more thing. You can go to the office from here whichever way you want, take hours to get there if you like, but at noon, promise me that you will get here as soon as possible.

NOVAKOVIĆ: But of course! Of course! *(At the door they kiss, and he goes.)*

RINA *(at the door)*: Ana, please see the gentleman off!

4. RINA, ANA

RINA *(standing at the door, waves for a while, then comes back in)*.

ANA *(enters)*.

RINA: The gentleman's gone?

ANA: Yes, he has.

RINA: Ana, I am going to get dressed and you get ready to go out. Oh, yes! When you go to the jeweller's, please call by at Mrs. Sloutski at Poincaré's Street; ask her – how much longer do I have to wait for my negligee. She's been promising to get it done for a week now. Please tell her . . . I'm cross!

ANA: Certainly.

RINA *(goes to the room on the left)*.

5. ANTA, ANA

ANTA *(a middle-aged man, slim, balding. He comes in panicking, looking behind him as if somebody is running after him. Sits down uninvited)*: Ana, a glass of water, please!

ANA: Certainly! *(Goes out and comes back straightaway with a glass of water.)*

ANTA *(drinks it all up)*: Thank you! Where is the lady?

ANA: She is getting dressed.

ANTA: Getting dressed? She's getting dressed at such a moment!?

ANA: She'll be ready in a minute!

ANTA: In a minute!? Women never get dressed in a minute. *(Remembers.)* Please, tell me, is the lady a bit unsettled this morning?

ANA: How do you mean unsettled?

ANTA: Well, you know what an unsettled woman looks like, you must've been unsettled at some point?
ANA: The lady is in the same mood as usual.
ANTA: She hasn't sort of heard anything that could have disturbed her?
ANA: Not as far as I know.
ANTA: Please go and call her, tell her it's very urgent, she doesn't have to button up every last button. Please go!
ANA *(goes)*.

6. ANTA, then RINA and ANA

ANTA *(fidgeting nervously in the chair and wiping his forehead and neck with a large handkerchief)*.
RINA *(dressed up, surprised and alarmed)*: What is it for goodness' sake, what happened?
ANTA *(to Ana, who follows behind)*: Ana, one more glass of water please.
ANA *(exits)*.
ANTA: Oh, it's nothing!
RINA: But you are so agitated?
ANTA: Of course I am agitated, you will be agitated as well when you hear what I have to tell you.
RINA: So something has happened. Speak for God's sake!
ANA *(brings in a glass of water)*.
RINA *(to Ana)*: You may go!
ANA *(exits)*.
RINA: Speak, speak for goodness' sake, is anyone ill?
ANTA: But, please, who would think of being ill in these circumstances?
RINA *(horrified)*: Or . . . maybe, dead?
ANTA: Dead? Yes, dead! That would be very good, but that's the point, he is not dead.
RINA: Who, for God's sake, who are you talking about? Please don't torture me like this.

ANTA: Do you have heart problems?
RINA: Yes.
ANTA: That's it, you see, that's why I have to tell you about it with great caution and from a distance.
RINA: All right! But please get on with it.
ANTA: I will, but I tell you, it's got to be with great caution. Please sit down.
RINA *(sits down)*.
ANTA *(after she's sat down):* Here is a glass of water.
RINA *(impatient, disturbed):* Please speak!
ANTA: Tell me, please, do you remember your youth?
RINA: What kind of a question is that?
ANTA: I told you, we have to approach this from a distance: so, do you remember your youth?
RINA: But of course!
ANTA: You were of course a girl, before you became a woman?
RINA: Really, sir!
ANTA: I know, you want to say that that's clear in itself, but I just have to state all the facts. So, once you got married, you were not a girl anymore?
RINA *(offended):* Please, sir, if this is a joke, it is very distasteful, and I –
ANTA: Be patient, we are almost there. You got married, and what happened then?
RINA: Then I became a widow.
ANTA: That's what I mean. You see, that fact is inaccurate.
RINA: What do you mean inaccurate?
ANTA: Listen, but please we have to treat this with great caution.
RINA: What's got into you this morning, sir: what are these riddles, what kind of a conversation is this?
ANTA: Please be patient. We shall bring the whole matter to the light of day presently. Let us see, on what basis do you claim that you are a widow? Your husband got cross with you one day, left

home and said he didn't know where he was going and when he was coming back. This is the statement you gave at the investigation.

RINA: Precisely!

ANTA: And he left, or rather . . . disappeared. The day after, his suit was found by the Danube, and all his papers were in it, even his identification card . . . and the whole matter was clear. The body was found six weeks later in the Danube, completely deformed, of course, but it was established that it had been in the water for six weeks, exactly the amount of time since the disappearance of your husband, also his initials were found on the shirt, and we proceeded with a ceremonial funeral. You were behind the coffin in the procession, and I was there too.

RINA: But please, why are you telling me all these things that have been repeated hundreds of times? I've had it all up to here, and I don't want to think about it anymore.

ANTA: OK, let's skip that for now. But there is one thing we cannot skip and that is: what did you do when you became a widow?

RINA: I got married again.

ANTA: That's where you went wrong, you see, you shouldn't have gotten married.

RINA: That is a personal thing, sir, and I do not permit such impertinence –

ANTA: Still you made a mistake. I can give you an example of a certain Saveta Tomić. She is an honourable, but poor woman. She cleans people's houses to support herself.

RINA: Please, sir, leave Saveta Tomić alone, what does some Saveta have to do with all this? You storm into my house like that, totally perturbed, start speaking in riddles, annoying me and frightening me and now . . . you tell me about some Saveta.

ANTA: That's not "some Saveta", dear lady, but an authentic Saveta, and after you've heard me out, you will understand.

RINA *(sits down, resigned)*: OK, speak!

ANTA: That Saveta Tomić lost her husband in the war. He was killed and they buried him at the front. She received an official report about his death, on the basis of which she became a widow. As such, as an authentic widow, she married some tram driver. She'd been suffering greatly on her own, so she needed some support to see her through. And she lived happily with her husband, and she would have lived happily ever after, but then one day, after three years . . . her first husband turns up alive, released as a war prisoner.

RINA *(is shocked, gets up and looks him in the eye).*

ANTA: And of course, the second marriage immediately fell through because Saveta wasn't a widow when she got married the second time. And she had to go back to the first husband.

RINA *(disturbed, pale):* Sir, do I understand you correctly?

ANTA: Take some water please, please!

RINA *(unaware of her actions, complies).*

ANTA: Sit down.

RINA *(sinks into an armchair, fidgeting with her hands):* Speak, in God's good name, please speak!

ANTA: I saw him!

RINA *(terrified, shrieks):* Whom?

ANTA: Him!

RINA *(desperate):* Whom, for God's sake?

ANTA: Your first husband.

RINA: This is terrible, this is a torture! Why did you come to torture me like this, who sent you? What is this you are talking about, who told you this rubbish; what do you want from me, speak, what do you want?

ANTA: I saw him.

RINA: Do you know him at all?

ANTA: How can I not know him, I owe him 10,000 dinars . . . God rest his soul!

RINA *(very disturbed):* That's . . . that's impossible . . . you are ill . . . that's . . . Oh, my God, I'm losing my mind!

ANTA: Please, don't! You mustn't do that now.

RINA: That can't be true. Say it's not true, please, please say it! Or if it's true, I don't know, I can't think.

ANTA: There you are! Just think what would have happened if I hadn't told you like this, with caution and from a distance?

RINA *(gets hold of the phone):* Hello, Hello! Mr. Novaković, please. He hasn't arrived yet!? Look, please, this is not possible . . . No!? *(She puts the phone down.)* Oh, God!

ANTA: Why are you bothering him?

RINA: Well, who shall I talk to if not my husband?

ANTA: True, that's very true.

RINA *(going to the phone again, but before dialling):* Listen, don't allow me to raise the alarm if it was just a joke or if you didn't see well –

ANTA: Well who would make such a joke! You think I'm happy that I saw him? And I saw him, I saw him very clearly. Ristić, the shopkeeper, was standing in front of his shop and he was terribly surprised when he saw him. He simply went white. The deceased approached him, they shook hands and talked for a long while in front of the shop. When they parted, I went to Mr. Ristić and asked him: Excuse me please, who was this gentleman you were just talking to? "That's the man" says Mr. Ristić "whose funeral you went to; that's Mr. Marić and he was just telling me how it all happened". There, that's what Mr. Ristić told me, and he personally spoke to him.

RINA *(dialling):* Hello! Hello! Mr. Novaković please? How come he hasn't arrived yet? *(She puts the phone down agitated.)* That's terrible! That's impossible! May I ask you a favor, can you please go personally to the Ministry of Building and Environment; it's not very far; can you please go, you know, he must be there by now; maybe he stopped at some other office on the way, but he must be there. Find him at all costs and tell him to leave everything – everything – and come home immediately.

ANTA: He will get to the office, he will, any time now, please be patient.
RINA: No, no, no I can't be patient, I can't bear this, I can't bear it, please go, go, please!
ANTA *(getting up):* OK! I'll go!
RINA: You can come back with him.
ANTA: Oh, yes, of course I will. *(Exits.)*

7. ANA, RINA

RINA *(rings the bell).*
ANA: Yes?
RINA *(confused):* Actually . . . what did I want, oh I don't know . . . I've forgotten . . . I'll call you again.
ANA: Certainly! *(Exits.)*

8. MILE, RINA

MILE *(a dandy, powdered and well dressed, approaches her, embraces and starts kissing her):* How is my little darling?
RINA *(rests her head on his shoulder):* Oh, Mile, I am so unhappy, so unhappy.
MILE: But why, my sweetheart?
RINA: You will not believe it when I tell you . . . I don't believe it, I don't want to believe it, I can't believe it. It is too terrible!
MILE: What on earth is the matter? You are so upset.
RINA: The matter is very unusual, unimaginable, and I can't deal with it, I can't compose myself, I can't think.
MILE *(strokes her hand):* Tell me, what happened?
RINA: Imagine, my first husband, the one that committed suicide by drowning, he's re-appeared, he is alive.
MILE *(surprised):* What do you mean? Alive? That's nonsense, that's impossible, you have a bit of a fever; there you are, you've got high temperature, you are just hallucinating a bit; must be fever.

RINA: I knew you wouldn't believe me. Well, no, it's not believable, still . . . you can imagine how distressed I was when I heard.
MILE: Calm down, darling; it can't be true.
RINA: It is true, oh, it is true; something tells me that it is true, I don't know why, but I'm sure of it.
MILE: But for goodness' sake, his body was found and identified.
RINA: There were some who doubted even then and who claimed that all the evidence was inconclusive, but he hasn't been in touch for three years, and that was the best proof.
MILE: You would be in a very difficult situation if that were true.
RINA: I'd have to go back to him; imagine, I'd have to go back. I've only just found true marital happiness and now I have to return to marital slavery? I would lose you as well, Mile! *(She falls into his arms and starts sobbing.)*
MILE: You must be strong, darling. We will find a way out of it, we have to seek some advice!
RINA: Seek advice? Who the devil can I seek advice from when I've been trying to contact my husband for the last half hour and he is not in the office; he left god knows how long ago, and he still hasn't got there.
MILE *(looks at his watch)*: He will not get there before ten.
RINA: You say it as though you know it for certain?
MILE: I know just as well as you know. At this time of day, just before going to the office, he always goes to Lidočka's for a coffee. That's been the same every day ever since Lidočka came back from Berlin.
RINA *(indifferent)*: Does he stay there long?
MILE: Till he finishes his coffee, until about ten o'clock.
RINA: Who can wait till then, I have to talk to him as soon as possible.

MILE: Madam Salev, Lidočka's neighbour, is on the same floor, and she has a telephone as well. If you wish –?
RINA: Oh, no, no. I don't want to disturb him like that. He mustn't know that I know either. That's where our marital bliss resides . . . we never disturb each other like that.
MILE: Then you must be patient.
RINA: Patient! As if it were that easy!
MILE: The best thing is . . . don't think about it. I can divert your thoughts to other things. My dearest darling, I have totally run out of money, and look I'm as thin as a winter mosquito. In a couple of days I'm getting some money in, but in the meantime, do you think you could lend me 200 dinars?
RINA *(takes some money out of her purse):* You always have financial problems.
MILE: What can I do, I'm trying my best, but life is so complicated!

9. Add ANTA

ANTA *(entering):* He's not there, I told you, he's not there!
RINA *(to Mile):* So, as I said, sir, my husband wouldn't be able to receive you even if he came back now; he has certain problems at the moment. In fact, it would be best if you made an appointment to see him in his office regarding your business; he seldom receives at home.
MILE *(kissing her hand):* That's what I'll do, madam. I do apologize! Good bye! *(Exits.)*

10. RINA, ANTA

RINA *(having sent Mile a kiss stealthily, to Anta):* I do not know why they've got offices when everybody always looks for them at home. So, he is not there?
ANTA: No. RINA: But he must be there!
ANTA: I've just been there.

RINA *(picks up the phone)*: Hello, Hello! Is that you Milan? Yes.
(To Anta) There you are!
RINA: Have you heard anything? You haven't? Please, come home at once! Please! You haven't sat down yet? Don't. Come home at once, the matter is very serious and very urgent; I'll go mad waiting for you . . . Hurry up, please! *(Puts the phone down.)* He's coming!

11. Add SPASOJE

SPASOJE *(a nuoveau riche)*: Good morning! *(Kisses Rina's hand.)* I'm sorry, I've knocked twice. I don't want to impose, I've just called by to ask you a favor. My daughter would like to look at some materials for her wedding dress, for as you know, her wedding day is drawing near. And she would very much like you to come with her, she trusts your taste immensely and she won't do it without you.
RINA *(impatiently)*: Yes, but not now, not today; I have some more important matters to attend to, which actually concern you as well.
SPASOJE: Me?
RINA: You haven't heard anything?
SPASOJE: I don't know; what was I supposed to hear?
RINA *(to Anta)*: How come, sir, nobody has heard anything apart from you.
ANTA: I haven't heard, I've seen.
SPASOJE: What the devil have you seen?
ANTA: I'll tell you. Do you have heart problems?
SPASOJE: Yes, a bit.
ANTA *(rings the bell)*: Of course, it's typical for a man of your age.

12. Add ANA

ANA *(enters)*: You've called!

ANTA: Ana, can you please bring a glass of water.
ANA: Certainly! *(Exits)*.

13. RINA, SPASOJE, ANTA

ANTA *(to Spasoje):* Please, sit down, I've got to tell you this with great caution and from a distance.

RINA: Please, enough with your 'great caution', sir. *(To Spasoje)* The gentleman takes forever. I'll tell you – the man whom we all know to be dead, deceased, the man whom we buried, is alive.

SPASOJE *(startled, shouts):* Who on earth are you talking about?

ANTA: The one whose house is in Terazije and whose entire estate you inherited.

SPASOJE: Come on, please; nonsense, childish nonsense. How can that be?

RINA: I can't believe it either.

SPASOJE: Who would believe anything like that, and who could invent such a thing, please?

RINA: I've heard it from our relative here . . . Anta.

SPASOJE: You?

ANTA: Me.

SPASOJE: What do you drink so early in the day?

ANTA: I don't drink anything, but even if I had a gallon of petrol now, it wouldn't make any difference.

SPASOJE: Please tell me, how can something so stupid occur to you?

ANTA: I saw him, I saw him with my own eyes.

SPASOJE: Who?

ANTA: The deceased . . . Pavle Marić.

SPASOJE: Which Pavle Marić.

ANTA: The one whose estate you've inherited.

SPASOJE: You leave the inheritance alone, and you tell me . . . In fact, there's nothing you can tell me. You'll only tell me the most stupid, impossible nonsense. I would understand if you said "I've heard", although then I'd punish you for spreading misinformation, but if you say "I've seen" . . . when you say "I've seen," that's simply a crime.

ANTA *(insists):* I've seen him!

SPASOJE *(irritated):* There he goes again!

RINA: Can you imagine how I felt when I heard it.

SPASOJE: OK, if you said . . . the Sun blacked out, OK, I accept it; every light must go out some time. I accept that! If you said, for example: the priest of such and such a church, swallowed the church spire; OK, I can accept that too. There are some priests who can swallow church profits, and when their stomachs expand, they may of course, be able to swallow the spire and all five bells. Very well, I can accept that. I can accept that the Danube changed its course and started running in the opposite direction; I can accept that the government decided to have free elections; all of the world's wonders I can accept . . . do you understand . . . all wonders, but that you've seen the man whom we buried three years ago . . . I can't accept that! And why on earth did you have to run here and terrorize this poor lady like that!? *(To Rina)* I can imagine how you felt when you heard.

ANTA: Can you imagine how I felt when I saw him?

SPASOJE: Listen to him, on and on!

ANTA: Honestly, when I saw him, my knees went weak and I couldn't even walk. And all of a sudden I began sweating, and then as if someone slid a piece of ice down my shirt, I started shivering with cold.

SPASOJE: I don't know what you have to shiver about?

ANTA: What do you mean "what"? And what about the 10,000 dinars?

SPASOJE: Well, you declared under oath in court that you'd returned that money to him.

ANTA: Well, yes, I declared it, of course I declared it, but he was dead then, and now he is alive.

SPASOJE: So, that's what it is?

ANTA: Well, yes of course.

SPASOJE: Wait a moment, I'll tell you . . . *(He takes a booklet out of his pocket and leafs through it.)* This is the criminal law book, I always carry it around. It's very useful, one can learn an awful lot from it. This is, so to speak, a guide through life. *(He finds the page.)* Ah, there we go: paragraph 144, perjury. *(Reads for himself.)* So, a year in prison and loss of national honour for a year. It can be more than that, but you can certainly book a year in.

ANTA: Who?

SPASOJE: You!

ANTA: Why me?

SPASOJE: For perjury, what else.

ANTA: What do you mean a year in prison? How can you just say it like that, as if you were weighing a bag of onions. Prison . . . that's all I need!

SPASOJE: And loss of national honour.

ANTA: I don't mind that. One can live very happily without national honour. But prison, my dear sir, that's a different kettle of fish. And what I don't understand is why you . . . what gives you the right to sentence me like this.

SPASOJE: I should actually be the one to sue you, because you have damaged me for 10,000 dinars.

ANTA: Well, really!?

SPASOJE: Of course! When your creditor committed suicide, they determined his estate, and you owed to that estate, and then I inherited that estate as his closest relative.

ANTA: Ah, now I understand why you were so happy earlier on to hear that Pavle Marić is alive. Of course, who else would be happy if not you, his closest relative?

RINA *(irritated by their conversation):* Gentlemen, for lord's sake, you are talking about everything, but the most important thing.

ANTA: Well, the gentleman cannot just tell me like that: a year in prison. Just like that . . . prison, as if there is nothing else in life but prison. And why doesn't the gentleman look into this life-guide of his, and see how many years are due to him.

SPASOJE: I damaged no one for 10,000 dinars.

ANTA: No, of course not. That's trifles for you, you don't want to dirty your hands with such things. But a three storey house in Terazije, a plot near the Railway Station and two shops in King Peter's Street, that's something!

SPASOJE: What do you mean to say?

ANTA: Well, perjury, seven false certificates, four solicitors and an inheritance. Look it up in that guide of yours.

SPASOJE *(extremely angry, goes towards Anta clenching his fists threateningly, but controlling himself at the last minute):* You said it now, and never again!

14. Add NOVAKOVIĆ

NOVAKOVIĆ *(enters agitated):* Oh, dear God, dear God!

RINA *(hurries to meet him):* You know?

NOVAKOVIĆ: Just now on my way back I bumped into Mr. Tadić and he told me that he had seen him and talked to him. Otherwise I would have had no idea why you had called me.

ANTA: I saw him too!

NOVAKOVIĆ: Really saw him?

ANTA: Just as clearly as I see you now.

SPASOJE: That means, gentlemen, we can no longer believe in death? Death has turned deceitful too. *(He pulls a piece of paper from his pocket.)* Please, is this a death certificate or is it not?

ANTA *(looking):* You were one of the signatories as well?

SPASOJE: No, YOU were! Is this a death certificate, I ask you; have we buried him –

ANTA: Allotment 17, grave 39.

SPASOJE: Hasn't he stayed there nicely and peacefully for three years? Hasn't he? So how can he all of a sudden be alive now?

And can it be that way? Can people just do what they like, just like that? All the progressive Western countries, I'm sure, must have a law regarding this, and according to that law . . . whoever is dead, is dead. In our country however –
ANTA: No country can force anyone to be dead.
SPASOJE: That means, I can't be sure that one day my deceased wife, who died eleven years ago, may not reappear one day? She reappears, comes home "Good afternoon", and we just go "Oh, good afternoon, please come in!"
NOVAKOVIĆ: The matter is not what might happen and what might not happen; the matter is . . . he is here!
SPASOJE: But how? Where from? Has he got up from his grave? Was he resurrected? Did he run away, did he fall down from a tree, from the Moon, or from Mars?
NOVAKOVIĆ: They say he returned from a journey.
SPASOJE: What journey? From the graveyard here? And how did he travel, pray? Dear God, I can't think anymore, and this is the first time in my life that I can't think. *(Sits down.)*
RINA *(to Milan):* Have you found out any details?
NOVAKOVIĆ: Yes, I've found out that he wasn't dead.
SPASOJE: Of course, he will now keep denying everything.
NOVAKOVIĆ: He was staying at the Excelsior.
SPASOJE: What kind of grave is that?
NOVAKOVIĆ: The Hotel Excelsior. That's all I know. *(Remembers)* Oh, yes, one more thing. He was asking around for my address, he wants to visit me.
ANTA: You?
NOVAKOVIĆ: Me, or . . . maybe my wife.
RINA *(terrified):* Me? Why me?
ANTA: Well, you are closest to him.
RINA: Me?
ANTA: Yes, because you are actually his wife.
RINA *(runs to her husband):* Milan, is it true what this gentleman is saying?

NOVAKOVIĆ *(confused)*: I don't know. *(To Anta)* On what basis are you saying this?
ANTA: On the basis of Saveta Tomić.
SPASOJE: There he goes again . . . who is Saveta Tomić?
ANTA: The one who married thinking that she was a widow, and when her first husband re-appeared, the Court moved her, in the name of law and order and without travelling expenses, from the second back into the first marriage.
RINA *(distressed, to Milan)*: Is that possible?
ANTA: That's according to the Law.
NOVAKOVIĆ *(wanting to console Rina)*: I don't believe that the law can serve barbarity, for that would certainly be barbarous.
RINA *(embracing Milan)*: I don't want us to part!
NOVAKOVIĆ: Calm down, Rina. There is no law that can destroy happy marriages.
SPASOJE *(having been thinking and listening to them)*: All that you say is completely secondary. Completely secondary. The most important question here is: how can a man whom we buried with all due rites three years ago, how can he and with what right.

15. Add LJUBOMIR PROTIĆ

LJUBOMIR *(carrying various newspapers, he is pale and very confused)*: What is this, what is this, for goodness' sakes!? *(Remembers)* I beg your pardon, madam! *(He goes to Rina and kisses her hand; addressing everybody.)* What is this?
RINA: Are you well?
ANTA *(rings the bell)*: Do you have heart problems?
ANA *(enters)*.
ANTA *(to Ana)*: A glass of water please!
ANA *(exits)*.
LJUBOMIR *(he sinks in an armchair)*: Oh, no, no, I'm fine . . . no, no. But what is this?

NOVAKOVIĆ: Who told you?

LJUBOMIR: Who? *(Hands out the papers)* All the papers are full of it!

ALL *(surprised)*: The papers? *(They all pick a copy each.)*

ANTA: Oh, the titles are so big!

SPASOJE *(reads a title)*: Just listen to this, please: "The Dead on the Rise".

ANTA *(reads)*: "And when the Day of Reckoning comes, the dead will rise from their graves".

NOVAKOVIĆ *(reads)*: "Allotment 17, grave 39 opened up and the deceased rose from the dead".

LJUBOMIR *(reads)*: "The dead rise, the dead speak".

ANA *(brings in a glass of water)*.

LJUBOMIR *(drinks up)*.

SPASOJE: I do not think that the matter is so interesting that all the papers should give it so much attention.

LJUBOMIR: Can you imagine how I felt when I found this out in the middle of the street!? I had no idea . . . waiting for the tram, I was just leafing through the papers and this title "The dead rise, the dead speak" caught my attention. As soon as I read the first few lines I felt sick!

RINA: Me too.

LJUBOMIR: I started sweating, my hands went cold, everything clouded up in front of my eyes and I had to lean against the wall.

SPASOJE *(takes him by the arm and to the side, confidentially)*: I don't understand, my son; why are you so distressed about it? I can understand everyone else, but you? What did you have to do with the deceased Marić?

LJUBOMIR *(still disturbed)*: We can't talk about it at the moment.

SPASOJE: It must be a big amount?

LJUBOMIR: Something like that.

NOVAKOVIĆ *(still engrossed in the papers)*: Ah, there we have it . . . a whole description of what happened. A full interview.

ALL *(huddling around Novaković)*: Please, read it out, please!

LJUBOMIR *(on the side, slightly worried, but listening).*

NOVAKOVIĆ *(reads)*: "In response to the question whether everything was carefully premeditated, Mr. Marić strongly denied that there was any deliberation in the matter. This is how he describes the event: 'It was a fateful decision, my wife was very unfair to me, which hurt me a great deal. For even then, even when I suffered because of her, I always –

RINA: Please, skip those banalities.

NOVAKOVIĆ *(reads)*: "I was very distressed and I didn't know what to do."

ANTA *(to Rina)*: Does he have heart problems too?

SPASOJE: Please, don't interrupt! Continue reading, please.

NOVAKOVIĆ *(reads)*: "Since I had to make a decision, I got frightened of myself. I realized that I could make a rash decision which I could then regret all my life. Then it occurred to me to go away, to leave this place where everything seemed to me then to be working against me; I decided to be on my own for a while so I can think and make decisions. I went away not telling anyone where. In fact, even I didn't know where I was going. When the ticket inspector asked me for the ticket and I didn't have one, he asked me where I was going and I finally settled for Vienna. I knew Vienna very well, so I thought I'd be quite comfortable over there."

ANTA: Exactly. And if he'd returned after a couple of days, everything would have been fine.

SPASOJE: But, please, don't interrupt! *(To Novaković)* Please, continue!

NOVAKOVIĆ *(reads)*: "In Vienna I checked into a hotel near the University, and spent a few days in there immersed in my problems. On the fourth day I went to town, hoping that I might bump into someone I knew in those bars frequented by our people. I didn't meet anyone, but I found some Belgrade dailies. I took one of the papers, opened it up and got really surprised when I found my own picture in it. Reading the titles I immediately learnt that I'd committed suicide by drowning in the Danube, and I proceeded to read the details of my own suicide. At first I was really amused; it made me laugh, and then it occurred to me . . . this could actually be the best solution to the situation. Being officially dead, but being alive at the same time."

SPASOJE: He considers that the best solution? Well, thank you very much!

ANTA: Well, that's from his point of view.

SPASOJE: Of course, from his point of view! But we have our point of view as well. *(To Novaković)* Please, continue!

NOVAKOVIĆ *(reads):* "I decided to go along with it. As Vienna is a bit inconvenient . . . you can bump into someone you know any time . . . I took the first train to Germany. Happily I found a nice job straightaway in a place near Hamburg, and I stayed there for three years, unnoticed, hardly ever going anywhere."

SPASOJE: And what I don't understand is: why did he have to leave such a nice job, he could have stayed there happily and everything would still be fine.

ANTA: Maybe he wanted to come back and check on his estate?

SPASOJE: Maybe! And maybe he wanted to claim his money back from his debtors.

RINA *(anxious):* I can't, I just cannot regain my composure and calm down.

SPASOJE: So, who did we bury?

NOVAKOVIĆ: He gives an answer to that question as well.

SPASOJE: And what does he say, pray?

NOVAKOVIĆ *(reads):* "In response to the question about the possible identity of the body found in possession of his clothes and documents," Mr. Marić says: "I think that must have been my building supervisor, a Russian immigrant, Aljoša."

SPASOJE: Aljoša?

NOVAKOVIĆ *(continues reading)*: "That day, just before I left, Aljoša told me that he had suicidal thoughts, he even told me he was going to throw himself into the Danube. He was wearing an old suit of mine that I gave him and he also had some of my documents on him. It could only have been him."
SPASOJE: Aljoša?
ANTA: And you put the wreath on Aljoša's grave.
LJUBOMIR *(desperate)*: Now we know everything. As you can see the situation is very bad.
SPASOJE: Of course, it's bad!
LJUBOMIR: At this moment of general shock, we are not even able to consider all the potential consequences.
ANTA: No, we are not! *(To Novaković)* For example, you could lose your wife.
RINA *(embraces Milan)*: Oh, no! Not that!
ANTA *(to Spasoje)*: And then you'd lose your estate.
SPASOJE: And then you'd go to prison for a year.
ANTA: There he goes again! I told you I was sensitive to that word.
SPASOJE: I only wanted to highlight all the potential consequences, you see. But there is one that is the worst of all . . . Mr. Đurić. What will Mr. Đurić say about it all?
ANTA: Who?
SPASOJE: The man who invested all of his experience, his reputation and his connections into our enterprise, into which we had invested our capital and knowledge, what will he say? For if we accept this state of affairs, if Mr. Marić is found alive, our whole enterprise would come tumbling down.
ANTA: Oh, that's the least that could happen.
SPASOJE: The least? What do you mean the least? Have you ever heard about the great techno-financial conglomerate Illyria Ltd?
ANTA: Of course I have.

SPASOJE: This company, sir, has applied to the Government for a concession to drain all the marshes, swamps, lakes and in fact all the aquatic sediments in this kingdom. That's one big job that will take twelve years to complete and will include some big construction work: at least ten iron bridges, around a hundred concrete bridges and a lot of tunnels. That's something very big, do you understand?

ANTA: I don't see what that's got to do with anything?

SPASOJE: What that's got to do with anything!? We have all invested all we had into this project. Mr. Novaković has invested around half a million in cash at the planning stage. Mr. Protić, my future son-in-law and the fiancé of my daughter, has been elected technical director of the company. Yes, sir, and not because he is my son-in-law, but because he is an expert. Two years ago my son-in-law published a great scientific thesis "Amelioration and Terrisation". That publication caused a great sensation. And on the basis of it, my son-in-law became an associate Professor at the university, because, sir, this is not just any scientific thesis, but a great scientific revolution in the field of hydro-technology.

ANTA *(amazed):* How come you speak with such knowledge about it?

SPASOJE: I learnt it all, my dear sir, I learnt it all off by heart so I can talk about the matter.

LJUBOMIR *(to Spasoje):* I do implore you, father, do not speak about it anymore, speak about something else.

SPASOJE: I wanted to explain it to him.

ANTA: And what does this have to do with you?

SPASOJE: First of all, that big techno-financial consortium doesn't have a basic capital of its own. The consortium's only capital is the fact that its general director, Mr. Đurić happens to have a minister for a brother.

ANTA: And Schwartz and Rosendolph?

SPASOJE: Schwartz and Rosendolph are mere mercantile agents: one is the agent of some automobile tyre factory, and the other an agent of a factory of combs and celluloid products. Why did we involve them in the consortium if they are just mere agents, you might ask? Because, my dear sir, our country, our banks and our city do not like enterprises without at least one Schwartz or Rosendolph and we don't consider them mere agents. We've promoted them into representatives of big foreign capital. Schwartz is the official representative of Belgian and Rosendolph of British capital. However, we do not require their capital anyway, for when we get the concession, we'll sell it on, but what we need is a recovery of the deposit and of all our expenses. Mr. Novaković paid for most of the expenses and I mortgaged my three-storey house in Terazije for the deposit.
ANTA: I thought you were giving that house to your daughter as a wedding present.
SPASOJE: Yes, but in the meantime I mortgaged it for the deposit. There, do you understand? And then in the middle of all that, one dead man turns up and swallows up the deposit and the whole of the Illyria enterprise. Can we allow that, please, can we?
NOVAKOVIĆ *(irritable):* That's what we should be speaking about, instead of Illyria.
SPASOJE: About what?
RINA: About him, the deceased. He could be here any minute now. Every time I hear the door my heart misses a beat.
SPASOJE *(confused but composing himself):* Well . . . let him come.
NOVAKOVIĆ: Yes, but how are we going to behave around him?
SPASOJE: How? It's easy. We simply musn't acknowledge that he is alive; it would be against our interests if we behaved as though he were alive. We will behave, therefore, as though he were deceased.

ANTA: What do you mean? Should we cross ourselves when we see him?
SPASOJE: You can cross yourself if you like, but as far as I'm concerned, he doesn't exist for me. If he comes, he's not here for me, if he greets me, I won't greet him back, I can't be shaking hands with dead people. No, thank you very much!
ANTA: And if he speaks?
SPASOJE: I won't talk to him.
RINA: I'll turn my back on him . . . I don't even want to see him.
SPASOJE: And do you think I want to see him.
NOVAKOVIĆ: You think therefore, that it's best to ignore him, totally ignore him.
SPASOJE: As if he didn't exist.
ALL *(agreeing)*.

16. Add ANA

ANA *(bringing a visiting card, hands it over to Novaković)*.
ALL *(terrified):* Is it him?
NOVAKOVICH: It's him!
ALL *(nervous, looking at each other)*.
NOVAKOVIĆ *(turning the card over in his hand and thinking; finally decides):* Let him in.
ANA *(exits)*.
SPASOJE *(with bravado):* For me, he doesn't exit.
ALL: Same here. *(They take up various positions. Spasoje folds his hands on his stomach and looks up at the ceiling; Rina hides behind Novaković; Ljubomir sits in a deep armchair and covers his eyes; Anta pulls a handkerchief to wipe his nose and freezes like that.)*

17. Add PAVLE

PAVLE *(enters, looking at everyone):* Good afternoon!
ALL *(frozen)*.

PAVLE *(he observes them for a while, and after a long pause)*: Good afternoon, I say.
SPASOJE *(still frozen, in the same position, but overpowered by his short temper)*: We heard!
PAVLE: I thought . . . I expected –
SPASOJE *(forgetting himself)*: What the hell did you expect; you didn't think we'd all faint when we saw you?
PAVLE: Oh no, my dear heir, I thought I would be welcomed by my family as it normally befits such situations. I've returned from the dead, for heaven's sake, haven't I?
SPASOJE: That's your problem!
PAVLE: Not only mine; what about my family. Wouldn't a wife cheer up at the sight of her husband whom she presumed dead?
RINA *(protesting and hiding behind Novaković's back)*.
PAVLE *(to Spasoje)*: Or yourself, for example, as my relative? I understand that you proved in Court that you were my closest relative; and I see *(he pulls out a death certificate)* you also signed my death certificate as a bereaved member of the family. Such a close relative as yourself must surely be happy to see me again.
SPASOJE *(confused)*: Of course, I don't deny that, but I can't allow you to play with my feelings like that. One moment you decide to die and I have to cry, and the next you decide to come back to life and I have to be happy. You could be changing your mind like that all your life, and then I wouldn't have anything else to do in my life but cry one moment and laugh the next!
PAVLE *(looking around)*: And then these other gentlemen. My best friend and business partner, for example?
NOVAKOVIĆ: You and I, sir, parted ways whilst you were still alive!
PAVLE: Oh, yes, and Mr. Anta, the relative of my wife's! However, let us skip him for the moment.
ANTA: Precisely, let us skip me.

PAVLE: But my dear young friend, Mr. Protić, for whom I had so much affection and so much trust and to whom –

LJUBOMIR *(broken up, approaches him):* I implore you, sir, let us talk about it face to face.

PAVLE: Certainly! Would you prefer us, Mr. Anta, to talk face to face as well?

ANTA: We said we would skip me.

PAVLE: And my wife, perhaps?

RINA *(turns as if stung, then experiencing a difficult moment; finally with a lump in her throat):* You may address my husband, please.

NOVAKOVIĆ: Sir, your former wife is now legally married to me and we now have a very happy life together. I don't see how you can take the liberty to harass my wife like this, and what gives you the right to address her in such a manner?

PAVLE: The fact that I am alive.

SPASOJE: You will have to prove that, sir! One can't just turn up like that and declare: I am alive! The investigation established that you had committed suicide and according to it you are dead; you are dead in the eyes of the legal system, and you are dead in the eyes of all of us here. We buried you, and ceremoniously at that. The lady and I walked behind the coffin in the procession, my son-in-law gave a speech, my daughter was in mourning for six weeks and I laid a wreath on your grave . . . now what else do you want; what more could you expect?

PAVLE: I am very grateful to you for such consideration!

SPASOJE: We gave you two memorial services as well.

PAVLE: I really do appreciate it.

SPASOJE: Then what else do you expect from us? We did everything that was in our power. What else do you want?

PAVLE: I do not want anything, I came to say thank you for everything you've done.

SPASOJE: Oh, no, you needn't have bothered.

PAVLE: So you reckon there is nothing else to discuss?

SPASOJE: I don't see that there is anything else we could discuss.
PAVLE: Don't you see that my return changes everything? That in fact the current state of affairs changes fundamentally? Surely there is a lot more to discuss around here.
SPASOJE: I don't see that anything can change, and if by any chance you find that the state of affairs is different, I shall give you a friendly piece of advice as to how to deal with it.
PAVLE: Please, it would be my pleasure to hear it.
SPASOJE: If your arrival is meant to be a threat to us all, I have to warn you to not delude yourself. You think it's easy to destroy everything that has been built after your death? You are wrong! The only solution for you would be to return wherever you came from and accept the fact that you are dead.
PAVLE: Yes that would be one solution, but there is another one and I've opted for the latter.
SPASOJE: And that is?
PAVLE: To stay here amongst you!
(General commotion.)
NOVAKOVIĆ: That means not amongst us, but against us!
PAVLE: If you wish.
SPASOJE: That means, sir . . . think again, please think again!
PAVLE: I've been thinking for three years.
SPASOJE: For such matters even thirty years of thinking may not be enough.
PAVLE: I do apologize, gentlemen, if I have disturbed you. I needed this meeting before we proceed. I was going to make a visit to everyone separately –
ANTA: You may skip me, though.
PAVLE: But it's even better that I found you all in one place. I wish you all a good afternoon. *(He starts to go.)*
SPASOJE: Please, just a minute, is this your last?
PAVLE *(stops):* My last? I am alive and I want to live! *(Exits.)*
ALL *(shocked looking at each other).*

SPASOJE *(the first to pull himself together, shouts after Pavle although he has already left)*: But we want to live too! Anta, please run after him and tell him: we want to live, we want to live too!

CURTAIN

ACT 2

A nice room in Spasoje's house.

1. VUKICA, SPASOJE

VUKICA *(wearing a nice dress, rich lipstick, bright nail-varnish, thinly shaped eyebrows. She is sitting languidly on a sofa, legs crossed and smoking a cigarette)*: I do not understand why everybody is hiding the reason from me?
SPASOJE: Nobody is hiding the reason from you, it's just that the reason is of such nature –
VUKICA: It must be a very strange reason indeed. To arrange the wedding day, to announce it to the whole world, print the invitations and then suddenly call it all off. Well, that's nothing short of a scandal! And why, why?
SPASOJE: Some great unexpected worries have befallen us.
VUKICA: Worries, worries, you always have them.
SPASOJE: Yes, that's right, but these are . . . how shall I put it, exceptional worries. To do with this consortium. We came across a big unexpected obstacle, and we are all very worried, including your fiancé.
VUKICA: Yes, my darling fiancé. Until a few days ago he'd be visiting several times a day every day, gazing into my eyes like a kitten, whispering sweet nothings in my ear, and painting our future life together in the brightest of colours. And now suddenly he hardly ever comes by, and when he does he is always somehow perplexed and absent-minded, he can hardly speak.

SPASOJE: I tell you, we've got big worries, that's why we can't think about the wedding now. I want the wedding day of my only daughter to be the happiest day of my life. *(He strokes her hair.)* Be a little patient and you'll see everything will be fine.
VUKICA: And on top of all that you bring me auntie-Agnija.
SPASOJE: But it wasn't me who brought her! She bumped into me yesterday exclaiming: "I have to come and see Vukica tomorrow!" I couldn't tell her: "Don't come, Vukica can't stand you."
VUKICA: Well, I can't stand her and that's it!
SPASOJE: But, darling we have to be able to stand her. First of all, she is my cousin, a second cousin, that's true, but she is my cousin, and then she is a wealthy spinster.
VUKICA: So? Is it my fault she never got married?
SPASOJE: I know, but she is wealthy. However, she is thinking of leaving all her money to a charity; all of those old spinsters, you know, they are all diseased with charity, but I think she might think about leaving something to you as well.
VUKICA *(determined and capricious):* I can't stand her!
SPASOJE: I don't understand why you can't stand her? What has she done to you?
VUKICA: She is just unbearable. Can you understand that she never speaks of anything else but the wedding night. Always about that and only about that, and she is so affected, and just keeps sighing.
SPASOJE: Well you should try to understand her, everybody sighs after their ideals.
VUKICA: What kind of an ideal is the wedding night?
SPASOJE: An ideal, my dear girl, is everything that one can't achieve.
VUKICA: So now I have to suffer because she hasn't achieved her ideal!

2. Add ANTA

ANTA: Good day! Good day, miss!

VUKICA: Good day!

SPASOJE: Please, darling, give us a moment, we have to have a talk regarding those worries of ours.

VUKICA: Of course! *(Exits)*

3. ANTA, SPASOJE

SPASOJE: Have you found him?

ANTA: Finally! He is not just a journalist for a particular newspaper, you know, or an owner, so you can't find him so easily.

SPASOJE: What is he then?

ANTA: He is something like a flying journalist; he says he is a publicist. He writes, you know, like that, in an underhanded way.

SPASOJE: That's just what we need! Have you got his name?

ANTA: Yes, I have! Mladen Đoković. They say, nobody can write like him: he is so sharp and so dangerous that he can ruin anyone he takes under his pen. He can turn white into black, and black into white like nobody else.

SPASOJE: Will he come by?

ANTA: Yes, today already.

SPASOJE: You haven't told him why I called him?

ANTA: No way. I've as much as found him, but, to tell you the truth, I'd rather not get involved in anything. You know very well that I've been skipped, so what do I want getting involved with it all?

SPASOJE: Don't you rely too much on being skipped; if we go down, we'll all go down together, and don't you worry you'll get your year too.

ANTA *(startled):* There you go again! Can't you bloody well leave that year alone for once!

SPASOJE: Well I just mention it like that, in passing.

ANTA: Not even in passing, please!

4. Add AGNIJA

AGNIJA *(dressed in youthful attire and made up; she carries a beautiful bouquet of flowers):* Good morning, gentlemen! *(She holds out her hand to Anta and then to Spasoje.)* How come you are the only one at home?
SPASOJE: Oh, no, Vukica is at home as well. *(Goes to Vukica's door)*. Come on, darling, hurry, hurry, auntie-Agnija is here!
ANTA *(having already got up):* I should go really.
SPASOJE: He'll be here today, won't he?
ANTA: Any time now.
SPASOJE: All right, come again some time.
ANTA: I will; goodbye Miss Agnija!
AGNIJA: Goodbye!
ANTA *(exits)*.

5. SPASOJE, AGNIJA

SPASOJE: I wonder what she is doing? Darling?
AGNIJA: Don't call her, I'd like to talk to you.
SPASOJE: What on earth do you have to talk to me about, there's Vukica you can talk to.
AGNIJA: I wanted to ask you about this wedding cancellation. Do you realize that it is very badly perceived out there?
SPASOJE: I don't care how it is perceived! Please, leave that alone, we'll talk about it some other time. Vukica, darling!

6. Add VUKICA

SPASOJE *(when Vukica enters):* Where have you been all this time?
VUKICA: Good morning, auntie-Agnija!
AGNIJA: Good morning, sweetie! *(She kisses her.)* This is for you. *(She gives her the flowers.)*
VUKICA: Thank you.
AGNIJA: Tell me, how are you, are you getting tired of all the excitement yet?

VUKICA: Oh, yes! *(Looking at the flowers.)* Those are very nice flowers!

AGNIJA: I chose them myself at the florist's. I wanted it to look like a particular bouquet I remember.

VUKICA: From your youth, certainly?

AGNIJA: Yes . . . yes . . . from some years ago. I received a bouquet just like this one, and it had a card attached to it which said: "To a flower – flowers."

VUKICA: That's very nice! And what was written on the other side of the card?

AGNIJA: Nothing! Just a name: "Sima Tešić, artillery captain".

VUKICA: Oh, I can imagine, it must be a sweet memory.

AGNIJA: But of course! I still have the stems from that bouquet.

VUKICA: And what did you do, dear auntie, to reward this gift-bearer for his attention?

AGNIJA *(confused, affected)*: What? What could I have done?

VUKICA: Oh, please tell me, do admit it, you must have done something to reward him.

AGNIJA *(confused)*: Well, really . . . I rewarded him with a nice smile. What else can a girl give to her admirer? But let us leave the pleasant memories aside, let's talk about you, about the future. Have you chosen your wedding dress yet?

VUKICA: No, I haven't but I'm not thinking about it now as the wedding has been postponed.

AGNIJA: Well, it's only temporarily postponed, but it will take place, won't it, Spasoje?

SPASOJE *(until then engrossed in some kind of a letter; startled)*: Yes, of course!

AGNIJA: And you should think about the wedding dress well in advance. There are so many fashion magazines around these days; it's very difficult to make up your mind. And then all the materials! Come around, I told you so many times, come round to my place, I've got more than three hundred samples of various materials for wedding dresses. Come and see.

SPASOJE: And what do you need all those samples for?

AGNIJA: Well, I just like choosing the samples, I wanted to have a collection. Why not? Some people collect stamps, some collect old coins, or pipes, or clocks or hunting trophies, why shouldn't I have my own hobby? I collect wedding dress samples, and that's my pastime.

VUKICA: Yes, why do you reproach auntie-Agnija, father? At least she is not collecting cats like auntie-Jovanka.

SPASOJE: I don't reproach her, I just don't understand how she doesn't get bored going to all the shops and asking for pieces of cloths?

AGNIJA: Don't speak like that, Spasoje, there are nice things about it. I go into a shop and I address the oldest shop assistant: "Sir, I would like to see some materials for a wedding dress!" And the shop assistant's face immediately lights up, and he really enjoys serving me, thinking that I'm the happy bride-to-be. And it goes on like that for half an hour. Real pleasure!

SPASOJE: Indeed.

AGNIJA *(to Vukica):* Come on, sweetie, I'd really like to see the underwear and the going away clothes you've prepared.

VUKICA: But I have shown them to you already.

AGNIJA: Never mind, I'd like to see them again. *(Whispering to her)* To tell you the truth, I don't think it's a good idea to wear white pyjamas on the first night; I much prefer the pale blue night-dress.

VUKICA *(desperate, to her father):* You see!

SPASOJE: What?

VUKICA *(confused):* You see, my fiancé is not here yet. *(She looks at the watch on her wrist)* Look at the time, and he is not here yet.

SPASOJE: He'll come. Don't be impatient.

AGNIJA *(embracing Vukica and taking her to the room):* Oh, sweet impatience! Let's go!

VUKICA *(going past her father):* You see!

AGNIJA and VUKICA *(exit)*.

7. ĐOKOVIĆ, SPASOJE

ĐOKOVIĆ *(a robust man, slightly scruffy)*: Good day, sir! I hope I've got the right address?
SPASOJE: And the gentleman is?
ĐOKOVIĆ: I am Mladen Đoković.
SPASOJE: Oh, yes, you are the journalist!?
ĐOKOVIĆ: No, not a journalist, a publicist, sir!
SPASOJE *(gesturing to him to sit down)*: I thought it was all the same.
ĐOKOVIĆ: No, sir. A journalist is tied to a paper, to an editor, to a publisher, I am a freelance writer, I write when I like and what I like: brochures, leaflets, pamphlets and things like that in general.
SPASOJE: Yes, that's just what we need and that's why I wanted to talk to you.
ĐOKOVIĆ: Please!
SPASOJE: They say that you are able to prove in any debate that black is white and white is black.
ĐOKOVIĆ: It is possible to affirm or contest anything, my dear sir, thanks to the power of logic. What else is the philosophy of the old Greeks, Protagoras, Isocrates and Aeschylus about? Its essence is in the premise that every 'yes' contains in itself its 'no', and every 'no' carries in itself its 'yes'. Everything depends on the power of logic.
SPASOJE: And they say you've got that.
ĐOKOVIĆ: Yes, logic is my skill! You see, god gives something to everyone; for example, he gave you money, and he gave me logic. He doesn't give everything to one person and nothing to another. He can't give you both money and logic, can he, because those two things don't go together. He gave me one and you another and he said: There you are, now you trade with what

you've got. You put your logic at Mr. Spasoje's disposal, and he'll put his money at your disposal.
SPASOJE: What do you mean put his money at your disposal?
ĐOKOVIĆ: I mean I'll nicely write up what you need and you'll nicely pay me for it, won't you?
SPASOJE *(holding back):* Well, yes!
ĐOKOVIĆ: So, having in principle agreed on the practicalities, will you please proceed with your requirements and give me all the details. *(He pulls out a pen and paper and gets ready to take notes.)*
SPASOJE: The matter is this: one man died three years ago and we buried him. I was personally at the funeral.
ĐOKOVIĆ: Lord rest his soul.
SPASOJE: Yes, but now we have to prove that he is dead.
ĐOKOVIĆ: Easy! If you could only tell me what style you want that in?
SPASOJE: What do you mean what style?
ĐOKOVIĆ: Do you want it in high style such as: "The departure of an individuum from a living environment is a result of an inevitable process which all natural phenomena are subjected to" or do you just want me to tell him straight: "You've snuffed it, mate".
SPASOJE: Well, this is much clearer.
ĐOKOVIĆ: So I shall tell him: You've snuffed it, mate, and these are the proofs: first, you're not alive.
SPASOJE *(interrupting):* But he is alive.
ĐOKOVIĆ: Who is alive?
SPASOJE: Well, the one that died.
ĐOKOVIĆ: I don't understand?
SPASOJE: So, he actually died as I told you, and we buried him three years ago, but now suddenly he reappeared alive.
ĐOKOVIĆ *(shaking his head):* Hm! Hm! Hm! That is a bit of an unusual case! I've been in a situation where I had to prove that a man who had been dead for a year was alive. It was necessary for

the dead to vote in the local elections, but that's an altogether different matter. It's one thing to have to prove that a dead man is alive, but it's a different thing to have to prove that a living man is dead.

SPASOJE: I know, but what about all the proofs, the death certificate, the funeral, the grave.

ĐOKOVIĆ: The grave? A grave is not a proof of whether the man exists or not. Does he exist?

SPASOJE: Well, he says he exists.

ĐOKOVIĆ: Well, that's it, you see, and we must believe him in this case.

SPASOJE: Well, can't this power of logic of yours prove somehow that he doesn't exist?

ĐOKOVIĆ *(thinking):* Hm, it's a really difficult problem, unless we resort to Einstein's theory.

SPASOJE: What theory is that?

ĐOKOVIĆ: According to Einstein, everything is relative. Therefore, we could argue that this man is only relatively alive.

SPASOJE: Wouldn't it be possible to use some other theory?

ĐOKOVIĆ: OK, let's get onto another theory. You tell me honestly, sir: you don't want this man around? He spoils your plans too much, is that right?

SPASOJE *(embarrassed):* Well, how shall I put it?

ĐOKOVIĆ: You've said it already; I understand. Well, yes, it's difficult to give back what one has inherited already.

SPASOJE *(sighing):* It is!

ĐOKOVIĆ: Fair enough! Now we are out in the open and I understand the whole situation. And if we carefully think about it all, it will be too early to write anything yet. I beg your pardon, that's just my opinion, but if you wish, I shall write. Only, you know, if I write now, that will provoke a response, and if we totally expose the whole thing, you might very quickly end up in court; and it seems to me that you have every reason to avoid the court in this case?

SPASOJE: Well, yes, what do I need the court for.

ĐOKOVIĆ: So, you see, it's better that you do this thing away from the public eye. As far as I'm concerned, it really is not in my favor to give you such advice, for if I wrote something now I could charge you more. As it is, I can only charge you for this piece of advice for the moment, and that'll be one thousand.

SPASOJE *(shocked)*: What!? One thousand for not writing!?

ĐOKOVIĆ: Yes, and that does not include the royalties for my discretion.

SPASOJE: What discretion?

ĐOKOVIĆ: Well, dear sir, now that I've got in on your secret, please tell me, what would prevent me now from publishing a little leaflet saying "The dead have risen, the living are getting ready to bury them again!"

SPASOJE *(petrified)*: You won't do that!?

ĐOKOVIĆ: So, you see how valuable my discretion is, and I ask for no more than a thousand altogether.

SPASOJE: All right, all right, agreed!

ĐOKOVIĆ: Very well, we've got a deal. I have warned you not to mess about with this and not to publicize it yet. OK? Now, on the other hand, you can't just sit around doing nothing, can you? You can do other things –

SPASOJE: Of course!

ĐOKOVIĆ: And in that respect I shall give you another piece of advice.

SPASOJE: Another thousand!?

ĐOKOVIĆ: It could be another two, or three or four . . . but, dear sir, I won't blackmail you, I will be happy with a thousand, which in addition to the other thousand, makes two thousand.

SPASOJE *(sighing)*: Two thousand!

ĐOKOVIĆ: Two, indeed, but listen to me first, and then you'll see that it's worth it. You, the family . . . I presume you are related to the living dead man?

SPASOJE: Yes.

ĐOKOVIĆ: You and the rest of the family should get together and declare this man a lunatic who uses his physical resemblance ... does he look like him?

SPASOJE: A spitting image.

ĐOKOVIĆ: Therefore you announce him mad and send him for a psychiatric investigation. Then you can make relevant arrangements, I don't have to tell you how to do these things, and he will be certified mentally ill. Believe me, in this country it is easier to declare someone mad than sane. And the proof of that, my dear sir, is the fact that I spent three months in a lunatic asylum myself too.

SPASOJE: You?

ĐOKOVIĆ: Yes, just before the local elections I was found mad, and then just after the elections I was found sane again.

SPASOJE *(worried):* Yes, it is worth considering this suggestion of yours.

ĐOKOVIĆ: Of course it is, and I hope you agree now that my price is reasonable?

SPASOJE *(remembers):* Oh, yes! *(With great remorse he takes two thousand out of his wallet and gives the money to him.)*

ĐOKOVIĆ *(getting up):* Thank you very much, sir, and whenever you need me I am at your disposal, whether you need some writing done or some good advice.

SPASOJE: Thank you!

ĐOKOVIĆ: I won't take anymore of your time. Goodbye, sir!

SPASOJE: Goodbye.

ĐOKOVIĆ *(exits).*

8. AGNIJA, VUKICA, SPASOJE

AGNIJA *(coming out of Vukica's room):* Such taste, such style! Every little detail has been chosen with remarkable discernment, indeed.

VUKICA: Now, you can't say I haven't shown you everything?

AGNIJA: Oh, yes, everything, everything, everything! I say, dear, you will be such an exceptional bride, so well prepared. And you've prepared it all on your own, you wouldn't even let me help you.
VUKICA: I didn't want to bother you.
AGNIJA: But why, why, when you know that wedding preparations are my favorite pastime.
SPASOJE: Well, we will call you, there are a lot more preparations to make, and a lot of time left.
AGNIJA: Of course there is a lot of time left, when the wedding has been postponed.
SPASOJE: Well, why do you insist so much on this postponement!
VUKICA: Please, auntie, don't even mention this to me. *(She goes to a table and finds something to do there).*
SPASOJE: Yes, it's best not to mention it.
AGNIJA *(goes to Spasoje, confidentially):* You know Spasoje, I can't tell you in front of her, but people are saying some strange things out there.
SPASOJE: And do you know what kind of things they are saying about you?
AGNIJA *(shocked):* Oooh!
SPASOJE: If you don't, I do, but I never came to tell you what they are saying about you, so you don't need to tell me what they are saying about me either.
AGNIJA: I meant it with the best of intentions.
SPASOJE: Not even with the best of intentions.
AGNIJA: Very well, very well, never again! *(Goes to Vukica)* Don't forget to call me, darling, when that cream dress is finished, I'm dying to see what it looks like.
VUKICA: Certainly!
AGNIJA *(kisses her, then stretches her hand to Spasoje):* Well, do forgive me, Spasoje! Goodbye! *(Exits).*

9. VUKICA, SPASOJE

VUKICA *(having seen Agnija off, drops into an armchair exhausted):* Ah!

SPASOJE: You are right: ah!

VUKICA: I absolutely can't bear it.

SPASOJE: It's not easy for me either, but what else can I do –

VUKICA: If you only knew what kind of questions she asks, it's terrible.

SPASOJE: Darling, I'm expecting the minister's brother. We have some serious matters to discuss so I'd like to ask you to leave us on our own when he comes.

VUKICA: Of course, you know that I never bother you in such situations. And anyway I've got a lot of writing to do. *(She gets up to go, but at that moment the door opens and Ljubomir enters. She stops.)*

10. Add LJUBOMIR

VUKICA: Oh, what a surprise! What a surprise!

SPASOJE: It's very good that you came as I've completely run out of excuses on your behalf before your fiancée.

LJUBOMIR *(having kissed Vukica's hand and shook Spasoje's hand):* Have I made a big faux pas?

VUKICA *(to Spasoje):* Do you hear him, daddy, he calls it a faux pas!? *(To Ljubomir)* That's not a faux pas, it's a crime. To neglect your fiancée as you do, to get your fiancée used to two or three visits a day and suddenly stop coming, to get your fiancée used to tender words and love promises and suddenly slip into academic absent-mindedness, you will agree that that's nothing short of a big crime!

LJUBOMIR: For goodness' sake, father, why do you complain that you can't excuse me any longer when you very well know why that is the case?

SPASOJE: I tell her, I tell her we've got big worries at the moment, worries that concern all of us, but they will pass, I tell her they will pass. I never go in great detail. And why should I?

LJUBOMIR: I wouldn't like to stay in my fiancée's bad books.

SPASOJE: You know what, you go over there into her room and defend yourself; fiancés can always defend themselves better in private.

LJUBOMIR: You are right. *(Takes Vukica's hand and they go to her room.)*

11. SPASOJE, SOFIJA

SPASOJE *(rings a bell)*.

SOFIJA *(enters):* Yes, sir?

SPASOJE: Sofija, I'm expecting a certain gentleman. When he comes, can you please make sure that no one interrupts us. Whoever comes, tell them I'm not in.

SOFIJA: Of course. *(She goes but comes back straight away)* Mr. and Mrs. Novaković.

SPASOJE: Oh, they? You can let them in.

SOFIJA *(lets them in and exits)*.

12. NOVAKOVIĆ, RINA, SPASOJE

NOVAKOVIĆ: Good afternoon.

SPASOJE: Good afternoon! *(They shake hands)* What a surprise!

RINA: Not a surprise at all. I promised Vukica to come round so we can go shopping together.

SPASOJE: Oh, yes, she very much trusts your taste, only –

NOVAKOVIĆ: And just imagine, dear sir, now I have to go shopping too.

SPASOJE: How come?

NOVAKOVIĆ: My wife wouldn't cross the threshold on her own.

RINA: Imagine if I bump into him, I wouldn't know what to do.

SPASOJE: Well, you will both be spared the hassle. I have postponed the wedding and all the preparations. There'll be enough time for that. But you are always welcome, Vukica will be very happy to see you.

RINA: Let's go to see her, then. *(She wants to go.)*

SPASOJE: Just a moment. I wanted to ask you. You said you would see your solicitor for a consultation?

NOVAKOVIĆ: I've seen him.

SPASOJE: And?

NOVAKOVIĆ: He says that our marriage is indeed annulled with the re-appearance of the first husband, and that my wife has to return to him.

RINA: That would be terrible, that would be a most cruel punishment!

NOVAKOVIĆ: The solicitor says the only solution would be if the first husband sought divorce, got divorced and if I then remarried my wife. And to tell you the truth, I intend to make such a proposal to him.

SPASOJE: To who?

NOVAKOVIĆ: To the deceased.

SPASOJE: To ask him to seek divorce!?

NOVAKOVIĆ: Well, yes, why would he need a wife who doesn't love him?

RINA: I couldn't survive it if I had to go back to him.

SPASOJE: Wait a minute! It's not so simple as it seems. In order to seek divorce he has to be alive.

RINA: Well, he is alive!

SPASOJE: He is alive, I know he is, but we mustn't admit that. Do you know what it would mean if we recognized him as legally alive? That would mean that we would all end up in court; all of us god-fearing and innocent people would have to suffer the humiliation of standing in the dock.

RINA: You know how it is, Mr. Blagojević, when the ship is sinking, everyone fights for their own survival.

SPASOJE: Ah, that's how you see it? Each for themselves? All right then, let everyone fight for themselves. But don't be sorry if I find my rescue first.

NOVAKOVIĆ: You seem to be threatening us, Mr. Spasoje?

SPASOJE: I am not threatening anyone, but you say 'when the ship is sinking', and you are forgetting that that ship will pull half a million of your own cash with it.

NOVAKOVIĆ *(startled):* You don't mean?

SPASOJE: I do mean, yes I do. You're forgetting that in this whole affair your marriage is not the most important thing.

NOVAKOVIĆ: I'm not forgetting, but –

SPASOJE: Well, if you are not forgetting, than you must be patient. I, for example, have an important meeting today with one very prominent gentleman. I very much hope that he will be of great assistance to us.

NOVAKOVIĆ: Well, of course, we will be patient.

SPASOJE: You go now to Vukica's room; her fiancé is in there, and you have a good time, I'll take care of your worries. Please. *(To Rina, following her.)* I implore you, madam, please exercise your influence over Vukica and calm her down; she is very upset that the wedding has been postponed.

RINA: Oh, yes, yes, of course!

RINA and NOVAKOVIĆ *(exit to Vukica's room).*

13. SOFIJA, SPASOJE

SOFIJA *(enters):* One gentleman to see you, sir.

SPASOJE: Did he say who he was?

SOFIJA: I think it's the gentleman you were expecting.

SPASOJE: Oh, yes! Please, let him in immediately!

SOFIJA *(exits).*

14. PAVLE MARIĆ, SPASOJE

SPASOJE *(when he sees Marić at the door, unpleasantly surprised):* Oh, it's you?

PAVLE: Does my appearance still take you by surprise?

SPASOJE *(slightly confused):* I didn't expect you.

PAVLE: I felt the need to talk to you in person once again, before I proceed with particular action.

SPASOJE: I don't see what we have to talk about.

PAVLE: If you don't see what we could talk about, I see much less point in it myself. I only wanted to avoid scandal.

SPASOJE: If you wanted to avoid scandal, why did you come back at all, why didn't you stay where you were?

PAVLE: I did intend to stay there anyway. I only came back to arrange the management of my estate and sort out certain relationships.

SPASOJE: As regards the management of your estate, that has been arranged.

PAVLE: Oh, yes, I see, you have arranged it well for yourself, but it is necessary that I arrange it from my end as well.

SPASOJE: Please tell me, since we are already talking like this, face to face, would you be prepared to discuss the situation honestly and openly?

PAVLE: Why not?

SPASOJE: Then, please sit down. *(He offers him a cigarette.)*

PAVLE *(sits in an armchair looking at it):* That's the armchair from my study.

SPASOJE: Oh, yes, will you say that these cigarettes are yours as well? *(Lights a cigarette; sits down.)* Would you like to reveal your intentions to me, but honestly? I mean, could you tell me what you intend to do and which actions you intend to take?

PAVLE: I will tell you, why not? There is nothing in my intentions that I should hide. For example, as regards Mr. Milan Novaković who dispossessed me of my wife, and as regards my wife, who so deeply offended me –

SPASOJE: You will seek divorce, I know that already.

PAVLE: No, I won't seek divorce, I'll leave it open like that; I'll let them live in a marriage without a legal basis.

SPASOJE: You'll leave them to fret about their marital happiness?
PAVLE: Are they happy, really?
SPASOJE: That's what they say.
PAVLE: Well, why should I spoil that?
SPASOJE: And regarding the one about the ten thousand dinars?
PAVLE: That's least important, I'll think about it later.
SPASOJE: Well, you are right, he hasn't really robbed you but me.
PAVLE: How do you mean 'you'?
SPASOJE: Well, after your death, the court determined your estate and invited all the debtors to come up with what they owed. If he had come up with his debt, that amount would have gone to me as an inheritor of the estate.
PAVLE: All right, I'll leave him to you and you can pursue him if you like. It really is not fair that he should damage you like that.
SPASOJE: Fine, and . . . *(he can't find the right words)* . . . I mean . . . How shall I put it? And what position do you take towards me?
PAVLE: That matter is most simple and clear. You've inherited my estate because the court was led to believe that I was dead. As I am actually alive, the inheritance will be reverted and you will vacate this house as well as hand back the ownership of everything else.
SPASOJE: Well, really!
PAVLE: That is, of course, if I encounter your good will and collaboration; if not, then I'll pursue it another way. I shall accuse you of being a false successor. My solicitor is already gathering information on all the false documents and false witnesses you brought into court to prove that you are my close relative, although we are only related, and you know this very well, because your mother married some distant relative of my

mother's. Then, of course, the case will acquire a completely different standing.

SPASOJE *(worried, thinking):* Hm! So that's what you intend to do?

PAVLE: Yes, it is!

SPASOJE: But, sir, to say the least, that would be a crime. Do you know that I am a respectable and important member of the society, do you know that –

PAVLE *(interrupting):* I beg your pardon, I don't mean to take away your respectability, only your estate; I leave your respectability to you.

SPASOJE: Please tell me sir, are all dead people as naive as you are, or are you a special case! What else is respectability if not estate? If you take away the estate, you've taken away my respectability.

PAVLE: Yes, actually, I remember: before you appropriated this estate you were a nobody.

SPASOJE: Of course I was a nobody.

PAVLE: Yes, yes, I remember.

SPASOJE: And now you understand why I dislike your intentions and why I can't recognize you as a living man.

PAVLE: Yes, I understand, I do, but what can we do, it is difficult to find any kind of solution which would be suitable for you.

SPASOJE: Oh, but there is something, and if by any chance you'd come straight to me, the matter would have been resolved well before now.

PAVLE: Oh, I'm very curious?

SPASOJE: We said we would talk openly. So I'll tell you. I've got a very good plan where neither you nor I would suffer any losses.

PAVLE: Let's hear it?

SPASOJE: First of all you should seek divorce from your wife. We'll all help you; I can give you enough material for three divorce petitions.
PAVLE: And then?
SPASOJE: Then, when you get divorced, you will ask my daughter's hand in marriage, and I shall give it to you. Why are you looking at me like that? You'll ask for my daughter's hand in marriage, I shall give it to you and I'll give you the estate that used to belong to you in dowry.
PAVLE: A very interesting proposition; that way I would become my own son-in-law.
SPASOJE: That way both you and I can keep both the estate and respectability.
PAVLE: And in that case you would recognize me as a living man?
SPASOJE: Yes, in such an exceptional case.
PAVLE: I don't understand only one thing, you offer me your daughter who is already engaged?
SPASOJE: Yes, so you can see how great my sacrifice is! Imagine, I could have a son-in-law who is a university professor, a celebrated scientist, and a great scientific writer, and I am prepared to sacrifice him for you; you must agree that it's quite generous of me.
PAVLE: I think that the sacrifice is so much greater given that these two young people are obviously in love, and you are prepared to ruin it for them.
SPASOJE: Well, yes, that too!
PAVLE: For if you lost the estate that you promised to your son-in-law in dowry, he would certainly stay engaged to your daughter anyway?
SPASOJE *(a little confused):* Well, yes . . . certainly, for he is such an honourable man, believe me, he is such a rare man of quality.

PAVLE: I believe you! And if that 'rare man of quality' lost his professorship and the name of a great scientist, your daughter would certainly stay engaged to him?
SPASOJE: Well, I'm not so sure about that.
PAVLE: Then you are in a really difficult predicament for that can very easily happen to you.
SPASOJE: What can happen to me?
PAVLE: Well that . . . that you lose your son-in-law, not because he would leave you but because your daughter would leave him.
SPASOJE: I don't understand.
PAVLE: Hasn't your son-in-law ever told you anything about the crime he committed against me?
SPASOJE: Not a word! What crime, what crime are you talking about?
PAVLE: I can't find another word for his behaviour.
SPASOJE: Does he owe you a lot?
PAVLE: Much more than you can imagine.
SPASOJE: What on earth did he do with all that money?
PAVLE: It's not money, it's something else that cannot be estimated in monetary terms.
SPASOJE: I don't understand.
PAVLE: Your son-in-law should have acquainted you with this because you should know the entire complexity of your predicament at the moment.
SPASOJE: My predicament? Why my predicament?
PAVLE: I'll tell you why. Your son-in-law was once a protégé of mine; I helped him along from school days into adulthood; he acquired my affection and my trust. Just before I took my journey I entrusted the young gentleman with a manuscript for safekeeping . . . a scientific thesis, which I had worked on very hard for seven years. And as soon as he saw me off to the cemetery, and made sure that I was dead, he came home after the funeral and printed my thesis under his own name.

SPASOJE *(losing his balance with shock):* What? That publication!?!?
PAVLE: Yes, that publication on the basis of which he has obtained his professorship and the status of a scientist, on the basis of which he has become a director of this Illyria of yours, on the basis of which he became your son-in-law and on the basis of which you have promised him all the dowry.
SPASOJE *(sighs with despair, sinks in an armchair and covers his face in his hands; after a pause he lifts his head and without confidence, quietly):* Can you prove this?
PAVLE: Yes, of course!
SPASOJE *(gathering himself together):* That means you are quite resolved?
PAVLE: Yes, I am resolved to go the right way about it.
SPASOJE *(thinking for a moment, then with bravado, gets up):* Are you aware that you could encounter obstacles even if you went the right way.
PAVLE: We will deal with those obstacles in court.
SPASOJE: You think so? *(Walking back and forth, agitated, wants to say something but can't think of anything)* I just don't know what to say.
PAVLE: I don't think anything else can be said on the matter, both you and I are sufficiently informed!
SPASOJE: Well, yes, I'm informed, of course I am –
PAVLE: Then there is no need for any further discussion. I've kept you too long as it is anyway; goodbye cousin!
SPASOJE *(hardly audible):* Goodbye!
PAVLE *(exits)*.

15. LJUBOMIR, SPASOJE

SPASOJE *(looking after him in utter confusion and frustration; then goes to the door of Vukica's room):* Ljubomir, Ljubomir!
LJUBOMIR *(enters)*.
SPASOJE: Marić was here, he's just left.

LJUBOMIR: What did he want?
SPASOJE: He told me some very strange things, very strange.
LJUBOMIR: Probably something interesting from the world beyond the grave.
SPASOJE: No, something from this world. Your scientific name and status: he claims that you stole them.
LJUBOMIR: I don't understand how one can steal one's name or status, one's status is not a cigarette case or an umbrella.
SPASOJE: It's not. But he claims that he has a proof that he gave you his manuscript for safekeeping and that as soon as you returned from the cemetery, you printed it in your own name.
LJUBOMIR *(cynically):* What else should I have done, put it in the grave with him?
SPASOJE: So, you don't deny it, you actually admit it.
LJUBOMIR: And you find that it is a crime? Believe me, it's not, for everybody takes everything they can from a dead man. Somebody takes his wife, somebody takes his work and somebody his house and the whole estate. Catch what you can.
SPASOJE *(bites his lip):* Well, yes, but this is different. On the basis of your catch you became a university professor; and on the basis of your professorship I gave you my daughter and a big dowry –
LJUBOMIR: It's all the same, there is no difference at all. On the basis of your catch you became a wealthy man, and on the basis of your wealth you looked for and found a son-in-law with a status.
SPASOJE: You are so impertinent, you forget all about the dutiful respect you owe the father of your fiancée.
LJUBOMIR: Oh, no, father, I never forget about due respect; but I think this is strictly a business conversation.
SPASOJE: Well yes, a business conversation, of course. *(Remembers)* And Illyria?
LJUBOMIR: What about Illyria?

SPASOJE: Well you are the director. The company has an international standing. If they take away your professorship, if you lose your reputation?
LJUBOMIR: That would be a much smaller loss than if you lose the house you mortgaged to the government.
SPASOJE *(dejected)*: Well yes, that's true! *(Sighs)* That's true! *(He keeps quiet, his head down.)*
LJUBOMIR *(after a pause)*: Do you have anything else to discuss with me?
SPASOJE: No, nothing else.
LJUBOMIR: In that case, if you need me, I shall be with my fiancée. *(Exits.)*

16. SPASOJE, SOFIJA

SPASOJE *(sitting in an armchair, deep in thought)*.
SOFIJA *(entering)*: A gentleman to see you, sir.
SPASOJE *(perks up with hope)*: Ah, that's him. *(With great hurry)* Let him in immediately, let him in.
SOFIJA *(exits letting Mr. Đurić in)*.

17. ĐURIĆ, SPASOJE

ĐURIĆ: Good afternoon, sir!
SPASOJE *(all blissful)*: Good afternoon, Mr. Đurić! You've come just at the right moment, at the right moment! Please, please, sit down!
ĐURIĆ: So? I'm curious how far you've got with the matter?
SPASOJE: Not very far. With that man you cannot get anywhere the nice way.
ĐURIĆ: You've talked?
SPASOJE: Yes, he was here earlier, he came as if god sent; we talked in great depth and quite openly.
ĐURIĆ: What did he say?
SPASOJE: Not only does he refuse any proposition of a compromise, he even intensifies his attacks.

ĐURIĆ: He's threatening you?

SPASOJE: That he's threatening to take my estate, that's nothing new, but now he is threatening my son-in-law.

ĐURIĆ: What does he say?

SPASOJE: You won't believe it; he says: I'll topple him, I'll take away his professorship. He wants to portray him as a false scientist. Please! That man claims that he wrote the thesis which my son-in-law then printed under his own name.

ĐURIĆ: Oh, that's a big accusation, and at the worst moment possible. The matter of Illyria is being discussed at the cabinet as we speak; any moment now we could get the concession, and that means millions, millions!

SPASOJE *(entranced):* Millions!

ĐURIĆ: And at such a moment when we can already see all those millions –

SPASOJE *(continues):* A bully comes along to take away my estate and my house, which is mortgaged for the cause, and he wants to topple my son-in-law! I mean the director of my company.

ĐURIĆ: We should think it through carefully.

SPASOJE: I ask you, please, can you think on my behalf, I am not able to think any longer.

ĐURIĆ: You see, one shouldn't just approach this thing from one's own narrow point of view, as you do. The matter demands to be approached from a much broader, shall we say, from the perspective of the state. Can't you see that within this whole phenomenon there is a system, a system with destructive intentions? That man has been living in some secretive corner of Europe, working for some company as he says, but I would venture a guess that he might in fact have been working for some subversive international unit. Who knows what he has learnt over there, who knows what kind of ideas have entered his head and affected his powers of reason? Can't you see what he is up to? He attacks everything that is holy. He intends to destroy everything that makes up the basis of a society? Start from the beginning, please, and look at what he is doing. He wants to destroy a marriage –

SPASOJE: And a happy marriage, at that!

ĐURIĆ: And marriage, my dear sir, is one of the first pillars of society. What else . . . he wants to rob someone of their estate, a private estate!

SPASOJE: That is, my estate!

ĐURIĆ: And finally, he wants to demean, dethrone and trample down an authority. In his destructive rage he wants to take down a respectable scientist.

SPASOJE: Oh, my god, I'm only just realising it now, only now can I really see the real intentions of this man!

ĐURIĆ: Oh, yes, yes, sir, that's how we should look at this matter. And when we look at it this way, we can see that this phenomenon contains a danger of broader significance.

SPASOJE: A danger . . . of course, it's a danger!

ĐURIĆ: And this worry of yours, sir, cannot and must not remain a private matter; this should be the worry of an entire society, the worry of the state, if you'd like.

SPASOJE: Well, yes, of course, I'd like! Let the state deal with this worry!

ĐURIĆ *(a thinking pause):* Now, you tell me: should we in such a case give way to the legal system to deal with it? Is the legal system able to see through the apparently legal exterior of those destructive forces?

SPASOJE: No!

ĐURIĆ: For what will the legal system do? This is what: This is my rafter and I ask for it back. The legal system such as it is has no alternative but to say, "it is your rafter, take it back!" But what if this rafter supports the whole house, so now, in order for you to have your rafter back, the whole house has to fall apart? What is bigger, what is more important, I ask you: the rafter or the house?

SPASOJE: The house!

ĐUIRĆ: Exactly! And now imagine Illyria as a house, for it is one big organization of great importance, and then suddenly somebody comes along and says: give me my rafter. Yes, your rafter, but if we pull your rafter out, the whole of Illyria falls on its head!

SPASOJE: Terrible!

ĐURIĆ: And in addition, if . . . have you got a telephone by any chance?

SPASOJE: There it is at your hand.

ĐURIĆ *(picks up the phone and looks for a number):* Hello, hello . . . Is this the cabinet? Is it you Mr. Marković? This is Đurić. So? *(Having heard something, his face lights up with joy.)* Thank you! Thank you, very much! *(He puts the phone down and goes to Spasoje with his arms open.)* Illyria! Illyria! *(Embraces him tightly.)*

SPASOJE: Yes?

ĐURIĆ: Yes!

SPASOJE: Agreed?

ĐURIĆ: Yes!

SPASOJE *(falls into his embrace):* Illyria! Millions! *(Suddenly he remembers)* And the rafter?

ĐURIĆ: What rafter?

SPASOJE: The one that can be pulled out to destroy the house?

ĐURIĆ: Don't you worry; we are safe now. We'll sort that out, come round later today! I'm off to the Ministry; I want to see the ministerial signatures with my own eyes. You come by my place later today, and I'll figure something out till then, or should I say: I already have a plan; don't worry! Goodbye! *(Exits).*

SPASOJE: Goodbye. *(Follows him to the door.)*

18. SPASOJE, RINA, NOVAKOVIĆ, LJUBOMIR, VUKICA

SPASOJE *(returning from the door, rubs his hands with pleasure, whispering):* Illyria! Illyria! *(Goes to Vukica's door.)* Children, ladies and gentlemen, over here, please!
ALL *(entering):* What is it?
SPASOJE *(joyful):* Illyria! Illyria! Illyria!

19. Add ANTA

ANTA *(runs in out of breath):* Good afternoon! Ladies, gentlemen, an important announcement! Does anyone here have heart problems? *(Goes to the door, to Sofija.)* Five glasses of water, please! The news is, ladies and gentlemen, very, very good, but I have to start from a great distance, just in case –
SPASOJE: You want to tell us that we've got the concession for Illyria?
ANTA *(disappointed):* So you know? *(Goes to the door.)* Sofija, no need for the water!
SPASOJE: Yes, ladies and gentlemen, we've got the millions, that is, we've got the concession. Come on, come on, everybody, let me embrace you.
ANTA *(runs to his embrace).*
SPASOJE *(pushes Anta):* Not you; shareholders only . . . let me embrace you, brothers and sisters, shareholders. *(He embraces as many as he can, shouting.)* Illyria! Illyria!

CURTAIN

ACT 3

Spasoje's study.

1. SPASOJE, SOFIJA

SPASOJE *(standing next to a desk, opening his mail).*
SOFIJA *(brings a letter in).*
SPASOJE *(taking it):* Who from?
SOFIJA: I don't know, a boy's brought it in.
SPASOJE *(opening the letter, reading it and frowning; reads it again, muttering):* Of course! I knew it! Of course I knew it! *(To Sofija)* Is the boy still here?
SOFIJA: Yes, he is waiting for a reply.
SPASOJE: Well, of course he is waiting for a reply, of course he is, and that means I have to reply, doesn't it?
SOFIJA: I don't know, sir.
SPASOJE: Well, of course, who else can reply but me? I have to reply; I may not like it, but I have to reply. *(He takes 500 out of his wallet, puts the money in an envelope and seals it).* There, give him the reply since I have to reply.
SOFIJA *(takes the letter and leaves, stops at the door):* A gentleman to see you, sir.
SPASOJE: Who?
SOFIJA: I don't know, I've never seen him before.
SPASOJE: Let him in!
SOFIJA *(withdraws letting Mile in).*

2. SPASOJE, MILE

MILE *(carrying a leather bag under his arm, bows and hands out a letter).*
SPASOJE *(opening the letter):* Another letter! Goodness, can't breathe for the letters this morning! *(Reading the signature)* Oh, this is from Mrs. Rina Novaković!
MILE: Yes, the lady has sent me to you.

SPASOJE *(having read the letter)*: Ah, I see? Well, glad to meet you, please, please sit down, young man.

MILE *(sits down)*.

SPASOJE: And you are, the lady writes, a clerk at the Petrović Solicitors'.

MILE: Yes!

SPASOJE: And certain Pavle Marić has approached Mr. Petrović to represent him.

MILE: Yes, to start court proceedings against you.

SPASOJE *(startled)*: Against me!? How do you mean against me!? Why against me!? You seem to be closely acquainted with the matter?

MILE: Yes I'm working on the case.

SPASOJE *(unsettled)*: What are you doing? How are you working on it? Please, tell me, what is going on? He is suing me, you say? OK, let him sue, but why me? Please tell me that, why me?

MILE: Not only you, he has lodged four petitions.

SPASOJE *(offering him a cigarette)*: Four petitions?

MILE: He is suing you for using false evidence in court in appropriation of his property. He demands return of his property and charges you on criminal grounds.

SPASOJE: Oh, really! Criminal grounds? And the other three?

MILE: One against Milan Novaković for adultery and an intrusion upon marriage.

SPASOJE: Yes, I thought so; the third?

MILE: The third against the university professor, Ljubomir Protić, for the theft of a manuscript and publication of the same under his name!

SPASOJE: Well, does he ever have enough of it! And the fourth?

MILE: Against some Anta Milosavljević for perjury.

SPASOJE: So he hasn't skipped him either? And you, I mean . . . what did I want to say . . . so are these charges really serious?

MILE: Actually, I have to say, when my boss looked at the material he exclaimed: "Oh, I'll sort them all out like a bag of worms!"

SPASOJE: Sort who out, what worms?

MILE: Well, you!

SPASOJE: What does he have to sort me out for, and why sort me out, please! Like worms.

MILE: He means, metaphorically.

SPASOJE: I don't like it even metaphorically. And anyway, you tell me, please, has he submitted his case?

MILE: No, he hasn't, he is just working on it at the moment, and then I'll type it all up.

SPASOJE: Very good! Very good! You will be typing it up, then! And you could kind of procrastinate with this typing, couldn't you? We could do with a bit of procrastination in this.

MILE: Oh, yes, yes of course, I have already given my word to Mrs. Novaković that I shall procrastinate.

SPASOJE: Very good! Very good! Believe me, dear young man, we shall be very grateful and we shall make sure that we show you our gratitude somehow.

MILE: I was saying to Mrs. Novaković, I would be very happy with, say, a position in your company Illyria. You will, I presume, need some clerical staff?

SPASOJE: Of course! And your qualifications are?

MILE: Yes . . . well, I've got . . . I've got an incomplete baccalaureate; I've got an incomplete mercantile apprenticeship; some incomplete technical training and an incomplete law degree.

SPASOJE: Generally . . . incomplete? Well, anyway, what do you need it for, your best qualification is your acquaintance with Mrs. Novaković.

MILE: That is, you understand, quite an accidental acquaintance.

SPASOJE: Well, of course it's accidental, that's what I thought anyway. So, I can very gladly promise you a position in the company; only of course after we actually open. That won't be very soon, but as soon as we open.

MILE: And in the meantime?

SPASOJE: In the meantime? In the meantime, patience!

MILE: Yes, certainly; only you know, I have a very modest salary at the solicitor's, and life is very expensive.

SPASOJE: Oh, yes! Now I understand. You would obviously like a reward for your favor?

MILE: Oh, goodness, no; not at all! I only do it out of respect towards Mrs. Novaković. It would be different if you offered me a small loan, that would be quite acceptable, but a reward would be an insult.

SPASOJE: And what would be the amount constituting this insult?

MILE: You mean the loan?

SPASOJE: Yes, that's what I mean.

MILE: I never ask for more than what I really need. At the moment I would need about five hundred.

SPASOJE *(taking the money reluctantly out of his pocket)*: That's just as much as I can give you at the moment. *(Gives him the money.)*

MILE *(taking the money)*: But, please, Mrs. Novaković mustn't know anything about this.

SPASOJE: Of course. I mustn't know what you and Mrs. Novaković know, Mrs. Novaković mustn't know what you and I know. In mathematics, I think, this is called the rule of the three.

MILE *(laughing)*: Yes, yes! So, I shall keep you informed about the state of affairs at the solicitor's. *(Goes.)*

SPASOJE *(following him)*: And please, procrastinate, procrastinate as much as possible.

MILE: I am at your disposal, sir! *(Exits.)*

3. ANTA, SPASOJE

SPASOJE *(reading Rina's letter again and smiling)*.

ANTA *(at the door):* Here I am!
SPASOJE: Have you found it?
ANTA: Yes, I have, of course!
SPASOJE: Is it the way I wanted it?
ANTA *(hands over a small envelope):* There!
SPASOJE *(taking a photograph out of the envelope):* Yes, very good! How on earth did you find it!
ANTA: Don't ask, it wasn't easy. I went to all the photo-shops, the ones that do passport photographs, and I spent ages roaming through all those boxes of photographs, and finally, somehow, I found it.
SPASOJE: Very good!
ANTA *(sitting down):* But I was thinking . . . such a big house and you couldn't find a single photo of his anywhere around.
SPASOJE: There were some, but I need this passport format.
ANTA: Also, on the way I was looking around for commercial premises and office-space for Illyria. I've found a couple of premises but with only two rooms each.
SPASOJE: That's too small, we'll need three or four rooms only for the clerical staff.
ANTA: And you will have a lot of clerical staff?
SPASOJE: Oh, yes, there'll be a lot of work to do.
ANTA: Well, won't there be some work for me to do there, then?
SPASOJE: You don't have the money, you see, and money's very important. There you are, had you not swallowed those ten thousand, you could've bought shares with that money –
ANTA: Well, I don't have to be a share-holder.
SPASOJE: What else?
ANTA: Well, some kind of a position. I am the only unemployed pensioner in this country, and you can't say I'm not capable.
SPASOJE: You are capable, I can't say you aren't, and you are always ready to run around when necessary, but to tell you the

truth, you would be a bit unsuitable for employment in such a company.

ANTA: Why?

SPASOJE: Well . . . because of that thing.

ANTA: Which thing?

SPASOJE: Because of your perjury.

ANTA: Oh, yes, that's right, you are right there, you and I are not the most suitable ones for such a company.

SPASOJE: You, you are unsuitable, and that has nothing to do with me.

ANTA: Well, I mean, you know, given those forged certificates and false witnesses.

SPASOJE *(angrily):* I told you once and for all not to mention that anymore.

ANTA: Well, why do you mention it to me?

SPASOJE: I am one thing, and you are quite another. You lied under oath, and so what? Who and what are you now!? A nobody; you've got just as much money as you need for your tram ticket, and that's your capital. It would've been different if you'd made those ten thousand that you swallowed into a hundred thousand, and those hundred into two hundred, and four hundred and so on! That's different. Had you done that, I would have taken my hat off to you and never mentioned any perjury. What is a perjury when you've a capital of eight hundred thousand? The whole world would've taken their hat off, and forgotten the perjury.

ANTA: That's true, you can see that the whole world is taking their hat off to you.

SPASOJE: They are, of course they are, and that's the difference between you and me.

ANTA: All right, that's all right; but I thought, you see, you might also need some people like me in the company.

SPASOJE: We might need people like you, but let me tell you, you are not lucky enough, there you are, you are just not a lucky man.
ANTA: And why not?
SPASOJE: Well, for example, you found me that publicist!
ANTA: And?
SPASOJE: And he robbed me of two thousand dinars the day before yesterday, and look at what he says today. *(He pulls a letter out of his pocket and reads.)* "Dear Sir, I've found out from reliable sources that soon all papers will be reporting the matter, in great detail and at great length. They have got the material from the very person who, in your opinion, is not alive. If the papers publish this they will rob the money from my hand, or should I say, they'll take away the bread from my mouth. To avoid this, I must either write a pamphlet to be released tomorrow afternoon or I can keep quiet, which means a great sacrifice on my part, and sacrifice nowadays is a very expensive affair. I would, in all modesty, be very happy with a thousand dinars." There!
ANTA: And what did you do?
SPASOJE: I cheated on him. I sent him five hundred.
ANTA: Would that be enough for the sacrifice?
SPASOJE: Of course it would be enough, what else? You would sacrifice yourself for two hundred, so why wouldn't he for five.
ANTA: Well, what he says about the papers is true, I've heard it as well.
SPASOJE: What have you heard?
ANTA: I've heard that Marić called all the journalists and –
SPASOJE: And you haven't heard that he called the solicitors?
ANTA: Why solicitors?
SPASOJE: He lodged a case, he's suing you.
ANTA: Why me?
SPASOJE: For perjury.
ANTA: Why only me, isn't he suing anyone else?

SPASOJE: He's suing all the rest of us, but not on criminal grounds. He's suing one for taking his wife, another for taking his money, but those are not criminal charges. He's suing you for perjury, and that's at least a year in prison.
ANTA *(annoyed):* I know, you told me. How many times have you told me already? *(Worried.)*
SPASOJE: As you can see he hasn't skipped you.
ANTA: No, and he could have, really.
SPASOJE: He could've, of course he could've; he could've skipped me too, but there you are, he didn't!
ANTA *(scratching his head):* To hell with it, I really don't feel like going to prison.
SPASOJE: I don't feel like going either, my friend! You think it's easy? This year I'm off to Carlsbad, this year I'm off to Bled, and this year . . . off to prison. I don't feel like it, either!
ANTA: So what shall we do now?
SPASOJE: We'll have to work hard. I'll deal with the court, and you deal with the papers. Go to them straightaway, see everybody from the editor to the printer, tell them to be patient, tell them to wait just for another 24 hours, and tomorrow, they'll get some truly sensational material. Go tell them, and as soon as you're done, report back to me.
ANTA *(getting up to go):* And you know . . . this thing with the court?,,, I really wouldn't like to have anything to do with it.
SPASOJE: I told you, I'm going to deal with that, I've put it in motion already.

4. Add AGNIJA

AGNIJA: Good afternoon, everyone. Oh, it's you dear Mr. Anta, I'm so glad to see you. I was going to try and find you anyway, I've got to tell you . . . I've heard a completely different version of what you told me the other day.
ANTA: It might be, it might be, but that doesn't change anything.

AGNIJA: Basically, it is not true that the late Mr. Marić had a birthmark above his left lip.

ANTA: OK, I accept it, he didn't; only please excuse me this time, I really haven't got the time to chat, I've got some very important business to attend to. Isn't that so Spasoje? I've got some very important business, haven't I?

SPASOJE: Yes, yes! You must go this moment!

ANTA *(to Agnija):* Please, excuse me! *(Exits.)*

5. AGNIJA, SPASOJE

AGNIJA: And I have to talk to you too, Spasoje.

SPASOJE: What about?

AGNIJA: About what they are all saying outside. I have to tell you, we are family, and I'm worried.

SPASOJE: What do you have to worry about, and why on my behalf, please!?

AGNIJA: But how can I not worry? For instance, I met Mrs. Draga Mitrović yesterday and she asked me straight away: "Please, tell me, why did Mr. Spasoje call his daughter's wedding off so suddenly, when all the invitations had been printed already? There must be something there!"

SPASOJE: My daughter will get married when I want it, not when Mrs. Draga Mitrović wants it, and the invitations can very easily be printed again.

AGNIJA: And it's not only Mrs. Draga Mitrović. Ah, if you only knew what people were saying not only regarding the wedding but also regarding many other things.

SPASOJE: I told you already, once and for all, I don't care what they are saying.

AGNIJA: I've also been round to Nasta's, who read my cup.

SPASOJE: What cup, for god's sake, woman!?

AGNIJA: A coffee cup! Listen to me, Nasta has told the fortunes of many ministers by reading their coffee cups, and she's always guessed, so they say, precisely when they were going to become "former ministers". I tell her: it's a big problem, a big worry for me. And do you know what she said?

SPASOJE: I don't know, I don't want to know, do you understand; all I need now is to start believing in some coffee cups.

AGNIJA: What? You don't believe in fortune-telling from a cup?

SPASOJE: I don't.

AGNIJA: Then you don't believe in God either.

SPASOJE: What does God have to do with coffee cups?

AGNIJA: Well it's all about destiny; God decides on your destiny and the coffee cup only tells you about it in advance.

SPASOJE: Please stop with this claptrap . . . but since you are here you can do me a favor which I'll be grateful to you for. I need to get Vukica out of the house for at least an hour. I will have some meetings here today which could be pleasant, but they could also be unpleasant, and I wouldn't want her to be around.

AGNIJA: Well, that's not difficult; I'll take her to look for the wedding dress material. Only you should've let me know in advance so I could bring my collection of samples, but never mind, I already know very well what can be found in which shop.

SPASOJE: That could be a bit tricky. You know that we've just postponed the wedding and I've asked Vukica not to look for the wedding dress as yet; I can't go back on my word now. Can you think of something else you could look for.

AGNIJA: How about this: I could ask her to come with me to choose a silver dining set. I've seen several 24 piece sets in some shops; I'd like to give her one as a wedding present, and it would be good for her to make her own choice.

SPASOJE: Yes, that's a good idea. She'll like that. *(Goes to the door on the left.)* Vukica? Vukica, darling, come along, auntie-Agnija is here. *(Coming back)* Please, keep her as long as possible.

6. Add VUKICA

VUKICA: Oh, hello, auntie, what do we owe this surprise to?

AGNIJA *(kissing her):* Business, darling, very important business. I came by to pick you up, we're going out together.

VUKICA: Out? Where?

AGNIJA: So you can help me, darling, to choose your wedding gift.

SPASOJE *(to Vukica):* Yes you should help auntie-Agnija, darling.

AGNIJA: I'll tell you what it is. You see, I wanted to buy you a bedroom suite, but Spasoje was very much against it. He said he had ordered all the furniture already.

SPASOJE: Of course!

AGNIJA: And I wanted to buy you a bedroom suite according to my taste.

VUKICA: That would certainly be something really extraordinary.

AGNIJA: I've always imagined my own wedding suite in pale blue. All the walls would be painted in that colour, especially the ceiling. Now imagine a pale blue double bed spread, pale blue pillows and a sky blue chandelier. Oh god, that would be exquisite, the newlyweds would feel as though they were in heaven. That's how I always imagined my bedroom.

VUKICA: Oh, it's a real pity you haven't had a chance to get one.

AGNIJA *(sighing with real feeling):* Of course it's a pity! Anyway, as Spasoje was so much against it, I decided to get you a 24-piece silver set. Pure silver set.

SPASOJE: It sounds like a really nice gift.

VUKICA: And why do you need me?

AGNIJA: I've found three sets at three different jeweller's shops, and I can't choose between them. I would love you to choose yourself.

SPASOJE: Really, Vukica, since it's for you, it's best that you make the choice.
AGNIJA: I don't mind how much it costs; the most important thing is that you like it.
SPASOJE: Yes, go along, Vukica.
AGNIJA: You must. I really wouldn't like to get it without you.
VUKICA: Could we do it some other day, I have a really bad headache today.
SPASOJE: And who can guarantee that you won't have a headache next time?
AGNIJA: Yes, and believe me, as soon as you get out and get some fresh air, it'll go away.
VUKICA *(deciding with great difficulty):* OK, then. Let me get ready. *(Goes to her room.)*
AGNIJA: I'll help you. *(Goes with Vukica.)*

7. SPASOJE *(alone)*

SPASOJE *(goes to the phone and dials a number):* Hello! It's you, Mr. Đurić. I'm sorry to bother you, but the situation is very serious. You've heard, have you? They say, his solicitor is preparing a lawsuit. I've heard that from a reliable source, and he is also preparing a press campaign. That's what you've heard, isn't it? So tell me, can't we stop this somehow; can't we get someone to censor this, to prevent the papers from writing about it, for what is censorship for after all if it won't protect the interests of honourable and respectable citizens? And if it won't protect us as individuals, let it at least protect Illyria as an enterprise; that enterprise represents the pride of the state, and ruining us means ruining the enterprise. What's that? Sorry? Yes, I've done everything as you instructed, the police have been contacted, the witnesses have been named, everything, everything has been arranged. And more than that, I've asked the police agent, who you recommended, to be here at 10:30, which is when Marić will be here too. He will come because I said it was regarding a final proposal. With Schwartz? Yes, I've prepared everything and I've invited Schwartz.

8. Add SCHWARTZ

SCHWARTZ *(enters, elegantly dressed).*

SPASOJE *(having noticed him, waves to him to wait a minute and continues talking on the phone):* Here he is, Mr. Schwartz has just arrived. Yes, yes, of course, Mr. Đurić, that's what I'll do, I'll sort it out with Mr. Schwartz this moment. Yes, we mustn't take any more time over it, either-or, and as soon as today we'll see what happens! I'll keep you informed, oh, yes, I will! *(Putting the phone down.)* Where have you been, Mr. Schwartz, for heaven's sake, I've sent for you three times today?

SCHWARTZ: I'm sorry, I didn't know it was that urgent.

SPASOJE: It's extremely urgent. Please, sit down.

SCHWARTZ: Thank you. *(He sits down.)*

SPASOJE: Have you got a visa in your passport?

SCHWARTZ: Yes, you asked me to have it ready for travelling as soon as the concession is through.

SPASOJE: Have you got it on you?

SCHWARTZ *(taking it out of his pocket):* I never part from my passport.

SPASOJE *(taking the passport):* You will leave it with me for a while.

SCHWARTZ: What do you mean?

SPASOJE: You will leave it with me, and tomorrow you will go to the police and inform them that you have lost it or maybe had it stolen.

SCWARTZ *(protesting):* But, sir!

SPASOJE: It is to do with a very important matter, and it is completely in your interest to have this matter resolved the best way possible.

SCHWARTZ: But how can I be left without a passport?

SPASOJE: I told you already, tomorrow you will apply for another one.
SCHWARTZ: Will I get another one?
SPASOJE: You have just heard me talking to the minister's brother on the phone? You can see that I am doing everything according to his instructions, so what are you worrying about when there is somebody else taking care about everything.
SCHWARTZ *(uncomfortable)*: Yes, however . . . How shall I put it, it's not very pleasant. I don't know how my passport and my name will be used.
SPASOJE: Nothing unlawful. You don't have to worry about it. On the contrary, your passport will facilitate one good deed, do you understand, a good deed.
SCHWARTZ: I believe you, sir, but it is still a bit awkward.
SPASOJE: Shall I get you Mr. Đurić on the phone, so he can explain it to you in person?
SCHWARTZ: Thank you, I believe you . . . only . . . will I certainly get a new passport tomorrow?
SPASOJE: Tomorrow, or maybe the day after tomorrow.
SCHWARTZ: And you say I have nothing to worry about?
SPASOJE: Exactly.
SCHWARTZ: And I can go now?
SPASOJE: Wait! *(Opens the passport, peels off the photograph with a letter opener and gives it to him.)* You may need it.
SCHWARTZ *(even more disturbed)*: But, sir, this is –
SPASOJE: This is something I've explained already, therefore you may rest assured!

9. Add VUKICA, AGNIJA

AGNIJA *(coming out of Vukica's room)*: We are ready.
SPASOJE: What took you so long?
AGNIJA: Well, you know, girls' talk!
SPASOJE *(introduces them):* Mr. Schwartz, a member of the managerial board of Illyria, my daughter, my cousin.

SCHWARTZ *(bowing)*.
VUKICA: Daddy, is it all right if we stay out a bit longer?
SPASOJE: It's all right, I've got a lot of work to do today anyway*! (To Schwartz who is growing impatient):* So, Mr. Schwartz, we've agreed.
SCHWARTZ: Thank you. Goodbye, sir. *(Bowing to the ladies again, exits.)*

10. SPASOJE, AGNIJA, VUKICA

AGNIJA *(following Schwartz with her eyes):* A very noble gentleman!
SPASOJE: He is not noble, he is married!
AGNIJA: Ah, I see.
SPASOJE: What was it? *(To Vukica)* Oh, yes, don't you hurry home because of me. Take a good look at those sets, for you know those are the kinds of things you only buy once in a lifetime.
AGNIJA: That's what I said, as well! Let's go, Vukica.
VUKICA *(kisses her father on the cheek and exits with Agnija)*.

11. SPASOJE *(alone)*

SPASOJE *(turning around to see whether anyone is looking, takes out of the envelope the photograph that Anta had brought, then takes a bottle of glue out of the drawer and applies some on the back of the photo, sticks it on in the passport and presses hard with his hand)*.

12. SOFIJA, SPASOJE

SOFIJA *(enters):* A gentleman from the police.
SPASOJE: Let him in, let him in, straight away.
SOFIJA *(withdraws, letting the agent in)*.

13. AGENT II, SPASOJE

SPASOJE: How can I help you?

AGENT: I'm here to put myself at your disposal.
SPASOJE: You are acquainted with the matter?
AGENT: Yes.
SPASOJE: Have you got the instructions?
AGENT: They said I would get them from you.
SPASOJE: Good, very good. Are you being accompanied by anyone?
AGENT: I've got two policemen outside on the street.
SPASOJE: Don't leave them outside, it could look suspicious. Let them wait in the garden, and you will go into the adjacent room until I call you. The ones that I guarantee for are all right. Otherwise . . . you know.
AGENT: I understand, sir.
SPASOJE: You may go into the room on the right. *(He follows him to the door.)* Sofija, please take the gentleman into the small room. *(He returns.)*

14. Add LJUBOMIR PROTIĆ, ANTA

ANTA: I met Mr. son-in-law here; he had already visited the papers.
SPASOJE: You had?
LJUBOMIR: Yes, but it's very difficult to persuade them. It's a first class sensation, and they won't let it go.
SPASOJE: They'll write?
LJUBOMIR: I managed to postpone it for a couple of days; I've promised them an even bigger sensation by then.
SPASOJE: Very good, very good, that's just as much as we need, a couple of days.
LJUBOMIR: And Mr. Anta says he's already been to the solicitor's.
SPASOJE: Yes, he is suing Mr. Anta.
ANTA: He is suing all of us.
LJUBOMIR: On criminal grounds?

SPASOJE: I don't know, I think he is suing us on civil grounds, and Mr. Anta on criminal grounds.

ANTA: He is suing all of us on the same grounds, there's no difference.

LJUBOMIR: And what for?

SPASOJE: He is suing Mr. Novaković for taking his wife, me for allegedly taking his estate, you for –

LJUBOMIR *(interrupts with a gesture not to talk in front of Anta)*.

SPASOJE *(remembers)*: Ah, yes. He is suing you for you know what.

LJUBOMIR: And Mr. Anta?

ANTA: Me too for 'you know what'.

LJUBOMIR: That means we should employ a solicitor as well?

SPASOJE: My best solicitor is my clear conscience.

ANTA: Mine too!

LJUBOMIR: Still, clear conscience doesn't know the paragraphs, and paragraphs can be very dangerous things.

ANTA *(more to himself)*: Very dangerous!

SPASOJE: The only question is, should we take the same solicitor for all of us, or should we take one each! In any case we shouldn't be too rash. I will seek Mr. Đurić's advice on this, too.

LJUBOMIR *(wants to go to another room)*: Is Vukica around?

SPASOJE: No, she went out with auntie-Agnija, she will be a while.

15. Add NOVAKOVIĆ, RINA

SPASOJE *(having noticed them at the door)*: Well, thank god you've arrived!

RINA: I've had such a bad headache –

SPASOJE: My dear lady, we all have a headache today, but what can we do, the situation is very serious; we have to get through it together, for it's burning under all of our feet. That's why I've had to ask you to come over today at all costs. Marić has submitted his case to the solicitor, and in a couple of days' time, we shall all be charged.

NOVAKOVIĆ: Well, so what, we'll find a solicitor as well, and try to defend ourselves.

SPASOJE: Defend ourselves? It's easy for you to say we'll defend ourselves, for after all, what have you got to lose? Nothing.

NOAKOVIĆ: What do you mean nothing?

SPASOJE: Well, he is only suing you for taking his wife. Even if you lose the case, what have you lost? A wife and nothing else. That at least is not a big loss.

RINA *(offended)*: How do you mean this, sir?

SPASOJE *(realizing)*: That is, I beg your pardon, I mean the loss of a wife is not a material loss, and we are talking about material losses here. Then, taking somebody's wife is not a criminal act, nowadays that's just a sport and nothing else. Therefore, his charges against you are not at all dangerous, but take for example, this poor Anta.

ANTA *(protesting)*: Why me again?

RINA: Take yourself as an example, why don't you.

SPASOJE: Myself and all of us, for you are deluding yourself, Mr. Novaković, if you think that you've got a cheap deal here in losing only your wife to him. You'll also have to face a material loss. You've taken Mrs. Rina Marić thinking that Mr. Marić was not alive; if however, the court now returns his wife to him, that means that he is alive, and if he is alive, the whole of Illyria will go to hell. Everything will go, everything, including of course half a million of your cash which you have so far invested in the enterprise.

NOVAKOVIĆ *(frightened)*: Half a million!? Can it really be lost? If that happens, believe me, I have no choice but to commit suicide.

SPASOJE: There you see! Should we allow that to happen? You commit suicide, my son-in-law commits suicide, Anta commits suicide . . . and even if Anta doesn't commit suicide, what use is he to me. I can't defend myself on my own, we all have to do it together.

ANTA: Of course!

ALL *(agreeing)*.

SPASOJE: We have to fight, and it is a fight for life. We cannot afford to choose our means, for our very survival is at stake. You have to be prepared for everything, do you understand, everything!

NOVAKOVIĆ: How do you imagine this "everything".

SPASOJE: I'll tell you the whole plan. I've been thinking it through all day and all night. I'm not saying I thought of it entirely on my own; it's essentially Mr. Đurić's plan, I just developed it. Mr. Đurić has really tried hard to make sure that this plan is realized and he took certain necessary measures with the authorities. The authorities will be completely at our disposal.

NOVAKOVIĆ: Legal authorities?

SPASOJE: No, the point is that this should never get to the legal authorities. Marić has been reported to the police as a dangerous element, as a representative of a destructive organisation from abroad, which I will testify to, as well as you Mr. and Mrs. Novaković, my son-in-law and Anta. You will all have to be ready to make such a statement if necessary.

NOVAKOVIĆ: What statement?

SPASOJE: Any, any statement that will portray him as a destructive element, as a foreign agent, an anarchist, anything that can work against him, do you understand?

ANTA: Even if we've never heard or seen anything like that.

SPASOJE: Not *"even if* we've never heard or seen it", but precisely what you've never heard or seen . . . that is what you will testify to.

NOVAKOVIĆ *(uncomfortable):* That would actually be, how shall I put it?

SPASOJE: Please, say it!

RINA: That would perhaps be immoral.

SPASOJE: Immoral, of course, what else do you expect! You think morals will help you? I learnt about morals in religious education at school, but religious education is one thing and life is another. Please, tell me, Mrs. Novaković what would you prefer, morals or Mr. Novaković's suicide? Or you, Mr. Novaković, tell me, do you like morals better than your five hundred thousand, or maybe you, my son, do you prefer morals or . . . *(He stops himself.)* Or you, Anta, would you rather have morals or a year in prison? Come on, say it?

LJUBOMIR: Really, it is a very difficult position we are in.

SPASOJE: Of course it's difficult. Immorality is power, power, my dear sir, and a kind of power that is more powerful than the law itself. The whole world worships immorality nowadays, only Anta pretends to –

ANTA *(defending himself)*: What about me?

SPASOJE: You are frowning for some reason, maybe you'd like to represent virtue in our society?

16. Add SOFIJA

SOFIJA *(bringing a card in)*: A gentleman.

SPASOJE *(reading the card)*: Mr. Marić. Let him in!

SOFIJA *(exits)*.

SPASOJE: Gentlemen, I warn you, be ready for anything!

17. Add PAVLE

PAVLE *(enters, bowing; nobody returns his greeting; to Spasoje)*: I have come in response to your special invitation.

SPASOJE: Yes, I invited you to come.

PAVLE: You said it was going to be the final conversation between us.

SPASOJE: Yes, final.

PAVLE: Since I have made my final decision regarding the situation, I really don't find that there is any necessity for any more conversations, however, I've come to hear what you have to say.

SPASOJE: You've done very well to come; it is in your greatest interest that you have done so.

PAVLE: You think so?

SPASOJE: I don't think so, I know so. As we don't have much time for conversations, we'll proceed with the matter immediately.

PAVLE: And we'll talk like this, in public?

SPASOJE: Yes, in front of everyone. I invited them especially, for what I have to tell you is from all of us.

PAVLE: Fine.

SPASOJE: Do you know that you are being followed by the police?

PAVLE *(surprised):* The police?

SPASOJE: Yes, I wouldn't be surprised if there are some police agents in front of my house at the moment, or in my garden or, indeed, behind this door.

PAVLE: That's how dangerous I am?

SPASOJE: Much more dangerous than you think, all your movements, all your actions and all your intentions have been exposed.

PAVLE: That's very interesting.

SPASOJE: It's very interesting for the police, too.

PAVLE: Are you going to tell me anything more about these actions and intentions of mine?

SPASOJE: I'll acquaint you with all the material that has been gathered against you, so that you can assess your predicament for yourself.

PAVLE: I shall be grateful to you, sir.

SPASOJE: You, sir, are an agent and an exponent of an anarchist organisation which has for its aim the destruction of society, social system and the state.

PAVLE *(laughing):* Is that all?

SPASOJE: That's not all; you will be assured that that's not all as soon as I present you with the evidence. The beginning of the investigation leads to a certain theft of letters in your house –
PAVLE: Love letters?
SPASOJE: That's what you say but the investigation says otherwise. That was a theft of highly compromising letters which revealed your entire destructive purpose. As soon as those letters were intercepted, your close accomplice in action, a certain Russian immigrant Aljoša, committed suicide, and you ran away abroad and lived as an immigrant for three years.
PAVLE: This is the first I've heard of it. So those were political letters?
SPASOJE: Not political but revolutionary, anarchist letters.
PAVLE: We could say that if a woman's infidelity is described as marital anarchy.
SPASOJE: The police are acquainted with the content of those letters.
PAVLE: I see, so they've read them, have they?
SPASOJE: No, they haven't read them since the lady has destroyed all the letters wishing to save you.
PAVLE: I am very grateful for that! But how do the police know that those letters were revolutionary? Unless the lady claims so?
SPASOJE: Of course she claims so.
PAVLE: Really!? That means that she would even give such a statement if necessary.
SPASOJE: Of course she will give such a statement.
PAVLE *(addressing Rina):* I would very much like to hear the lady confirm this to me.
RINA *(confused, disturbed, almost sobbing):* I . . . I –
PAVLE: Yes, yes, the lady would give such a statement; it is entirely in keeping with her understanding of morals.
NOVAKOVIĆ: Sir, I do not permit you to insult my wife like this.

PAVLE: I am insulting my own wife; the lady is only your mistress.

NOVAKOVIĆ: As long as she carries my name –

PAVLE: Your name? I don't know whether that means anything to you, but obviously to her it means nothing! She carried my name too and she had her own views on morals; she now carries your name and still has the same views.

RINA *(overcome with feeling and momentary anger):* Enough! *(Spitefully)* I will give a statement, I will! *(She sinks in an armchair.)*

PAVLE *(calm and indifferent):* I believe you! *(To Novaković)* You will of course confirm this statement for you are also acquainted with the content of those letters?

SPASOJE: Yes, the gentleman will confirm. Not only that, the gentleman will also give a statement about the anarchist propaganda you were spreading at the building site, about the suspicious characters and the agents from various international organizations whom you had brought in from abroad and employed at the site in order to give them an alibi.

PAVLE: The gentleman will claim that?

SPASOJE: And much more.

PAVLE *(looks Novaković in the eye and when he lowers his eyes, Pavle turns his back on him with profound contempt, addressing Spasoje):* I presume the collection of such perfect witnesses can in no way exclude your respected son-in-law?

SPASOJE: Of course not, my dear sir. His statement will be one of the strongest against you.

PAVLE: Will it?

SPASOJE: Just before you emigrated you made sure that you removed all the evidence against yourself by giving this young man certain manuscripts of yours, which as you said, were very precious to you.

PAVLE: That's right.

SPASOJE: There you see, you don't deny the basic fact. Of course, no one can deny the truth. After your funeral, my son-in-law, not knowing what to do with your manuscripts, had a look, and to his great surprise found them to be a collection of most confidential revolutionary correspondence with various organizations abroad. The kind of correspondence which doesn't lead only to prison but straight to the gallows. The young man found himself in great trouble, he certainly didn't want to keep such documents, and didn't find it suitable to take them to the police, for what would be the point in that given that you were already dead? My son-in-law had a chat with Mr. Anta, since he is a man of great experience, and they made the decision to burn all that correspondence, in the interest of your peace and the peace of your soul.

PAVLE *(with great disgust):* Your son-in-law will give such a statement?

SPASOJE: Yes!

PAVLE: And Mr. Anta will confirm that?

SPASOJE: Mr. Anta? He will confirm it under oath if necessary.

PAVLE: A spineless worm!

ANTA *(underbreath to Novaković):* Now I'm a worm.

PAVLE: Mr. Protić, I would very much appreciate it if you could confirm that you are prepared to make such a statement?

LJUBOMIR *(keeps quiet).*

SPASOJE: Tell him, tell him, feel free to tell him!

LJUBOMIR *(tortured, whispering):* Yes. I will!

PAVLE *(angry):* A crook!

(General commotion.)

PAVLE: I thought you were a mere thief, but you are more than that, you are a criminal!

ANTA: Oh-o!

SPASOJE: Please remain calm, gentlemen, the gentleman has nothing else to defend himself with but insults.

PAVLE *(still agitated):* You expect me to want to defend myself? What from? Who from? From you, immoral vermin!

ANTA *(to Novaković):* There we go again, now we are all vermin!

PAVLE *(pulls himself together):* I shouldn't have allowed myself to lose my temper. These kinds of phenomena in this environment are not a sufficient reason for agitation. *(To Spasoje)* Let us, therefore continue our chat? Please tell me, then, my dear closest relative: Will you make a statement too?

SPASOJE: What kind of a question is that? Of course I will say everything I know. I can't be expected to be unscrupulous and hide what I know.

PAVLE: And what is it that you know and that your scruples prevent you from hiding?

SPASOJE: I know all about great amounts of money that arrived into your account in foreign currency from abroad –

PAVLE: And you will back this up with documents similar to those that you used in court to prove our kinship.

SPASOJE: I know how I'll back it up, that's my own affair.

PAVLE *(getting agitated again):* Dear god, is it possible that I'm hearing these things; did you really say all these things which I've just heard? It is unimaginable that so much iniquity can be found amongst such a small number of people. People, yes – for after all, you are all human, after all, you must have at least a seed of humanity in you.

SPASOJE: Of course we do, I'll prove it to you; I'll prove how humane we are and what great care I took to fulfil my family duties towards you, sir. *(He pulls out the passport belonging to Adolph Schwartz.)* I have prepared a passport with a visa for you, sir. According to this passport, your name is Adolph Schwartz, because you wouldn't be able to cross the border under your own name. Your picture is in the passport. *(He gives it to him.)*

PAVLE *(dumbstruck):* Passport? What for?

SPASOJE: So that you can leave the country without problems and in good time.

PAVLE: Leave? *(He grabs the passport.)* Give it to me, give me this invaluable document. *(He puts it in his pocket with great urgency.)* This is the biggest proof of your corruption. I won't give you back this document, I won't give it to you for anything on earth!

SPASOJE: I don't want it back, keep it, you'll need it. When you have to decide whether you are going to spend ten or fifteen years alone, unseen and unheard of, under somebody else's name in some German, Dutch or even Swedish town, or whether you are going to spend ten or fifteen years alone, unseen and unheard of in some prison cell, you will then realize the value of this passport.

PAVLE: Prison cell? What would I do in a prison cell, and why? Because I ask for robbers to return my honour, hard work and property? That's why I am an agent of an anarchist organization, because I want to expose you as the robbers and crooks that you are? Is that a destruction of society and the social system for you? Are one polygamous woman, one false friend, one bandit in a professor's chair, one robber and one perjurer, are those the pillars of that social system of yours? And I, the one who asks for his moral and material possessions to be returned to me, I am supposed to be a destructive element? Oh, you vermin, you don't even deserve to be spat on by an honourable man!

SPASOJE: We have allowed you to say everything you wanted, and you have heard what you needed to hear; now you only need to see that all of this has not been empty claptrap. *(He rings a bell. Pause. Silence.)*

18. Add SOFIJA

SOFIJA *(enters)*.

SPASOJE: Sofija, is there anyone waiting outside?

SOFIJA: Yes, there is a gentleman from the police waiting here and there are two policemen in the garden.
SPASOJE: Please, tell the gentleman to come in.
SOFIJA *(exits)*.

19. As before
PAVLE *(looking at everyone individually):* It is true, isn't it? It is true?
ALL *(keep quiet)*.
PAVLE: Speak, for god's sake, is this true? Mr. Spasoje, Mr. Protić, Mr. Novaković, Mr. Anta, speak, is this true?
ALL *(keep quiet)*.
PAVLE: You want me in prison, do you? In prison or in exile, so that you can live on my account? Is that it? Is that it? *(He looks at them, nobody raises their head; then with pain and bitterness.)* Oh how much immorality and how little courage . . . can't anyone speak up, does no one dare?

20. Add AGENT II
POLICE AGENT *(to Spasoje):* I'm sorry, I'm here on business.
SPASOJE: You've come to see me?
AGENT: We've been informed that there is a person in your house at the moment who is being sought all over the capital. Apart from you and the gentleman *(pointing at Novaković)*, whom I know personally, can I ask all the gentlemen present to show their IDs, please. *(To Anta)* Your ID, sir?
ANTA *(confused, looks through his pockets):* I'm . . . I'm sorry, I haven't got one on me.
SPASOJE: He is my relative, I can guarantee for him.
AGENT *(to Ljubomir):* You, sir?
LJUBOMIR *(has already prepared his ID, hands it out)*.
AGENT *(returning the ID to Ljubomir):* Thank you very much! *(Addresses Pavle Marić)* Yourself, sir? *(General silence with certain tension.)*

PAVLE *(after a moment of inner struggle; controlled)*: Who are you actually looking for?
AGENT: I am looking for the former engineer Pavle Marić.
PAVLE *(perturbed)*: You are looking for Pavle Marić?
AGENT: Can I have your ID, please?
PAVLE *(defeated, dejected and resigned takes out Schwartz's passport and hands it over)*: I am Adolph Schwartz!
(General exchange of discreet glances.)
SPASOJE *(quickly takes over)*: Mr. Schwartz is a member of the managerial board of the Illyria enterprise; he is travelling today on business on behalf of Illyria and he . . . *(he looks at his watch)* he has to catch the first train at 11:10 for Germany and beyond, maybe. As you can see he has a visa.
PAVLE *(taking the passport back)*: Yes, I'm leaving on the 11:10 train.
SPASOJE *(to Marić)*: You have got the main instructions, you will have to hurry up if you wish to catch this train.
PAVLE *(with contempt)*: I will hurry up, don't you worry, I won't miss the train. *(He looks at all of them one by one once again.)* Yes, I will hurry up, I will go.

21. As before without MARIĆ

AGENT: Have I finished my job?
SPASOJE: No, not yet. I'd like to ask you one more favor. My car is downstairs, please take it and go straight to the station. The train should leave in five or six minutes; can you, please, make sure that the gentleman has really left.
AGENT: Certainly. *(Exits.)*
SPASOJE *(following him out)*: And, please, inform me.

22. As before without the AGENT

SPASOJE *(coming back from the door)*: Gentlemen, you may relax.
ANTA *(takes a deep breath)*.

NOVAKOVIĆ: I can't, I tell you, I cannot relax anymore.

LJUBOMIR: Really, one could've expected anything else, but this.

SPASOJE: I believed in our victory all along, as I've always valued that great pearl of wisdom: "the good must win in the end".

RINA: So where is he going now?

SPASOJE: He is returning to the dead.

NOVAKOVIĆ: You really think that he's left the stage now?

SPASOJE: More permanently than ever before. In the past he had emigrated under his own name, and now under someone else's. This way he has himself accepted his own death.

ANTA: Yes, but what if . . . I mean . . . what if he reappears again in three years' time?

SPASOJE: In that case your year in prison is guaranteed. As far as we are concerned, we will have developed the business till then, we'll have secured ourselves with millions and nobody will be able to do anything to us.

NOVAKOVIĆ: Only . . . are you sure, he will leave?

SPASOJE *(looking at his watch)*: At this moment he'll be on the train. *(A long pause.)*

ALL *(keep quiet)*.

SPASOJE *(still looking at his watch)*: By now, the train is pulling out. *(Telephone; he goes to get it.)* Hello? Yes, this is Spasoje Blagojević . . . yes, yes so he has boarded the train and left? Thank you . . . thank you very much for letting me know! *(Puts the phone down; victoriously.)* You have heard the agent's report. And now, may god give the deceased eternal peace, and may we continue with our normal life!

23. Add VUKICA, AGNIJA

VUKICA *(to her father)*: Have I stayed out too long?

SPASOJE: No, you've arrived just in time. I have told you, ladies and gentlemen, we may continue with our normal life.

And we will start with joyful celebrations. The wedding will take place as soon as possible, tomorrow, the day after, not later than Sunday. *(He embraces Vukica.)* Yes, we can continue our life, we can continue our life!

(General celebration.)

(The director may leave out this last appearance if they wish.)

CURTAIN

Translated by *Duška Radosavljević*
Edited by *Dennis Barnett*

ĐORĐE LEBOVIĆ
(1928—2004)

Born in Sombor, Vojvodina, Serbia, in 1928, Lebović was taken to a World War II German concentration camp when he was only fifteen and was the only one in his family who survived. This experience left a lasting scar on his life. After World War II, he studied philosophy at the University of Belgrade and to earn a living he worked as a bricklayer, teacher, interpreter and journalist.

His acclaimed play *Hallelujah* takes place in a hospital for former World War II camp prisoners and it is based on his personal experience. His plays were performed throughout Europe and the USA. *Hallelujah* was produced at Hope College, Holland, Michigan. The production was selected for the regional College Theater Festival in Athens, Ohio in 1972.

HALLELUJAH

CHARACTERS:

Former camp prisoners:
  Pip
  Sipka
  Zero
  Yustus
  Zola
  Moishe
  Convalescents

Former combatants:
  Major, the head of St. Raphael's Hospital
  Sergeant
  Jello, a nurse—prisoner of war
  Dumbo, a nurse—prisoner of war
  Bertha, the head nurse
  Soldiers

People from the outer world:
  Nanita
  Pepi
  Coachman
  Priest

Man with Pipe
Boy with sword
Children

The play takes place immediately after the war, in the territory of the defeated country.

PART I

(The yard of the hospital is empty. The hospital clock tolls seven times. All of a sudden, the silence is broken by a sharp, metallic voice from the loudspeaker.)

VOICE FROM THE LOUDSPEAKER: Good morning! The command of the liberation army wishes a pleasant stay and a quick recovery in St. Raphael's Hospital to all its patients and ex-prisoners!
(The voice from the loudspeaker is replaced by loud, cheerful music.)

SCENE I
Hospital room

(The room is whitewashed with seven iron beds and one long table with benches around it. The stiff body of Yoyo lies on the bed in the corner, wrapped in a blanket. Music from the loudspeaker comes into the room. Pip comes in carrying a tray with bread and a big cup. Pip is only sixteen; his face is pale and thin, as if it were turned into two restless eyes.)

PIP (walking): Yoyo! Sleeping is over. Time for breakfast!
(Pip puts the tray on the table, takes up the cup and goes to Yoyo's bed.)
PIP: Come on, Yoyo, here is your milk.
(Pip puts the cup on the edge of the bed and comes back to the table. He is spreading the butter on a thick slice of bread with a spoon handle.)
PIP: You must eat if you want to recover.
(Zero comes into the room, unnoticed. Zero is strong, stout, with a strong neck and sun-tanned face. Vitality springs from him.

However, his behavior contradicts his appearance; he is depressed, confused and he is looking down all the time. Zero comes reluctantly into the middle of the room, as if he doesn't know what to do. Pip doesn't seem to notice Zero's presence. With a slice of bread he goes again to Yoyo's bed.)

PIP: Yoyo, shame on you! It's about time to get up. Yustus will be angry.

(Pip shakes the stiff body under the blanket.)

PIP: Will you wake up . . . ?

(Pip realizes, at last . . . He jerks his hand, suddenly. But his fingers brush the cup off the edge of the bed and it crashes on the floor, making a loud noise.)

ZERO *(Tonelessly)*: He is dead.

(It is only now that Pip notices Zero. In anger he shouts at him.)

PIP: Go away, Zero! Do you hear me? Get out of here!

(Dejected, Zero goes to his bed. He sits on it and vacantly stares at Pip. Pip indecisively takes up the cup, constantly looking at Yoyo's bed. Sipka appears at the door. Sipka is skinny, middle-aged, with a few gray hairs, wrinkled face and thoughtful look. A gray cigarette holder peers out from his mouth all the time.)

SIPKA: What's the matter, Pip? What are you staring at?

(Pip does not pay any attention to his words.)

PIP: Sipka . . . Come here . . .

(Sipka goes to Yoyo's bed.)

PIP: Yoyo has died.

(Pause.)

SIPKA: I thought he was sleeping.

(Sipka pulls the blanket over Yoyo's head.)

PIP: Why did you cover him?

SIPKA: This is what they do in the hospitals—when somebody dies.

PIP: And why did Yoyo die? Nobody is supposed to die anymore.

(Sipka lays a hand on Pip's shoulder.)

SIPKA: He did it by mistake; by sheer mistake.
(Yustus comes to the room. He is a tall man with oval head, pointed beard and glasses which are fixed with a string. Yustus has a dignified bearing, his movements are resolute, his steps are long and quick.)
YUSTUS *(Loudly)*: Why is this room in such a mess? Who is on duty today? You, Pip, I bet! When will you get used to order and punctuality?
(Everyone in the room is still.)
YUSTUS: What the hell is this? Yoyo hasn't eaten his breakfast? Where is he?
SIPKA: Nowhere.
YUSTUS: You are hiding again, eh. Yoyo?
(Yustus starts the "hide-and-seek" game. He is looking under the beds and the table, pretending full involvement.)
YUSTUS: Where are you, Yoyo? Is Yoyo here . . . Is Yoyo there . . . Where is Yoyo?
(He comes to Yoyo's bed on tiptoe.)
YUSTUS: Yoyo is under the blanket! Whoops!
(Yustus takes off the blanket from Yoyo with a sudden move. Then he falls silent, staring at the bed, stupefied. Yustus lets the blanket fall slowly.)
YUSTUS *(With incredulity)*: When did it happen?
PIP: Today.
YUSTUS *(Nervously)*: Today, today! But when? *(More calmly)* But how is it possible? He was cured. Sure, he has lost his memory, he's forgotten how to speak and walk—but otherwise he was in perfect health.
(Loud whistling is heard at a distance.)
YUSTUS: Pip, tell that lousy bastard . . .
(Pip is already at the door. He shouts . . .)
PIP: Zola, don't whistle!
(Zola and Moishe enter. Zola is still whistling the tune from the loudspeaker. Zola is a long-legged skeleton with untidy, red hair

and a freckled face. His movements are awkward, uncontrolled, and he talks loudly. Moishe is much shorter than Zola. He hides his head between his shoulders, his movements are slow; he is like a big turtle. He is lost in his thoughts. An almost invisible, sad smile is always on his lips.)

YUSTUS *(Sharply):* Shut up! Hear me?!

(Zola stops whistling.)

ZOLA *(Surprised):* Why?

YUSTUS *(Solemnly):* There is a dead man in this room.

ZOLA: How come? Who brought him here?

PIP: Yoyo has died.

ZOLA: You're kidding, eh?

(Zola bursts into laughter. But when he sees that everybody is serious and frowning, he swallows his laughter.)

ZOLA *(Pulling himself together):* Can't be. It's been almost a month since anyone has died!

MOISHE *(Touchingly):* Poor Yoyo.

(Zola sighs deeply.)

ZOLA: Poor devil. He hasn't had time to eat his breakfast.

(Yustus approaches him resolutely.)

YUSTUS *(Energetically):* Zola! You go and bring the nurses.

(Zola nods and goes to the exit. Having noticed a slice of bread which had been intended for Yoyo, he stops and takes it without the slightest hesitation. Zero is sitting motionless on his bed and at that moment Zola looks up at him. Then Zola throws the bread back on the table, looking scornfully at him and walks out in a hurry.)

YUSTUS *(Disapprovingly):* He'll never have enough to eat. He thinks of nothing but food!

SIPKA *(With a smile):* . . . Thanks, therefore—exists.

(Meanwhile, Moishe has been staring at Yoyo's bed. Finally, he speaks up absentmindedly, as if his words were addressed to someone who is invisible . . .)

MOISHE: I always said that he would die.

(Pip looks up at Moishe in surprise.)
PIP: You never said that, Moishe.
MOISHE: I was saying it to myself: Yoyo shall die! He was bound to die.
PIP: Who bound?
MOISHE: Because that was meant for him.
(Zola appears at the door, followed by the nurses, Jello and Dumbo. The worn-out uniforms of the defeated army can be seen underneath their white coats. They have the numbers of the prisoners of war on their chests. Slack and flabby, with a square head and goggle-eyed, Jello is carrying the stretcher. Dumbo is skinny and with desperately "dumbo" ears.)
DUMBO *(Harshly)*: We've come for the "package"! Is it ready?
(Pip, Yustus and Moishe make room for them. They put Yoyo's covered body on the stretcher.)
JELLO: The crazy one?
YUSTUS *(Angrily)*: Watch it! Yoyo was paralyzed.
(Zola approaches Jello and stares at his closely.)
ZOLA: Understand, Jello? Paralyzed, but not crazy.
(Jello shrugs his shoulders indifferently, as if to say, "It's all the same to me," and then he and Dumbo lift the stretcher. They head for the exit. Suddenly, Yustus shouts . . .)
YUSTUS: Dumbo!
(The nurses stop. Yustus approaches them.)
YUSTUS: Where are you taking him?
DUMBO: To the mortuary.
YUSTUS: And then?
(Dumbo looks at him in surprise.)
DUMBO: Why do you ask? Bup . . . into the pit.
(The nurses take Yoyo away. Yustus is frozen for a while, looking at the door, and then suddenly turns back.)
YUSTUS *(Loudly)*: Listen to me! We can't allow them to throw that man into the pit like a rotten potato!
ZOLA *(With resignation)*: But what else can we do?

(Yustus draws himself up.)
YUSTUS: We can bury him! *(With dignity)* The way it becomes us, as free men.
(Everyone looks at Yustus in surprise.)
ZOLA *(Amazed):* Bury him?
PIP *(Incredulously):* In the graveyard?
ZOLA: How?
YUSTUS: According to the custom of the outside world.
ZOLA: Look, Yustus. We don't know a thing about Yoyo. Who he is, what he is, where he comes from . . .
PIP: We don't even know his name.
YUSTUS: We know he is a man! *(Complacently)* What do you say, Sipka?
SIPKA *(Nodding his head):* It sounds good.
YUSTUS: Isn't it right?
SIPKA: It should be right.
YUSTUS *(Satisfied):* Then—we agree! *(Confidently)* Don't worry, boys. I'm sure we can do it.
(He points at Moishe.)
YUSTUS: Know where the mortuary is?
(Moishe rouses himself.)
MOISHE: In the cellar.
YUSTUS: Go over there and make sure nobody takes Yoyo away.
MOISHE *(Reluctantly):* Should I go in?
YUSTUS: Of course.
MOISHE *(He is scared):* It's dark in there . . . and cold.
ZOLA *(Scornfully):* Nonsense! You and your fairy tales.
MOISHE *(Seriously):* I was in the mortuary . . . in the concentration camp.
YUSTUS *(Fatherly):* This is not a camp, Moishe. Come on, get going.
(Moishe is looking desperately around the room.)
MOISHE: And what . . . what do I do if somebody takes Yoyo

away?
(Yustus thoughtfully scratches his ear.)
YUSTUS: Hm? Can you whistle?
MOISHE *(Amazed)*: Whistle? Me?!
PIP *(Readily)*: I can.
(Pip puts his fingers in his mouth and whistles loudly.)
YUSTUS: Great, Pip! Go with Moishe. If somebody comes to take Yoyo, you whistle as loud as you can!
ZOLA: Hurry up! The rounds will start soon.
(Moishe and Pip exit quickly.)
ZOLA: And now?
YUSTUS: Now we shall ask for permission to bury Yoyo. We must get it from the head of the hospital.
(Steps are heard from the outside. Zola peers out the door.)
ZOLA: Here they are! Bertha and the chief.
(Yustus and Sipka sit down on their beds. The Major comes into the room followed by Bertha. The Major is a gray-haired man, in his fifties, with a slack face and a tired look. He wears a white coat over his uniform. The head nurse, Bertha, is a flat, dry creature with teeth like haystack. The Major goes to Yustus' bed.)
MAJOR *(Professionally)*: Stomach?
YUSTUS: Works.
(Major nods and goes to Sipka.)
MAJOR: Cough?
SIPKA: Modest.
MAJOR: Did you give up smoking finally?
SIPKA *(Calmly)*: Eight years ago, Major.
MAJOR *(Remembering)*: Oh, yes.
(The Major addresses Zola . . .)
MAJOR: How's the leg?
ZOLA: The leg is fine. But the shoes are bad.
MAJOR: You should go to the quartermaster.
(The Major stops beside Zero.)

MAJOR: Why don' you shave?

ZOLA *(Bitingly):* It wouldn't do a thing for him.

BERTHA *(Sharply):* Silence! . . . (To the Major) Two are missing.

ZOLA *(Quickly):* On duty in the kitchen!

(The Major comes to Yoyo's bed, takes off the patient's record and crosses it with a large gesture. Yustus works up courage at last and goes to the Major.)

YUSTUS *(Out of the clear blue):* We've decided to bury Yoyo.

MAJOR *(Absent-mindedly):* Pardon?

YUSTUS: We won't let them throw Yoyo into the pit by the dunghill.

MAJOR *(Shrugs his shoulders):* That's where they're all interred.

YUSTUS: Yoyo is going to be buried in the graveyard.

(The Major looks up at Yustus.)

MAJOR: In the graveyard? When?

YUSTUS: Tomorrow.

(The Major waves with his hand.)

MAJOR: Impossible. The corpse must be interred immediately!

(Major goes to the exit, followed by Bertha. Yustus blocks their way.)

YUSTUS: Major, we are not pigs.

(The Major sighs.)

MAJOR: Since I've become the head of this hospital, hundreds of ex-prisoners have died. We buried them all without any ceremonies. What's so different now?

YUSTUS: We are free men.

MAJOR *(Spreading his arms):* Nobody denies that.

SIPKA: We trust you, Major, but we want to be sure.

(The Major hesitates for a moment, then he waves his hand.)

MAJOR: Well, well, let it be. But the burial must be tomorrow at the latest. According to the regulations, the corpse may not remain in the mortuary for more than a day.

BERTHA *(Briskly):* We don't want any disease in St. Raphael's.
YUSTUS: We accept your terms, the burial will take place tomorrow afternoon.
(The Major nods and starts to exit. He turns back at the door.)
MAJOR: Just one more thing: don't expect any help from us. We haven't got money for that sort of thing.
YUSTUS: We don't need anybody's help. We're not children!
MAJOR: Well then, that's the agreement; the burial must take place tomorrow afternoon . . .
YUSTUS *(Impatiently):* I said tomorrow afternoon and I'll stick to it!
MAJOR *(Conciliatory):* All right, all right . . . We won't argue over a trifle.
(The Major goes out, followed by Bertha. Yustus addresses the others.)
YUSTUS: Did you hear him? It's a trifle for him. As if we didn't know that the afternoon is the proper time for funerals. I mean, usually.

SCENE II

The yard of the hospital. Bertha and Dumbo enter. Bertha hisses angrily.

BERTHA: What burial! That's nonsense! This is their first step into life and they're already asking for things!
DUMBO: But Major said . . .
BERTHA: He gives in! If *our* Major were in his place it would be a different story.
DUMBO *(Mockingly):* Oh, if, if . . . If I had a horn instead of a nose I would be a rhinoceros.
BERTHA *(Sharply):* What are you saying? You should be ashamed. I spent the whole war in this hospital. And I can tell you that our soldiers were less demanding than theirs! They

never asked to be buried when they died.
DUMBO *(Shrugs his shoulders):* Well . . . *I don't blame them for not burying me in this war.*
BERTHA *(Scornfully):* Idiot! Don't you see they are making fools of us?
DUMBO *(Spreading his arms):* No, I don't . . .
BERTHA: Because you're blind! They want to humiliate us! Want to show us that they won. They should be happy to have heads on their shoulders! *(Resolutely)* You and Jello will take Yoyo's corpse and dig a hole and throw him in right away! Understand?
DUMBO *(Reluctantly):* But Major . . .
BERTHA *(Cunningly):* Don't you worry. It's according to their regulations.
(Bertha spreads her mouth into a wicked smile.)
BERTHA *(Wickedly):* I'll give them their burial!
(Bertha walks out energetically. Dumbo shrugs his shoulders and follows her.)

SCENE III

Mortuary. An empty cellar with vaulted ceiling. Yoyo's covered body lies on the table. A candle is flickering. Moishe is standing against the wall and humming quietly. Pip is sitting on the floor and watching Moishe with silent interest for some time.

PIP: Are you praying?
(Moishe rouses himself, embarrassed.)
MOISHE: Me? Oh, no . . . Just humming.
(Pause)
MOISHE *(Absentmindedly):* We used to have guests on the Sabath . . . They were drinking wine . . . Father was sitting at the head of the table singing . . . It was cozy and bright in the kitchen . . . (In a changed voice) Pip, do you believe in God?

PIP: Oh, no, Moishe. I know there is no God. There hasn't been for a long time. Yet I saw people in the camp praying. *(Inquisitively)* Moishe, why did they always cry?
MOISHE: Because God has left us.
PIP: You mean left you—the Jews?
MOISHE: Us as well as all others.
PIP: And an old man told me in the camp that God has been liquidated. He said: "God is dead. They killed him with all the rest."
MOISHE: No, Pip, nobody can kill him. It's only he who can kill others.
(Moishe points to Yoyo's body.)
MOISHE: There, look what he has made out of him! *(Irritated)* He has become unjust and wicked. *(Definitely)* I will never pray to him anymore.
PIP: And what if some other, better God comes along?
MOISHE: Psssst!
(Steps are heard from the outside. Moishe and Pip freeze, listening intently. Jello and Dumbo come into the mortuary. Moishe and Pip block their way to Yoyo.)
PIP: What do you want?
DUMBO: We've come to get the corpse.
PIP: Go away! Nobody is going to touch Yoyo.
JELLO: Come on, don't talk crap. We need that dead body.
PIP: Yoyo is *ours!*
DUMBO: Listen, fellows, there's been enough kidding around. Get moving. We've got to dig him in.
PIP: Yoyo shall be buried.
JELLO *(To Dumbo):* They've gone crazy, I swear.
DUMBO *(With brutality):* Get lost!
(Dumbo pushes Moishe away; Moishe falls on the floor. From the floor he catches Dumbo's leg and Dumbo loses his balance.)
MOISHE: Whistle, Pip! Whistle!
(Pip starts whistling like mad. Jello rushes to help Dumbo but

Pip takes him around the neck, whistling all the time.)

(Sudden noises around the mortuary: feet shuffling, whistling, cries . . .)
YUSTUS *(From the outside):* Here! Follow me!
(A group of convalescents, led by Yustus, rushes into the mortuary. With their white coats, the nurses are excellent targets. The convalescents fight with them. Leaning against the wall, Sipka watches the "battle" calmly. At last, the nurses manage to escape. They look terrible and retreat to the exit.)
YUSTUS: Leave them alone. Let them run away!
(The nurses disappear.)
YUSTUS: Thank you, men. You did a good job.
(Yustus is looking around him.)
YUSTUS: Sipka and Zola! And Pip. And you Moishe! You stay here! We have some important arrangements to make. The others will watch the entrance. If they come again, use force.
(The convalescents exit. Yustus, Sipka, Pip, Zola, Moishe and Zero stay in the mortuary.)
YUSTUS: Sit down.
(They sit on the floor, except Zero, who is hesitating by the door. Yustus is standing in the middle.)
YUSTUS: Since we have permission—the next thing to do is to set up the funeral committee.
ZOLA: That's right.
YUSTUS *(Solemnly):* Gentlemen, I am opening this first meeting of the "St. Raphael's Funeral Committee." First of all, we have to elect a chairman.
SIPKA: That should be you. You were a lawyer once and you will know best how to defend our interests.
ZOLA: I agree.
PIP: So do I.
MOISHE *(With a nod):* Yes.
YUSTUS: Gentlemen, thanks for your confidence. Now, to

work. First, we should define our responsibilities. Sipka, you will be our advisor.

SIPKA: Because I don't say much?

YUSTUS: Sipka, be serious. Zola—you will be our cashier and in charge of supplies.

ZOLA *(Delighted):* Great!

YUSTUS: Moishe, I appoint you commander-in-chief of our fighting unit. You and your men will guard Yoyo, day and night.

MOISHE: But . . . chairman . . . I am not good at fighting.

YUSTUS: So much the better! Everything should be settled without violence.

PIP *(Disappointed):* And me? What am I going to be? Nothing left for me!

YUSTUS: Who says so? You'll be my personal secretary. You will take notes of everything, I tell you.

PIP *(Surly):* Eh, takes notes . . . But how?

YUSTUS *(With dignity):* You forget that we have something to be proud of.

(With a grand gesture, Yustus takes two fountain pens from his pocket. He passes one to Pip.)

YUSTUS: Take good care of it!

PIP *(Delighted):* I will, chairman.

(At last, Zero comes forward.)

ZERO: Look, Yustus . . . I could also . . . lend a hand.

(With a studied gesture Yustus takes off his glasses and scrutinizes Zero.)

YUSTUS: Who is he?

ZOLA: The dead.

YUSTUS: The dead should be silent.

(Everybody turns his head away from Zero and they don't notice his presence anymore.)

YUSTUS *(Satisfied):* Now, then, we've done the most important thing.

ZOLA: Good. And what's next?

(Yustus thoughtfully scratches his beard.)
YUSTUS: Next? Hm? *(Painstakingly)* What do you think, Sipka?
SIPKA: I am wondering how we are going to prepare everything for the burial when we are not allowed to leave the hospital.
YUSTUS: Exactly. That's a good point! What do you suggest?
SIPKA: Getting permits for the outside world.
YUSTUS *(With confidence)*: Good, we'll have them.
(Yustus goes to the exit resolutely. When he gets to the door he stops and turns to Zola.)
YUSTUS: Zola, organize two meetings of the patients. We should inform them of our decisions.
(Zero comes to Yustus.
ZERO *(Ingratiatingly)*: I will call them.
(Yustus doesn't take any notice of him.)
YUSTUS: Come on, Zola. Quickly!
ZOLA: Let Zero go. *(Mockingly)* He is an expert at organizing meetings. And if we find him a club . . .
ZERO *(Revolted)*: I was not a capo.[1]
ZOLA: But you beat people.
(Zero is getting more and more angry.)
ZERO: I was a . . . That was my job. As you, Zola, had to peel potatoes. Or you, Yustus, had to make hand grenades in their factory.
YUSTUS *(Scornfully)*: That's of no importance whatsoever.
ZERO: But they killed people with those grenades on the front!
ZOLA *(Irritated)*: But not with his hands, eh!
ZERO: But due to his talents. That's the same thing.
(Zola approaches Zero with anger.)
ZOLA: When I was peeling potatoes, you were peeling human skin! Was that the same thing?
ZERO: But *they* ate that potato.

---

[1] A notorious corporal.

YUSTUS: Cut it! Why argue? Our court has pronounced the death sentence on you long ago.
(Zola grabs Zero by the shirt.)
ZOLA: You killed and you shall be killed.
(Zero pushes him off.)
ZERO *(Irritated)*: Then kill me! What are you waiting for? Why don't you kill me?
YUSTUS *(Calmly)*: You know very well we would do it gladly—what's to be done when nobody wants to . . . the hell with it! Everybody voted for your death, but nobody wants to be the hangman! Doesn't that make any sense? Everybody tries to get out of it!
(Zero is going to say something but Yustus interrupts him with a sudden gesture.)
YUSTUS: Enough! *(To Zola)* Call the meeting. I'm going for the permits. Pip, come along!
(Yustus walks out, followed by Pip. Zola goes after them, but he stops and turns back to Zero).
ZOLA: I'll give you a piece of advice. Kill yourself. That would be the best solution. At least, you can choose your own death.
ZERO *(Muttering)*: Crap.
SIPKA: Unique privilege, Zero. Normally, death makes the choice.
ZERO *(Defiantly)*: I've made my choice.
ZOLA *(Incredulously)*: Have you?
ZERO *(In a hoarse voice)*: Yes. Life.
(Sipka slowly shakes his head.)
SIPKA: That kind of death is too slow. It will be very hard for you to bear it.

SCENE IV
The hospital grounds

(Sipka, Zola and Pip, led by Yustus, walk to the barred gate. At a distance, dejected and with his hands in his pockets, walks Zero. An armed soldier is standing at the gate. Yustus shows him the permit with a large gesture.)

YUSTUS *(Proudly):* Here you are!
(The soldier opens the gate with an indifferent look. With self-importance and dignity Yustus walks through the gate. The others follow him, producing their permits. When Zero's turn comes, the soldier stops him. Zero is confused and he looks down. The soldier shrugs his shoulders and slams the gate. Zero leans his head on the bars. . . . With a sad look he is watching Yustus and the others who are going to the outer world. Then he suddenly turns back and goes to the hospital, in a hurry. Yustus and his men have stopped at the other side of the lawn.)
Yustus *(Satisfied):* Here we are. Outside. And now—everybody to his job!
ZOLA: What job?
YUSTUS: Pip, write this down.
(Pip takes the notebook and the fountain pen out of his pocket).
YUSTUS: First, a hearse, with little silver angels on the roof.
SIPKA: We'll look for one in the town.
(Sipka puts his arm around Pip's shoulder.)
SIPKA: The two of us.
YUSTUS: Then, a priest. *(Pointing at Zola)* You will supply him.
ZOLA: Why the hell do we need a priest?
YUSTUS: Don't ask stupid questions. Don't you know that at least one priest must be present at the burial?
PIP *(Taking notes):* Thirdly . . .
YUSTUS: Thirdly, an obituary with a nice black border.

(Like at school, Zola raises his hand.)
ZOLA: Leave it to me. I'll write it!
(Zola starts. Then he whistles loudly. Zero is coming from the other side of the lawn. Everybody is looking at him. Zero is smiling, making a gesture with his hand as if he wants to say: "Here I am.")
ZOLA: How did he get out?
YUSTUS *(Waving his hand):* Who cares.
(Yustus lifts up his hands over his head.)
YUSTUS: Off we go on the town.
(Sipka and Pip, followed by Zero, go first, Zola is hesitating for a moment, then he changes his mind and starts in the opposite direction. Yustus stays alone. He has some doubts. At least, he goes back unconvincingly. When he comes to the gate he shows the permit to the soldier. The latter is surprised but he opens the gate and closes it after him. Yustus walks in and then suddenly addresses the soldier.)
YUSTUS: And I . . . I am going to write a touching four-page eulogy!
(He walks to the hospital proudly. The soldier looks at him in amazement.)

SCENE V

Nanita's kitchen.
(A small, crowded room in utter disorder. The table is covered with the remnants of food and vegetables, there are dirty dishes on the old, sooty stove. In front of the chest there is a coarse rug. With his hands in his pockets Zero is leaning against the wall, by the door. Looking down, immobile and silent, Zero seems to prove that nobody wants him here. But he is listening to the conversation very carefully.)

MAN WITH PIPE: The hearse? No, there is no such thing . . .

Not in this village.

SIPKA: Hm . . . Strange. We were told . . .

MAN WITH PIPE *(Nodding his head):* Well, yes it's true, I used to have one. Once upon a time. But now? *(Spreading his arms)* What could I do with it now? The horses need to be fed . . . not much work going—as it used to be . . .

SIPKA *(Smiling):* . . . in the good old days.

(Man with Pipe winks at him)

MAN WITH PIPE: You mean during the war? God bless you, fellow, you are dead wrong. Never so many dead and so little work for me. There were corpses . . . O-ho! In the hospitals, prisons . . . and then in those . . . well, what'ye call em?

PIP: Concentration camps.

MAN WITH PIPE *(Approvingly):* Yes, there. *(Sighs sadly)* By George, there were corpses even in the streets. *(Spreading his arms helplessly)* But they didn't ask for me . . . Believe me, not a single time.

SIPKA *(With mild irony):* That surprises me, indeed.

MAN WITH PIPE *(With resignation):* Dear me, the world has changed. I am not surprised by anything anymore. *(With a nostalgic sigh)* Eh, in my days the war was a different thing. We had respect for the dead, at least. I always used to say: look, men, this will come to no good. Whoever doesn't respect the dead is committing a crime and we all know that one rotten apple spoils the barrel.

(He takes the pipe out of his mouth and shouts . . .)

MAN WITH PIPE: Nani! Tobacco.

(Nanita hands him a pouch, looking at Sipka the whole time. The man with a pipe taps out his pipe absent-mindedly and begins to fill it. Pip takes Sipka by the sleeve.)

PIP: Let's go see the town.

SIPKA: You go ahead.

PIP: What about you.

SIPKA: I'll stay here.

(Pip looks at Nanita, then at Sipka. He turns and leaves without a word. After a while, Zero starts to leave muttering . . .)

ZERO: I think I'll go too. *(He is not speaking to anyone in particular. He follows Pip out slowly. Man with Pipe lights his pipe).*

MAN WITH PIPE: Yes . . . Yes . . . I always used to say: Look, men, he may be your enemy a thousand fold, but he's dead and he deserves your respect. *(Shrugging his shoulders)* But, what could I do? They wouldn't listen to me. *(Bitterly)* And look where we are now.

(He notices that Nanita is still standing nearby and he shouts at her . . .)

MAN WITH PIPE: Come on, come on, time's a wasting.

(Nanita reluctantly goes to the stove. Sipka watches her as she goes)

SIPKA *(Quietly)*: Daughter?

MAN WITH PIPE *(With contempt):* Servant. *(Blows smoke out of his pipe)* Serves in bed as well. *(Stretches, stands up lazily and mutters . . .)* Humph . . . Hard times. *(Turns back to Nanita)* I think I'll go to the orchard. *(Pointing at Sipka with his pipe)* You might offer this . . .

(Man with Pipe is lost in thought looking for the appropriate term for Sipka. He puts his pipe into his mouth—to give him time.)

MAN WITH PIPE: You might offer a drink to our . . . guest. *(Goes to the door, but before he leaves he speaks to Sipka again.)* But I don't think you'll find a hearse. *(Shrugging his shoulders)* And what for . . . My god . . . what made you think of a burial at this time?

(Man with Pipe exits. Sipka doesn't move. He calmly watches Nanita. She is busy at the stove and pays no attention to him.) (Pause)

NANITA *(Casually):* Can you remain silent for a long time?

SIPKA *(Nodding his head):* Yes I can.

(Nanita goes to the shelf and takes down and earthen jug.)
NANITA: Do you like apple brandy?
SIPKA *(Shrugging his shoulders):* I don't remember.
(Nanita pours some wine for Sipka but she is not looking at him.)
NANITA: Camp prisoner?
SIPKA *(Simply):* You have beautiful eyes.
(Nanita looks up slowly. Sipka smiles mildly.)
NANITA: How long?
SIPKA: Let me see your hands.
(Nanita wipes her hands on the apron and then shows them to Sipka. He is looking carefully at her hands and after a while he closes his hand around two of her fingers.)
NANITA: Months?
SIPKA: Years.
(Pause)
(At last, Nanita takes her fingers out of Sipka's hand. She walks to the table and starts to peel potatoes.)
NANITA: They call me Nani. But my name is Nanita.
(The smile disappears from Sipka's lips.)
NANITA: You've never heard that name?
SIPKA: I was in the camp called—Nanita.
(Nanita's hands drop down.)
NANITA *(Helplessly):* You hate me now.
(Sipka is smiling again.)
SIPKA: The only nice word I ever heard in that place was Nanita.
(Nanita carries on with the peeling. She looks as if she is completely absorbed in it.)
NANITA *(Casually):* My husband was an officer.
SIPKA: There were lots of officers.
NANITA: Maybe he was commander of the camp . . . *(After a brief pause)* Maybe even of your camp.
SIPKA: There were lots of camps.
NANITA *(Tonelessly):* He is dead.

SIPKA: I know.
NANITA: How do you know?
(Sipka is looking around the room.)
SIPKA *(Significantly)*: I see.
NANITA: I am serving here for room and board.
SIPKA: Doesn't he pay you anything?
NANITA *(Shrugging her shoulders)*: The food is very expensive and then I have a roof over my head. For the time being. And after that . . .
SIPKA: And what?
(As if she did not hear his question, Nanita walks to the stove and pours the potatoes into the pot.)
NANITA: Are you happy?
SIPKA *(With a smile)*: It's become a habit with me.
NANITA: Why don't you stay for lunch?
(Sipka is looking at the door.)
SIPKA: It will make him angry.
NANITA: Go to my room and he won't see you.
(Nanita points to the door in a corner of the kitchen, Sipka stands up and goes to Nanita.)
SIPKA: Isn't he jealous?
NANITA *(With resignation)*: Well, he grew old.
SIPKA: Still, he is a man.
NANITA: Not very often.
(She pushes Sipka mildly towards the door.)
NANITA: I'll come as soon as I've finished my work.
SIPKA *(Indecisively)*: The fact is, I was on my way to find a hearse . . .
(Nanita is looking firmly at Sipka's eyes.)
NANITA: You've got plenty of time.
SIPKA *(Nodding his head)*: I know I've got time. *((Significantly)* And nothing else.

SCENE VI

The moor.
(Pip enters, looking tired. He sits on the ground. Some children pass by him in a file and he is watching them with interest. They are led by a little fatty who has a wooden sword in his hand. He is followed by three boys who have wooden rifles. They are leading a small boy whose hands are tied behind his back. Marching seriously, they approach the wall. The "prisoner" leans against the wall, and the soldiers assume their places for firing. The boy with the sword ties a handkerchief around the head of the "prisoner." Pip is leaning forward, constantly watching the children. He holds his breath. The boy lifts up his sword. The "soldiers" are shooting. They produce the following sounds: "dum . . . dum . . . dum . . ." and ra . . . ta . . . ta . . . ta . . ." The prisoner falls on the ground. Then he stands up. Pip sighs with relief. The children come to Pip. They are curious and size him up with great seriousness. Pip is smiling benevolently.)

A BOY WITH A SWORD: Where do you come from?
PIP: From "St. Raphael."
BOY/S *(Suspectingly):* You run away.
PIP: I've got a permit.
BOY/S *(Resolutely):* Stand up!
(Pip stands up and he is still smiling at them.)
BOY/S: What do you want here?
PIP: A hearse.
BOY/S: Yer' kiddin'.
PIP *(Proudly):* I am on the burial committee.
(Children surround Pip and make a circle.)
I BOY: Yer' a liar!
II BOY: A spy!
III BOY: A Castaway.
BOY/S *(Sharply):* Hey, quiet.

(The children fall silent but they still have an unfriendly look in their eyes.)

BOY/S: This is our castle.

PIP *(With a smile):* That's nice.

BOY/S: Why are you laughing? *(Threateningly)* You want to fight?

PIP *(In a conciliatory way):* No, I don't.

(The boy with a Sword stands aside and he points his sword at Pip.)

BOY/S: Grab him.

(The boys attack Pip. Reluctantly, he tries to defend himself, but he does not take it seriously. However, the boys are serious; they are beating him and presently he finds himself under a crowd of infuriated children. Suddenly, Zero shows up. He wants to help Pip and he starts to beat the children haphazardly.)

ZERO *(Infuriated):* You damn bastards!

(Scared, the children scatter and run away. Pip is lying on the ground. The boy with a Sword tries to run away, but he stumbles and falls to the ground. As he is falling, his sword is thrown out of his hand. Zero rushes at him madly and starts to punch him.)

ZERO *(Out of control):* You dog! You dirty dog! You son-of-a-bitch!

(Pip stands up quickly and jumps on Zero's back, punching him strongly with his fists.)

PIP: Leave him alone. You damn bastard. Stop it, I tell you!

(Surprised, Zero tries to throw Pip away, but Pip bites his shoulder. Zero cries painfully. The boy escapes Zero's grasp, stands up and starts to run. Pip leaves Zero at last. They are both panting. Pip's face is distorted by the unrestrained hatred.)

PIP *(Spitefully):* You damn killer.

(Zero is standing, looking down desperately.)

ZERO *(Depressed):* They were beating you . . . And I had to defend you.

PIP: All you can do is beat people.

ZERO: I didn't want . . . believe me I didn't . . .

PIP: We are not in the camp anymore! Hear me? You are no longer a capo.

(Zero's shoulders droop even more.)

ZERO *(Docile and ingratiating)*: Pip . . . forgive me . . .

PIP *(Disgusted)*: Get lost!

(Zero walks out slowly. Pip cleans the dust from his cloths. He notices the sword and picks it up. When he stands up again, he is face to face with Pepi. Pepi is 14: skinny, feeble, short haircut, bright, eyes on a pale, meager face. The two boys look at each other in silence.)

PEPI: You really showed him.

(Pip nods his head simply.)

PEPI: I am Pepi. And you?

PIP: Pip.

PEPI *(Surprised)*: What kind of a name is that?

PIP: None. A nickname.

PEPI: And your real name?

(Pip seems not to have heard the question.)

PIP: You belong to them?

PEPI *(Surly)*: I don't belong anywhere. *(Friendly)* Did they hurt you?

PIP *(Waving his hand)*: It's nothing . . . Nothing serious . . .

(Pip wants to give the sword to Pepi.)

PIP: Want it?

PEPI *(Scornfully)*: What for? *(Proudly)* I've got a real one. Want to see?

PIP: I'm thirsty.

PEPI: I live right over there, Let's go . . .

(Pepi walks out. Pip hesitates for a moment. Then he takes the sword and runs after Pepi.)

SCENE VII

Pepi's room.
(The room is furnished with a few simple items: a table, chairs, an old chest of drawers, a bookshelf. Two photos, of a man and a woman, hang on the wall. They are framed by a black ribbon. Pepi comes to the room. Pip follows him, hesitating.)

PEPI: What's the matter? Come in . . .
(Pip stops in the middle of the room. He looks around, as if spellbound.)
PIP *(Amazed):* It's nice here.
PEPI: The furniture is old. It's my granny's. Ours was much nicer.
(Pepi walks to the chest and takes out a steel sabre.)
PIP: It's heavy.
(Pepi puts the sabre on the table.)
PEPI *(In a low voice):* In my cellar. I've got something else as well. Something more terrifying.
PIP: What?
PEPI *(With a finger on his mouth):* Shh . . . My granny might hear.
(Pepi takes a jug from the shelf, pours water into a glass and then gives it to Pip.)
PEPI: Here's some water. *(Watching Pip drink the water)* Do you like milk?
PIP: Oh, God, yes. And you?
PEPI: Haven't seen any for a long time.
(Pip is embarrassed. Pause.)
PEPI: I've heard they give you chocolate in the hospital.
PIP *(Baffled):* Sometimes. *(Lively)* You want me to bring you some?
PEPI *(Unconvincingly):* Forget it. I don't like chocolate.
(Pepi turns his back to Pip.)

PEPI: If you insist, you can bring it for my granny.
(Pepi sits on the table.)
PEPI: Will you go home soon?
PIP *(Shrugging his shoulders)*: So they say.
PEPI: Do you have parents?
(Pip shows a sign of "no" with his head.)
PEPI: Relatives?
PIP: I guess not.
PEPI: Where are you going, then?
PIP: Well, just home.
(Pepi points to the photo of the man on the wall.)
PEPI: That's my father.
(Pip looks at the photo.)
PIP: Was he killed.
PEPI: In action. *(Proudly)* He had three medals. How 'bout yours?
PIP *(Embarrassed)*: I don't know . . .
PEPI: My dad was killed in a tank. How 'bout yours?
PIP: They shot him.
PEPI: Didn't want to make war?
PIP: Because he made it.
PEPI: Against us?
(Pip nods his head.)
PEPI *(Bitterly)*: Everybody was against us.
(Pepi stands up and walks to the portrait of the woman.)
PEPI: My mother. She was a nurse. Gone. How 'bout yours?
PIP *(Nodding his head)*: Mine too.
PEPI: At which front?
PIP: In the camp.
(Pause)
PEPI: Our teacher told us that there were only criminals and traitors in the camps.
PIP *(Dryly)*: He was lying.
PEPI *(Nodding his head)*: Yes, he was. I'll never believe

teachers any more.
(Pepi stands beside Pip.)
PEPI: When I grow up I'll be an inventor. I will build a tank which will be faster than the aircraft and no bullet in the world will break through it.
(Pepi walks to the bookshelf.)
PEPI: Look—this is all mine. You want to borrow some?
PIP: No, I am busy. We are preparing a funeral.
PEPI *(Surly)*: You like funerals?
PIP *(Confused)*: I don't know. Never been to one.
PEPI *(Frowning)*: You shouldn't go. It isn't nice.
PIP: It is true that there are always fallen leaves in the graveyards?
PEPI: What makes you ask that?
PIP *(Shrugging his shoulders)*: Just wondering. I would like to walk on fallen leaves.
PEPI *(Incredulously)*: In the graveyard? Aren't you afraid of the dead people?
PIP *(Surprised)*: Why be afraid?
PEPI *(In a low voice)*: My granny says that they come out of the graves at night and that they kill their murderers in revenge.
PIP *(Carefree)*: So what? You didn't kill anybody.
PEPI *(Scared)*: But they don't know that. They must think we are all murderers. *(In a subdued tone)* They should be buried far away.
PIP: Where?
PEPI: In another, unknown country. The further the better . . . So that they could never come back.

SCENE VIII

The room in the hospital.
(A long table is set for six persons. A big bowl is in the middle. Yustus is sitting at the head of the table. He is deeply absorbed in

his writing. Zero is sitting at the opposite end. He is picking at his food with a spoon slowly, watching Yustus out of the corner of his eye. Zola enters the room. Without a greeting he approaches the table in a hurry, pours the food into his plate and begins to eat greedily. Yustus is watching him reproachfully, playing with his spoon nervously. At last, Zola becomes aware that Yustus is watching him. He lifts up his head and shouts . . .)

ZOLA: The priest is not coming.
(Then he carries on with his eating.)
YUSTUS *(In disbelief)*: Pardon?
ZOLA: Forget about the priest.
YUSTUS: What? He rejected?
ZOLA: Yes, but very politely. Busy—he says. He has to decant wine.
(Yustus strikes the table with his fist.)
YUSTUS: For God's sake. I bet you didn't tell him that there is a real funeral in question.
(Zola stops chewing.)
ZOLA: Yes, I did. But the priest says he must decant wine. Otherwise, it will begin to stink of the barrel. And that is, he says, very unpleasant.
(Pip enters the room. He has muttered something as a greeting and then he sits at the table. Yustus is looking at him angrily.)
YUSTUS: Where have you been all this time?
PIP *(Pouring the food into his plate)*: With Sipka.
YUSTUS: And where is he?
PIP: He has stayed . . . *(Having bitten a piece of bread)* With a sort of girl.
(Yustus stops playing with his spoon. Zola lifts up his head, and his jaws, which were chewing industriously, freeze. Just about to put the spoon in his mouth, Pip notices that Yustus and Zola are watching him in amazement. He looks confused. He doesn't understand why his words gave rise to such a reaction, but he

thinks that it is better to change the subject.)
PIP: There is no hearse.
YUSTUS *(Disapprovingly)*: Impossible. Every civilized place must have a hearse!
PIP *(Shrugging his shoulders)*: But this one hasn't.
(Yustus puts his plate away, in anger.)
YUSTUS: Nice people, aren't they! *(Striking the table with his fist)* We must find some sort of hearse! We can't have a funeral without a hearse.
ZOLA: Yustus, I saw it in the shed. There was a cart in the shed!
YUSTUS: A cart? Nonsense! We can't drag Yoyo around as if we were dog catchers!
ZERO *(Looking down at his plate)*: How about a wagon?
(Nobody wants to pay any attention to him. Yustus taps his spoon on the table nervously.)
PIP *(Striking his forehead with his hand)*: That's it. A wagon!
YUSTUS: Great, Pip! Good idea! That's it. A wagon! No one will laugh at us if we use a wagon instead of a hearse.
ZOLA: Yustus, they don't give you anything free in this town. What if a coachman charges us for Yoyo's transport?
YUSTUS *(Casually)*: So what? *(Very officially)* Cashier!
ZOLA: Yes?
YUSTUS: How much do we have in the treasury?
ZOLA: Nothing.
YUSTUS: What's that? Spent everything?
ZOLA: What's the matter with you? We never had anything!
YUSTUS: All right. Perhaps we didn't. But we'll have something now. *(Briskly)* Pip, the pen!
(Pip looks at him in surprise.)
YUSTUS: What are you waiting for? Give it to me!
(Pip is trembling.)
YUSTUS *(Embarrassed)*: I feel sorry, too . . . but don't you see . . . we have no choice. We must pay somehow.
(Pip turns his back to Yustus, keeping the pen in his hand firmly.)

ZOLA *(Hesitatingly)*: I could contribute something . . .
YUSTUS *(Surprised)*: You?
(Zola puts his hand in his pocket and takes out a pen knife.)
ZOLA: This?
YUSTUS *(Surprisingly)*: Where did you get that?
(Zola is at a loss.)
ZOLA *(Embarrassed)*: Well, Bertha . . . that old bitch . . . in other words, the nurse . . . left it . . .
YUSTUS: And you've stolen it?
(Zola strikes the table with his fist.)
ZOLA *(Irritated)*: How long were we going to eat without a knife?
YUSTUS: Listen, Zola—we are free now and we have to accept the laws of the outer world. You'll give it back to Bertha right away.
(Zola wants to protest, but Yustus stops him with a firm look.)
YUSTUS: Not a word. Don't say a word!
(Zola throws the knife on the table, infuriated, Yustus stands up.)
YUSTUS *(To Zola)*: This afternoon you will go to the quartermaster and ask the sergeant to give us a coffin . . . or something like that. Understand? But first you will take Moishe's lunch to the mortuary. *(Significantly)* The whole lunch.
(Pip laughs cheerfully. Zola takes Moishe's plate and walks out of the room, grumbling. Yustus holds out his hand and Pip puts the pen in his palm. Yustus puts his hand on Pip's shoulder.)
YUSTUS: And we two will find the wagon. *(Addressing the empty table)* Don't worry gentlemen, we shall have a proper hearse!
(Yustus and Pip walk out. Zero is alone in the room. He approaches the table, takes the knife with a triumphant smile and puts it in his pocket. Then he goes to the head of the table, awkwardly imitating Yustus in his behavior and speech.)
ZERO: Gentlemen, don't worry . . . You will have a proper hearse!

(Zero begins to laugh in a strained, affected manner.)

CURTAIN

PART II

SCENE IX

The coachman's room.
(A small, dark room with a low ceiling and old shabby furniture. The coachman, Yustus and pip are sitting at a table. The coachman is over sixty. His gray, bristly hair is untidy and his face is covered by a beard.)

THE COACHMAN: No, you won't find a wagon. They've taken all the wagons to the neighboring village. They're carrying hay for the army.
YUSTUS: We know that . . . But we've seen a wagon and a horse in your stable.
THE COACHMAN *(Nodding his head):* Yes, Monique is my mare.
YUSTUS: Does that mean that you're not carrying hay?
THE COACHMAN: No. They left me alone because of sickness.
PIP: What's wrong with you, old man?
THE COACHMAN: Nothing with me, sonny. But my mare is somewhat short-winded. If I were sick—believe me, they wouldn't spare me. No fooling with this army. They know how to squeeze a man.
YUSTUS: What do you expect, old man? This is what happens when you lose a war.
THE COACHMAN: Monique and I didn't lose it because we didn't fight.
(The coachman takes a better look at his visitors.)

THE COACHMAN: You're from St. Raphael aren't you?
(Yustus nods his head.)
THE COACHMAN *(Surprised):* And what do you want the wagon for?
YUSTUS: One of our men has died. Tomorrow is his funeral . . .
THE COACHMAN: . . . and you want Monique and me to take him to the graveyard. Drop that, stranger. Monique is terribly scared of dead people. I remember, last year we were taking some of the ones who were shot. She was scared to death. She couldn't eat for three days afterwards.
YUSTUS: Don't worry, we won't show her the dead. *(Confidentially)* You know, it's very important for us to get our friend buried the way it becomes us as free men. Understand?
(The Coachman shrugs his shoulders sullenly.)
THE COACHMAN: Oh, boy . . . All of a sudden everybody wants to get their dead buried. And I am positive there won't be room for by Monique under the ground.
PIP: But Monique is a mare.
THE COACHMAN *(Offended):* So what, sonny? That mare has never bitten anybody in her life, or kicked for that matter, and still they wanted to eat her up a couple of times. It's a miracle that she has survived this war.
YUSTUS: But look. *(Significantly)* I didn't tell you the most important thing. We are going to pay nicely.
THE COACHMAN: Pay? You? Ha . . . What with?
(Yustus takes the pen out of his pocket, triumphantly.)
YUSTUS *(Grandly):* With this!
THE COACHMAN *(Amazed):* With that? *(Surly)* Don't be stupid, stranger. What could I do with it?
YUSTUS *(Angrily):* What do you mean, what could you do with it? It has fantastic value.
THE COACHMAN *(Shrugging his shoulders):* It may be valuable somewhere . . . but not here.
(The Coachman stands up. Yustus and Pip are still stunned.)

THE COACHMAN: Listen to me. Why don't you forget it? Who needs funerals these days? What's the use? *(Friendly)* We'd better have a glass of wine, eh?
(The Coachman puts a jug of wine on the table. Zero appears at the door at that moment. Yustus stands up.)
YUSTUS: Thanks, but we should be off now.
(The Coachman shrugs his shoulders.)
THE COACHMAN: It's up to you.
YUSTUS: Let's go, Pip. *(To the Coachman)* The best of luck.
THE COACHMAN: If there's any luck left.
(Yustus and Pip walk out, without looking at Zero. Zero comes to the table and begins to pour wine into the glasses without saying anything.)

SCENE X

A village road.
Pip and Yustus enter. Yustus is lost in his thoughts and Pip is angry.

PIP: The old codger is completely gone. He doesn't even know the value of a fountain pen, does he?
YUSTUS *(Absentmindedly)*: No . . . he can't know that.
PIP: What's important is that we can. *(After a brief pause)* Would you give it to me again?
(Yustus hands the fountain pen to Pip.)
YUSTUS: You can keep it as long as you want.
(Pip carefully puts the fountain pen in his pocket.)
PIP: Don't worry. I know how to take care of it.
(Yustus is thinking deeply.)
PIP *(Curiously)*: What are you thinking about?
YUSTUS *(Disheartened)*: It won't be easy, Pip. Not easy at all. Nothing seems to be going right. Where could Sipka be now?
PIP: Well, in town. Are you heading that way?

YUSTUS *(Shaking his head):* No, I'm not.
PIP *(Surprised):* But you haven't seen the town yet.
YUSTUS: What is there to see? How could I go like this? I look like a beggar.
PIP: So what? They don't look any better.
YUSTUS: Doesn't matter. I'll go for a walk in the woods. Would you like to join me? I bet you'll like it much better than in town.
PIP *(Hesitatingly):* I'd like to, but, you see, I promised somebody that I would come . . . in fact, a boy from town.
YUSTUS *(Seriously):* Be sure you don't get mixed up with the wrong people.
PIP: He's not bad, Yustus. He's only inexperienced. *(Expertly)* He's young.
YUSTUS *(Nodding his head):* Good. But come back by dinner time.
(Yustus lifts his head.)
YUSTUS: It's humid. Perhaps we'll get a storm.
(Yustus starts moving with tired steps.)
PIP: You want me to look for Sipka?
YUSTUS *(Turns back):* Why?
PIP: I'll tell him to come back.
YUSTUS: Doesn't matter, Pip. It's not necessary. He'll come back anyway.
(Pip waits until Yustus leaves, and then he starts with quick steps.)

SCENE XI

Pepi's room, Pepi is sitting at the table. He is reading. Pip enters the room. He steps at the door without saying anything. Pepi raises his head.

PEPI: Why are you so late?
PIP: We've been looking for a wagon—for a hearse. Couldn't

find one.
Pip falls, exhausted, into the chair.)
PEPI: What will you do now?
PIP *(Desperately)*: I don't know.
PEPI: Don't have a burial.
PIP *(Shaking his head)*: We've got to. *(After a brief interval)* By the way, are you coming?
PEPI: But I didn't know your friend.
PIP: Nobody knows Yoyo.
(His expression goes somber.)
PEPI: I don't like it when people die. How 'bout you?
PIP: Yustus says that nobody will die anymore.
PEPI: They will die in the war.
PIP: But the war is over.
(Pepi shakes his head.)
PEPI: Not quite. My teacher says we will have another war soon.
PIP: Your teacher always lies. He lied about the camps as well.
PEPI: Yes, but he's an expert about the wars.
(Pip is hesitating. Finally he pulls a chocolate bar out of his pocket. He hands it to Pepi awkwardly.)
PIP: For your granny?
(Pepi takes the chocolate without looking at it. He puts it on the table and covers it quickly with a book.)
PIP: And this.
(Pip puts a pack of cigarettes on the table.)
PEPI: My granny doesn't smoke.
(Pip takes a cigarette out of the pack and lights it. Pepi is looking at him in surprise.)
PEPI: They allow you to smoke?
PIP *(Surprised)*: Why shouldn't I be allowed? *(Pushing the cigarette box to Pepi)* Take one.
PEPI *(Suddenly)*: Why don't we become buddies, we two? You want to?

PIP *(Nodding his head):* Sure.
PEPI: We'll see each other every day. Okay?
PIP: When the burial is over they will take my pass away.
PEPI: Then don't go back to the hospital. Stay here. *(Significantly)* For good.
PIP *(Amazed):* Stay here?
PEPI: Well, yes!
PIP *(Unconvincingly):* I can't. I've got to go home.
PEPI: Yes, but you haven't got a home.
(Pip is looking down. An uneasy interval. Pepi is trying to make up for his mistake; all of a sudden he becomes artificially carefree. Pepi opens the chest. He takes out different toys. Most of them are broken.)
PEPI: See this: It's all mine!
(Pip is watching Pepi without any expression on his face.)
PEPI *(Taking the toys out of the chest):* We'll share everything I have.
(The chest is empty. Breathless. Pepi is standing beside a big heap of toys.)
PIP *(Surly):* I don't like toys.
(Pepi suddenly becomes serious. He comes to Pip.)
PEPI *(In a low voice):* If you stay I'll give you something nobody has.
PIP *(Uninterested):* What?
PEPI *(After a significant interval):* Hand grenades . . . and bombs. There are plenty of them in the cellar of that ruin.
(Pepi grasps Pip's arm.)
PEPI: Stay. Stay, Pip, please. I don't want to be alone.
PIP: Do you know Sipka?
PEPI: No, who is he?
PIP: He says he is afraid because he can never be alone.
(Pip goes to the door. Pepi holds him tightly by the arm.)
PEPI: Where are you going?
PIP: Back.

PEPI: Coming tomorrow?
PIP: Tomorrow is the burial.
PEPI *(Sullenly):* The sooner it is over the better.
(Pip is ready to start again.)
PEPI: Pip!
(Pip stops.)
PIP: Yes?
PEPI: I know you don't like the stuff in the cellar. You don't want to stay with me because of that. Isn't that so?
(Pip is silent.)
PEPI: Don't worry, Pip; I'll dig everything under ground. When I tell you . . .
PIP: Wait until I bring Sipka. He'll tell you what to do with it.
(With a friendly smile Pepi holds out his hand toward Pip.)
PEPI: See you.
(Pip is nodding his head and pushing off Pepi's hand mildly.)
PIP: I don't like partings.
(Pip walks out of the room. Tired, Pepi sits down on the floor beside a heap of scattered toys.)

SCENE XII

The mortuary.
(Moishe is sitting, leaned against the wall. He is humming quietly but he is constantly watching the table with Yoyo's body. Zola enters. He has a big piece of cardboard in his hand.)

ZOLA: Did you finish your lunch?
MOISHE: There is something left. Want it?
(Moishe holds out the bowl to Zola. But Zola wants to show good manners and he hesitates.)
MOISHE: No, I am not hungry. Take it.
(Zola takes the bowl and sits down opposite to Moishe. He begins to eat,)

ZOLA *(With his mouth full):* Is it dull here?
MOISHE: No, it isn't.
ZOLA: What do you do?
MOISHE: Look after Yoyo.
(Pause. Zola is busy eating.)
MOISHE: What's it like outside?
ZOLA: Cloudy . . . It looks like rain. *(Pointing at the cardboard with his spoon.)* Look, I've made the obituary. *(Moishe takes the cardboard. He looks closely at it.)*
ZOLA: Like it?
MOISHE: It's nice.
ZOLA: Keep it here until Yustus comes back.
(Zola has finished eating. He stands up and goes to the exit.)
MOISHE: Where are you going now?
ZOLA: To sleep.
MOISHE *(Surprised):* Aren't you going to town?
ZOLA *(With resignation):* I've already been there?
MOISHE *(Inquisitively):* What did you see there?
ZOLA: Oh, all sorts of things . . . Many shop windows . . . and, you know . . . everything. But they don't give you anything . . . I mean just like that. They ask for money. Even for the food. *(Waiving his hand)* I don't want to go any more.
MOISHE: What about people? What are they doing?
ZOLA *(Shrugging his shoulders):* Well, you know . . . they are walking . . . talking to each other . . . cating . . .
MOISHE: Like it used to be?
ZOLA *(Nodding his head):* Yes, just like that . . . As in the old days . . .
MOISHE: And is there . . . a church in the town?
ZOLA: Yes, there is. I was there. You know, I was looking for a priest.
MOISHE: Was it full?
ZOLA: The church? Oh, hell no! There wasn't a single a soul in it.

MOISHE: Nobody was praying?
ZOLA *(Indifferently):* I didn't see anybody.
MOISHE: And you? Did you pray?
ZOLA *(Stupefied):* Me? Nonsense! Who would I pray to?
MOISHE *(Significantly):* That's nice. You won the war, but you don't have coffins for your corpses.
(Bertha sizes them up and then walks to the exit. With the obituary in his hand, Zola blocks her way.)
ZOLA: I wanted to ask you . . . Where can I post this?
BERTHA: Nowhere. No notices are permitted!
ZOLA *(Offended):* This is not a notice, this is an obituary.
BERTHA: An obituary! Nonsense. Had we put obituaries up for everybody who died, our walls would have been covered with such scribbles.
(Bertha is walking out. When she comes to the door, she turns back again.)
BERTHA *(With a sneer):* But don't forget it: This is not an asylum, this is a hospital.
(Bertha walks out energetically.)
ZOLA *(Sullenly):* She's laughing at us.
MOISHE *(Calmly):* When it is so difficult for God to bear defeat, why should it be easy for people?

SCENE XIII

Nanita's room. It is a small room in the attic: light barely penetrates through a small window; it is tidy, but very modestly furnished: an iron bed covered with a blanket, a small table, a dresser, a shabby armchair and a small shelf. Nanita is sitting in the armchair and Sipka is sitting beside her on the floor.

NANITA *(Nostalgically):* I used to have a servant once . . . big apartment . . . nice furniture . . . lots of dresses . . .
SIPKA: You were pretty?

NANITA *(Proudly)*: Oh, yes, very much so.
SIPKA: You are not bad looking now, either. You have beautiful eyes. *(Uneasily)* Have I already told you that?
NANITA *(Smiling)*: Yes, you have.
SIPKA: And about the hair?
NANITA: Yes.
SIPKA: And the breasts?
(Nanita stretches back in the armchair.)
NANITA: When did you sleep with a woman last?
(He stretches on his back on the floor. He's looking at the ceiling. A pause.)
NANITA: Don't you remember?
SIPKA: I remember some women.
NANITA: You love them?
SIPKA *(Smiling)*: Not all of them.
(Nanita slips from the armchair and sits down on the floor beside Sipka.)
NANITA: Could you love—me?
SIPKA *(Still looking at the ceiling, simply)*: I do love you.
(She is bending over Sipka.)
NANITA: Why do you lie?
SIPKA: You gave me food and drink.
NANITA: Do you love me only for that?
SIPKA: For that, as well.
(Nanita's head comes closer to Sipka's.)
NANITA: You don't know me. You've never seen me before.
SIPKA: Oh yes I have. Very often.
NANITA: Where?
SIPKA: Everywhere.
NANITA: But that wasn't me.
SIPKA: It was a woman. Why not you?
(Pause)
NANITA: What do they call you?
(Sipka sits.)

NANITA: Old name.
SIPKA: A camp name.
(He takes the cigarette holder out of his mouth and puts it on his palm.)
SIPKA: It means—a cigarette holder.
NANITA: How long have you had it?
SIPKA: For a long time.
(Nanita holds out her hand.)
NANITA: Give it to me.
(Sipka's face darkens. He is holding the cigarette holder in his fist and he stands up.)
NANITA: You won't?
(Sipka's puts his hand with the cigarette folder into his pocket and turns his back to Nanita.)
SIPKA *(Surly)*: No, I won't?
(Nanita leans her head on the armchair.)
NANITA: You like that cigarette holder better than me.
(Sipka goes to Nanita and puts his hand on her head.)
SIPKA: I like both of you the same.
(Nanita takes Sipka's hand and holds it on her head.)
NANITA: I love you, too . . . Sipka.
SIPKA: I know that. You gave me food and drink.
NANITA *(Warmly)*: I would like to give you much more . . .
(Sipka takes his hand out of Nanita's.)
SIPKA *(Mildly)*: One shouldn't exaggerate.
(Sipka goes to the shelf and looks at the objects which are arranged on it: a piece of stone, a piece of wood and a piece of cloth.)
SIPKA: What's this?
(Nanita stands up and walks to Sipka. She takes the piece of stone in her hand.)
NANITA: This is what is left . . . from our home . . . *(Pointing at the piece of wood)* from our furniture . . . *(Taking up the piece of cloth)* and my favorite dress . . .

SIPKA: You keep these remnants?
NANITA: Why don't you throw your cigarette holder away?
SIPKA: I've brought it from the camp, Nanita.
(Nanita's face takes on a cunning expression.)
NANITA: Okay, Sipka. I'll throw it away! I'll destroy this garbage when I get everything back again!
SIPKA *(Cynically):* Furniture, servants, dresses!
NANITA: No. Not only that.
SIPKA: What else?
NANITA: Everything!
SIPKA: What?
NANITA *(Embarrassed):* I don't know . . . how to say . . . (Insisting) But I've got to get everything! I've got to have a new start! *(After a brief pause)* We've got to have a new start.
(Sipka walks to the window.)
SIPKA: Look.
(Nanita turns her back to the window.)
NANITA: That's not true. We two are in nobody's way!
SIPKA *(Nodding his head):* No. Not until we posses something . . . and until we live together.
NANITA *(Defiantly):* Still, we shall stay together!
SIPKA *(Cynically):* Forever?
NANITA: Forever.
SIPKA: And what shall we do when our eternity is over?
NANITA *(Bravely):* It won't be over. It mustn't.
SIPKA: My eternity has passed once. And yours, too, Nanita?
(Nanita bows her head in silence. She goes to her bed and sits on it. Pause. Finally Nanita manages to control her sadness. Her face is cheerful again.)
NANITA: Why do we keep talking about the past? There is no past, anymore . . . and we are here . . . together.
(She holds her hand out to Sipka.)
 NANITA: Come here . . .
(Sipka comes close to the bed. Nanita lies back.)

NANITA: Here . . .
(Sipka sits down on the bed.)
NANITA: Lie down . . . here, beside me.
(Sipka doesn't move.)
NANITA: You don't want to sleep with me?
SIPKA *(Coldly):* I'm not sleepy.
(Nanita raises herself on her elbows.)
NANITA *(Depressed):* Is this revenge?
SIPKA: What for?
NANITA: For "Nanita."
(Nanita hides her head behind Sipka's back.)
NANITA: I didn't know what they were doing to you. I couldn't even believe it.
(Sipka lifts Nanita's head tenderly.)
SIPKA: It's not your fault.
(Pause)
NANITA: Don't you want me?
SIPKA *(Nodding his head):* Eight years.
NANITA *(Upset):* I would like so much . . .
(Sipka puts his finger on her lips tenderly.)
SIPKA: No, Nanita. Let's not push it.
(Nanita pushes Sipka's hand away, tenderly.)
NANITA: I want to make you happy. I want you to accept happiness.
SIPKA: You want me to worry about it?
NANITA: It pays. You'll see for yourself.
SIPKA *(Surly):* I've already seen.
NANITA: Don't you want to forget?
SIPKA *(Points at the shelf):* And you?
(Nanita lies back on the bed again. Sipka lies on the floor, beside the bed.)
NANITA: Help me. Try . . . Help us to forget . . .
SIPKA: You mean Nanita and Sipka?
NANITA: Sad Nanita . . . and unhappy Sipka.

SIPKA *(Tonelessly)*: Sad Nanita doesn't exist anymore . . .
NANITA: Unhappy Sipka doesn't exist either . . .
(Pause)
NANITA: I would like so much for you to be tender.
SIPKA: I would like that too.
NANITA: Give me your hand. Caress me . . . my face . . . my hair . . .
(They are both lying, immobile.)
NANITA: My hair is coarse.
SIPKA: My fingers are coarse, Nanita.
NANITA *(Exhausted)*: I used to be pretty . . .
SIPKA: Yes, I remember.
NANITA: But I am old now . . .
SIPKA: Centuries have passed . . .
(A long pause. Suddenly, lightning illuminates the dark room. A strong thunder wakes Nanita. She jumps from the bed, terrified.)
NANITA: Sipka! Do you hear!
SIPKA: Yes, the thunder.
NANITA *(Relieved)*: I was scared.
SIPKA: Me too.
(Nanita is kneeling beside Sipka with her head on his shoulder.)
NANITA: I had a dream.
SIPKA: A nice one?
NANITA: It was a holiday. The shadows disappeared into the crevices, and glittering light was pouring into the streets. Flowers burst through the asphalt, and dappled petals covered the roofs . . . We were walking hand in hand, crossing the glimmering bridge.
(Nanita lifts up her head.)
NANITA: Sipka, why don't dreams last forever?
SIPKA: There are bad dreams, too.
(Sipka stands up.)
NANITA *(Upset)*: No, Sipka . . . don't go.
SIPKA: I must. My friends are waiting for me.
(Sipka walks to the window. He is looking outside . . . Nanita

stands up from the floor.)
NANITA: You're coming again?
SIPKA: It looks like a storm.
(Sipka turns back and walks with quick steps toward the door. He exists without looking back at Nanita.)

SCENE XIV

(The office. A gray, cold room with a writing desk and few chairs. The Major is standing by the window with his back turned toward the door. He's smoking. There is lightning every now and then and the sound of thunder. Moishe enters. He is awestruck. He stops by the door, embarrassed and confused. He blinks his eyes, not being accustomed to the light. Dead silence. Moishe doesn't move. Finally the Major turns surround and notices him.)

MAJOR: Oh? You've come?
MOISHE: Me? *(Nodding his head)* Yes.
(The Major goes to the writing desk. He hesitates. At last he points to a chair.)
MAJOR: Well, sit down Mr. . . . uhm *(Pause)*?
MOISHE: Moishe.
MAJOR: Mr. Moishe, sit down.
(Moishe takes the nearest chair and sits on its edge. He smiles.)
MAJOR *(Drumming his fingers on the table, absentmindedly)*: How are you?
MOISHE: Healthy.
MAJOR: That's good.
(The Major sits at the writing desk.)
MAJOR: You will be able to go home soon.
MOISHE *(Nodding his head)*: That's good.
MAJOR: What are you?
MOISHE: A camp prisoner.

MAJOR *(Waiving his hand):* No. I mean before . . .
MOISHE: My father was a rabbi.
MAJOR *(Absentmindedly):* Uh huh . . . Your father?
(An interlude. The Major holds out his cigarette box to Moishe, with an obliging smile. Moishe goes to the table and takes a cigarette. The Major gives him a light. Moishe sits again on the edge of his chair. He puffs clumsily. He smiles constantly. The Major doesn't know how to begin.)
MAJOR *(With an effort):* About that funeral of yours . . . you know . . . hm. . . ? Well, I can understand you . . . but you should understand me.
MOISHE *(Nodding his head):* Sure.
MAJOR *(Encouraged):* I'm a doctor, first of all. But I am a soldier too. I've got to carry out the orders.
MOISHE: You are supposed to.
(With a sudden gesture the Major opens the drawer in the writing desk, takes out a big heap of files.)
MAJOR *(Striking the files):* Here, look at them. These are all orders! And this . . . *(Taking up a sheet of paper)* a written order that all the corpses in the hospitals should be interred immediately, so that infection doesn't spread, disease . . . and the like. Understand?
(Moishe coughs. He waves the smoke out of his face.)
MAJOR: Now. There was a military inspection in a nearby place. They are likely to come here tomorrow. And what shall I do if they find a corpse in the mortuary? A corpse more than a day old?
(The cigarette has a long ash, and Moishe doesn't know what to do with it. The ashtray is on the other side of the writing desk. He looks around embarrassed.)
MAJOR: I promised you . . . but you see . . . don't you . . . that inspection. *(Shrugging his shoulders)* What can I do?
(The Major stands up.)
MAJOR: You will explain to your friends, won't you?

MOISHE *(Readily)*: I will.

MAJOR *(Relieved)*: Well, then . . . I will send the nurses for the corpse.

MOISHE: Why?

MAJOR: The corpse should be interred today. Right away!

MOISHE *(With a benevolent smile)*: The burial is tomorrow.

MAJOR: The control might come tomorrow! If they find the corpse, I will be punished.

MOISHE *(Surprised)*: You?

MAJOR: Me, of course! Is that clear, now?

MAJOR *(With relief)*: I'll send for the nurses.

MOISHE: Why?

(The Major is becoming infuriated.)

MAJOR: But listen, Mister . . .

MOISHE: Moishe.

MAJOR *(Sharply)*: Mr. Moishe, if you don't deliver the dead to the nurses, I'll call the guard! Know what that means?

MOISHE: The guard? *(Nodding his head)* I know.

MAJOR: We'd better not argue about it.

MOISHE *(With a broad smile)*: Better not.

MAJOR: It's okay then?

(Moishe stands up. He starts for the door. When he reaches it, he turns around. The smile has disappeared from his face.)

MOISHE: Yoyo is *our* dead.

(He knocks off his cigarette ash onto the floor and then walks out.)

SCENE XV

The Coachman's room. A faintly glowing light bulb barely illuminates the room. Zero and the Coachman are sitting at the table which has a jug of wine and two glasses on it. The Coachman is tipsy, but he doesn't show it much. However, inexperienced Zero is almost drunk.

ZERO *(Beating on the table with his palm):* I say, and I will repeat it a hundred times, there is no survival for the weak! *(With disgust)* And your mare is phooey! She's a real cream puff!
COACHMAN: Oh, leave the poor thing alone. Didn't she suffer enough?
ZERO: You should be stern with the animals, to make them tough!
COACHMAN: I don't like a whip, stranger. You won't find one in my place.
(Zero stands up and pushes the chair away with his legs. He staggers and he supports himself with his fists on the table.)
ZERO: Don't want to beat her, heh?
(Zero goes around the table and stops beside the Coachman.)
ZERO: And if they came and said . . . *(Emphasizing each word)* . . . We shall beat you, old codger, if you don't beat your mare! *(Triumphantly)* What would you do then?
COACHMAN *(Calmly):* Well, if it couldn't be otherwise, let them beat me.
(Zero laughs loudly. He sits on the table and sneers at the Coachman.)
ZERO: Did they ever beat you, old man?
COACHMAN: I don't remember.
(Zero jumps off of the table.)
ZERO: They didn't. I bet they didn't. You would have remembered otherwise. I bet you would have . . .
(Zero takes the glass of wine and guzzles it.)
ZERO: But me? You see, me . . . There is not a thing they didn't do to me!
COACHMAN *(Shrugging his shoulders):* Well . . . That was the war.
(Zero is calm again; his anger disappears suddenly.)
ZERO: Yes, of course . . . you're right . . . the war.
(Zero goes back to his chair and falls into it.)

ZERO *(Dully)*: What kind of war would it have been if they hadn't beaten anybody?
(The Coachman takes up the jug and pours wine into the glasses.)
COACHMAN: Well, why should it be that way?
(Zero strikes the table with his fist.)
ZERO: When it's war, it's war! *(More calmly)* Somebody beats you because he likes it, and somebody because he must. Isn't that the same thing? Tell me. Isn't it the same?
COACHMAN: If they beat me, it would be the same.
(Zero stands up and pats the Coachman on the shoulder.)
ZERO *(Smiling grotesquely)*: You're a wise old man. You should help us. *(The Coachman drinks a gulp of wine and wipes his mouth with his sleeve. Then he shakes his head.)*
COACHMAN: I won't.
ZERO: Come on, rent us that wagon. Come with Monique to the burial.
(The Coachman puts down the glass sullenly.)
COACHMAN: What's wrong with you people? It seems you are all after that poor mare. Leave her alone! The war is over.
ZERO: The war is over you say? Over . . . huh? You're wrong, old man, you're dead wrong. The war is still going on!
(The sound of thunder is heard. Zero holds out his hand towards the door.)
COACHMAN *(Calmly)*: A thunderstorm, stranger.
ZERO *(Scornfully)*: What did you say, a thunderstorm? They don't shoot anymore? The shooting is over? The cannons are silent, huh? *(With artificial pathos)* The war is over! No more war! *(Lifting his glass)* Let's forget the war! Let's forget everything! Cheers!
(Zero empties his glass. Then he walks to the Coachman and puts his finger on his lips . . .)
ZERO: Sh! If somebody asks you, you don't know anything. You didn't see anything. Got it? We shall pretend that nothing

happened . . .

COACHMAN *(Nodding his head):* That's right, stranger. You are right: One should forget the ugly as soon as possible.

(Zero strikes the table with his glass.)

ZERO: And who is the first to forget? Who? The victors their victory, or the defeated their defeat?!

(Zero becomes depressed all of a sudden. He looks down desperately, lost in his thoughts . . .)

ZERO: And I? What shall I do? Am I to forget something?

(Pause. For some time Zero is staring vacantly. Finally he is himself again. He goes to the table and falls into the armchair. His face takes on a repenting look.)

ZERO *(Ingratiatingly):* I beg you, old man . . . do me a favor . . . do it for my sake. Please come to the burial . . .

(The Coachman loses his patience. He strikes the table with his fist angrily.)

COACHMAN: Enough with that burial! Enough! I don't want—I don't—that's it!

ZERO: Think it over . . .

COACHMAN *(Stubbornly):* No! Monique is not going to drag that dead body! *(Striking the table with his empty glass)* No, no, no!

ZERO: But I will explain to you . . .

COACHMAN: I don't want to listen. Get lost!

(Zero walks to the window and looks outside.)

ZERO: I can't. The storm . . .

COACHMAN: Well, there you are; we shall have rain and there won't be any burial!

(Zero goes back to his place.)

ZERO: You don't know anything! A burial is much nicer when it rains . . . Rain and a burial—they go together.

(Zero holds out the empty glass to the Coachman.)

ZERO: More!

COACHMAN *(Snarling):* You can't have it.

ZERO: Just a drop.
COACHMAN: Not a bit.
ZERO: Then give me something to eat.
COACHMAN: I don't have anything.
ZERO: Only a bite.
COACHMAN: I don't have anything.
(Zero is thinking for a moment and then walks to the Coachman with a heavy step. He has a pen knife in his hand. The blade is pointed toward the Coachman's breast.)
ZERO: You don't have—or you don't want to give me?
COACHMAN: Listen, stranger, you know what hunger is?
(Zero's hand with the knife drops down. For some time he watches the Coachman stupefied.)
ZERO: Hunger? Did you say—hunger? You hungry? You?
(All of a sudden, zero bursts into laughter.)
ZERO *(Laughing)*: Starving. You people starving.
COACHMAN *(Surly)*: That's not funny.
(Staggering, Zero walks to his chair, laughing all the time.)
ZERO *(Still laughing)*: It is funny. Damned funny.
(Suddenly Zero becomes serious. He stands up and strikes the table with his fist.)
ZERO *(Triumphantly)*: You will come to the burial. I swear you will.

SCENE XVI

The hospital yard.
(Occasionally, there is lightning in the sky. The wind is getting stronger. A regiment of soldiers, led by a sergeant, is marching across the moor, towards the gate. They come into the yard. In front of the mortuary a file of the convalescents. Yustus, Moishe, Sipka, Zola and Pip are among them. They are standing in silence, motionless—as if they were dead. They resemble funny, shaggy scarecrows as if someone had sloppily dressed them in

their hospital gowns. The squad of soldiers stops a few steps from the silent file. Jello and Dumbo stand behind them. They have the empty stretcher in their hands. The sergeant comes forward and gives a sign to the nurses. Jello and Dumbo walk carefully toward the entrance of the mortuary. When they reach the file they come to a standstill.)

SERGEANT *(Sharply):* Make way for the nurses!
(There is lightning and thunder. The file doesn't give way.)
SERGEANT: I have orders to use force in case of disobedience.
(Sergeant turns back to his regiment and gives a sign with his hand. The soldiers take up their "front" position. The soldiers advance slowly. The convalescents don't move. A few steps in front of the file, the soldiers stop, hesitating. They look at the sergeant, and then the stormy sky. Jello and Dumbo are hiding carefully behind the soldiers. The convalescents remain motionless. The wind is getting wild.)
SERGEANT *(Impatiently):* One minute . . .
(Dead silence. The Sergeant wipes his sweating forehead with his arm. He watches the time nervously. Finally, he gives a sign with his hand.)
SERGEANT *(Dully):* Well?
(There is a sudden clap of thunder. The storm breaks over them.)
DUMBO: Rain!
JELLO: Let's get out of here!
(The nurses run first. The Sergeant sighs with relief. He lifts up his hand cheerfully and then runs to a shelter with long steps. As if they waited for his sign—the soldiers run away with their heads hidden between their shoulders. The file of convalescents stays immobile. The storm reaches its climax. It is obvious now that the whole scene was a kind of mime. Perhaps it could be performed that way.)

CURTAIN

PART III

SCENE XVII

The mortuary.
(The members of the Burial Committee, wet from the rain, are crouching in the dark mortuary. The sounds of the stormy weather can be heard from time to time. Yustus is the only one who moves. He paces back and forth nervously.)

YUSTUS: Well, then: What's the matter? What are you—deaf and dumb?
ZOLA *(Surly):* And what are we supposed to do?
YUSTUS: We should do something! Tomorrow is the burial and we have a hundred things to do yet. I bet you didn't even write the obituary.
ZOLA: You're wrong about that! *(To Moishe)* Where did you put it?
(Moishe brings the obituary from the corner. Zola lifts up the big pieces of cardboard triumphantly.)
ZOLA *(Proudly):* Have a look!
YUSTUS *(Angrily):* To hell with it! Why didn't you put on the black border?
ZOLA: There wasn't any black ink. After all, what's wrong with the green ink? It matches the red letters nicely.
YUSTUS: Garbage! An obituary should have a black border and black letters. Black is the color of mourning. Isn't that so, Sipka?
SIPKA: It used to be that way.
YUSTUS: Well, I admit that the border . . . but, the red letters. . .
ZOLA: What could I do? Pip didn't want to lend me the fountain pen.
YUSTUS: Okay, okay . . . read the text.
ZOLA *(Stands to read):* "To morrow at 4 p.m. there will be a

grand burial of the late Yoyo, a former prisoner in the concentration camp who has died here unexpectedly. All who are healthy and can walk are kindly requested to take part in the burial. The burial will take place in the graveyard. The Burial Committee of St. Raphael's Hospital. *(After a significant pause, complacently.)* Well, how do you like it?

YUSTUS: Terrible. *(Zola sits.)* It's irreverent to the dead. Tell him, Sipka.

SIPKA: No, I like it, as a matter of fact.

YUSTUS *(Waving his hand):* All right, all right, better something than nothing. The important thing is that we have an obituary. *(To Zola)* Zola, go and put it in a prominent place!

ZOLA: Yes, but how? I can't go out as long as we are besieged!

PIP: You think the soldiers will come back? Again?

ZOLA: Don't you worry! They'll be here as soon as the storm is over!

PIP *(Gives a low whistle):* That will be something!

(Yustus takes off his glasses and starts to wipe them carefully.)

YUSTUS: Hm . . . Yes . . . But I am afraid they are stronger than we are. What do you think, Sipka?

SIPKA: Stronger than us, yes, but against us . . . I doubt it.

YUSTUS: In any case, we can't fight them.

PIP *(Disappointed):* That means we'll give them Yoyo.

YUSTUS: Not at all!

ZOLA: Well, what else?

YUSTUS *(Angrily):* What else? What else? Why do you ask me? I am not a general but a chairman of the Burial Committee!

(Moishe moves uneasily in his chair.)

MOISHE *(Embarrassed):* Chairman . . . may I say something?

YUSTUS *(Benevolently):* Go ahead.

MOISHE: Let's organize a hunger strike.

(Zola jumps off his chair.)

ZOLA: What? Are you crazy, Moishe?

(Yustus begins to scratch his beard thoughtfully.)

YUSTUS: Well, you know . . . it is not such a bad suggestion.
ZOLA: Oh, damn it! Not to eat? Us? Not one of us will accept such foolishness! We'd be better off fighting than starving.
(A sharp whistling is heard from the outside. Everybody falls silent.)
MOISHE: Who is it?
VOICE: The guard leader.
MOISHE *(To Yustus)*: The guard leader.
YUSTUS: What's up?
VOICE: The Major is coming.
YUSTUS *(Excited)*: With the soldiers?
VOICE: By himself. What shall we do?
MOSIHE *(To Yustus)*: By himself. What shall we do?
(Yustus looks at Sipka. Sipka nods his head, calmly.)
YUSTUS: Let him come in!
MOISHE: Let him come in!
(Everyone is looking at the door. Presently the Major appears. He steps into the mortuary and looks around.)
MAJOR: Yes, gentlemen, you really put me on the spot, didn't you?
YUSTUS *(Sharply)*: We stuck to the agreement. But you didn't, did you? You—an officer!
MAJOR: Mister, I am not only a soldier.
YUSTUS: But we are not animals anymore!
MAJOR *(Patiently)*: If the inspector discovers the corpse, I shall be punished, not you. I shall be refused my leave, not you.
YUSTUS *(Coldly)*: It's not your fault.
MAJOR: Mister, I thought you would believe me: I haven't seen my family for three years.
YUSTUS: I haven't seen mine for five years.
MAJOR: Still, you'll see yours before I see mine.
SIPKA *(Calmly)*: It's not that everybody even has a family, sir.
(The Major looks at Sipka and then takes out a cigarette box thoughtfully. He lights his cigarette carefully.)

MAJOR: All right, I understand you, but I don't see any reason why you could not bury the corpse this evening. You can pay the last respects to your friend that way, can't you?
YUSTUS: Yoyo's place is in the graveyard, not on the dunghill.
MAJOR: That doesn't make any difference to him that we are alive . . . and should go on living either! And to you, sir? Does it make any difference to you?
(The Major and Sipka look at each other in silence. Drops of rain are heard from the outside. At last, the Major throws his cigarette with a sudden gesture and steps on it, energetically.)
MAJOR: After all, that won't be my first punishment fine . . .
(Sipka smiles in a friendly way. The Major smiles back. He goes to the entrance, but Yustus blocks his way.)
YUSTUS: I will take care of your defense!
MAJOR *(Surprised)*: You? Are you a lawyer?
YUSTUS *(With dignity)*: Yes, I am.
MAJOR: Thank you. Unfortunately, I won't be in a position to use your legal advice.
MAJOR *(Addressing everyone)*: You can destroy the barricades.
(Pip jumps up carefully. The Major goes to Yustus and holds out his hand. Yustus looks at the hand in surprise. Then, he shakes it firmly.)
MAJOR: Well, it seems I kept my word. It's your turn now. But don't forget tomorrow . . .
YUSTUS: . . . at four sharp . . . not a minute later!
(The Major nods his head and goes to the exit. He stops at the door.)
YUSTUS: Something else?
(The Major hesitates. It seems as if he could not find the right words. Finally he speaks up . . .)
MAJOR: Well . . . I would like to wish you a happy burial.
(He walks out quickly. Yustus clasps his hands.)
YUSTUS: Gentlemen, we've made it! *(To Pip)* Go tell the others. They should all come back to the rooms.

(Pip goes out quickly. Zola shouts after him . . .)
ZOLA: Don't forget dinner!
(Pip walks out. YUSTUS rubs his hands with satisfaction.)
YUSTUS: That's it. Everything settled.
ZOLA: The hell it is! And what about a hearse? And a priest? And a coffin? *(Waving his hand)* If we carry on like this we won't do anything.
YUSTUS: That isn't so. The burial will take place. It is a question of honor.
ZOLA: Yes, but they give us short notice.
YUSTUS: Well, we have come this far and there is no turning back.
ZOLA *(Depressed):* We won't make it.
(It seems that nature wants to confirm Zola's portentous words: a lighting flash illuminates the mortuary, followed by strong thunder. Zero appears at the door at that moment. He is wet both inside and outside. The water is dripping along his unshaven face. Zero makes a sweeping gesture with his hand.)
ZERO: Gentlemen, the hearse is ready!
(He stumbles into the mortuary.)
ZOLA *(Disdainfully):* Wet as a sponge. Dead drunk.
YUSTUS: Drunk dead.
(Zero hold out his hand to Yustus.)
ZERO: Dead—as you are, Mr. Yustus. *(Staring at Zola.)* And as you, Zola! *(Holding out his hand to Yoyo's table)* As Yoyo . . . *(Making another sweeping gesture)* All of us! We are all just dead bodies. Dead on leave, gentlemen . . .
(Yustus turns his back to the drunken Zero.)
YUSTUS *(To Zola sharply):* Throw him out!
(Zola does not like this order. He makes reluctant movements.)
ZERO *(Putting a finger to his lips):* Shhhhhhh . . . A special hearse for you . . . a wagon on for wheels . . . with a mare . . . *(Laughing hysterically)* . . . with a neurotic mare . . .
(Zero stops laughing. He puts the finger to his mouth again.)

ZERO: Shhhhhhh . . . the poor thing is scared of dead people . . . She mustn't see any of us! She will get a shock!

(Zero bursts into laughter again. Then he becomes serious all of a sudden.)

ZERO: You know who found a hearse! Zero! Hear me? Your lousy Zero! Gentlemen . . .

(Zero comes close to Yustus who turns his head away disgusted.)

ZERO: You are stupid, "chairman." You forget this!

(Zero puts his hand on his stomach.)

ZERO *(Patting his stomach)*: This! This! *(Addressing the others)* Eating, gentlemen! *(To Yustus)* Food, that is the thing! *(Scornfully)* And not a fountain pen!

(Zero's words arouse the attention of the others. They are waiting impatiently to see what he will say next. Although drunk, Zero is aware of the impression he has made on them.)

ZERO *(Scornfully)*: What's the matter? Maybe you don't want to listen to me? Maybe you want me to shut my big mouth? Well, well . . . let it be . . . *(To himself)* Shut up, Zero! Back to your corner, you lousy dog!

(Staggering, Zero walks to Yoyo's bier. Pause. Nobody moves. Finally, zero speaks up . . .)

ZERO: Shhh . . . Everyone is silent as the dead—as, the dead would have it.

ZOLA *(Infuriated)*: I'll kill him!

(Zola rushes at Zero. Suddenly the pen knife glitters in Zero's hand. Zola stands back . . . Zero bursts into laughter. He throws the knife away and it falls beside Zola's feet. Zola hesitates. Zero walks toward him . . . Zola crouches, takes the knife, and wants to throw it at Zero . . .)

SIPKA *(Icily)*: Stop it!

(Zola freezes. The knife falls from his hand to the floor. He turns his back to Zero. Zero bursts into laughter again. Pause. Nobody moves. Zero walks to Yoyo's bier.)

ZERO: You are wiser dead than they are. Look . . . the price is in

barter. Everything eatable. Got it? Everything. We should take everything to the old codger in the morning . . . right?
(Suddenly Zero turns his back. His face turns into an ugly grimace.)
ZERO: Here you are! You've got your hearse! Now you can spit on the late Zero!
(Zero staggers to the exit, and then he turns back again.)
ZERO *(Scornfully)*: My dead gentlemen . . .
(Zero walks out. They remain silent for some time.)
YUSTUS *(Excited)*: Well, what's the matter? Why are you silent? Take that damn cigarette holder out of your mouth and say something.
SIPKA: Hm, it seems that the coachman's stomach is growing.
YUSTUS: So what?
(Sipka spreads his arms.)
SIPKA: Perhaps we can help him.
(Zola jumps to his feet.)
ZOLA *(Revolted)*: Do you think that we can accept the services of a former capo?
SIPKA *(Calmly)*: Even a wild beast might be useful. *(Smiling mildly as if he were apologizing)* Sometimes.
YUSTUS *(He has made up his mind)*: Cashier!
ZOLA *(Reluctantly)*: Yes.
YUSTUS: Tomorrow morning you will start to collect contributions! Look mainly for chocolate, biscuits, cheese and cans!
(As if he has done a difficult and important job, he falls into his chair exhausted.)
YUSTUS *(Having a sigh)*: Well, we've solved this problem as well.
ZOLA: Like hell! If we don't find a coffin, we won't have a burial.
YUSTUS: Didn't I tell you to go to the Quartermaster . . .
ZOLA: I did go there! But the Sergeant doesn't want to hear of

it. He says that nobody gives a coffin as a present these days. You buy it or you requisition it.
YUSTUS: This is a nice game. We have neither permit nor money. Sipka, what do you think?
SIPKA: Zola, are there any bars on the Quartermaster's windows?
ZOLA: No, there aren't.
SIPKA: Hm . . . very interesting . . .
(Yustus is looking at Sipka surprised.)
YUSTUS: Wait a minute, Sipka . . . what are you thinking of . . . that sort of thing wouldn't be very fair either.
(Sipka walks out.)
YUSTUS *(After a brief hesitation):* Okay. We have no choice. But look, let's understand each other: we won't steal, we'll just borrow.

SCENE XVIII

The Quartermaster's quarters.
(A long room with high shelves along the walls. All sorts of things are arranged on the shelves in an orderly fashion, and every bit of the space is being used. Complete darkness. A loud crash breaks the silence, as if plenty of metallic objects had fallen down.)

ZOLA: Damn it! Light that candle, will you?
(A weak flame illuminates the dark. Zola is sitting on the floor, under the window in the midst of scattered mess kits. It's obvious that he did not choose that place to sit down. He stands up, making an effort.)
ZOLA: Oh, God! A real mess.
(Zola is lighting his candle from Pip's. The objects in the quartermaster's quarters get clearer outlines.)
PIP *(Delighted):* So many things over here!

ZOLA *(Disappointed)*: But I can't see anything in the way of food.

PIP: Look, Zola! Look at this!

(Pip lifts up his discovery from the floor, triumphantly: a bugle with a big decorated ribbon.)

PIP: Isn't it nice?

(Pip blows as strongly as he can. The sharp sounds of the bugle scare Zola.)

ZOLA *(Scared)*: Shut up! You want them to hear us? Give me that monster!

(Pip holds out the bugle to Zola, obediently. Zola is scratching his head thoughtfully.)

ZOLA: Hm? Do you need this thing for the burial? *(Shrugging his shoulders)* Well . . . who knows? *(Putting the bugle aside)* We've got to ask Yustus.

PIP: Zola!

(Zola walks to the shelf whose contents surprised Pip so much. Cardboard boxes with medals are on the shelves. Zola puts his hand into one box.)

ZOLA *(Delighted)*: Aren't they shiny! *(Sadly)* It's a pity Yoyo isn't alive. He would have liked to play with them. Shall we take a few with us, uh?

PIP: What for?

(The medals fall from Zola's hands to the floor. Pip walks further on.)

PIP: Hey look!

(Zola's candle throws light on a big heap of uniforms. They are the uniforms of the defeated army. Helmets are piled beside them.)

ZOLA: Uniforms—I'll be damned.

(Zola touches the uniforms with his fingers.)

ZOLA: They are brand new. Shall I try one? Hold it for me.

(Zola gives Pip a candle and takes one jacket. He begins to put it on.)

ZOLA: Ready?
(Pip lifts up both candles high above his head . . . Zola has an officer's jacket and the loose belt hangs around his skinny hips. The helmet comes to his nose. Wrinkled trousers and old slippers complete Zola's uniform.)
ZOLA *(Proudly)*: How do I look?
PIP: Stupid.
(Pip goes along and then he comes to a stop.)
PIP *(Stupefied)*: Look!
ZOLA: What?
(Pip is staring silently. Zola, whose helmet is still on his head, takes Pip's candle and lifts it up. With the candles high above their heads, Zola and Pip are standing immobile beside a big heap of the concentration camp clothes: wrinkled, striped jackets, trousers, caps . . .)
ZOLA *(Stupefied)*: The hell with it! Concentration camp clothes.
PIP: Where did they get them?
(Zola moves the helmet back on his head.)
ZOLA: Come on, Pip, take a cap.
PIP: Wait a minute. Don't you remember what the Sergeant said?
(Zola begins to imitate the Sergeant's stern, decisive way of speech.)
ZOLA: "The commission will take inventory, enumerate, and arrange everything which is in the hospital stores, so that everything can be used again—when it's needed."
PIP: There it is: we mustn't touch anything.
ZOLA: I'm sorry, but I need a cap. Come and choose one for me.
(Pip steps on a heap of clothes, and shuffles through it with his foot.)
ZOLA: It should be clean, though.
PIP: Here you are!
(Pip throws a cap to Zola. Zola catches it in the air.)
ZOLA *(Satisfied)*: Great! It's a nice one! Yustus should buy us a drink.

PIP: Why?

ZOLA: Why? Hell—haven't you seen a military burial before? You haven't? Now listen: first—a caisson, on the caisson a coffin, and on top of the coffin—a military cap.

(Putting the cap on his palm, Zola begins to march with a bowed head, imitating the sounds of the funeral march.)

PIP: Yoyo wasn't a soldier.

ZOLA: Doesn't matter. He was a camp prisoner. *(Solemnly.)* The cap which he used to wear will lie on his coffin.

PIP: What coffin? We haven't got one yet.

ZOLA: Easy . . . take it easy . . . *(Lifting his handle)* Give me some light.

(Pip lifts up his handle. Zola is looking at the furthest corner of the Quartermaster.)

ZOLA *(Excited)*: Look!

(The candle illuminates a few coffins in the corner. They are just coarse, wooden boxes, painted black.)

ZOLA: We can choose now!

(Zola starts to knock on the planks expertly, as if he were testing their quality.)

ZOLA: This one, uh?

PIP: I guess it fits.

(They take one coffin and carry it to the middle of the room.)

ZOLA: It's heavy, isn't it?

(They put the coffin on the floor. Pip is panting. He takes out a package of cigarettes and holds it out to Zola.)

PIP: Want one?

ZOLA: Give me one.

(They light their cigarettes on the candle flame.)

ZOLA: Shall we sit for a minute.

(They sit on a coffin.)

ZOLA: Oh, look—I've still got this helmet on my head! I wondered why I felt so depressed.

(Zola takes the helmet off. He plays with it.)

ZOLA: And what if I took this piece of junk home . . . just imagine! My friends are sitting in the tavern . . . and boop, all of a sudden I drop in with a helmet on my head! *(Laughs)* The'd fall off their chairs!
(Pip laughs as well.)
ZOLA: We will drink wine out of the helmet . . . Everybody! Not a drop will be left at the bottom! Then we'll put the helmet in the corner and throw our glasses at it . . . crash, crash, crash!
(Zola suddenly falls silent. His hand drops down. The helmet slips to the floor. His body is crouched on the coffin.)
ZOLA *(Depressed):* Will she wait for me? What do you think?
PIP *(Simply):* The wife has to wait.
(Zola is staring vacantly.)
ZOLA: She couldn't do everything by herself . . . take care of the kids . . . and land . . . for so many years. She doesn't know that I am alive. To her I've been dead for a long time.
PIP: She'll be surprised when she sees you.
ZOLA *(Desperately):* Oh yes, damn surprised . . .
ZOLA: Do you have a girl?
PIP: Yes, I have.
ZOLA: Will she wait for you?
PIP: She doesn't know I like her. Didn't have time to tell her.
ZOLA: Well, doesn't matter. You'll tell her now. *(Pause.)*
PIP: You know what, Zola? I've made up my mind: I'm going to live on the floor . . . high, high above, on the top floor, in a big city. I'll be on my own, all on my own. I'll be standing at my window and looking down at people . . . lots of people . . . as they walk down the street . . .
(Zola steps on his cigarette, and then he pats Pip on the shoulder.)
ZOLA: Let's go, Pip. They are waiting for us.
(Zola and Pip stand up. Pip extinguishes the candle. The Quartermaster's quarters are dark again.)

SCENE XIX

The mortuary.
(The shivering candle illuminates Yoyo's bier and Moishe who is standing nearby with his head bowed. Yustus comes into the mortuary, dragging his feet; Zero follows him. Moishe raises his head. His face shows the traces of a sleepless night.)

YUSTUS: Are you sleepy, Moishe?
MOISHE: Me? Oh, no . . . I'm not. I can go on like this till morning.
(Yustus laughs.)
YUSTUS: The morning is already long on its way.
MOISHE *(Surprised)*: Is that so?
(Yustus walks to Moishe and puts his hand on Moishe's shoulder.)
YUSTUS *(Solemnly)*: Moishe, there is good news; you will be our priest at the burial!
MOISHE *(Firmly)*: No, I won't.
YUSTUS: But listen: maybe Yoyo was of your religion. Oh, well, yes, according to probability calculus, I'm almost certain of it. It would be ideal if you could be our rabbi at the burial.
MOISHE *(Tonelessly)*: If I have to sew something . . . I could do that.
YUSTUS: Come on, Moishe. If the prayer is too long, you don't have to say all of it. Understand? Only the beginning and the end.
MOISHE: If I have to cut wood . . . I could do it.
YUSTUS: You're afraid that you will make a mistake? Doesn't matter! Who on earth knows Hebrew?
MOISHE: If I've got to carry something heavy . . . I could do that as well.
YUSTUS *(Nervously)*: But we need a rabbi now! Understand, a rabbi! We can't have a burial without a priest!

MOISHE *(In the same voice):* If I've got to . . .
YUSTUS *(Angrily):* Cut it. That's enough. We don't want anything! Anything from you.
(Moishe walks slowly to Yoyo's bier.)
YUSTUS *(Sternly):* Where are you going?
MOISHE: To take care of Yoyo.
YUSTUS: It isn't necessary! You let us down and you are not on the committee anymore.
(Moishe bows his head.)
YUSTUS *(Relentlessly):* You're dismissed.
(Yustus walks out of the mortuary with energetic steps. With a bowed head, Moishe stands still for some time. Standing at the door, Zero is looking at him inquisitively. Moishe walks to the exit without looking at him.)
ZERO: They don't know what mercy is.
(Moishe is looking at him as if he were surprised that Zero could talk. Zero approaches him.)
ZERO: You see, that's their gratitude. And they say that I am the one who is lousy and wicked.
MOISHE *(Nodding his head):* You used to be that way.
ZERO: Others beat as well.
MOISHE: They were wicked too.
ZERO: But they gave me the orders. Understand? They gave me the orders! What else could I do?
(Moishe watches him closely. His face is without a smile, stern and threatening.)
MOISHE *(With hatred):* You should have defied God!
(Suddenly, Moishe holds out his hand and strikes Zero in the face. Pause. Zero stands silent, with a bowed head. Moishe looks vacantly at his hand. Finally, Zero makes a move. He takes Moishe's hand with a somewhat awkward tenderness.)
ZERO: You and I are not like the rest of them . . . That's why they hate us.
MOISHE: Nobody hates you!

ZERO: Oh, yes. They hate me. Everybody hates me. Everybody.
(Moishe shakes his head.)
MOISHE: No. They despise you. No salvation for you and no use looking for it.
(Moishe is looking down.)
MOISHE: And as far as I am concerned let them hate me. I am not afraid of hatred, either divine or human. I am used to hatred both divine and human.
(Moishe wants to walk out but Sipka appears at the door.)
SIPKA: Where are you going?
MOISHE *(Indifferently)*: I don't know.
SIPKA: Aren't you supposed to stay with Yoyo?
MOISHE: Yustus said . . .
SIPKA: He's changed his mind. We shall get a real priest.
(Sipka addresses Zero.)
SIPKA: And where is your secret pass to the outer world?
ZERO *(Suspiciously)*: You want to turn me in?
SIPKA *(To Moishe, as if he didn't hear Zero's remark)*: Find ten volunteers—right away. *(To Zero)* You'll take them out to the hospital.
ZERO *(Stupefied)*: You want help. You want my help?
SIPKA: Why? Aren't you going to help?
(Zero's face is overwhelmed with happiness.)
ZERO *(Readily)*: We shall wait for you on the lawn behind the hospital.
SIPKA: Make sure you'll be there in an hour.
ZERO: Where are we going?
(Jello's head appears at the door before Sipka can reply.)
JELLO: Patient Sipka—which one is he?
SIPKA: Yes?
JELLO *(Suspiciously)*: You?
(Jello steps into the mortuary and sizes Sipka up. He scratches his ear as if something was not quite clear to him.)
JELLO: Well . . . if you are him . . . you have a visitor . . .

(Silence. Moishe and Zero are staring at Sipka in surprise.)
JELLO: I'll be damned if I am kidding . . . I saw her myself.
ZERO *(Stupefied)*: Her?
(Jello makes a sign of the cross.)
JELLO: It's female, so help me, Saint Raphael.

SCENE XX

The hospital yard.
(Sipka is walking toward the gate quietly. The convalescents follow him in silence. There are plenty of them as if everybody wanted to see something unique. Sipka stops at the fence and the convalescents stop as well. Nanita is standing behind the bars and they all look at her indifferently. Divided by the bars, Sipka and Nanita look at each other in silence.)

NANITA *(Embarrassed)*: Hi . . .
SIPKA *(Simply)*: Hi.
NANITA: You are not angry?
SIPKA: What for?
NANITA: I just wanted to see you.
(Pause. Nanita is embarrassed.)
NANITA: They won't let me in.
SIPKA *(Shrugging his shoulders)*: A regulation.
(Nanita is watching the convalescents who are standing behind Sipka's back. They all look serious and expectant.)
NANITA: I would like to talk to you.
SIPKA: Talk.
NANITA: Not here.
SIPKA: They are all right.
(Pause.)
NANITA: Perhaps you might come out?
SIPKA: Well, yes . . . I might indeed.
(Sipka takes the pass out of his pocket and shows it to the soldier.

With a lazy gesture, the soldier opens the gate. Sipka walks out and stands beside Nanita.)
SIPKA: You look nice.
NANITA *(Stammering, embarrassed)*: Oh . . . well . . . I thought . . . I'd dress up a little . . .
(Nanita falls silent. She does not know what to do with her hands. Pause.)
NANITA: Shall we go for a walk?
SIPKA: No. Better stay here. I have to wait for my friends.
(Sipka sits down. Nanita hesitates for a moment. Then she sits beside Sipka. She looks at the hospital yard through the bars of the fence. The convalescents are gathered by the fence. With their faces to the bars, they watch Sipka and Nanita.)
NANITA *(Whispering)*: Why are they looking at us?
SIPKA: They like you.
NANITA: They are all silent.
SIPKA: They want to be polite.
(Pause.)
NANITA: Why are you so cold?
SIPKA: No, I'm not.
NANITA: You didn't even touch me.
(Sipka takes Nanita's hand carefully.)
SIPKA: Better?
(Nanita turns around quickly.)
NANITA: Kiss me!
SIPKA *(Surprised)*: Now?
NANITA: Right now!
(Sipka looks at her in silence. She is looking at the fence.)
NANITA *(Challenging him)*: You are ashamed?
(Sipka kisses Nanita's eye. Nanita leans her head on Sipka's shoulder.)
NANITA *(After hesitating for awhile)*: I wanted to tell you something. I gave notice to the old man.
SIPKA: Why?

NANITA: Because I've decided to leave.
SIPKA: Where to?
NANITA: Where are you going?
SIPKA: You have chosen a fellow traveler with paralyzed legs.
NANITA: I have chosen something I have never had before.
SIPKA *(With mild irony):* What? A cigarette holder?
NANITA: Yes, Sipka.
(Sipka stands up.)
SIPKA: I must go.
NANITA *(Disappointed):* Already?
SIPKA: I have things to do. This afternoon we have a burial.
(Nanita stands up . . .)
NANITA: When you finish, will you come? We shall have lunch together. Will you?
SIPKA *(Nodding his head):* I will.
(Nanita holds Sipka's hand.)
NANITA: Be sure you come. We have to talk.
SIPKA *(Tartly):* About Nanita and Sipka?
NANITA: No.
(Nanita walks out. Sipka waits until she disappears and then he starts walking slowly in the same direction. The convalescents turn their back to the fence. The hospital yard is empty.)

SCENE XXI

The priest's room, overlooking the yard.
(It is a room with thick carpets and heavy curtains. It breathes a solemn and heavy atmosphere. The crucifix is hanging on the wall. The priest is an elderly, gray-haired, plump man with a benevolent look. The priest is looking at the crucifixion. He seems to be addressing the figure of Jesus.)

PRIEST: It is most unfortunate to die . . . *(Turning around, he lifts up his hands as if he was giving a sermon.)* To die in long awaited freedom.

SIPKA: Oh, yes, it's very unpleasant.

(The priest goes to the table where Sipka and Pip are sitting.)

PRIEST *(His eyes are closed, and his voice is sad)*: Lately, we have gotten used to the idea that we could at any moment leave this world. *(Straightening up, cheerfully)* But today we believe in life again!

SIPKA *(Calmly)*: And somehow we'll manage to get used to that as well.

(The priest doesn't know what to say next.)

PRIEST: Hm . . . yes, yes . . . *(After a brief interval, as if he were stimulated by an unexpected idea)* Oh, yes! I could offer you some wine. *(Going to the dresser)* I hope you like it. *(He takes out a bottle of wine and lifts it up to the light.)* *(Sympathetically)* It's a good old wine. *(Pouring some wine into Sipka's glass.)* I'm sure you couldn't get anything like this in the concentration camps.

SIPKA *(With mild irony)*: No, not like this.

(Pip takes the empty glass and holds it out to the priest.)

PRIEST *(Surprised)*: You drink, too, my son?

PIP *(Surprised)*: Why not?

PRIEST *(Lifting his index finger, fatherly)*: When I was your age, I didn't drink . . . *(Pouring the wine in Pip's glass, accusingly)* Nor did I smoke. *(Pip takes a cigarette out of his mouth, quickly. He doesn't know what to do with it.)*

SIPKA: You shouldn't blame him, Father. He was in the camp.

PRIEST *(Surprised)*: I didn't know they put children in the camps, too. *(Putting his hand on Pip's head)* I'm sure there were only a few of you over there?

PIP: Only a few of us are left.

PRIEST: Hm . . . yes. *(The priest sits down and pours the wine into his glass.)*

(He looks at his glass) They say you had a hard time of it in the camps.

SIPKA: So they say.
PRIEST: They say you were starving.
SIPKA: Sometimes.
PRIEST: Did they beat you?
SIPKA: Now and then.
PRIEST *(Playing with his glass):* You know . . . I used to see the camp prisoners. They were taking them through our village. They were quite skinny and fairly dirty. When they were passing through, I always closed my windows and even the shutters. *(Addressing Sipka as if he were revealing an important secret)* And I tell you, there were people who were standing at their windows and staring at those wretched creatures.
SIPKA: They were heartless, Father.
PRIEST *(Stands up. He takes a few steps and then stops in the middle of the room):* They stopped near my house once . . . It seemed to me they were tired. I had my servant give them a bowl of milk. Know what happened? They drank it all.
SIPKA: The milk must have been fresh.
PRIEST: I did what I could. *(Spreading his arms.)*
SIPKA: Many didn't do that much, Father.
PRIEST *(The Priest beginning to walk again, clasping his hands absentmindedly):* Well, you see, I'm very sorry, my dear friends . . . but I can't help you this time. I told your friend: so many things to do, to think of, to worry . . .
SIPKA: I understand you. We came to apologize.
PRIEST: Oh . . . it's all right.
SIPKA: Still, you ought to know. You see, that fellow who was here last time, he's not very bright. *(Sipka stands up and walks to the terrace; opening the curtains he looks through the window.)* Well, you see . . . even before he saw you, he had told everyone in the hospital that you had accepted to come to the burial . . . *(Turning his back to the window)* And everyone was excited at the news.
PRIEST: That's unfortunate. But it's not my fault, my son.

SIPKA: Of course, it isn't. That's why we want to apologize for everything that might happen through no fault of your own, of course.

PRIEST *(Walks to Sipka):* And what might happen?

(Zero appears with two convalescents in the yard. They stop in front of the terrace.)

SIPKA *(Calmly):* Well, you see, they are the camp prisoners, they are short-tempered . . . rash . . . coarse . . .

(A group of convalescents appear in the yard and they join the others in silence.)

PIP: They fight very often.

SIPKA: Especially if they feel cheated. *(The priest looks at them. Immobile accusing figures of convalescents have covered the yard. Sipka goes to the priest. Behind the priest's back.)* And so, if something happens, you will forgive us, our reverend Father. We are sorry indeed.

(Pause. Everyone is looking at the priest. He turns his back to the terrace slowly.)

PRIEST *(Thoughtfully):* And when . . . what time is your burial?

SIPKA: At four in the afternoon, Father.

PRIEST: Did you say at four? Well, it seems I could manage to come. Let me see . . . oh yes . . . the time suits me-

SIPKA: Thank you, Father, you are very generous. *(Sipka gives a sign to Zero. Zero walks out of the yard, followed by the convalescents. Sipka turns to the priest again.)* The only thing I've got to tell you—we are very poor people.

PRIEST *(Takes Sipka and Pip by the arm and leads them to the door in a friendly manner):* I know, I know . . . you don't have to pay anything. I won't charge you. And I will tell the sextant to toll the chapel bells during the funeral. *(Suddenly the Priest stops dead; he is addressing Sipka confidentially.)* But tell me. Why such a fuss over this funeral? Was he an important person?

SIPKA: Not important, Father, but a person. *(Sipka and Pip walk to the door. Sipka turns back at the door.)* One more thing: our

late friend, you know, may not have been a Christian.
PRIEST: Doesn't matter, my son. *(With pathos)* We are all equal in death.
SIPKA: Yes, Father, you are right—in death . . .

SCENE XXII

The yard of Pepi's house. Sipka and Pip enter. They stop. Pip whistles a few times. Nobody answers.

PIP: Pepi.
(Silence)
PIP *(Shouting)*: Pepi.
(A boy appears behind them. He has a sword in his hand and a cap made of newspapers on his head.)
BOY: Nobody's in.
PIP: Where is Pepi?
BOY *(Confidentially)*: He has real bombs, you know that? *(Scornfully)* The miser! He was hiding them from us and now they took them all away.
PIP *(Excited)*: Took them? Who?
BOY: Well, them guys . . . the soldiers. Moron! He wanted to bury them.
PIP *(To Sipka)*: You hear that? The soldiers got a hold of Pepi.
SIPKA *(Addressing the boy)*: Know where they've taken him?
BOY: Well, to the hospital.
PIP *(Stupefied)*: But why?
BOY *(Shrugging his shoulders)*: How should I know? He was gone in a minute. *(Expertly)* He was gone in a flash.
(Pause. Finally, Pip pulls himself together. He comes to the boy with the sword.)
PIP *(Angrily)*: It can't be true.
BOY *(Defiantly)*: I say it is. *(Proudly)* I know how it looks when a real bomb explodes.

(Sipka puts his hand on Pip's shoulder.)
SIPKA *(Calmly)*: When did it happen?
BOY: Yesterday evening, during the thunderstorm. We thought it was the thunder.
(An interval. Pip stands depressed, with a bowed head.)
PIP *(Surely)*: Shall we go . . . to Pepi?
SIPKA *(Shaking his head, mildly)*: No use.
(Pip sits down. Sipka sits beside him. The boy with a sword shrugs his shoulders and walks out dragging his wooden sword behind him.)
PIP: I feel like crying, Sipka.
SIPKA: Nobody is watching. You are free to cry.
PIP *(Hopelessly)*: But how?
SIPKA: Try.
PIP *(Shaking his head)*: I can't.
(Sipka and Pip are silent for some time.)
PIP: Yustus said that no one would die anymore—like before.
SIPKA: Still, it means that people will die.
(Pause)
PIP: Sipka, is there such a world where people can live as long as they want to?
SIPKA *(After hesitating a while)*: There is life here as well, Pip.
PIP *(Nodding his head)*: It's hard . . .
SIPKA: Yes, sometimes.
(Sipka stands up.)
SIPKA: Let's go, Pip. The burial will begin soon.
(They start walking. Suddenly Pip stops and pulls Sipka's sleeve.)
PIP: Oh yes, Sipka! You promised to introduce me to that girl. Don't you remember?
SIPKA *(Surely)*: I've changed my mind.
(Pip shades his eyes with his head and looks toward the sky.)
PIP: We shall have nice weather for the funeral.
(Pip lifts his hand suddenly.)

PIP: Look, Sipka! Birds! *(Excited)* So many of them . . .
(Sipka looks up too.)
SIPKA: Summer is coming again . . .
(They watch the birds for some time.)
PIP: Sipka, are there poisonous birds?
SIPKA: Poisonous birds? Oh no, Pip.
PIP: Are you sure?
SIPKA: Positive.
PIP *(Sighing)*: I would like to be a bird. *(After a brief pause)* And you?
(Sipka puts his hand on Pip's shoulder.)
SIPKA: I would like to be you, Pip . . .

SCENE XXIII

(The path to the graveyard. The procession of convalescents is passing by. The church bells are heard. The priest goes first, followed by Yustus, Moishe, Sipka, Zola, and Pip who are carrying Yoyo's coffin. A striped cap of the concentration camp prisoner is lying on the top of the coffin. Far away Zero is walking by himself. Nanita is standing alone and when Sipka passes by she takes his hand. Sipka leaves the funeral procession and comes to Nanita. The convalescents pass by them and disappear. The sound of the church bells is replaced by the sound of the cemetery chapel bells.)

NANITA: I was waiting for . . . Couldn't you come?
SIPKA: Didn't want to.
(Nanita is looking down.)
NANITA: I thought you loved me.
SIPKA: I do.
(Suddenly Nanita grasps Sipka's hand and holds it tightly.)
NANITA *(Excited)*: Come, Sipka, let's run away!
SIPKA: No, Nanita! It's too late.

(Nanita steps aside. Her shoulders droop down.)
NANITA *(Defeated)*: You are still hoping . . .
SIPKA *(Indifferently)*: Hoping for what?
NANITA: That you will meet your wife . . . and children . . .
SIPKA *(Sullenly)*: If I could only believe in the life to come . . .
NANITA *(Bitterly)*: You don't even believe in this life!
SIPKA: Would I have come back if I hadn't believed in it?
NANITA: Then you hate it!
SIPKA: Yes. Part of it, yes.
(Nanita comes closer to Sipka.)
NANITA: But that part has gone . . . Vanished . . .
SIPKA *(Unyielding)*: Yes! Never to return again!
(Sipka caresses Nanita's head.)
SIPKA: You are of brave stock.
NANITA: And you? Are you afraid?
SIPKA *(Nodding his head)*: Very often.
NANITA: Afraid of what?
SIPKA: That Nanita will be taken away just like everybody else.
(Nanita puts her head on Sipka's shoulder.)
NANITA: But if you leave me, I will be taken nonetheless. *(Makes one more attempt)* Let's leave this place , Sipka! Let's run far away!
(Sipka shakes his head.)
SIPKA: We are not fast enough, Nanita. Not anymore.
NANITA *(Closes her eyes)*: Is this a farewell?
SIPKA: It's all I can give you.
(Pause, Sipka starts out.)
NANITA: You remember my dream?
SIPKA: I remember all dreams.
NANITA *(As if spellbound)*: The shadows retreated into the crevices . . . Oh, yes, love was my only hope . . . The flowers burst through the asphalt.
(She doesn't notice that Sipka is leaving her.)
NANITA: And hand in hand we were crossing the bridge . . .

(She is alone now. Pause. Finally, she turns around and when she sees that Sipka has left, she walks slowly in the opposite direction. The stage is empty for a while. The sound of the bells becomes stronger . . .)

SCENE XXIV

The graveyard. A small country churchyard, with only a few untidy graves. The convalescents are standing around Yoyo's grave. Sipka joins them in silence. Yustus is finishing his speech.

YUSTUS: Naturam expelas furca, tamen usque recuret—You can fight nature even with a hay fork, but it will come back again. Rest in peace forever. What happened must never happen again.
MOISHE: Amen!
EVERYBODY: Amen!
(They disperse slowly. Yustus, Moishe, Pip and Sipka are still standing beside Yoyo's grave. Zero is sitting on a nearby grave, watching them. Suddenly, Moishe raises his head.)
MOISHE: But wait!
(They all look at him, scared.)
MOISHE: Yoyo has gone!
(They are all paralyzed by Moishe's final words. They stand silent, with their hands bowed. Very softly, the final part of Handel's oratorio "Hallelujah" from the Messiah is heard. Yustus, Sipka, Zola, Moishe, Pip and Zero are leaving the graveyard slowly. They are going along the path. The music is getting louder. Yustus is first, then Zola, Sipka and Moishe. Sipka puts his hand on Pip's shoulder. Far behind them Zero is marching slowly with his hands in his pockets. The music is loud now, the graveyard is empty. In the middle of it a grave with a simple wooden cross and a cap on it can be seen.)

ĐORĐE LEBOVIĆ

CURTAIN

Translated by *Nikola Koljević*

ALEKSANDAR OBRENOVIĆ
(1928—2005)

Aleksandar Obrenović was born in Belgrade. He studies at the University of Belgrade in the department of drama. Upon graduation, Obrenović worked as a dramatist for Radio-Television Belgrade. In cooperation with Đorđe Lebović, he wrote a play, *The Heavenly Squadron,* which won the first prize at "Sterijino Pozorje," a Serbian theater festival. This festival has been held yearly in Novi Sad, a city with a distinguished and long Serbian cultural tradition. In 1960, Obrenović's play, *The Return of Don Juan,* was acclaimed.

Obrenović's drama, *Variations,* consisting of four scenic miniatures, was written in 1958; it's third part, *The Bird,* received "Prix Italia" as the best radio play in 1958. In *Variations,* Obrenović concentrates on the existence of "the little man" in contemporary conditions, often with satirical colors. The play exposes the intimate and basic situations of an individual; it is a presentation of a happening, an event.

Variations was performed in the U.S. at the Center for Soviet and Eastern European Studies and Performing Arts at Southern Illinois University in Carbondale, Illinois, in 1971. Obrenović's plays have been translated into fifteen languages.

THE BIRD

CHARACTERS:

OLD MAN, seventy

OLD WOMAN, a bit younger

NEIGHBOR, fifty-five

THE BIRD

(A beautiful afternoon in April. The OLD MAN and the OLD WOMAN are outdoors with their bird cage and bird trap. On one side of the stage—an overturned tub propped with a stick—the bird trap. The OLD MAN is holding one end of a rope; the other end is tied to the stick. The OLD WOMAN is holding the cage door open. It grows darker as the play progresses.)

OLD WOMAN: You won't catch it.
OLD MAN: I will!
OLD WOMAN: Maybe it won't come.
OLD MAN: I must catch it today. I must!
OLD WOMAN: Maybe it won't come.
OLD MAN: I must catch it. It's now or never.
OLD WOMAN: The sun was coming up when we set the trap. It will be getting dark soon.
OLD MAN: I set it a long time ago. A very long time ago. I was still a boy.
OLD WOMAN: That was this morning. The neighbor asked us: „Where to, so early, neighbors"?
OLD MAN *(Angrily):* He always asks irrelevant questions, though he's a good man. I wandered aimlessly through the woods and through sheaves of sun rays . . . Every dewdrop was a sun.
OLD WOMAN: I've never seen so much sun.
OLD MAN: That's because you've never been in such a forest.
OLD WOMAN: A nice forest?
OLD MAN: It had blackberries and hawthorns and ferns, trees of all kinds, deer, rabbits, flowers, and foxes. It had everything.
OLD WOMAN: And then?
OLD MAN: Suddenly . . . suddenly from high above, from the very top of a poplar tree, I heard its song. I couldn't see it. It was hidden in the crown. I knew right away that was it.
OLD WOMAN: How could you tell?

OLD MAN: I don't know. But I realized right away that that was it.
OLD WOMAN: Have you seen it ever again?
OLD MAN: Never. Something always kept hiding it from me. And, I could hardly ever hear it sing, but already then, in that forest, I had made up my mind to catch it.
OLD WOMAN: You made up your mind. Lucky you. I've never succeeded.
OLD MAN: Early this morning I had the feeling it was somewhere here, above us, very near, and then, I heard it. It never sang so beautifully.
OLD WOMAN: And if I hadn't asked you now, you would never have told me about it?
OLD MAN: Once I thought I had caught it.
OLD WOMAN: You thought? It flew away?
OLD MAN: No. Yes and no. That was you.
OLD WOMAN: Me! Me? But I can't sing. Have you ever, ever heard me sing?
OLD MAN: I said I thought.
OLD WOMAN: I don't have this much of an ear for singing, A-a!
OLD MAN: I realized that too late.
OLD WOMAN: Anyway, it was nice.
OLD MAN: Sometimes.
OLD WOMAN: I am sorry . . .
OLD MAN: Psst! There it is! Granny, there's the bird! It's the bird, Granny! Granny!
OLD WOMAN: Where?
OLD MAN: Not so loud. There! There . . . hovering . . . hovering. . .
OLD WOMAN: I can't see. Should've taken my glasses. Let's move away so it won't notice us.
OLD MAN: It's not suspecting anything. Oh, I lived to see it!

THE BIRD

OLD WOMAN *(Pointing to the cage door):* I've opened the door.

OLD MAN: That's clever of you. It's hovering . . . it's coming lower now . . .

OLD WOMAN: What does it look like?

OLD MAN: It's much prettier than I imagined. It's head is completely white . . .

OLD WOMAN: And the wings? The wings are the most important. What color are they?

OLD MAN: Golden.

OLD WOMAN: Golden. A nice color!

OLD MAN: No, the wings are blue. Blue like the sea.

OLD WOMAN: Golden or blue?

OLD MAN: And, what if they're red?

OLD WOMAN: You're lying to me. Why?

OLD MAN: It's flying up again.

OLD WOMAN: Don't let it go. Please, don't!

OLD MAN: It's mine. Remember that!

OLD WOMAN: Then I won't hold the door open. *(She shuts the cage door)* Let it be mine too. Your bird is my bird.

OLD MAN: No, it's mine!

OLD WOMAN: I don't know how to find mine. I am not capable of doing that.

OLD MAN: That's not my fault.

OLD WOMAN: Just remember . . . that summer. We were coming back to the city and I told you . . .

OLD MAN: You have to forget that. Forget it! You always keep reminding me . . .

OLD WOMAN: I've already forgotten. After sharing your bed and board for fifty years, haven't I deserved to share your bird too?

OLD MAN: All right, all right, all right . . . we can try. It will be ours.

OLD WOMAN: Thank you. Thank you very much. *(She opens the cage door.)*
OLD MAN: But, I'm the one who found it.
OLD WOMAN: You found it and now it's ours.
OLD MAN: It's still up there. It looks like a butterfly now. Granny, the sky is so blue today!
OLD WOMAN: Oh, I love blue so much. The blue sky and the clouds slowly, very slowly, white, floating, floating . . . Where are they floating?
OLD MAN: There. *(Pointing in one direction.)*
OLD WOMAN: Where?
OLD MAN: There *(Pointing in another direction.)*
OLD WOMAN: That's the only way it can be.
OLD MAN: Psst!
OLD WOMAN: Psst!
OLD MAN: It saw the decoy. It's coming down . . . Do you see it?
OLD WOMAN: Aha, aha! It's beautiful. I still can't see the colors, though.
OLD MAN: It's coming lower! It's coming lower, lower!
OLD WOMAN: Psst! Lie down!
(Both of them lie down. The Old Woman falls on her stomach and covers herself and the Old Man with old newspapers. The Old Man accepts it with meek resistance.)
Why don't you tell me the color of its wings? Is that some kind of a secret?
OLD MAN: You'll see when we catch it.
OLD WOMAN: And if it changes color by then?
OLD MAN: What a question! How can it change color? That's the way it was born.
OLD WOMAN: I'd like to see its colors now.
OLD MAN: I can't help you there. Everybody's got to see that for himself.

OLD WOMAN: And anyway, you can't distinguish colors at dusk either. You can't!

OLD MAN: Be quiet! It's going for the trap.

OLD WOMAN: I can't look! I'm afraid to. *(She pulls the newspaper over her head but, nevertheless, keeps the cage door open.)* Tell me when you catch it.

OLD MAN: Be quiet now! Aha! Aha!

OLD WOMAN *(In the softest whisper)*: What is it doing now?

OLD MAN: Oh, it's so beautiful! So beautiful! It's flying toward the fence. It's jumping along it! It has a green tail.

OLD WOMAN *(In a whisper)*: And the wings, the wings?

OLD MAN *(Screams)*: A hawk!

OLD WOMAN *(Quickly comes out from under the newspapers)*: A hawk?

OLD MAN: A hawk is attacking it!

OLD WOMAN: Oh, that's awful! Awful! Use a stone! Shout! *(Shouts)* Shoo! Shoo!

OLD MAN *(Shouts)*: Shoo! Shoo! Shoo! Shoo! You darn bird!

OLD WOMAN: Save the greentailie!

OLD MAN *(Jumps to his feet, grabs a stone and flings it into the air)*: Shoo!

OLD WOMAN: Save it!

OLD MAN: Where are they now? I can't see them. Where are they?

OLD WOMAN: Aren't they there?

OLD MAN: They disappeared in the clouds. It's getting dark.

OLD WOMAN: Oh, what will happen to our bird?

OLD MAN: My bird. All right . . . our bird.

(They sit on the ground and look at the sky. A long pause.)

OLD WOMAN: I feel like eating pears.

OLD MAN: Why precisely pears?

OLD WOMAN: Just like that. Only a tiny bite! I love pears so much. You know, the big ones . . . the yellow ones. They're juicy. I love them because they're juicy and they smell heavenly.

OLD MAN: But why would you want pears right now? Why pears, in the first place?
OLD WOMAN: I feel like eating them, oh, just a bite!
OLD MAN: It's still early for pears. It's only April.
OLD WOMAN: That's why I don't like April.
OLD MAN: You're looking up at the sky, you want to find out about our bird and then, all of a sudden you start thinking of pears.
OLD WOMAN: Why, is it a crime to like pears? To like them even if you're looking for greentailie in the sky?
OLD MAN: It's a crime.
OLD WOMAN: Then I hate pears. All pears. Is the hawk . . . do you see anything?
OLD MAN: Only the sky and the clouds.
OLD WOMAN: And the wings . . . what color are they?
OLD MAN: So, it happened when we were coming back to the city?
OLD WOMAN: I forgot, I don't remember anything.
OLD MAN: It was then you said it.
OLD WOMAN: I don't remember anything.
OLD MAN: Did I hit you after that?
OLD WOMAN: I don't remember anything.
OLD MAN: How long was it before we spoke to each other again? Two years?
OLD WOMAN: I don't remember anything. *(She tears one page of the newspaper into tiny pieces.)* Daily events.
OLD MAN: But, at that time you weren't right.
OLD WOMAN: You know, we, you and I, we are the clouds . . .
OLD MAN *(Ominously):* I am sure you weren't right.
OLD WOMAN: We float there *(Motions with her hand)* and there *(In another direction)* and then we disperse . . .
OLD MAN: It was a mistake going to that spa. If we hadn't gone, that wouldn't have happened; there would have been no slaps and a two-year silence . . . But still, you weren't right.

THE BIRD

OLD WOMAN: Or we condense more and more and snow, rain and hail fall from us . . . and then they either praise us or curse us. I imagine us exactly like two clouds, there above the tower.

OLD MAN: Those two?

OLD WOMAN: You are the bigger one, and I'm the one spreading after it, like a hand, trying to reach it, but the wind is between them.

OLD MAN: So what if you were right? So what? I am not infallible.

OLD WOMAN: I forgot. I don't know what you're talking about. I forgot everything. I can't remember anymore.

OLD MAN: Can you forgive me now? It's past time you did that; you've tortured me long enough—thirty-five years of torture is quite enough for such a crime. Forgive me. Now we have a bird together. I even agreed to that. Forgive me, please!

OLD WOMAN: Tell me the color of our bird's wings.

OLD MAN: You're impossible!

OLD WOMAN: I'd like them to be a color I love. I think that would bring us luck.

OLD MAN: What color is that?

OLD WOMAN: Say the color of the wings and I'll know.

OLD MAN: You . . . you don't know what color you like.

OLD WOMAN: I like the color of our bird's wings. What's strange about that? One must know with what colored wings his bird flies, right?

OLD MAN *(With great difficulty):* The wings are . . . the wings are blue . . .

OLD WOMAN: Oh, blue! Blue like the sea?

OLD MAN: Yes.

OLD WOMAN: I like that! Blue! Thank you! I really forgot everything. Really.

(The neighbor comes by, chewing on a chicken leg. All the time they are talking with him, the Old Man and the Old Woman never forget to look at the sky.)

NEIGHBOR: Hello. Good evening neighbors. I've been watching you all day long. What are you doing here, on the ground? Playing?
OLD MAN: Yes, this is a very serious game.
OLD WOMAN: We're trapping.
NEIGHBOR: Like that?
OLD WOMAN: We're trapping our bird.
OLD MAN: My bird. All right, ours.
NEIGHBOR: You have a bird?
OLD MAN and OLD WOMAN *(In a significant and assured tone):* Hmmm.
NEIGHBOR: Oh. Does that mean it has escaped?
OLD MAN: No, we haven't caught it yet.
OLD WOMAN: We've been waiting for it since this morning . . . No, much longer.
NEIGHBOR: So.
OLD MAN: We already have a cage. I made it myself. Every year I'd buy some bamboo sticks; bamboo is best for cages; it's very expensive, though, and you see, now we have a cage.
NEIGHBOR: What's the name of that bird of yours?
OLD MAN: We don't know.
NEIGHBOR: Is it a nightingale?
OLD MAN: No.
OLD WOMAN: It isn't.
NEIGHBOR: A titmouse?
OLD MAN: It isn't.
OLD WOMAN: No.
NEIGHBOR: A parrot, a pheasant, a peacock, a cuckoo, a black grouse?
OLD WOMAN *(To the Old Man):* Is it one of those?
OLD MAN: It isn't.
OLD WOMAN: It isn't.
NEIGHBOR: A woodpecker?
OLD MAN: Another wrong guess. That's our bird.

OLD WOMAN: Our bird, and I also call it greentailie, because it has a green tail. Its head is all white, and its wings are blue. Blue, imagine.

NEIGHBOR: Well.

OLD MAN: It was just reaching for the bait . . .

OLD WOMAN: When a hawk suddenly attacked it . . . this big, believe me. And awful! He wanted to kill it, but it wouldn't give up. They disappeared into the sky, but its wings are really blue like the sea.

NEIGHBOR: Oh? I came for my basket. *(Plays triumphantly with his chicken bone)* You've got it.

OLD MAN: Which basket are you looking for?

NEIGHBOR: My basket.

OLD MAN: Hmm, yes. *(To the Old Woman)* Give the neighbor his basket.

OLD WOMAN *(Gets up):* Right away. *(She takes the cage with her but then comes back)* Let it stay here, just in case. Don't put it inside without me.

OLD MAN: All right. *(The Old Woman leaves)* I'm sorry you had to come and get it yourself.

NEIGHBOR: You believe you'll catch that . . . that . . . what do you call it? Gree . . . green . . .

OLD MAN: Greentailie. I will. It's never been so close.

NEIGHBOR: Childishness! Catching a bird! Childishness!

OLD MAN: Don't say that, dear neighbor. This isn't an ordinary bird.

NEIGHBOR: You are childish. Even if you do catch it, what do you need it for?

OLD MAN *(Thunderstruck):* What do I need it for? What . . . what do you mean what do I need it for? Well . . .

NEIGHBOR: There, see, you don't know! You don't know!

OLD MAN: Well . . . it . . . I need it . . .

NEIGHBOR: In a cage?

OLD MAN: Last night I dreamed that I died. Understand now?

NEIGHBOR: Understand what?
OLD MAN: That . . . I want to see it up close, touch it . . .
NEIGHBOR: Oh? And why do you want to do that?
OLD MAN: Just today I told Granny you always ask the wrong questions, though you're a good man.
NEIGHBOR: Isn't it better for the bird to stay up there?
OLD MAN: Maybe, for the bird, but not for us. I'm afraid of last night's dream. I want it beside me, in my hands; I want to know what it was I loved so madly and sought so madly . . .
NEIGHBOR: Let it fly, let it be free.
OLD MAN: I can't believe it will keep on living and flying when I'm under the ground.
NEIGHBOR: Oh, it will, of course it will. Then it will really be free. Nobody will try to trap it. Is it a pretty bird?
OLD MAN: The prettiest of all!
OLD WOMAN *(Coming back):* You want a basket; that means you lent us one?
OLD MAN: Oh, you gave us your basket?
NEIGHBOR: Well, of course! I gave you my best basket. Best, do you hear? I could keep anything in it.
OLD MAN: Granny, this is serious. Have you looked everywhere?
OLD WOMAN: Everywhere.
OLD MAN: We have to return the basket to our neighbor.
NEIGHBOR: You must.
OLD MAN: By all means. *(To the Old Woman)* Look again.
OLD WOMAN *(Leaving)*: All right. *(Stops)* But I don't remember his giving it to us . . .
OLD MAN: Neither do I.
NEIGHBOR: I did. My best basket.
OLD MAN: When?
OLD WOMAN: Yes, when?
NEIGHBOR: Twelve years ago.
OLD MAN and OLD WOMAN: Aha!

NEIGHBOR: Twelve years ago. A big woven basket with handles like this *(Shows with his hands),* almost new, no, no, completely new, still firm, with painted flowers on it.
OLD MAN *(Desperately):* Granny, I don't remember it at all.
OLD WOMAN: Neither do I. I'll go and look for it. *(Leaves)*
NEIGHBOR: If you've ruined it, beware!
OLD MAN: If we've got it, don't worry! Besides, we can always buy you a new one.
NEIGHBOR: Oh? I don't agree! You can't get such baskets anymore, they've stopped making them. I want my basket!
OLD MAN: I understand. There it is! It's alive! Oh! There it is! Look! Alone, the hawk's gone! Oh! Oh! *(Throws himself to the ground)* Lie down! Lie down! Please!
NEIGHBOR *(Hesitates but finally does so and looks at the sky):* I can't see a thing.
OLD MAN: What? You can see it so well; there it is, beneath the clouds.
NEIGHBOR: You're imagining things.
OLD MAN: Take a better look. See, it's coming back again. It's so beautiful.
NEIGHBOR: I can't see a thing. All I see are stars and circles dancing before my eyes . . . That's from anemia . . .
OLD MAN: How come you can't see it? There it is, over the house.
NEIGHBOR: Aha, aha-aa now I see. Well. So, that's it?
OLD MAN: That's it. It's singing! It sings beautifully! Hear it?
NEIGHBOR *(Laughs raucously):* The bird? No-ooo . . .
OLD MAN: Why are you laughing?
NEIGHBOR *(Cannot control his laughter):* It . . . it . . .
OLD WOMAN *(Coming back with an old, dilapidated basket):* Did you catch it? *(Changing the tone of her voice)* I could hardly find it. It was up in the attic with all the junk. It's so dusty.
NEIGHBOR: That is not my basket. That was my basket . . .
OLD MAN: It's still yours.

NEIGHBOR: I gave you a new basket. My best basket. It was the pride of my house. I want it back the same as I gave it to you. You have to give it back. I could keep everything I had in it; all my best things.
OLD WOMAN: Here is your basket, but I swear I don't remember your ever giving it to us.
OLD MAN: Maybe you never really did.
NEIGHBOR: That's the trouble! That's the worst thing about it—you've forgotten that I ever gave you my best basket. That's absolutely disgraceful!
OLD MAN: What can we do now?
NEIGHBOR: And I thought—I had finally found somebody, people I can trust; that's what you looked like. I thought—since they've asked me so nicely, since they need it so badly, I'll lend them my best basket; with them it'll be as safe as with me, maybe even safer; let it stay at their place. When I need it, I can always ask for it and get it back the same, maybe even hand-decorated . . . However, you turned out to be only ordinary neighbors and nothing more.
OLD MAN: Granny, how can we help him?
OLD WOMAN: But what does he want? We've been neighbors for so long and he hasn't even noticed that we have a bird!
OLD MAN: Yes, and he wasn't even able to remember its name for more than five minutes, but anyway . . .
OLD WOMAN: He's only an ordinary neighbor too.
OLD MAN: Anyway, anyway . . . we should do something to help him.
OLD WOMAN: Because of a basket . . . No. I don't understand.
OLD MAN: I knew a man who couldn't believe that certain people live and are quite happy, without ever having a button-hole in their coat lapel. He would become really desperate when he saw that some others not only don't know anything about buttonholes on lapels, but also haven't got the slightest idea of what a coat is.

THE BIRD

NEIGHBOR *(Angrily tearing the basket and throwing the pieces all around)*: I don't exist anymore! Neighbors!

OLD WOMAN: What's he talking about? What's the matter with him?

OLD MAN: He is dead, can't you see?

NEIGHBOR: Well, good-bye!

OLD MAN: Good-bye. We are so sorry . . .

OLD WOMAN: We are so sorry . . .

OLD MAN: Believe us . . .

OLD WOMAN: Believe us . . .

OLD MAN: If we could only do something.

NEIGHBOR: Good-bye, neighbors. *(Leaves rapidly)*

OLD MAN: Today he put his foot in his mouth.

OLD WOMAN: Why, we forgot all about the trap! Look at all the birds that came.

OLD MAN: But ours isn't among them.

OLD WOMAN: That means, those birds belong to somebody else.

OLD MAN: They'll peck at everything! Shoo!

OLD WOMAN: Shoo! *(Goes to the tub waving her hands around)* They went away. Are you sure we set the right bait?

OLD MAN: Yes. It has to be the right bait. It would be awful if we'd made a mistake.

OLD WOMAN: And what should we feed it?

OLD MAN: Everything it wants to eat. We'll buy all the best bird food and let it choose.

OLD WOMAN: But then we'll spend all our savings.

OLD MAN: We've been saving up for the bird anyway.

OLD WOMAN: You're a real man. *(She sits beside the Old Man)* I can't help loving you. *(Tears the newspaper again)*

OLD MAN: Love me.

OLD WOMAN: You're afraid?

OLD MAN: If we catch it, what will happen to me . . . with us?

OLD WOMAN: Just let it come. I'll put the cage beside the window. It will have sun enough.
OLD MAN: It'll have everything.
OLD WOMAN: And we will have it. That's so nice! And there will be no more secrets between us.
OLD MAN: There will be no secrets.
OLD WOMAN: I started thinking of pears again. I feel just like eating them; what can I do? Damn me!
OLD MAN: The neighbor laughed when I showed it to him.
OLD WOMAN: He laughed?
OLD MAN: He almost choked from laughter.
OLD WOMAN: What does he know about birds? Basket-maker!
OLD MAN: True, that's the reason. Listen! It's singing!
OLD WOMAN: I can't hear it.
OLD MAN: Up there.
OLD WOMAN: I can't hear a thing.
OLD MAN: He couldn't hear it either. No one hears but me.
OLD WOMAN: I'm afraid to look.
(They lurk by covering themselves with newspapers. The Old Woman covers her head. The Old Man watches attentively.)
OLD MAN: It's hovering! It's coming down . . . now, it's ours!
(The Neighbor appears from behind, gun in hand. They do not notice him.)
NEIGHBOR: Is that your bird?
OLD MAN *(Still looking at the sky)*: Yes.
NEIGHBOR: The one that's hovering?
OLD MAN: It's hovering now.
NEIGHBOR: So, the one that's going for the tub?
OLD MAN: That's it, that's it, that's it. Oh, just listen to its song! Granny, it will be ours! Look!
(His eyes follow the bird coming down. Granny would like to peek out from under the papers, but she is afraid.)

NEIGHBOR: So. *(Raises his gun and aims for a long time. Just before the gun fires, Granny gathers enough courage to peep out.)*
OLD WOMAN: I can see it!
(Immediately after, a shot echoes and a crow falls to the ground.)
OLD MAN: What happened? Who fired?
OLD WOMAN: Who killed our bird?
NEIGHBOR: The basket. *(The Old Man and the Old Woman run over to the bird.)* No use. It's dead. A dead crow. A stinking crow. A vulture. Thank me. *(Laughs)*
OLD WOMAN: Really, a crow . . . and you said it sang beautifully.
OLD MAN: To me it was beautiful.
OLD WOMAN: It's so skinny! God, so skinny; only skin and bones! Look, look, and its wings aren't even blue.
OLD MAN: No, they aren't. Give it to me. *(The Old Woman hands him the bird. They look at it for a long time.)* And it looked so beautiful high up in the sky!
OLD WOMAN: That was the most . . .
OLD MAN: Now it's a dead crow, the vulture is dead. Hey, its heart is still beating! Feel it.
(The Old Woman touches the bird.)
OLD WOMAN: It's beating.
OLD MAN: Can you really feel it beating?
OLD WOMAN: Yes. It's beating very softly.
OLD MAN: Just like mine. Mine.
OLD WOMAN: Really, like yours. It won't last long.
OLD MAN: A little at least. At least a little bit. A bit longer . . . before night comes . . .
(He takes the cage and puts the crow inside. The Old Woman shuts it. They squat beside the cage and stare at the bird. The Neighbor stands behind them, watching thoughtfully. It suddenly grows dark. Only a ray of moonlight illuminates the group around the cage. The Old Man and the Old Woman rise slowly;

they look at the Neighbor in silence, and then disappear into the darkness, taking the cage with them. When they are out of sight, the Neighbor recoils. He is ready to go, too, but sees a piece of his basket, takes it, wants to put it in his pocket, then changes his mind and throws it into the night. He tightens his grasp around the gun and leaves. The ray of moonlight does not accompany anyone out. For a long time it remains alone on stage, and then slowly, very slowly fades.)

CURTAIN

Translated by *Daša Drndić*

ALEKSANDAR POPOVIĆ
(1928—1996)

Popović was born in Ub, Serbia. He started writing in 1950 and was the first author to introduce light humor and Serbian slang into his works. He is considered to be the founder of contemporary Yugoslav satirical plays.

Popović's works marked a new direction in satirical writings. He introduced personages from everyday life, people from the streets who dealt with ordinary matters. His satire is framed within his plays, similar to burlesque and vaudeville, complete with low comedy and vulgarity. While Popović's satire is based on the idea that one learns easily when one laughs, Popović's Hats Off! (1967) is a protest against mechanization, bureaucracy, and automated life and sex.

The popularity and effectiveness of Hats Off! lies in Popović's ability to use current and proverbial expressions. Popović rapidly alters his themes and subject matter, with little regard for the form or content, stressing only the values of the humorous and the satirical.

HATS OFF!

Theatrical Vespers in Two Acts
(Waste and Halter)

CHARACTERS:

Macabre—All-Power
Two-Ton Honey
Adagio—The Court-Bawdy-0
Flirty-Gertie
Eugene—Man of Mystery
Artie Fartie
Seven Maids Who've Never Been Laid
There's more guessing than messing, but it all goes up in smoke anyway.

ACT I: WASTE

(On by Day—Off by Night)
(MACABRE'S *Court. Nightmarish confusion.*)

THE SEVEN MAIDS (Singing and dancing):

> On my coat a hundred patched,
> Every debtor has his snatches! . . .
> People think that it's a joke,
> That I'm absolutely broke,
> But I have one hundred grand—
> Grains!—pure Adriatic sand!

MACABRE: Wham! . . (*The confusion abates.* THE SEVEN MAIDS, MACABRE, *and* HONEY *exit.*)
ADAGIO (*Stays behind with* GERTIE *to clean up the mess.* ARTIE *droops on the throne*): I feel as if I'd been raped by the Seventh Fleet.
GERTIE: That's what I call wishful thinking!
ADAGIO: We work our fingers to the bone, and they plunder us in our own house!
GERTIE: The floor boards creak under their feet!
ADAGIO: And the pillow reeks under their cheeks, like rotten fish in a porcelain dish!
MACABRE: Give me your hand!
GERTIE: Yeah! . . . as they say "Right makes might!" But why waste breath. Just let everything follow its own fine course, right down to rack and ruin!
ADAGIO: Come on, let's have it, bandmaster! Toast each in turn! Music! . . . (*Music.*) First toast to the host! (*Music.*)
GERTIE: And his wife—but not for life! (*Music.*)

ADAGIO: To the brass on their ass, and the cops in heat on their beat. *(Music.)*
GERTIE: And the tinker, tailor, soldier, sailor! *(Music.)*
ADAGIO: Rich man, poor man, beggar man, thief! *(Flourish of trumpets, pompous gallop.)*
MACABRE *(Enters doing the gallop):* Come on now, let old Dad take you for a little walk through history!
GERTIE: That's Macabre, the head-codger around here!
MACABRE: Give me some skin!
ADAGIO: And get your knuckles rapped!
MACABRE: Adagio!
ADAGIO *(Jumps forward and dances about* MACABRE*):* At your service, Right Reverend!
MACABRE: You sinner, you! *(Exits.)*
ADAGIO *(Jumps off after* MACABRE*):* My only sin is that I'm forever longing for your whip!
HONEY *(She appears at the same moment and looks back at* ADAGIO*):* What are you prancing about for, Adagio?
GERTIE: That's Two-Ton Honey—Macabre's second wife in order of running, but now she's the apple of his eye. They call her Cunty-Honey as a pet name.
MACABRE *(Enters,* ADAGIO *saunters after him):* Cunty-Honey, I can't stand to look at him doing a jig like that!
HONEY: Like a cat on a hot tin roof. . . phooey! *(Exits.)*
MACABRE *(To* ADAGIO*):* You heard her, first go pee on a tree, and then come!
ADAGIO: I won't! I like to struggle with nature.
GERTIE: In the daylight, he can face anything; I should know! For me he's a real man! But as soon as it gets dark, he wets himself. He goes all to pieces from one caress . . . and I'm like his wife, humph! *(Exits.)*
MACABRE *(To* ADAGIO*):* You're laying yourself wide open, Adagio. I hope you can hold out!

ADAGIO: Even if I have to help myself a little with my hand, I won't let you down!
MACABRE: And now go ask if he wants anything.
ADAGIO: I know Artie's answer without even asking him: he loves silk pants better than a silk gown.
MACABRE: Keep knowledge like that to yourself. You'll need it, and ask him like I told you to! *(GERTIE enters. ARTIE comes on the ramp accompanied by a gallop.)*
GERTIE: That's somebody called Artie. Actually he's Macabre's son by wife number one, but he's in the doghouse here now!
ADAGIO *(Bows before* ARTIE*)*: Is there anything the young bull desires?
ARTIE: You must help me exterminate them all! *(Exits.* ADAGIO *dances out after him.)*
MACABRE *(Enters with GERTIE)*: You must persuade him to run off with you!
GERTIE: Who'll inflame your old blood if I go?
MACABRE: I'll watch dirty movies! In the meantime disown him by surprise. He won't be my son any more! *(Exits, followed by* GERTIE.*)*
HONEY *(Enters with* ARTIE*)*: Macabre is on his last legs . . . he'd like to, but he can't. . . .
ARTIE: It doesn't matter, I can do it for the both of us. You don't lose a thing!
HONEY: I know, but then he strains at it all day long . . . and he has monkey glands implanted, and he pushes, gets all red in the face, the veins in his neck almost burst . . . and he pants like a dog in the sun. . . .
ARTIE: Well, if all bugs were to shit honey, what would happen to the bumble-bee?
HONEY: That's it! We just have to catch him spent on the mattress with that bitch. Then it's a bullet in the forehead for her, and a muzzle and a leash for him! *(Exits, followed by* ARTIE.*)*

MACABRE *(Enters with* ADAGIO): You're young, and she's an old woman!
ADAGIO: You don't get it for nothing—even from an old bag!
MACABRE: You're wrong; an old woman takes what she can get. She won't turn anything down. That'll be my corpus delicti, to get rid of her! *(Exits, followed by* ADAGIO.*)*
HONEY *(Enters with* GERTIE*):* What about making love with both the father and the son!
GERTIE: And the Holy Ghost! He left me heavy once, and nobody ever believed me!
HONEY: Don't worry: you've got sex coming out of your ears! They'll tear each other to pieces over you, like wild boars in heat! *(Exits, followed by* GERTIE.*)*
MACABRE *(Enters, followed by* ARTIE*):* You've got to help me liquidate these conspirators, Son!
ARTIE: Which ones?
MACABRE: Honey is thick with Gertie. And Adagio is worming his way into her confidence! They're all in cahoots! They ought to be shot! *(Exits, followed by* ARTIE.*)*
HONEY *(Enters with* ADAGIO*):* Kill the bastards when they least expect it, and you'll have a place in my bed guaranteed!
ADAGIO: Don't think that I'm haggling, but I've had better offers.
Honey: Don't get excited: let me finish. . . . On top of that you'll get an apartment and a warm bed, all for free!
ADAGIO: What about my commission?
HONEY: Well, it all depends on the service rendered, what kind of showing you make. *(Exits, goes off, followed by* ADAGIO.*)*
ARTIE *(Enters, followed by* GERTIE*):* Adagio is cheating on you, Gertie. . . . He could very well get you in big trouble. Better to kill him today than to kill someone else's crabs on you tomorrow! As for me, I'll bump off Honey—and then we can get to the elections with an easy mind!

GERTIE: Macabre is sure to be the top candidate anyway, and we know that the masses always blindly go for the first man. And then he'll be sitting pretty.... A lot of good that will do you.... And you, you'll stand on the sidelines, green with envy!

ARTIE: But if we just light a firecracker under his seat, that'll make things hot for him. The old man has one foot in the grave already. One more shove and he'll topple into the hole, and then we two are left to run the show. *(Exits, followed by* GERTIE.*)*

HONEY (Enters with MACABRE): Well, are you deaf and dumb?

EUGENE *(Peers out):* Mooooo!

MACABRE: Concentrations of motorized birds of prey have been observed around the borders. And the beast in me has been ominously gnashing its teeth for three days now. I must take a look into this. *(Exits.)*

EUGENE *(Peers. out):* Mooooo! *(Charges* HONEY, *she steps aside and he runs past.)* Mooooo!

HONEY: Let's see if it'll make him wiser if he knocks his head against the wall?

EUGENE *(Rushes at* HONEY*)* Mooooo! *(She dodges him. He runs past and hits his head on the wall.)*

HONEY: That should calm him down now!

EUGENE *(Hops about):* Mooooo!

HONEY: What a thick skull! *(Takes off her red skirt and remains in her panties.)* Maybe he'll chase a skirt on a stick? *(Puts her skirt on a stick and leads* EUGENE *through a Veronica with a Flourish of Brass.)*

EUGENE: Mooooo! . Mooooo! . . . *(In the end* HONEY *conquers him.)*

HONEY: Who are you?

EUGENE: A big ox. Mooooo!

HONEY: Just as I thought: a nobody. Raw potential! But put you in the big time. Just let them get used to you, and then you'll weave spider webs around them after my pattern!

EUGENE: What do I get for it? What's in it for me?

HONEY: A higher standard of living.

EUGENE: I'll fight for my bacon and for my butter! I'll fight for my car and my TV set! I'll fight to the last gasp! *(HONEY exits and he obediently follows her.)* Mooooo!

MACABRE *(Enters):* The tourists have swarmed all over, and all they do is click-click with their cameras. They shoot at everything they see!

HONEY *(Enters):* Even the birth rate has gone out of control; everything is going down the drain; pretty soon we'll be eating one another!

MACABRE: Everybody's gotten into a uniform; you can't tell her from him anymore!

HONEY: The worst of all is that everyone has his heart set on your speedy end—I must tell you that, though I know it's not pleasant to hear.

MACABRE: Well, we'll have to see about that!

HONEY: All right, but don't forget afterwards, when spoils are shared out, who first warned you about what can happen.

MACABRE: I'll give everyone his measure.

HONEY: That's precisely what I'm saying, this is where you're wrong: you don't measure your friends with yardsticks across their backs! *(Exits.)*

MACABRE *(After her):* Would you, Cunty-Honey, be the only one to wish me well? I'm a bit suspicious about your unnatural interest in all this. *(Exits.)*

ADAGIO *(Enters with* GERTIE*):* My poor little Gertie, just look at it! Why here it's all for none and nobody for all! Who'll live through all this? *(Exits.)*

GERTIE: Me—that's who! Because, when it comes to a free-for-all, I'm all for free! Let there be music, and let the wine flow: come on . . . music! *(Music.)*

MACABRE *(Enters with* ARTIE, HONEY, *and* EUGENE*):* The old clock on the wall says it's time for bed!

EUGENE: Mooooo! *(Everyone undresses. Striptease.)*
MACABRE *(To* ARTIE, *who is already in his underpants)*: You've already got your pants off?
ARTIE *(Embarrassed)*: Well, someone asked me:

"Artie, my boy,
Show me your toy.
Don't be so coy!"

HONEY *(She and* GERTIE *quickly gather up their things and cover themselves in embarrassment)*: Is there no love without insult? *(Exits.)*
GERTIE: This is an insult! He offered me his life if I would be his wife! *(Exits.)*
ARTIE: I was pulling their leg, honest, Dad!
MACABRE: I believe you, my boy, but, nevertheless, I ask you, where's your honor, where's your dignity?
ARTIE *(Gets dressed quickly)*: It's all because of them! I could easily catch cold!
MACABRE: If she's as naked as a jaybird, your pants won't be in the way! Besides, you and I must still appear on the rostrum.
GERTIE *(Enters)*: Where's the pail?
ADAGIO *(Enters, bringing the pail)*: Have I got to be a chambermaid now? *(To* HONEY.*)* Your grace has expressed the desire to ease herself before going to bed. *(*HONEY *goes off,* ADAGIO *follows her with the pail.* MACABRE *and* ARTIE *mount the two rostrums at either side of the stage.)*
MACABRE *(From the rostrum)*: Why? . . . but why? . . . but why does man live?
ARTIE *(From the rostrum)*: Why? Why? Why, so he can give!
MACABRE: But if he's to give and give, how will he get rich?
ARTIE: By walking on water and avoiding the ditch!
MACABRE: And the wind is strong! But in case, there's a wind blowin'?

MACABRE AND ARTIE *(Sing the end in a duet)*: And there's nothing to throw in? No use rowin'—try floatin'! *(They slowly descend from the rostrums. Music.* GERTIE *enters quietly, bringing along* THE SEVEN MAIDS.*)*
GERTIE *(To* THE MAIDS*)*: Come on now, girls, open up!
THE SEVEN MAIDS AND GERTIE *(Dance and sing like fairies around* MACABRE, *who acts as if it were all just a dream.* ARTIE *slumps down on his throne)*:

> None but the brave
> Deserves to rave.
> None but the slave
> Deserves to crave.
> Down at the altar
> One dons the halter,
> God help who falter!
>
> Fire, fire, we desire
> Love and life to acquire.
> Dance, dance, now's our chance!
> Breeze, breeze, will you please
> Give us wings to fly and tease!
> Dance, dance, now's our chance!

(They ply their charms on MACABRE.*)*
MACABRE: You're like will-o'-the-wisps; you don't excite me a bit!
GERTIE AND THE SEVEN MAIDS *(In a frenzy)*:

> Earth, earth, for all it's worth
> Give us love to foster birth.
> Dance, dance, now's our chance!

MACABRE: You send chills down my spine! But so do snakes!

GERTIE AND THE SEVEN MAIDS *(Still more furiously)*:

> Water, water, the earth's daughter,
> That old codger almost caught her!
> Dance, dance, now's our chance!

MACABRE *(Manages to escape from them and flees off stage)*: make you sorry—you'll see! *(THE MAIDS become silent.)*
ARTIE *(Rouses himself on the throne)*: Gertie!
GERTIE *(Rushes to him)*: Just say the word and I'm yours, but be nice to me.
ARTIE: Listen to me, Gertie, and I won't beat you.
GERTIE: But, if you're a friend, don't try to get something for nothing.
ARTIE *(Sharply)*: What are you hiding in your slip?
GERTIE: Two bunches of grapes.
ARTIE: And I'm a wine-press! Come on; let's go!
GERTIE: I don't feel like it!
ARTIE: You want new love, but won't give up the old one!
GERTIE: I can't give up what I've never had!
GERTIE AND THE SEVEN MAIDS *(They dance seductively, in order to overwhelm* ARTIE*)*:

> Sun, sun, mighty sun!
> Pop your gun—have some fun!
> Dance, dance, now's our chance!

*(*ARTIE *acts as if it were all just a dream. He tries to catch* GERTIE, *but she always eludes him.)*
ARTIE: Don't try to escape, my little witch! *(*THE MAIDS *settle down.)* Come here and let me kiss you! . . . Why are you running away?
GERTIE: Because it's not very far from here to there! From the lips to the hips!

ARTIE: You're very edgy this morning; I know who's to blame!
GERTIE: He hasn't made love to me for over a week!
GERTIE AND THE SEVEN MAIDS *(They dance seductively, in order to overwhelm* ARTIE*):*

> Lonely and forsaken,
> Lips that aren't taken!
> Lonely and forsaken,
> Lips that aren't taken!

*(*ARTIE *acts as if it were all in a dream, tries to catch* GERTIE, *but without success. Then all at once he stops and "wakes up.")*
ARTIE.: That's enough!!! *(*THE MAIDS *scatter.)*
GERTIE: What's the matter with you?
ARTIE: What's the matter with you? You dance, you sing, and in the cupboard there's not a thing! Like sparks: now you see them, now you don't. . . . And me, overcome with sorrow. . . .
GERTIE: You should be, but it's all the same to me.
ARTIE: What's garbage today will burn green with life tomorrow!
MACABRE *(Suddenly appears on the rostrum):* But this green fire will wane! *(*ARTIE *quickly climbs up on the other rostrum.)* Just ashes and cinders will remain!
ARTIE *(From the rostrum):* Autumn and frost will come!
MACABRE: And I won't be on this platform anymore.
MACABRE AND ARTIE *(Sing the end in a duet):* And belong to the long, long past oblivion—oblivion. . . . *(*ARTIE *disappears from the rostrum, and* MACABRE *slowly descends to the stage. The* MAIDS *quietly leave the stage, and* GERTIE *comes forward to meet* MACABRE.*)*
GERTIE: Do you know what's good for marble, Macabre?
MACABRE: No, unless it's a good woman's warm bottom?
GERTIE: A good try, but off the mark! I'll tell you, but the one who does it should think of me when I'm no longer here.

MACABRE: Are you talking about your tombstone or mine?
GERTIE: About yours, Macabre! About yours! Just state in your will that your tombstone is to be rubbed with a linen rag and turpentine—and it'll shine like crystal! And, as for me, just let them say: "Gertie taught us that once a long time ago." *(ADAGIO runs across the stage.)* Why is that man flitting around like a mad-man again?
MACABRE *(ADAGIO runs across the stage again):* Adagio, is that you in the depths of nocturnal stillness?
GERTIE: Is he rushing about again because of the chamber pot?
ADAGIO *(Rushes to them):* Dan's been killed! . . . fishing in the river. . . . Someone must have shortened the fuse!
GERTIE *(Whispers to ADAGIO):* Not like that, for heaven's sake, sugar the pill!
MACABRE: Send a deputation and, in token of humility, let them wash dishes over the open grave!
ADAGIO: But in what connotation?
MACABRE: In the spirit of—my nose is clean.
ADAGIO: So he died of a natural accident!
MACABRE: And every delegate must wear a black band on his heel!
GERTIE *(Softly to ADAGIO):* Take it easy, man. Never mention horns in the home of a cuckold! *(Exits.)*
ADAGIO: And, as I was saying, a grenade went off in his hand. He didn't have time to throw it away in the river.
MACABRE: I smell sabotage, Gertie!
GERTIE *(Enters):* If my vote counts for anything, I say get the fool out of here! *(Exits.)*
MACABRE: But this must be done with style. Get the bastard out!
ADAGIO: Let's not be hasty! We might break the ceiling!
MACABRE: I won't deny myself anything. When I talk about tightening the belt, that only goes for other people.
ADAGIO: Well, put the thumb on your boys.

MACABRE: Sure, but how can I be happy if everyone around me is unhappy? They'll turn everything sour!

ADAGIO: All right, but we've got to get some idea. We'll need approximately about a hundred odd skewers. At least there's no shortage of poltroons. And with astronomical figures, one more or less won't make any difference!

MACABRE: Gertie! *(*GERTIE *enters.)* Have you pulled down the fence?

GERTIE: Fanny fell off the fence on a phallic fish!

MACABRE: Good thing it didn't fracture its fins! Come on, bring a glass for Adagio and a bottle of rot gut. Let's drink to the ratification and set our minds at ease. *(*ADAGIO *goes off.)*

ADAGIO: And throw the hay to the winds, lay your head in the shade, and your bum in the sun to sizzle. What more do you want?

MACABRE: On condition it's all done quickly, for money comes on one leg and leaves on a hundred! What scares me is ending up in the red, and Artie could burst in any minute now. You know how picayune he is! He wants everything in black and white!

ADAGIO: Why didn't that idiot go back where he came from, just like you told him in front of everybody in parliament?

GERTIE: Huh, not even a dog who followed a peasant's cart goes back to the farm if he's so much as licked a butcher's block in town. Much less Artie . . . and that's that! *(Exits.)*

ADAGIO: If there were as many epistles as there were apostles, a prophet would be hard put to be born!

MACABRE: Gertie says: "A hen will hatch ducklings, but she doesn't lay them!" You listen to her, because there's always more to her wisecracks than meets the eye. *(Exits.)*

ADAGIO: Hey, isn't Macabre a smart one! Every one of his words is pregnant—with at least twins and sometimes even triplets—all of them with curls. I bet everyone is worth between six months and sixteen years, according to circumstances. No matter which way you take them, they're always heavy.

GERTIE *(Enters):* How did you manage to get here in this blizzard?
ADAGIO: On a white horse.
GERTIE: Where did you manage to find ice and snow August?
ADAGIO: The same place you found the blizzard!
GERTIE: And how did you find the big wide world in which we live?
ADAGIO: Well . . .

> In this big world
> We call our house,
> Everyone kowtows,
> And everyone bows:
>
> The mass to the class,
> The class to the brass,
> The brass to the ass,
> And the ass to the grass!

GERTIE: Shhh!. . . speak a little softer. He may have left his ear under the threshold as he went out.
MACABRE *(Enters):* I forgot to tell you, Gertie! Carve up the sirloin and wrap it up in rhubarb leaves for him to take for bait! *(GERTIE goes off)*
ADAGIO: All the meat to the foxes again?
MACABRE: To each his own, according to his merit!
EUGENE *(Enters and makes straight for* MACABRE*):* Please, sir, Eugene here.
MACABRE *(Pushes* EUGENE *away):* Later, I don't have time now! *(*EUGENE *bows and goes off.)*
ADAGIO: What about us, Macabre?
MACABRE: For the likes of you: bread!
ADAGIO: Well, I'm sorry, but I think you're wrong there. Man doesn't live on bread alone!

MACABRE: I know . . . when he has enough of it . . . but when it gets scarce, then you should see how man lives on hard, soured crusts! What do you say to that?
ADAGIO: I say: "Don't talk when your mouth is full."
MACABRE: You're forever chewing the cud!
ADAGIO: It's just that my mouth is full of pain, and I just can't swallow it. . . . And I don't dare spit out!
GERTIE *(Enters):* The beds are ready!
MACABRE: Come with me, Gertie, to tuck me in . . . Will you?
GERTIE: Why not, Macabre? A woman is like water: where she's lain once, she'll come again.
MACABRE *(To* ADAGIO*):* And you, Adagio, remember: Don't spit in the pot you eat from! *(Starts off but* GERTIE *does not follow him.)*
ADAGIO: He doesn't give me much credit.
MACABRE: Why?
ADAGIO: I wasn't born yesterday! But now I think it's your turn to answer one of my questions! *(Approaches and swings a door, which squeaks.)* What is this door doing?
MACABRE: It's squeaking.
ADAGIO: Oil it, and it won't squeak.
MACABRE: Here, take it, you glutton, and have your fill! Let's go, Gertie. Why have you stopped halfway? You look at me as though I'll eat you up?
GERTIE: We won't eat up each other, that's for sure! But I'm afraid that the dark might swallow us both up?
MACABRE: There's a cure for that, too: let's have a candle! *(*ADAGIO *with a candle.)* Where are you going?!
ADAGIO: Why, to hold the candle for you, just like you said? *(*MACABRE *goes off.)*
GERTIE *(To* ADAGIO*):* As soon as we get in, you blow it out! *(*ADAGIO *exits.)*
MACABRE *(Returns):* Now I've had enough of him! *(Exits.)*

ADAGIO *(Returns)*: Listen, let's throw a blanket on him and beat him up! I'll go get the blanket! *(Exits.)*

MACABRE *(Returns)*: You blow out the candle, and I'll take him in hand. He'll be my trial balloon in the market; he's come along just in time! There hasn't been a better decoy in all history! He'll bring down eleven big mountains.

GERTIE: And dry up eleven bountiful fountains. . . .

MACABRE: And when the slugs and worms start writhing in the sun, I'll just smile and wink at the road menders: roll your steam rollers over them and flatten out the ground! *(Exits.)*

GERTIE: Just you roll; everything good will die forever, but weeds will pop up again after the first rain!

ADAGIO *(Enters)*: When he doubles you up, you scream loud enough to deafen him! And be careful how you wriggle at your job; kick him with your heels down his back, enough to knock out his kidneys! *(Turns around.)* Are you coming, Macabre?

MACABRE *(Offstage)*: Like a calf to the slaughter! Baaaaaa!

EUGENE *(Enters)*: Mooooo!

ADAGIO *(Shoves* EUGENE*)*: Later, we don't have time now!

EUGENE *(Obediently leaves)*: Mooooo!

MACABRE *(Offstage)*: Baaaa!

GERTIE: I thought he'd get away at the last moment; now look at him: he's bleating! He won't show himself for anything!

MACABRE *(Offstage)*: Baaaaaaaa!

GERTIE: We'll fry his hide at tonight's meeting.

ADAGIO: It's damned tough, you can be sure! We'll have to cook it two or three times. *(Turns around.)* Are you coming soon, Macabre?

MACABRE *(Offstage)*: You go on ahead, I'll be right with you!

GERTIE: Just enough time to set up an ambush . . . come on! (GERTIE *and* ADAGIO *go off)*

ARTIE *(Appears on the rostrum)*: This waaay! This waaaaay! This waaaay!

MACABRE *(Enters)*: Some pull that way, others pull this way . . . each pulls his own way, and the cart doesn't budge.
GERTIE *(Offstage)*: This waaaay! This waaaay! This waaaay!
ARTIE *(From the podium)*: This waaaay! This way! This way!
MACABRE *(Does not know which way to turn)*: I'm coming. Wait a minute, till I get my bearings!
GERTIE *(Enters)*: What's the hitch this time?
MACABRE: I'm wanted urgently on the telephone. *(Goes off, ARTIE disappears from the rostrum.)*
ADAGIO *(Enters)*: They tease you and tease you! It's always like that . . . they hold out a morsel and just as you open your mouth to take a bite, it's jerked away!
GERTIE: You've got a cursed hand. Whoever you kill turns into a ghoul. *(Goes off, followed by ADAGIO.)*
ARTIE *(Appears on the rostrum)*: This waaaay! This waaaay! This waaaay!
MACABRE *(Enters)*: Who was that, Son?
ARTIE: A traveler!
MACABRE: In other words: a human submarine! . a wandering vampire . . . a blood sucker! I just wonder what kind of fish he's trying to catch in these troubled waters of ours?
ARTIE: He got lost in the dark thick forest and wants us to give him quarters.
MACABRE: Quarter him then!
ARTIE: Six feet square, a little corner, he says.
MACABRE: He's lying!
ARTIE: There's no end to Asia! . . . and to integration . . . and to unconditional surrender, he says!
MACABRE: He's lying!
ARTIE: He says restoration! Liberte, Egalite, Fraternite! Silk purses out of sows' ears! It's the twentieth century, he says. . . .
MACABRE: Lies, all lies! He's a lying bastard!

ARTIE: Who the hell would know? Maybe he's asking for political asylum? I can't understand his language very well. It's neither left nor right.

MACABRE: Twelve percent, just in case . . . or, if it comes to the worst, a dime on the dollar! Our unselfish sense of oneness and our willingness to forget about insignificant slaughters—that's what it'll cost him. You tell him that, and I'm going to lie down. I feel like turning in.

GERTIE *(Offstage):* This waaaay! This waaaay! Over here.

ARTIE *(Macabre starts to leave):* Wait, Dad! *(Macabre halts)* Have you forgotten the vows that we carved in sand?

MACABRE: How was that tune again? I forget it now?

ARTIE: When saints go marching out,
> Virtue at last cops out,
> And peasants become a little redder,
> We'll no longer be together!

MACABRE: Well, Son, it's either a rich life or death! Even if it is on credit! Grab what you can. Don't worry about repaying! But the installments keep accumulating!

ARTIE: That's how our vows stand, written in the sand!

MACABRE: Yes, that's how it stood once, as if carved in water, until we got squeezed from all sides! No more credit! No more vows! The water washed it away, and the wind blew it off!

ARTIE: I suppose some pretty wench erased it from your heart, Dad?

MACABRE: No, Artie, my son, no! It's because of strong winds and rough water that it's not worth making any vows. Everyone is forgiven for it!

ARTIE: Much is forgiven, Macabre, but nothing is ever forgotten! When you need it, up it comes!

MACABRE: So what if it does! Maybe it won't. Who can tell? One thing remains: you can't always live in fear of death! It's

always better to die once and for all than to die a little each day and rot in life!
ARTIE: So you say, death, is not the worst?
MACABRE: I only said that there are degrees to it!
ARTIE: Will you at least come to the funeral?
MACABRE: Yes, if you'll dig into your pockets for the taxi fare!
ARTIE: Maybe I can get time's chariot for us? *(Leaves the rostrum.)*
MACABRE: Wait a minute! I want to give them instructions on how to behave while we're away.
GERTIE *(Enters)*: If one of your cronies is making interventions again by telephone because of poor business, you can tell him from me that all of the most important seats in the quorum are already taken!
MACABRE: What if he offers us a fair swap?
GERTIE: Leave him alone, man. A beggar is no giver! *(Exits.)*
MACABRE: Fine, then, you cook an egg on the fire, break it in half, and, hot as it is, rub it on his nose!
ADAGIO *(Enters)*: What is this I hear? Are things tightening up again?
MACABRE: The bastard will never think of stealing eggs again! *(Exits.)*
ARTIE *(Appears on the rostrum)*: This waaaay! This waaaay! Hurry uphill, Macabre! Run! The taxi driver is impatient! He's cursing us with bell, book, and candle and wishing himself long life and good health at our expense!
MACABRE *(Enters)*: The help here has gone to rack and ruin: they feed the cat, let the mice take over, and the cops go on shooting crap. They keep score with their billy-clubs—on the skin! They've lightened our purses, the motherland's breasts are dangling like empty bags, and hunger-maddened turkeys fly across the sky, like birds of doom!
ARTIE: If they carry on this way, they'll end up down the drain!

MACABRE *(Mounts the rostrum):* I agree with that, unconditionally! *(*MACABRE and ARTIE *leave the rostrum.)*
ADAGIO *(Enters with GERTIE):* What's all this? Wherever you look you see them reading psalms. Is it some saint's day today?
GERTIE: Yes. St. Pugnacius! If he should get into my bed just once, he'll be coming around more often. He'll turn his coat and change his vote. He'll leave that goat, or I'll cut his throat. *(Exits.)*
ADAGIO: Yeah, you could give him the works—but no matter how you heal the wounds, the scars will still remain. And, remember, there's no coat or cloak that'll hide a leper. No, we'll be damned till the end of our days!
HONEY *(Enters):* What are you doing here at this time of the day?
ADAGIO: I'm spying on the spies, as it were. I watch you and you watch me, and whoever informs on the other first, he gets the merit. Hell, your left hand can't trust the right these days. Humanism's gone whacky! Everyone has started keeping tabs on everyone else. I'm sick of it; I wish I were far away from it all!
HONEY: Cool down, Adagio. The further you go, the closer to death you'll be. I think you're on your last legs.
ADAGIO: What about you, Cunty-Honey?
HONEY: I can't sleep a wink. I keep dreaming of mangy sheep in brambles. They sort of bleat.
ADAGIO: Like in heat!
HONEY: Maybe, I don't know. But I can clearly hear something smacking hungrily all night . . . . as if walking through mud and minding its step. And I wish I could hear it here, in my heart, because I fear it would be over all too soon in my dream. Like Prince Charming and Cinderella. No sooner do I shut my eyes, than something like a film spreads over my eyes: like yellow paisley patterns, red fish bones, and a kind of pepper-and-salt color. And I keep waking, and even in my dream I keep an ear slightly ajar, to hear the weather forecast for the next classification period. *(Groaning and muttering.)* Shh come, come

. . . but on your tiptoes, so we don't scare him away. There he goes; now you see him, now you don't! *(Exits after the sound, followed by* ADAGIO.*)*

ARTIE *(Appears on the rostrum)*: They'll be playing cards all night! All kinds of them: Punch cards! Credit cards! Party cards!

MACABRE *(Appears on the rostrum)*: And there'll be stars galore! Shooting stars! Generals' stars! Film stars! Water will gush upon the sand!

ARTIE: Chains will clank upon the concrete. And, out of the walls of fortresses, mother's milk will continue oozing for centuries to come! *(Both disappear from the rostrum.)*

HONEY *(Enters)*: Who is it? Who shattered people's dreams?

ADAGIO *(Enters)*: The juggler!

HONEY: Do you mean Macabre?

ADAGIO: I'm not suggesting anyone. No names have been mentioned! All I know is that he juggled with dreams just like a juggler tossing plates in a circus. So long as his hands were firm, the magic worked.

HONEY: And the mouth moved up to the top of the head! And, all at once, everybody started talking through his hat!

ADAGIO: And their eyes got too big for their heads! And they gazed at the stars, and suddenly everyone stopped saving. The few remaining monuments are pissed on by dogs . . . and the janitor rolled off the roof into the septic pit, from which a snake, yellow as an egg, crawled out!

HONEY: And their noses dropped down to their chins! And everyone's hair started growing out of his eyebrows, as if the fashion had come for low brows and high asses. *(Exits.)*

ADAGIO: The thumb, too, as I told you at the beginning, slipped under the index, and two fingers on the map are like two thousand miles on the earth. The pilgrims wore their feet to a nub and never got anywhere. And so . . . and so . . . they held on grimly, breathing as their last words: we are near, almost there.

And drunken dreams grimaced in warped mirrors, until his hand shook. *(HONEY enters.)*

HONEY: Whose, the juggler's?

ADAGIO: I'm not insinuating anyone. No names have been mentioned. All I know is that the mirror fell on the stone . . . and shattered. Now nobody knows how to put together the shattered dream, so everyone lives piecemeal . . . . Get what you can!

HONEY: Would you sing something nice and sensible so that I can fall asleep on your shoulder?

ADAGIO: How do you pay?

HONEY: In kind, according to the service rendered . . . since nowadays no one will do anything without payment. All right, get on with it! But if you've ever lighted a cigarette, you'll know that it's useless to start puffing before the match is fully aflame. Don't be impatient, the flame might just flare up and immediately go out.

ADAGIO *(Music for Sexual Act. ADAGIO sings):* There was a fat gal named Honey . . .

HONEY: Easy, easy, don't burn me up!

ADAGIO: Whose past was far from sunny . . .

HONEY: Keep that up and I'm through!

ADAGIO: She spat on the floor . . .

HONEY: I can hardly wait!

ADAGIO: And swore like a whore . . .

HONEY: My cup runneth over!

ADAGIO: Now its fun-on-the-run Honey-Cunty!

HONEY: Sing it, Sam!

ADAGIO: Honey-Cunty, Cunty-Honey!

HONEY: Just a little more. Go on! *(ADAGIO stops singing; the music ceases.)* Why did you? Why? Why did you stop just now?

ADAGIO: I like to tease you, Cunty-Honey.

HONEY: So that's the thanks I get for having brought you from rags to riches overnight!

ADAGIO: You mean to the gallows!

HONEY: You know what happens to slimy characters. I'll kill you!
ADAGIO: I'm not the kind of man that women could kill with their charms. *(Exits.)*
HONEY: If you're going to sell me out, I'd rather you kill me with your own hands! *(Goes off after* ADAGIO.*)*
ARTIE *(Enters carrying* GERTIE *in his arms)*: I like white, Gertie. Your white body! *(Sets* GERTIE *down on her feet.)*
GERTIE: Yes, but white may also be forbidding in its purity. Just don't get the wrong idea, Artie! You don't dare touch it for fear of getting it dirty! *(ARTIE throws her down on the ground.)*
MACABRE *(Appears on the rostrum):* You know what the smell of a white oleander blossom is like, Son? *(ARTIE starts.* GERTIE *flees.)* At first it's delighting and exciting, but afterwards your head feels like bursting! *(Disappears from the rostrum.)*
ARTIE: The crimson poppy in the glare of the sun blinds you! And the six-petalled field flower makes you vomit! Whatever is beautiful can do you harm! Gertie, where did you go? I need you! Where are you?! *(Exits.)*
ADAGIO *(Enters with* HONEY*)*: Kill yourself, yourself!
HONEY: My heart is torn and bleeding, Adagio. At least comfort me.
ADAGIO: Comfort today, comfort tomorrow. Every day you just want to come fart, no wonder your heart is torn apart!
HONEY: Even a priest's cassock can get torn. Never mind people's reputation! Everything gets patched up and mended. The main thing is that it lasts.
ADAGIO: Nothing lasts forever.
HONEY: I know that better than anyone.
ADAGIO: What do you know?
HONEY: I know that even green wood burns along with the dry wood.
ADAGIO: What's that? What's that?

HONEY: You can't feed a bonfire with sawdust, that's what . . . *(Cries.)*

ADAGIO: What are you crying for? Wait, think about it: and loosen your girdle a little! *(Strip tease.)*

HONEY: Eh!

ADAGIO: Fill your lungs with fresh air; it'll bolster you up!

HONEY: Ah!

ADAGIO: Relax! Your straps are biting into your shoulders!

HONEY: Oh!

ADAGIO: And loosen the laces on your girdle by a few inches. *(HONEY ends up with nothing on. For how long? That's up to the director.)* Now do you see? No use lecturing a hungry man about food; rather give him something to bite into . . . like this!

HONEY: Quite true! With no clothes on, I do breathe much more freely, naked like this!

ADAGIO: Like the naked truth.

HONEY: The ugly truth.

ADAGIO: The easily accessible truth.

EUGENE *(Enters):* Mooooo! Mooooo!

ADAGIO *(Pushes* EUGENE *away):* Later, I don't have time now! *(*EUGENE *bows and leaves obediently.)*

EUGENE: Mooooo!

HONEY: Take me, if it's like you said just now. Match your words with deeds!

ADAGIO: You're sure looking for trouble. You want to let the wolf guard your sheep!

HONEY: It's not trousers that makes a man!

ADAGIO: In any case we'll leave it as arranged. But tell me first, without any rush or nervousness, I really am curious to know: if someone doesn't want you, won't you yourself lure someone into your embrace after I've gone my own way?

HONEY: Yes, my dear, here they say that what a woman slaughters for meat is bound to be uneatable.

ADAGIO: And you put a pestle between your legs and hold it there while you kill your chickens!

HONEY *(Sobs):* There indeed would be meat, but it wouldn't be so sweet! I'd rather nestle or wrestle than squeeze a pestle!

ADAGIO: Go ahead and cry! When you wake up from your love dreams, it'll become quite clear to you, Cunty-Honey, that man is man and woman is woman, and ever the twain shall have meat!

HONEY: All meat goes the way of our life hopes and illusions—to the dogs.

ADAGIO: Yes, but the pot remains!

HONEY: What's the use if it's licked clean! Today it no longer matters . . . but once upon a time!

ADAGIO: You asked your mother what you'd be!

HONEY: Oh, for heaven's sake, don't start that now! What's over is over and done with!

ADAGIO: Oh, do tell me, why the hell not! You'll make Macabre pay for it through the nose once he's down! *(Starts to leave.)* He'll stone for his own sins and ours, too! Come over and take a peek! Shhh! Gertie is carrying on diplomatic relations in bed with him! *(ADAGIO and HONEY go off.)*

MACABRE (MACABRE *enters carrying* GERTIE *in his arms):* Why should other people's happiness distract us from our own despair? For how long are we going to look as if we live for other people's progress? *(Pushes GERTIE down On her feet.)*

GERTIE: I don't know, Macabre; but even if I knew, I wouldn't be believed, because it's up to you to decide. All I have to do is keep clear of any perversity! Because you're just great!

MACABRE: Tell me, now, tell me honestly: am I clever? *(Enter HONEY and ADAGIO.)*

ADAGIO: Your intellect shines down upon us like the sun!

MACABRE: Tell me, now, tell me without beating around the bush: am I popular?

HONEY: The goodness of your heart is only matched by the splendor of your soul! The world worships the wisdom of your words! *(HONEY and ADAGIO exit.)*

MACABRE: And what about my strength? Tell me without embellishment, is it declining?

GERTIE: You're terrific, Macabre! You're certainly still very strong!

MACABRE: And you're pretty!

GERTIE: You're rich, too!

MACABRE: And you're raw! I'll have to invest some capital in you to see some returns on raw material.

GERTIE: The beauty of my body comes to me from my father and mother, and there is nothing anyone can do about it. Even when I have given what you are yearning after, Macabre, it'll still remain my own! *(MACABRE throws her on the ground.)*

ARTIE *(Appears on the rostrum):* Cold memories conceal their fingers under other people's hearts. They're all lying to you because they hate you, but I'm your son! I both love you and hate you. I both want you and don't want you. I'll tell you, though: if it's true that history is our teacher, then the teacher is the only one that you should lie with, because only her children live forever!

MACABRE: I'm sick of my power! And I'm sick of sycophants! I'm not going to keep running after my desires like a greyhound after a mechanical rabbit. Gertie, where are you? I want you!

ARTIE: No use looking for her. She'll smother you with the charms of her everyday banalities and inanities!

MACABRE: Gertie, where are you?

ARTIE: No good looking for her, I told you! She's a young thing. Even if you could understand her, what good is it to you, if you, old as you are, can't keep up with her? The frustration will kill you!

MACABRE: Gertie, where are you? I waaaaant you! *(MACABRE exits.)*

ARTIE: They're all lying to you because they hate you, but I'm your soooon! I both love you and haaate you! Oh, you specter with vicious serpents oozing fire instead of milk! Oh, you monster! Are you going to pour the venom of your lust over my father?! *(Disappears from the rostrum.)*
EUGENE *(Runs across the stage):* Mooooo!
ADAGIO *(Enters with* HONEY*):* We'll become famous by dragging him through the mud after he's dead.
HONEY: Yes, we'll alter his past until it's tailored to suit us!
ADAGIO: But leave wide seams, because a man has a way of growing and filling out. Everything becomes too small for him!
HONEY: No, I still won't do it!
ADAGIO: You don't dare!
HONEY: Even if I don't dare, it's still your fault. I smell a conspiracy between the brass and the class. Their collusion causes constant confusion! Remember, Adagio, you've got to keep in with God and the rod if you want to get a return on your wad . . . and that's what's most important of all. So what are you waiting for? Why hesitate? Go ahead!
ADAGIO: I'm not hesitating, just being cautious. I want to catch up with my fortune, but I'm careful not to run past it in my hurry.
HONEY: Are you going to start doing anything before the autumn rains? Hurry, man, life is short!
ADAGIO: I will, but I want you to tell me . . . tell me about your secret-most self, concealed right at the bottom, that only belongs to you!
HONEY: Wouldn't you like to know?
ADAGIO: Speak up, then!
HONEY: Look how impudent he is! Go away then, go!
ADAGIO: Who, me?
HONEY: How many times have I told you not to sit on my desk in my office when a stranger calls!
ADAGIO: Aren't we kind of family?

HONEY: Familiarity breeds contempt. We can't have that sort of thing going on at work! Otherwise you'd be throwing paper clips into my neckline in front of everybody, wouldn't you? Or making paper darts out of top secret files? Or rummaging through my handbag in front of the whole staff? Or ramming your cigarette into my mouth? Or making balloons out of contraceptives and leaning across six rows of chairs to tap them against my bottom—while I'm making a speech, no less!

ADAGIO: I did it out of boredom, without any ulterior motives!

HONEY: Well, I don't tolerate any familiarity or vulgarity which you assume in order to show the crowds that you are in with the V.I.P.'s. And in the end you'll be cruelly punished for it, just like any old flunkey! Once he's done his job he gets a kick in the ass! Go away!

ADAGIO: How? On foot?

HONEY: Take the Rolls-Royce.

ADAGIO: It's hardly possible, milady! The chauffeur has his day off today!

HONEY: Oh, don't be a fool! You ought to be given a good whipping!

ADAGIO: Mummy's going to whip me!

HONEY: I'm not wet behind the ears. You're not going to take me for a ride. Get out of here, d'you hear me? All right, I forgive you, you big boob! Clear out now, you nincompoop! Scram! I don't want you near me! *(Pushes him toward the edge of the tower.)* You've just upset me, I can hardly breathe; Beat it now, before I kick you!

ADAGIO *(Resists):* You want me dead, do you? *(Springs away from her.)* O.K., then, thanks for your neighborly solicitude! I'll go without your help, but the other way!

HONEY: Do you at least know where you'll be going?

ADAGIO: I'll follow my nose!

HONEY: To the East?

ADAGIO: Into life!

HONEY: To the West?

ADAGIO: As far away from here as possible! *(Runs toward the first passage.)*

THE SEVEN MAIDS *(They block the first passage)*: Come! Come!

ADAGIO: Farther, still farther! *(Takes a step back, then rushes to the second passage.)*

THE SEVEN MAIDS *(They move away from the first passage to block the second one)*: Come! Come!

ADAGIO: Farther, as far away as possible! *(Takes a step back, then rushes to the third passage.)*

THE SEVEN MAIDS *(They move away from the second and block the third passage)*: Come on! Come on!

ADAGIO *(Runs back)*: I'm surrounded! Encircled with red ink!

HONEY: Ha, ha, ha, ha, ha!

ADAGIO: Honey, I've stepped into the trap which I laid myself! You told me that I was setting up a trap for someone else!

HONEY: Ha, ha, ha, ha, ha! *(HONEY exits.)*

ADAGIO: You can have the sirloin! And the bait! Take the snare off my feet! And the weight off my mind! And the veil from my eyes! And the blot off my record! And the stripes off my sleeve! I'm content with dry bread! Life means more to me than the standard of living!

HONEY *(Offstage)*: Ha, ha, ha, ha, ha!

ADAGIO: From now on obey you blindly, Honey . . . you give the orders! Humiliate me as much as you want! I'm no longer a man . . . arf, arf, arf! *(Exits like a dog.)*

HONEY *(Offstage)*: Ha, ha, ha, ha, ha!

MACABRE *(Enters with* ARTIE*)*: What does she find so funny tonight?

ARTIE: Tickle-tickle!

HONEY *(Offstage)*: Ha, ha, ha, ha, ha!

MACABRE: I wouldn't say so, judging by the sound . . . tickle-tickle is tinkling . . . like a bell. . . .

HONEY *(Offstage):* Ha, ha, ha, ha, ha!
MACABRE: That sound could be caused by gas pains. *(ARTIE starts to leave.)* Where are you going?
ARTIE: I'm going to ask them if they can carry on their argument across the fence in a more civilized manner! *(Exits.)*
MACABRE: O.K., but come around afterwards to check if my blanket is still on me! *(Lies down and covers himself.)*
HONEY *(Offstage):* Ha, ha, ha, ha, ha!
ADAGIO *(Enters):* How am I going to escape? Someplace where no one will think of looking for me. What about the wardrobe! *(Rushes toward the wardrobe.)*
ARTIE *(From the wardrobe):* Occupied!
ADAGIO: Now you see, Adagio, what it is not to make the necessary reservation! But I know where I'll go! I'll shove Macabre under the bed and I'll get into his own place! *(Drags* MACABRE *off the bed, onto the floor, and under the bed. Gets into bed himself.)* When I pull the blankets over my head, not even my own mother will recognize me! *(Covers himself.)*
HONEY *(Enters):* Ha, ha, ha, ha, ha! My dream bust is a bust dream!
ARTIE *(Enters):* Everything looked much better while I was still able to retreat, but now . . . now it looks as if the die's been cast. An epoch is smashed on a diceboard. You ask me if I'm afraid? I'm half dead with fear! And I have no more choice.
HONEY: Don't be stingy, and it'll come true. It's unlucky to be tight-fisted!
ARTIE: What brings bad luck is a busybody pestering you with good advice!
HONEY: You pay someone from outside to get rid of him, and there'll be time for you to insult me. There's still a lot of haggling to be done. But this thing I told you, it'll come out cheaper in the end, and you won't have to dirty your hands.

ARTIE: But we should also make a showing in the community. We should prove that the Almighty's grace has passed from the mighty to the mightier, as prophesied.
HONEY: So, it means both: the crime in public and the public in crime. What matters is to save face . . . although there are even some who don't mind cutting off their nose to spite their face. Rather that than face the wall!
ARTIE: And with mourning widows behind the wall, planted on brass bedsteads, as in school books . . . sniffing and humming the "Marseillaise," as though they were about to lay an egg.
HONEY: As you so rightly pointed out: it's the present beat generation that tomorrow will lead the nation. . . . "Make love, not War!" *(Starts off.)*
ARTIE: Wait, don't go! *(She stops.)* It's late, Cunty-Honey!
HONEY: Too late to add insult to injury! *(Starts off)*
ARTIE: Wait, Honey, don't go! *(She stops.)* I've already instructed the constable how to force the rejoicing in the public squares!
HONEY: Let them strike up military marches and deadly classics, with announcements during the intervals that something very important will happen but that not much notice should be taken of all that. So, the matter is an urgent one, but not such as to give rise to anxiety. In other words, it is a life and death issue, but there is no need to worry or hurry.
ARTIE: Except that janitors are becoming landlords and vice-versa. Barbers and those who are shaved . . . vice-versa and opposite of the other way around. The higher you fly, the harder you fall. And polluted market places are ploughed up by troubleshooters harnessed to the plough instead of oxen!
HONEY: What about the oxen?
ARTIE: They have the day off.
HONEY: And Macabre?

ARTIE: Death for the old and feeble! At last we've come to the crux of the matter! There, we'll kill him according to our ancient custom.
HONEY: Will he go to the ritual?
ARTIE: Like sheep to the congress!
HONEY: He's like the man who sows the wind—he always hopes that the whirlwind might change direction!
ARTIE: I'm now going to issue last instructions . . . Gertie!
GERTIE *(Enters):* I'm sorry I'm so late. I would have come much earlier, but some eunuch called Eugene stopped me. Do you know it?
ARTIE: You mean her?
HONEY: No, him!
GERTIE: Well then, what sex does it belong to?
HONEY: Middling: neither here nor there, always in the middle. Whatever happens, he's always placed right. You do as you like, but I'll take care of him. It may be important in the future.
ARTIE: I should never have overlooked him! We met so many times at different places, yet I never cultivated him. I thought he was just a local yokel. Thanks for the tip. I'll send him my visiting card with expressions of my highest esteem . . . and you, Gertie, wash his feet on my behalf . . . and walk his shoes around the table . . . offer him full comfort! *(She starts to leave.)* Wait, I haven't finished dictating., At the crack of dawn, make some cornbread for Macabre's death ritual. What are you waiting for?
GERTIE: Initial it here so we know who dictated. All I do is to put things down—you're the dictator! *(Exits.)*
ARTIE: What bothers me now is that fellow Eugene.
HONEY: You're right. Things aren't so simple.
ARTIE: Are you trying to frighten me?
HONEY: I'm trying to cover you from all sides, because a riddle is a riddle, like an embryo in a mother's womb.
ARTIE: Do you find it hard to make up your mind?
HONEY: No, never!

ARTIE: Give me proof or I'll write you off!
HONEY: I'll get the seven maids who've never been laid, in their petticoats inside out, to keep watch around the house all night!
ARTIE: Let them say anathema.
HONEY: Is that when you address all kinds of oaths, threats, and accusations at someone, but fail to state his name?
ARTIE: That's it, Cunty-Honey! Frightening propaganda! Whether you like it or not! As they say: the situation is unclear and gives cause for utmost caution, which in turn calls for quiescence. So, as I said, I'm going to take a walk around the lobbies in the hope of bumping into Eugene! *(Exits.)*
HONEY: It seems to me that confusion has grown. Artie is whistling in the dark, and his flanks are unprotected. All he needs is a prod. Hey you! What're you waiting for? Where's your atmosphere of mutual respect, notwithstanding misunderstandings and disagreement on an insignificant part of the issue? (ARTIE *goes off. Music.)*
THE SEVEN MAIDS AND GERTIE *(Sing and act out a ceremony of Anathema—the weird dance of damnation):*

Molly mocks
Prickly pricks
Kooky cock,
Someone sticks.
Knock, knock!

ADAGIO *(Peers from beneath the blanket):* Who's there?
THE SEVEN MAIDS AND GERTIE:

High and mighty,
High and mighty!

GERTIE: I'm a specter with vicious dragons!
THE SEVEN MAIDS AND GERTIE:

Molly mocks
Prickly pricks.
Kooky cock,
Someone sticks.
Knock, knock!

ADAGIO *(Peers from beneath the blanket):* Who's there?
THE SEVEN MAIDS AND GERTIE:

High and mighty,
High and mighty!

GERTIE: Kiss them, and you'll see they're the only breasts which give fire instead of milk!
ADAGIO: Would you say that it's a court messenger's fault that the scales of justice are weighted with lead on the side of the rulers? Have you ever known a ship to sail in spittle? I'm not going to spit. What the hell am I, an earthling, doing here among you fairies? Why are you picking on me?
GERTIE: Because the rain-dancers, until yesterday gaily kicking their heels in boudoirs, are now croaking in swamps! Snow frills in the ditches but can only cover the mountains! Because what's big is big, whether it's hot or cold . . . whether it's white or black . . . whether by hook or by crook.
THE SEVEN MAIDS AND GERTIE:

Molly mocks
Prickly pricks,
Kooky cock,
Someone sticks.
Knock, knock!

ADAGIO *(Peers from beneath the blanket):* Who's there again?

THE SEVEN MAIDS AND GERTIE:

> High and mighty,
> High and mighty!

ADAGIO: Look, what angels! . . . And I have to go tomfooling with a tomboy like Gertie!
ARTIE *(Enters)*: Where's Adagio? *(THE SEVEN MAIDS and GERTIE exit.)*
HONEY *(Enters)*: Adagio is at my bedside table. And Eugene?
ARTIE: He's completely vanished, but maybe he's hatching something—I'll have to stop him! *(Comes to the bed.)* Macabre, it's time for you to take off your mask! Throw off the blanket!
ADAGIO (From beneath the blanket): I dare not tell you the truth. I can't, either; my eyes smart from the bright light. What is it that keeps shining from the river?
HONEY: It's the reflection of faraway lightning.
ARTIE: Like your former glory.
THE SEVEN MAIDS *(Off stage)*: Better stalemate than checkmate, better peace than police, better right than might, better . . .
ADAGIO: Hear it rolling, hear it rolling. . . thundering. . .
HONEY: All hell has broken loose! The earth is thirsting for justice! Get up!
ADAGIO: I can't. I feel as if I'm drunk.
ARTIE: You're drunk from boredom, Macabre! To hell with you! *(Exits.)*
ADAGIO: And a current, my good friends. I feel a current in my body, as if ants were crawling all over me. Take off the electrodes. And you, Cunty-Honey, come to me. I feel sad. . . . Come lie next to me!
HONEY: I won't, Macabre, because you're sad out of spite! There are also other reasons.
ADAGIO: What reasons are those?
HONEY: You'll drown and yet there'll be no flood! *(Exits.)*

ADAGIO: I'm yearning for freedom!

GERTIE *(Enters bringing cornbread):* Well, you can't buy freedom in the market place! *(ARTIE comes in wearing a butcher's apron. GERTIE speaks to ARTIE)* Here's the cornbread.

ARTIE: Put it on his head!

ADAGIO: Don't bring anything to me! Go away! I'm not hungry! Shoo! Scat!

GERTIE *(To ARTIE):* He wants to die contemptuous of life!

ARTIE: But I don't want to live appreciative of death! Put it on his head, before Eugene comes to mess things up!

ADAGIO: What are you trying to do, Gertie? You, too, Gertie?

HONEY *(Enters carrying an axe, which she hands to ARTIE):* Strike while the cornbread is hot! *(Exits.)*

ADAGIO: Where I expected the sun to shine on me, I got an axe on the head instead! *(ARTIE hits him on the head with the axe through the cornbread.)* Gertie! You, too, my lovely . . . my sweet . . . *(ARTIE hits him again, he sways and falls on the floor by the bed.)*

ARTIE: I'm not responsible for your death, Macabre. The cornbread is what killed you! *(Throws away the axe and exits. GERTIE exits on the other side of the stage.)*

MACABRE *(Drags himself out from under the bed.)* Was that for me? *(Enter HONEY. MACABRE goes up to her.)* You're killing with boredom . . . suffocating with red tape! You're killing indiscriminately whatever positive trend you manage to lay your hands on!

ADAGIO *(Revives):* They've killed all that's human in me. Arf, arf, arf! *(Falls back again.)*

MACABRE: And you even forget to advise me by postcard of the train of events! What are you thinking?

HONEY: We ourselves don't know anymore what to think. It looks as if your soul has hardened inside you.

MACABRE: Ha! I'll have to take a purgative . . . *(Exits followed by* HONEY.*)*

ARTIE *(Enters with* GERTIE): My hands are clean. Try now, Gertie, with all due pomp and honors to remove him from public life as soon as possible and get him off the political scene. But you must watch your step. We're not yet quite clear about Eugene. Do the job according to the system of thin air.

GERTIE: As they say: watered down.

ARTIE: Yes . . . so that we get the spirit of the message between the lines. Jot it down if you find it hard to remember. The bully that beats up your bull is a hero! And, if you get a few hours overtime on this job, put it down in your notebook. You'll get fifty percent, only hurry up! But if Eugene arrives unexpectedly, act dumb. I'm going to rifle the works to get some ideas! *(Exits.)*

GERTIE *(After* ARTIE*)*: People know this very well, Artie! Where might is master, justice is its handmaiden. It's better to keep your mouth shut. We don't have to pour water over an extin-guished fire! *(Exits.)*

MACABRE *(Enters with* HONEY): All this trouble . . .

HONEY: A cannonball . . .

MACABRE: Yes . . . just to kill a sparrow. What a comedown!

GERTIE *(Enters)*: A ghost! *(Swoons.* HONEY *catches her. At the same moment,* ARTIE *enters and rushes to the bed where* ADAGIO *is lying dead.)*

MACABRE *(To* HONEY*)*: What's the matter with her? What did she say?

HONEY: All she said was, "The mindless fool sells wisdom" . . . and she died of fright!

GERTIE *(Revives)*: You've killed my personality . . . Ga, ga, ga! . . . *(Collapses.)*

ARTIE: Well, cornbread is what killed poor Adagio!

ADAGIO: Arf, arf, arf!

MACABRE: It's only the poor man that's killed by cornbread, Son.

GERTIE: Ga, ga, ga!

ARTIE *(Swoons):* Taxes impoverish everyone, Father . . . *(Drops to the floor;* HONEY *supports him.)*

MACABRE *(To* HONEY*):* What did he say?

HONEY: All he said was, "When the horse is dead, everyone knows the right cure." And he died of failure!

ARTIE *(Revives for a minute):* You've killed all that's beautiful in me . . . *(Collapses.)*

THE SEVEN MAIDS:

> Molly mocks
> Prickly pricks.
> Kooky cock,
> Someone sticks.
> Knock, knock!

MACABRE: Who's there?

EUGENE *(Enters):* Eugene!

MACABRE *(Shoves him away):* Later, I haven't time now! *(*EUGENE *bows servilely and leaves.)*

HONEY: Do you realize what you've done, Macabre! For heaven's sake, that was Eugene!

THE SEVEN MAIDS *(General confusion):*

> High and mighty,
> High and mighty!

HONEY *(Leaves and everyone in confusion rushes after her):* Eugene, come back! Wait! Wait, don't go! Let there be peace among the mighty! *(Only* ARTIE *remains on stage, acting the part of a monument.)*

ACT II: HALTER

(Everything as in Act I, except for ARTIE'S *statue under canvas. Nightmarish confusion.)*

THE SEVEN MAIDS *(Singing and dancing)*:

> Words are wasted on the dead,
> Try to praise the quick instead.
> Gold and dollar are the same.
> Never mind the country's fame!
> Every shepherd feeds his herd.
> Leaders could, too, if they cared!

(They exit.)
ADAGIO *(Henceforth acts as a dog)*: How are we to look dignified on an empty stomach! An empty sock can't stand upright!
EUGENE *(Enters)*: Fetch!
ADAGIO *(Comes to him quickly)*: Arf-arf-arf-arf! *(Gets a lump of sugar.)*
GERTIE *(Henceforth acts as a goose)*: Our schools can't be very good, since those in charge of them send their children to parochial schools!
EUGENE: Goosie-goosie!
GERTIE *(Gabbles)*: Ga-ga-ga-ga-ga! *(Gets a tidbit from EUGENE.)*
ADAGIO: He who uses other's people's money to build his fortune will soon be dragging stones to the political graveyard!
EUGENE: Fetch!
ADAGIO: Arf-arf-arf-arf!
GERTIE: Too many cooks spoil the broth!
EUGENE: Goosie-goosie!

GERTIE: Ga-ga-ga-ga-ga!
ADAGIO: A warm coat on your back is worth a million hot words on paper!
EUGENE: Fetch!
ADAGIO: Arf-arf-arf-arf-arf!
GERTIE: I wonder who looks after the governess' children?
EUGENE: Goosie-goosie!
GERTIE: Ga-ga-ga-ga!
ADAGIO: The only remedy against mass drowning is for the masses to learn how to swim!
EUGENE: Fetch!
ADAGIO: Arf-arf-arf-arf-arf!
GERTIE: What's the good of propaganda's pearl necklaces if they're meant to strangle you!
EUGENE: Goosie-goosie!
GERTIE: Ga-ga-ga-ga!
ADAGIO: We've wised up: foreign economic aid feeds you with the spoon and gouges your eyes with the handle!
EUGENE: Fetch!
ADAGIO: Arf-arf-arf-arf!
GERTIE: That's why it's better to give up halfway than to keep going along the wrong road to everlasting failure!
EUGENE: Goosie-goosie!
GERTIE: Ga-ga-ga-ga!
ADAGIO: Because a poor society spends little but costs a lot!
EUGENE: Fetch!
ADAGIO: Arf-arf-arf-arf!
GERTIE: Humph, wise men tell others how to work, but they're wise enough not to work themselves!
EUGENE: Goosie-goosie!
GERTIE: Ga-ga-ga-ga!
ADAGIO: But what good is it when one's career is never quite enough!

EUGENE: Fetch! Goosie-goosie! *(All three hide on the stage when they hear someone coming.)*
MACABRE *(Comes in hunched over and shuffling.* HONEY *helps him along.)* Honey, I still haven't been able to figure out why we're chasing after that Eugene?
HONEY: You're slow in catching on.
MACABRE: At my age, I'm lucky to be catching at all!
HONEY: We'll still have to go more to the right.
MACABRE: There's an abyss to the right!
HONEY: No, there isn't. Your bearings are all wrong. *(Starts off)*
ADAGIO *(Barks at them):* Arf-arf-arf-arf!
HONEY *(To* MACABRE*):* Let's go; why've you stopped?
ADAGIO: Arf-arf-arf-arf!
MACABRE: Don't you hear how he's barking!
ADAGIO: Arf-arf-arf-arf!
HONEY: His bite is worse than his bark. Get away! *(*ADAGIO *sits down.* HONEY *and* MACABRE *start off, but now* GERTIE *attacks them.)*
GERTIE: Sssss! Sssss! Sssss!
MACABRE: Hey, tease, stop it, please!
HONEY: She teases when she pleases!
GERTIE: Ssss! Sssss! Sssss!
MACABRE: Her tease gives me no peace!
HONEY: You don't hear good, Macabre. That's a goose! Shooo! *(*GERTIE *exits.)* And don't jump at every sound! You'll loosen your screws!
MACABRE: At my age what's one screw, more or less?
HONEY: Your nerves are shot, lean on me! *(They exit.)*
THE SEVEN MAIDS *(An orgy in song and dance):*

> Legs run around,
> Feet beat the ground.
> Behinds shake about,
> And bellies stick out.

And souls quake,
Backbones break!
Hearts will bleed—
There's no need!
Pfft!

(They dance out.)

MACABRE *(Enters with* HONEY*)*: And what's that sticking out there?

HONEY: The reapers are reaping.

MACABRE: What are they reaping?

HONEY: You know what you sowed.

MACABRE: Discord?

HONEY: Uh-huh. And now people are spitting at each other, shitting on each other, and hitting each other.

MACABRE: But it seems to me that they're biting off more than they can chew!

HONEY: You don't see good.

EUGENE *(Enters):* Please, sir, Eugene here. . . .

MACABRE (Pushes him): Later, I don't have time now! *(Eugene bows and leaves.)* Wait! What did he say his name was?

HONEY: A common one; he doesn't warrant attention. *(*EUGENE *returns.)*

MACABRE: Didn't he say: "Eugene?"

EUGENE: Yes, "Eugene."

HONEY: He said: "Routine."

EUGENE: Yes, "Eugene."

HONEY: He said: "Guillotine."

EUGENE: Yes, "Eugene."

HONEY: He said: "A rude teen."

MACABRE: And I would interpret what he said as: "Eugene."

HONEY: You don't interpret very well. Lean on me. *(They start off)*

ADAGIO *(Barks at them):* Arf-arf-arf-arf!

HONEY: And be careful where you walk; you stepped on his tail! *(They leave.)*
ADAGIO: Arf-arf-arf-arf!
GERTIE: What is this I hear, that you're a dog?
ADAGIO: Yes, unfortunately. What about you?
GERTIE: It depends. Throughout history they have given me or taken away from me all kinds of properties.
ADAGIO: Why, I had a lot of different treatments, too. We have the same fate.
GERTIE: I was all sorts of things—just imagine! A fox—sly, and a skylark—gay, and a caterpillar—crawly . . . and now I'm a goose: Now I'm a complete fool . . . Ga-ga-ga-ga!
ADAGIO: And I used to be a billy goat: wild and strong-headed . . . Baaaa-baaa! And later in my heyday, a wild boar: passionate and ferocious. Grrr-grrr! Those are also my happiest memories of the time I sowed my wild oats. All the rest is thin and pale. It almost faded out completely when I was a worm, a catfish, a chameleon, and so forth.
GERTIE: Why, how many faces do you have?
ADAGIO: I don't even know myself! At first I kept a record. I hoped to be able to pay back the debt, but soon I lost both the accounts and every hope.
GERTIE: And, as for me, from cherry-red dreams, I cooked an ideological jam.
ADAGIO: In my case, I think the decisive factor in everything was the large traffic in my spiritual domicile. Not a single change passed me by.
GERTIE: At least you've never had a dull moment.
ADAGIO: There's almost no spice I haven't been seasoned with. But I tried with all my might. I was always fired up! But still I never succeeded in being a man.
GERTIE: They say that pride is what adorns a man.
ADAGIO: I've heard that, though I've never come across it.
GERTIE: Well, real men are rare.

ADAGIO: And they say that they're characterized by wisdom.

GERTIE: Yes, so they insist, but I don't understand why at the same time there's twice as much talk about human stupidity.

THE SEVEN MAIDS *(Come in from all sides):* About scientific idiocy!

ADAGIO: About human obtuseness!

THE SEVEN MAIDS: About unnatural materialism!

GERTIE: About drastic humanism!

THE SEVEN MAIDS: About sexual imperialism!

ADAGIO: About infanticidal aestheticism!

EUGENE *(Enters):* Fetch! *(THE MAIDS go off)*

ADAGIO: Arf-arf! *(To* GERTIE.*)* Pardon me for a moment, my master is calling.

EUGENE: Goosie-goosie! *(Exits.)*

GERTIE: And mine is calling me, too.

ADAGIO: Maybe we're fellow-treavellers. What's your master's name?

GERTIE: I don't know. But, at this particular moment, that's not of historical importance.

ADAGIO: Absolutely right. I don't know the identity of mine, either. And what does yours do?

GERTIE: Who knows?

ADAGIO: Mine is an enigmatic personality, too.

GERTIE: A gray eminence.

ADAGIO: A figure cast to the forefront by enigmatic coincidence. Scumfloats. But let's hurry to report before our master gets lost on the foggy horizon. Arf-arf! *(Exists.)*

GERTIE: Ga-ga! *(Exits.)*

HONEY *(Enters):* Things are developing as well as could be desired.

EUGENE *(Enters):* Please, Eugene here . . .

HONEY *(Shoves him):* Later, I don't have time now!

EUGENE: But when you do have . . . just wait! Then I'll be the one who has no time.

HONEY: First of all, you're invented, but not for me!
EUGENE: I am Eugene.
HONEY: Why, you don't even exist.
EUGENE: What do you mean I don't exist, when I'm Eugene!
HONEY: Don't lie to me when I'm the one who thought you up!
EUGENE: My sweet little mommy!
HONEY: Later, I don't have time now!
EUGENE: I'll try to see that you never get hungry. I have a goose, and I have a dog!
HONEY: And underneath the canvas?
EUGENE: I don't know, that's a secret. People say there's a monument underneath and that it's covered up so that no one would be reminded of the past.
HONEY: All right, then, be careful.
EUGENE: Of what?
GERTIE: Deformation. Because, even though I invented you, sometimes fabrications, get away, and, like tattered clouds in a strong wind, begin to change into the weirdest shapes!
EUGENE: That means, there's no pleasure without leisure!
HONEY: Later, I don't have time now! *(Exists.)*
EUGENE: But when you do have time, Mother, just you wait! Then it'll be me who won't have any! You're kidding yourself: my love isn't blind! Fetch!
ADAGIO *(Enters):* Arf-arf-arf-arf-arf!
EUGENE: Goosie-goosie!
GERTIE *(Enters):* Ga-ga-ga-ga-ga!
EUGENE: Are you dying of thirst?
THE SEVEN MAIDS *(Enter from all sides, excitedly, in song and dance):*

> Legs run around,
> Feet beat the ground.
> Behinds shake about,
> And bellies stick out.

All souls quake,
Backbones break!
There's no need!
Pffft!

(They falter.) Waaater! Waaaater! *(Exit.)*
EUGENE: What do you mean, "Water!" you son of a bitch?
ADAGIO: It wasn't me who asked for it!
THE SEVEN MAIDS *(Offstage):* Waaaaaater!
GERTIE: That's our parched, cracked mother earth crying for water.
EUGENE: I asked you: are you dying of thirst for revenge?
ADAGIO: Arf-arf-arf-arf!
GERTIE: Ga-ga-ga-ga-ga!
EUGENE: Stop yelping into the wind! Your teeth will fall out, and you won't have anything to bite with!
ADAGIO: I'm dying of thirst for knowledge . . . Arf-arf!
GERTIE and ADAGIO *(In one voice):* Why! Why! Why does man live? Grrrr! Sssss!
EUGENE: That sounds more like death agony and wheezing than rebel cries!
ADAGIO: Yeah, mind you don't sneeze too hard; you might give up your ghost . . . Arf-arf!
GERTIE: I can't hold it any longer! *(Exits.)* Ga-ga-ga-ga-ga!
MACABRE *(Enters):* What are you doing here? (EUGENE *and* ADAGIO *sit up and beg like dogs.)*
EUGENE: Nothing in particular, Right Reverend. We're sitting on our haunches before you.
MACABRE: It's all right for him to beg; he's a dog.
ADAGIO: Arf-arf!
MACABRE: But what are you doing with him?
EUGENE: That's what I'd like to know myself!
MACABRE: All right, dismissed! *(They run wild.)* But that doesn't mean that now you should run and piss on me!

EUGENE: Fetch! *(They calm down.)*
MACABRE: Now what are you doing?
EUGENE: We're spreading ourselves out
MACABRE: I appreciate your kindness, but with one small reservation. Namely, a big, wise father-regime must be very careful about whom he marries his beautiful, rich careers to. *(Kicks them.)* Scat! Shoo!
EUGENE *(To* ADAGIO*)*: Get out of my way! Fetch! His Reverence is not in the mood for any nonsense! Out! *(ADAGIO goes off.)*
MACABRE *(To* EUGENE*)*: And you stay to listen!
EUGENE: I hope it'll be worth it?
MACABRE: I'll give you a shako. *(Gives him a shako.)*
EUGENE: Unh-unh. Would an ox head be too little for a cat to eat?
MACABRE: I'll give you a sash. *(Gives him a sash.)*
EUGENE: I'd do it for a lot less, to tell the truth. Why are you so generous?
MACABRE: I'm old and worn out.
EUGENE: You're never too old to kick!
MACABRE: There's no future for me, while the past is all mine—including our unforgettable love.
EUGENE: Maybe so, but you can't really see it.
MACABRE: Time conceals the truth, but I'll uncover it.
EUGENE: And what shall I do?
MACABRE Why, you'll chew on the canvas!
EUGENE: Until we chew memories down to the bone?
MACABRE: You'll find out in due course. Now go!
EUGENE: Where?
MACABRE: Upwards. Now you're a nobody, but when you get up with a sash around your shoulders and the shako around your ears, you'll be somebody! All doors will open before you because of the amulet you took with you, and, thus, you'll become somebody! *(EUGENE starts to leave.)*

GERTIE AND ADAGIO *(Enter)*: Don't forget us! Ga-ga! Arf-arf! *(EUGENE, GERTIE, ADAGIO, and MACABRE exit.)*
THE SEVEN MAIDS *(Enter and in a frenzy)*: Who's to keep us? Who's to feed us? When you're gone, who's to beat us?
HONEY *(Enters)*: You wanted to bypass me, but you didn't know that the round robin goes clockwise! *(After her comes EUGENE dressed as a convict.)* And for that reason you've now been severely punished! Just as all doors opened before you when you kept your shako and sash as amulets, so now iron doors will slam shut behind you! *(Thunder. HONEY goes off)*
EUGENE (GERTIE *and* ADAGIO *enter)*: It's me, my goosie! My doggie! *(They exit.)* Your Eugene! *(MACABRE enters with HONEY who helps him along.)* Don't forget me! Tell my mother what's happened to me! *(Exits.)*
MACABRE: Cunty-Honey, why is it that there's always somebody here reminding somebody else to remember? And then they try not to forget?
HONEY: They're forever going up and down, up and down, and you can't make out anymore where the circle's head or tail is.
MACABRE: Let's stop then.
HONEY: Don't try! Your brakes are bad.
MACABRE: You're right, Honey, because everything in me is worn out and weak, just as you keep saying. I want to get stronger! *(Enter EUGENE dressed as a convict; ADAGIO, no longer a dog; GERTIE, no longer a goose; and THE SEVEN MAIDS.)*

THE SEVEN MAIDS *(Confusion)*:

> I'm a seamstress,
> I sew up backs!
> My man's plain black!
> He lays down tracks!

ADAGIO: Visitors are coming: get the footstool ready for lunch!
THE SEVEN MAIDS (Confusion):

I'm a beautician,
And hair's my curse!
My man's got a mission—
He males each nurse!

MACABRE: Right you are, my dear children; your words are gold!
HONEY: No, Macabre! Don't do anything you haven't consulted me about beforehand! Don't be a mean old man! *(MACABRE snatches off the covering from the monument. All present are astonished and frightened.)*
ARTIE *(Stands like a statue—his own monument)*: First of all, don't run away just because I've begun to speak! Naturally, I know the human heart rather well from before!
MACABRE: Vanity is the only thing that fills them with fear.
ALL: And poverty! And poverty!
ARTIE: Never fear, I won't demand a feast in memoriam! But if you just happen to have a boiled egg or chicken drumstick on you.
GERTIE: I have an egg, Macabre, the one you told me to bake on charcoal, as a cure for egg-sucking!
MACABRE: It's the same thing; peel it and feed him. *(She peels the egg and feeds* ARTIE.*)*
ARTIE: *(With his mouth full)*: It's true that I'm made of iron, all hard and everlasting, but that doesn't mean much. Even cotton is sometimes harder than bone . . . and poverty is the hardest thing of all. Nevertheless! You should see the lonely head of a man on a pillow in a darkened room.
MACABRE: With twitching lips!
HONEY: And words that drip like venom!

ARTIE: No, that's no longer a talk; that's a conversation. And those aren't words like words in the light and the ears of others!
ALL: What is it? What is it?
ARTIE: That's more like sniffing around your own life . . . like a dog sniffing around a rubbish heap, where, if he's lucky, he may find a bone. . . .
MACABRE: And a stone!
ARTIE: In their dreams and delirium, many cry over the grave of their homeland; but what really goes on in this world when we're awake?
MACABRE: Don't we see it, even though we look?
HONEY: Don't we hear it, even though we listen?
ADAGIO: Don't we spit it out, even though it disgusts us?
ARTIE: You, who sit at home, at conferences, and in offices!
MACABRE: Everything is done in the proper manner: by telephone interventions, official acts, diplomatic channels!
ARTIE: You're all wrong! *(All except* MACABRE *slowly go off.* MACABRE *and* ARTIE *from now on act as if in a dream.)* I'm always outside and I see when something rustles in the weeds, at the bottom . . . slowly seethes, like lava! . . . and overflows! It boils, and not one of you notices it! But on my pedestal the footsteps of history reverberate like gun salvoes! Thunderbolts shall still rip asunder these morasses of hot air. And all the illusions that you have woven over your heads shall scatter like scum!
MACABRE: Oh, my past! I may have made mistakes. Maybe I haven't done all that should have been done! Oh, my past. Maybe I went astray! Maybe I parted company with myself, and what I wanted to do went one way, while what I was able to do went the other way. Tell me!
ARTIE: No, it doesn't matter whether the hatter can play the bagpipes; people want to know what kind of headgear he's able to cut out for them! And when they hear that he's good and that he's made a lot of people happy, they all rush to him!

MACABRE: Oh, my past! Did I neglect you, poor dear, for the sake of others? Did I like them better than I did you, who have always been behind me, faithful as a shadow, with one end attached to my feet? Tell me!
ARTIE: Well, the master-hatter who's made caps for many people, pretty ones and expensive ones and thinking ones—he usually goes around wearing his own work-cap . . . because, if someone knows how to make a hood for a wise man, it doesn't mean that he himself can become a wise man by putting on a thinking cap! You must remember one thing: that whoever doesn't get what's his own might as well not have had anything at all!
MACABRE: Oh, my past, I'm not tired of you! And when I look at myself in you as in a mirror, I seem to be as young as a lily. Oh, my past, you give me strength, and I'm indebted to you for the entire future! *(MACABRE slowly sinks and falls asleep by the statue.)*
ARTIE: Don't touch what's not yours; take what belongs to you; otherwise it won't be acknowledged as such. And lives, those wasted as well as those fulfilled, will fill history, just as small drops of water fill a big river.
HONEY *(Enters with GERTIE)*: Shhh . . . Tippytoe . . . Let him get fast asleep before we fulfill his last wish. You know what his favorite dish is?
GERTIE: Stew of lies.
HONEY: But not like last time; it didn't turn out very well.
GERTIE: I oversalted it, but you know how he is: his mouth is always watering for that dish. He likes it whether it's got too much salt or too little.
ADAGIO *(Enters)*: Goose!
GERTIE: Mongrel!
HONEY: All right, Adagio, didn't we say that we wouldn't mention the past anymore?
ADAGIO: But the statue is a permanent reminder.

HONEY: We'll turn it inside out like a glove! . . . that dark past, never fear! *(*MACABRE wakes up.*)* Quiet!
MACABRE: Has it gotten dark again?
HONEY, GERTIE, AND ADAGIO *(All together):* It has.
MACABRE: Hasn't the sun come up?
HONEY, GERTIE, AND ADAGIO *(All together):* It has.
MACABRE: Is it raining?
HONEY, GERTIE, AND ADAGIO *(All together):* It's pouring.
MACABRE: But I thought the sun was shining?
HONEY, GERTIE, AND ADAGIO *(All together):* It's broiling.
MACABRE: How do I look this morning?
HONEY, GERTIE, AND ADAGIO *(All together):* Fresh.
MACABRE: Oh, my past! Am I still able to make judgments when people are lying to me? Tell me, am I wise?
ADAGIO: Your mind warms up as light warms a man lost in darkness!
MACABRE: Oh, my past! I've destroyed you because of those who have never loved me. Tell me, am I popular?
HONEY: Your heart is like a lamb, meek and mild, and your soul is like a love bird during mating season; wherever you appear things come alive. Even the rocks start pulsating and breathing joy!
MACABRE: For years you poisoned me with the futility of stale water, and that corroded me like rust. Tell me, hasn't my strength been sapped?
GERTIE: Wherever you appear, even today, the earth opens up under your feet! And where you point your finger, the mountains are rent asunder!
MACABRE *(Metamorphosis. Becomes erect, strong, and vigorous):* You lying sycophant. I've never been able to find out from you what's day and what's night! You lie to me because you hate me, and you hate me because you're afraid of me! And you wanted to poison me with lies! And you did poison me, but I've gotten over it. Look! *(Presses finger on the castle. The walls fall*

apart, something crashes. Thunder and lightning.)* I'm still powerful! Hats off! *(More thunder, all are petrified.)*
EUGENE: Please, Eugene here. . . .
MACABRE: You've come, just at the right time!
EUGENE: No, I can come later. I'm used to being put off.
HONEY *(Pushes* EUGENE *forward):* Now! Now! Now or never!
MACABRE: You've been wanting a chance to say something for ages, so there you are. You're finally free to say what's on your mind!
EUGENE *(More to himself):* For so many years now this has been my winning card. Must I really get into a mess so near the end?
MACABRE: Don't mumble; quickly say what you have to say!
EUGENE: I don't have anything to say.
MACABRE: What, then?
EUGENE: I've been leading everyone up the garden path for years now. I've been living on my own mysteriousness. I'm a figment of the imagination.
MACABRE: You wretch, off with your hat, too!
EUGENE: But I don't own a hat.
HONEY: So much the worse for you! Instead of your hat, it'll be off with your head! Hit him! Let him be the scapegoat! *(Confusion. Scuffling. Crowding, they close the circle around* EUGENE.*)*

COLLECTIVE SPEECH

MACABRE: The only truth for me is my path and those who go along this way, to the hills far away!
ADAGIO: If I'm ever again a regime son-in-law, I'll know how to arrange my cherished career!
HONEY: Give me a salt pestle!

ARTIE: And the past is as true as it is false!

GERTIE: And they'll choke me again like a goose, in bed—that's for sure!

MACABRE: Oh, my past, I'm never tired of you! *(Separates himself from the crowd and sits on the throne.)*

ARTIE: Don't touch other people's property. Just take what belongs to you, or else you won't get any credit for it.

(The end of the collective speech. The crowd opens up and EUGENE *comes out of the circle, again as a general with an officer's cap and sash.)*

HONEY *(To* EUGENE*)*: Come on now, report!

EUGENE *(Goes before* MACABRE *on the throne)*: All the wolves are satisfied, Right Reverend, and no goats are missing!

MACABRE AND THE REST *(Rises from the throne and goes to the footlights, followed by all the others. In one voice)*: And thus, we've finished our walk through history. . . . *(The lights dim.)*

THE END

Translated by *E.J. Czerwinski*

LJUBOMIR SIMOVIĆ
(1935—)

Born in 1935 in Užice, Serbia, Simović is a well-known poet, short story writer, playwright and screenwriter. An electronic version of his poems has been published in France, and his famous play, *The Šopalović Traveling Theatre,* a study of human relations of a group of travelling actors, which is still attracting audiences in Serbia and abroad. He received his BA in 1962 in South Slavic Literature. As a student, he was an editor at the literary magazine *Vidici* and spent his whole career as an editor of the Art section of Radio Belgrade.

Simović's plays were translated into almost all European languages and performed in Hungary, Bulgaria, Mexico, Germany, Russia, Switzerland, Poland, Belgium, Canada as well as other countries.

LJUBOMIR SIMOVIĆ

THE TRAVELING TROUPE ŠOPALOVIĆ

CHARACTERS:
Occupying forces
MEITZEN – a „Volksdeutscher," officer in the Siecherheits polizei – SIPO, „coordinator" in the District Police headquarters
Collaborators
MILUN – a sergeant in the Municipal Guard
DROBAC – the prison „flogger": behind him he leaves tracks of blood
Townspeople of Užice
BLAGOJE BABIĆ – with his bottle
GINA – his wife, „tied" to the wash-tub Simka, the young widow of the late Major ADZIĆ (artillery command); she is dressed in black
DARA – a loom-worker
TOMANIJA – her „shadow"
Actors in the Traveling Troupe Šopalović
VASILIJE ŠOPALOVIĆ – leader of the troupe
JELISAVETA PROTIĆ – the actress dressed in golden yellow
SOPHIA SUBOTIĆ – the actress in violet
PHILIP TRNAVAC – the actor with two masks, beneath which there lies perhaps a third woman from the crowd.

The action takes place in Užice, during the occupation. One hot summer.

PART ONE

Scene One

THE ARREST OF THE ACTORS AT THE „RAKIJSKA PIJACA" IN UŽICE

The „Rakijska pijaca" (the „Brandy Market"), round the sides of which can be seen some of the following shop-signs: KAFANA „KOD PEVCA" („The Rooster Café"), SODA-VODA (Soda Water). SAJDZIJA PETROVIĆ. (Petrović – watchmaker), PEKARA (Bakery), RAKIJSKI PODRUM (Brandy Cellar). In front of the brandy cellar – several barrels and a few crates of bottles, hanging from the walls – two or three siphoning tubes. The walls are covered with various German notices, proclamations, announcements: BEFEHL! WARNUNG! BEKANNTMACHUNG! VICTORIA! In several windows and doorways black flags can be seen. On one wall – a prominent swastika. At the center of the marketplace, facing the crowd, are the traveling actors: they are performing a „stylized version" of a scene from Schiller's The Robbers, as advance publicity for their evening performance.

SOPHIA: Never! I would sooner go dead into my grave than lie in your incestuous bed!
VASILIJE: So, princess – you will not be won by gentleness? My ugliness disgusts you, does it? I am not well-built and handsome like Karl, even the peasant girls on our estate look in dread upon my ugliness. But for all your love of Karl, and for all the loathing you feel towards me – I shall have you!
SOPHIA: Never!
VASILIJE: I shall drag you – by force if need be – into my bed, I shall brutally take from you your virginity, and I shall cast your beauty into the mud!

SOPHIA *(slapping his face):* In that case – take this for dowry!
VASILIJE: That's your way, is it? Then fling you into the abyss of humiliation, I'll wipe my boots with your fair hair, and I'll drive you to love with the whip! And when I've satisfied my lust, throw you to the drunken soldiers and let the bloodthirsty brutes enjoy the last morsels of your virginity! You might have been a queen – now you'll be a whore!
SOPHIA *(embracing him):* Ah, Franz, forgive me, Franz – it was just one of my little jokes: *(As she embraces him, she draws his sword and, holding it pointed towards him, quickly backs away.)* Evil brute! – see what I'll do to you now! I may be a helpless woman, weak and gentle, but desperation gives me a giant's strength! Fiend – I dare you now to touch with your perverted hands this body, sworn to your honorable and foully slandered brother! Touch me, I dare you! And this steel will pierce your lustful breast! *(The scene is broken off by Jelisaveta, who climbs lip onto a barrel to address the assembled crowd.)*
JELISAVETA: Will the virtuous and unfortunate Amalia succeed in defending her honor and her virginity? Or will the brutal Franz, who has deceived his father and slandered his brother, triumph in his corrupt intent? Or will the wronged and banished Karl return at the last moment to defend his beloved Amalia and, like a thunderbolt, strike to punish his wicked brother?
PHILIP: All this you will learn if you come this evening to the opening of *The Robbers,* a tragedy by the famous Friedrich Schiller, presented to you by . . .
VASILIJE: . . . The Traveling Troupe Šopalović!
JELISAVETA: The part of the unfortunate and virtuous Amalia is played by the beautiful young actress, the great hope of the Serbian theatre – Miss Sophia Subotić *(Sophia steps forward and bows.)*
JELISAVETA: The part of the honest Karl, so treacherously deceived, is played by the celebrated Romeo, Hamlet, and Pera

Segedinac, the interpreter of so many unforgettable roles – Mr. Philip Trnavac! (Philip steps forward and bows.)
JELISAVETA: The role of Karl's brother, the despicable Franz, will be performed by the leader of our troupe, the renowned Vasilije Šopalović. *(Vasiije steps forward and bows.)*
PHILIP: In the part of the old count, the unfortunate father of Franz and Karl – and here performing exceptionally, in a male role – is our great tragic actress, Jelisaveta Protić *(Jelisaveta bows.)*
VASILIJE: On account of the curfew regulations, the performance will begin somewhat earlier than usual. At six o'clock tonight, in the cafe of the brothers Todorović, there begins an unrivalled, unforgettable, unbelievable theatrical spectacle – a performance rich in intrigue and blood and love! You will see killings!
DARA: We can see killings here, too, every day!
VASILIJE: Ladies, gentlemen! Do not miss the chance of seeing the flower of Serbian theatre appearing in one of the greatest performances of all times!
FIRST WOMAN: Not the flower – the dregs!
SECOND WOMAN: A fine time you've chosen for theatre!
THIRD WOMAN: You should be ashamed!
FOURTH WOMAN: The town's blackened with black flags!
DARA: Every day – raids, arrests, shootings, and you come here to play theatre!
TOMANIJA: Serbia's seething with Bosnian refugees. How would you like to play to them?
DARA: Have you seen the gallows on the corn market?
SECOND WOMAN: Do you realize there's a war on?
JELISAVETA: Do we have to give up our art just because there's a war on? Never! Even if it costs us our life!
THIRD WOMAN: You have no shame!
TOMANIJA: If eggs didn't cost ten thousand a piece I'd give you a fine sendoff!

JELISAVETA: Who are you to threaten me?
FIRST WOMAN: Just you dare to start your acting!
JELISAVETA: And who are you to stop me?
VASILIJE: We also have to live off something, don't we?
DARA: If you want to live, try grave digging. There's a job at least that'll give you plenty of work today!
JELISAVETA: I don't need you to tell me what work to do!
SOPHIA: Jelisaveta!
JELISAVETA: I didn't cultivate my beauty to trade it for a spade!
FIRST WOMAN: What she needs is a sound thrashing!
JELISAVETA: I've had enough of our complacent provinces. Enough of blind fools!
SECOND WOMAN: I'll show you who's blind!
DARA: Go and do your acting somewhere else – not here!
THIRD WOMAN: The blood's like rainwater. We're ankle-deep in it!
FOURTH WOMAN: For every German killed, they're shooting a hundred Serbs!
DARA: Half of Serbia is swathed in black and they're acting!
FIRST WOMAN: Shameless whore!
JELISAVETA: Such primitivism – I've never seen it anywhere before!
SECOND WOMAN: I'll give you primitivism – right on the arse!
DARA: Did you hear what she said?
TOMANIJA: She put herself up on that barrel just to spit at us!
FOURTH WOMAN: German hirelings!
JELISAVETA: Tar-boilers!
FIRST WOMAN: Do you see this black I'm wearing – black as your soul?
DARA: Are we going to let whores insult us to our face?
TOMANIJA: I'll get you off that barrel! *(The shouts and insults grow louder. Milun rushes on.)*

MILUN: Who's causing all this trouble?
THIRD WOMAN: Ask them!
SECOND WOMAN: Traveling rabble!
MILUN: Move away!
VASILIJE: We are the Traveling Troupe Šopalović. I am Vasilije Šopalović, leader of the troupe.
MILUN *(to the crowd):* Break it up!
JELISAVETA: It was time somebody stepped in to help us!
MILUN: Let me see your permits.
SOPHIA *(still holding Franz Moor's wooden sword):* But don't you realize, sir, we are actors!
MILUN: Drop your weapons!
SOPHIA: What weapons?
MILUN: Drop your weapons when I tell you, or I'll shoot!
SOPHIA: Really sir, this is absurd.
JELISAVETA: These aren't weapons just stage props.
MILUN: I told you to put them down. And note – I'm saying it again. Hands up! Hands up, when I tell you!
VASILIJE: We are the Traveling Troupe Šopalović!
MILUN: I told you to lay down your arms!
JELISAVETA: Put them down – the fool really means it!
MILUN: All of you over there! Against the wall! Who told you to draw your hands? Over there, d'you hear and not a word out of any of you! Have you got your permits or not?!
JELISAVETA: I really don't see what we, actors, have to do with such things.
MILUN: I'll show you what you have to do with them. Get moving!
SOPHIA: Where are you taking us?
MILUN: You're not here to ask questions. Move, when I tell you!
JELISAVETA: Vasilije, for God's sake, do something!
VASILIJE: Sergeant, this can all be easily explained. I think . . .

PHILIP: Aah! That confusion in your head – you call that thinking? Thinking? With a head like yours? Do you really believe that what passes through your head is some kind of thought? If that's what you think, you must have a very high opinion of yourself! What did he say – „I think". No less! Can anyone, with such a head, „think"? Have you any idea of what that means – that process, that verb, that verbal action: to think? Aristotle was a thinker, Stefan, so too were Plato and Descartes – but you, Stefan, are not!

MILUN: You told me your name was Vasilije.

VASILIJE: Yes, Sergeant, Vasilije. Vasilije Šopalović.

MILUN: How can you be Vasilije, when he calls you Stefan?

VASILIJE: You don't understand!

MILUN: I've understood enough. You have no permits. You're carrying arms. And you're using false names!

JELISAVETA: For God's sake, Vasilije. Explain to him!

MILUN: He can do his explaining at the police headquarters! Now, get moving, or do I have to explain to you, Stefan, with a rifle-butt?

VASILIJE: But, sergeant, I am not Stefan!

MILUN: Are you going to move – or do I have to hit you?

JELISAVETA: But Philip was just speaking his lines! *(To Philip)* You get so caught up in your part; it's quite unnatural.

SOPHIA: It's not just Philip's fault; Vasilije gave him the cue.

VASILIJE: When did I give him the cue?

SOPHIA: When you were talking to the sergeant, you said: „This can all be easily explained, I think . . . ,, D'you remember where that's from?

VASILIJE: It just slipped out. Anyway, I can't always be watching what I say in front of Philip! You see, sergeant, this is the text of a play. I have the part of Stefan, and when I say „This can all be easily explained, I think," here Philip, who is playing the part of Uroš, breaks in with the words you have just heard.

It's all quite simple. *(To Jelisaveta)* It seems he doesn't understand . . .
JELISAVETA: All it needs is a single gesture, just one word, a tiny detail and straight away he imagines he's on stage! *(To Sophia)* You try and explain to him.
SOPHIA: What Philip said, he didn't say to Vasilije but to Stefan, and he didn't say it as Philip but as Uroš – d'you follow?
MILUN *(After brief reflection)*: Stefan – get moving!
JELISAVETA: His stupidity is beyond belief! *(Milun, with his gun pointed, leads the actors off stage. The crowd begins to disperse. Dara and Tomanija are left alone on stage.)*
TOMANIJA: I don't remember ever seeing you so angry.
DARA: As when?
TOMANIJA: As now, when you shouted at the actors.
DARA: How could I not shout at them? Putting on a play today – why, that's open collaboration!
TOMANIJA: Do you think the underground should do something about it?
DARA: I certainly do! And I'm sure they will!
TOMANIJA: What do you think they'll do?
DARA: Nothing, for the moment. Nothing, until our comrades have carried out the action they planned.
TOMANIJA: Won't you tell me what it is?
DARA: The less you ask, the less you know, and the less you know, the easier you live!
(Fade out)

Scene Two

THE INTERROGATION OF THE ACTORS AT POLICE HEADQUARTERS

A gloomy, empty office: a desk, chairs, and a metal stove. On the walls are various notices and announcements. And on one wall, maps of the world, of Europe, and of the regions bordering on the river Drina, and the district of Užice.

MEITZEN: You say, then, that you are the leader of the troupe?
VASILIJE: Yes, sir, I am. And if you'd kindly let me explain . . .
MEITZEN: There'll be time for that as well – first the facts. The rest of you, sit down, first things first. Name?
VASILIJE: Vasilije, Sir!
MILUN: He's lying. This fellow calls him Stefan.
MEITZEN: I'm asking him now. Vasilije, you say?
VASILIJE: Yes, Sir, Vasilije. Vasilije Šopalović.
MEITZEN: Stop calling me „Sir", will you! Father's name?
VASILIJE: Miloš, sir. Miloš Šopalović, a grocer from Velika Plana.
MEITZEN: Sex?
VASILIJE: Whose?
MEITZEN: Male. There are four of you, are there?
VASILIJE: Four.
MEITZEN: Are you perhaps married couples?
PHILIP: Those three are – I'm a free man.
MEITZEN: What do you mean, those three?
JELISAVETA: He's so stupid; sometimes it drives me to despair. You see . . .
VASILIJE: It's all been a simple misunderstanding, sir, right from the start.
MEITZEN: With you lot it's nothing but misunderstandings! I have a whole pile of charges against you here. You have no permits! You use false names! You hold gatherings in public places! You're carrying weapons! What kind of weapons, sergeant?
MILUN: Side-arms, Herr Meitzen!
SOPHIA: What your sergeant calls weapons, sir, are merely ordinary stage props.

JELISAVETA: You must know, surely, what weapons actors use? Wooden swords, like this one, stove-pipe cannons, imitation guns!
SOPHIA: We wear armor and crowns of cardboard, our beards are wool, our moustaches and eyebrows blackened on with coal, we play stringless violins, we limp on sound legs, our pregnant bellies are rounded out by cushions, and the tears we weep over dead mothers are brought to our eyes by onions!
JELISAVETA: Our gold sovereigns are metal tokens.
VASILIJE: We live in painted houses
PHILIP: Well, so what?
SOPHIA: Please, Philip, don't you start explaining anything!
PHILIP: You're not going to tell me, surely, that a wooden sword is not a serious weapon?
VASILIJE: Please, pay no attention to him!
PHILIP: Or that with a wooden sword you cannot slay dragons or put tyrants to death? Or that with a wooden sword you cannot parry the thrust of a blade of steel?
JELISAVETA: After your parrying and thrusting you can use your sword for kindling-wood!
PHILIP: Surely you're not going to tell me that with token money you cannot bribe a witness, or a judge, or a minister? Or that gold ducats are worth more than tokens? Or that stone houses last longer than painted houses? Or that they are safer? Or that a painted house is not a proper house?
JELISAVETA: Pay no attention to his fantasizing!
PHILIP: And you call yourselves actors!
SOPHIA: You don't mean to say you think we're not?!
VASILIJE: Please, sir, don't take Philip seriously. He alone is responsible for the tragic misunderstanding which has led to this arrest!
MEITZEN: Why do you think he's responsible?
VASILIJE: Why? Because he lives in the clouds, in his illusions, his dreams. Because he confuses life and theatre; he himself

doesn't even know when he's in life and when he's on stage. Nor when he is really Philip Trnavac, and when he is a character from a play!

JELISAVETA: Give him a skull, and he becomes Hamlet. Hand him an enema, and he becomes M. Fleurant. Offer him a pouch of tokens and he becomes transformed into Kir Janja![1] Make head or tail of that, if you can!

VASILIJE: You see, sir, Philip is simply not aware of reality!

PHILIP: But you are?

VASILIJE: You're a fine one to be asking me!

MEITZEN: Enough!

PHILIP: What did he say? „aware of reality"! What reality?

VASILIJE: This reality! This one – this, in which you are right now! This reality into which you've led us through your stupidity! The reality of this room, this desk, this stove! This waxed floor! This gentleman, this sergeant, Jelisaveta, Sophia, me!

PHILIP: You don't surely mean to say that you are – reality?

VASILIJE: You surely don't mean to say that we aren't?

PHILIP: You are my bad dream, nothing more!

VASILIJE: Did you hear that?

PHILIP: All I need to do is wake up, for you to disappear!

VASILIJE: And one day you will wake up, but things won't appear as you dream and imagine them to be! Reality is not theatre, nor is it living in the clouds!

JELISAVETA: For him, even this war would exist only if it took place on the stage!

VASILIJE: That wooden sword will cost you your head!

MEITZEN: You can leave your arguments for later!

VASILIJE: Excuse me, I couldn't control myself.

JELISAVETA: We were just trying to explain!

---

[1] Kir Janja: a character from the eponymous play by J. Sterija Popović the epitome of the miser. (Translator's note).

MEITZEN: To explain what?

VASILIJE: What you were asking about – the weapons! Don't you see that it's just a matter of a wooden sword?

MEITZEN *(after glancing at the sword):* What fools I have to deal with!

JELISAVETA: I'm amazed at how you put up with it all!

SOPHIA: If you're going to arrest people for being in possession of wooden swords, which could be used only as firewood for frying eggs or boiling tea – that is, provided you happen to have any eggs or tea! – what on earth do you do with people who have real guns and real bombs?

MEITZEN: Who's asking the questions here – you or me?

SOPHIA: Are we not even allowed to speak our thoughts aloud here?

MEITZEN: It says on the charge – sheet that you also use false names!

SOPHIA: False names!

JELISAVETA: This sergeant of yours has mixed up our real names with the names of the characters we play!

MEITZEN: Could you try to explain?

MILUN: This one says his name's Vasilije – and this one here calls him Stefan!

VASILIJE: In the production, I'm Stefan, but in private life I'm Vasilije. For goodness' sake, any intelligent person could distinguish between the two!

JELISAVETA: If you intend by any chance to start arresting actors you should have police with at least a minimal grounding in theatre!

SOPHIA: Then tragic misunderstandings like this wouldn't happen!

MEITZEN: It says here that you've been causing people to gather in a public place!

MILUN: They were holding speeches at the Brandy Market. This one here was addressing the crowd from the top of a barrel!

VASILIJE: We did not hold any speeches. We were just performing an extract from one of the scenes, for advance publicity.
MEITZEN: Publicity for what?
VASILIJE: The performance!
MEITZEN: And do you have a permit for this performance?
JELISAVETA: You dare tell him that you don't have that permit and I'll hand in my resignation this very moment!
VASILIJE: I think our reputation is sufficient authorization.
JELISAVETA: Just as I feared.
MEITZEN: So – you don't have a permit either?
VASILIJE: If you think that some bureaucratic, administrative scrap of paper with a few purple stamps and scrawled initials is more important than our artistic acclaim, then I really don't know what on earth we're talking about here!
MEITZEN: I am not holding any kind of talk with you here! This is a police hearing, not a private chat!
VASILIJE: We just can't seem to find a common language . . .
MEITZEN: I am not trying to find a common language with you: I am here to question you! I am the one who asks the questions. And it is your duty to answer my questions!
JELISAVETA: And not to argue!
MEITZEN: Are you at all aware of the situation you are in? This is not a madhouse, it's a police-station! Or would you perhaps like me to give you a somewhat more tangible idea of where you are?
MILUN: We ought to bring Drobac in to see them!
MEITZEN: Quiet, you! And you – sit here!
VASILIJE: Well, since you insist . . .
MEITZEN: If you have no authorization, it means you are working illegally! Don't you realize, man, there's a war on! Your country is under occupation! Here, the laws of occupation are in force! Wartime regulations!
VASILIJE: If you think a permit's so very necessary . . .

MEITZEN: If I think it's necessary? And you don't think it is? There's nothing whatever to think about! These are the orders of the German military commander for Serbia! And you, as actors if at all you are actors – must be aware of this fact!

JELISAVETA: Above all the leader of the troupe.

MEITZEN: Will you stop interrupting? Just as you must also be aware of the fact that the performance of plays without the personal authorization of the German military commander is punishable at the very least by imprisonment! In the „Banjica",[2] in case you didn't know! That's the first point!

JELISAVETA: Now just try telling him you didn't know! *(She slits on Meitzen's desk and lights a cigarette.)*

MEITZEN: The second point is this: I'm not going to ask you how you managed to get by in other parts of Serbia without a permit – that's a matter for the local authorities, not for me! But on the territory of the District Command for Užice, every illegal performance will be treated in accordance with occupation law! And you – get off my table! That's the second point.

JELISAVETA: Don't say later, you weren't warned!

MEITZEN: And put out that cigarette in my office! The third and last point is this: all these charges are more than enough for me to put you into jail until the first transports leave for the prison camps! And into jail you'll go, right now!

MILUN: I'd let Drobac take over from here!

MEITZEN: Go and see if there are any free places in jail!

VASILIJE: Could this perhaps be the document you needed?

MEITZEN *(taking the paper from Vasilije and scanning it):* Office of the Supreme Military Command for Serbia . . . *(Sitting down)* . . . Traveling Troupe Šopalović. in the troupe, neither Jews nor Gypsies . . . nor persons married to Jews . . . permission granted . . . performance of *The Robbers* by Friedrich Schiller . . .

SOPHIA: Who, in case you didn't know, is a German writer!

---

[2] Banjica: a top-security Concentration-camp in Belgrade. (Translator's note).

JELISAVETA: As if the gentleman didn't know that!

MEITZEN *(reading further):* . . . in the towns of inner Serbia, including the region of Banat regular fire precautions. For: Military Commander for Serbia, General.

VASILIJE: General von Schroeder, antiaircraft artillery division!

MEITZEN: Lieutenant-Colonel. . . . Why didn't you show this to me right away?

VASILIJE: You asked first about the wooden sword!

MEITZEN: You may leave.

JELISAVETA: Excuse us for thrusting ourselves upon you like this, unannounced!

MEITZEN: Just a minute: one more question!

VASILIJE: Go ahead.

MEITZEN: Have you seen the gallows on the Corn market?

VASILIJE: We have. Why do you ask?

MEITZEN: It doesn't bother you?

VASILIJE: What?

MEITZEN: Having to perform in the shadow of the gallows?

(Fade out)

Scene Three

QUARREL IN THE COURTYARD OF THE ADZIĆ HOME

Directly facing the audience is the inner facade of the one-floored house of the late Major Adzić. A spacious verandah runs along the full length of the upper floor. Stage-right is the low, bungalow-style house of Blagoje Babić. In front of the house, Gina is washing clothes in a tub supported by two stools. In the yard is a water pump; washing-lines, not yet in use, can be strung across the yard. Stage-left, beneath a large linden tree on a gentle slope lading towards the river is an oak table flanked by benches. The exit to the right leads out onto the street.

VASILIJE: And now, now that we've somehow managed to get out of the hands of the police, and when we still have to prepare for this evening's performance – they're not around! Sophia seems to have nothing better to do than to go swimming!

GINA: What else should she do in this heat! She isn't tied to the wash-tub like me!

VASILIJE: And as for Philip – I don't know whether he's in Ellsinore, or Venice, or on some landowner's estate in Russia!

GINA: In Russia?

VASILIJE: I didn't mean it literally, in real Russia . . . But there was something I wanted to ask you: we'd like to hold our rehearsal here in the yard, if it wouldn't disturb you . . . You see, we don't want to pay extra for rehearsal time in the café. It's not just that the cost of hiring the place for the performance has turned out rather high, but also that we have to pay in advance! In short, we haven't a dinar left! We really wouldn't get in your way . . .

GINA: You'll have to discuss that with Simka; she rented you the rooms, not me!

VASILIJE: She said she didn't have anything against it, provided we didn't bother you . . . *(Without a word, Drobac comes in. In spite of the heat, he is wearing thick peasant trousers and a jerkin; soft leather sandals on his feet. He is flicking an ox-hide whip. Still without a word, he crosses to the pump, leans his whip against it, pumps water, drinks from his hands, splashes his face and wipes it with his cap. He breathes slowly out.)*

DROBAC: I hanged those corpses on the Corn market. Just by the weighing scales.

GINA: So I heard.

DROBAC: It'd have been better if you'd seen.

GINA: As if I hadn't seen more than enough already . . .

DROBAC: It's harder to hang a corpse than a live body.

VASILIJE: Who are these people who've been hanged?

DROBAC: Trouble-makers.

VASILIJE: Did you really have to hang them like that?
DROBAC: Like what?
VASILIJE: Like that – naked, without sandals or trousers.
DROBAC: If I'd have had my own way, I'd have stripped off their underpants as well! Don't bloody stare at me! That's the quickest way to root them out – understand? You don't understand. If you were, let's say, a trouble-maker . . . And if you were thinking of going off to shoot the Bosch, but you knew that you'd have to swing stark naked on the marketplace, tell me, would you shoot?
VASILIJE: That's not my business. I'm an actor.
DROBAC: If you set off somewhere, and you knew you might have to die, you'd think twice at least before you went! And when you'd thought it over, either you'd go or you wouldn't go! But if you knew that you'd be humiliated you wouldn't think about it twice, but ten times over! And you wouldn't go! Men are strange cattle! They're more afraid of shame than death!
VASILIJE: You know what you're doing.
DROBAC: What did you say you were?
VASILIJE: An actor.
DROBAC: You ride a bike round the wall-of-death?
VASILIJE: I'm in the theatre, not the circus!
DROBAC: You're not a tramp are you? Or a gambler?
VASILIJE: Do I look to you like a gambler?
DROBAC: Just asking. On account of the Regulation on Corporal Punishment. According to Article 3, tramps, vagrants, gamblers, drunkards, and persons guilty of disseminating false information are all liable to corporal punishment. The fact that you're an actor is no guarantee that you're not also a drunk and a vagrant. And according to Article 5, the sentence of corporal punishment by beating may stipulate anything from 5 to 25 strokes upon the rear portion of the body, where the flesh is thickest. That's why I'm asking.
VASILIJE: I'm an honest, decent citizen!

DROBAC: Well, since you're a decent citizen . . . do you respect me?
VASILIJE: Sorry?
GINA: Of course he respects you!
DROBAC: I'm asking him!
VASILIJE: Naturally, I respect you!
DROBAC: When I go into the „Hotel Paris", all fall silent! Whatever table I sit at, all stand up to leave! Out of respect! When I go down to the market stalls, people cross to the other side! Because they respect me! Old women cross themselves in my path, as if I were an icon! Understand?
VASILIJE: I understand.
DROBAC: You lie. You do not understand! *(To Gina)* He won't know my name.
GINA: Drobac.
DROBAC: Right. Drobac. And he won't know what I'm going to ask him now! *(To Vasilije)* D'you know why I'm called Drobac? *(To Gina)* He doesn't know. *(To Vasilije)* Because I flay them to the bone! And get their guts![3] That's why I'm Drobac! Make sure you remember – for next time! *(He goes off, right, leaving his whip by the pump.)*
GINA: Always the same. Never a good-day or a good-bye. Nothing! He strays in, empty-eyed, like a young bull strays out again! And in those sandals, you never hear him come! *(She rinses out the clothes).*
VASILIJE: Well, who is he?
GINA: The flogger – who else?
VASILIJE: The flogger?
GINA: D'you see this?
VASILIJE: What's that?

---

[3] Drobac in Serbo-Croatian drob means intestines. (Translator's note).

GINA: Wherever he goes, he leaves tracks of blood! *(She wipes the cobblestones with the cloth.)*
VASILIJE: It's hard to believe. Look, he's forgotten his whip!
GINA: That means he'll be back for it! And have to mop up after him again!
VASILIJE: That's what he beats them with?
GINA: Anything will do. Clubs, boots . . . but mostly he uses the whip. That's what hurts most: it cuts right through to the bone!
VASILIJE: If I'd have met him on the street, I'd have taken him for just an ordinary peasant.
GINA: Before the war, up in the hills round Sinjevac, he was – excuse the expression – raping the goats!
VASILIJE: And today he's in power!
GINA: He shows no mercy to anyone! Not even the young, the old, or the sick. He won't show mercy even for money! He's been offered gold watches not to use the whip. But he's too evil to be bought off with a gold watch!
VASILIJE: How can a man be such a brute?
GINA: He's not a brute. He's worse. He's inhuman! *(Blagoje comes on, carrying a bottle in his pocket.)*
BLAGOJE: What was Drobac looking for here?
GINA: What about you, Blagoje? Where have you been all this time?
BLAGOJE: I went to hear the news from the fronts.
GINA: You've brought back a bottle full of news, I see!
BLAGOJE: What does our actor say to a drop for the road?
VASILIJE: Thanks, but I can't take it in this heat. And until the performance is over I'll have to stay quite sober. Some other time perhaps. *(He goes into the house.)*
BLAGOJE: Can't take it because of the heat! It's not the heat, it's the empty stomach. These actors never have enough money for food!
GINA: It's the stink of your drink that made him run!
BLAGOJE: It has the scent of ambrosia!

GINA: Fine ambrosia! You'd think lizards had been pickled in it over winter! . . . Will I ever live to see you five minutes sober in the day?
BLAGOJE: It's not out of anger I drink, but out of pain!
GINA: It's hard for you, isn't it, to find an excuse for drinking!
BLAGOJE: For hell's sake woman, the Germans have broken through to the Volga!
GINA: That doesn't mean you have to drink a river of rakija.[4]
BLAGOJE: I've told you before – don't nag!
GINA: If I nag, I'm only nagging for your own good! . . . Who says they've broken through to the Volga?
BLAGOJE: Who says? The newspapers! Read for yourself. The Volga for God's sake – that's half of Russia!
GINA: When they got through to the Dnieper, you didn't sober up for a week! As if you had your own water-mill on the Dnieper!
BLAGOJE: I'm tired of your nagging. I've been tired for a long time! And I'm not a child – you don't have to be always preaching me!
GINA: When you get started on the rakija, you're no longer a man!
BLAGOJE: Someday you'll make me a man out of clay!
GINA: To make a man such as you are, I need no other material!
BLAGOJE: Brain! That's what Adam was made of too!
GINA: I know you've got a quick tongue! . . . You swill and you guzzle, and you don't see what our Sekula is rushing into.
BLAGOJE: What's he rushing into?
GINA: Is it really possible that you don't see anything?
BLAGOJE: To you, I've always been blind. But I was blindest when I married you.
GINA: And you found your sight when you started spending my dowry! *(Simka, Jelisaveta, and Vasilije come out onto the*

---

[4] rakija: brandy, spirits.

verandah. Jelisaveta drapes the stage costumes over the verandah railing to give them an airing.)
SIMKA: You can get out onto the verandah from both rooms.
JELISAVETA: So I saw.
SIMKA: There are also some easy chairs – feel free to use them! And from here you have a wonderful view of the river! *(To Vasilije)* Did I show you the oak table under the linden tree? You can have lunch and dinner there – as long as the summer lasts!
VASILIJE: What shall we have for lunch? Beef soup with noodles and boiled beef with horseradish sauce? Or roast lamb with salad? Grilled fish? Or perhaps roast goose or roast duck?
SIMKA: Goose did you say? And duck? . . . Before the war the river was all white with geese and ducks! You couldn't even doze after lunch from the cackling! Now there's not a feather to be found, not even one white flake *(To Jelisaveta)* Have you seen how close the river is? When my husband, the late Major, was still alive we used to sit here after lunch eating apricots, and he would throw the stones from the verandah into the river!
JELISAVETA: Was your husband a major?
SIMKA: In the artillery.
VASILIJE: Did he die in this war?
SIMKA: No, he died of inflammation of the lungs. That's the advantage of having a room upstairs: you don't have to shut the windows at night, and you get clean air coming up from the river! In summer you can hear the crickets all night long. The Major didn't close the windows even in winter, and he regularly slept without pajamas! But he had an iron constitution!
GINA: God rest his soul!
SIMKA: And where were you performing before you came here?
JELISAVETA: I was acting in Belgrade, at the „Manege". We were rehearsing Puget's *Happy Days.* Those really were happy days. I had a wonderful female role . . . *(She breaks off at the sound of heal / firing: several bursts from a machine-gun).*
GINA: God what was that shooting?

BLAGOJE: Machine-guns!
GINA: I'd feel easier if Sekula was at home!
BLAGOJE: You're always imagining things!
JELISAVETA: Do you know where Philip is?
VASILIJE: Off somewhere provoking Polonius perhaps, or counting golden thalers . . . How should I know?
JELISAVETA: I hope the fool hasn't got himself into another mess somewhere.
GINA: I wish I knew what that firing was about!
VASILIJE: You don't seem the least bit frightened?
SIMKA: I, sir, am from an officer's family! . . . Well, I think you can manage without me now; I hope I've shown you everything? Get your things unpacked, settle in, and make yourselves at home! I'm leaving everything there for you; I know I can trust you! *(She goes into the house.)*
JELISAVETA: Sophia could at least lend me a hand! But no, her ladyship goes straight off to the river! And I haven't even had time to do my nails, or put up my hair, or have a massage, or fix my make-up – nothing! *(She and Vasilije go back together into the house.)*
GINA: You'd think they weren't in a war but out on an excursion!
BLAGOJE: Actors are bohemians, and artists, and men of the world. They're not to blame if you don't know that!
GINA: I don't need any great knowledge to recognize who's a whore and who's a thief!
BLAGOJE: You've never seen anything further away than Zabučje yet you want to pass judgment on the whole world!
GINA: As if I could have seen anything more with you around! Home – market, washing – ironing – cooking – sewing! That's been my whole life with you! Though, God knows, you've promised me the moon!
SIMKA *(comes into the courtyard carrying a covered tray)*: Gina, could I leave the silver cutlery with you?

GINA: Are you worried the artists might pocket it?

SIMKA: It's better to leave it with you then have to worry about it! There's twelve silver forks, twelve knives, twelve tablespoons and twelve teaspoons! *(Gina wipes her soapy hands on her apron, takes the tray from Simka and carries it into the house.)* It was our wedding present from the officers' corps! *(To Blagoje)* What could that firing have been?

BLAGOJE: All I know is it was a machine-gun!

SIMKA: It seemed to be coming from the town center.

BLAGOJE: Somewhere between „Foto Lazić" and the Debeljević bookshop, I'd say.

SIMKA: Up till now, the shooting's been mostly at night . . . But Gina's worried about Sekula.

BLAGOJE: Screech-owl!

SIMKA: Who knows what he might have got led into?

BLAGOJE: Who could lead him into anything?

SIMKA: I'm afraid Gina may have good reason to be frightened.

BLAGOJE: Frightened of what?

GINA *(returning from inside):* The people you let into your house, my God!

SIMKA: If you haven't seen a soul for seven days you're glad to see the devil on the eighth!

GINA: You'll be right glad when they fill your house with bed-bugs! God knows what sort of places they've been dossing down in! *(Sophia, wearing a violet-colored swimming costume, comes back from the river, drying her long loose hair.)*

SOPHIA: D'you see that building behind the bridge?

BLAGOJE: The steel construction? That's the first electric power-station in Serbia.

SOPHIA: I swam right up to there!

BLAGOJE: You must be in good shape, then!

GINA: What do you expect!

SOPHIA: What a wonderful place you have here – a house by the river!

GINA: That's why we don't often swim – we're right by the river!
SOPHIA: I thought I heard some shooting!
BLAGOJE: Don't worry. I'm here!
GINA: That's a great reassurance!
BLAGOJE: I fought under Commander-in-Chief Stepa! On the slopes of Cer we were covered with the same greatcoat!
GINA: You and the donkey were covered by the same roof!
SOPHIA: You can't imagine how wonderful the water is! I couldn't resist getting my hair wet! And it'll take me two hours to get it dry! But if I don't go right in, if I don't get wet all over, I don't feel I've had a proper swim!
BLAGOJE: I agree. You can't call it swimming without diving in, going right under!
SOPHIA: The river has the smell of watermelons, have you noticed? And such wonderful rocks for sunbathing, and beautiful trees! The banks are full of dandelions and chamomile! You must live as if you were always on an outing.
GINA: Not quite always!
SOPHIA: I could spend all summer without getting out of the water! Would you mind rubbing down my back, I can't reach round! I could swim all the time! I'd swim to the sky, if only I could!
BLAGOJE: Swimming is the healthiest sport of all – and particularly good for a fine figure! I'm always ready to go swimming, at any time – just say the word!
GINA: Don't forget your water-wings, we don't want you to drown!
BLAGOJE: I can swim all styles – breast-stroke, back-stroke, crawl, butterfly, 4x100 meters mixed style, underwater diving, diving from the board – head first, feet first from various heights!
GINA: You forgot to mention the dogpaddle!
SOPHIA: Thanks all the same; I can manage on my own now! I must nip in and get out of this wet costume! (She runs into the house).

GINA: Mind you don't get your ovaries chilled! Wonderful water, wonderful rocks for sunbathing, everything's wonderful to her! She sees the chamomile, but she doesn't see the war all round her!
SIMKA: Actors, actresses . . . they've always lived outside the world!
GINA: She's not ashamed of going around naked!
SIMKA: If I told you, you wouldn't believe me!
GINA: And I haven't taken my hands out of the wash-tub all morning.
SIMKA: She even puts rouge on her nipples!
GINA: She wouldn't think twice about displaying all her goods on the marketplace! Help yourself, gentlemen! First come, first served!
BLAGOJE: I suppose you'd have her tied to the spinning wheel with her legs apart, so she could sit by the window and spin her you know-what!
GINA: When it comes to siding with whores you're the first to stick up for them! *(Sophia, having changed into a lilac-colored dressing-gown, comes out onto the verandah. She drapes her wet costume over the railing, and looks out towards the river.)*
SOPHIA: Jelisaveta!
JELISAVETA *(from inside)*: What is it?
SOPHIA: You didn't tell me what a wonderful view there is from here.
JELISAVETA *(coming onto the verandah)*: When did I have the time? I've had to do all the unpacking by myself!
SOPHIA: But have you seen the wheat all heavy with golden ears?
JELISAVETA: When could I? I've spent all morning airing the costumes!
SOPHIA: Like waves of pure gold!
JELISAVETA: I'm so tired I've got spots in front of my eyes!

SOPHIA: I adore the summer! Days filled with the buzzing of bees, evenings with the chirping of crickets! And how wonderful the silence is here – just listen! . . .
JELISAVETA: What must I listen to?
SOPHIA: You can hear a bee buzzing in a glass!
JELISAVETA: I can hear a buzzing in my head . . .
SOPHIA: You really ought to have a swim. It's a shame not to!
JELISAVETA: And when, may I ask?
SOPHIA: I can't remember ever feeling as wonderful as I do today! *(She goes inside)*
JELISAVETA *(following her)*: Now that you've had a good long swim, and a good lie in the sun, and you feel so wonderful, you might get changed and come and help me . . . *(She goes into the house with Sophia.)*
GINA: I didn't even know it was so „wonderful" here! Looking at the view from over the wash-tub, you wouldn't say so!
SIMKA: They're different, Gina, different to us!
GINA: I can see they're different.
SIMKA: How many times do you rinse the clothes?
GINA: Five.
SIMKA: They spend their whole life as if they were on a ship: here today gone tomorrow!
GINA: All my ships have sunk in this tub! *(Sophia comes out of the house and strolls towards the river).*
JELISAVETA *(from the verandah)*: Sophia! Where are you off to now?
SOPHIA: To get a bit more sun!
JELISAVETA: Do I have to take all these things out by myself?
SOPHIA: It's a shame to spend a day like this indoors! *(She runs down towards the river. Jelisaveta goes bock angrily inside.)*
GINA *(to Blagoje)*: Since you're standing around with nothing to do, you could pump me some water for rinsing . . . D'you hear me, Blagoje?
SIMKA: He stands there as if he was miles away!

GINA: Blagoje!
BLAGOJE: When I see her, I feel like a room . . .
GINA: Like what?
BLAGOJE: Like a room filled with violets!
GINA: You shouldn't even drink boza,[5] let alone rakija!
SIMKA: Men just have no standards at all!
GINA: All they want is what's new and different!
BLAGOJE: I can't stop wondering: what's the purpose of so much beauty? It can't be just there for loving . . .
SIMKA: The only good thing about her is her hair!
GINA: If I was to wear her clothes, and she mine she'd no sooner stand next to me than next to a slut!
BLAGOJE: I can well imagine!
GINA: But I wear a man's shoes, a man's coat, I sweat and I slog – with a rope for a belt! I'd have done better to string the rope round my neck than try to live an honest life!
BLAGOJE: It's easy to live an honest life with beauty like hers!
SIMKA: You could at least show some consideration!
GINA: He shows consideration when he needs something! Cook Gina, wash Gina, fetch Gina, Get up Gina – Sekula's wet himself, Camphor Gina – I've got a pain in my back! Rent Gina, electricity Gina, firewood Gina. Let him die – of angina!
(Jelisaveta comes out to shake clothes out on the verandah.)
GINA: Don't you shake your filth out onto my clean washing!
JELISAVETA: Are you talking to me?
GINA: Do I have to do my washing for you to make it dirty again?
JELISAVETA: I was just hanging out my nightdress. What's dirty about that?
GINA: That's where the slut's filth is thickest!
JELISAVETA: You might choose your words a little more carefully!

---

[5] boza: a sweet drink made from millet. (Translators note).

GINA: For twenty years, this has been a decent house. And in one hour you've turned it into a brothel!
JELISAVETA: I've never been so insulted in my life!
GINA: Pity your father didn't use a corn-cob on a bitch then you wouldn't be as you are now!
JELISAVETA *(to Blagoje):* If you have no way of silencing this woman . . .
GINA: Who's going to silence me?!
BLAGOJE: Gina, shut up!
GINA: And who do I have to shut up for? Shut up for a whore? And who are you that I should shut up for you? If you were someone who could give the lead, be of use, someone who could dig, and scythe, and lend a hand, someone I could look up to! Then I might „shut up"! But why should I shut up for an aging whore!
JELISAVETA: What are you babbling about?
GINA: You heard! You're an old whore!
JELISAVETA: Me? Old?
GINA: Find a mirror. Take a look!
JELISAVETA: She keeps her teeth in a glass. Now she wants to bite!
BLAGOJE: Shut up, Gina – or I'll give you a taste of the whip!
GINA: Go on, take it! Just like you! That's Drobac's whip. Take it! You're his spitting image! Go on, hit your son's mother! Go on! Strike out for the slut!
JELISAVETA: Just wait till I come down!
GINA: Just wait till I come up!
BLAGOJE: Have you gone mad, Gina?
GINA: Yes, I have! Give me something to kill the bitch!
SIMKA: Don't be crazy, Gina!
GINA: Give me something heavy so I don't have to hit her twice!
(Dara and Tomanija come in from street, through the entrance)
DARA: Easy, Gina, calm down. We know how it is for you!
GINA: How do you know how it is for me?

DARA: We came as fast as we could, because we know it's hardest for you now.
GINA: Hardest for me?
TOMANIJA: Do you still not know?
GINA: Not know what?
DARA: But didn't you hear that shooting a while ago?
BLAGOJE: Why do you ask?
SIMKA: Who was shooting?
TOMANIJA: They killed them on the spot! With machine-guns!
SIMKA: Who was shot?
BLAGOJE: Who shot who?
GINA: I can't bring myself even to ask.
DARA: Any chance of a glass of water in this house?
SIMKA: Who shot who?
TOMANIJA: They killed the district commander!
BLAGOJE: Domazet?
SIMKA: Good riddance!
GINA: Who killed him?
DARA: Whoever it was, may his hand turn to gold!
TOMANIJA: They also killed Anda . . .
SIMKA: Karamarković?
DARA: It was a masterly action!
BLAGOJE: What action?
SIMKA: Why did they kill Anda?
DARA: Why, you're not sorry for her are you? German whore she was.
SIMKA: How can anyone shoot at a woman?
TOMANIJA: She wasn't a woman, she was a witch!
BLAGOJE: Does anyone know who did the shooting?
TOMANIJA: It's like a hornet's nest in town!
GINA: Oh God, where's Sekula!
TOMANIJA: But don't you know? Shall I tell her?
DARA: Sekula's been arrested!
GINA: What did you say?

DARA: I thought you'd already heard about it! They suspect him of the shooting.
BLAGOJE: Not Sekula?
DARA: They're holding him at police headquarters!
TOMANIJA: By now he's surely in the clutches of Drobac!
GINA: I'd rather you'd told me they'd killed him!
SIMKA: Are you mad!
GINA: That they'd killed him – so I might thank the Lord!
BLAGOJE: Do you realize what you're saying!
DARA: Enough! What matters now is that he's alive! And as long as he's alive, he could still get out of it!
GINA: He'd sooner get himself out of hell! I've seen what they look like those poor wretches who know nothing, nothing at all! So what will Sekula look like tomorrow, my Sekula who does know something and they know he does!
BLAGOJE: How do you know what he knows?
GINA: A mother doesn't need to see to know!
SIMKA: Here – drink a little.
GINA: It would be easier to bear if I knew what those brutes were doing to him in those blood-spattered cellars of theirs! Like this, I know nothing; I can only imagine, and I imagine him even worse and more bloody than they in their evil could conceive!
DARA: For the moment, it's sure that they're not beating him!
SIMKA: How do you know?
DARA: I didn't say I knew. But I know who does know!
GINA: If they're not beating him that means it's worse still!
BLAGOJE: How can it be worse if they're not beating him, you idiot!
GINA: Because it means he's started confessing.
BLAGOJE: What has he got to confess?
TOMANIJA: You must know Sekula, you're his mother after all!
GINA: How can I say I know him, when I don't know what tortures he's going through?

DARA: For the moment, nobody's putting him through any tortures! They need Sekula alive and fit!
TOMANIJA: They think he might have a lot to tell them!
GINA: That's just what I'm afraid of!
BLAGOJE: What can he tell them, when he knows nothing?
DARA: Go and search Sekula's room, burn all papers!
BLAGOJE: What papers?
TOMANIJA: For God's sake man, don't be such a moron!
DARA: Don't just stand there gaping! Every second is precious!
(All suddenly fall silent. Enter Drobac.)
DROBAC: I forgot my whip. Somewhere here I left my whip. Where's my whip? Meitzen's calling me to work – and the whip's not around! Without my ox-hide whip I'm like a man without hands! I was hunting up and down for it, then remembered it would be here. Without the whip I'm not decent!
SIMKA: Surely it's not you who's going to interrogate him?
DROBAC: I don't do the interrogating. I merely help.
GINA: Help? How? By beating? With this whip?
DROBAC: Don't touch that whip when I'm talking to you!
SIMKA: Sekula's done nothing wrong!
GINA: Surely you don't want the blood of an innocent child on your hands?
BLAGOJE: He knows nothing. Nothing about anything!
DROBAC: None of them ever does. At first. But what at first they didn't know, in the end they do!
BLAGOJE: Upon my head be it – I swear he knows nothing!
DROBAC: Some know, some don't know. As they choose!
GINA: What do you mean, „as they choose"? *(All this time, Jelisaveta has been standing on the balcony watching what is happening below. After the arrival of Dara and Tomanija, she was joined by Vasilije. During Drobac's monologue, Philip comes in from the street. He crosses to the oak table and remains there till the end of the scene. The actors observe the entire scene in silence.)*

DROBAC: I'm not like some of those agents who beat, and beat and beat, then go away and start all over again! They beat for five hours, for six, for seven, three to a shift – and no result! They beat and beat, and he keeps his mouth tight shut! All he can tell them is, I don't know! But hand him over to me for quarter of an hour and one mouth won't be enough for him! He doesn't know for the chief of police, he doesn't know for the secret agents, he doesn't even know for the SS! But you should see how much he knows for me! There are many who come to me in „number seven" all puffed up and cocky when they arrive! But I cut them down to size. I knock the stuffing out of them! By the time they leave they know even what they didn't know they knew!

GINA: Dear God . . .

DROBAC: But for all this you have to know where to hit and you have to know how to hit, and you have to know where his nerve-ends are, and where his kidneys lie! D'you understand? You don't understand! If you lash him to the whip ping-post and if his skin doesn't splay apart, you might as well not have tied him up! If you flog him and the blood doesn't spatter your forehead, you might as well not have flogged him, D'you understand? You don't understand. You don't make stools with two legs!

SIMKA: Gina! Give her water! Unbutton her blouse!

TOMANIJA: Splash her face!

SIMKA: Gina! Gina!

TOMANIJA: No use calling her. She's fainted!

DARA: Slap her cheeks. Go on. Harder! *(To Blagoje)* What are you standing around for like a lost sheep? Have you got a lump of sugar in the house?

BLAGOJE: Sugar?

SIMKA: She's coming to!

DROBAC: But when I went to pick up Jevrem at Tatinac, and when Jevrem heard who was coming to call! I came across him

in the yard. He had hanged himself! From a huge pear-tree, that gives wagon loads of fruit! By the time they'd cut him down from the rope, I'd picked three kilos off it! *(On his way out, Drobac almost walks into Sophia, who is coming back from the river. Both are surprised and confused. For a moment, Drobac stares at Sophia with astonishment. In the end, his exit looks more like flight. The outcome of his meeting will be shown in scene seven.)*
SIMKA: Is there anything that could turn that brute into a human being?
TOMANIJA: He's left traces of blood everywhere!
DARA: Well, actors, what is it? Are you watching our bloody theatre?
(Fade out)

Scene Four

ROAST PUMPKIN ON THE OAK TABLE UNDER THE LINDEN
Or
THE REHEARSAL OF SCHILLER'S ROBBERS

The courtyard, as in the last scene. shortly before midday. It is a very hot, bright day. Seated around the table are Sophia, Jelisaveta, and Vasilije, rehearsing a scene from The Robbers. Jelisaveta, in the role of the old count is sleeping at the table. Sophia, as Amalia, comes up to her. Vasilije is directing.

JELISAVETA: My son!
VASILIJE: You have to say that three times!
JELISAVETA: My son! My son! My son!
VASILIJE: Now, you run up to his side! That's right! And take his hand.
SOPHIA: Listen. Listen. He's dreaming of his son!

JELISAVETA: You're here? . . . Now what do I say?
VASILIJE: You ask: Are you here? Are you really here?
JELISAVETA: Are you here? Are you really here? Ah, how wretched he looks! . . .
VASILIJE *(prompting):* Don't look at me . . .
JELISAVETA: Don't look at me with eyes so full of sorrow, I am unhappy[6] enough as it is!
VASILIJE: For God's sake, Jelisaveta, you're a man not a woman. Speak like a man!
JELISAVETA: I am UNHAPPY enough as it is!
VASILIJE: You don't have to stress it quite so much!
JELISAVETA: I am unhappy enough as it is!
VASILIJE: That's it. Now, you waken him . . .
SOPHIA: Open your eyes, dear old man! You were only dreaming! Come, now, wake up slowly!
JELISAVETA: Was he really not here? Did I really not clasp his hand?
VASILIJE: Same again. Did I not clasp – as a man, not as a woman. Can't you get into the part enough to persuade yourself that you're playing the count, and not the countess? You're a man, Jelisaveta, not a woman!
JELISAVETA: I'm trying my best, but it's no good!
SOPHIA: If she'd just give the minimum of concentration!
JELISAVETA: Since you know how the Count ought to be played, why don't you take the part?
SOPHIA: And who would play Amalia, then? Vasilije?
JELISAVETA: You're not the only woman in the troupe, are you?
SOPHIA: Don't be silly!
JELISAVETA: And don't you be so cheeky!
SOPHIA: We can't go on working like this!

---

[6] unhappy: Jelisaveta uses the feminine from (nesretcha) instead of the masculine (nesrećan). He makes the same mistake later. (Translator's note).

JELISAVETA: I don't see what sort of a repertoire this is.
VASILIJE: What's bothering you all of a sudden about the repertoire?
JELISAVETA: A troupe of four actors can't be expected to perform a play with fifteen or twenty characters!
VASILIJE: We manage as best we can.
JELISAVETA: We manage beautifully, don't we! Out of the twenty characters, you cut half. And out of what's left, you give us two or three roles each to play! The women play men, the men women. Instead of concentrating on the job, we split our minds in all directions. And the play-writers turn in their graves!
VASILIJE: The best thing we can do is take a rest and relax. A touch of first-night nerves is quite normal.
JELISAVETA: But it doesn't suit my temperament at all to play a man!
VASILIJE: Now you tell me, just before the opening night! . . . A true actor should be able to be a bench or a broom if necessary!
JELISAVETA: And I don't really understand why we're performing this Robbers!
VASILIJE: Because Schiller is a German writer. Who else would they let us perform? And also because our audience, our people – with their freebooting, freedom-loving, rebellious traditions, their refusal to submit or to be bribed, their pride and their resilience – like to see rebels such as Karl Moor! The descendants of Miloš Obilić don't come to the theatre for art but for heroism! Nor do they go to church to see Christ and the Virgin Mary, but to see their own holy kings and warriors! *(From the door of her house, Simka breaks in on them.)*
SIMKA: Could somebody give me a hand?
VASILIJE: But of course! What is it you need?
SIMKA: I've roasted the pumpkin, but I can't bring it out on my own.
VASILIJE: Let me help . . . Where did you find such a big one?

SIMKA: And if someone could lay the table-cloth . . .
VASILIJE: Jelisaveta! *(Jelisaveta spreads the cloth over the table under the linden-tree. Vasilije carries out the huge roast pumpkin and lays it on the table.)*
SIMKA: Since this is all we have, let's call it lunch!
JELISAVETA: For some, it's breakfast, lunch and dinner.
SOPHIA: Indeed, so it's been for the past few days!
SIMKA: What was that?
JELISAVETA: I can tell you, it smells wonderful!
SIMKA: Our occupation banquet! . . . Would you mind playing the host and doing the „carving"?
VASILIJE: I'd be delighted.
SIMKA: Please sit down and help yourselves. Where's Mr. Philip?
JELISAVETA: Perhaps in Gloucester's castle.
SIMKA: Where?
VASILIJE: This is no time for joking. He's down by the river, probably rehearsing his part.
SIMKA: Why don't you call him up?
VASILIJE: Jelisaveta will call him.
JELISAVETA: Who else! *(She goes off towards the river.)*
SOPHIA: How do you manage for food in these wartime conditions?
SIMKA: In summer we just scrape but winter's impossible! In summer you can cook pears, grill peppers . . . Dip onions in salt . . . But when the black winter comes round again . . . you go to the market, and there's snow on the counters!
SOPHIA: Summertime is holy to me!
SIMKA: I prefer autumn.
SOPHIA: Autumn?
SIMKA: Autumn brings peace to the house. *(Jelisaveta returns from the river with Philip.)*
SIMKA: Come and sit down, Mr. Philip. I've baked a pumpkin . . . Some people like it sugared . . .

JELISAVETA: Where can you find sugar today?
SIMKA: I saw you were having a rehearsal.
VASILIJE: We had to go over the scene between the Count and Amalia once again. Jelisaveta's been having some technical difficulties with the part . . .
JELISAVETA: That's a nice way of putting it: „technical" . . .
SIMKA: Please don't get me wrong but . . . I'm afraid it won't be convenient any longer for you to hold rehearsals here . . .
VASILIJE: But you yourself said we could!
SIMKA: I know, I did say so . . . But now, as you've seen, Gina's son has been arrested, and I don't think it would be right to perform in front of her door, so to speak . . . It would seem as if we were mocking her.
JELISAVETA: Everything bothers that Gina – art most of all!
SIMKA: You shouldn't hold it against her. She doesn't have an easy time!
JELISAVETA: I don't think I've ever heard such foul language!
SIMKA: She's drowned her life in that wash-tub!
JELISAVETA: And because of her, her husband's drowned his life in the battle! . . . What else can the children do, from marriages like that, except go out into the street and shoot people?
SIMKA: It's not so! Sekula's a fine young man – and I'm certain he's not the kind to go shooting at anyone. Particularly not at a woman! If anyone's the soul of gentleness, then he is.
VASILIJE: You're not crying, are you?
SIMKA: What's got into your head, why should I be crying? . . . It's just that, ever since you arrived, things have been turning around in my head.
VASILIJE: Won't you tell us?
SIMKA: Well . . . You can see there's a war on. And yet you . . . dress up in all sorts of costumes, put on make-up, and go on play-acting . . .
VASILIJE: And you find that somehow improper?

SIMKA: I don't really know myself.
VASILIJE: Tell me . . . where is your baker now?
SIMKA: Stanimirović or Slavić?
VASILIJE: I'm asking in principle . . . Where do you think the baker should be?
SIMKA: Why, in the bakery, of course!
VASILIJE: And the chemist?
SIMKA: In the pharmacy. I don't understand why you're asking.
VASILIJE: And the teacher?
SIMKA: In school!
VASILIJE: And where's the blacksmith? Where's the miller?
SIMKA: The blacksmith's in the forge. The miller's in the mill. What strange questions!
VASILIJE: And where, by the same reasoning, should an actor be?
SIMKA: I know what you want me to say: in the theatre! But is this really the time for theatre? Besides, you can't compare a baker and an actor. The baker at least helps us somehow to keep body and soul together, but an actor . . .
SOPHIA: Perhaps an actor can show just why it's worth trying to keep body and soul together!
JELISAVETA: You can't measure theatre in terms of a loaf of bread.
SIMKA: I didn't actually say . . .
VASILIJE: Have you any idea what theatre is? You're sitting here in Užice, and only ten yards away – England begins! Ten seconds' walk from here the ninth century begins!
SIMKA: That England of yours, believe me, lies in the shadow of the Užice gallows! And from the stage, in that ninth century of yours, you can hear shooting from the twentieth century!
JELISAVETA: You ought to take off your widow's black, Mrs. Simka,
SIMKA: What's got into you – I'm in mourning!

JELISAVETA: That's why I suggest it because you're in mourning! Put on something white, right away! And bring out the white with a touch of red! And put a white flower in your hair!
SIMKA: Why?
JELISAVETA: Because you're in mourning, because it's war, because of the arrests, because of the killing, because of the burning! Put on a white hat, wear white gloves, carry a white sunshade!
SIMKA: Do you want Užice to stone me?
SOPHIA: I know some people might think I was joking, but this was a really pleasant meal as good as a banquet!
PHILIP: The rabbit was completely unsalted!
SIMKA: Rabbit!?
PHILIP: On the other hand, your venison was over-salted!
SIMKA: I fail to see the point of all this irony . . .
VASILIJE: The same old story!
PHILIP: And why did you serve red wine with the fish?
SIMKA: What fish are you talking about?
PHILIP: I'm talking about this sturgeon! As if you'd baked it in sawdust. The rooms haven't been aired for months, the whole house is covered in dust, white all over with dust, and cobwebs everywhere! Autumn's already on the way and you still haven't scraped the mud of spring off the shoes! The window-ledges are full of dead flies! There are buttons missing on your dress, and you fix the gaps with safety-pins. You leave dead hairs and hair pins all over the house, and the saucers are overflowing with cigarette-ends!
SIMKA: Perhaps my house is a bit run down, perhaps there is dust, perhaps there are cobwebs, but I haven't neglected the house because I'm lazy but because I'm in deep mourning! And also, perhaps, because I no longer care for life. And perhaps I wasn't able to cook for the Major as he liked – I know all the

tales they tell in the neighborhood! – but if anyone's going to reproach me for anything, it won't be an outsider!

JELISAVETA: What Philip was saying had no connection with you.

SIMKA: You heard what he said to me. What right has he?!

SOPHIA: He wasn't saying it to you, but to Simona.

SIMKA: My name is not Simona, it's Simka!

JELISAVETA: Philip was talking to Simona, the widow in the comedy Last Summer.

SIMKA: But the whole time he was turning to me!

VASILIJE: When he looked at you it wasn't you he saw.

SIMKA: And he was talking about my house! If there are dead flies in some of the rooms, it's because I live alone, and I can't manage!

SOPHIA: The house he was talking about is in Bourgogne, in France!

SIMKA: Where?

JELISAVETA: Philip gets these sort of fits of theatrical madness! Give him a spade and he'll be transformed into a gravedigger. But take away his spade and give him a scepter, and in a flash the gravedigger will be turned into a king!

SIMKA: I don't need a king, or a grave-digger!

JELISAVETA: You don't understand . . . When you see Philip . . . for instance, when he's eating . . . he isn't eating, but acting someone eating. Or when he's reading, he isn't reading but acting someone reading.

VASILIJE: In other words, he's not quite all there!

SOPHIA: He gets us into terrible misunderstandings.

VASILIJE *(to Philip):* This behavior of yours is becoming unbearable. Because of you we're always out of the frying-pan into the fire! Because of you we got ourselves arrested, and now because of you again we're likely to be thrown out into the street – right before the performance! How can I act when I don't know where I'm going to sleep? If you have to be forever acting, then at least act what's needed – Karl, the person you're supposed to be playing tonight! I never know from one moment to the next who you are and what you are! Could you – I beg you! please try to be Hamlet in Hamlet, to be Karl in *The Robbers,* and to be Trepljev or Trigorin or whoever you like in *The Seagull* – but during the day, outside the performance, in your ordinary life, to be like everyone else, the person you really are, Philip Trnavac?

JELISAVETA: You're wasting your breath! We simply have no sense of reality!

PHILIP: People are always going on at me about reality!

JELISAVETA: It seems to me that's what you're determined to escape from!

PHILIP: I can't find my way into this reality, can't become part of it, alone. I can only enter reality through all the means of the art to which I belong.

VASILIJE: All the means of a full production, with wings, and wigs, spot-lights and extension cables!

JELISAVETA: I'd love to see how that would look!

SOPHIA: I don't see why you're making fun of him.

VASILIJE: An actor is one person in life, another on the stage – and no-one with any sense ever confuses the two.

SOPHIA: But where, in fact, is this boundary between life and theatre? Is it where the footlights begin? Or does this boundary simply not exist?

VASILIJE: And should we be glad – as perhaps Philip is – or horror-stricken – as perhaps I am – if this boundary does not exist?

SOPHIA: And what if this boundary can exist only when it's removed?

VASILIJE: If the boundary is removed, where then would theatre be? In the market-place, in the blacksmiths forge, in the pharmacy? Then even basket-weaving could be a performance!

SOPHIA: Then let it be.

VASILIJE: „Then let it be!" It's so easy to say. But who is going to watch this basket-weaving, and pay for it, as a performance?
JELISAVETA: I wouldn't know where I was without the boundary.
VASILIJE: Theatre, we know, is here and life is there! I never confuse one with the other. I am Hamlet only on stage, and that's that!
SOPHIA: That's why there's a strong touch of Aleksa Žunić[7] in your Hamlet!
VASILIJE: Well, surely you don't expect me to go searching for the ghost of the King of Denmark in the markets of Užice? For me, theatre begins and ends at the footlights.
SOPHIA: The two aren't divided by the sword!
VASILIJE: I didn't say they were, for hell's sake! . . . Besides, Philip isn't even saying that there's no boundary between theatre and the world. He simply behaves as if the world didn't exist!
JELISAVETA: Don't you think it's time you gave him a chance to speak?
VASILIJE: Who's stopping him?
PHILIP: If an actor is to succeed in creating . . .
VASILIJE: What?
PHILIP: And in expressing . . .
VASILIJE: Expressing what?
PHILIP: What do you, as an actor, want to achieve, to create, with your art, in this so-called world?
VASILIJE: I want to help people to understand life.
PHILIP: And what else?
VASILIJE: I want to help them to forget!
PHILIP: And what else?
VASILIJE: Isn't what I've said enough?

---

[7] Žunić: a character from the *Suspicious Character* by Branislav Nušić – a „spy".

PHILIP: In this world in which we transform sheep into woolen linings bears into busbies, and pigs into boots, who, if not you, will make the wool bleat, the busby growl, and the boots give birth to a litter of piglets! *(The transparent back-drop of the traveling troupe Šopalović is lowered. The following INTERLUDE is performed in front of it.)*

INTERLUDE

VASILIJE: This curtain hides a poverty dearer than gold, an age contained in two hours, infinity in ten square yards!

JELISAVETA: In front of this curtain lies the dark in which are burnt the saviors of cities, wooden chests, boats, and washing-tubs!

SOPHIA: In the dark beyond this curtain wise men have out-fooled the fools, and the fools outwitted the wise men!

JELISAVETA: In front of this curtain the war cooks turnips and bandages, and peace pays for a hole in the head with a hole in the pocket!

PHILIP: Behind this curtain, Rome is transformed into the Alps, the Alps are turned into the fish-market and the fish-market becomes the steppes!

SOPHIA: Behind this curtain the deep-blue evening wind furrows the sea on which there sail ships bigger than the sea itself!

VASILIJE: This curtain divides the world into the seas of fire and ice, into the stage and the dank hole from which all watch!

PHILIP: This curtain does not divide gold into black and white, behind it the blacks and the whites and the blues unite – in gold!

VASILIJE: The bell rings from cap sounding the wise man's thought: behind the curtain shines the light of the world that goes dark before that thought!

The lights gradually go out on stage and come on in the auditorium.

(CURTAIN)

Scene Five

THE BANNING OF THE PERFORMANCE

The courtyard, as in the previous scenes. Late afternoon. Vasilije and Sophia, packing the costumes into trunks, continue their conversation from where they left off before the curtain.

VASILIJE: We should be glad to have even this theatre.
SOPHIA: What a theatre! Three planks on top of two barrels!
VASILIJE: Do you think that's little?
SOPHIA: A stool would be enough for you!
VASILIJE: You don't know what one can do with just a stool! You can hold a whole fete on top of a barrel!
SOPHIA: And you can present the entire Hundred Years war from the top of a trunk! I know those stories!
VASILIJE: You don't need a lot of bits and pieces to produce good theatre!
SOPHIA: Just plenty of talent and a lot of good sense. I know!
VASILIJE: In many theatres, in many different places, I've seen splendid displays of stage technique – but I've never been very taken by it all. To me a fish is a greater wonder than a ship! A swallow more miraculous than an airplane!
SOPHIA: You can't make a production out of nothing!
VASILIJE: Every stage-prop you use has to be thoroughly studied.
SOPHIA: I study as much as I can when I can!
VASILIJE: You have to try to go to the very limit of your own resources. Once you've succeeded, you can do wonders even with an ordinary pot!
SOPHIA: A pot?
VASILIJE. Whatever you like. When I was a young actor, in Ivanjica, preparing the part of Kir Janja, I used to think for days about some of the props I would use. At the same time, without

being really aware of it, I would observe all the things a peasant does with his cap. He wears it on his head; when he goes to a funeral, he takes it off as a mark of respect to the dead; he uses it to wipe his face after washing; to shake the dice in when he's gambling with the railway man; to fan the fire in the stove; to sit on; to carry letters in; he sticks marigolds into it; he uses it to kill flies; or to protect his fingers when he's carrying a hot dish; he puts it under his head and sleeps on it; when the grocer has weighed out a kilo of cherries, into the cap they go; and when he has eaten the cherries, the peasant shakes out his cap and puts it back on his head. D'you see what I mean?
SOPHIA: The way you talk one would think you could set out in this wash-tub and sail away to discover America!
JELISAVETA *(from the verandah):* Sophia!
SOPHIA: What's the matter? Is the house on fire?
JELISAVETA: D'you know where the swords are?
SOPHIA: How should I know?
VASILIJE: Aren't they in the wicker basket?
JELISAVETA: That's where the wigs are kept. *(Simka comes out of the house.)*
VASILIJE *(to Sophia):* Help her find them. They must be in one of these crates. *(Sophia goes back inside.)*
SIMKA: Are you getting ready for the performance?
VASILIJE: Yes, for the performance. We've reserved a free ticket for you.
SIMKA: I've no time to go to the theatre today. Besides, it wouldn't be right. I need to be here to help Gina. You've seen what's happened . . .
VASILIJE: That son of theirs . . .
SIMKA: Sekula?
VASILIJE: How old is he?
SIMKA: Twenty at Christmas – if he gets through this alive!
VASILIJE: Why do you say „if he gets through this alive"?

SIMKA: Do you happen to know of anyone who came back from those cellars?
VASILIJE: D'you think they'll shoot him?
SIMKA: If he's lucky!
VASILIJE: And if he's not?
SIMKA: Have you not seen the tracks of blood that Drobac leaves behind him?
SOPHIA (from *the verandah*): Vasilije! I can't find them in the chests!
VASILIJE: Where are they then?
JELISAVETA *(from the verandah)*: If you don't find them, you're going to do your sword-fighting tonight with leeks! And the audience will applaud you with tomatoes!
VASILIJE: Without me, you don't know whether you're coming or going! *(He goes inside. Sophia and Jelisaveta withdraw from the verandah.)*
SIMKA *(to herself)*: I don't know why all this had to happen to me! *(She goes over to the table).* They're looking for the swords, and here they are on the table! *(She is about to shout to the actors, but Gina comes in from the right.)*
SIMKA: Have you calmed down?
GINA: I'll calm down when I die.
SIMKA: Did you manage at least to get a nap after all this?
GINA: A nap! With you and your actors around?
SIMKA: I kept them as quiet as I could . . . They're all on edge – tonight's the performance.
GINA: I was burning Sekula's papers.
SIMKA: Did you find anything among them?
GINA: I found this! *(She holds out a letter to Simka. Simka glances through it, turns pale, sits down on the step, and covers her face with her hands. In a short while, Philip will come back from the river and will follow their conversation with great care.)*

GINA: You had already started this when the Major was still alive?
SIMKA: Does it matter now?
GINA: You, our closest neighbor with my son?
SIMKA: Please, Gina!
GINA: Do you know how old Sekula is?
SIMKA: I know. You don't need to tell me!
GINA: How could you have deceived such a man?
SIMKA: Such a man!
GINA: You wanted all you could get and still you were crying for the moon!
SIMKA: I had everything! And it all smelt of army cloth and officer's boots!
GINA: And there I was going for those whores from the road-show . . .
SIMKA: When you had a whore right at your own door? Is that what you wanted to say?
GINA: This thing, between you and Sekula . . . how did it happen?
SIMKA: It didn't happen . . . it blossomed!
PHILIP *(bursting in on them dramatically):* Yes, blossomed! That's the right word! Like millions of buds all at once! Dear mother, embrace this woman, just as she embraced me upon her flowering breast!
GINA: How did you manage to pet him in your arms as well?
SIMKA: Him?
GINA: You deceive your husband with Sekula, and Sekula with the actor! Who are you going to deceive the actor with tomorrow?
PHILIP: Mother!
GINA: What the hell's got into you, man? Cut it out!
PHILIP: Do not be cruel, mother, listen to me!
GINA: I am not your mother! *(Blagoje enters. Philip runs up to him.)*

PHILIP: Come, father, and see how a mother disowns her one and only son!

BLAGOJE: Are you mad? Disowning him now, in his most difficult hour?

GINA: And who's this I'm supposed to be disowning?

BLAGOJE: You're disowning your son, now that he's in prison!

GINA: Me? Disowning my son? You're out of your mind!

BLAGOJE: You heard what he said!

GINA: He can say what he likes – it isn't true!

SIMKA: Just as it isn't true that I had anything to do with him!

GINA: I wouldn't swear to it!

SIMKA *(to Philip):* Tell me, why have you spent all day interfering in my life? I've given you no cause to do so!

PHILIP: Where am I?

BLAGOJE: Are you asking me?

PHILIP: Are you not my father, Megaron? Is this not my mother, Megara?

GINA: Highly likely!

PHILIP: If you are not my parents, who then am I?

BLAGOJE: What's he babbling on about?

PHILIP: And who, in that case, are you?

BLAGOJE: Me?

PHILIP: You do not have a hunchback?

BLAGOJE: Why should I have a hunchback?

PHILIP: You do not have a disfigured face?

BLAGOJE: What?

PHILIP: Nor do you have a crippled arm? Nor a lame leg?

BLAGOJE: What do you imagine I am – a monster?

PHILIP: You are not Richard!

BLAGOJE: Who said I was?

PHILIP: I do not recognize any of you here . . . You are not deformed . . . and without deformation there can be no Richard! Nor do you have a large nose . . . and without a large nose there can be no Cyrano! Who are you? Lear? If you are Lear, where is your fool? How can I recognize you, Fortinbras, if you come without drums and flags? I do not know where I am . . . How can I find my bearings? If I could see a skull, or a spade . . . a bag of thalers, or a helmet and sword . . . If at least you were holding a fan, or a spray of flowers . . . I do not know who I am, I do not know what I am to say! Is there not a prompter in this theatre? Is there a director for this production? Is there a stage manager here? *(He goes of towards the river.)*

GINA: It would be doing him a service to immerse him again and re-christen him! *(She goes over to the wash-tub and carries on with her washing.)*

BLAGOJE: He must have been hitting the bottle somewhere! In a big way!

SIMKA: What could he drink when there isn't even anything to eat?

BLAGOJE: I couldn't understand one word of it all!

GINA: D'you think I could?

SIMKA: It's all a mix-up of bits and pieces from various plays. He says that boots have to give birth to piglets, and woolen linings have to bleat . . .

GINA: His mother's milk will start bleating in him, poor fool!

BLAGOJE: Boots give birth to piglets?

SIMKA: He means pigskin boots.

BLAGOJE: Give birth to piglets?

SIMKA: Don't make fun of me – I'm hopelessly lost! Let the actors explain to you; I am not able.

BLAGOJE: What are they to explain? *(To Gina)* And why did he say that you disowned your son?

GINA: Because he's not quite in his right mind!

BLAGOJE: He's what?

GINA: He calls me mother, and you father! When I see him crazy and you drunk, I wouldn't be surprised if it was true!

BLAGOJE *(going off towards the river):* Of course, if I am not drunk, then I must be mad! But if I am not mad, then I'm drunk!

(He notices the blood traces left by Drobac, and follows them carefully.)

GINA: What are you looking at there?

BLAGOJE: Has Drobac been slinking round here again?

GINA: What would he be round here for?

BLAGOJE: These are his tracks . . . I wish I knew what brought him back! . . . Did you burn all the papers?

GINA: I burnt them! If only I'd been clever enough to read what I was burning! Like that at least I'd never have found out . . .

BLAGOJE: Found out what?

SIMKA: Gina, I beg you!

BLAGOJE: Why are you begging her?

GINA: Leave that bottle alone for a while. Give it a rest!

BLAGOJE: I am not drinking because I feel like drinking!

GINA: But because you're worried about Sekula?

BLAGOJE: Perhaps you think I'm trying to find an excuse, do you?

GINA: And what's that dahlia doing all of a sudden in your buttonhole?

BLAGOJE: I put it there to pick your eyes!

GINA: My eyes have long since cried themselves out! And leave that bottle when I tell you! The last thing we need is your drunken rambling!

BLAGOJE: Unlike you, I can control myself! And I know what I am saying.

GINA: Well, if you can control yourself, why do you fuddle your senses with that rakija? *(Milun enters from the street.)*

MILUN: I hear there are some actors staying here!

SIMKA: Temporarily, yes.

MILUN: I have an order to announce to them!

SIMKA: They're here, in the house, packing for the performance. Do you want me to call them, or will you go in?

GINA: Are you the jail-keeper?

MILUN: Why do you ask?

GINA: My son was arrested today!
BLAGOJE: Her son was arrested! And not my son?
GINA: His name is Sekula. Sekula Babić.
MILUN: The assassin?
GINA: He's been arrested, and he's completely innocent!
MILUN: I know. Those are the only ones that get arrested!
GINA: You could help me!
MILUN: Will somebody call those actors?
SIMKA: Mr. Vasilije!
MILUN: Help you? And how?
SIMKA: Mr. Vasilije! I don't know why they don't hear! *(She goes inside.)*
GINA: By telling me how he is, giving him my greetings, slipping a little something into his cell!
MILUN: And what's that „little something"? A file, perhaps!
GINA: A file – what are you talking about? No, something warm to wear, he was dressed so lightly when he left. To keep him from freezing at night, till he gets out. And something to eat!
MILUN: He'll get his prison food there!
GINA: But you must surely be a father, you'll understand! Blagoje, give the man a drink! As much as you help us may God help you and yours!
MILUN: Rough stuff this rakija of yours . . .
GINA: And we'll certainly repay you!
MILUN: It hasn't been properly natured! *(Vasilije and Simka come out onto the verandah.)*
VASILIJE: Were you looking for me, sergeant?
MILUN: I was! Come down from there!
VASILIJE: Is it urgent?
MILUN: Couldn't be more urgent!
VASILIJE: I'm just tying up the last of the packing eases. I'll be right down!
MILUN: Don't keep me waiting. I've got other work to do! *(Vasilije and Simka go back inside.)*

GINA: If you could just take him a blanket and some bread!
MILUN: Listen, for that I'd risk being sent to the front!
GINA: You won't be running any risk. I'll wrap the bread in the blanket for you, nobody will notice anything!
MILUN: I'm sick of the front!
GINA: If you could just slip him something warm!
BLAGOJE: There'll be a bottle of rakija for you!
MILUN: Get the bottle, then we'll see!
GINA: Thank you a thousand times! *(Simka returns to the yard.)*
BLAGOJE: Perhaps you could knock up a quick bite to eat?
GINA: What, for instance?
BLAGOJE: Anything . . . an apple tart.
GINA: And when am I going to roll the dough? And what am I to make it from? Ashes? Where am I to find the time for making a tart? Madman! *(She hurries inside.)*
BLAGOJE: And bring the mana bottle of the strong stuff!
MILUN: You said two!
BLAGOJE: Did I? Make it two!
MILUN: Is that man thinking of coming down or not?
SIMKA: He said he'd be right down . . . Mr. Vasilije! *(Philip returns, looking as confused as when he left. He listens with increasing attentiveness to the conversation which follows.)*
SIMKA: Do you know what actually happened this morning?
MILUN: Haven't you heard?
SIMKA: We've heard something, but everyone tells a different story.
MILUN: The district chief was slaughtering a calf, in the yard! He'd just finished – skinned it, slit it open – and he was bending down to get out the liver when along he comes and – bang! The chief didn't even let out an ah! Just sank down into the calf's blood!
BLAGOJE: There's another story that he was killed in bed!
MILUN: Who says that?
SIMKA: And Anda, what happened to her?

MILUN: Karamarković? Well, they got her later! She was getting ready to go and see her daughter, at the maternity-ward. They burst in on her! You could hear her from outside, screaming for help! Later, the guards took away that man of hers! *(Philip comes suddenly to life, as though he had been given a message. He notices the wooden sword on the table, grabs it, and strides firmly off-stage. What he made of this conversation will be revealed in scene ten.)*
SIMKA: Sekula?
BLAGOJE: Sekula had nothing to do with this crime!
MILUN: That remains to be seen! They're still on the spot, carrying out the inquest. We haven't even taken out the corpses yet! *(Gina returns)*
GINA: Here, give him this. And, please tell him . . . What should you tell him? Tel! him not to worry! And tell him . . . tell him that they'll soon let him out! And tell him to look after himself! And not to be afraid. Tell him we know he's not guilty!
BLAGOJE: That won't be much help to him that we know he's innocent!
MILUN: What the hell's all this you've stuffed in here?
GINA: Just the essentials!
MILUN: You said just a blanket and bread!
GINA: Here. That's for you to spend in the café.
MILUN: This is dangerous, you know!
GINA: And don't forget the rakija that's for you! It smells like ambrosia!
MILUN: You might as well have brought out the horse and cart!
GINA: And just one more thing, I beg you! For God's sake, please try to keep him out of the hands of Drobac!
MILUN: Not even God can help you there! People have offered him gold watches not to be beaten, but the fool won't even take a gold watch!
GINA: What can I do, then?

MILUN: Do what all the others do, nothing! . . . What's happened to that Stefan?
BLAGOJE: Which Stefan? *(Carrying cases in both hands, and packets under his arms, Vasilije comes out of Simka's house.)*
VASILIJE: Sorry to keep you waiting, we're late for the performance!
MILUN: You're not late!
VASILIJE: We are, we are! It's nearly five already, and the performance begins at six!
MILUN: It does not begin at six!
VASILIJE: But it does. We've announced it on the posters!
JELISAVETA *(from the verandah):* Wait, Vasilije! You've forgotten the wig and the boots!
VASILIJE: I haven't got two pairs of hands!
MILUN: It doesn't begin at 6, or at 7, or at 8! It doesn't begin at all! Now do you understand – Stefan?
VASILIJE: I am Vasilije Šopalović, not Stefan!
MILUN: Do you intend to interrupt me the whole time – Stefan?
VASILIJE: All right, call me what you will – only hurry up! What's the matter now?
MILUN: You have a message from Meitzen: your performance is banned!
VASILIJE *(putting down the cases):* Banned?
MILUN: The district commissioner has been killed! This is a time for mourning, not for theatre! If you had any sense, you'd have realized it yourself. Instead of leaving us to do your thinking for you!
VASILIJE: But we have a permit! A police officer can't just cancel an authorization from the supreme military commander!
MILUN: Show me that permit! *(Sophia returns.)*
VASILIJE: Herr Meitzen has seen it!
MILUN: I want to see it!
JELISAVETA *(from the verandah):* Why don't you show it to him? He won't eat it!

VASILIJE: There you are . . . Written in Serbian and in German!
MILUN: I see . . . And which is the Serbian?
VASILIJE: On the right, in Cyrillic . . . With the proper signatures, and the stamps. Everything that's needed! *(Milun, with exaggerated care, folds the permit, and slowly tears it into bits, which he places in his mouth, and swallows.)*
VASILIJE: Why did you do that?
MILUN: What did I do?
VASILIJE: You tore up my permit!
MILUN: What permit?
VASILIJE: Why are you suddenly pretending you don't know? What permit? The permit for the performance, which I gave you in front of these people!
MILUN: You gave it to me?
VASILIJE: And you tore it up and swallowed it!
MILUN: I did? What are you saying? Have you any proof for what you're saying?
VASILIJE: You swallowed the proof but I have these witnesses!
MILUN: Did you see this man give me any permit?
GINA: We didn't!
MILUN: Has any permit whatsoever been shown here?
GINA: None!
MILUN *(to Blagoje):* Did you see me tearing up a permit here?
GINA: He didn't!
MILUN: And, when I tore it up, did I swallow it?
GINA: He didn't see anything. No permit of any kind!
JELISAVETA *(from the verandah):* Why don't you let him answer for himself?
GINA: I'm not holding his tongue! Go on, tell him yourself that you didn't see it!
BLAGOJE: I didn't . . .
GINA: Does that make you feel easier?
JELISAVETA: How are you not ashamed?

MILUN: And now, listen to me! You've got until tomorrow to get the hell out of here!
VASILIJE: And go where?
MILUN: I couldn't care! You're free to go – wherever you want. Go wherever your eyes lead you and your legs take you! While you still have eyes and legs left! But don't let me find you here tomorrow: And one thing more: if I ever have to come for you again, there'll be no way out! And it won't be paper you eat, but stone! And don't wait for Drobac to decorate the gallows with you . . . Stefan! *(He leaves the stage. Gina, not without a certain uneasiness, goes back to the wash-tub and carries on mechanically with her washing. Blagoje is confused and ashamed.)*
SOPHIA *(to Vasilije):* Is that what you have in mind when you talk about „our people"?
JELISAVETA *(to Blagoje):* Do you still feel like a room . . . ?
BLAGOJE: Like what?
JELISAVETA: Like a room filled with violets?
(Fade out)

Scene Six

THE TRACKS OF DROBAC

The courtyard, the same evening. A full moon.

GINA: No, I don't have the least twinge of conscience. Not the least! For a son's sake, a mother would testify even against the Father!
TOMANIJA: Sometimes, that holiest thing of all, a mother's love, can turn out terribly wrong!
GINA: When it comes to a child, I'll not only lie, but even kill if necessary!
DARA: Show me where you saw his tracks.

GINA: I didn't see them. It was Blagoje. Here they are, come over here! And from here they go on . . . on towards the river!

DARA: That they would have trusted Drobac to shadow someone – that I can't believe! That would be too complicated for his mind.

TOMANIJA: So why is he skulking around?

DARA: That's what I wonder.

GINA: I feel easier knowing he's here.

TOMANIJA: Why easier?

GINA: At least I know that, as long as he's here, he's not at the jail! And that Sekula can rest from the beating!

DARA: If you don't mind my saying so, that's what frightens me most of all!

GINA: Why?

DARA: You know that when Drobac gets hold of his victim, nothing will make him let go!

TOMANIJA: Nothing will tempt him away!

GINA: What could have tempted him away from Sekula then?

DARA: We'll have to face up to the truth. If at this moment Drobac is not at the jail, and if he's prowling around here, that can only mean one of two things: either that the torture's over, or that Sekula has been beaten to death . . .

GINA: Stop!

DARA: . . . or, even worse, that he's confessed, that he's given all away, and that they've nothing more to get out of him!

GINA: You think it's worse if he's confessed than if he's died?

DARA: If he's died, at least he's died as a man – for a holy cause! And at least he's come through his torture honorably. But, if he's confessed, it means he's stained his honor, and the worst torture is still to come! It also means that the whole organization is in danger! That's why we must find out what's happened, so that we can act in time! If it isn't already too late.

GINA: You have no feelings at all!

DARA: Emotion will get us nowhere. *(Blagoje comes in.)*

TOMANIJA: What do you think we should do now?
DARA: First we must follow the tracks, and see where they lead!
BLAGOJE: They lead along the river.
DARA: I know. I've seen them. They might even lead us to something. Have you got any weapons?
BLAGOJE: Nothing, except this pen-knife!
GINA: And the bottle in your pocket. And the flower in your lapel!
BLAGOJE: This bottle serves me as proof.
GINA: Proof of what?
BLAGOJE: Proof that you've made a dish-rag of me!
GINA: I couldn't make anything of you that you weren't already!
BLAGOJE: But the dahlia – you don't ask about that! The dahlia is to show you that I'm not going to be a dish-rag any longer!
GINA: But a vase, instead?
BLAGOJE: I'm going to get rid of this bottle – and of you!
GINA: You may get rid of me – God willing! – but you'll never rid yourself of the bottle, not in a lifetime!
BLAGOJE: You think I can't? Just look how I can't! *(He throws the bottle far out into the river).* Now do you see how I can't? Did you hear that splash it made – splash! It'll float down the Đetina, into the Morava, into the Danube, and from the Danube into the Black Sea, and from the Black Sea into nothingness! I'm finished with drink – for ever and ever!
GINA: For ever and ever – until the next occasion.
BLAGOJE: You kept my soul corked up in that bottle!
GINA: Then along came the actress, the enchantress, the Djinn, and uncorked the bottle!
BLAGOJE: Uncorked it. And released me!
GINA: Your sweet „Liberator"! She wouldn't stop even Drobac from plugging her!
BLAGOJE: Go on, rant away! Your ranting won't get up to her!
GINA: I know it won't – she's very high-up! The only one who can't get up her is someone who doesn't want to!

BLAGOJE: I can tell a silk purse from a sow's ear!
GINA: I'll ask you what difference you can tell when you're sober!
BLAGOJE: I am sober! Sober as a judge.
GINA: So I see!
BLAGOJE: Even if a whole ocean of rakija rolled past me, I wouldn't even sniff at it!
GINA: know you!
BLAGOJE: Never again!
GINA: You'll be swimming after that bottle – crawl and butterfly!
BLAGOJE: That's something you'll never have to see!
GINA: A dish-rag's a dish-rag! That's all you are a sponge, an old soak! As for that little cock-teaser of yours, that so-called actress – she'll have you twisted round her little finger, she'll fix you! She'll go for the soft spot. She'll wrap herself round you like a brandy poultice! Nice and tight!
DARA: How long are you two going to go on squabbling? Till Drobac gets away!
GINA: The menopause of the male is even worse than the female!
DARA: Leave your arguments for later! We have to go carefully – there's no fooling with Drobac! And there's no knowing what we might run into. Gina, you wait for us here!
GINA: If you want to give orders, give them to someone else! Not me! It's my son who's at risk!
TOMANIJA: There are things even higher than a mother's love!
GINA: Not for me, there aren't!
DARA: All right, come with us then since you're so set on it! But remember this: I'm not going to let anyone's personal emotions interfere with our action – not even yours! *(They set off towards the river. Jelisaveta and Vasilije come out of the house.)*
JELISAVETA: That witch! – she never stops squabbling! I don't know how she doesn't tire herself out!

VASILIJE: Just you mind your own affairs!
JELISAVETA: What do you make of these tracks of blood?
VASILIJE: I'm telling you, mind your own affairs!
JELISAVETA: May I ask where you were thinking of moving on to tomorrow?
VASILIJE: You may.
JELISAVETA: Well, what did you have in mind?
VASILIJE: Nothing. Without the permit we won't be allowed anywhere!
JELISAVETA: But the permit's only required for Serbia!
VASILIJE: What of it?
JELISAVETA: Well, we could go across into Bosnia, and play in Višegrad and Goražde . . .
VASILIJE: Being a Serb today in Bosnia is worse than being a cornered fox!
JELISAVETA: D'you think it's any better for Serbs here?
VASILIJE: We've been divided and separated by the Drina. Separated again by the Sava! I fear the time is not far off when the Ibar and the Morava will also come between us!
JELISAVETA: The way we are, we could be cut off even by the Gluvački stream! . . . As for money need I ask we don't have any?
VASILIJE: You know we don't. We spent our last penny on renting the cafe.
JELISAVETA: Wouldn't the cafe owner give you anything back?
VASILIJE: He didn't even give me the chance to ask! I hardly managed even to get our things out . . . Now we won't have anything to pay Simka for the rent, either.
JELISAVETA: Well it's just too bad if we haven't got it, we haven't got it! I'll give her one of my costumes from The Cherry Orchard. We anyway won't be doing Russian plays!
VASILIJE *(acting):* „I love life on the whole, but this life of ours – this petty, provincial, Russian bourgeois life I hate and despise

from the depths of my soul!" . . . I played Astrov in *Uncle Vanya.*

JELISAVETA: In *The Three Sisters,* you played Kuligin, Masha's husband.

VASILIJE: In Shakespeare, winds blow, storms rage, hurricanes spout, blood spatters from wheel to wheel of the grinding, blood-driven machinery, all the cogs and wheels of heaven and earth screech as they turn, the planets revolve, crowns and heads roll! But in Chekov, we find people weary of all this. They have gathered together, after all their lost battles, in some sheltered nook in the feeble autumn sun to warm themselves in the weak rays, to gossip, yawn, and die . . .

JELISAVETA: What time could it be?

VASILIJE: I don't know. I had to pay with my watch for our overnight stay in Požega.

JELISAVETA: That pumpkin we had for lunch has whetted my appetite so much that I'm hungrier now than if I hadn't eaten at all! *(Simka comes in from the right.)*

SIMKA: Resting in the moonlight?

VASILIJE: We're packing up. Just taking a short rest.

SIMKA: It's a lovely night, so still. As if there was no war at all . . . D'you know where you'll be going tomorrow?

VASILIJE: We still don't know. But I think: it would be best if we set off this evening.

SIMKA: Why suddenly this evening?

VASILIJE: I might as well be straight with you . . . As you know, our performance has been banned. We spent our last dinar on renting the cafe.

SIMKA: So you won't have any money to pay my rent?

VASILIJE: That's what I wanted to say. And that's why we'd better be leaving right away.

SIMKA: We're not going to make a fuss about the rent! You stay the night, and don't think of the money! Besides, once the curfew begins you daren't go anywhere! I've enough on my mind as it is without having to answer for what happens to you! Is there nobody in at Gina's?

JELISAVETA: Nobody. They're down by the river, following the blood track.

SIMKA: I don't know why Drobac is prowling around here so much! I'm frightened to leave home even during the day, let alone at night! *(She goes inside.)*

JELISAVETA: And I thought she'd claw our eyes out for her last dinar!

VASILIJE: Well, at least that's one problem solved! But our situation's so bad, even this can't do much to improve it. D'you know where Philip is?

JELISAVETA: How should I know? Sometimes I envy him; his craziness! Who knows how far away he is from all this!

VASILIJE: And Sophia? Surely she hasn't gone swimming this evening as well?

JELISAVETA: I'm afraid she has. She put on her bathing costume.

VASILIJE: Let's hope she's not fool enough to go far away! Shall we go on with the packing?

JELISAVETA: I don't only have to play men's parts, it looks as if I also have to do men's jobs as well!

VASILIJE: I don't know what I'd do without you!

JELISAVETA: You'd just fade away, like the snows of yesteryear!

VASILIJE: We'll be finished in no time.

JELISAVETA: If only I could just sit here in the moonlight, thinking of nothing in the whole wide world! If there were no yesterday, no tomorrow, no words, nothing! . . . When I look up at the stars like this, it seems to me that this world is just the threshold! . . .

VASILIJE: It's not the threshold, just an ordinary bottle. We're all corked up inside it. And the moon up there, that's the cork!

JELISAVETA: Whether we're in a bottle or not, tomorrow we have to travel. Travel, without knowing where we're going! No sooner do we finish unpacking than it's packing again!
(Fade out)

INTERLUDE

Flourishing the wooden sword, Philip appears on the darkened stage.

PHILIP: Downtrodden, crushed, oppressed, I shall stand up
and with my wooden sword resist the soldiers' steely might!
To whimpering babes and weeping mothers
I shall bring freedom with the wooden sword!
I shall conquer England, Poland and Bourgogne with a wooden sword,
on a wooden horse!
I shall show the world the steel-black log wrought asunder
by the wooden sword!
Through dark lands
past the roaring from chains
I shall set out to slay the dragon with my wooden sword!
In the shape of a cloud,
Red-hot and glowing,
to impale the beast
on the point of my wooden sword!
Into the shadow, into the foam
I shall bear from the cloud
the maiden won
by the wooden sword!
Borne on by lamentation by wailing and by tears
into the flaming blaze I fly
with the wooden sword!
(He rushes off.) (Fade out)

Scene Seven

THE SCARLET PIMPERNEL
or
THE SHAVING OF SOPHIA'S HEAD

The river bank. Moonlight. A humid summer evening, full of flowers, crickets, fireflies. Sophia is drying her hair after swimming. To one side, standing in the dark – at first invisible to the audience – is Drobac. Without blinking, without stirring, he stares at Sophia. One cannot tell whether he is spying on her or whether he is entranced by her. Sophia senses that she is being observed, turns towards him, catches sight of him, and cries out. Drobac walks slowly over to her.

SOPHIA: You gave me such a fright!
DROBAC: You go swimming even at night?
SOPHIA: Who are you?
DROBAC: Aren't you afraid?
SOPHIA: What should I be afraid of?
DROBAC: You never know who might turn up in the dark.
SOPHIA: What if anyone does? . . . You haven't told me who you are!
DROBAC: You might be mugged. You might get beaten. You might . . . might be suddenly attacked . . . Do you understand? You don't understand!
SOPHIA: How can you think only of such terrible things? Where do you get the imagination?
DROBAC: There'd be no point in your shouting here.
SOPHIA: I don't see why I'd need to shout.
DROBAC: And if anyone did hear you, they wouldn't dare to come to your help!
SOPHIA: But surely you would take me into your protection?
DROBAC: Me?

SOPHIA: Would you not?
DROBAC: I would. I would take you.
SOPHIA: There, you see! So what have I to be afraid of?
DROBAC: And you're not afraid of me?
SOPHIA: Why should I be afraid of you – you haven't got horns! I was only frightened because I didn't hear you coming!
DROBAC: These sandals are made of calf-skin. When you walk in them, nobody hears.
SOPHIA: You still haven't told me your name.
DROBAC: I'm called . . . Drobac.
SOPHIA: First name or family name?
DROBAC: Both. That's all I have. You haven't heard the name?
SOPHIA: Lord, how lovely the scents are!
DROBAC: That's savory. It's good against rheumatism.
SOPHIA: And this?
DROBAC: That's verbena. The best herb of all against pains in the joints! And that's sage, it's good against flu.
SOPHIA: Even I know what this is. It's mint!
DROBAC: Mint's good against heavy oppression.
SOPHIA: What's that: „heavy oppression"?
DROBAC: That's when . . . when you have difficulty in breathing!
SOPHIA: And this?
DROBAC: That's heliotrope – against cramps. *(Sophia gives a shriek.)* What's the matter?
SOPHIA: I got stung!
DROBAC: Why don't you look where you put your feet!
SOPHIA: Damn nettles!
DROBAC: It's not the nettles' fault if you go around barefoot!
SOPHIA: It burns horribly. Damn thing!
DROBAC: Why do you curse the nettles? They're not to blame for stinging you. Nettles are also herbs, you know. They can cure inflammation of the intestines. And TB.

SOPHIA: Nettles? Really? I'd heard they can be cooked and eaten, but never that they can cure . . .
DROBAC: Even the worst plants have their use.
SOPHIA: Even weeds?
DROBAC: Weeds cure the kidneys.
SOPHIA: And do you know what this is?
DROBAC: That's edelweiss.
SOPHIA: How can you tell which is which in the dark?
DROBAC: By their scent.
SOPHIA: But they don't all have a scent.
DROBAC: So you think . . . But, anyway, it's bright tonight. Look how much moonlight there is!
SOPHIA: And do you know the names of all these little plants?
DROBAC: I should think so.
SOPHIA: You must be a herbalist?
DROBAC: A herbalist?
SOPHIA: You cure sick people by means of flowers!
DROBAC: Me?
SOPHIA: If someone has a headache, you give him mustard-seed, chamomile, and thyme. If he has spells of dizziness, you give him Klamath leaves and peony roots. If he has bad blood, you give him roots of violet and sage-leaf. And on boils and bruises you place plantain leaves – is that right?
DROBAC: Plantain leaves.
SOPHIA: And for jaundice, you gather horse's tail and immortelle! If someone has heartburn, you give him wild flowers, ginger-root, and walnut leaves! Blue, violet, yellow, white, red, golden, mottled . . . the whole summer, and autumn too, you are up in the hills gathering herbs . . . You dry some of them in the sun, some in the wind, some in the moonlight . . . And all are made healthy by your plants!
DROBAC: I am not a herbalist.
SOPHIA: How do you know all the names then?
DROBAC: And how do you know them?

SOPHIA: And how do you know which plant is for which cure? Where did you learn all this?
DROBAC: These were things every child knew in Sinjevac!
SOPHIA: And did you have baked pumpkin in that . . . Sinjevac?
DROBAC: Pumpkin? Yes, we baked them. When we were watching the goats. We also roasted corncobs. And we made magic lamps out of pumpkins!
SOPHIA: Out of pumpkins?
DROBAC: You slice the top off the pumpkin. Take out the seeds from inside, clean it out. Then you cut holes into the sides – for the eyes and mouth, or just for decoration. And you put a candle inside. You light the candle. Put back the top. And the candle inside glows through all the holes!
SOPHIA: It must be lovely!
DROBAC: Sometimes we'd have five or six of them, all aglow!
SOPHIA: I love the way you talk. I could listen to you for hours!
DROBAC: To me?
SOPHIA: And can you guess what this plant is?
DROBAC: The blue one? Mouse-droppings!
SOPHIA: Where I come from, we call it the scarlet pimpernel. It cures the sight.
DROBAC: I got my sight back this morning without it. . . If only I hadn't!
SOPHIA: Got your sight back?
DROBAC: When I saw you this morning . . . When your hair brushed against me this morning . . .
SOPHIA: Oh, was it you who came in as I was coming back from the river?
DROBAC: It was as if you'd wiped the blood from my eyes!
SOPHIA: As if I had wiped the blood from your eyes! Well, I never! . . . Now that you can see clearly. Now that your eyes have been opened. Tell me what you see!
DROBAC: I see . . .

SOPHIA: Go on, tell me!
DROBAC: I see your beauty!
SOPHIA: See what he knows! But, of course, you see nothing but my beauty?
DROBAC: I see . . . I see my own ugliness!
SOPHIA: Ugliness? Why ugliness?
DROBAC: You don't know what I use to earn my bread!
SOPHIA: What do you use? A hammer? A pack-axe? A needle and thread? A baker's oven-shovel?
DROBAC *(showing her the ox-hide whip):* That's what I use!
SOPHIA: You're a coach-driver?
DROBAC: A flogger.
SOPHIA: A what?
DROBAC: A flogger . . . I flog people . . . I tie them to the post and beat them . . . Do you understand? You don't understand!
SOPHIA: You're lying!
DROBAC: It's a great pity I'm not!
SOPHIA: You're just trying to frighten me!
DROBAC: If I'm lying, look at these hands – they don't lie. Water won't wash It away, nor benzene, nor brandy.
SOPHIA: Is it possible!
DROBAC: Look at the tracks I leave.
SOPHIA: Keep away from me!
DROBAC: Now you are afraid of me!
SOPHIA: I'm not afraid of . . . I am afraid!
DROBAC: I'm more afraid of you than you are of me . . .
SOPHIA: Is there no other work you could have done?
DROBAC: What other work?
SOPHIA: It doesn't matter what . . . You could have gathered herbs, and everything around you would have smelt wonderful! . . . You could have been a grave-digger, or a stone-mason; you could have cleaned stalls and stables. However bad the work . . . anything would have been better than this!

DROBAC: I could have worked the land, tanned the goat-hides . . . I could have spun wool and dyed it, to make cloth . . . I could have learnt the locksmith's trade, with the brothers Pecović . . . I could have cast pots and jugs, baked bread . . .
SOPHIA: Why didn't you, then?
DROBAC: I could have, just there was something missing . . .
SOPHIA: What was that something that was missing?
DROBAC: That little something which, when you don't know at the time what it is, becomes something big! It's too late now to talk of it!
SOPHIA: It's never too late.
DROBAC: Even if I had a thousand tongues, there'd be no point in talking. This will stay with me, till it drives me under!
SOPHIA: Why don't you get away from it all, while you still can?
DROBAC: The snake can't crawl back into the egg . . . nor the louse back into the burrow from which it came!
SOPHIA: You must escape, as soon as you can!
DROBAC: From what?
SOPHIA: From everything. But firstly, from that whip!
DROBAC: I can't escape even from my own tracks. And where should I escape to?
SOPHIA: Some place can be found, even for you . . .
DROBAC: What place? A louse-hole? A wasp's nest? A snake-hole? A cockroach-nest?
SOPHIA: For heaven's sake, you too are a man!
DROBAC: What kind of man? I even envy the louse, because it's a louse! Is that a man?
SOPHIA: If you mean to be a man, throw away that whip! Throw it into the river! What are you waiting for?
DROBAC: I can't.
SOPHIA: You can't, or you don't dare, or you won't?

DROBAC: This whip and me, it's as if we were married – in the eyes of the world, and of the icons! It wouldn't help even if I cut off my own hand with it!
SOPHIA: Heavens, how dark it is!
DROBAC: Moonlight outside, and inside dank and dark! But we must wonder through that dankness and darkness . . .
SOPHIA: Where to?
DROBAC: Who knows?
SOPHIA: Wait! . . . Take same of that scarlet pimpernel. Perhaps it will help to lighten . . .
DROBAC: What?
SOPHIA: Perhaps it will lead you out of . . .
DROBAC: What?
SOPHIA: Out of this dark! And into . . .
DROBAC: What?
SOPHIA: I don't know! *(Drobac, carrying a spray of scarlet pimpernel and his ox-hide whip, goes of left, towards the water. Dara, Tomanija, Gina and Blagoje come in from the right.)*
DARA: What's happened, little actress, has your darling gone away?
SOPHIA: What darling?
TOMANIJA: Did you bump into the flogger?
SOPHIA: Into who?
GINA: She doesn't know who! The flogger, who's killing my son!
SOPHIA: What are you talking about?
TOMANIJA: Was it really God who gave you so much beauty?
DARA: Do his bloodstained hands really not bother you?
GINA *(to Blagoje):* Drobac has crumpled your bit of silk in his great paws!
DARA: Did you come here to go riding with that bloody brute!
SOPHIA: What are you saying! Have you no shame?
DARA: Shame? In front of whom? A shameless woman?
GINA *(to Blagoje):* There – that's your Liberator!

TOMANIJA: She decked the murderer with scarlet pimpernel!

GINA *(to Blagoje)*: Look how high she's climbed!

DARA: This must have been some great love! Look at all the herbs and flowers they've been rolling in!

BLAGOJE: You great slut!

SOPHIA: Let me go!

GINA: What's made you so bloodthirsty all of a sudden?

BLAGOJE: The blood's come to my eyes!

TOMANIJA: Found someone to cover with floppers, did you! A sodomite!

BLAGOJE: Is that why you were swimming so much – for him?

SOPHIA: That hurts!

BLAGOJE: Is that why you were painting your face – for him?

GINA: Whore! She even puts rouge on her nipples!

SOPHIA: Are you mad! That hurts!

DARA: They should send you to Siberia!

SOPHIA: What are you doing! Let me go! It hurts!

DARA: We know what to do with German whores! Blagoje – start cutting!

SOPHIA: That hurts, man!

BLAGOJE: Of course it hurts! And there's more hurting to come!

SOPHIA: Let go my hair!

BLAGOJE: Struggling will get you nowhere!

SOPHIA: Leave me – scream! It hurts!

GINA: Go on – scream! Drobac will come riding up to rescue you on his white broomstick!

TOMANIJA: She bites – the bitch!

BLAGOJE: Hold her tight! Catch her arms!

DARA: I can't when she's twisting!

BLAGOJE: Slap her face then!

TOMANIJA: She struggles like a wild-cat!

BLAGOJE: Let her go! . . . Now she can fly, if she wants to! *(They draw back from Sophia. With shaven head, she kneels in the middle of the stage. All regard her wordlessly for a moment.)*
GINA: Why did we do this?
DARA: She needs to remember how the people judge!
GINA: What people?
DARA: She can thank God she got off without being tarred!
TOMANIJA: And feathered!
GINA: Lord, what's left of all that beauty?
BLAGOJE: Here, have this dahlia – to make yourself pretty!
TOMANIJA: D'you realize how much you'll save on combs and hair-pins and curlers? No more hair-washing and plaiting and wasting time!
GINA: Do we really need to make fun of her as well?
BLAGOJE: Don't tell me you're going to stand up for her now? The flogger's bed-mate!
GINA: And what have you got against her all of a sudden?
BLAGOJE: She lets herself be rolled by Drobac!
GINA: And d'you think you're any better than Drobac? You'd have done just the same yourself!
DARA: Here we are wasting our time – and Drobac is getting away!
BLAGOJE: I'll find him by his tracks. He won't get away from us!
TOMANIJA: Dara!
DARA: What is it?
TOMANIJA: All the way up to here, up to her, he left blood tracks . . . but look, from where she is . . .
DARA: From here, no more tracks!
TOMANIJA: As if he'd flown away!
DARA: He didn't turn into an angel by any chance!
GINA: That raven?
DARA: Blagoje, look round, will you? *(Blagoje searches for the tracks.)*

TOMANIJA: Stop, Blagoje!
BLAGOJE: What is it?
TOMANIJA: Walk on! . . . Another step! . . . Oh, Lord! . . . One more step!
BLAGOJE: What is it?
TOMANIJA: Gina, look!
GINA: Black Blagoje!
BLAGOJE: What is it?
DARA: You're leaving tracks of blood behind you!
(Fade out)

Scene Eight

CONTINUATION

The same place, a few moments later. It has suddenly grown dark, the moonlight has gone. The wind is rising. All except Sophia have left the stage. Alone, her head shaven, she wanders along the bank, sobbing hopelessly. Out of the wind and the dark, Philip, in great excitement, flourishing his wooden sword, appears before her. He blocks her way. She does not recognize him, and tries to run away.

PHILIP: Stop, poor wretch! Have no fear of my hand!
SOPHIA: O, Lord! Don't kill me, I beg you!
PHILIP: I shall kill others, more detestable than you!
SOPHIA: Leave me alone! Do not touch me!
PHILIP: There is no-one I should touch with greater right than you! *(Sophia breaks free from him and runs away. Philip stands amazed. The wind grows stronger.)*
(Fade out)

Scene Nine

CARRYING OUT THE CORPSES

Late evening. The corner of two streets, in which can be seen the signs APOTEKA (Pharmacy), BIOSKOP „LUKSOR" („Luxor" Cinema), KNJIŽARA DEBELIEVIĆ (Debeljević's Bookshop). A crowd has gathered outside the house of the district commissioner waiting for the corpses to be carried out. The wind of the previous scene is still blowing.

FIRST WOMAN: Did they kill them here in the house?
SECOND WOMAN: They did!
THIRD WOMAN: In bed, what's more!
FOURTH WOMAN: I'm surprised that Domazet didn't shoot back!
FIRST WOMAN: What's a naked man to shoot with?
SECOND WOMAN: Don't tell me you don't know!
THIRD WOMAN: We won't see anything from your hat!
FOURTH WOMAN: We're not at the theatre!
TOMANIJA: Domazet wasn't killed inside the house, but in the yard. While he was slaughtering a calf! And Anda was killed after him – inside!
FOURTH WOMAN: She was getting ready to go and see her daughter, at the maternity-ward.
FIRST WOMAN: Who are you talking about?
FOURTH WOMAN: Anda.
FIRST WOMAN: Karamarković
TOMANIJA: She got what she deserved, the whore! *(Jelisaveta comes on. She is visibly upset.)*
JELISAVETA: What's going on here?
SECOND WOMAN: Nothing much – the devil's come to fetch his own!

THIRD WOMAN: We're waiting for the corpses to be brought out!
JELISAVETA: Is this where it happened then?
FOURTH WOMAN: Right here!
JELISAVETA: Does anyone know who killed them?
FIRST WOMAN: They say he shot right from the doorway!
JELISAVETA: Who?
THIRD WOMAN: With a pistol!
TOMANIJA: It wasn't a pistol – it was a machine-gun! The bullets knocked half the plaster off the walls. That couldn't happen with a pistol!
FIRST WOMAN: They've arrested a young man from Međaje!
SECOND WOMAN: Have you heard when they're going to give out the ration books?
THIRD WOMAN: Why?
SECOND WOMAN: For soap
FOURTH WOMAN: They say tomorrow.
JELISAVETA: Who's inside now?
FIRST WOMAN: Meitzen – with the police commission.
SECOND WOMAN: They're holding the inquest.
TOMANIJA: The inquest was already held in the afternoon – now they're taking them to the mortuary.
SECOND WOMAN: Why only now?
FIRST WOMAN: You tell me!
THIRD WOMAN: Will you take your hat off! I can't see a thing!
FOURTH WOMAN: If I didn't have sinus trouble, I would.
FIRST WOMAN: Have you seen this morning's paper by any chance?
SECOND WOMAN: No. Why do you ask?
FOURTH WOMAN: Look, here they come!
THIRD WOMAN: Are they carrying them out?
SECOND WOMAN: Yes, they are – on two stretchers!
THIRD WOMAN: You can't see a thing from here!
FIRST WOMAN: We should have taken a better place!

THIRD WOMAN: I can't bear to watch it!
TOMANIJA: Why did you come, then, if you can't bear it?
FIRST WOMAN: God delivers his justice when the moment comes! *(The guards carry out the bodies on stretchers covered with blankets. They are followed by Meltzer. They lower the stretchers to the ground. Brandishing, his sword, Philip rushes out of the darkness and steps before them.)*
PHILIP: Look at this deed, this great blood, look at these two bodies here on the ground! Slain by the blows of my right hand! Just retribution for my pains! *(General consternation and dismay. The following exchanges all take place simultaneously, in panic and great urgency.)*
MEITZEN: Guards!
JELISAVETA: Philip!
MEITZEN: Don't let him get away!
FIRST WOMAN: Can he be the killer?
SECOND WOMAN: May your hand turn to gold!
FOURTH WOMAN: Innocent people die for the likes of them!
THIRD WOMAN: I can't see a thing from your hat!
FIRST WOMAN: Is that the actor?
SECOND WOMAN: Run! They're going to shoot!
FIRST WOMAN: Why doesn't he run, the fool! *(The guards fire. Philip falls dead.)*
(Fade out)

Scene Ten

THE DEPARTURE OF THE ACTORS

The road, outside the town. On the empty stage, far left, can be seen a signpost: KOSJERIĆ 22 km. POŽEGA 21 km. VALJEVO 69 km. Mid-morning. The actors have stopped for a rest. They are carrying a great deal of baggage – wooden boxes leather cases, canvas bags and wicker baskets. Vasilije wipes his brow, lights a cigarette. Jelisaveta is sitting on one of the cases, motionless, as if she were staring at a point which did not exist.

JELISAVETA: I wasn't upset for nothing, then! We were busy packing up, and all the time I felt restless, something was worrying me, literally driving me out into the street! It was as if someone had taken me by the hand and dragged me right up to that house!

VASILIJE: You've been talking about nothing else. Now stop!

JELISAVETA: It just won't go into my head! That Philip, half-crazed and all excited, should suddenly appear! And that they should kill the man like that, in cold blood! To think that he would go all the way up to the house and kill the woman! And after all that, come back and publicly, in front of everyone, confess! I still can't believe it . . . it's as if I'd been dreaming!

SOPHIA: If I hadn't remembered Philip last night, I might have lost my head, not just my hair!

VASILIJE: Why Philip?

SOPHIA: It wasn't Philip himself, but his way of acting! When Drobac came up on me like that, I nearly died! If I'd run away, he'd have caught me up! If I'd cried out, who would have heard me? If I'd tried to defend myself . . . but how could I, against a madman? Then, luckily, I remembered I could hold him at bay!

VASILIJE: How?

SOPHIA: I remembered the part of the herbalist in *The Exiled King*. We played it last autumn in Despotovac. So I talked to him about plants and herbs, repeated everything I could remember of the text! And the lines I didn't know, I made up! I was acting as if it was a matter of life and death! In the end, I felt almost sorry for him.

VASILIJE: For who?

SOPHIA: That flogger.

JELISAVETA: Then maybe it was all calculated!

SOPHIA: What was calculated?

JELISAVETA: The whole thing with Philip.
VASILIJE: The same story all day!
JELISAVETA: I can't get it off my mind. Maybe he had a double mask. First, the actor's mask. And under the actor's mask, the mask of the Fool, but what was under the Fool's mask?
SOPHIA: What do you think it might have been?
JELISAVETA: He might have been in the underground resistance!
VASILIJE: That madcap?
JELISAVETA: As a member of a traveling troupe – particularly as a madcap and a Fool – he could move all over Serbia without anyone suspecting him of anything!
SOPHIA: Do you think we just served as a screen for him?
VASILIJE: Why a screen?
SOPHIA: He's asking me!
JELISAVETA: I just remember that, over the corpses, he said that that was retribution for his pains!
VASILIJE: What pains?
JELISAVETA: You ask me a lot!
SOPHIA: Actually, he had said earlier that he would kill them. Only I didn't pay any attention to it! . . .
VASILIJE *(becoming interested):* When did he say so?
SOPHIA: Last night, when those brutes shaved off my hair! I was left alone. Somebody surprised me, and I was so desperate, so frightened in the dark that I didn't recognize who it was – I thought he wanted to kill me . . . I hardly heard what he said, half his words were carried away by the wind. But I think what he said was: „I shall kill others more detestable than you!" Something like that!
VASILIJE *(now deeply interested):* Was that after they had cut off your hair?
SOPHIA: Why do you ask?
VASILIJE *(to himself, as though recollecting):* My heart in pain, my head shorn . . .

JELISAVETA: What's that?

VASILIJE: And from the head with a blade I shaved the hair . . .

SOPHIA: What are you talking about?

VASILIJE: When Philip appeared before you, did he by any chance say; „Stop – have no fear of my hand"?

SOPHIA: How do you know?

VASILIJE *(to Jelisaveta):* And when they brought out the corpses, and when Philip saw them, did he say: „Look at this deed, this great blood, look at these two bodies here on the ground . . . "

JELISAVETA: „Slain by the blows of my right hand, just retribution for my pains!"

SOPHIA: Surely you don't think? . . . But that would mean . . .

VASILIJE: Of course that's what it means! When he met you, your hair had been cut off! He thought you were Electra! What he said to you were the words Orestes spoke to Electra after her head had been shaven! And when he saw the corpses being brought out, for him those were the bodies of Aegistes and Clytemnestra!

JELISAVETA: But you don't mean, surly, that he thought all this was theatre?

VASILIJE: Philip, when he confessed in public to the police, was not admitting that he had killed the district commissioner and his mistress – he had probably never heard of either of them; he was then Orestes, announcing to the citizens of Argolida that he had killed his mother and Aegistes!

JELISAVETA; Can it be possible?

SOPHIA: But why of all things should Electra have come to his mind?

VASILIJE; Everything that happened seemed like a scene from Electra. The commissioner, like Aegistes, was killed while he was slaughtering a calf! And Clytemnestra was lured to her death by being called to see her expectant daughter! And then you appeared before him with your head shaven! And the corpses

were carried out, just as in a performance . . . Strand by strand the story of Orestes began to enmesh him like a net!
JELISAVETA: So, it was theatre that killed him?
VASILIJE: But that also spared the real killer!
JELISAVETA: And what you took for a mask was in fact his real face?
VASILIJE: Which mask do you mean: the mask of the actor, or the mask of the Fool?
JELISAVETA: I mean the mask of the Actor-Fool!
SOPHIA: Something else occurs to me . . . Perhaps Philip sacrificed himself to save Sekula?
VASILIJE: Why should he have saved him? What was Sekula to him?
SOPHIA: And what was Hecuba to him or he to Hecuba?
JELISAVETA: If any of those policemen had had at least a scrap of knowledge of theatre, it wouldn't have come to this!
SOPHIA: Whatever he was, Philip was, above all, an actor!
VASILIJE: Whatever he was, he's now a corpse!
SOPHIA: Philip held high the wooden sword!
VASILIJE: Better to say that life used him and played with him! And he . . . He didn't even know which role he was playing, or why, or in which performance! *(Simka, almost running, rushes in from the right. She is wearing a white muslin dress, with a red belt. In her hair, a sprig of white chamomile.)*
SIMKA: I thought I'd never catch up with you!
VASILIJE: What brings you here?
SIMKA: Sekula was released from prison this morning!
JELISAVETA: Is that why we're dressed in white?
SIMKA: He was released on account of Mr. Philip's confession last night . . . Gina wanted to come with me to thank you, but she has a heavy load of washing to do!
JELISAVETA: She'll end up being buried in that wash-tub!
SIMKA: She really does it to hide her shame!
JELISAVETA: Gina – shame!

VASILIJE: What's she ashamed of?
SIMKA: Everything, everything! Sophia saved her Sekula from torture . . .
SOPHIA: I saved him?
SIMKA: Drobac went after you like a man bewitched, he didn't even lay a finger on Sekula! And Mr. Philip saved him from the death sentence!
JELISAVETA: Philip liberated him with his wooden sword!
SIMKA: So you see how in the end you're being repaid for everything. We were really all to blame for the way you were treated! I most of all, perhaps.
VASILIJE; Why you?
SIMKA: If I hadn't pressed you to stay overnight . . . if I had let you go on your way last night . . .
SOPHIA: Philip wouldn't have lost his life, or I my hair!
JELISAVETA: Whatever happened, and however it happened – it might have been far better, but it might also have been far worse than it was!
SIMKA: I fear you'll never forgive us!
VASILIJE: We have nothing to forgive you! Everything that happened is all part of our work – and our fate!
SOPHIA: I could forgive everyone – but Blagoje, never!
SIMKA: Blagoje's back at the bottle again. He'll do himself in! . . . *(To Sophia)* But didn't they shave your head?
JELISAVETA: They did! That's just a wig.
SIMKA: It's even lovelier than your natural hair!
SOPHIA: Nice of you to say so!
SIMKA: When they let Sekula out of jail this morning, they gave him this envelope to take to you. They found it in Philip's pocket.
SOPHIA: What is it? A letter?
VASILIJE: It seems to be Philip's will!
JELISAVETA: His will!
SOPHIA: What did he have to leave in a will?

VASILIJE *(reading):* „When I die, whether it be of natural causes or by violent means, if there is any money to be found in my pockets let it be given to the actors to drink my farewell."
JELISAVETA: Was there anything?
SIMKA: A handful of tokens.
VASILIJE: „I have no fixed property nor moveable assets, except this sinful body, which anyway never belonged to me and which will be returned to mother earth: dust unto dust! I beg only that my head may not share the fate of my body . . . "
JELISAVETA: What does he mean?
VASILIJE: „ . . . and that my skull may be donated to a theatre company, as a stage-prop."
SOPHIA: A stage-prop?
VASILIJE: „Whenever the gravedigger, as he digs and sings, throws up Yorick's skull from the grave, and whenever Hamlet takes it in his hands and says: 'That skull had a tongue in it and could sing once', that will be my resurrection!"
SOPHIA: Is that all?
VASILIJE: That's all.
JELISAVETA: Poor Philip!
SOPHIA: Does anyone know where he's buried?
SIMKA: Probably somewhere in Krčagov. Nowadays they throw them all into mass graves, cover them with lime and pack them down!
SOPHIA: So, we'll never find his grave. His grave or his skull!
JELISAVETA: How can we fulfill his last wish, then?
VASILIJE: Even though dead, that mad head of his will find its way from the mass grave into the hands of some Falstaff playing Hamlet!
SIMKA: And you? Will you carry on with the theatre?
VASILIJE *(picking up the cases):* We'll carry on – what else can we do?

SOPHIA: Along comes the great flood, sinking boats, covering mountains and continents! And we try to save ourselves from the floodwaters by climbing up on chairs!
JELISAVETA: As if the flood was a mouse!
SIMKA: And now, where will you go?
VASILIJE: Fifty yards from here – and we might be in England! And in five minutes, we might be back in the sixteenth century!
JELISAVETA: Through wastelands filled with weeping we shall head for the flames with the wooden sword!
SIMKA: May the Lord protect you! *(The actors pick up their baggage and set off slowly into the distance, towards the blue backdrop of the sky. The transparent curtain of the traveling troupe Šopalović drops behind them.)*
SIMKA: Stop! Wait! I nearly forgot to tell you. They found Drobac, the flogger hanged! He hanged himself at Tatinac, on a pear-tree! A huge pear-tree that gives wagon-loads of fruit! He hanged himself with the same ox-hide he used for beating! He was holding a scarlet pimpernel! They don't hear . . . *(The lights are slowly dimmed.)*

CURTAIN

THE END

Jelova Gora, 6 April 1985

Translated by *Alan McConnell-Duff*

DUŠAN KOVAČEVIĆ
(1948—)

Kovačević was born in Mladenovac, Serbia in 1948. He is a playwright and director who also served as Serbia's ambassador to Portugal. He received his BA degree in dramaturgy in 1973 from the University of Belgrade. He worked at TV Serbia as a dramaturge and since 1998 has been the artistic director of Zvezdara theatre.

One of his best plays, *Balkan Spy*, which is included in this anthology, is a story of political intrigue and deceit. A dedicated royalist, he is a member of the Crown Council of Prince Alexander Karađorđević and member of the Serbian Academy of Arts and Sciences.

DUŠAN KOVAČEVIĆ

BALKAN SPY

Balkan Spy is protected by copyright.

Copyright © 1997, 2016 Dennis Barnett

All rights reserved.

Translator's Aknowledgments

Special thanks to Cheryl Spasojević for her invaluable help. I would also like to thank the following people: Simone Genatt, Jennifer Raguz, Mirko Spasojević, Gordona Crnković, Željko Đukić, Natasha Đukić, Lawrence Pavlinovich, Penny Pavlinovich, Aron Aji and members of the Literary Translation Workshop at the University of Iowa, and of course, Susan Millar, Lucas Barnett, and Gus.

CHARACTERS:

ILIJA ČVOROVIĆ[1], the owner of the house, the property, and his wife. He believes in freedom for all mankind.

DANICA[2] ČVOROVIĆ, Ilija's wife.

SONJA[3] ČVOROVIĆ, Ilija's daughter

ĐURA[4] ČVOROVIĆ, Ilija's twin brother

The TENANT, Peter Markov Jakovljević,[5] a Parisian tailor

---

[1] Pronounced "Ee'-lee-ya Chvo'-ro-veech."
[2] Pronounced "Dah'-neet-sah."
[3] Pronounced "Sohn'-yah."
[4] Pronounced "Jew'-rah."
[5] Pronounced "Peh'-tehr Mahr'-kohv Yah-koh'-vlee-yeh-veech."

Act One

1.

The TENANT

(DANICA ČVOROVIĆ, a 50-year old housewife, sits at the kitchen table peeling potatoes and listening to the radio. Having aged prematurely long ago, she is always worried, absorbed in thought and preoccupied with her endless troubles. From time to time, she looks out the window of her small, cramped kitchen.)

RADIO VOICE: Today we will feature your favorite Argentinian tangos from the series, "The Music of Your Youth." *(With the first measures of an Argentinian tango, we hear the front door open. Her husband, Ilija Čvorović, a short, powerful, broad-shouldered, man getting on in years, enters the kitchen. He is out of breath as if he has been running for days; he leans on the armchair in the corner, next to the coat rack. He wipes his perspiring forehead and removes his shoes. He puts a hand over his chest as if holding his heart. The music upsets him; he crosses to the radio and turns it off. He takes out a pack of cigarettes and a matchbook. He lights up anxiously. Finally, his wife dares to speak.)*
DANICA: Why did they call you? *(Ilija is silent. He shakes off the ashes, nervously, high above the ashtray. He pulls on his moustache with his fingers.)* Did they call you because –
ILIJA: Because what?
DANICA: Well, you said, maybe they were checking –
(Ilija stares at her, shaking his head)
ILIJA: You are going to drive me into my grave. Is he at home?
DANICA: Who?
ILIJA: My dead father! Who do you think? Our Tenant!

DANICA: No.

ILIJA: Where is he?

DANICA: I don't know. He left this morning . . . hasn't come back. What happened?

ILIJA: Nothing. But . . . it's just the beginning. *(His wife shrinks and sits, staring at her worried husband.)*

DANICA: Why did they call you?

ILIJA: Because of him.

DANICA: Because of him?

(Danica shifts on the chair, not knowing what to say, or how to continue.)

ILIJA: I was such a fool. I said we didn't need a Tenant. Didn't I?! Do you hear what I'm saying?

DANICA: Yes, you did.

ILIJA: Yes, yes, a hundred times I told you, but you insisted, as if we were starving, barefoot and naked. As if our life depended on his worthless money: "We have to let a room! We have to let a room!" And you let it all right, but it wasn't a room, it was me. You let me down!

(The woman looks with terror at her hysterical husband. She watches him as if she were seeing him for the first time. Ilija pounds on the table to make his point.)

ILIJA: Nobody listens to me! I'm always the last to be asked, and the first to get hit by it all! Our whole life together I've had to explain everything to you!

DANICA: For God's sake, Ilija –

ILIJA: You don't listen to me. Do you know who that man is?

DANICA: His profession?

ILIJA: What?

DANICA: What do you mean?

ILIJA: What do I mean? Who is that man?

DANICA: Well, he said he studied at some school and twenty years ago he went to France and became a tailor. His brother is a tailor too. At least that's what Sonja says. She says that for now

his stay is temporary, but he hopes to come back to Belgrade for good. He is trying to open his own shop –
ILIJA: Yes. And?
DANICA: What, and?
ILIJA: Well, who is he? What's he doing now? What's his job? How does he survive?
DANICA: How do I know? He doesn't talk. I don't ask him. I see him once a week. He pays his rent on time.
ILIJA: Pays on time? Honest to God? Pays on time?
DANICA: Yes.
ILIJA: But do you know where the money comes from? How he pays "on time"? Isn't it suspicious that in the eight months he's lived here, he hasn't worked a single day? Yet he throws his money around and lives just like anyone else who slaves away and labors. You've never wondered who's supporting him?
DANICA: Ilija, please, tell me what's going on?
ILIJA: That man, that Peter Markov Jakovljević, that evil and dangerous man with his three names! They've had him under surveillance for a long time. They asked me what I knew. When did he arrive? What's he done? What's he told us? Who visits him? Does he have many friends?
DANICA: Who'd you talk to?
ILIJA: An inspector. He said he was only "collecting information," but I know what that means, "collecting information."
DANICA: The inspector said he was dangerous?
ILIJA: No.
DANICA: Well, how do you know if he is?
(Ilija looks at his wife, tightens his jaw, and moves as if he would like to hit her.)
ILIJA: Why did they ask me about him?! Was it just a whim? Since when are the police so interested in an honest man?
(His wife timidly gets up and moves away from her enraged husband.)

DANICA: Well it's nothing, as soon as he returns we'll give him his notice. Let him pack his things, immediately and get lost.

ILIJA: I said I'd get rid of him, but he told me not to panic or make a fuss. He said he is "only under investigation." I know what that means, "under investigation."

DANICA: All sorts of things.

ILIJA: Do you know what he was doing in France? He was sharing our country's secrets. If he was just a thief or a common criminal, they'd have already nabbed him.

DANICA: The inspector told you that?

ILIJA: No, but you don't have to be a genius to figure it out. I've had my eye on him from the start: he's so quiet, puts black canvas over his windows, brings men with beards to his room, goes for walks when normal people are sleeping, keeps his light on until two or three each morning, locks himself in, disappears for days.

DANICA: Did you ask the inspector if he's dangerous?

ILIJA: Yes.

DANICA: And what did he say?

ILIJA: Nothing. He said: "No one is dangerous, as long as there is no evidence to the contrary." A brilliant answer. When they say to us: "That so-and-so lives at your house," it tears me apart.

DANICA: Did you tell him you have a bad heart?

ILIJA: You are not normal! I wasn't there for a medical exam. I asked him: "My friend, what should I do *while* there's no evidence to the contrary? He could be doing all sorts of things." "He isn't," he said, "let that be our worry." I thought to myself: your worry will break my back.

DANICA: What else did he ask?

ILIJA: Nothing. He told me not to tell anyone we spoke. If he moves, or goes on another trip, I'm to let the inspector know. But I could tell he hadn't said everything he was thinking, so I asked him – "my friend, do you suspect me? You know I did two years' time." "I didn't know," he said, and on his table sat this large blue folder with lots of coffee rings on it. My file, undoubtedly.

DANICA: What kind of a question was that? Why would he ever suspect you?

ILIJA: What kind of question? Haven't we had this man in our home for eight months? We've protected him for eight months.

DANICA: We haven't protected him.

ILIJA: No, of course, you're right, we reported him, didn't we?! How do they know we don't know what he does? Why did he come to our house?

DANICA: I ran an ad. Anybody who wanted to could have come.

ILIJA: Anybody could have come, but he's the one who did! Why couldn't an honest man come instead?

DANICA: How are you supposed to tell who a man is the first time he shows up at your door?

ILIJA: *We* know that we knew nothing about him when we took him in, but they don't know that! That's why I asked. I want to sleep in peace. I've had enough.

DANICA: And what did he tell you?

ILIJA: He laughed. And I know what it means, this laughter of his. In the beginning, everything's funny to them. In the end it's all misery. I know their ways.

DANICA: God, Ilija, how could they think you're connected with him? You didn't know him and never saw him before. You've only left the country once, when you went to Romania –

ILIJA: Then he offered me coffee and cigarettes. When I calmed down, we chatted a little. He said, as though he didn't know: "When did you do your two years?" Forty-nine. Eighth of September, 1949. "And for what?" And I told him the whole story. He listened. Pretended it was something he didn't already know. You wouldn't be able to tell he's an inspector: nicely dressed, light suit, bright shirt, longish hair. In my time you could recognize them from miles away. They did that on

purpose, to frighten everyone. You knew who they were, as soon as you saw them. Today, they go to the other extreme: When you see them, you don't know who they are. That must be why there are so many of them around. He asked me: "Have the recent price increases been difficult for you?" I think, I didn't spend two years in prison for nothing.[6] So, I told him, "yeah, things *have* been tough, but they were stable for a long time. And that time was nearly sacred to us." As I'm leaving, in the hallway, as if beside the point, he asks me: "Does he get calls from Paris?" I assured him that, so far, that's not been happening.
DANICA: What do you mean? Yes it has.
ILIJA: When?
DANICA: Several times.
ILIJA: Why didn't you tell me?
DANICA: Why does it matter?
ILIJA: Why does it matter?! If the police know that they called him, and I didn't say so, then . . . then it looks like I'm protecting him, like I lied. Do you and I live under the same sun? You're not normal. You're going to drive me right back into hard labor. *(Ilija goes to the phone, lifts the receiver, dials the number.)* Hello . . . Please give me Mr. Dražić[7] . . . Yes . . . Is this Mr. Dražić?. . . Inspector, this morning I was at your place for the interrogation . . . the interview, I'm sorry . . . you see, I've gone to so many interrogations . . . Well, I told you that . . . that . . . you know who I mean . . . that they never called him from Paris, and now my wife says . . . I didn't know – she thought that it wasn't important – but it seems they called him a few times . . . I'm sorry?. . . Yes, yes . . . Naturally . . . Goodbye . . . *(Slowly, unhappily, he puts down the receiver.)*

---

[6] Ilija is referring to approximately three years during the late 1970's when inflation was under control. In 1982, when this play was written, according to Mirko Spasojević, the price increases were "outrageous." Presumably, here Ilija has been smart enough to keep his criticism of the government to himself.
[7] Pronounced "Drah'-zhee-ch."

DANICA: What did he say?

ILIJA: That I shouldn't get excited; that I shouldn't call him; that he'll call me if he needs something. He said: "Our conversation was for information only." It's easy for him to talk, he doesn't have a criminal under his roof.

DANICA: Don't get upset, please, you'll make yourself sick. Now go. Sit down.

They're just being careful. They just don't want to see any more of those gangs, blowing up railroad tracks and bridges. You immediately think the worst.

ILIJA: When was the last time you cleaned his room?

DANICA: Yesterday.

ILIJA: What was there?

DANICA: Nothing special. A few clothes, one suitcase, some books. He's not exactly tidy.

ILIJA: Give me the key!

DANICA: What for?

ILIJA: Give me the key! *(Danica takes the key from the bureau and gives it to Ilija, who approaches the window and pulls back the curtains.)* Stay here, make sure no one comes. *(Ilija quickly unlocks the door to the Tenant's room. He enters. His wife peeks through the window. Ilija returns carrying a rather large suitcase; puts it down on the table, opens it, and removes the things. He looks at all the objects, turns them, weighs them, studies them. He leafs through a journal. Removes a small box.)* "Petit pakuet." Looks like some medicine.

DANICA: His brother sends it to him every month. He's diabetic.

ILIJA: *(Reading off the box.)* "Not subject to customs inspection." He told you that he was diabetic?

DANICA: Sonja told me. *(Ilija finds a checkbook in a compartment of the suitcase. He leafs through it. He smiles, shaking his head.)*

ILIJA: How much do we have in our savings?

DANICA: What savings?

ILIJA: Do you know how much he's got? $142,000. That's like . . . like . . . five times. . . one hundred times five . . . five hundred, five times - that's over eight hundred million dinars. And on the black market - a billion!
DANICA: So, he's been at it for twenty years.
ILIJA: For twenty years?! I've been working my whole life!
DANICA: They pay well, there.
ILIJA: Where there?! You think this comes from honest business? The French pay with their shitty Francs, not with dollars! *(From outside we hear the hum of a motor. Ilija crosses to the window.)* Were they driving a car earlier?
DANICA: Yes. *(Ilija quickly returns the things to the suitcase, closes it and carries it into the Tenant's room. He returns, locks the door. Crosses to the window.)*
ILIJA: Make coffee. No sugar for him. He's got friends here. Do you know why he chose our house? Because we're not in the center of town. We're not in plain sight. Now, when he's here, act normal: simple, peaceful, friendly. Don't blurt out anything stupid. *(Ilija opens the front door. He calls to the Tenant who has started around the house towards his "separate entrance").* My friend Jakovljević! Good day . . . Drop in for a moment . . . Come on in, we haven't seen you for months . . . Come on in, come on . . . *(Ilija lets the Tenant, a hard-shelled, tall man, into the room. He smiles, fixes his glasses on his hooked nose, and in confusion, he looks back. Ilija offers him a chair.)* Sit down. You never stop by.
TENANT: Thank you. You know, I'm in a hurry. *(Speaking to his friends outside.)* Wait for me.
ILIJA: Have some coffee. Just a little while ago, I was saying to my wife: That Jakovljević! It's like he's avoiding us. He never drops by.
TENANT: Thank you, Mr. Čvorović. It's so pleasant here. These last few days, though, have been quite difficult. *(Danica begins to speak, but Ilija shuts her up with a look.)*

ILIJA: How is your illness? Sonja told us.

TENANT: Oh, I'm doing fine. Everything else, it seems though, is going wrong. Your heart?

ILIJA: It keeps the beat, so I keep marching. Otherwise, how's your work going?

TENANT: Badly. They send me from one office to the next, from one door to the next, from window to window. Each day I get certificates and documents, copy applications, wait for secretaries. Some days I'm ready to chuck it all. You know, it's impossible the way things are done here. Everybody promises, and nobody does anything. If only they'd tell me no, it won't happen. Then I'd say: Fine, goodbye, and go back to Paris. But instead it's – "You'll see. It'll happen. It'll happen. Don't worry. It just needs approval. Drop in next month." Believe me, I can stand anything but this loss of dignity.

ILIJA: What exactly is the problem? Maybe we could help you.

(The Tenant smiles, takes out his wallet, where he finds a piece of paper.)

TENANT: It's been exactly nine months since they found a space for my business on Banov Ban's hill. Everything was all set. I called my brother and had him pack my sewing machine for shipping. I'd already found designers and craftsmen who were interested here, then a few days ago, everything fell through. They said the space "was zoned commercially" for a store. "A store, my friend, is more important than a tailor's salon." "But you should have told me that nine months ago!" I said. Thank God I didn't fall into a coma. I think my sugar level was over three-hundred. I've squandered a year begging from scruffy clerks.

(Danica walks past her broad-shouldered husband, sits opposite the Tenant and begins to speak angrily.)

DANICA: That's nothing. You know how long we waited for our apartment? Twenty years. For twenty years we were supposed to move "in the spring." Meanwhile we lived in shacks and basements, waiting for this so-called "spring." The only paycheck we had was his; we had a daughter, then she went to dental school.

ILIJA: Danica, we've solved our problem. Get the man his coffee. He's in a hurry.

DANICA: How have we solved it? We solved it when your heart went bad, and I got rheumatism. We're in debt up to our ears over this house. We have squandered this life. *(Handing the Tenant a cup of coffee.)* Here, without sugar. This isn't a home, it's a grave.

ILIJA: Danica –

DANICA: I've got one more thing to tell you: we may have solved the problem about our living arrangements, but our daughter is still unemployed and she graduated five years ago. A grown woman, ready for marriage, who suffered like Jesus to get through that school. She tells me, in this country, we have the worst teeth in Europe. We have people with no teeth at all, others with only two teeth in their head, but there aren't any jobs for a dentist. It's because we have a hundred thousand politicians –

ILIJA: There's work! There was work for her! It's not the politician's fault –

DANICA: What work? She's applied to forty-six clinics. I have a huge pile of applications and rejection notices.

ILIJA: Little Miss Precious won't work anywhere outside of Belgrade. Didn't they offer her a job in Upper Rakovac![8]

DANICA: Do you know where Upper Rakovac is?

TENANT: No.

DANICA: No one else will say it, but Upper Rakovac is a hundred kilometers away from Lower Rakovac. It's a place where the sun rises once a week and sets twice a day.

ILIJA: Danica –

---

[8] Pronounced "Rah-ko-vats". A small village about ninety minutes from Belgrade.

DANICA: She was born in Belgrade. Her boyfriend, her family, all her friends are here. Let somebody work there that comes from there. Let them fix their own mother's teeth, their own father's teeth. You can go to Upper Rakovac to see the dentist, but my daughter will fix my teeth here. Do you think the children of wealthy people have to wait for employment? For them, first they hire them, and then they create the job.

ILIJA: Danica –

DANICA: Are you going to deny it? Everybody knows, but they pretend they *don't* know, and those in power, they know that everybody knows but pretend they don't know, but *they* pretend that they *don't* know that everybody pretends they don't know. Well, we all pretend; it's the only way to keep the peace.

ILIJA: I'm sorry, she has weak nerves. Ever since the war.[9]

(From outside a siren is heard. the Tenant rises. He feels uncomfortable, as if he were the cause of this quarrel.)

TENANT: Ma'am, don't be upset. That won't help. Thank you for the coffee. I forgot my friends are waiting in the car. Goodbye.

ILIJA: Well, stop by again. It was nice to see you. *(The Tenant leaves the house. Ilija returns, approaches his wife, grabs her by the shoulders; he speaks angrily, quietly, hissingly.)* You stupid woman, what did you say? Couldn't you see he was provoking us, testing us? Why were you yapping when nobody asked you a thing?

DANICA: What I said. Wasn't it true?

ILIJA: Shut up. Stop. *You* know what the truth is?

DANICA: Yes, I do.

ILIJA: If you ever speak like that again, I will scorch you like the fucking sun! Who made the truth your business? It's not your concern. *(From the Tenant's room can be heard steps and the sound of things being moved. Ilija goes to the door, tries to listen, stoops down and peers through the keyhole. His wife sits*

---

[9] World War II

at the table, takes out a handkerchief from the pocket of her apron. Ilija suddenly stands, looks back, feels the pockets of his jacket.) Where are the keys for the Moskvitch?[10]

DANICA: Here. Where are you going?

ILIJA: I'm going to find out what's going on. This "tailor's salon on Ban's hill?" He thinks I bought into it. Nothing about this to anyone, not Sonja, not even my brother. Let's keep Đura[11] out of it for now. No one.

(Outside we hear the sound of a car moving away. Ilija runs out. Soon we hear the departure of another car, following. Danica is motionless as she sits at the table.)

---

[10] A Russian automobile.
[11] Pronounced "Joo-rah."

2.
Ilija's First Day of "Work"

(Sonja, their daughter, who is nearly thirty, is eating lunch and talking between mouthfuls. She's in a smiling, excited mood. She wants to say everything at once.)

SONJA: . . . then doctor Bošković[12] calls me and says: "Everything should work out, as long as that witch doesn't go crazy again." So far, she's retired five times. Then I call Dragan,[13] and we have dinner with Bošković and his wife. And it turned out the doctor is Dragan's uncle from Kruševac[14], or some sort of cousin by some aunt. Dragan promised the doctor he would bring some auto parts back from Libya for him.
DANICA: What a coincidence. If you hadn't gone to his house last week –
SONJA: Nothing would have happened. And I grumbled because I didn't want to go. But that evening Bošković promised he would hire me, although he had been drinking a bit, and I thought maybe he'd promise anything, but . . . I still can't believe it.
DANICA: Take some butter. And just this morning, I fought with your father. We haven't talked about you getting a job for two years, and today, as if I was psychic. To tell you the truth, I won't believe it, either. Not until I see you in a labcoat . . . Doctor Čvorović! *(The daughter laughs, stands and firmly hugs her mother.)*
SONJA: Oh, is that what's most important to you? Huh?. . . Is it?
DANICA: Let go of me . . . I can't . . . Sonja, please . . .

---

[12] Pronounced "Bohsh'-koh-veech."
[13] Pronounced "Drah'-gahn."
[14] Pronounced "Kru'-sheh-vahts."

(Danica turns her head, hides her face. Sonja gives her a long hug. Playing and joking with her mother.)
SONJA: Of course, I knew that was going to happen: half an hour of being happy followed by half an hour of crying.
DANICA: If I could cry because you weren't working, I can cry now, too. That Bošković better deliver. And Dragan better bring something back from Libya for his fiancée, too.
SONJA: I hated using a personal connection to find a job, but what could I do? It's the way things are. On Sunday, we're taking you and Dragan's parents to lunch. It's time you got acquainted.
DANICA: We've been talking to them on the phone, for years. We actually get to meet them? Are you . . . Are you planning something?
SONJA: We'll see.
DANICA: You can stay with us. You'll have your own part of the house, too. Our Tenant will be leaving, soon. *(From the yard, we hear the hum of an automobile. Danica goes to the window to look.)* Here's your father. Don't tell him right away. After what he said this morning, I want to rub it in a little. He mentioned Upper Rakovac, again – *(Ilija enters, dusty, wrinkled, shaken up. He is barely standing. His wife and daughter run to help him get to the armchair, where he drops.)*
DANICA: Is it your heart?
SONJA: Daddy, what is it? Your heart?
ILIJA: It's nothing . . . I fell . . . I hurt myself a little.
DANICA: Where did you fall?
ILIJA: On the ground! Where did I fall. Come on, you're looking at me as if I was a ghost. Give me some brandy. This is nothing.
(He lifts his trouser leg slightly, looks at his injured knee . . . Danica brings a flask of brandy and three glasses. She pours the drinks.)
SONJA: Mama, tell him. It'll make him feel better.

DANICA: The only time in my life I have ever had brandy was at our wedding, when he made me. But today, I will drink on my own. Cheers!

ILIJA: What is today? Our thirtieth anniversary?

DANICA: For that I wouldn't drink.

ILIJA: What is it then? Are we drinking because I fell?

SONJA: I got a job.

(ILIJA looks at his daughter, as if what she announced is impossible or unintelligible. He is silent for a long time, glaring at her fixedly.)

ILIJA: You got a job?

SONJA: Yes. I got a job. I start on Monday. What daddy? Why are you looking at me like that? I got a job. I really got a job.

(The father stands, extends his hand and excitedly congratulates her. Then he takes money out of his wallet.)

ILIJA: Here, go celebrate. I'd do more, but I've not been paid, yet. *(To Danica)* And you, today, in front of that man – running your mouth. Do you see? Sonja, here's to your good fortune. Here's to us!

SONJA: Can I take the car?

ILIJA: Take it. Drive, but be careful. There are maniacs out there - running through lights. *(Sonja takes her things.)*

SONJA: Daddy, why don't you sell that Russian car? It guzzles gas like the devil.

ILIJA: And what would I buy? They're all the same.

(Sonja kisses her mother.)

DANICA: When will you be back?

SONJA: When I want to. Tonight I am – what should I say? "My own person." Goodbye, Daddy.

(Sonja leaves the house. From the yard, we hear her rev the engine then depart. Ilija gets more brandy for himself. He takes off his unlaced shoes and loosens his tie.)

ILIJA: Is it true she found a job, or is she jumping the gun?

DANICA: It's true, thank God.

ILIJA: Well, then, to your health! And for something good to happen to me.

(Ilija drains most of his glass. What's left he pours on his injured knee. His wife looks at him, worried.)

DANICA: What happened, Ilija?

ILIJA: Be quiet. Don't ask. Did he return?

DANICA: No. Where did you fall?

ILIJA: In Dorćol.[15] *(He stands and pulls a small piece of paper from his pocket. He goes to the telephone, lifts the receiver, and dials a number.)* Hello . . . Inspector Dražić, please . . . You are . . . Yes . . . Hello . . . Comrade inspector, this is Ilija Čvorović. This morning I was at your place, in connection with that . . . Yes . . . Well, I want you to know he had a meeting in Zmaj - Jovino[16], an hour ago. Five of them. They exchanged dollars for marks and some sort of plans . . . I just happened to see them . . . Yes . . . Well, you know, it's not exactly nothing to me. He lives in my home . . . Yes . . . of course . . . Goodbye. *(He angrily puts down the receiver.)* These criminals. They're running loose right under his nose, exchanging foreign money and making plans, in the center of town, and all he can say is: "don't worry." He doesn't give a fuck that this guy lives under my roof. You should see what they look like, criminals, thugs, murderers. They pulled down the blind in the middle of a bright day, gathered around a table, took out a pile of bills, some papers, some plans, locked all the doors, bolted the gate. Is this the way friends gather? The way honest and honorable people act?

DANICA: How did you see all that?

ILIJA: Easy: I jumped over the neighbor's wall and climbed up to a balcony next to a lightning rod –

DANICA: Ilija, you poor man, are you alright?

---

[15] Pronounced - "Dor'-cho-lah," a section of Belgrade.

[16] Pronounced - "Zmy - yo'-vee-noh".

ILIJA: No, I'm not! Not when I have to deal with this! I wouldn't give a damn what he's doing, where they're meeting or what they're planning, if only that . . . that criminal didn't live in my house! Tomorrow, my name will be dragged through the news, when they report where he's been hiding out, making his plans. And he organizes it all. The others looked at him as if he was God. He talks, he explains, he orders – the others sit and listen.

DANICA: Calm down, Ilija. You need your medicine.

ILIJA: I have lived honorably and I will die honorably. He is not going to turn my life into shit, so that people can look at me and point their fingers. These are hostile groups, organized from outside the country. He's got plenty of money to bribe people with. And he's going to open a tailor shop – he can tell that story to his dead father.

DANICA: What's the matter with your leg? Did you break something?

ILIJA: No. I fell, as I was getting down. The lightning rod broke. Luckily, I fell on a bed of flowers. If I'd fallen on the pavement . . . I got all their license plates. And I can pick him out of a million. Oh, and it's an international gang; there was a black man there, too. When they left, they went one at a time. Our Tenant locked the gate. You realize that because he hides here, makes his plans here, they're going to think we are his accomplices.

DANICA: Do you want lunch?

ILIJA: Why do you ask? Don't I deserve it it? Well, fuck him. He doesn't know who he's dealing with. Their own mothers' milk will make them sick, using my house for their hideout. *(Danica brings out a plate of bread. Ilija shakes his head and continues to mutter threats to himself, as he breaks the crust and angrily chews.)*

3.
An Annual Vacation

(From the radio comes quiet, sleepy music. Sonja sits at the table, putting on her makeup. The doorbell rings. Sonja leaves her makeup, and goes into the hall. She is only wearing a short nightgown, so on the way, she puts on a house dress.)

SONJA: Please.
(The Tenant enters. He carries a bouquet of flowers. An eternally restrained, careful, and quiet man, he hands them to her. The girl looks at him, excitedly.)
TENANT: Congratulations on finding a job. A little late.
SONJA: Thank you. You didn't really go all the way into town just for flowers?
TENANT: I was just happy when I heard. I know what it's like to be out of work.
SONJA: The roses are divine. Thank you.
(The Tenant sits down, crosses his legs, and observes Sonja, who has been touched by his gift. She looks for a vase, finds one, and puts water in it.)
TENANT: I was on a trip. When I got back last night, your mother told me.
SONJA: Did she cry? *(The Tenant laughs, nodding his head in agreement.)* If I knew she was going to cry that much, I wouldn't have taken it. I want to treat you to something. Would you like a cognac?
TENANT: I shouldn't . . . but for this I can. How is the job?
SONJA: Great. I get to work with children, and it makes me sing. My colleagues look at me like I'm crazy. But I waited five years. I was at the end of my rope. I was thinking all kinds of things. If this hadn't turned up, I'd have gone to Libya.
TENANT: Libya?

SONJA: My boyfriend's a contractor and does some work, there. They have a clinic there, too. Please . . . I can talk to you . . . this day has begun so nicely for me.
(The Tenant rises, clicks his heels, as if he were saluting, and raises his glass.)
TENANT: To a long and successful job. *(They drink. The Tenant looks at the clock.)*
SONJA: Please stay a little longer . . . What is happening with your shop?
TENANT: It's beginning to come together, knock on wood. I purchased a share of the building on that property in Dorćol. And now, again they're lining up: council members, commissioners, planners, tradesmen. It's starting all over, but I'll endure it. I'm a born masochist.
SONJA: Does this mean you'll be leaving us soon?
TENANT: Maybe, a month or two, a year . . . two years. When I left for Paris, I was going to stay for one night, and I returned here – a year later. And then the most curious thing was that everyone asked me, "why have you come back?"
SONJA: Would you like some coffee?
TENANT: No thank you. I'm in a hurry.
SONJA: You're always in a hurry. Looking at the clock . . .
TENANT: The concept of rushing was invented by those of us who have nothing better to do. People who have jobs, sitting and working, they don't hurry anywhere. In Paris, I sat from morning till dusk behind my sewing machine. Here, the hurry-mania gets me. But I guess it takes more than rushing to be successful. Have you ever been to Paris?
SONJA: I haven't. I don't travel much. First, it wasn't possible, and now my boyfriend, Dragan, when he gets back from Libya, he won't want to go anywhere. He wants to build a house in some village. Anything I might want in a village I can find in Belgrade. But even Belgrade's getting boring to me. I'd love to go to Paris for two or three weeks.

(The man pulls a handful of keys from his pocket. He picks out two and sets them on the table.)
TENANT: Please, it's yours – a two-room flat. Stay two, three years.
SONJA: You're joking. I can't just take your keys. *(Getting suspicious.)* What is this apartment for? Huh? In case of a secret rendezvous?
TENANT: *(Laughing.)* No, it's for my son. He's a musician in New York. Paris was too small for him. An intelligent, good young man, but unfortunately, he inherited many of my traits. And in the end we quarreled. *(The Tenant becomes silent. He returns his glass to the tray. The girl observes him, expecting him to continue the story. The man gestures that it is all senseless and unimportant.)* You know, in families things move in a cycle, return to their origin. A friend of mine refers to it as "the heredity problem." I told you I left the university, where I studied philology without graduating. And I went to Paris, where I expected to become a world class poet. I thought I'd conquer the world writing modern poetry. I was dying of hunger and yet nearly all I did was write. I published two collections at my own expense.
SONJA: Nothing happened?
TENANT: Oh, yes, something happened, but it was just the opposite of what I'd intended. You see, I could only write what I liked to read. So, I became the most exquisite plagiarist. One day, nearly dead with hunger, I went to my brother's shop, who, up until then, I had despised. I sat behind a sewing machine and it all became clear: I am a really good tailor. Believe me, with linens, with wools, I can do anything. Before the war, my father ran a large tailor shop in Niš.[17] We did everything, the whole family, and we were all quite good at it, but I ran from it like the plague. I used to dream of setting that shop on fire. My father,

---

[17] Pronounced "Neesh.

my uncle, even my brother had to beat me to keep me working. Even when I was studying in Belgrade, if I saw a tailor's shop, I'd cross the street to avoid it. I thought it was wearing my family down, and I was afraid I would get trapped, entangled. Do you know why I'm telling you this?
SONJA: No, but I like listening to you.
TENANT: Everyone asks me about that apartment, thinking I'm using it for romantic adventures. But really, I'm hoping, eventually, my son will return. And yet, someday soon, I'm sure I'll hear from him: "I'm doing great, Dad. I opened a tailor's shop."
SONJA: Is that what you want?
TENANT: No, God help me. And yet, he is nearly tone deaf. He has just enough ability to fool himself into thinking he's a good musician. Of course, I watched him sew a button on a shirt once, too.
SONJA: A really good tailor?
TENANT: What a joke! He couldn't even hold the needle! Still, I've wanted to say to him: son, if you forget the trumpet, I'll buy you a sewing machine. But then I remember my father and the way he beat me. Before he died, I told him I was going to be a poet, and he lifted a little from his pillow, looked at me and said: "You idiot, don't you know all the good poems have already been written?"
SONJA: What do you think? Was he right? Here, have a little –
TENANT: No, no more, I must hurry.
SONJA: Alright, together, we'll both hurry. Cheers.
(Danica enters the house: She carries two rather large bags. She stops and observes her smiling daughter and the Tenant, with raised glasses.)
DANICA: Good morning.
(Sonja stands up, takes the bags from her mother.)
TENANT: Good morning.
DANICA: How are you?

SONJA: We're fine. We're in a hurry.

DANICA: Where are you going? *(Sonja laughs. She is playing with her confused mother, who isn't in on the joke.)* You've had a little to drink it seems. Have you been to the grocery store, lately?

TENANT: I've stopped in.

DANICA: Have you seen the prices? They're not normal! In one month everything went up 50%. These two bags cost two-hundred thousand dinars! Look what's in them. There's nothing in there that this should cost two-hundred thousand dinars! I want to know who's stealing my money? I hope somebody is keeping track of all this. This is terrible. The price of one detergent has gone up four times. And you know what's worse? People are grateful to even have detergent. That it's come to this.

SONJA: Sit down Mama, everything works out in the end. Sit.

DANICA: Don't say that. When you have your own home to run, then I'll ask you. Beans, three seventy-five. Soon they'll be selling them by the bean, the motherfuckers. This used to be a farmer's world. Cabbage, two-fifty. Where I came from, even if you couldn't take care of the fields, there was still beans and cabbage. There's no meat, no oil, no decent white light bulbs, only red ones, made for a whorehouse. There's no milk. Where are the cows? Have they all died? Are they on strike? *(The Tenant stands up. Sonja tries to keep him.)*

SONJA: Sit down –

TENANT: No, I really have to be going now.

DANICA: I always drive you away with my chatter. But I get so frustrated, I have to speak my mind.

TENANT: That's a problem we both have.

(Sonja returns the keys which the Tenant has offered her.)

SONJA: Please. When I decide to take a trip, I'll call you. And thank you for the flowers. Drop in this week, I'm working afternoons.

TENANT: Goodbye, Ma'am.

DANICA: Goodbye, goodbye.
(The Tenant leaves the house. Sonja shows him out, returns, and speaks to herself as if making a joke.)
SONJA: Too bad he isn't a little younger.
DANICA: What did you say?
SONJA: Nothing. I said he is a fine man.
(The doors of the bedroom opposite from the Tenant's open. Danica, frightened, stands next to her daughter. From the doors emerges Ilija. He is depressed, gloomy, and angry.)
DANICA: Ilija . . . You scared me . . . You went to work this morning. When did you come back? How did you get in the room?
ILIJA: Through the window.
DANICA: Through which window?
ILIJA: I know what I'm doing.
DANICA: What is all this, didn't you work today?
ILIJA: No. Tomorrow, neither. I'm taking my vacation for the year.
DANICA: You're doing what? What will you –
SONJA: He's probably going to build something in the yard again.
ILIJA: No, this time, I'm going to tear something down.
DANICA: You didn't tell me you were going to take a vacation.
ILIJA: If I'd told you, you'd just yap. You never shut your trap.
SONJA: Daddy . . .
ILIJA: What is it?
SONJA: How can you talk like that to Momma?
ILIJA: Because she deserves it. I've told her a hundred times not to say stupid, foolish things in front of people, and she just goes on yapping and yapping! She knows everything about everything, she has all knowledge. She can solve all the problems of the country. *(Ilija wants to keep "screaming", but stops to turn off the radio. He crosses to the window and looks out from behind the drapes. Satisfied that no one is snooping, he*

turns and continues tearing into his wife, who is petrified with fright.) The whole world grins and bears it, but she runs at the mouth and won't stop. She blabs all day long.

DANICA: Well. What did I say? I'm worried. It's so expensive. You don't do the shopping. Soon, you'll be screaming "where's the money?" Here, look, you just spent two-hundred thousand dinars! *(Ilija notices something suspicious. He moves the drapes, looks. Quickly he goes to the foyer, slips on laced shoes, and puts on a jacket.)*

ILIJA: You've been told. Just watch what you do. *(He leaves the house. Danica sits at the table.)*

DANICA: He insults me. He just insults me, screams and threatens.

SONJA: What is it with him?

DANICA: Sonja, ask our Tenant to move out, as soon as possible. Tell him you're getting married and that we're going to need his room. Tell him to go.

SONJA: Why? What happened?

DANICA: Will you tell him?

SONJA: I will, if you'll tell me. Mama, what happened?

DANICA: Nothing. It's nothing.

(Danica turns her head and looks at the floor. Sonja sits near her mother and silently watches her.)

4.
Counter-Espionage

(Danica sits at the kitchen table, peeling potatoes and as she does listens to the radio. A red bulb lights the room. The blurry, dim light bothers Danica.)

RADIO VOICE: . . . and that remains our greatest debt, our greatest duty. Our coverage of the news will return at 7:30. Now it is time for music to dance by from our series "The Music of Your Youth."

DANICA: Who's there?

(With the first sounds of a waltz, Ilija enters the house: He puts his umbrella in the corner, removes his shoes, and puts on his slippers, shakes his beret and hangs it on the clothes tree. He crosses to the table and looks at his wife. Against his chest, he has concealed a rather large object, which creates a bulge beneath his topcoat. His wife looks at him for a second, then returns to her potatoes.)

ILIJA: You're going to go blind under this light. Are there no white bulbs? *(Danica is silent, turning her head. Ilija squints, looking at the red bulb.)* It's like a whorehouse. You don't want to speak to me? Huh? Do you hear me? Danica? Answer me, don't just sulk! You don't even say "hello" to me. Like I'm some bum who just walked in! Danica! *(Ilija grabs one potato and lets it drop into the pan. Water splashes the grey-streaked woman who calmly, without speaking, wipes her face with the end of her apron. Ilija unbuttons his topcoat. On his chest hangs a rather large camera with telescopic lens. He removes the camera and sets it down on the table. He goes to turn off the radio.)* There's time. You'll talk to me. You won't be able to keep your mouth shut when you see these pictures. All day I thought, "maybe I am making a mistake, not being fair. I'm just imagining it." But today, when I saw what they were doing, how they got together and made their plans, it all came clear to me. I've recorded everything here. Twenty photographs. Now, when I testify, if they call me a liar, say I made it all up, I've got proof. Here it is in black and white. They lunched at the "Intercontinental" with two others. I've got pictures of them arriving, eating, talking.

DANICA: Did you have lunch today?

ILIJA: You can talk! I did. Why?

DANICA: So, he had to eat somewhere, too.

(Ilija is astonished: he doesn't know whether to laugh in desperation or to hit his wife.)

ILIJA: Oooo, I will fuck you with the hot sun, you're not normal! What do you think? I'm a fool, an idiot? Don't you find it suspicious where he chooses to eat, where he meets his friends? He went to lunch but he didn't eat. This meeting was just to exchange some plans. Afterwards, one of the others flew to London, taking everything with him. He walked right by the police and right through customs without inspection. He passed through without a trace of suspicion. But me? They saw me taking pictures, so they grabbed *me* and questioned *me*! There are thieves right under their noses, but they grab me! I'm always suspected of something. Listen to me, if you don't like what I'm doing, then you can pack up and leave. I got screwed once for believing in people, but never again. *(He crosses to the Tenant's door, tilts his head, trying to listen.)* They know what they're doing in the East, shutting down their borders, not letting somebody else's riff-raff wander freely through their country. That way they know who they're doing business with. *(He peeks through the keyhole.)* By the way, he spotted me at the airport. I told him I was picking up a friend from London. So, if he asks you . . . you know? In the meantime, he's destroying a marriage, having an affair with a journalist who has two children. He drove her to a friend's apartment. And why? Huh? Not for what you think. He's telling her what to write. At the same time, I'm sure they . . . well . . . you know . . . what you're thinking, but you'll

see what I mean about the article. I'll show it to you. She attacks everything living and dead. Of course, he snuck his own ideas in wherever he could. Just as he was ordered to do. Just as his handler planned. *(The telephone rings. Danica crosses to it, lifts the receiver.)*
DANICA: Yes . . . Who?. . . Please, which number did you call?. . . No, no you are mistaken . . . Yes . . . *(She puts the receiver down, and returns to the chair.)*
ILIJA: Who was that?
DANICA: Wrong number.
ILIJA: A man's voice?
DANICA: Yes.
ILIJA: Who'd he ask for?
DANICA: Who?
ILIJA: I'm asking you! Who was he trying to reach?
DANICA: Some Popović.
ILIJA: Popović?
DANICA: Yes.
(The man stares at his wife, smiles weakly and shakes his head.)
ILIJA: Oh, Danica, Danica, I knew that you were naive and –
DANICA: Stupid? Go ahead and say it, you've already said it a thousand times!
ILIJA: What else can I say when you act so abnormally? They were calling me!
DANICA: You?
ILIJA: Yes, me! They were checking to make sure I'm home. Today, he saw me at the airport, and last week in Košutnjak.[18] They were in a hurry, so they called to see if I would answer. If I answered, they'd say nothing, and they'd know they could do what they wanted. They'll call again, too. I am their biggest threat. I wouldn't be surprised if they show up here someday to take me out of the picture. *(The telephone rings. Danica recoils,*

---

[18] Pronounced "Ko-shoot-n-yak

dumbfounded. Ilija, with a triumphant look, smiles, shakes his omniscient head, and, slowly picks up the receiver.) What did I tell you? I knew it. To stay a step ahead of them, you have to know how they think and what they'll do. Hello?. . . Speak louder, I can't hear you . . . Yes . . . Who?. . . Did you call a little while ago? Yes, yes . . . That's right. The operator can make a mistake, but not a hundred times . . . Comrade, listen to what I'm telling you. The number may be wrong, but you got what you wanted anyway, didn't you? That's not clear to you? It will be clear, it will be! I will fuck each one of you, right down the line. I am talking to you! You remember what I'm telling you! You mangy . . . *(Ilija angrily slams down the receiver, crosses towards the table, stops suddenly and grabs his chest. Danica jumps up to help her husband. She leads him to the armchair.)*
DANICA: Is it your heart? Sit. What is it? Ilija?
ILIJA: I'm worn out. There must be a hundred of them . . . and I'm alone . . . I said they'd call again. They really get to me. I can't handle it all. I've had to run, to rush places. *(Danica brings his medicine from the bureau.)* They won't call me anymore. He's been suspecting me now, for ten days or so. He knows I'm on his trail. Listen, Danica, and remember, remember well, what I am about to say to you: if something happens to me, he did it. Either he or someone from his gang. I think they're preparing something ugly for me. *(He swallows his medicine without water. Danica sits on the arm of the chair, concerned about her tired husband. She puts her hands on his shoulders.)* Did you recognize who was calling?
DANICA: No.
ILIJA: It was his him, speaking through his sweater. He's going to try to get me out of the way, soon.
DANICA: "Get you out of the way?" What do you mean?
ILIJA: He's going to kill me.
DANICA: For God's sake, Ilija, what are you saying?

ILIJA: I'm saying what I know is true. So far, everything I thought would happen, has happened. I'm telling you, if I disappear for two-three days, you have to call the police and accuse him of murder. *(The doorbell rings. Danica, frightened, looks at her husband. He calmly signals to open the door. Danica goes into the foyer. Ilija crosses to the bureau and picks up a large knife. He hides it behind his back and peeks out into the corridor, from where he hears an unintelligible conversation. Danica is upset as she returns.)* Who was it?
DANICA: A beggar. I'm scared.
ILIJA: A beggar?
DANICA: I gave him ten dinars.
ILIJA: You're sure he was a beggar?
DANICA: He looked like one.
ILIJA: It's begun. They'll visit us now as beggars, umbrella salesmen, farmers with cream, people looking for an address. Our house will be under surveillance. Someone will be on duty, round the clock, ready to let him know whenever we leave the house. They'll try everything they can to neutralize me, but I'm afraid they've fucked themselves. They're prepared for anything – except me. We're going to have it out, my friend, and we'll see who gets killed. We will sell our lives dearly. I don't have to do this alone, do I? I'll get my brother. *(Ilija dials the telephone.)* Hello Đura . . . Get over here . . . Right away, it's important . . . I can't on the phone . . . Yes . . . Uh, I can't . . . It isn't that . . . Just come . . . Hurry! *(He puts down the receiver.)* Have you told anyone anything?
DANICA: No.
ILIJA: Not Sonja?
DANICA: No.
ILIJA: Well, don't! I'll tell Đura, just in case anything happens to me. He'll always be here to help you. Do we have beer?
DANICA: No, there's wine.

ILIJA: He drinks beer. Get me the bottles. If it's not too much trouble, make some cheese streudel.

DANICA: It's not safe for you. Where are you going? Here, here. *(She gets the beer bottles from the bureau and puts them in a bag.)* Buy a little sausage and cheese too. Oh, I almost forgot: Your boss, Dragoslav[19] called and asked when you'd be returning to work?

ILIJA: I don't know. When my vacation comes to an end. If I have to, I'll take sick leave. This is the most important thing right now. Lock the door and don't open it until you hear who's there. Both locks. They could be after you as well. I worry about Sonja. I thought I'd give her money to take some trip. Get her out of here, until this is over.

DANICA: She just started to work.

ILIJA: We'll discuss it. Come on, lock the door. *(Ilija leaves the house. Danica locks the door, twice.)*

---

[19] Pronounced "Drah-go-slahv."

5.
Attempted Murder

(That same night, a half hour later. While Danica prepares the table for dinner, she keeps an eye on the pastry rolls she is baking. A muffled knocking is heard at the door. Danica is frightened as she crosses into the corridor.)

DANICA: Who is it? Who is it? *(From outside is heard the sound of Ilija's "It's me!" Danica opens the door and screams. Ilija enters the room with his face and hands covered in blood. His clothing has been torn. He is missing his right shoe. He falls into the armchair, almost unconscious. Danica lifts her arms as if to resist the horror.)* Ilija!
ILIJA: Just as I thought.
DANICA: Oh, dear God. Should I call an ambulance?
ILIJA: What did I tell you half an hour ago? I told you he'd try to kill me. Don't call anyone. I'm OK. Fuck that shitbag's mother! My whole life they've been trying to kill me. My whole life.
DANICA: Well, they haven't really . . . *(Danica, flutters around her husband, takes his jacket, and wipes his face with a handkerchief.)*
ILIJA: Give me some brandy. Đura's not here? I just hope they didn't get him too. He carries a pistol, but that's no good when they attack you from behind. I knew it. I didn't expect it again today. Liquidation, murder, assassination – one right after the other. That's the western system. They don't have prison camps, they don't have anyone left to lock up. Instead of camps, they have graves. In the war, they wounded me, after the war they imprisoned me, now they are trying to murder me. *(Danica gives him a bottle of brandy, thinking that her husband will drink, but he holds out his hands.)* Pour it. Disinfect, more, more. They'll return. If we don't fight, they'll kill us all.

(Danica pours the brandy, Ilija splashes his face, jumps up and screams in pain. Danica pulls the white tablecloth from the table and gives it to her husband, who applies the linen to his face. Danica cries and holds her "blind" husband. Finally, Ilija calms down and sits, takes a swig of the brandy from the bottle, takes out a cigarette and with trembling hands, begins to smoke.)

DANICA: What happened?

ILIJA: He ran me down in front of the supermarket. I tried to avoid him, but he turned straight for me. It was my luck thatbefore he reached me, he grazed this van.

DANICA: Was he in the car?

ILIJA: Who?

DANICA: Our Tenant.

ILIJA: No, it was one of his men. He doesn't do the killing, himself. I didn't think he would. He just funds it and organizes it. The others kill. This one that hit me, I think he's in one of the photographs.

DANICA: Did he run away?

ILIJA: He would have if he could have, but instead he's in the hospital. I was just crossing the street, and he drives right at me, catches my leg, then bounces off the van and crashes into a wall. The police came and I had a real fight with them. They hassled me, said I was jaywalking. This guy tries to kill me and I'm the one who's guilty. I guess I'll be guilty as long as I live.

DANICA: Were you jaywalking?

ILIJA: Sure, but that's not important! He was going to hit me even if I if was on the sidewalk. He was parked there, waiting for me, and when he saw me step into the street, he drove straight at me. While they were putting him in the ambulance, I told him, "I'm going to drink your blood for this. Sooner or later, you'll pay with your head."

DANICA: Didn't they want you to go to the hospital too?

ILIJA: Yeah, but I wouldn't let that happen. I've crossed myself off as if I didn't exist. They can't do anything to me. Has that bastard been here?

DANICA: No. He told Sonja that he was going to Niš to visit his aunt.

ILIJA: Then by Sunday, I'll be in Niš, too. I'll go see just what kind of home bred such a criminal. That must be where he grew up. *(The doorbell rings. Danica goes to answer it, but Ilija stops her. He takes the knife from the bureau and crosses to open the door. He returns with his twin brother, Đura. Đura is a small, stocky, bow-legged man in a black worn-out suit. He is petrified, frozen, as he observes his unfortunate brother. He carries a pound of coffee and a several packages of toilet paper.)*

ILIJA: Come in.

DANICA: Hello, Đura.

ĐURA: Poor Ilija. What is it?

ILIJA: Nothing. Put that down. Sit.

ĐURA: Where did it happen?

ILIJA: In front of the market, a little while ago. A car hit me.

ĐURA: Ooh! Did you break something?

ILIJA: I don't think so. My shoulder hurts a little, my head aches. Sit.

ĐURA: You should go to the hospital, get an x-ray. Who knows what might be wrong. Get ready, I'll take you.

ILIJA: No, it's nothing. He just caught me across the knees and I ended up on the sidewalk. Sit. I was lucky that a passerby cushioned my fall.

ĐURA: You could have been killed.

ILIJA: I still could be. This is just the beginning. That's why I called. If something happens to me, I need you to look after my family. I don't want them to be alone in the world.

(Đura looks first at his brother, then his sister-in-law. He is still holding the gifts. Ilija pulls up a chair for him to sit.)

ĐURA: I can't sit down when I see you in such a way. Why is she crying?
ILIJA: I can't tell you until you sit down. I can't explain it all in just a few words. Give him some brandy. Crying doesn't help. What did you bring? You shouldn't have. Sorry about this light, the white one burned out. Sit.
ĐURA: Danica, what's happened? Will someone tell me? Why are you crying?
DANICA: Ilija will tell you. Sit Đura, listen to him. You are reasonable. You tell him what he should do.
(Danica pours brandy into a glass. Đura finally sits, but immediately stands again: from his back pocket he pulls a pistol, which bothers him – he transfers it to an inside pocket of his jacket.)
ILIJA: Cheers! All kinds of evil can find a man. You never know what a day will bring, or the night will bring, but this . . . I just can't think straight. A great evil has found me.
ĐURA: Are you sick?
ILIJA: I should be so lucky.
ĐURA: Tell me already, I'm in a cold sweat.
ILIJA: You know we have a Tenant.
ĐURA: I know. I heard from Sonja.
ILIJA: Are the pastries burning?
DANICA: They're fine.
ILIJA: Well, you see, he moved in eight months ago. And everything's been peaceful, on the surface at any rate: good day - good day, hello – hello. He there, we here. He has his own entrance. We almost never see him. Anyway, he looked suspicious to me from day one: always hiding something, sneaking, inviting these dark figures and tramps into his room, going out for walks at all hours of the night. *(Ilija cautiously stands, crosses to the Tenant's door, puts his glass against the door, and his ear against the glass, trying to listen in. Then he crosses to the bureau and turns on the radio. He turns the music*

up louder. He returns and sits across from his brother.) Sorry we don't have any beer. When he hit me, he broke all the bottles. A month ago or so, I received a call from the police.
ĐURA: From the police? What did they want?
ILIJA: I'll tell you everything. First I thought they called because of me. You yourself know that when you've done time, you're never at peace. You think someone is always checking up on you. And I knew I hadn't done anything. But I thought, with this world in such a situation – well, a lot's been written about that.
ĐURA: Did they mention me?
ILIJA: Why you?
ĐURA: Well, because of prison. If they've called you, they'll probably call me.
DANICA: Tell him what's happened. Your only avoiding the -
ILIJA: Will you shut up? When I said we didn't need a Tenant, you wanted to pluck out my eyes.
ĐURA: Ilija! Are you going to tell me what happened?!
ILIJA: I will, if she'll let me talk. Not another word! She knows everything! So, I went to the police, I greet them. Good day - good day, you are so and so, I am so and so. Danica, turn up the radio, someone could hear us . . .

(As the music on the radio drowns out Ilija's story, Đura numbly stares at him.)

ACT II

6.
Brothers

(It is nearly dawn. Danica sits in the armchair, drowsy, tired, worn out. Ilija pours another drink for Đura, who paces, patrolling the room.)

ILIJA: There. I've been talking all night, and I've only begun. When you see the pictures, it will all be clear.
(Đura stops, looks through the window, and rocks on his heels. He crosses to Danica and puts his hand on her shoulders.)
ĐURA: Danica, go, lie down. Don't torture yourself.
(Danica rises, turns, and heads towards the door.)
DANICA: Do you need anything?
ĐURA: You just rest. We've got this covered.
(Danica exits into her bedroom. She shuts the door. Đura returns to the window, and silently looks outside. Ilija is impatient. He fidgets and looks at his brother, who is lost in thought.)
ILIJA: Well, what do you say?
ĐURA: Nothing.
ILIJA: How "nothing"?
ĐURA: Easy. Nothing. What am I supposed to say? You've been acting like I'm your enemy, lately. Why'd you call me now?
ILIJA: Well –
ĐURA: If "something happens" to you, I am supposed to take care of Danica and Sonja? You should talk to my Smiljka.[20] She'll help them. But I swear, I'm ready to walk out of here and never come back. You know how you've been treating me? Like I was a distant aunt or something, instead of a twin brother. That's bullshit, Ilija.!

---

[20] Pronounced "Smeel-ka."

ILIJA: I thought –

ĐURA: What did you think? What did you think? Ah, Ilija . . . I don't know what to say to you. For the last month your head's been in a bag. I sensed that something had happened, that something's not right. I call, I ask questions, I get in touch, you lie, Sonja lies, everyone's lying, and I start to think something evil must have happened to you. Fuck it all, if we've come to the point where you have to hide from your own family. If that's the way it is, let's just put an end to it, each to his own life. But then what would I tell everyone? That you've been ruined? That I know nothing about my own brother? Here you are, dragging me into this situation, with me completely in the dark. Why couldn't you come to me as soon as you knew and tell me it's like this and that, then we coulda got organized. All I can say is thank God you've got me to break this shit up. How could you think of starting a war on a gang of imperialist pigs like this all by yourself, and hiding it from me?

ILIJA: Đura, brother . . . I didn't think . . . I wanted . . . *(Ilija stands, crosses to his brother, spreads his hands helplessly. He is silent. They look at each other. They hug, as if they hadn't seen each other for a hundred years. The reconciliation is interrupted by the sound of the doorbell. Ilija peeks into the corridor, and turns. Đura takes out his pistol and cocks it. He motions to his hesitant brother. Prepared for anything, he crosses towards the corridor. From outside we hear the sounds of Sonja's voice.)* Sonja doesn't know anything. Not a word in front of her.

(Đura unlocks the door. Sonja enters smiling, in a good mood. Đura hides his pistol behind his back and sticks it in his belt after Sonja passes.)

SONJA: Good morning, Uncle Đura.

ILIJA: Where've you been all night?

SONJA: I was on call.

ĐURA: Ilija, drive me home. I need to get some things.

ILIJA: Of course. And I've got work in town. Don't wake your mother, she didn't sleep all night. Her gout was acting up.

ĐURA: Bye, Sonja. I'll see you later. Come on, Ilija.

(The brothers hurriedly leave the house. Sonja waits for the car to leave, following them through the window. She then crosses to the telephone and a dials a number.)

SONJA: Please, can you get Peter . . . Yes . . . You're so kind . . . Hello . . . I am well, never better . . . Maybe . . . *(She smiles.)* Yes . . . I'll take you to lunch . . . Why? Because I'd like to have lunch with you. If you want I can invent another reason. *(The door to the bedroom opens. Tired, exhausted, and sleepy, Danica listens to her daughter's conversation.)* Can I drop by?. . . It won't be too uncomfortable? *(Smiling)* OK . . . Bye . . . Hey! Bring those books . . . Yes . . . Bye . . .

(Sonja hangs up and turns.)

DANICA: Who were you talking to?

SONJA: Did I wake you? I'm sorry . . .

DANICA: Never mind me. I asked: Who were you talking to?

SONJA: Mama, what is it?

(Danica returns to her room. She stops at the door, turns and says with scorn and disgust.)

DANICA: It's a disgrace. I'm ashamed of you. He's old enough to be your father. *(Danica closes the door.)*

7.
Everything is Contrary to How it Appears

(Ilija has set up a screen and plugged in a small projector next to the chairs as if in a movie theater. He shows Danica and Đura to their seats. He turns off the red light and returns to the projector.)

ILIJA: Now you'll see who's in this mafia, where they meet, and how they are organized. *(The screen lights up and the FIRST SLIDE appears. It is the Tenant, with a man and a woman, walking along the river front. Ilija reads his information from a rather large notebook. Đura takes notes.)* Gypsy Island, March 5, at 11:20 AM. I took these pictures from the car while I was driving, because it was a clear shot. Danica, what would you say if someone showed you this picture, and you didn't know what they were doing?
DANICA: Nothing. People walking.
ĐURA: That would be what my Smiljka would say, too.
ILIJA: Đura, anyone who's not familiar with the world of espionage would say that. You notice nothing. They do whatever they want, they make their plans right in front of you. You're simply blind and deaf. In this work there is one basic rule: everything is contrary to the way it appears. Danica, what would you say, if you met that man on the street, who is he?
DANICA: Well . . . just a man . . . .
ILIJA: A clerk, an employee, a teacher. But he is a scientist who works in Vinča.[21]
ĐURA: In Vinča? *(Clucks his tongue.)* Now it's all clear to me.
ILIJA: Do you know what Vinča is? Danica?
DANICA: I've heard of it.

---

[21] Pronounced "Veen-cha."

ILIJA: You've heard of Vinča, like you've heard of the Taj Mahal.[22] Vinča is our biggest nuclear plant.

ĐURA: The powers-that-be have hidden that place beneath impassable mountains, one hundred meters underground. This is a top state secret, for everyone – except us.

ILIJA: The scientist and the spy walk together, sharing stories.

ĐURA: No one watches this scientist to see who he meets with, comrade?

DANICA: And who is the woman?

ILIJA: The scientist's lover. Also a mother of two children. *(SECOND SLIDE. The Tenant, the scientist, and the lover lunch together at one of the boat restaurants. The scientist holds a rather large piece of paper, which the Tenant carefully inspects, leaning in a little. The lover converses with the waiter.)* Same day, two hours later. The scientist is showing him the Vinča plan. He explained it for half an hour. Our Tenant just watched and listened. In their training, these terrorists and spies are taught to remember everything. There are some who, after only one reading, can memorize ten pages of tiny written text.

DANICA: And the waiter?

ILIJA: What . . . the waiter?

DANICA: There is a waiter.

ILIJA: Yes, of course there is. They work in public like this so it won't look suspicious. Just like this – the people sitting, having lunch and chatting. What spy would have a meeting in such a public place? Remember, I said: Everything is contrary to the way it appears. After they studied the plan well, the scientist crumpled it up and threw it in the river. As if it was just an ordinary piece of paper. After all, burning it would have drawn too much attention. Instead, they throw it away like an empty

---

[22] In the original, Kovačević uses the "Tosin well." I'm told this refers to a tourist site in Belgrade with no great significance. The point is that Danica doesn't recognize the implications that can be drawn from Vinča.

box of tobacco. *(THIRD SLIDE. The crumpled piece of paper floating in the Sava River.)* The river then carried the plan towards the tip of the island. I followed it and next to one little houseboat, I went down into the water, and just as I was about to grab it, twenty meters from the shore, some cretin in a boat comes and runs right over it. The paper was gone.
DANICA: Ilija! You went swimming in March?
ILIJA: Of course I did. I would have plunged into a kettle of boiling water for that kind of proof. *(FOURTH SLIDE. The Tenant, the scientist, the lover and another woman, enter the National Theatre.)* That night they went to the opera, and the Tenant's girlfriend, the journalist, joined them. He's surrounded, you see, by people of such importance. These are not ordinary people. Anybody he shakes hands with is a well-known someone or something. There are spies all around us. We just need to know how to recognize them. Now, when I see one, I know exactly what he is. When they entered, I bought a ticket and followed them. Their seats were in the orchestra. I was in the balcony.
DANICA: You went to the opera?
ILIJA: Yes.
DANICA: What did you see?
ILIJA: Them. The opera didn't matter!
ĐURA: What a man has to endure because of these criminals.
ILIJA: I wondered why they went to the opera, but when the performance began, I understood everything; there, they could whisper in peace because on stage they never stop bellowing. But the real reason they were there, I learned during intermission. *(FIFTH SLIDE. The four of them, looking suspicious alright, in the lobby conversing with another three visitors – two men and a woman. Đura points his finger at one of the new people.)*
ĐURA: I know him!
ILIJA: Doctor Stanisavljcvić.[23] A surgeon.

ĐURA: Do you know him too?
ILIJA: I've learned a lot about him.
ĐURA: He operated on me.
ILIJA: And that man is a professor from the Philosophy Department. This is the professor's lover.
DANICA: They all have lovers?
ILIJA: All of them.
DANICA: If they'll betray their wives, why not their country? My God, my God, what kind of people are they?
ILIJA: I took pictures of them on the steps, from behind a pole. When you see them like this, you might say they met by chance. I mean, they pretended to be surprised and, then kissed one another. Why would that shitass get kissed by a professor and a doctor? How are they connected? Why did they meet there? What did they talk about? The latest style of underwear?
ĐURA: Leave the doctor to me. He lives in my district.
ILIJA: Of course, they stayed through the end of the performance so it wouldn't look suspicious. *(SIXTH SLIDE. The whole group from the theatre is in a cafe. They are seen in the middle of a toast, holding their glasses up.)* Afterwards, they went to The Three Hats,[24] which was where they were headed all along. The opera was just a diversion, so later they could go to the café without being seen. They didn't plan on having me to deal with.
DANICA: Who paid for all that? Lunch on the island, dinner at The Three Hats.
ĐURA: Whoever he's working for. The CIA, probably the CIA. They've destroyed half the world!
ILIJA: That's the last picture I got that night. Some horse of a waiter kicked me out. He thought I was a street photographer. That's how we protect spies in this country. Anyway, they split up around two in the morning. They pretended to be drunk. As

---

[23] Pronounced "Sta-ni-sahv-lee-ya-veech."

[24] A very popular, traditional Serbian restaurant with outdoor seating.

they left, the Tenant and the scientist hugged again. What a diabetic! He drank and ate like an animal. He's lied to us about everything.

DANICA: What do they have to do with Vinča? Do the people in Vinča know anything?

ILIJA: They're going to. I've written to warn them. They need to secure their defenses, to tighten their controls of the installation and the people there. I told them to be on the lookout for sabotage. *(SEVENTH SLIDE. The Tenant, the scientist, and the doctor, in hunting garb, with rifles "at ready", walking through expansive fields. A bird dog runs in front of them.)* Sunday, March, 7, in the fields below Kosmaj,[25] he leads them out for a military drill pretending it was a pheasant hunt. First: They shot at things all day long, but killed nothing. Clearly, they were there just to practice. They weren't hunting. Next: They worked on their conditioning; they must have walked fifteen, twenty kilometers. Third: They broke up into groups of three. Everybody knows that's the general operating procedure for saboteurs. And fourth: The whole point of this day's outing was to get more familiar with the terrain around Belgrade. Today, he hunts here; tomorrow, he hunts there; the day after, somewhere else. Little by little, hunt after hunt, they learn what they need to know about Serbia. They see what's going on, what people are planning, and they speak with villagers about the mood of the country.

(EIGHTH SLIDE. An angry dog, baring his teeth.)

ĐURA: What is this? Did he attack you?

ILIJA: He did. I followed them about a hundred meters behind. And I was hiding in this bush when this dog turned and came straight towards me. There was nothing to do. He couldn't do anything to me. I could have smothered him like a chicken, but I was afraid to blow my cover. So I escaped by squatting low to

---

[25] Pronounced "Koh'-smigh."

the ground and rushing through the woods. Of course, they shot at me. I plunged into some ravine, through a stream, I had water up to my neck. Finally, I got away on the other side. They must have shot at me for half an hour.

DANICA: Ilija, they could have killed you.

ĐURA: They wanted to, I'm sure. They can't charge you with murder, you know, if it happens during a hunt. And there is no hunting without murder. It's just all written off as an unfortunate accident. In our village, if you hated somebody, you invited him to hunt. That's how it used to be. In those days, we killed one rabbit for every two villagers. Eventually, our village got hunted out. What we saw then!

ILIJA: I remember.

ĐURA: When the hunters came back from the hunt, all the kids, we'd run into the street to wait for them. First, three or four of them came along, carrying hares and pheasants on their belts, and then came the car carrying the dead hunters. Always more hunters than there was hares and pheasants. And they knew exactly which year to hunt which family. Do you remember when the Marković[26] family invited the Babić[27] family to hunt for wild boar?

ILIJA: In November, 1948. It divided the village – for and against.[28]

ĐURA: They all go out one morning, and in the evening the Marković's returned with one pig and all the Babić's. They said it was an accident, a wayward shot. How did one shot kill five people? But the next winter, the Babić's went hunting for wild geese, and they killed one goose and six Marković's. What is that?

---

[26] Pronounced "Mar'-ko-veech."
[27] Pronounced "Bah'-beech."
[28] Thinly veiled reference to those who believed Tito should line up with Stalin (including Ilija and Đura) and those who approved of his break from the Soviet hegemony.

(NINTH SLIDE. The Tenant is leaving the French Embassy with another man.)
ILIJA: It's the next day, around noon. At the French Embassy. He stayed for half an hour. Went into the Embassy carrying a bag and, as you see, he came out without one. Everything was delivered to the French secret service. Facts are transmitted by diplomatic channels to Paris, and from Paris to Washington, those cowboys. Fascism is child's play next to these criminals.
(Ilija turns off the projector, turns on the light. Đura stands, putting his hands behind his back. He walks, thinking. Danica dares to remind him.)
DANICA: Đura, you'll be late for work.
ĐURA: Don't worry, I'm on sick leave. Listen Ilija, we need to discuss this, seriously, the two of us. This isn't the best way to go about this. All these pictures, you can send them to him as a memento. You don't have any material evidence. You have nothing tangible to back-up those pictures. And, what's more, what are you doing? You attacked a murderer with a camera! If you ask me, we should have grabbed him, by now.
(The doorbell rings.)
ILIJA: See who it is!
DANICA: I don't dare.
ILIJA: Go see! Why be afraid with us here? *(Danica exits to the foyer. We hear her unlock the door and a garbled dialogue. Ilija takes out a knife and Đura draws his pistol. They move forward. Danica returns – petrified with fear.)* Who was it?
DANICA: Some man. He was looking for the Davidović[29] family. He said they live on our street.
ILIJA: There is no Davidović on our street.
DANICA: That's what I thought.
ILIJA: Give me the pistol. I know who he's looking for. *(Ilija grabs the pistol, cocks it and exits into the hall. We hear his*

---

[29] Pronounced Dah'-vee-do-veech."

furious voice.) Who do you want? Listen friend, if one more of you enter my yard I will start shooting without thinking! Now get out! Get out! What, are you threatening me? Stay! Stop! *(Two shots ring out. Danica shrinks, goes to Đura, who hugs her, calmingly, patting her on the shoulder. Ilija returns, firmly holding his pistol.)* He'll think again before spying on me. Undoubtedly, they're preparing something.
ĐURA: Let's go Ilija! Hurry, I'll take care of him.
DANICA: Where are you going?
ILIJA: Go to bed, sleep.
ĐURA: Sister, call Smiljka. Tell her not to wait up for me.
ILIJA: Lock the door well.
(Ilija and Đura quickly leave the house. From the yard, sounds are heard of the car starting and pulling away, Danica dials a number on the phone.)
DANICA: Sonja. . . Please come see me . . . If you can, immediately, please . . . Yes . . . As soon as you finish work, come straight here.

8.
A Discussion About Father

(Danica and Sonja are sitting at the table at the end of a long conversation. They are silent. Sonja is observing her tired and tortured mother. From the yard, we hear a barking dog.)

SONJA: I can't believe . . . How long has this been going on?
DANICA: What?
SONJA: Well this, with our Tenant and all this spying?
DANICA: Forty days . . . feels like forty years.
SONJA: Daddy doesn't go to work anymore? Is he on sick leave?
DANICA: No. Now he's just not getting paid, but Đura is still on sick leave.
SONJA: Why doesn't he retire? He could have retired five-six years ago.
DANICA: And what would we live on? Do you know how much his pension would be? It used to be he'd never admit to being sick. We were already in debt up to here, and now, even more so. Everything is financed. Our debt is over five million dinars.
SONJA: Because of this?
DANICA: Yes. First, he bought a camera with a telephoto lens. Then, a slide projector and a tape recorder. For the German Shepard, he paid eight thousand.
SONJA: For that mutt in the yard?
DANICA: That is a trained, thoroughbred dog. Đura got him through his connections.
SONJA: Why did he go to Niš?
DANICA: To visit our Tenant's family. He learned that his father and brother were in prison, after the war. He's gone to find out why. He thinks the whole family are criminals.
SONJA: Is Đura with him?
DANICA: No. Đura stayed to tail our Tenant and to get another loan. They're going, next week, to Paris. *(Sonja lights a cigarette.*

Her mother looks at her worriedly.) Why is your hand shaking? Are you tired?
SONJA: A little. I have work.
DANICA: Look. He's strictly forbidden me to tell you, but I couldn't endure it any longer. I was ready to crack.
SONJA: Mama, what do you think of all this? *(Danica shrugs her shoulders, helplessly and anxiously.)* We can't get Daddy to a doctor, can we?
DANICA: Because of his heart?
SONJA: I'd tell him it was because of his heart.
DANICA: But it would be . . . ?
SONJA: Because of his head.
(Danica stares at her daughter, surprised and perplexed.)
DANICA: What do you mean, "because of his head"?
SONJA: He'd go to see the cardiologist "because of his heart," but I'd get a psychiatrist friend to examine him, too. Daddy wouldn't even notice.
DANICA: And?
SONJA: And – he could get treated.
DANICA: For his heart?
SONJA: Mama . . .
DANICA: Tell me quickly and clearly what it is he would be treated for?
SONJA: Do I have to explain it all to you as if you were a little child? He's had a nervous breakdown. He's gotten it into his head to drive our Tenant away, in fact he is driving him away. And tailing people he doesn't even know. He doesn't go to work, he's going into debt, he's buying stupid things, hauling in useless equipment and dogs. He'll kill someone. He'll end up in a mental hospital. It's urgent that he gets treatment.
(Danica stands up. She observes her daughter calmly, coldly.)
DANICA: You think your father is going crazy? *(Sonja is silent.)* You hear me? Do you think your father is going crazy?
SONJA: I think he is.

DANICA: A crazy father?
SONJA: Yes. And it's going to get worse.
DANICA: Then, if that's what you think, we have nothing else to say. I called you to help him, to advise him what to do, how to be done with all of this. And you, you want to put him in an asylum, to declare him insane. They'll tie him up and keep him with people who *are* crazy! You want –
SONJA: Mama –
DANICA: You want to humiliate him, to laugh at him, see his friends deny him. So, his family will talk about how Ilija went crazy. And I know why you're doing this! Don't think I don't know! Now I believe Ilija even more, you see? Did you have lunch with this criminal on Thursday?
SONJA: Yes . . . and you know what?
DANICA: We know everything my dear child. We know that the two of you have been secretly planning something for months.
SONJA: You're not serious. Mama, please, be reasonable. He invited me and Dragan to lunch on Thursday, but Dragan couldn't come because –
DANICA: Because you didn't tell him.
SONJA: I told him.
DANICA: You did not tell him!
SONJA: Well . . . no.
DANICA: Don't lie to me!
SONJA: He invited me to lunch to ask me what was going on here. He said some strange things had been happening. I didn't know what to tell him.
DANICA: And now you'll tell him everything?
SONJA: No, as long as father stops tailing him and trying to scare him away.
DANICA: If we leave him in peace, he'll carry out his plans. He might destroy the whole country. Sonja, let me ask you something. Do you think your father is corrupt, evil?
SONJA: I don't think that. I never said that.

DANICA: Has he ever done something bad to anyone? Hasn't he gone out of his way to help everyone who needs it, even people he'd only just met? Hasn't he always done that from his heart, without a trace of dishonesty?

SONJA: Yes.

DANICA: It's nice of you to acknowledge that much, at least. While he worried about us, about the house, about your education and your job situation, then he was sane, but now, when he's worried about all people, because you don't get anything out of it, now he is crazy. He's supported you for five years without complaining. Not even once! And now, as soon as you begin making your own money, you want to thank him by shutting him up in an asylum. What do you think will happen to his heart when he learns that you've fooled him into taking a psychiatric examination! He'd die in an instant from such torment. I don't know what you've got going with this criminal, let your shithead boyfriend worry about that, but I warn you, if you talk to him again, you're not to say a word about any of this.

SONJA: Mama –

DANICA: If you say one word to him, you'll never be welcome here again. Don't even call me. Your father's had a very difficult life. He's lived like a dog for ages, working his butt off.[30] He's endured insults, humiliation. Never complains. Never feels sorry for himself. He's used to the torment, the suffering. But right now, he's facing his most difficult struggle, a struggle for others, for his country, his people. You realize he may be killed? It's him and Đura up against hundreds. His greatest support must come from this house. No one attacks him here, you understand? Only the dog. Your father is sacred to me, like God, and if sometimes he makes a mistake, it's only because he wants what's best for people.

---

[30] In the original, Danica uses a derogatory term here, meaning "black person," referring to the Gypsies.

(Sonja gathers her things, puts her lighter and cigarettes into her bag. She pulls out a rather large piece of paper. Apathetically, miserably, she shows it to her mother.)

SONJA: You haven't seen my marriage certificate.

DANICA: I haven't and I won't.

SONJA: Is it that you think Dragan's family came to the wedding?

DANICA: I know they didn't.

SONJA: Only the witnesses were there.

DANICA: Dragan certainly wanted to invite all of us.

SONJA: Yes.

DANICA: But you didn't.

SONJA: I don't like ceremonies.

DANICA: Well, evidently there's something else you don't like.

SONJA: What?

DANICA: Your father. You think he's mad. You've been thinking that for a while now. I've seen you watch over him, check him out. That's why you didn't invite us. You were afraid he might do something crazy at your wedding, and that Dragan's family might worry. Because if the grandfather's crazy, who knows how the grandchildren will turn out? That's why you didn't call us . . . even though you said you didn't want to plan the wedding meal without us. All right, child, all right, keep it simple, maybe you think we didn't deserve to be there. Only, you're going to regret it bitterly when you realize your father's been right, and how much suffering and torment he's gone through. Bitterly you'll repent, but it'll be too late. And Sonja, I beg you don't get too close to these criminals. Your father has enough evidence to put them in prison. And the last thing I want to say is that he knows why you've avoided us, yet he swallows that poison in silence, getting out of your way like he owes it to you, as if you didn't owe him a thing. Your father is a great man. I knew that from the beginning. What I didn't know was that you could be so small, so miserable and so lost! *(Sonja grabs her purse, looks back at the house as if she forgot something, bursting into tears, she rushes outside, crying. In the yard, she is greeted by the barking dog.)*

9.
From Bad to Worse

(Danica helps her husband out of his overcoat. Ilija is tired, but content after visiting Niš.)

DANICA: I haven't slept a wink. You could have called. What happened in Niš? Why were you there so long?
ILIJA: Turns out I didn't even have to go. I already knew everything. Give me some brandy. Not from the bureau. I have a bottle in my bag. I brought some of his uncle's homemade batch. Has Đura been here?
DANICA: He dropped by last night for twine.
ILIJA: What kind of twine?
DANICA: Clothesline. He came at midnight, took the twine and ran off. He was crazed that you hadn't called. You know that dog barks and attacks everything that moves. Bloodthirsty.
ILIJA: He's a purebred. His grandaddy was a border guard.
DANICA: *(Clucking her tongue.)* His grandaddy guarded the country and now he's betrayed it.
ILIJA: The grandaddy of the dog. The dog's grandaddy.
DANICA: Well, at least you returned safe and sound.
ILIJA: To tell the truth, it wasn't that easy. And yet, his uncle is an uncommonly fine man. He welcomed me like I was a close relative. He told me everything. His family quarreled in 1946. There was a trial.
DANICA: The uncle was on trial?
ILIJA: No, the uncle testified and exposed them. *(Takes a sip.)* Homemade brandy. The Tenant's father and his brother, those dogs, collaborated with the Germans. They betrayed our country. They sewed clothes for them. His father was in prison for six and a half years, and his brother for four. I don't have proof that they sewed uniforms, but that's what his uncle said. As soon as his father got out, he escaped to Greece, and then from Greece to

France. The uncle swears he took at least ten kilos of gold. That's how he could afford to open his shop. Another rotten capitalist. And he didn't leave the uncle a cent. I knew trash like our Tenant must have come from a house of thieves. He couldn't have become a great criminal spontaneously on his own; he must have inherited something. It's all blood and upbringing. That trait doesn't come from money or coercion; one has to be born, raised and taught to be trash, a traitor, and a criminal. Then the money starts to come. That's what I was thinking before I went there. But it's even worse.

DANICA: Terrible. Just let somebody try and tell me you're wrong, now.

ILIJA: Who would say that?

DANICA: Anybody. How did you get him to talk to you?

ILIJA: I pretended I was a newspaper reporter. I said that I wrote a column about domestic spying. When he heard that, he invited me into the house, and brought out pictures and newspaper articles about the trial, one thing after another. The aunt was a problem, however. She said none of it was true – she's always taken our Tenant's side – but the uncle chased her out of the house. We talked two nights and two days without stopping. When I was leaving, he said to me: "For money, he'll betray us, our country, the whole world, a world too small for such a big traitor. His father was the same." He then told me that his aunt, who he's still friends with, he wouldn't write her just because they lived on Lenin Boulevard.

DANICA: What's the connection?

ILIJA: He refuses to write the name Lenin on an envelope. That's how far he takes it! His uncle said that if we were living on Roosevelt St. or Churchill Avenue, he'd write twice a day. Everyone knows. Nobody's fooled. Dirty trick! A disgrace! Oh, did you read today's newspaper? *(He takes from his pocket a rolled-up newspaper. He leafs through it and finds the article.)* Now I'm sorry I didn't kill that bum. Read this.

DANICA: "New increase in the cost of living . . ."

ILIJA: Not that, this: "Maniac Loose on the Streets!"

DANICA: That happens every day. They attack women, children.

ILIJA: Read it, woman! I'm the maniac! It says I shot at an innocent man who was looking for an address.

DANICA: Look, here, your full name and address.

ILIJA: And do you know who wrote that? His lover, the journalist. They think they can use the newspaper to harass me until they can find a way to lock me up. They want to throw me into prison, so they can work in peace. A newspaper that works for spies. Nowhere else on earth.

DANICA: How do you know that she wrote it? There's no by-line.

ILIJA: She didn't dare assign her name to it. She knows I'd recognize it. Soon, she'll be attacking me on radio, television.

(From the yard, the German Shepard howls. Ilija stands, grabs his pistol from his bag, and exits into the corridor. He returns with his panic-stricken brother, Đura, who is carrying in his arms several blue light bulbs.)

ĐURA: Don't tell me anything! Not a word! You could have at least kept in touch by code. Have you forgotten the code? Have you? Ah, Ilija, why did I waste a week teaching you all about conspiracies? It's no use.

ILIJA: Sit down. I have all sorts of documents and information.

ĐURA: I was tailing them, and all I could think of is how they've caught you and killed you. Sister, here, I found blue light bulbs. They are almost white. White will arrive next month.

DANICA: Thank you, Đura.

ĐURA: Look I'm completely grey. I'm already mourning for you. Tonight I picked up the professor. I figured if they'd hurt a hair on your head, I'd kill him. So, I've arrested him, temporarily.

ILIJA: Arrested him?

ĐURA: That's right. I was afraid they killed you, and were getting away. Who else in this world is going to arrest them? This way if I had one of them in custody and you disappeared, at least I could take an eye for an eye.
ILIJA: So, where is he?
ĐURA: My house, in the basement. I tied him up with a clothesline. He's got a sock stuffed in his mouth, so he can't move or make a sound.
ILIJA: That wasn't necessary. Now, they'll be on alert.
ĐURA: I had no choice. I asked him: What'd you do with Ilija? And he acted dumb, like he didn't even know you. And what about his Tenant, Jakovljević, do you know him? "I know him," he said, "he's my friend." I told him, "if he's your friend, then Ilija is your enemy." Then I blacked out, and hit him a couple of times, and when he fought back, I grabbed a shovel from the coal pile and I hit and hit –
ILIJA: Calm down. Đura. Sit down. Come on, calm down.
ĐURA: Then I grabbed an axe –
ILIJA: You didn't!
ĐURA: But then he admitted everything: how they're organized by a foreign power, which is where their orders come from, and that they're planning several actions next month. That's why this mongrel is flying to New York.
ILIJA: Who is flying to New York?
ĐURA: Jakovljević. Your Tenant.
ILIJA: Flying to New York? When's he flying?
ĐURA: Tonight at 9:20.
ILIJA: Do you see what you've done here? Because of one professor, a hundred of them will get away. Instead of grabbing them all at once in a pack, now we need to chase them all the way to New York, all because you blacked out. So much for stopping the conspiracy!
ĐURA: You didn't call me. I thought that they had you –

ILIJA: You are not normal! I've told you a hundred times not to be stupid and go off half-cocked! That's why I didn't call you earlier; I knew how quickly you'd turn everything to shit! Your whole life has been about nothing but brute strength: shovels and axes! Don't you have any brains?

ĐURA: Thanks a lot, brother.

ILIJA: I followed them, I stayed in control, I took great care. I tightened the circle around them, and then, when they were almost within grasp, you run in and chase them away with a shovel and an axe! Where is he now?

ĐURA: At the doctor's for lunch. The journalist is there, too.

ILIJA: Let's go. If he gets away, we've failed. Đura, Đura, what you have done to me . . .

(The brothers leave the house. In the yard, they are greeted by the barking dog. Danica turns, not knowing what to do.)

10.
Interrogation

(DANICA sits at the table, peeling potatoes. The room is illuminated now by a light blue bulb. We hear the radio.)

RADIO VOICE: . . . There are various opinions about this so-called "enchanted" circle, its causes and its consequences. Many of those interviewed, though, stated that they couldn't take a position regarding such unpredictable results. They declared that the consequences could be easily foreseen, but that it's useless to speak about them. When these consequences become reality, the very representatives who are responsible for the circle to begin with will attack them, and the results begin to pile up. In this way one can see how the consequences then become their own cause, blurring any insight presumably gained by the so-called experts. According to them, based on that principle, the current time is always time gone by. Great mistakes in the running of the economy never happen today, rather they are only the consequences of what happened yesterday, but of course yesterday it was forbidden to talk about them. Is it any wonder that our well-intentioned politicians describe our situation as hopeless? After all, you don't get very far when you're chasing after your own tail.

Coming up next will be arias from a variety of different operas, in the broadcast, "The Music of Your Youth."

(Danica starts at the sound of the front doorbell. She listens closely, then, frightened, she rises and exits into the hall. She asks, "Who is it?" and when she is answered, she unlocks the door. The Tenant enters the house. He is pale, confused, and exhausted.)

TENANT: I'm sorry to disturb you at this hour, but I must. I am leaving on a trip this evening.

DANICA: I know, I know. Please . . .

TENANT: How did you know?

(The woman is dumbfounded and embarrassed. She tries in vain to escape from her error.)

DANICA: I don't know, rather I thought –

TENANT: Don't apologize; you're not to blame. I came for my things and to pay you for the last month. I am leaving you today, and I agreed to give you thirty days' notice. I wouldn't want to break our agreement. Please. *(Danica takes the money. The Tenant observes her wearily.)* Madame . . .

DANICA: What?

TENANT: I have to ask you something before I leave.

DANICA: Yes?

TENANT: Why has your husband been following me?

DANICA: My husband . . . following you? Why do you . . . think that?

TENANT: He hasn't told you that he's been following me for the last twenty days?

DANICA: No . . . really . . . I didn't know.

TENANT: And just last week another man joined, whose resemblance to your husband is unbelievable. Do you know nothing about this?

DANICA: No.

TENANT: He hasn't told you where he's been going, where he's been staying, or what he's been doing?

DANICA: My husband?

TENANT: Yes.

DANICA: No . . . that is, he tells me . . . but he didn't say that you . . . Why would he?

TENANT: For the first few days, I thought it was just a coincidence that our paths were crossing, and then I realized it was intentional, that he'd been on my heels the whole time. Do you know where he's been the last four days?

DANICA: On a business trip.

TENANT: To where?

DANICA: To . . . Skoplje.[31]

TENANT: He wasn't in Skoplje, he was in Nis. He stayed at my uncle's home, inquiring about me, and my father, and my brother. The whole time, my aunt says, he took notes, made copies of photographs . . . documents. He said he was a newspaper reporter, who specializes in stories of espionage. Do you at least know where he was last Sunday? In Karlovac, in Srem.[32] You didn't know?

DANICA: No. He didn't mention Srem or Karlovac. And so what he went to Srem or Karlovac?

TENANT: I was there, too.

DANICA: Well, then he was with you.

TENANT: He was not with me, he was following me.

DANICA: I don't know. Are you're certain it was Ilija?

TENANT: I saw him, just as I see you now. While I was having lunch at my friend's house, he took pictures of us from a tree in the next yard. When I went out to ask him what he was doing, a branch broke, and he fell head first from the top of the tree. He fell on his back – I thought he'd never get up again – and then, he jumped up and climbed over the fence. He was limping and moaning. He just missed killing himself.

DANICA: Excuse me . . . I don't know . . . what I can say to you?

TENANT: My dear madam, if he hasn't revealed to you what he's been doing outside the house, certainly you know what he does here, inside the house. Have you not noticed the cord running beneath the carpet?

DANICA: What cord?

(The Tenant lifts the carpet slightly and pulls the cord. He opens the bureau and pulls out a tape recorder.)

---

[31] Pronounced "Skoh'-plee-yeh."
[32] Pronounced "Kar'-loh-vahts" and "Srehm."

TENANT: The microphone is plugged in under my bed. When someone comes to visit me, it is recorded here. He presses the button on this tape recorder, and then climbs into the attic. He drilled a hole above my room. He spies from above. I can see his eye on the ceiling. All I could think, all last week, was that he must be a voyeur. Do you know what that means? Someone who likes to watch others through keyholes.

DANICA: That's vulgar and it doesn't interest me. I know nothing about any of this.

TENANT: Meanwhile, madam, my friends told me, that there was some man persecuting them. He photographs them, he photographs their families, writes anonymous letters, telephones them, records their license plate numbers. Then, I froze when I saw both of them a few days ago.

DANICA: Who?

TENANT: Your husband and his double. One was sneaking around up ahead, while the other lurked behind. How many of him are there, anyway? Tell me, please, why is he doing this? Why is he behaving this way? What have I done to you?

(Danica stays silent, trying to escape his looks and his questions, but the interrogation for a moment makes her nauseous. She turns and wildly attacks the Tenant.)

DANICA: You don't know what you have done? You don't know?

TENANT: No.

DANICA: Then I'll tell you! You've destroyed our lives! You've ruined our home. Ilija's lost his job because of you. My daughter won't call us anymore, because you've made her crazy, forcing her to leave us! We're up to our ears in debt because of you! You should be ashamed of the mess you've made. Don't you see that everything is collapsing because of you? You've destroyed all of us.

(The doors to the bedrooms open: Ilija and Đura emerge. Danica, hysterically, with a tear-stained face, crosses to her

husband and hugs him. Ilija is smiling, grinning at the Tenant, who looks at them, surprised, confused and frightened.)
TENANT: You're home?
ILIJA: Yes. You know I am always with you or just behind you. Đura, turn off that howling.
(Đura turns off the radio. He watches the Tenant carefully.)
ĐURA: At last it is time for a little chat.
ILIJA: Calm down, Danica. What is it with you?
DANICA: I can't look at him anymore! I can't . . . I'd love to see him . . .
ILIJA: *(Restraining her)* Now, now, now, prepare a pot of coffee for us, then go.
DANICA: I'm leaving now! You prepare it for him! I . . . I . . .
ĐURA: Sister, go visit my Smiljka. Have her give you something to calm you down. Go on.
(Danica slips on her shoes, takes her bag and overcoat, starts to leave, then returns to spit on the Tenant. Then with a moan, she turns and leaves the house. Ilija shakes his head, crosses to the Tenant, and wipes him with a handkerchief.)
ILIJA: Her nerves are getting worse. It hasn't been easy for her. You know my brother, Đura.
ĐURA: Pleased to meet you. Đura.
TENANT: We've seen each other.
(Đura gives a heartfelt laugh. He hits the Tenant on the shoulder.)
ĐURA: Old friends. *(The Tenant begins to speak)* Quiet. *(To Ilija)* Finish what you're doing.
(Ilija hands over a jug of water in a rather large pot, he pours in several spoonfuls of sugar and coffee, mixes it all with a ladle and puts it on the stove.[33] From the bureau he takes a bottle of brandy and three glasses.)
ILIJA: At last, we've reached the end. Let's have a drink.

---

[33] Ilija is making Turkish coffee.

TENANT: I fly out tonight, as you know. I've still got to pack, yet I must ask you –

ILIJA: Cheers. Drink freely, drink. You know, I'm on to you. You don't have to pretend anymore that you're a diabetic.

ĐURA: Cheers! We know all about you.

ILIJA: So, how long have you been doing these things?

TENANT: What things?

ILIJA: We know everything. We've been watching you.

TENANT: Watching me? You've been intimidating and harassing me. Isn't that more like it?

ĐURA: That's only part of the picture.

TENANT: I know you have been tailing me for twenty days, but I don't know why?

ILIJA: Ah-ha! Today makes forty-five days! Forty-five days. Then, I went undetected for twenty-five days. But it wasn't easy. You're a cunning man, but you have to admit, you've finally met your match. And I did this without your intelligence or your special training. I just used my raw experience and instinct. It is much easier, though, now that Đura is helping.

ĐURA: I've only just gotten into this. And you have to admit, you are a real snake of a man. I told you, Ilija, this man is a professional. A first rate professional! Aren't you?

ILIJA: Before we get to specifics, tell me: did you suspect for a second that I would discover what you were up to? I'm just an ordinary, naive, insignificant man, aren't I?

TENANT: I don't understand you, sir?

ĐURA: He's asking you – earlier, did you know we knew anything before you learned how much we know?

TENANT: What do you know, gentlemen?

ILIJA: First: I am not a gentleman to you. If I was a gentleman I'd never catch you. To you, I am "comrade". Now answer my question.

TENANT: What can I say to you?

ILIJA: When did you realize that I knew it all?

TENANT: Please, let's not play this anymore. Just tell me why you've been following me. I have to leave. I'm going to be late.
ILIJA: Your son is in a hospital in New York?
TENANT: How did you know? Who told you my son is in a hospital?
ILIJA: You see, we do know everything. They called to tell you that he's in the hospital, and you've got to attend an urgent consultation. You've involved your own son in this crime. First, you sold yourself to them, and then you sold your son. *(He is at a loss for what to say. He stares at the brothers: as the twins stroll in circles, crossing the room. He wants to stand, but Ilija pushes him back down.)* Sit.
TENANT: Are you ordering me? What gives you the right to–
ILIJA: Sit! Sit and don't move! You're not going to tell me how to do this. You will leave here when you answer these five questions and confirmed them in writing, letter by letter.
(Ilija takes a folded sheet of paper from his pocket; he throws it in the Tenant's lap. Đura points a small lamp, illuminating the blinded man.)
TENANT: What is this? Turn the light off, please.
ILIJA: The light bothers you? It bothers you, the light? I'm sure the dark suits you better. You've become so accustomed to living in the dark, now the light bothers you.
ĐURA: Look mister, you'd better start making sense if you know what's smart. Ilija has a bad heart. He doesn't dare get upset. It could make him sick. It wouldn't be good for him if something happened. Ilija, calm down. Come on, let's take it slowly. We will all conduct ourselves calmly and quietly. He is an intelligent man. He is a professional. He knows that in a situation like this, he better not fuck around. Just take it easy.
(The Tenant lowers his head, shielding himself from the light, and reads the paper with a growing smile. By the end he is laughing.)
TENANT: Who came up with these wise and intuitive questions?

ILIJA: I . . . And what is so funny to you? What's so funny?

TENANT: No one helped you? I believe you wrote these, but somebody had to talk you into this, or force you.

ILIJA: No. I've used my own experience, my own intellect, my own suffering, my own nerves, and my own money. All-mine. Nobody's paying me, I am a free man. That's where we differ. I'm not a mercenary, or a criminal, or a traitor!

(Ilija once again becomes wild. His brother grabs him, smiling.)

ĐURA: Ilija . . . Ilija . . . Calm down man, we will not accomplish anything this way. Calm down. And this is the last time I'm going to warn you, if something happens to him, I will chop you up into little pieces! He is all I have in this world! I am only interested in getting him out of this shit alive! So be careful, or I will butcher you! You don't know who Đura is!

(The screaming and threatening is interrupted by the telephone. Ilija lifts the receiver.)

ILIJA: Yes? Yes . . . He left . . . I don't know . . . He took his things, got into a cab and left . . . Yes.

(Putting down the receiver, he runs to the stove. Đura pours a drink for himself and his brother.)

ĐURA: The journalist?

ILIJA: A woman who is concerned where her man is. Why did you pull her into this filthy business? Why are you destroying her career and her life? I've written to her editor and informed him what she's been doing, for whom she's working, and who is paying her. Isn't it obvious to you what I'm talking about? *(Ilija uses a ladle to pour three rather large cups of coffee out of a pot. He puts down the ladle, crosses to the bureau, opens a drawer and pulls out a wad of clipped articles. He brings them to the table and puts them down in front of the Tenant.)*

ILIJA: Did she write these? Look! Look!

ĐURA: You're going to get beaten, mister, heavily beaten. Look.

TENANT: Please . . . Did she write . . . What's the problem with them? All this is well known. These are just reports on government, banking . . . the economy. You know the kind of a situation our world's in and why. You knew that before these articles.

ILIJA: And how is it that after visiting you, every day – she suddenly takes an interest in the "problems of our country".

TENANT: If you know it all, then you obviously know she's on an editorial board set up to deal with economic issues.

ILIJA: We know that, but what isn't clear to us is why you chose a lover who's a journalist writing about "economic issues"? Why not a seamstress, or a saleswoman, or a street cleaner – someone of your class? Huh?

ĐURA: Mister, your schools and your training are of no use, when you meet up with a man like this. It's not just that he's my brother . . .

(Đura, satisfied and proud, claps his brother on the back. Ilija pulls out the tape recorder.)

ILIJA: Do you know what she wrote about? Do you forget? All she did was copy a conversation you had with that professor. Do you remember what bullshit you told him in your room – under my roof? You told him how terrible the situation was; how our economy is on the verge of collapse; how certain people put us in debt to the West just so they could live in luxury; how our grandchildren will spit on our pictures, because our own children won't dare do it while we're still alive; how it makes perfect sense that we have a double standard; how young people today ask questions only when they're faced with a sense of real responsibility.

(Ilija presses the button on the tape recorder, We hear the Tenant's voice.)

VOICE OF TENANT: Everything could have come together towards the end of the fifties. It couldn't have happened earlier, but in fifty-eight, nine, it could have, and it would have created a great turning point in our economy. Today, instead, we're in the same condition in Vojvodina, Mačva, Slavonia, and Šumadia.[34] We should have been the first to export food to Europe.

Voice of Professor: I'm afraid we had no experts, though, not even in economics. *(Sarcastically)* And of course they insist that our village households are still an important economic unit.[35]

VOICE OF TENANT: But nationalizing everything? Is that the solution? I'm not asking just because they took everything my family owned, but –

VOICE OF PROFESSOR: Yes, I know, but I'm not talking about a simple administrative nationalization, rather I'm interested in the creation of a great economy, in which the farmer would stay the owner of his property, legally, though essentially, it would still be overseen by the government. The farmer has to feel the land belongs to him, or else, he'll move to the city where, as always, he becomes a real social problem. I know because like all progressive young people in those days, I was part of the rush from village to factory. We hurried through villages in a Jeep, talking about the future of industry. And people believed us, abandoning the land and all their property. Do you realize what percentage of the land is uncultivated?

(Ilija turns off the tape recorder. He is silent, motionless, observing the Tenant. He points to one article.)

ILIJA: "We could have fed Europe!" And? What did she write there? She wrote down every turd you two shit that day. That's what she wrote. And what's at the bottom of all this? Are these yours?

(Ilija pulls from his pocket two badges with word "Solidarnost" [Solidarity] written on them.)

---

[34] Pronounced "Voy'-vo-dee-nah, Slah'-vo-nee-yah, Mahch'-vah, Shoo'-mah-dee-yah"

[35] The Professor quotes a turn-of-the-century author named Janko Veselinovic, unknown to English speakers. I chose to leave the reference to him out of the text. An exact translation of what the Professor says would be - "'And the village household is an economic unit' - Janko Veselinovic."

ĐURA: Did you hear what he asked you? Are those yours?
TENANT: No. They are Polish.
(Đura crosses to the Tenant, with his fists clenched, but his brother grabs him and stops him.)
ĐURA: You motherfucker –
ILIJA: Đura, calm down. Now, slowly. Sit down. Now, those young people, who carried this message into Marx and Engels Square. Who organized them? Huh? Isn't it obvious? It was your friend, the professor. And isn't it also obvious who's responsible for the first foreign Pope in 600 years on the throne of the Vatican? Huh? He's not just a foreigner, he's a Polack! Huh? And isn't it obvious why you didn't write your aunt for twenty years? And why you got my daughter to collaborate with you, move out of our house and join the underground?
(The Tenant stands, shouts.)
TENANT: You're not normal! You are a deranged lunatic! Lunatics!
(Đura pushes his brother aside and hits the Tenant in the face with his fist. Afterwards, he begins on his arms and legs, screaming before each punch.)
ĐURA: Who's a lunatic? You mother fucker! I'm gonna kill you! He *is* a lunatic, he mistook you for a human being! Give me my pistol!
(Ilija grabs his brother, tries to drag him off to the side.)
ILIJA: Đura . . . Đura . . . Enough! Calm down. Alright, calm down . . .
ĐURA: There are one-hundred and twenty on our list, and I am going to murder every one of them! Let *me* ask him a few questions. With these criminals, you can't talk that way. You gotta grab'em by the throat, hit'em in the balls with your knee, and then . . .
(Đura again tries to get to the Tenant, who is wiping his bloody face with his hands. Ilija stops him, holding him tightly around the waist.)

ILIJA: Enough. Stop. Now, take the keys, go get the professor, we'll confront him with that. Did know your friend confessed? Yes, he confessed to everything. Go Đura, bring him back.

ĐURA: I'm not going anywhere. This criminal will take you by surprise. He knows many tricks.

(Ilija takes the pistol out of his pocket, cocks it and pushes it in his belt.)

ILIJA: Yes, but I know this "trick". He won't try anything.

ĐURA: Wait till I handcuff him, just in case.[36] *(Đura takes handcuffs from his pocket. He crosses to the Tenant and handcuffs one of his hands to the arm of the heavy chair.)*

ĐURA: Don't get near his feet. If he tries something, empty the whole clip. At least we have bullets. I'll be back in fifteen minutes. Then they will sing together.

(Ilija succeeds in dragging his brother to the door. Đura turns, threatening to return and "complete the work," but he leaves the house. In the yard the dog waits for him. The car moves away quickly. Ilija returns, helplessly throwing up his hands. He smiles with indifference, as if to excuse Đura's attack. He takes a cup of coffee and sets it on the arm of the chair. He turns off the table lamp.)

ILIJA: Please. Excuse us. I didn't expect that kind of "conversation". Have some coffee. You know, I know everything, and for every charge, I have material evidence. I'm sorry about what happened here, but you are guilty. And you continue to provoke, to insult, to degrade us. Everyone has their limits. And Đura's nerves are weak. I know your handlers told you when you moved into my house, that I spent two years in prison. This you know. I don't know if they mentioned Đura. Probably they did. But he spent over three years there. The

---

[36] In the original - "tie him up". Because he must have one hand free later to dial the phone, I have chosen to change the text to adhere to the way it was done in the film. An alternative would be to go back to using a rope and having the actor work one hand free during the struggle.

coffee has sugar in it. You can drink freely. You see, what they told you, it's true. I admit it whenever someone asks. I place my hands over my heart, like this, and I say: Yes, I loved him like someone loves God, or let's say their children or their mother. Stalin was everything to me. Today, they write all kinds of things about him: what's true and what isn't. They charged him with crimes he never committed. Some he did. That is known, and I admit it. Nonetheless, at that time, I thought he was sinless. I was young, stupid, angry. I would have taken up my rifle and fought. I would have been killed, thinking I died for a great earthly right. I needed to sober up, and sober up good so I could stop and think and recognize that those who put me in prison did so for my own good, so I wouldn't roam or suffer. And today I am grateful to them. Today I know exactly where I made my mistakes, and where I didn't.

    Does your jaw hurt? Đura has a heavy hand. I've told you all this for one primary reason: I think today you're in a very similar place to where I was many years ago. Except, my friend, you don't have the excuse of being young and not knowing what you're doing. At your age, there is no excuse for betrayal. Now collect your thoughts, consider, and pour them out to me. If you try, I swear, by my Sonja, what you tell me man to man, in trust, will always remain within these four walls. I know, you're like a child who wants to stay on the side your father and brother chose. But at the moment, for you, this is the wrong way to think. You've turned off the path. You are lost in the dark woods, where the foreign agents, who roam through our world, wait for you. The English have organized it, and as usual, they've informed the Americans, and they're waiting for you in Paris, where your brother is already working for them, just as my brother is working for me – and so they drew you into the game. That's how it is, right? Right. And it's understandable. You were young, you needed money to go out, for girls, for a car, for clothes, for parties, and they've got everything in the West – but it's expensive. They offer everything, and it's all beautiful at first glance, in fine wrapping. A man from here flies to it. He wants to drink, to eat, to fuck, and that costs money. Then an agent from a foreign power shows up, takes out a check and asks: "How much? Five thousand, ten thousand, twenty thousand?" And you find yourself in a pickle, in a very sticky situation. The landlady wants her money, the merchant wants his, the whores want theirs, everybody . . . and where will it come from? The agent, then increases your pay and says: "It's nothing really – just a little of this, a little of that. Just a trifle. Only two facts." You look at him. And you want to punch him in the mouth, but then you think: Wait, that much money, and I'm only going to tell him what everyone here already knows? So you take the check – and that's the end of it. Now you're in the game, and he starts asking for bigger, more important secrets about our country, our problems. You resist, saying "we didn't agree to this." And he smiles and says: "As you wish. We could keep working together, or we could tell your embassy about you." And just like that, little by little, you become stuck in your betrayal, up to the neck. And to calm your conscience, you start to believe everything they tell you. They fill you with propaganda and lies. They meet emigrants and mercenaries from other socialist nations. They organize meetings with well-known traitors, who persuade you that even if they need you to work for free, you must do it. You return here, get involved with local gangs, people who hate everything, and who shit all day long in order to publish their "theories." You think that most people are unhappy, that you can create a revolution. You imagine yourself as the future president of the country, and, then . . .

TENANT: And then? This is really interesting – then?

ILIJA: Then, I appear. Believe me, I've spent long nights thinking about you. I'd welcome the dawn, staring at the ceiling. Finally, weighing the pros and cons, my friendly advice to you is, and I'll tell you what I'd tell my own brother, Đura, if he were in a similar situation: first, confess everything to me, and then, we'll get into my car and go to the police, where you can stand tall and face the music and say: "That's right, brothers, everything is true and I am shit" – just like that, with those words, with no self-pity or crying – "I ate shit, I was wrong, I was a rat, I was garbage, I did this and that, my eyes were blind, but here, today I can see. Judge me so that I can repent my sins, stand on my own feet and once again be a man. I ask you to consider all my reasons. It isn't easy for me, I have undergone a terrible trial. I didn't have a wise man to advise me, to rouse me, to pull me from this hell."

TENANT: Nice, very nice. I really must thank you. I didn't know that because of me you "welcomed the dawn, staring at the ceiling." That touches me . . .

ILIJA: Can I ask you something?

TENANT: Certainly.

ILIJA: Can you help me keep from killing you.

TENANT: And . . . how, how can I help you?

ILIJA: Listen, I'm afraid you're going to provoke me, and I'll take out my pistol and shoot you. Understand? My whole life, I've been on the verge of killing someone. And what's more, I've had good reason. Nobody would begrudge me. But *you* shouldn't pay the price for all the others, for those who offended me, humiliated me or persecuted me. No, no, no . . . *(The Tenant has become small and quiet; he sees and senses that Ilija could really kill him. Ilija drains his glass of brandy, then continues to talk.)* So, you'll tell them these things, and they'll decide what to do. Then, from my experiences, they'll take an hour or two to talk about it, then they'll return and offer you cigarettes and coffee, to have a friendly chat. Of course, they'll say to you: "You're a little late in realizing all this, but what can be done? It's better late than never." Then, we'll all drink together. I'll return to my work; after all, I've been tied up with more important matters. And you'll return to Paris and then, you can start working for us,

as you should. But, before that, we'll come back here. Danica will prepare lunch. We'll invite your uncle. You'll make peace with Đura – he'll forgive you for fighting, we'll sing, dance if we have to. And as for me, well, if you remember me during the holidays[37] – you might remember – but if you don't, it's nothing – everything I did was in the line of duty. They don't need to pay me or reward me with decorations. My biggest satisfaction will be the thought that I guided a man onto the correct path.
TENANT: Please, if I can interrupt you for a moment without helping you kill me. I'm not about to shoot myself, you know –
ILIJA: Let me finish. I don't have two countries, like you. I have one daughter and one country, and when you only have one of something – your feelings about them are much stronger. You – with your two worlds – you don't know such a feeling. So, Mr. Jakovljević, have we come to an agreement?
TENANT: About what?
ILIJA: What – about what?! Haven't you heard what I've been saying for the last half hour?!
TENANT: I heard.
ILIJA: Well?
TENANT: I'm grateful to you for your advice. I feel you really want what's best for me –
ILIJA: Of course I do! You're from Niš. You're one of our own. I can tell, everything you do, you do with indifference, I can see how guilty you feel about being pulled into this underground world. Once, when you were sitting in the park,[38] alone, gazing across the river,[39] I watched you among the pine trees; I could easily see that you were tormented, struggling, eating away

---

[37] The playwright here specifies the Day of Security, a federal holiday.
[38] In the original text, Ilija specifies the park at Kalemegdan ("Kah - leh - mehg - dahn"), a fortress that was originally built in the Middle Ages by the Celts. It sits at the intersection of the Sava and Danube rivers in Belgrade.
[39] In the original text, he refers to Zemun ("Zeh - moon"), a small town across the river from Belgrade.

inside. I thought about running up and telling you all this then, but . . . Let's drink. It's homemade. It's your brandy, you know. I got it from your uncle. Splendid man, quite a fellow.
TENANT: Pardon me, sir, dear Mr. Čvorović, can I suggest something to you, just as you did for me? From the heart?
ILIJA: Of course, you're from Nis! Please.
TENANT: Unlock me, then put your shoes on, and we'll go together to the hospital. I'll confess to everything, in written form, verbally, on tape, however you want it.
ILIJA: God be blessed, thank you. But why the hospital? Do I look ill?
TENANT: Very ill.
ILIJA: I've been tired. I've been running around now for two months. I've been upset. You know, my heart.
TENANT: And your nerves. They're shot. I have a friend, a doctor, who can help you. We'll call your daughter, as well.
(Ilija begins to move, then stops, stares at the Tenant with a smile. Then he laughs and spreads his arms.)
ILIJA: Mister Jakovljević, you are not normal! Here, I swear to you, on my daughter who betrayed me, you are not normal! What do I look like to you? Do I really look that feeble-minded? Huh? I should go to the hospital with you?
TENANT: Yes. I'm advising you . . . as your friend.
ILIJA: And why? It's not my heart, is it? You think I'm mad, don't you? You've already said as much. You've repeated it openly. So now you'll persuade Sonja to have me committed. Undoubtedly, there is a doctor there who will examine me, decide I'm a dangerous lunatic, put me in a straightjacket, and lock me in a cell. Since you haven't managed to lock me up in the usual way, you've hired this doctor to help you. What's more - you think I'm going to go along with it. Well, Mr. Jakovljević, you're not even a man. I've seen *women* more brave than you, women who stood up straight and died in silence. But you're a lowly and common cockroach, a piece of trash, an animal turd.

Well, it's not going to work the way you planned, Jakovljević. I would have thought with your training, that you knew to be more cautious, thoughtful, more subtle. But, you're just like my brother, Đura - shovel and ax, and whatever is left. Come on, gather your courage and say it to my face. Am I mad? You motherfucker, be a man!

TENANT: I'm going to be late. Please, do something. Or take me to-

ILIJA: First we settle this. I find it very interesting. You think that I am mad?

TENANT: You are certainly sick.

ILIJA: And what kind of sickness is it? Describe it for me? I can't see myself like you do, maybe I really am sick. I don't know, you've confused me. It wouldn't be good if I was crazy and didn't know it. To look at me, I am an altogether common, normal man. Like most people, I have a family, I've sent my daughter to school, I've built a house, I try to help others, I'm in debt, I'd love to have grandchildren and take them to Košutnjak. So far, that's alright, isn't it? No, I'm only crazy to you - to other people I'm normal. You think everything can be alright for sixty years, and then all at once, I go crazy - because of you? No, you aren't someone people go crazy over. You have to use your imagination a little to give yourself that much significance. I am, Jakovljević, a perfectly healthy and normal man! Listen to me! I am healthy and normal! I'm not sick, insane, or mad! I am healthy!

TENANT: Then this is terrible.

ILIJA: What's terrible?

TENANT: You're not mad and yet you behave like this? That's worse than if you were mad. That's, that's –

ILIJA: That's what? Tell me, tell me what it is? You want me to tell you? It's hate! It's hate and disgust! My whole life, I've fought against all of you, and over and over again you've torn me down, I have barely survived.[40]

TENANT: All of us? Who are "we", dear Čvorović?! Who do you mean?!

ILIJA: You traitors! You, your father, your brother, all those we killed, all those who got away. When you realized I survived the war, survived your efforts to tear me apart, you locked me up, gave me hard labor. You couldn't stand all of us being equal; you couldn't bear that there weren't any differences between people. My wounds hadn't even healed properly and then, you returned. You came by the thousands, and soon it will be your brother's friends and their "honestly earned" capital, who will once again build castles and traps! To again destroy and step on people! To again make us slaves! They forced me to believe in their cause, and for that I was put in jail – and you who have fought them every step of the way – they let go free. What does this mean, you motherfucker?! Does it mean that I've been a fool my whole life? That I have fought against my own principle and conviction? Does it mean that that when I'm in a wheelchair I'll watch capitalism once again rise up; watch again as people are consigned into slavery?! That I was imprisoned only because I screamed: Long live Stalin and equal rights?! Is that why I was imprisoned?! I should have screamed: Long live capitalism? Stalin killed you, but that wasn't enough! I held his picture up for

---

[40] In this speech and what follows, Ilija is referring to the difficulties experienced within the former Yugoslavia by anyone who tried to maintain an ideological position. Ilija and Dura fought Hitler as Partisan soldiers under Tito's leadership. Throughout the war, the Partisans were dedicated Stalinists, but in 1948, Tito broke with Stalin, and any of his followers that maintained their allegiance to the Soviet leader were sent to a gulag known as *Goli Otok* (Bald Island), where they summarily had Stalin beat out of them. They were released once they could prove they had been rehabilitated. They accomplished this by taking a fellow prisoner and beating Stalin out of him, similar to what Ilija is doing with the Tenant. In the meantime, without Stalin's support, Tito needed capital. For this reason, he allowed those who had left the country when Communism took over to return. The Tenant's family - capitalists who had initially fought Tito – were welcomed back, and Ilija, and others like him, felt betrayed.

five years, like an icon, and sooner or later, I will hold it up again! Remember: sooner or later! You won't succeed, not with me here, not with my brother here, not while there are a hundred thousand others, you won't . . . You . . . won't . . .

(Ilija stops, crosses towards the Tenant, his mouth open as if in short supply of air. He staggers, and leans on the bureau, and slowly, choking, slides to the floor. His hands tear at his shirt collar, as if it were strangling him. The Tenant gets to his feet, as much as his "chains" will allow. He pulls the heavy armchair over to where Ilija is. With his free hand he unbuttons his shirt.)

TENANT: Where is your medicine? Where are your pills? Do you hear me?

ILIJA: I will die . . . They're . . . in the drawer . . . You've killed me . . .

(The Tenant searches the drawer. He tosses aside piles of drugs.)

TENANT: Where is your nitroglycerin? These aren't going to help. Where is it?

ILIJA: I don't have . . . The pharmacy was out . . . You've killed me . . .

(The Tenant drags the armchair to the telephone; he dials a number.)

TENANT: Hello . . . Emergency? . . . Send an ambulance to number 22, Dobravska Street. . . Heart attack. A man has fallen . . . No, there's no medicine . . . Yes . . . *(He puts down the telephone, and with great effort, lifts the chair.)* They'll be here in five minutes. I'll leave the door open. I'd stay with you, but when your brother returns . . . I'm sorry, I have to go. I wish the best for you . . . I've taken your pistol.

(Ilija attempts to rise. He grabs the cord of the telephone, pulling it off the table. The Tenant has to turn the armchair sideways to leave the house. In the yard he is met by the barking dog. Ilija dials the phone.)

ILIJA: Hello . . . Smiljka . . . I am . . . Where is Đura? . . . Tell him to leave everything . . . He must get to the airport, right

away . . . Tell him that he's escaped . . . Someone has to stop all flights . . . Tell him to block the runway . . . I'm right behind him . . .
(Ilija leaves the receiver, tries to get up, but again he doubles over in pain. Crawling on all fours, fighting for his life, moving his arms and knees with difficulty, he exits into the yard, where he is welcomed by the barking dog.)

The End

Belgrade, 1982

Translated by *Dennis Barnett*

SINIŠA KOVAČEVIĆ
(1954—)

Born in 1954 in the village of Šuljam in Serbia, Kovačević graduated from the Faculty of Dramatic arts in Belgrade. He writes for theatre, film and TV.

One of his best known plays is the award winning drama, *The Times Have Changed*, which depicts a farmer, as the main character, who is trying to adjust to the new communist social order and mentality of his countrymen. Kovačević's works were translated and performed in Russia, Great Britain and Germany.

TIMES HAVE CHANGED

A Play in 96 Images

Dedicated to Mother and Father

Dear Director!

Don't be disturbed by the fact that in this play horses are shod and wild pigeons and white oxen appear. I only imagine this in some theatre of my own. I know very well that instead of a horse, a bicycle will be taken to the blacksmith, and I know there will be no wild pigeons, and that the oxen will bellow from offstage. But it's a pity.

S. K.

CHARACTERS:

ILIJA PEVAC, *33 years old, villager, plowman, farmer*
NEVENA PEVAC, *30 years old, Ilija's wife*
MILOŠ PEVAC, *65 years old, Ilija's father*
ILIJA JEŠANOV, *33 years old*
DUŠAN GOLIĆ, *50 years old, the second highest-ranking, and later the highest-ranking man in the new government*
PAVLE DOBRENOV, *35 years old, a tradesman before the war*
VELINKA BELIĆ, *25 years old, a good comrade, an enthusiastic activist*
BRANISLAV RADAKOVIĆ, *also called*
TUJTA and, more recently, DEAF TUJTA
BRANA KOVAČEVIĆ, *22 years old, teacher, nicknamed* PAVLE KORČAGIN
RADOJA BELEGIŠKI, *blacksmith, 42 years old, known as* BIG RADOJA
ĐORĐE BELEGIŠKI, *17 years old Radoja's son, member of the Communist Youth League*
FATHER JOVAN, *50 years old, fat and ponderous*
ČAVKA, *50 years old, party member and activist*
DOCTOR, *known as* DOC, *permanent secretary*
GRANDPA VASA THE REACTIONARY, *70 years old*
RADULE, *a Bosnian, 40 years old, colonist*
CVIJETA, *his daughter, 16 years old*
JOVIŠA ERAK, *22 years old, also a colonist*
HANS, *33 years old, German prisoner of war . . . and others, many others.*

The action takes place in Srem in 1945 and 1946, from July to July.

1.

(The month of July. The broad plain of Srem. The great expanse of grain is turning yellow, the cornfields are green. In the middle of the fields is a dusty dirt road. Thick layers of dust reveal the long absence of rain. In one grain field there are reapers. The men cut the grain, the women tie it in sheaves. On the horizon two figures come into view. The two horsemen approach the reapers. Both wear English shirts, with remnants of military boots. They have haversacks on their backs. They come up to the harvesters. Both have several days' growth of beard, both are thirty-three years old, both were captured the first day of the war as soldiers from the same unit. After five years as prisoners-of-war, they are returning to their homes, to their families. Ilija Pevac and Ilija Ješanov. Fellow soldiers. The year is 1945.)

PEVAC: Good morning. How is it going?
JEŠANOV: You're working hard. *(The reapers gather around the newcomers, answering their greetings.)*
PEVAC: Could we get something to drink?
REAPER: Of course. You, little one, give them the jug. *(A young girl jumps up to get the water. She hands it to the unexpected visitors. Pevac takes a long swig from the bottle.)*
FIRST REAPER: Oh my God . . . Ilija, is that you? *(Pevac laughs and nods.)*
FIRST REAPER: I thought so, but I'm still not sure. Ilija Pevac and Ilija Ješanov, of course. They always went together like Tuesday and Wednesday. Oh my God.
SECOND REAPER: Well, how was it?
JEŠANOV: It's over. And here?
FIRST REAPER: Don't ask. It's hard to say who was worse, the Ustaše[1] or the Germans.

SECOND REAPER: Well, it's over now.
PEVAC: What about our people?
FRST REAPER: They didn't touch yours. Not a one. The houses where someone had been taken prisoner they left alone.
PEVAC: Thanks for the water. Let's go, namesake.
JEŠANOV: So long. *(The two namesakes start towards the village. They are followed by a malicious remark.)*
SECOND REAPER: I hope Ilija Pevac doesn't find his mare saddled, eh, gramps? *(The old man laughs. He cuts a wide swath in the grain. Ilija Ješalov and Ilija Pevac move hurriedly towards the roofless white church steeple in the distance.)*

2.

(Forgetting his friend completely, Ilija Pevac runs towards the gate of his house. In the courtyard is a white, undamaged house. Ilija Ješanov continues along the street. Pevac opens the door and goes inside. An eight-year-old boy who was playing around the well slips away into the house. A huge grey dog strains at his chain.)

PEVAC: Murat! *(The dog calms down. It howls and tries to wrench itself free of the chain.)*
PEVAC: Quiet, Murat. It's me. *(Finally, the chain breaks. The enormous Murat jumps on his master. Blood gushes out. Pevac's young wife, Nevena, runs out of the house. Pevac and the dog are rolling in the dust. The wife shouts.)*
NEVENA: Murat! Sit. Into the house! *(Like a lamb, the dog goes into the house. Pevac straightens up. His hands and face are bloody from the bites of the dog. He wipes the dust and blood from his face. Nevena's knees begin to shake; she stumbles and

---

[1] "Ustaše" refers to the Croatians who collaborated with the Nazis during WWII.

sits comically down in the old metal trough containing water for the chickens.)

3.

(Pevac sits at a table full of food. His mother puts still more food on the already overloaded table. Then she starts to cry uncontrollably. Pevac chews with all his might. In the courtyard under a huge mulberry tree, old Stojan Ješanov is digging a hole. From it he takes a moldy barrel. Pevac comes out with two large tin mugs. The old man draws the cork, and Pevac holds the mugs under the spout. Wine gushes out. Father and son sit on the pile of earth. They clink glasses forcefully, then drain them. Next to them is a large puddle of wine.)

4.

(Ilija Pevac, Nevena, Ilija's father Miloš, and the doctor. The doctor is bandaging Pevac.)

DOCTOR: You got cut up pretty well. *(He prepares an injection.)*
PEVAC: And I was lucky.
DOCTOR: Luckier than those who didn't come back. How was it?
PEVAC: Rough. I missed home, my family. The work was hard.
DOCTOR: They didn't beat you?
PEVAC: Never, What about you, Doctor?
DOCTOR: Comrade Doctor.
PEVAC: How are your people?
DOCTOR: I don't know. *(Pevac looks at him in amazement.)* They're all dead.
PEVAC: Oh my god . . . but how?
DOCTOR: By the knife, my boy, by the knife.

5.

(Night. Nevena and Pevac are in bed. Next to them their son is sleeping. Pevac moves closer, and Nevena responds willingly. Then Pevac gets a cramp. He has waited four and a half years for this night and it is over before it has begun.)

6.

(The stables. Pevac and Nevena.)

NEVENA: We have plenty of poultry. There were three hatchings this spring. *(Proudly)* Twenty from each chicken. The cow is fine. You'll see when Miloš brings her back.
PEVAC: Rumenka?
NEVENA: Her calf. The Ustaše took Rumenka in '43. But I hid the calf in the cupboard.
(Pevac laughs.)
PEVAC: And the horses?
NEVENA: Soko and Vidra. Grandpa kept them. What all he had to do in order to keep them, you have no idea. *(Nevena picks up the pitchfork and digs away the straw in the corner. A square hatch appears, covering a hole.)* And here's where I hid the comrades.

7.

(Ilija Pevac is cleaning his threshing floor. A neighbor, seventy-year-old Grandpa Vasa, squeezes through a gap in the fence. He comes over to Pevac.)

GRANDPA VASA: How's it going, Iko?
PEVAC: Grandpa Vasa! Hello.

GRANDPA VASA: Welcome home. *(They kiss each other on the cheeks.)* I'm glad you made it back.
PEVAC: How are you?
GRANDPA VASA: Oh, working hard. It's going all right, huh?
PEVAC: All right.
GRANDPA VASA: Slow and hard, eh? Who had it easy in prison?
PEVAC: There were some who did.
GRANDPA VASA: I'm glad you got back safe and sound. Well, I have to go.
PEVAC: Where?
GRANDPA VASA: To work. I only stopped by to welcome you home. I really have to go.
PEVAC: Tell Đorđe to drop by.
GRANDPA VASA: There is no Đorđe anymore. *(Silence.)*
PEVAC: And nobody tells me. How long ago?
GRANDPA VASA: Two years ago.
PEVAC: Oh, no. What about Spasa?
GRANDPA VASA: She took the boy and went back to her family.
PEVAC: Oh, no. I'm sorry, Grandpa Vasa, believe me.
GRANDPA VASA: Me too.
PEVAC: A lot of people are dead. And all of them young.
GRANDPA VASA: The young fall. Look at Đorđe.
PEVAC: Who killed him? The Germans?
GRANDPA VASA: I'm afraid my Đorđe died on the wrong side. I have to go.
PEVAC: Stay a while so we can have a drink.
GRANDPA VASA: I'm going. It's not good for you to be seen with a reactionary. *(Someone shouts to Pevac from the courtyard gate. Grandpa Vasa quickly runs away to his own yard, and Pevac goes to open the gate. A girl of fifteen is waiting for him, all out of breath.)*
GIRL: Comrade Pevac, report at once to the local council. Death

to fascism! *(She turns and runs up the street. Pevac closes the gate behind her.)*

8.

(The office of the new government, characteristically bare except for a few objects, also typical. An induction telephone. Two "desks." There are two men in the office. A policeman conducts Ilija Pevac in. One of the men is a rather short fifty-year-old with a short neck and a powerful build. He is called Golić. The other is Pavle, thirty years old, slender, with a foppish mustache. He strokes it frequently, straightening it along the line of his upper lip in a mechanical, unconscious movement.)

GOLIĆ: All right, Pevac, where have you been? Do you think we've got nothing better to do than wait for you? *(Pevac greets Pavle warmly. They kiss each other.)*
PEVAC *(To Golić.):* I only wanted to change my shirt.
GOLIĆ: Next time don't bother. *(Pevac looks at him in amazement.)*
PAVLE: Sit down, Ilija. *(Pevac sits down.)*
GOLIĆ: Listen, Pevac. You know why we sent for you.
PEVAC: I can guess.
GOLIĆ: Well, just so you don't have to guess . . . *(Pavle obviously does not approve of Golić's way of speaking to Pevac.)*
PAVLE: Listen, Ilija, we went for you in order to explain a few things to you, in a friendly way.
PEVAC: Well, here I am.
GOLIĆ: I would like to do this in the official way, according to regulations.
PAVLE: That's not necessary in this case.
GOLIĆ: What do I know? I just like to be able to sleep at night. *(He takes a sheet of paper and begins to write.)* Last name Pevac, first name Ilija? Date of birth?

PEVAC: May seventh, 1911.
GOLIĆ: Profession kulak? *(Pavle looks at him.)*
PEVAC: Farmer.
GOLIĆ: Fathers name Miloš. Now tell us, Pevac.
PEVAC: What?
GOLIĆ: Everything in order. It's very important that what you tell us agrees with what we have here.
PEVAC *(Irritated)*: What is it you want, Golić?
GOLIĆ: Comrade Golić. First of all, I want the truth, because we know everything anyway . . . Second, I want everything from the day you were captured until yesterday. As for last night, I can imagine it. *(He makes a graphic gesture with his hand.)* Ha, ha, ha, there must be singing around the house this morning.
PAVLE: Ilija, just so we don't have to go through all this—you were called in for a conversation, not an investigation and so we could, first of all, explain a few things to you. A lot has changed here, it's a new order . . .
GOLIĆ: Comrade Pavle, I'd like to go by the rules just the same. So I can sleep well at night.
PEVAC *(Nervously and mechanically)*: I was captured on the thirteenth of April, along with my whole battalion. Major Vasić killed himself with a hand grenade. We were taken on foot to Romania, and from there to Budapest by truck. *(Golić is writing the whole time.)* From Budapest we were taken to Vienna by train, from Vienna to Munich by truck, and from Munich to a prisoner-of-war camp on foot. Is that how you want it, boss?
GOLIĆ: That's fine. *(Pavle turns towards the window.)* Go on.
PEVAC: What else?
GOLIĆ: What was the name of the camp?
PEVAC: Stalag A2. *(Someone knocks on the door. Pavle is grateful for the interruption.)*
PAVLE: Come in. *(A villager enters.)*
VILLAGER: Death to fascism, comrades. Well, here's Ilija. When did you get back? *(Pevac does not answer.)*

VILLAGER: Comrades, I need two men today, I'm making a pigsty.
GOLIĆ: Go see Čavka.
VILLAGER: Thanks, comrades. So long.
GOLIĆ: Who else from our village was with you?
PEVAC: Ilija Ješanov and Gligor.
GOLIĆ: How did they conduct themselves there?
PEVAC: Like everybody else.
PAVLE: Let's speed this up, in spite of the fact that comrade Golić wants to sleep well. Ilija, big changes have taken place here. For the better, of course. Right now things are still difficult, but it will get better, do you see? The people have taken things into their own hands. That's how it should be, right? Among other things, the biggest plot of land you can own is twenty hectares, which is enough, don't you think? Even too much. That means that your fifty-two hectares have been divided among comrades who have no land. Some land has not been divided up and has been left fallow. You'll find out why when the time comes. That's the fairest way, right? We know you're an honest man . . .
GOLIĆ: As far as a kulak can be.
PAVLE: No interruptions in the future, is that clear, Comrade Vice President?
GOLIĆ: It's clear.
PAVLE: Pardon me?
GOLIĆ: It's clear, Comrade Captain.
PAVLE: That's better. *(To Pevac.)* We know you didn't compromise yourself in Germany and we expect you to be a loyal member of this new society and to help as much as you can and to be a good comrade, for Christ's sake. Now let's go have a beer. *(The two of them go out. Golić finishes his meticulous notes. There is not a single letter on the paper. Instead there is a crude sketch of Ilija Pevac. Someone knocks on the door.)*
GOLIĆ: Come in! *(Ilija Ješanov enters.)*

JEŠANOV: Death to fascism! You sent for me, Comrade Golić?

9.

(Ilija Pevac and Pavle in the street. A group of captured Germans are working on one of the buildings, unguarded. Pevac and Pavle pass close to them. Pevac looks closely at the unshaven faces. Pavle notices this.)

PAVLE: They're repairing the school. They can fix everything they fucked up. *(Pevac does not answer.)*
PAVLE: There are two hundred of them in our village alone. *(They arrive in front of the Cooperative. In front of it several people are squatting around some bottles of beer. When they notice Pavle, they start to get up. Then they recognize Pevac and greet him.)*
PAVLE: What are you doing, comrades?
VILLAGER: We're waiting for Germans.
PAVLE *(to Pevac):* We didn't tell you that. Whenever you need some help, go see Čavka, okay? And you'll get two or three Germans. Of course, on condition that you return them in one piece.
PEVAC: Are we still going to have that beer?
PAVLE: Sure. They've rationed us beer now, and who knows when it'll be our turn again.
PEVAC: Who's tending bar here? *(The proprietor comes over.)* Bring us beers all around. *(The proprietor brings several liter bottles of beer from behind the improvised bar, and gives one to each of them. Pevac pays.)*
VILLAGER: Well, how was it?
PEVAC: How do you think it was? Like it is for them. *(He nods towards the Germans. At that moment a man of Pevac's age passes on the other side of the street. Pevac jumps up. Shouting.)* Tujta! Tujta! Isn't that Brana Tujta? Brana! *(The man goes*

through the door of the church.)
PAVLE: You can shout until tomorrow, for all the good it will do you.
PEVAC: Has he gone crazy?
VILLAGER: Deaf. Deaf as a post.
PAVLE: A mine exploded a meter in front of the trench he was in.
VILLAGER: He's completely changed. Avoids everybody.
PEVAC *(Looking at Tujta for a long time):* The hell.

10.

(The church door. There are neatly piled pieces of the roof of the bell tower lying on the ground. A large cross which once stood on the peak of the bell tower is leaning against the wall. The walls are scorched, the windows contain only a few fragments of stained glass. Tujta goes into the bell tower. On the floor, almost buried in bricks, beams, and tiles, is a huge bell. Tujta carefully inspects it. He tries to move it, but does not succeed. He looks it over again, centimeter by centimeter. He does not find any cracks. Then he starts to remove the debris from the bell. The broad hulk of Father Jovan blocks the doorway of the bell tower.)

FATHER JOVAN: How goes it, Branislav?
TUJTA: Don't bother, Father. I can't hear you at all.
FATHER JOVAN *(Shouting):* How goes it?
TUJTA: Could be better. *(The monk laughs.)* We have to raise the bell.
FATHER JOVAN: It won't work. The tower will collapse. *(Tujta shakes his head. Gesturing.)* The tower will fall. It's cracked. It won't hold the bell. *(Tujta finally understands. He stands there for a few moments, then bends down and continues his work.)*

11.

(Ilija Pevac with an old couple. On the wall is an icon and the picture of a twenty-year-old youth in the uniform of the old army.)

OLD MAN: Please don't lie to me, Ilija.
PEVAC: I'm not lying, Uncle Sreta, I swear.
OLD MAN: If he's dead, it's better if you tell me, tell me right away.
PEVAC: He's not, I tell you.
OLD MAN: But then why . . . for the love of God.
PEVAC: They always told us everybody was fed in communal kitchens that they set fire to the churches, that the women belonged to everybody . . .
OLD MAN: But none of that is true. Except for the churches. And those were set on fire by the Germans.
PEVAC: He wasn't the only one who believed it. Quite a few left.
OLD MAN: Oh, what's happening to us, Spomenka? *(The old woman does not move.)*
PEVAC: The Americans liberated our camp. Whoever wanted to could go with them. *(For a few moments no one speaks. Then Pevac stands up.)*
PEVAC: That's how it was. He said he'd get in touch as soon as he could. Goodbye. *(Pevac goes out. The old woman finally breaks down and begins to wail. The old man hides his tears in his white mustache.)*
OLD WOMAN: Who will light candles for me, Gligor?

12.

(A building site. Captured Germans are at work. Golić stands in the shade with another man. Tujta comes up to them.)

TUJTA: Hello.
GOLIĆ: Hello.
TUJTA: Can you give me three Germans tomorrow?
GOLIĆ: Sure. Eh, Čavka? *(Čavka nods.)* What are you doing?
TUJTA: I can't hear. *(Golić asks again, gesturing and shouting. Tujta understands.)* I'm going to raise the bell.
GOLIĆ: For that I won't give you any. I can't. I won't! *(Tujta turns and starts to go. Golić grabs him by the sleeve.)* And I wouldn't advise you to do that, either. And you an ex-soldier. Shame on you.
TUJTA: I don't hear a word you're saying. *(He turns and leaves.)*

13.

(A grain field. The sun stands high above three reapers. They finish a swath and go off towards a tree and shade. We recognize Ilija Ješanov. He approaches the tree. Two German military jackets are hanging from it. The reapers sit down. Ješanov takes a bottle and some food out of his bag. He takes a drink, then offers some to the Germans. He takes a loaf of bread out of a white towel and divides it into three equal parts.)

14.

(Dusk. Nevena is driving the last chickens into the coop. Her son is helping her. Pevac comes out of the stable. He closes the door behind him. He takes the washbasin, which is leaning against the wall and fills it with water from a can. Old Miloš Pevac is

patching a harness. Nevena goes into the house.)

PEVAC: Come on, Miloš, pour for me. *(The boy takes a tin pitcher and starts to pour water over his father.)* Faster. *(The boy obeys, almost fearfully. Nevena comes out of the house. She has put on a new apron and is wearing a new scarf on her head.)* What are you all dressed up for?
NEVENA: I'm going to a meeting.
PEVAC: Where?
NEVENA: I'm a WAF. The president.
PEVAC: WAF?
LITTLE MILOŠ: Women's Anti-Fascist Front. W. A. F.
PEVAC: Do you know what time it is?
NEVENA: Seven-thirty.
PEVAC: What will people say? Out in the town at eight in the evening!
NEVENA: What's wrong with that?
PEVAC: To hell with W. A. F! You're not going anywhere.
NEVENA: But the comrades will . . .
PEVAC: To hell with the comrades. Take off your things.
LITTLE MILOŠ: Go ahead, mama.
PEVAC: You be quiet, shrimp. *(In a tone that does not permit any argument.)* Nevena, take off those things at once.

15.

(Ilija Pevac is cleaning out the stables. With a powerful motion he throws forkfuls of refuse a long ways. From the neighboring courtyard the blows of an axe can be heard. Old Vasa is mending his barn. He works like an old man, awkwardly and with great effort. Pevac goes through a gap in the fence.)

PEVAC: How's it going Grandpa Vasilije?
GRANDPA VASA: The way it does when you're old.

PEVAC: Here, give me that. I'll do it. *(He takes the axe from Grandpa Vasa.)*
GRANDPA VASA *(Disconcerted.)*: It's all right. Don't. It's all right.
PEVAC: What do you mean it's all right? Let me do it.
GRANDPA VASA: Get out of here, boy. Someone will see you.
PEVAC: So what? Let them see me.
GRANDPA VASA: Go on, Ilija. I'm being boycotted.
PEVAC: You're what?
GRANDPA VASA: I'm being boycotted. Now go. You'll get into trouble.
PEVAC: Forget about your goddamn boycott and give me that board. *(Grandpa Vasa hands him the board. Pevac quickly hammers it into place with a few powerful and skillful blows.)*

16.

(The courtyard of Ilija Pevac. Ilija Pevac and Ilija Ješanov are at work, transferring bags of grain from a wagon to the barn.)

JEŠANOV: How much do you have, namesake?
PEVAC: Eleven cubic meters and an acre.
JEŠANOV: Not bad.
PEVAC: That's nothing. In Germany we harvested twenty from land that wasn't as good.
JEŠANOV: It's still not bad, namesake. Next year we'll get that much. And why didn't you get two or three Germans to help you? Wouldn't Golić give you any?
PEVAC: I didn't ask for any. *(Ješanov laughs.)*
JEŠANOV: I remember when he wasn't such a big shot. *(They continue in silence.)*
PEVAC: Golić – the top man in town. Good God.
JEŠANOV: We were away for a long time namesake. In five years the first can be last and vice-versa. You know how long

five years is, don't you?
PEVAC: Okay, with Pavle, I can understand. But Golić. The lowest man in the village. Nothing but a day-laborer and a sharecropper, and a bad one at that.
JEŠANOV: You'd be better off not thinking like that.
PEVAC: He didn't even have enough fat on him for a dog to bite. *(Again they continue in silence.)*
JEŠANOV: Does it bother you about the land? *(Pevac laughs.)*
PEVAC: Does it hurt when they pull out one of your teeth? It's not the money that bothers me, it's the land itself, do you understand?
JEŠANOV: What do you have to complain about? You have enough left.
PEVAC: For Christ's sake. You see someone else plowing your land, it bothers you.
JEŠANOV: Who got yours?
PEVAC: Jova Koviljac, Đorđe Belgiški, Mika Belov, who knows, a lot more. Some is still fallow. They are probably keeping it for someone . . . Yesterday I was in the fields. Jova Koviljac had his team in there plowing. Plowing my grandfather's land, for God's sake. I said, "Hello, Jovan, are you plowing?" He doesn't say anything. He doesn't speak to me anymore. He's offended—as if they'd given me his land. *(Ješanov laughs. He looks around him. Then in a whisper.)*
JEŠANOV: Do you ever think of Greta? *(Silence. Pevac answers after a long pause.)*
PEVAC: And how. *(They stop working.)*
JEŠANOV: That was a woman! In every sense of the word!
PEVAC: Do you know how close I came to staying there?
JEŠANOV: I know, namesake, I know.

17.

(The office of the new government. Pavle and Golić are in their

places. Ilija Pevac is sitting before them.)

PEVAC: Listen, Golić . . .
GOLIĆ: Comrade Golić.
PEVAC: Listen, comrade Golić. This is my business and nobody else's. It's no skin off your ass if I don't let my wife go wandering around at night.
GOLIĆ: Pevac . . .
PEVAC: Comrade Pevac.
GOLIĆ: Pevac, I've got three things to say to you. First, this isn't some cheap dive; you've been swearing about a hundred years too long. Second, comrade Nevena is a real comrade, a hardworking activist, and that's not just your business. Third, a meeting of the W. A. F. isn't wandering. If this happens again, we'll bring you up before a meeting, in front of the whole village. Just so you know.
PEVAC *(Irritated, people from Srem would say furious)*: Why would you bring me up before a meeting? Why? Why would you do that? What does the village have to do with my family affairs?
PAVLE: Comrades, we can talk about this calmly. *(At that moment, an uproar is heard outside. All three look out the window. Two rather old men are fighting violently. Pavle runs outside.)*
PEVAC: That's Mlađa and Milenko. What are they fighting about, for Christ's sake?
GOLIĆ: Sensible people, aren't they? There was a war on here for four years, comrade Pevac. We killed each other, you know? *(In the meantime, Pavle has separated the two antagonists.)* And I don't want to hear any more of "That's my business." Those times are past, brother, understand? And another thing—Vasa Koviljac is a reactionary and he's being boycotted.
PEVAC: First you'd better explain to me, comrade Golić, what a reactionary and what a boycott is.
GOLIĆ: His son is a traitor.

PEVAC: Then his son is a reactionary, so boycott him. *(Someone knocks. A youth of about seventeen enters, with the marks of his first shave.)*
YOUTH: Death to fascism! Comrade Vice-President, National Youth Brigade has completed its mission. Grandma Koviljka's kitchen has been whitewashed.
GOLIĆ: Have all the mothers of soldiers who died in action been taken care of?
YOUTH: Yes. What should we do now?
GOLIĆ: Now you can rest a little. You've earned it.
YOUTH: Give us a job to do. We don't want to rest.
GOLIĆ: You don't have to overdo it. Rest a little.
YOUTH: No. Uncle Golić, give us something to do. We're not tired. *(Golić laughs.)*
GOLIĆ: Okay, report to Čavka.
YOUTH *(Happily):* Yes, sir, comrade vice-president. *(He goes out.)*
GOLIĆ: Do you know whose son he is?
PEVAC: Whose?
GOLIĆ: Radoja the blacksmith's.
PEVAC: Big Radoja's. So big already?
GOLIĆ: Kids change. And the times too, Pevac. Shape up while there's still time. Times have changed.

18.

(The interior of the bell tower. Tujta has nearly finished cleaning the bell. All the rubble has been taken out of the tower. The huge bell is turned on its side. Ilija Pevac comes in. Tujta notices him. Pevac extends his hand. They shake hands firmly.)

TUJTA: The door is too narrow. I'll have to make it wider.

19.

(The office of the new government. Pavle and Golić are in their usual places.)

PAVLE: He's an honest man, so treat him that way.
GOLIĆ: I treat him the same way I'd treat any comrade.
PAVLE: I'm not so sure. Make sure nothing like that happens again.
GOLIĆ: There won't be any more of it, Pavle, word of honor.
PAVLE: You know it would be bad if anyone said anything.
GOLIĆ: I don't understand at all.
PAVLE: Try a little harder. I don't want any more quarreling between you two. You know that the whole village . . .
GOLIĆ: . . . knows that before the war I was a hired hand for Ilija Pevac.
PAVLE: Very good!
GOLIĆ: I'm proud of that, Comrade Captain.
PAVLE: As you should be, Comrade Vice-President.
GOLIĆ: Just let me tell you one thing, Comrade Captain. If he tries anything at all, he'll get what he deserves.
PAVLE: And what might he try, for example?
GOLIĆ: I don't know. I'm only warning you. *(Pavle gets up and starts to leave.)*
PAVLE: A little more tolerance and everything will be all right. The man was away for five years. You have to understand it, if he acts a little strange. *(Golić is silent.)* And one more thing. I want you to recommend Comrade Nevena for party membership. Is that clear?
GOLIĆ: It's clear, Comrade President. *(Pavle goes out and leaves Golić alone.)*

20.

(The courtyard of Ilija Pevac. The door to the courtyard opens. A girl from the Communist Youth League and a German come in.)

GIRL: Pevac! *(Murat starts to bark. Old Miloš comes out.)* Grandpa Miloš, is Nevena or Ilija here?
MILOŠ: They're up on the threshing floor. They're stacking hay.
GIRL: Here, they sent this fascist to help you. And tell Nevena and Ilija they have to come tomorrow, without fail. There's a meeting at eight. Goodbye.
MILOŠ: Goodbye! *(The girls leaves. Gesturing)* Go up there.
GERMAN: I understand everything. I'm Hans, a farmer too.
(The German starts towards the threshing floor. Miloš continues mending sacks.)

21.

(The courtyard of Ilija Ješanov. A metal drum is attached to the large walnut tree in the courtyard. Ješanov taps a little around the barrel. Then he climbs down the ladder. He takes a pail already filled with water and climbs back up. He pours the water into the barrel. He comes down and stands under the barrel. He pulls the wire. Water falls onto his head. An improvised shower. Ješanov's father Stojan appears.)

STOJAN: What are you doing, you idiot?
JEŠANOV: This, father, is called a shower.
STOJAN: Take it down, the whole village will laugh at it. *(Ješanov laughs Water runs down his face.)* It's understandable that you have to make this kind of junk, when you don't have anyone to pour water on you when you come back from the fields. Get married, then you won't need that shower of yours anymore. *(He goes away across the courtyard, laughing. Ilija*

Ješanov is standing under the shower. He is laughing.)

22.

(Ilija Pevac stands in front of the Cooperative with another farmer. They are tipsy.)

PEVAC: Let's go to Jocika's for some wine now. *(The farmer shakes his head.)* Let's go. Jocika always has the best wine in town. *(The farmer again shakes his head.)* We'll go for one at my godfather's and then home, eh?
FARMER: I haven't spoken to him for two years.
PEVAC: Why not?
FARMER: Don't ask.
PEVAC: Jesus Christ, are there three people in this village who talk anymore?

23.

(The overcrowded hall of the Cooperative. On the rostrum sits the presidential committee. The table in front of them is covered with a rug. There are slogans on the walls. The son of Radoja the blacksmith shouts "Long live Comrade Stalin!" The hall thunderously takes up the cry. "Long live Comrade Tito!" shouts a Young Communist near the door. Again the hall echoes the cry loudly. Golić stands up. Pavle looks at him.)

PAVLE: Wait. I'll do it. *(Golić sits down.)* Quiet, Comrades. Here is the agenda for today's meeting. I will report on the renovation and rebuilding of the damaged houses. Comrade Golić will report on land distribution and agrarian reform.
VOICE FROM THE ASSEMBLY: Long live agrarian reform!
PAVLE: And then, the third item on the agenda—the receiving of new members into the party. Followed by miscellaneous

business and then dancing. *(Applause.)* I can proudly say that in our village there is not a single mother of a fallen soldier who has not been taken care of.

VOICE FROM THE ASSEMBLY: Long live the fallen soldiers! *(Only a few voices take it up. There are a few long moments of silence. Pavle is also confused. Then someone shouts "Long live Marshall Tito!" The hall echoes with the cry "Long live Tito!")*

THE SAME VOICE: We don't want the king! The king isn't worth a damn!

THE ASSEMBLY: No king! *(Applause.)*

VOICE: Tito fought, the king got married!

THE ASSEMBLY: That's right!

PAVLE: Young people, farmers, and . . .

24.

(Brana Tujta passes beside the Cooperative. Across his shoulders is a pickaxe. He enters the portal of the church. From there he goes into the bell tower. He swings the pickaxe in powerful movements. He tears the door apart and widens it. A flock of pigeons flies out of the bell tower. An agitated Father Jovan rushes out of the church.)

FATHER JOVAN: What are you doing that for, you wretch? *(Not answering, Tujta continues to swing the pickaxe.)* You'll kill both yourself and some innocent bystander.

TUJTA: I don't hear you, Father.

FATHER JOVAN: What are you doing that for, you fool? *(He begins to shake Tujta.)* The tower is shaking, it's going to fall. *(Tujta swings the pickaxe some more.)* Every time you hit it, it shakes right down to the foundations. One of these times will be one too many and you'll kill somebody.

TUJTA: Get out of here, Jovan. Don't bother me. *(He starts to swing the pickaxe again. Father Jovan is frightened and runs out. Tujta continues to make the door wider, the bell tower indeed shaking dangerously with every blow.)*

25.

(The meeting room of the Cooperative. There is an ovation. Golić sits down.)

PAVLE: Following that detailed report by Comrade Golić, let's pass on to the third item on the agenda, the receiving of new members into the ranks of our honored party. You all know what a Communist and revolutionary should be like. Please, Comrades, who will report from the committee on candidates for the party? *(A girl of around twenty-five stands up. We have already seen her as a Young Communist in the courtyard of Ilija Pevac, conversing with old Miloš.)*
PAVLE: Go ahead, Comrade Velinka. *(Velinka climbs onto the platform.)*
VELINKA: Unfortunately Comrades, today we have only one candidate to recommend. And that is Comrade Nevena Pevac. *(Pevac, astonished, looks at Nevena.)* You all know how during the war Comrade Nevena was active in aiding our struggle. You all know how she kept wounded fighters in her own house, you know that in her house, at the risk of her life, she sheltered many members of the underground, couriers, and even some very important comrades. We also believe that Comrade Nevena Pevac has matured politically, and has broken completely with religion and other remnants of the unenlightened past. *(Applause. Pavle leads it.)*
VELINKA: So much for that, Comrades.
PAVLE: You have heard, Comrades. Now we shall vote. All for, raise your hands.
GOLIĆ: Only Communists can vote. No one else should raise his hand. Only Communists.

PAVLE: Is anyone against? *(No one raises his hand.)* Then it's unanimous. Comrade Nevena, please come onto the stage. *(A little confused, Nevena goes onto the stage.)* Congratulations. You know what a responsibility is now yours. *(Congratulations are given. After Pavle, Golić and the others. Then Nevena leaves the platform and goes back to Pevac, accepting congratulations on the way.)*
PAVLE: Now on to new business, Comrades. Doesn't anyone want to speak? *(Behind Pavle, a tamburitza orchestra begins tuning their instruments.)*
JEŠANOV: I would like to speak, Comrades.
PAVLE: Go ahead.
JEŠANOV: Comrades, yesterday I was in the forest. It's terrible how many gypsy moths there are. One caterpillar after another. Comrades, our forest is going to be completely ruined. Just look at the mulberry trees around the village. There's not a single leaf left on them. It's a shame that our forest is being ruined, Comrades. I suggest that we form a brigade to combat these gypsy moths.
PAVLE *(To the doctor, who is keeping the minutes)*: Take that down, Doc. Comrades, I agree completely with Comrade Ješanov.
JEŠANOV: But we can't afford to wait.
PAVLE: And now, young Comrades, clear away the benches for dancing. *(In a few moments the table disappears from the rostrum. All of the benches are placed along the walls. The tamburitza players begin to play "Beautiful is the Guilded Srem." The first couples begin to dance, Nevena and Pevac among them, after so many years.)*

26.

(It is a clear night. Nevena and Pevac are walking along the street. The music reaches them from the Cooperative behind

them.)

NEVENA: How long has it been since we've danced?
PEVAC: God only knows.
NEVENA: Five years. Even more. *(They continue in silence.)* You know, now I'll have to go to meetings more often.
PEVAC: I see. Follow the crowd.
NEVENA: You're not unhappy that I joined the party?
PEVAC: Why should I be unhappy? But are you going to be able to do everything at home and there too?
NEVENA: Don't worry about that. You know, I'm really happy tonight. *(Pevac smiles.)* I'm proud, you know. *(They go a few steps without a word.)* We haven't been alone since you came back. *(Pevac lights a cigarette.)* Tell me how it was.
PEVAC: In Germany?
NEVENA: Yes.
PEVAC: I've already told you a hundred times.
NEVENA: Go on anyway.
PEVAC: You should see how they work the land. I spent my last year there on one of their farms, as a farmhand for a German. His sons were in Russia. Quite a few of us were assigned to farmers as farmhands. The way they work, and what they have to work with my God!
NEVENA: But what about the crimes they committed here? *(From behind a gate a dog suddenly barks. Nevena jumps back and grabs her husband's arm.)*
PEVAC: Down! Quiet!
NEVENA: My heart missed a beat. *(Hand in hand, Nevena and Ilija Pevac continue down the street. Towards their house.)*

27.

(A village street. A row of mulberry trees. In every treetop there is a young person or two. Ilija Ješanov is also there, removing

gypsy moths from the trees. The young girls work as hard as the boys. A song resounds as they work.)

At dawn when the sun is rising,
On Tito's boats the sailors sing.
Onward, onward, Tito's sailors.
Onward, onward, partisans.

28.

(The office of the new government. Golić is inside. Knocking before he enters, Ilija Pevac goes through the open door.)

PEVAC: Hello.
GOLIĆ: How's it going?
PEVAC: Fine. Listen, can you give me another German today? I'm spreading manure. GOLIĆ: Take two, brother.
PEVAC: One's enough.
GOLIĆ: Go see Čavka.
PEVAC: I'd like to get that little one I had before, if that's possible. Hans, his name was.
GOLIĆ: Ask Čavka about it. If someone hasn't already taken him.
PEVAC: He's a good worker.
GOLIĆ: No problem.
PEVAC: See you.
GOLIĆ: Bye.
PEVAC: Thanks.
GOLIĆ: Don't mention it. *(Without closing the door behind him, Pevac goes out and heads for the construction site.)*

29

(A long line of diggers stretches across the entire village. They

are digging a drainage ditch. Ilija Ješanov is working with all his might. Velinka passes by him with a water can.)

JEŠANOV: Give me some, Velo, let me drink my fill.
VELINKA: You're not from our group. You've got your own water carrier.
JEŠANOV: Yours is colder and sweeter.
VELINKA: It's all from the same well.
JEŠANOV: Well, you can't tell. Give me a cup. *(Velinka gives him a cup. Ješanov drains it in one gulp and holds out the cup for more.)*
VELINKA: No more for you.
JEŠANOV: Come on, give me some. I'll pay you back a liter this evening. *(Velinka laughs. Whispering.)* Come out in front of your house at eight tonight. I'll bring you the water. *(Velinka nods her head. Then she runs off with the water. Ješanov strikes a powerful blow with his packaxe.)*

30.

(A vineyard. The sun is high over the vines. Pevac and Nevena are under a cherry tree, making love slowly and tenderly. Then they both come at the same time, together. Nevena gets up. She shakes the dirt from her apron. She laughs and look at the sun.)

NEVENA: It's past noon, and we haven't pruned the vines yet. *(They both burst into laughter.)*

31.

(Ilija Ješanov's courtyard. Ješanov is there holding two pails of water. Old Stojan comes out.)

STOJAN: Where are you going with that water, you idiot?

JEŠANOV *(Through his laughter):* Father, I'm going to get married.
STOJAN: Who is this madman I'm living with, for God's sake? *(Ješanov leaves the courtyard, leaving his astounded father behind him. It is dusk.)*

32.

(Ilija Pevac's courtyard. Pevac and Hans are at work. Pevac stops and lights a cigarette. He offers one to Hans. Hans speaks with an accent.)

PEVAC: You're a good worker, Hans. Very good.
HANS: Thank you, Mr. Pevac. *(He lights his cigarette from Pevac's.)*
PEVAC: Where are you from?
HANS: Jena. From a village near there. I'm farmer too. I work the land.
PEVAC: Are you married? *(Hans nods his head.)*
HANS: I have left a big family at home. Wife, children, brothers, mother . . .
PEVAC: Are they still alive?
HANS: I don't know, sir. I don't think so. *(He speaks with certainty.)* The Russians are there.
PEVAC: So what? *(Hans looks frightened.)*
HANS: I didn't mean anything bad, Mr. Pevac.
PEVAC: You don't have to be afraid of me, Hans. Not at all.
HANS: The prisoners from the American occupation zone receive letters. We, others, don't. Their families write to them that there are massacres, that there is no more marriage . . . just think, Mr. Pevac, they burned the church and hung the priest.

33.

(Ilija Pevac is walking down the middle of the street, leading a horse by the halter. On the horse is Pevac's son, Miloš. They arrive at the blacksmith's. Pevac shouts.)

PEVAC: Radoja! *(Out of the blacksmith shop comes an enormous man with sooty cheeks and mustache.)* Where have you been, big fellow?
RADOJA: Ilija! *(They greet each other warmly. Pevac takes his son off the horse.)* Fuck you, you slut! How the hell are you?
PEVAC: The two hind shoes came off while I was spreading manure.
RADOJA: We'll take care of that. So how are things?
MILOŠ: Daddy, can I go to the playground?
PEVAC: What for? We're going right home.
MILOŠ: There's a football match between us and the Germans.
PEVAC: Go on, then. *(The boy runs off. Pevac and Radoja begin to work on the horse. They work quickly and skillfully.)* I never see you at the Cooperative, and you're never at the cafe.
RADOJA: I don't have anything to do with that bunch. *(Pevac says nothing.)* It's all nothing but bullshit. Golić and that gang. Those bums want to build a country – in two years they'll ask the king to come back. *(Pevac raises the horse's leg. Radoja puts down the hot shoe. Then he starts to harden the hoof.)* I hear your wife is one of them. Listen, Ilija, it seems to me that you don't know about anything. *(Pevac looks at him questioningly.)* I'm going to tell you something, because I'm more honest than all of them put together. I'll be surprised if you have a better friend than me in this village.
PEVAC: So tell me.
RADOJA: There's not much to tell. Your wife was unfaithful. To say the least. *(A long pause. All that can be heard is the horse's hoof being hardened. Perspiration appears on Pevac's*

face.)
PEVAC: Radoja, this isn't anything to joke about.
RADOJA: I had to tell you. And it's the truth, I swear. Your father knows about it, too.

34.

(Ilija Ješanov is going along the street. In his hands he has the jugs of water. It is dusk. Then in the shadow of a gate he sees Velinka and Pavle in intimate, almost tender conversation. Velinka gently straightens the medal on Pavle's chest. Ješanov hides behind a mulberry tree. He stands there a few moments. Then be pours out the water and goes away. Velinka notices him, but says nothing to Pavle.)

35.

(The house of Ilija Pevac. Nevena is at the stove, cooking supper. Pevac rushes in through the open door, bewildered and frantic.)

PEVAC: So that's how it was. *(He begins to strike Nevena immediately, as soon as he comes, through the door. He hits her with both his hands and feet, paying no attention to where the blows land.)*
NEVENA: Ilija, what's wrong with you? Ow! *(She starts to wail loudly.)*
PEVAC: What's wrong with me, you motherfucking whore, what's wrong with me? *(He hits her wildly, as if he were beating himself as well. Nevena falls, and Pevac continues to beat her.)*
NEVENA: Ilija, don't please.
PEVAC: You hid comrades . . . Goddamn it . . . *(He stands astride her and continues to beat her. Little Miloš comes to the door. He starts to fight with his father. Pevac shoves him away roughly and the boy falls. Then he runs outside stricken with*

fear. Pevac begins again where he left off. He grabs Nevena by the hair and begins to beat her head against the floor. Just then the boy runs in with an axe. He swings it. Nevena cries out.)
NEVENA: Don't, Miloš. *(Pevac turns around, then raises his arm. The axe glances off his arm and strikes him on the shoulder. Pevac whimpers. He slaps his son with all his might. The boy falls. Blood gushes from his nose and mouth, splattering the floor.)*
MILOŠ: I'll kill you. I'll kill you one day. *(Pevac picks up the axe and begins to yell. He swings the axe, striking the stove with all his might, frantically. Bricks, ashes, and coals fly about the room.)*

36.

(A party meeting at the Cooperative. Present are Pavle, Golić, Velinka, the Doctor, Čavka, and a few farmers whom we have already met in earlier scenes.)

PAVLE: Comrades, I call this meeting of the Manđelos cell of the party to order. Doc, keep the minutes as usual. Now don't frown. Who's missing?
VELINKA: Only Nevena.
PAVLE: I propose the following agenda.
GOLIĆ: We should check and see why Comrade Nevena isn't here. Write that down, Doctor.
PAVLE: So I propose the following agenda. The arrival of our comrades the colonists, meeting the teacher, and miscellaneous business. Agreed? Then you know, Comrades, what kind of people are involved here, right? They are hardened fighters and Communists. Revolutionaries, not smugglers. The people who bore most of the burden of our revolution. I think it's fair to say that the largest share of that burden, figuratively speaking, was on their shoulders. Of course, I don't mean by that to belittle the

contribution of people in other parts of the country, but it's well known what role Bosnia played in the war, especially the Bosnian borderlands. So we must welcome these people accordingly. To quote Comrade Kidrič "resettlement colonization is one of the basic tasks in the reconstruction of the country. It is a shortcut to socialism." End of quote. *(Applause.)* All that for my editorializing? Thank you. *(More applause.)* Excuse me, Comrades, but I have one more thing to add. We have to do everything in our power to welcome the colonists. I suggest that Comrade Velinka take upon herself everything concerning the cultural and artistic program. We should mobilize the young people, get them to put on a sketch or something, or a patriotic reading, by Branko Ćopić, for example, and folk music and dancing . . .

GOLIĆ: I definitely think we should get an accordion player from Mitrovica. People from the borderlands don't like our tambouritzas . . . And we should definitely practice a few Bosnia songs, like . . . well, I don't know. There are plenty of them.

PAVLE: All those in favor, Comrades. *(Everyone raises his hand.)* There are twenty-six houses in our village which belonged to Germans and four belonging to Ustašas, isn't that right? That means thirty families will be arriving here in Manđelos. Most of them are from villages around Banja Luka.

GOLIĆ: There's one that goes, "Oh Banja Luka, you have burned down and the girl has gotten pregnant . . ." We could learn that one.

PAVLE: We'll distribute the houses and land according to the number of members in each household. Families with officers will get an extra acre. One acre more, I think. You'll do that, Comrade Vice-president. Keep accounts-the bigger the family, the bigger the house, and vice-versa.

GOLIĆ: I'll take care of it.

PAVLE: And as for the welcoming party, everything should be festive and happy. With singing. We should definitely put up a stage. We've got red crepe paper. Velinka, choose the sketch from Socialist One-Act Plays. There are twenty-three of them there. And at the end we'll dance a kolo. That's obligatory, Comrades.

GOLIĆ: We all know that, brother.

PAVLE: Any questions? *(Velinka raises her hand.)* Yes, Comrade Vela?

VELINKA: None of the young Communists are going to want to play capitalists or fascists in the sketch. I guarantee it.

PAVLE: Just explain to them that it's a party assignment and there'll be no problem. So much for that, Comrades. That means, number one, Comrade Golić will assign the houses. Two, the stage and posters. Three, folk dancing and music and the sketch. I'll say a few words of greeting to the colonists at the beginning.

GOLIĆ: And the accordion and tamburitza players.

PAVLE: Right. And we have a picture of Comrade Tito. What about Stalin?

GOLIĆ: I'll bring one from home.

PAVLE: Doctor, have you written that all down?

DOCTOR: Yes.

PAVLE: Is there anything else in connection with the first point, Comrades? *(Everyone is silent.)* Then let's go on to the second. So, the arrival of the teacher. You all know that we're getting a teacher. When exactly?

GOLIĆ: The twenty-ninth of September.

VILLAGER: Is that definite? The children are already a month late starting school.

PAVLE: It's definite. *(To Golić.)* When did you say?

GOLIĆ: The twenty-ninth.

PAVLE: And the Bosnians?

GOLIĆ: The twenty-seventh.

PAVLE: Fine. That means we can use the same stage. You know, Comrades, in the new socialist school, the children are going to be taught new things: integrity, the socialist morality,

the value of work, optimism, and so on. To teach those things you need the right person. Well, we've got such a person, Comrades. In fact, we've got the best. What's his name?
GOLIĆ: Brana Kovačević.
PAVLE: Also known as Pavle Korčagin. And when someone has a nickname like that, Comrades, you know what he's like, don't you?[2]
VELINKA: Right.
GOLIĆ: We've all read *Tempered Steel*. Korčagin, eh?
PAVLE: Comrades, the person we've got is a young Communist from Belgrade, a member of the underground before the war. We have to give a proper welcome to a man like that, don't we?
VILLAGER: There's no problem there, Comrades. Even before the war the village teacher was all-important, let alone now. Before the war half the village met him at the edge of town, and the other half waited for him in front of the school. Don't worry about the welcome.
GOLIĆ: The comrade teacher is a Communist from before the war, one of the first to fight, do you see, man?
PAVLE: One of the young people should prepare a speech. You can help with that, Velinka. *(Velinka nods.)*
PAVLE: Which of them could do that?
DOCTOR: Radoja the blacksmith's son.
PAVLE: We have posters and a stage. Everything is taken care of. Great. Is there anything else in connection with the teacher?
VELINKA: Lodgings.
PAVLE: Good thinking, Vela. Čavka, send some Germans over tomorrow.
ČAVKA: Right.
GOLIĆ: The comrade teacher is single. Send a couple of young people to get a bed and a table from some German house . . .

---

[2] Pavle Korčagin was a fictional Bolshevik hero from Ostrovsky's novel, *How the Steel was Tempered*.

whatever they find. Act with moderation, yet find everything that's needed.

PAVLE: Is there anything else, comrades. *(No one speaks.)* Then on to miscellaneous business. Speak up. *(All are silent. Then, after a few moments, the doctor raises his hand.)* Yes, Doc?

DOCTOR: I have something, Comrades—the mistreatment of Comrade Nevena Pevac by her husband.

37.

(The blacksmith shop. Radoja is working at the forge. His son enters. We have already met him at Golić's office, after the whitewashing of Grandma Koviljka's kitchen. His name is Đorđe.)

ĐORĐE: I'm going.

RADOJA: Is that so? You could say that a little less often—"I'm going."

ĐORĐE: I'm, going to help make the stage for the welcoming party for the colonists.

RADOJA: Really, for the colonists?

ĐORĐE: For the colonists.

RADOJA: Those are those Bosnian hicks?

ĐORĐE: You might watch what you say a little.

RADOJA: Oh? Why?

ĐORĐE: Those Bosnian hicks made this revolution.

RADOJA: Well, screw them and their revolution.

ĐORĐE: Watch what you say or you'll be sorry for it later.

RADOJA: To hell with them and the revolution and the stage and everything else.

ĐORĐE: Comrade Belegiški, you can get thrown in jail for that.

RADOJA: No, I can't.

ĐORĐE: You'd better believe you can.

RADOJA: I can't, because they're already full. Jammed.

ĐORĐE: Watch what you say.
RADOJA: And who will send me there. You? You aren't going to report me yourself.
ĐORĐE: I will, personally. Even if you're my father a hundred times over.
RADOJA: Well, fuck you all one more time. The revolution, the Bosnians, Stalin . . . *(The son slaps his father hard. There are a few seconds of silence.)* Here you go. *(He returns the blow even more fiercely. The son answers it. Then Radoja. Then his son. Then Radoja again. They stop.)*
ĐORĐE: Reactionary! *(He goes out, slamming the door.)*
RADOJA: To hell with everything. And the ones who made the revolution, too. When they throw away their peasant shoes, getting too big for their britches . . .

38.

(The office of the new government. Pavle is sitting at the desk. Ilija Pevac comes in.)

PEVAC: You sent for me.
PAVLE *(Not raising his head):* Yes. *(Pevac stands silently for a long time. So long that he begins to shift his weight from one foot to the other. It is as if Pavle is keeping him waiting intentionally. This continues. Finally Pavle begins to speak.)*
PAVLE: You know why I sent for you.
PEVAC: No, I don't.
PAVLE: You know all right. Don't play the fool with me. *(He falls silent again.)* Sit down. *(Pevac sits. Pavle takes out a cigarette. He offers one to Pevac. Pevac shakes his head. Another pause. Pavle lights up.)* Don't do it again *(Again neither of them speaks.)* A family man. It doesn't become you. And in front of the child. You've been here before and you've seen that I don't approve of Golić's methods. But you ought to know that I

can be three times as bad as he is. A hundred times. *(He becomes more and more incensed.)* Don't do it again, If you value your head. That's all finished, my friend. Forever. A tight rein and the whip. Women aren't the same anymore, either, understand? Those are remnants of a dark past, and we've broken with that. I know it's not easy for you. You have the biggest burden of all. It's as if you were dropped here from an airplane. But it's time you finally realized how things are. You're no fool, for God's sake. Look at Ilija Ješanov. He's in the same situation and he's a model comrade. But with you it's one fuck-up after another. Golić told you that times have changed. Get that through your head, brand it there if you have to. Don't let me hear that you even raised your voice to you wife, let alone anything else. Do you realize, you blockhead, that you hit a member of the party? Do you know what that means, Pevac? The party knows how to defend its members, don't doubt that for a minute. Not for a minute. Get that into your head once and for all. Two can play this game, Comrade Pevac. *(He stops, out of breath, and gets control of himself. He reaches for his tobacco again. Again, Pevac shakes his head.)* Don't do this again. Remember that, Ilija. Don't be a fool. You can consider this either a friendly warning or a threat, whichever you prefer. *(He stops again. Both are silent. Pavle again picks up the package of cigarettes.)* Go ahead and light up, for Christ's sake. *(Pevac takes a cigarette. Pavle holds out a match for him.)* And all this because of what—village gossip. Who knows why they told you all that crap. If I knew who it was, I'd skin him alive, you know what I mean?

39.

(The village square. A stage is decorated with red crepe. There are pictures of Tito and Stalin side-by-side. The words "Tito-Stalin, Stalin-Tito," are pinned to the stage in white letters made of paper. There are posters of welcome all over Mandelos

"Welcome, Comrade colonists," "Bosnia-Srem," "Welcome Heroic Bosnia," "Socialism Through Colonization." The tamburitza band is tuning their instruments and practicing "O Banja Luka, you Have Burned Down." The folk ensemble is on the stage, along with Pavle Golić, Čavka, and the Doctor. Velinka is listening to the speakers practicing their speeches. Then someone shouts "They're coming!" The tamburitza players strike up "O Banja Luka, You Have Burned Down and the Girl Has Gotten Pregnant." Shots and shouting can be heard in the distance.)

PAVLE: First. Vela will propose members for the honorary presidential committee. Second, I'll say a few words and Golić will read the house assignments. Third, the youth group members will take everyone to their new houses and get them settled. Then everyone will come back for the cultural and artistic program. Vela, it's Tito, Stalin, Marx and Engels, in that order. Then dancing.

40.

(The house of Ilija Pevac. Nevena and Pevac are not speaking to each other. Nevena is putting on a new scarf. Pevac is setting the burners in the newly rebuilt stove. Grandpa Miloš comes in from outdoors. He sits down. Everyone is silent. Outside shouts can be heard.)

NEVENA: *(To the old man.)* Dad, I'm going to the reception. Goodbye.
MILOŠ: Goodbye, daughter. *(Nevena goes out without looking at Pevac.)*

41.

(A prisoner of war camp on the edge of town. The sound of gun shots and accordion music, naturally, can be heard in the distance. The captured fascists are resting. Some are lying in the sun, others are playing a game that consists of joining hands and turning in a circle until one member of the pair becomes dizzy. Hans is shaving, his face covered with lather with a folding mirror in front of him. Čavka goes by and notices the mirror.)

ČAVKA: Hans.
HANS: Yes, Mr. Kafka.
ČAVKA: Where did you get that mirror?
HANS: I don't understand.
ČAVKA: Spiegel. Yours?
HANS: Mine. From Jena. From home.
ČAVKA: Lend it to me, Hans . . . for a couple of days. *(Hans, not yet finished shaving, hands the mirror to Čavka. The lather is still on his face.)*
ČAVKA: I'll return it to you . . . soon.
HANS: I don't doubt, Mr. Čavka. I don't doubt it at all. *("Bastard", he mutters in German.)*

42.

(Đorđe conducts the family of Radule Erak into a house. We will meet Radule on several occasions later. That is, Radule and his wife, small children, and grandmother.)

ĐORĐE: Leave the goat outside, granny. There's plenty of room for it there. *(They go inside, confused and frightened. The room is huge, with a parquet floor, a tile stove in the corner, and a chandelier above their heads. The old woman starts to cry, then wail loudly.)* Here you are, Comrades. Make yourselves at home!

(He opens the doors to the remaining rooms.)
WIFE: All this?
ĐORĐE *(Laughing)*: Everything. Well, Comrades, don't forget to come back, you know. I have to be going. Get settled in and then come to the celebration. *(He goes out. The Eraks stand there, lost amidst all the rooms. Then the wife opens a window and then the shutters. Light pours into the room. Radule Erak slowly takes off his cap, as if he were standing before an icon.)*

43.

(Night. The house of Ilija Pevac. The child is asleep. Old Miloš and Pevac are sitting in the darkness. The light of a bonfire shines in. They are silent. Outside there is the sound of singing and gunshots.)

OLD MILOŠ: Someone's going to get killed tonight. The people have risen in Bosnia, the people have risen. They are led, they are led by Simela Šolaja. They're not singing, they're bellowing, for god's sake. *(Rain begins to beat against the window, then falls harder and harder. In a moment it becomes a real summer shower. "Hold it. Where are you going? What's a little rain to a real man," is heard outside. "Cousins, let's make the circle bigger." The rain lashes against the window and the bonfire grows dimmer and dimmer.)* They're rough and tough. It's a different world from ours. *(They fall silent again.)* We're not going to have it easy with them, nor them with us. Well, good night. *(He gets up and goes out. As soon as he closes the door, Nevena rushes in soaking wet. She does not greet Pevac. Pevac gets up from his chair, undresses and goes to bed. Nevena also undresses. She lies down next to her son. Neither Nevena nor Pevac speak, but they do not sleep, either. In the distance can be heard "Look little one, the paper's turning white, where we ate caramels last night." For a long time yet, these echoes of Bosnia* will resound over the farmland of Srem. The rain lashes against the window.)*

44.

(The door of the church. Tujta is working. He is trying to take out the huge church bell. He is trying to move it from the bell tower to the door, unsuccessfully. His shirt is soaked with sweat. He has obviously been working at this for a long time. Then he puts a beam under the bell, as a lever. The bell moves a little. Father Jovan appears with all of his two hundred and twenty pounds.)

FATHER JOVAN: How is it going, Branislav?
TUJTA *(Looking at Jovan):* I don't understand a word you're saying, Father.
FATHER JOVAN *(Laughing):* Could be better, huh?
TUJTA *(Reading the priest's lips):* That's about right.
FATHER JOVAN: Just be careful you don't wreck the bell tower.
TUJTA: You have to speak slower if you want me to understand.
FATHER JOVAN *(Indicating what he means):* Be careful!
TUJTA: Don't worry.
FATHER JOVAN *(Taking off his coat):* Together we can do it. Everything is easier with two. *(He puts his shoulder to the bell. The bell moves.)* OK, now push. It's moving, it's moving. It's hot to trot now. *(He laughs.)* There's something I have to tell you, Radaković.
TUJTA: Could be . . .
FATHER JOVAN *(Laughing):* . . . better. *(He takes Tujta's hand.)* I'm glad you came back to the fold.
TUJTA: I don't understand, Father. *(He looks the priest in the eye.)*
FATHER JOVAN *(Speaking distinctly):* I'm glad you returned . . . to the church. *(Silence. A long pause.)*

TUJTA: Get out! *(He seizes the pickaxe. The priest backs away.)* Move! Get out! *(He starts towards Jovan, and the priest beats a hasty retreat.)* Don't let me see you around when I'm here. Not even accidentally. *(He goes back to work. As if shrinking from his wrath, the bell moves more easily. Then a ten-year-old girl enters the bell tower. She puts her hand on Tujta's shoulder. He turns around.)*

GIRL *(Softly, syllable by syllable):* Daddy, let's go home.

TUJTA: Go ahead, I'll come later.

GIRL: Come on, daddy. Please. Let this be and come. You've been here the whole day. The fields aren't plowed and everyone's laughing at us. You've dropped everything because of this stupid bell. *(She starts to cry.)* Let's go, daddy. They're all laughing at us. I can't do everything by myself . . . Please . . . We're way behind everyone else. *(She stifles a sob. Brana puts the pickaxe on his shoulder and puts his arm around the child.)*

TUJTA: Let's go, daughter.

45.

(Big Radoja's house. Radoja's son is in front of the mirror. He has a copy of his speech in his hand.)

ĐORĐE: Honored Comrade. Welcome to Manđelos, a rich and fertile revolutionary village . . . You've overdone it, Vela. We are happy to have in our village a stalwart Communist, a member of the Belgrade underground, a man whose nickname says it all . . . *(He looks at his copy of the speech.)* Pavle Korčagin. Applause. Comrade teacher we wish you a pleasant stay in our village . . . our revolutionary village, and we hope that all your pupils will be honor students. Long live General Stalin, long live Marshall Tito, death to fascism, freedom to the people. Applause. *(He breathes a sigh of relief. Then he tries out some poses in the mirror. On the last few words he raises the clenched fist of his left hand. Then he tries it with the right. That seems like the best way to do it.)* Long live Marshall . . . Long live General Stalin, long live Marshall Tito. *(Another sigh of relief. That's it.)* Honored Comrade, welcome to . . .

46.

(On the stage we've already seen at the colonists' reception. The whole village has again assembled. In the villages of Srem, the teacher has long been more than just a servant to the community.)

ĐORĐE *(To himself)*: Long live Comrade Stalin, long live Comrade Tito! *(Velinka is next to him.)* *("Here comes the carriage! Here's the teacher!" Excitement, applause, shouts . . . then the teacher gets out of the carriage. It is a girl, barely more than a child, dressed in the uniform of the partisans, with a cigarette in her hand. When she steps out of the carriage and the villagers see that she is missing a leg, shock takes the place of silence.)*
VELINKA *(Nudging Đorđe with her elbow)*: Go ahead . . . *(Đorđe does not react. Velinka whispers.)* Begin. *(Silence. Đorđe fails to begin. Golić urges Velinka on with a look. Velinka shrugs her shoulders. Pavle gives her a questioning look. There is a long, uncomfortable silence.)*
TEACHER: Well . . .
PAVLE and GOLIĆ *(Simultaneously)*: Comrade schoolmaster. *(Another pause.)*
PAVLE: Comrade Brana, welcome.

47.

(A classroom of the village school. Or more simply, the lawn of the schoolyard. The teacher, Pavle Korčagin, is standing in front

of the pupils.)

TEACHER: That's how we'll vote, Comrade Pioneers. That way and no other. Why am I telling you all this? You don't vote yet, but sometime you will, and you'll vote in a new, socialist country. This doctor, Milan Grol, who is not even a real doctor, doesn't have a chance. Not the slightest. And why not? Because he doesn't have the people behind him. Instead he has the English and other capitalists and the despicable king. But the people know who has given them freedom. They will vote for those who bled during the war and not for those who spent the war in hotels, castles, and mansions, surrounded by servants and lackeys. And that, Comrade Pioneers, is why that miserable Doctor Grol has no chance at all. We'll show the world where we stand and what we stand for. Isn't that so?

KIDS: Yes! Yes!

TEACHER: The whole world is watching us. The rotten capitalists are already spreading rumors that the elections will be rigged. Do you know what rigged means? They're sending observers. Well, let them come. There'll be something to see, all right. They will see the triumph of truth and the defeat of the reactionaries.

LITLE MILOŠ: And what is triumph?

TEACHER: Victory, Miloš, victory. And that's why we're all—I mean your parents—are going to go to the polls with the slogan "Class consciousness now." Comrade Pioneers, get up that morning earlier than your mother and father, wake them up and say, "Go and carry out your duty as citizens."

MILOŠ: Why citizens? We're villagers. *(Pavle Korčagin laughs. She ignores the question.)*

TEACHER: There's no going back to the old ways, Comrade Pioneers. For us the king is dead. Long live Josip Broz!

KIDS: Long live Josip Broz!

MILOŠ: Excuse me, teacher, I have a question.

TEACHER: Go ahead, Miloš.
MILOŠ: Why are you called Pavle Korčagin, when you're a woman?
TEACHER: Do you know who Pavle Korčagin was?
KIDS: No.
TEACHER: Well, then your teacher will tell you about that now.

48.

(Night. The house of Ilija Pevac. Everyone is sleeping. Then little Miloš jumps out of bed. He starts to shake old Miloš.)

LITTLE MILOŠ: Grandpa get up. Wake up dad and mom!
OLD MILOŠ: What is it, little pal? What's the matter?
LITTLE MILOŠ: Get up, grandpa. It's time to carry out your duty as a citizen. *(Old Miloš looks at the clock on the wall.)*
OLD MILOŠ: Go back to sleep. It's not time yet.
LITTLE MILOŠ: Then when will it be time?
OLD MILOŠ: Just go to sleep. It's not even midnight.
LITTLE MILOŠ: Don't be late, grandpa, please.
OLD MILOŠ: Go to sleep. It's the day after tomorrow, not tomorrow. We'll be the first ones there, don't worry.

49.

(A pre-election meeting. The presidential committee is the usual one, but there is one new party member, the teacher, Pavle Korčagin. There are posters and the usual slogans: "Long live Marshall Tito," "Long live General Stalin," "Everyone to the polls," and "No Monarchy, We Want a Republic." Someone in the crowd shouts, "We want King Peter." And the crowd answers, "String him up.")

GOLIĆ: There's no reason to hem and haw, Comrades. They'd

like to pass him off on us, but we're better off without him. Let him stay in London and spend our gold, which he took with him. We don't need that, either. While we were bleeding, he was screwing Elizabeth and sending messages to his beloved people. This is the final attempt by the rotten capitalists to dictate the wishes of the people. Never again. Comrade Pavle said it well with the slogan "Class consciousness now!" We're all going out to show everyone what the wishes of the people are. As for the results of the elections, no need to worry—we know what they will be!

VOICE FROM THE CROWD: Tito fought while the king got married! We don't want the king—he's no good! *(The crowd answers in unison, "Hear! Hear!")*

GOLIĆ: Comrades, this is the final attempt of the English capitalists to go back to the old ways. If they need another king, they can have ours. Let him join hands with Queen Elizabeth. They're birds of a feather. So let's not hesitate, Comrades. Let's go to the polling place as early as possible—no exceptions. The youth group will bring older people and those who can't get around. Let's show the reactionaries who we are and what we're made of. *(Applause, ovations, cheers.)*

PAVLE: And now the comrade Doctor has the floor.

DOCTOR: I'll be brief, Comrades. I would rather not speak today, but I must. And this is why. Comrade Ilija Pevac beat his wife so badly that I wanted to send her to the hospital in Mitrovica, but she refused. I have never in my life seen anyone beat his wife so badly. I therefore suggest that we publicly condemn this deed of Comrade Pevac as a throwback to the unenlightened past, and that if he does it again we boycott him.

GOLIĆ: Call him onto the platform. Come up here and be a hero like you were when you beat up your wife. *(Pevac turns and hurries away.)*

GOLIĆ *(After him)*: Now you run away. But when it was a question of . . .

TEACHER *(In a tone which silences everyone):* That's enough!!!

50.

(The voting. The office of the new government, festively decorated and hung with slogans. "Class consciousness now" dominates. It is dawn. Pavle and Golić, the Doctor, Velinka and of course the Teacher, Pavle Korčagin are present. People enter and vote in silence. The atmosphere is celebratory. The voters each take a ball, put a closed fist in each of two boxes, the blind and the correct one, and then immediately display their empty fist. Ilija Ješanov immediately shows his empty fist, without putting his other hand in the blind.)

PAVLE: Don't do it that way, Comrades. We explained clearly how to vote, for God's sake. Otherwise your vote doesn't count. Write that down, Doc. Ilija Ješanov's vote is in invalid. He didn't cast his ballot properly. Don't do it like that, Comrades. Please. *(The villagers continue to vote. A long column of people votes in silence. Two men carry in an old woman on a stretcher.)*

51.

(The office. Balls are being counted. Golić, Čavka, Velinka, the teacher, Pavle, and the Doctor are present.)

GOLIĆ: No other place will finish counting before eight o'clock, or I'm the thinnest person here.
PAVLE: Let's count, Comrades!
GOLIĆ: And there's no other place where one-hundred percent of the people voted, I guarantee it. *(Pavle takes the correct box and begins to break the seal.)* What are you doing there? Why don't we count this handful in the blind, then you'll know right

away what the outcome is.
(He picks up the blind and breaks the seal. He shakes out the balls. There are nine of them.)
GOLIĆ: Nine. *(Silence. No one speaks.)*
VELINKA: Nine out of one thousand and twenty voters. That's an insignificant percentage of reactionaries.
GOLIĆ: Screw those nine. *(He sits down.)*
VELINKA: That's not bad, is it, Comrades?
GOLIĆ *(Picking up a ball):* This is yours, isn't it, Pevac. It is. It is. *(He puts the ball aside. The teacher Korčagin opens her mouth to say something, then changes her mind and goes out.)* And this is his father. *(He puts this ball next to the first.)* And this one is our Father Jovan, and this one is Big Radoja. And deaf Tujta.
PAVLE: How do you know all that?
GOLIĆ: In this village I know more than just the time of day, Comrade Captain. You can hang me if those aren't the ones. And this one is Grandpa Vasa. No, no, it's not him. It's Mika Parćaš, and this is his wife. I'll shit my pants if it's not, I promise you. Write this down, Doc. Report of the Commission of the Manđelos Electoral District. One hundred percent of the voters turning out. Nine for the ticket of Milan Grol, One thousand eleven for the Popular Front.
PAVLE: One thousand ten. Ilija Ješanov's vote doesn't count.
GOLIĆ: And send that to the Committee in Mitrovica right away.
PAVLE: No, don't. I'll take it. Okay, Comrades, you're free to go. You stay, Comrade Golić.
(The others leave. Pavle and Golić remain.) Are you sure that those are the ones?
GOLIĆ: I guarantee it.
PAVLE: Then put a little pressure on them. On condition that you're sure. See you.
GOLIĆ: Something else is bothering me.

PAVLE: What?
GOLIĆ *(Picking up the remaining balls)*: Whose are these two, for Christ's sake?
PAVLE: I'll see you.
GOLIĆ: Say hello to the comrades on the Committee. *(This sentence throbs with a strange sort of irony. Pavle goes out. Golić remains with the balls in his hand. He looks at them for a long time. Čavka enters.)*
ČAVKA: He went to skim off some cream.

52.

(The house of Ilija Pevac. Pevac and the Bosnian, Radule, are present. Pevac pours drinks.)

RADULE: No more.
PEVAC: This won't give you a headache.
RADULE: Don't pal. That's enough. And the same goes for you, Ilija. We have to get off our asses and do some work.
PEVAC: That's easy to say.
RADULE: If we could stand it in Germany everything else should be easy.
PEVAC: It's hard. Didn't you see? You were there. In front of the whole village. What does the village have to do with my stove and my bed? I wanted the earth to swallow me up. In front of a thousand people.
RADULE: Why don't you wait for him somewhere?
PEVAC: Who?
RADULE: In the dark somewhere . . . a few words, you know?
PEVAC: The Doctor?
RADULE: Oh, the Doctor. Your troubles aren't coming from that direction, Pevac. You know who I mean.
PEVAC: As if that would change anything. I can understand that there won't be a king anymore, okay, and that the government

has changed, that's okay, too. But even the language is different, for God's sake. We weren't away for a hundred years. Boycott, reactionary, obstructionist . . . they talk different. You left somebody a shepherd, you come back and now he's driving around in a jeep like a goddamn general. Half your friends are dead, the other half are in prison Brothers don't speak to each other. Twin brothers. The teacher couldn't even tell them apart.
RADULE: Who's that?
PEVAC: Mitar and Pitar Čamprag. They don't speak to each other.
RADULE: There was a war here, for Christ's sake.
PEVAC: I left behind a wife and came back to a comrade. My son avoids me like the plague. I left behind two hundred acres of land and returned to get thirty-five, which is a lot, they say, a lot. I'd like to adapt, but how, for the love of God?
RADULE: My friend, I have to put up with all that, too. But I've got a new house and new neighbors, and new customs . . . and a new country. Everything. You can see who has it worse. Pour another one, goddamn it. *(Pevac pours. They drink in silence.)*
PEVAC: Erak, listen. *(He continues in a whisper.)* Don't say anything about Greta to anyone, for god's sake.
RADULE: Pevac, what are you talking about? What do you take me for, goddamn it? It's safe with me, I swear it on the heads of my children. Don't mention it again. *(Pevac pours another drink. He empties his glass without clinking glasses.)*

53.

(The office of the new government. Pavle, Golić, Čavka and another villager are present. We have already seen the latter at a party meeting.)

PAVLE: Comrades, I have to pass along to you the compliments of the Committee in connection with the organization and the

results of the elections. The comrades are very satisfied. Second, it may be quite some time before the property records are in order. We are a young nation but a nation nevertheless. And a nation with no taxes isn't worth a shit. So a directive has come down which says that until the property records are complete, taxes will be determined not by units of land but by production, that is, approximately. The comrades higher up, since they have the greatest confidence in you, have appointed you three to the tax commission. (*He gives them some papers.*) Here are the quantities of foodstuffs which are to be supplied by Manđelos. That's how much the tax has to raise. Keep accounts so that tax brackets can be determined according to property, in other words fairly and within tolerable limits. Is that clear? You may go. Just two more things. Keep accounts so that no one's personal quarrels or disagreements affect the tax assessments. Is is clear what I'm talking about?
ČAVKA: And the second thing?
PAVLE: The second thing is that it wouldn't be bad if Manđelos contributed a little more than its share, would it, Comrades?

54.

(The cafe. There are several people inside, some from Srem, some Bosnians. Some of those present are Ilija Pevac, Big Radoja, Tujta, Ilija Ješanov. Tujta is alone at the bar. A Bosnian, we'll call him Joviša, comes up to him.)

JOVIŠA: Hey, deaf guy. *(The Bosnians laugh at Tujta. He doesn't hear. Joviša repeats his words behind Tujta's back. More laughter.)*
RADOJA: Do you think that's something to joke about?
JOVIŠA: What are you butting in for? Nobody asked you to. Deaf guy, have you raised that bell yet?
TUJTA: I don't hear a word you're saying. *(Joviša begin to*

gesticulate.)
JOVIŠA: Are you still trying to lift that bell? Pull on this. *(He grabs his penis.)* Maybe it will ring. What are you staring at, you jerk? Huh?
PEVAC: Boy, leave the man alone.
JOVIŠA: Nobody asked you, kulak. *(To the café owner.)* Listen, you. How long are you going to serve everyone who comes in here? You can't let just any kind of trash drink with people who were the first to fight and free the country.
TUJTA: What are you saying?
JOVIŠA: Whatever I feel like saying. *(The Bosnians make signs of approval.)* I'm telling you we're fed up. Who told Jablan Dukić that his tile stove was a monument to Hitler, so that he wrecked it with a pickaxe? Who gave Mila Erak popcorn seed to plant instead of ordinary corn? Who told that same Mila that the wheat he planted should be plowed under again? Fuck the lot of you. *(He gets angrier and angrier.)* Who told me that you build a fire in the oven of the range, so that I almost set fire to the house? Who, so I can tell you to go fuck your mother. Don't make me put half of the village in mourning.
RADOJA: Whose mother are you talking about?
JOVIŠA: All of yours, and yours most of all, you and that pious deaf guy, and Pevac. *(He seizes Tujta by the ear. And so it begins. Tujta slaps him hard, and in a moment it turns into a melee. They all jump up and reach for chairs, bottles, and a few knives. Someone catches a chair on the lamp and the fight continues in darkness. The fight is heated and long. Ilija Ješanov jumps onto the bar.)*
JEŠANOV: Peace, people, have mercy. What is wrong with you? Are you crazy? Calm down. *(To the café owner.)* Run and get Golić. You're not children, what's wrong with you? *(The café owner runs out. No one pays any attention to Ilija Ješanov or his words. The fight doesn't let up, but continues more violently and furiously.)*

55.

(The office of the new government. It is night. Present are Pavle and Golić, still sleepy and bewildered, along with the café owner and an excited Ilija Ješanov.)

JEŠANOV: Then Tujta hit Joviša, and first one and then another jumped in.
CAFÉ OWNER: Nothing is left in one piece, not even a salt-shaker.
GOLIĆ: We should call a meeting right away, tomorrow.
PAVLE: There won't be any meeting at all. Go get them right now, get them out of bed. Every last one of them. Get them all here in ten minutes. I don't want anyone to say a word about this. Anyone who opens his mouth is in the shit, I promise you. Is that clear?
CAFÉ OWNER: Yes.
GOLIĆ: Yes.
PAVLE: This imply didn't happen. Are you aware of what this means, Comrades? Of what political consequences it could have? We can't let a word of this get out. Consider that your duty to the party. Got it?
JEŠANOV and GOLIĆ: Got it.
CAFÉ OWNER: What about the café?
PAVLE: It has to be as good as new by morning.
CAFÉ OWNER: But how?
PAVLE: I don't know and I don't care. Let the brawlers worry about that. OK; let's go. I want them all here in ten minutes. In their shorts.

56.

(The bell tower of the church. Brana Tujta is at work. He is polishing the bell with sacking and ashes until in gleams. Outside

a north wind is howling. Tujta blows on his frozen fingers.)

57.

(The house of Ilija Pevac. Dinnertime. All four of the Pevac family are at the table, old and young Miloš, Nevena and Pevac, who is carving slices from a huge loaf of bread. He hands slices to both Miloses. Then he cuts a piece for himself. He puts the bread and knife on the table. Nevena starts to reach for them. Pevac changes his mind, cuts off a slice of bread and offers it to his wife. For a few long moments, Nevena hesitates. Then she puts out her hand and takes the slice of bread from her husband.)

58.

(In a huge room with a parquet floor an old woman sits in front of the fireplace spinning. Joviša, in the corner, is getting dressed and ready to leave. He straps on his pistol.)

OLD WOMAN: Are you going? That's a bad business, son. You're always drunk. Don't do it anymore. *(Joviša does not answer.)*
OLD WOMAN: It's no good. We have to live here, Joviša. *(Joviša still does not answer.)* Stay here, Joviša. And protect me from nasty neighbors. How long are you going to carry that pistol? Don't be rough and arrogant, son. And leave the brandy alone.
JOVIŠA: But mother, when I'm sober, I'm scared to death of them.

59.

(The house of Ilija Pevac. It is night. Pevac and Nevena are in bed. They are talking.)

PEVAC: I don't know how to tame him.
NEVENA: You have to be patient.
PEVAC: That an eight-year old child should remember things for so long . . .
NEVENA: Go slowly. Little-by-little it will take care of itself.
PEVAC: Tomorrow, I'll send him to invite people to our saint's day celebration.
NEVENA: Go ahead. Who are you thinking of inviting?
PEVAC: The usual people. Godparents, neighbors, friends, the priest the teacher.
NEVENA: Do as you like. But, I'm not sure you're doing the right thing.
PEVAC: What's wrong with it?
NEVENA: I don't know. I'll get everything ready, but I won't be around that day, just so you know.
PEVAC: Where will you go?
NEVENA: I don't know, to Velinka's or I'll go out somewhere.
PEVAC: Well, if you have to . . .
NEVENA: I don't have to, I want to. If I said in front of a thousand people that I've broken with all that, then I've broken with it. If I'm a party member, and if those things are relics of the past, then they don't go together. And don't get mad about it. *(Pevac laughs resignedly. Nevena gets up. She starts to get dressed.)*
PEVAC: It's still early.
NEVENA: It will get light while I'm doing the milking. And I have to go see Pavle.
PEVAC: What about?
NEVENA: About the taxes. Enough is enough. Even half of that would be a lot. You just can't do it that way.
PEVAC: Like a tyrant who decides on the shares. *(Nevena is already fully dressed. Pevac starts to get up too.)*
NEVENA: Don't. Sleep a little longer. *(She starts to leave. At the*

door she turns around.)
I think I'm pregnant.

60.

(The courtyard of Branislav Radaković, also known as Tujta, and more recently as deaf Tujta. The three-member tax commission comes in. They shout for the household. Tujta's daughter Ceca comes out.)

GOLIĆ: Is your father here, Ceca?
CECA: Yes
GOLIĆ: Call him, will you? *(The child goes inside. Shortly afterwards, she returns with Tujta.)*
TUJTA: What do you want?
GOLIĆ: As a veteran, you ought to be ashamed of yourself, Radaković. If we had to visit everyone three times, we'd never finish. Cant' you see that?
TUJTA: I can read your lips, but you'll have to speak a little slower.
GOLIĆ: I don't have to do anything. *(Angrily)* Don't hold us up, do you hear?
TUJTA: I told you nicely. Reduce the tax to a reasonable amount and I'll pay it. The way it stands I won't pay.
GOLIĆ: Who do you think you are not to pay it, are you out of your mind? When I say that's how much it is, that's how much it is. I want to have that tax by morning, or else I'll take it myself. I'll take the roof tiles off your house if I want to. Do you hear me, you deaf, crazy fool? I'll take the tiles from your roof, and the blankets from you and your kid.
TUJTA: Want a second. *(He turns and goes into the house. The members of the commission become uneasy. Čavka grabs his pistol.)*
ČAVKA: Let's go.

GOLIĆ: Are you afraid, Comrade Čavka?
ČAVKA: No, I just think . . .
GOLIĆ: All we need is for him to come out with a rifle. If he does, we'll shove it up his ass for him. *(To Ceca.)* Go and call him. We haven't got all night. *(She goes inside again. At that moment Branislav Radaković, also known as Tujta, and more recently as deaf Tujta, appears in the doorway in the uniform of a major in the People's Liberation Army of Yugoslavia. He is armed with a pistol and is wearing his medals. There is silence.)*
TUJTA: Commission for Apportioning Taxes, attention!
(Hesitation on the part of the commission.) I called you to attention. *(After a moment the commission falls into line.)* Daughter, open the gate. The big one. *(The child runs to do so.)* Right, face! *(The commission turns.)* Now beat it!

61.

(The house of Ilija Pevac. A lamp is burning beneath an icon of Saint Nicholas. The scene is the living room, in which stands a large table covered with a white tablecloth. The table is set for sixteen, and there are an equal number of chairs. At the head of the table is Father Jovan, to his right is old Miloš, and to his left, Radoja. No one else.)

FATHER JOVAN: And where is the lady of the house?
MILOŠ *(Clumsily):* Her mother is a bit ill. She went to see her.
RADOJA *(Ironically):* Today of all days. *(A rather long pause.)*
MILOŠ: Well, guests, cheers! *(They drink up. Then, Radoja stands up.)* Where are you going?
RADOJA: To get Ilija. He can wait all day, no one else is going to come. I'm sure of it.
(He goes out.)
MILOŠ: Cheers, sir!
FATHER JOVAN: This is good. Strong.

MILOŠ: From Banija. *(The fall silent again. Pevac and Radoja come in. They sit down.)*
RADOJA: It's no use, brothers! No one else. You can spit in my mustache if anyone else comes. *(Pevac is in a bad mood.)*
MILOŠ: Welcome, guests. *(They clink glasses.)*
RADOJA: In the time when God walked the earth, the house was always full. I remember it as if it were yesterday.
MILOŠ: Times change. What can you do?
FATHER JOVAN: But there has never been a time like this one.
RADOJA: You don't know how it was under the Tatars.[3]
MILOŠ *(To Pevac)*: Go on, bring out the food.
PEVAC: Someone else still might come.
RADOJA: Who all did you invite?
PEVAC: The usual people.
RADOJA: Those who would have come are afraid to, and those who aren't afraid don't believe any more.
FATHER JOVAN: I'm afraid that's just how it is, Radoja.
RADOJA: You can be sure there's someone hiding out there, watching who goes into this house. *(They are silent once more. Then they reach for their glasses. Drinking justifies the lack of conversation.)*
RADOJA: They get you coming and going. That tax, it's as if Aganlija and Kučuk Alija[4] each took a bite. What one doesn't get, the other one does.
FATHER JOVAN: For the love of God, let's not talk about that.
RADOJA: Why not?
FATHER JOVAN: Don't spoil this holy day, Radoja.
MILOŠ: Why don't you talk to Pavle about it?
RADOJA: What for?

---

[3] Radoja is referring to either the pre-Ottoman tribes that invaded the Balkan's in the Middle Ages, or to the Ottomans themselves.
[4] Two of the renegade janissary leaders who defied the Ottoman sultan in 1801 and took control of a region called Smederovo. Their rule was brief as the First Serbian Uprising in 1804 brought it to an end.

MILOŠ: Nevena talked to him and they let us off without paying.
FATHER JOVAN: I went. It didn't work.
MILOŠ: Of course, they only let us off because of Nevena.
PEVAC *(To Radoja.):* Why don't you send Đorđe?
RADOJA: He went on his own. If it weren't for him, I'd have paid half as much. My son. He's no son, he's a Judas. He went to complain that the tax was too little.
FATHER JOVAN: I don't know what I'll do, brothers. Even the bishop of Novi Sad doesn't have as many marriages, funerals, and christenings as they put down for me. I just pray to God to send down a plague. Either that or I'll take a machine-gun and shoot them myself.
PEVAC: What?
RADOJA: You'll hear about it. There'll be a stink like you never seen before. I promise you that. They'll ring it from every church bell.
PEVAC: Has Tujta raised the bell yet?
FATHER JOVAN: He's waiting for spring. But he comes every day to polish it. With ashes. It shines like new.
RADOJA: And him one of the first to fight, eh? Before the war there was no bigger Communist than him, and now he's turned into a turkey and gone back to the church.
FATHER JOVAN: It's not a question of that.
RADOJA: Then what is it?
FATHER JOVAN: I don't know, but it's not that. That's for sure.
MILOŠ *(To Pevac):* Let's start, son. No one else is coming, can't you see that? *(Pevac gets up.)* When I remember how it used to be on days like this. My God. *(Pevac comes in with the saint's day cake in one hand and a serving bowl full of soup in the other.)*
RADOJA: What a good housewife, only her apron isn't starched. *(No one laughs. Pevac approaches the table. He stumbles, drops the cake and spills the soup.)*

PEVAC: Fuck this whole goddamn world.
MILOŠ: Forget it. It's all right.
RADOJA: All we need now is for the icon lamp to go out. *(He stoops to help Pevac. He takes the pieces of the cake off the floor and puts them on the table. Pevac gathers the fragments of the serving bowl. He stands up.)*
FATHER JOVAN: Our Father who art . . . *(All four stand and murmur the Lord's Prayer. The atmosphere is unpleasant, as if all of them are conscious of the bad omens. Then two or three seconds later the teacher, Pavle Korčagin, appears in the doorway. Everyone falls silent. The silence drags on.)*
TEACHER: Hello. *(The teacher stands in the doorway. No one invites her to enter.)* Happy saint's day. *(The confusion among the men continues.)* Well, I was invited to a saint's day celebration, for God's sake.
MILOŠ: Daughter, I'll remember this forever, even in the grave. *(And as if they arrived with the teacher, Branislava Kovačević, also known as Pavle Korčagin, rays of sunlight enter the room.)*

62.

(The office of the new government. There is a telltale creaking and heavy breathing. It ends. Pavle gets up from behind the desk. He buttons his fly and his uniform, then picks up his pistol from the table and buckles it on. A woman also gets up buttoning her clothes. Only then do we recognize her as Velinka . . They finish dressing. Silence.)

PAVLE: Say, Comrade Belić, would you be willing to change your name?
VELINKA *(Thrilled):* Pavle?!
PAVLE: What would you think of Dobrenov? Velinka Dobrenov, eh? It doesn't sound too bad.
VELINKA: Pavle!

PAVLE: In a month or two. But don't tell anyone. *(Velinka just nods. If she has ever been happy, it is at this moment.)* A nice small wedding. Without any hoopla or anything. Just you and me and the witnesses. No reactionary relics. We'll go to Mitrovica for a day, then to work.
VELINKA: My Pavle.
PAVLE: No drums, no gypsy bands, no carousing.
VELINKA: Do you know how much I love you?
PAVLE *(Spreading his arms like a small child):* This much.
VELINKA: Almost as much as I love Comrades Stalin and Tito, Pavle dear.
(She tenderly straightens the medals on his chest.) Take them off next time, will you. They all dig into me. *(Both of them burst into laughter.)*

63.

(Radoja is in some sort of office. There is a man behind a desk.)

MAN: I still don't understand what you want, Comrade.
RADOJA: I want to sign everything over to my son.
MAN: A will?
RADOJA: Not a will. I want to sign it over right away, tomorrow. Today, if possible. I want everything to be his.
MAN: A contract for a gift, then?
RADOJA: That's it, brother.
MAN: What's your name, Comrade?
RADOJA: Radoja Belegiški.
MAN: And your son?
RADOJA: Đorđe Belegiški.
MAN: From?
RADOJA: Manđelos. *(The man notes everything officiously.)* Twelve acres of land, a vineyard, a plum orchard, and a house. Everything except the blacksmith shop.

MAN: All right, Belegiški.
RADOJA: How much do I owe you?
MAN: Quite a bit. But the giver doesn't pay.
RADOJA: That's okay I'll pay, I'll pay.
MAN: All right, Belegiški, then we'll take care of it Monday, when everything is ready.
RADOJA: So on Monday everything will be his?
MAN: On Monday.
RADOJA: Right down to the last fucking nail. *(Radoja exults and the clerk is completely dumbfounded.)*

64.

(The office of the new government. Golić is at his desk. Čavka enters.)

ČAVKA: You sent for me?
GOLIĆ: Why is Joca Stepanov wearing a German jacket?
ČAVKA: Well . . .
GOLIĆ: Where did Joca's wife get a German jacket and where did Mila Erak get German boots? *(Čavka bows his head.)*
GOLIĆ: Where did Ljuba Radičević get the blankets that he uses to cover his horses so they don't get wet, huh, Čavka?
ČAVKA: From the prisoner-of-war camp.
GOLIĆ: Yes, from the prisoner-of-war camp. You should be ashamed of yourself, Čavka. A Communist, or rather a former Communist.
ČAVKA: Don't do that, Dušan. I beg you.
GOLIĆ: Return your party booklet tomorrow . . .
ČAVKA: I didn't sell any of it. I swear.
GOLIĆ: Settle your accounts at the camp and turn it over to Ilija Ješanov. I don't want to send you to prison for lying.
ČAVKA: I didn't sell anything. You have my word as a party member. I took from the fascists and gave to the people. Joca

was barefoot and the fascist was wearing boots.
GOLIĆ: Shame on you.
ČAVKA: Don't disgrace me, Dušan. I swear by the party. Those criminals destroyed everything you had. They burned your grandsons in the cradle, so I took that stuff from them.
GOLIĆ: Go outside.
ČAVKA: Go and ask. If I took a single dinar, send me to prison. I won't say a word. Don't, Dušan, for the love of God . . .
GOLIĆ: It's too late, Čavka. Get out. This is a decision of the entire party and I have to enforce it. Starting today you're boycotted by order of the party.
ČAVKA: What about your soul, Golić? Is this my thanks for—
GOLIĆ *(Interrupting):* Get out.
ČAVKA: Just let me tell you one thing. Until today you had a cousin. At least you had someone for your whole life. Well, as from today you don't have that cousin any more. *(He takes his booklet out of his packet and throws it on the desk. he goes out. Golić buries his head in his hands and stays like that for a long time.)*

65.

(The house of Big Radoja. Radoja and his son Đorđe are there.)

ĐORĐE: You're the only one in the whole village. Not counting the priest, he's a professional reactionary. He was there as an official duty. No one else's father went to the saint's day celebration of the biggest kulak in the village, only mine. Obstructionist dupe! Taken in by a deliberate provocation. Deliberate.
RADOJA: Then the teacher was taken in too.
ĐORĐE: Leave her out of this. Completely, do you hear? She can do that. Only she, nobody else. She's different.
RADOJA: I've been going to saint's day celebrations at that

house for thirty years.

ĐORĐE: And this was the last one, I'm telling you.

RADOJA: Do you intend to abolish saint's day celebrations, too?

ĐORĐE: No we don't, but that was the last one for you.

RADOJA: You've abolished everything but the air.

ĐORĐE: You really are a fool and a reactionary. You're surrounded and you don't even see that you're beaten.

RADOJA: And you and Golić have won. And Pavle Dobrenov.

ĐORĐE: That's right, we have. Don't you see that we want everyone to be equal. For Ilija Pevac to be just like Radoja Belegiški. Do you understand that?

RADOJA: Why don't you make Radoja Belegiški just like Ilija Pevac? There's a job for you.

(They are both silent for a moment. Then Đorđe begins again, slowly.)

ĐORĐE: You know that the village hasn't got any other blacksmith but you. *(Radoja is silent and laughs sneeringly.)* You know that the village can't get along without a blacksmith. *(Radoja again is silent.)*

RADOJA: Why don't you open the blacksmith shop again? *(Radoja gives a cluck of refusal. Đorđe again explodes in anger.)*

ĐORĐE: You'll open it, all right.

RADOJA: The hell I will.

ĐORĐE: You'll open it up like a good boy. As a member of the Young Communists, I have the job of making you open it, and open it you will.

RADOJA: I will if you and Golić are the first to come and be shod.

ĐORĐE: You'll open it, you'll open it. Comrade Stalin also had this kind of problem and he solved them. And worse ones as well.

RADOJA: And just what problems did he solve?

ĐORĐE: He solved them, he solved them. And war came and he defeated his internal enemies, and he built socialism and the

economy and everything.
RADOJA: *(Ironically.)* Is that so?
ĐORĐE: It is, it is. From one hive they got two hundred kilos of honey, and potatoes, two or three to a kilo.
RADOJA: And cooties as big as turtles. *(Someone bangs on the door.)* Who is it?
VOICE FROM OUTSIDE: Grandpa Vasa's house is on fire. Quick! *(Both Belegiškis run out pell-mell.)*

66.

(The house of Ilija Pevac. It is evening. Little Miloš and old Miloš are present, along with Nevena, who is bandaging and treating a singed and sooty Grandpa Vasa, the Reactionary. From outside, an uproar of people shouting reaches them, and the flames are reflected in their faces and on the window panes. Grandpa Vasa is sitting next to the window and Nevena is crouching next to him. They are all looking out the window. Everyone is silent.)

VASA: Everything is going up. *(He starts to cry.)*
OLD MILOŠ: Look at him, the old man is crying. Everything will be all right.
VASA: Why didn't I stay in that house? *(They fall silent. Outside something collapses with a shudder.)*
OLD MILOŠ: A good house-raising party in the spring and in a couple of days the place will be like new. *(Grandpa Vasa, the Reactionary, continues to cry.)* There's hardly anyone in this village who hasn't been burned out, if that's any consolation. *(To little Miloš.)* Come on, scamp, pour us one. *(Little Miloš obeys, bringing Grandpa Vasa a glass of brandy. Vasa shakes his head.)* Drink it, it will give you strength. And why did you cry, like some kid? You'll spend the winter with us, and in spring we'll have a work party and fix everything up.

VASA: What do you mean a work party, with me boycotted?
OLD MILOŠ: The whole village is here putting out the fire, there's no one who didn't come running. The boycott is over. What boycott?
VASA: I hope you're right. Do you know what it means to go eight months without speaking to anyone, Miloš?

67.

(The café. The two Ilijas.)

JEŠANOV: How did the fire start?
PEVAC: He piled the straw too close to the house. He did it himself this summer. He couldn't drag it into the garden. A spark from the chimney fell on it, the straw caught fire and it spread to the house.
JEŠANOV: When there's a fire, straw is always closer than the well. *(They fall silent. They sip their drinks.)*
PEVAC: Where have you been? I haven't seen you in a long time, for Christ's sake.
JEŠANOV: Oh, hell, I don't know.
PEVAC: Couldn't come on Saint Nicholas' day?
JEŠANOV: Have we ever lied to each other, namesake?
PEVAC: Not as far as I know.
JEŠANOV: Well, then, do we have to talk about your saint's day celebration?
PEVAC: No, we don't, namesake. *(Both are silent.)*
JEŠANOV: Bartender, what do I owe you? *(To Pevac.)* I should be going.
PEVAC *(Laughing ironically):* The teacher was there. *(Ješanov does not answer.)* I'll pay. You can go. I don't want to keep you. *(They are silent again.)* I haven't congratulated you.
JEŠANOV: What for?
PEVAC: You've been accepted into the party.

JEŠANOV: How do you know?
PEVAC: Nevena told me last night.
JEŠANOV: Is it for sure?
PEVAC: I don't know. That's what she said. On Pavle's recommendation. Last night at the meeting.
JEŠANOV: Bartender, drinks all around!

68.

(The village square. Joviša and Đorđe are riding Father Jovan and old Miloš Pevac. A number of young onlookers are laughing. The teacher, Pavle Korčagin, comes up. The laughter stops. Đorđe and Joviša get down.)

TEACHER: *(Beside herself.)* What's this supposed to mean?
ĐORĐE *(Trying to be witty):* The new order has reined in the old. It's symbolism, Pavle. Religion and Capital. *(He does not finish. The teacher begins to rain blows on the two of them, using both her cap and her fists. Đorđe and Joviša stand there motionless, as if rooted to the spot.)*

69.

(The house of Big Radoja. Đorđe is alone. Outside someone shouts, "Is anybody home?" Đorđe opens the door and lets Cvijeta in, the seventeen-year-old daughter of Radula, the Bosnian.)

ĐORĐE: Come in, Comrade.
CVIJETA: My father sent me to ask if Radoja will shoe our horse.
ĐORĐE: Sure.
CVIJETA: Has he started to work again?
ĐORĐE: Not yet, but he will. Tell Radule he'll do it. Because of

you.
CVIJETA *(Laughing):* Why because of me?
ĐORĐE: Like that. *(They are silent.)* What is Joviša doing?
CVIJETA: How would I know?
ĐORĐE: If his girlfriend doesn't know, who does?
CVIJETA: I'm not anyone's girlfriend.
ĐORĐE: Joviša says you are.
CVIJETA: Let him say what he wants, but it's my affair.
ĐORĐE: Okay, Cveta.
CVIJETA: I'm Cvijeta, not Cveta.
ĐORĐE: And whose are you, if you're not Joviša's?
CVIJETA: Nobody's.
ĐORĐE: A girl like you, nobody's? That can't be.
CVIJETA: Oh, you . . .
ĐORĐE: Would you like to be somebody's?
CVIJETA: That depends.
ĐORĐE: On what?
CVIJETA: On whose.
ĐORĐE: Mine, for example. *(They both fall silent. After a few moments, Cvijeta laughs, turns around, and runs out.)*

70.

(The jail in Sremska Mitrovica. A man in a prison uniform and the teacher, Pavle Korčagin, stand facing each other. A step or two behind the teacher is a guard with a pail in one hand and a spoon in the other.)

TEACHER: You don't recognize me. *(The man shakes his head.)* In Belgrade, in '41, when you made me eat salt, I said I'd make you eat shit.
MAN *(Terrified):* Korčagin.
TEACHER: That's right, Crepajac, it's Korčagin. I came to keep my promise. *(Both of them are silent. Then Crepajac goes down*

on his knees and clasps his hands in supplication. He begs mutely, like a cocker spaniel. Korčagin looks at him for a long time.)
TEACHER: So, after four years of waiting, the pleasure isn't there.
GUARD: Excuse me, I didn't hear.
TEACHER: Nothing, nothing. Let's go. *(She turns and leaves, with the puzzled guard behind her. They leave Crepajac on his knees in front of the bucket of shit.)*

71.

(The office of the new government. Golić is at his desk. Nevena enters.)

GOLIĆ: Sit down.
NEVENA: What do we have to do?
GOLIĆ: Just make yourself comfortable and listen closely. Negotiations are underway with Germany for the payment of reparations and the repatriation of German prisoners-of-war and who knows what all else. I won't bore you with all that now. But they asked us about the conduct of their prisoners, the ones we have here, you know, and we requested the same information about ours. We've already got something from the Russians and the Americans, and we had already received something from our own people even earlier. Then we asked the Germans for something. This morning it arrived. *(He takes three dossiers from a drawer.)* This is Gligor's, this is Ješanov's, and this one I have to read to you, as a comrade of the party. I'll report it at the meeting tonight. I have to. But I wanted you to hear it first.
NEVENA: Go ahead and read it.

72.

(A woman, or rather an old woman, is at the stove. Someone knocks. Nevena enters.)

NEVENA: Hello.
WOMAN: Hello.
NEVENA: I've heard that you know how to do abortions.
WOMAN: I've changed my ways. Who told you that, poor child?
NEVENA: That's not important.
WOMAN: These days it's strictly forbidden. I wouldn't do it for a hundred dinars.
NEVENA: And for a thousand? *(Pause.)*
WOMAN: What month are you in?

73.

(The Cooperative, overflowing with the people of Manđelos. The same table is on the stage, the same carpet on the table, the same people on the table, the same slogans and shouts in the hall. Đorđe and Cvijeta are side-by-side.)

GOLIĆ: Comrades, today I will open the meeting, not Pavle, although he is here. This is the reason. Our Comrade Pavle is going on to new duties, with the Committee in Mitrovica. He has been promoted, you might say, so I congratulate him, both on my own behalf and on behalf of all of you. *(Applause.)* I give the floor to Comrade Pavle.
PAVLE: My dear fellow citizens of Manđelos, let me just say a few words of farewell to you. It has been easy to be the leader of this village and to govern people like you. You all know where the Committee is, and Mitrovica is not far, just down the road. So just drop in, my door will always be open to you. I would like to

stay here with you, but I am a soldier of the party. My place is where the party sends me. Let me conclude with a few lines from one of our poets. ''I will always keep you in my heart, I will always think of you with pride.''*(Applause.)* Comrade Golić has been appointed in my place, and Ilija Ješanov has been named vice-president. Thank you once more.

GOLIĆ: Just a few more words before the dancing, Comrades. I want to express public thanks to the youth brigade, who in just two days' time fixed up a temporary room here in the town hall for Grandpa Vasa Brnjaš. They have promised to repair his house sometime in the future. *(Applause.)* Just a little more, Comrades. We still have among us some hidden reactionaries, but we also have some who are out in the open. One of these, Comrades, is Ilija Pevac. Comrade Pevac was a prisoner-of-war, and suffered horribly. He was a servant for a German, whose sons were at the Russian front. Is Pevac here?

VOICE FROM THE HALL: No.

GOLIĆ: That's too bad. He wasn't in fact a servant for a German whose sons were at the Russian front, but for one Greta, whose husband was in Russia. And he stayed there, Comrades, under Russian soil. While we were spilling our blood here, Comrades, Pevac was warming the back of a German woman. I don't need to tell you what else he was keeping warm. There's even a suspicion that he has a child there. Just so we know who is who and who is what. I give the floor to Comrade Ilija Ješanov.

JEŠANOV: Comrades, I propose that the youth brigade build sidewalks throughout the village. There's mud up to your knees. You can't walk. Volunteers should report to Đorđe Belegiški and Joviša Erak. And now for some dancing.

74.

(The office of the new government, in half-light. As soon as our eyes are accustomed to the darkness, we recognize Pavle and

Velinka. Pavle is sitting on the floor, leaning against the wall. Velinka is beside him, her head on his chest. They are silent.)

VELINKA: You spoke well tonight. Very well. *(The sound of music playing reaches them from the Cooperative. Tamburitzas are heard playing "Beautiful is the Guilded Srem.")*
PAVLE: I have something to tell you, Velinka. Look at me. *(Velinka looks at him.)*
PAVLE: The most important thing in the world for me is that you understand completely what I have to say. *(Pause.)* I've been thinking about the two of us for a long time. We're Communists and revolutionaries, right? *(Velinka looks at him doubtfully and simply nods her head.)* And Communists have to build a new state, not a family. We are soldiers of the revolution, Vela. You're a good comrade and a good Communist, you can understand your Pavle.

75.

(The house of Ilija Pevac. From the Cooperative can still be heard the sounds of "Beautiful is the Guilded Srem." Nevena is delirious. She is lying in bed. Pevac is beside her.)

PEVAC: Should I go for the doctor? *(Nevena does not answer. Pevac takes a cloth, moistens it, and puts it on Nevena's forehead. She throws it aside.)* What's the matter with you?
NEVENA: You beat . . . the hell . . . out of me because of . . . gossip, and you . . . and you . . . had a child . . . there. Shame on you. I don't want . . . to see you . . . any more . . . ever. *(Pevac suddenly understands and uncovers Nevena. The sheet beneath her and her nightgown are soaked in blood.)*
PEVAC: So you . . .

76.

(The café. Ilija Pevac is drinking. It is apparent that he has been doing so for some time. Radule Erak comes in and sits down at the table.)

RADULE: I've been looking for you. I just want a word or two with you. I didn't tell her, I swear to God, Ilija? *(Pevac does not answer. Radule sits uncomfortably on his chair.)*
RADULE: I want you to believe me. More than anything. How is Nevena?
PEVAC: She's all right. She is up and around. *(Big Radoja rushes into the café.)*
RADOJA: Hey, everybody. Gligor has arrived from America. He's back.
RADULE: When?
RADOJA: Last night. He brought some Indian.
RADULE: He wasn't in India, you dope. He was in America.
RADOJA: So what? If there are Serbs there, why can't there be Indians? She's an immigrant, too, no doubt. They came into the house last night. The girl kissed her mother—and father-in-law on the hand. I kiss the hand of my father, I kiss the hand of my mother, she says, and in Serbia. But he can't say a word in American. I just talked to them. Uncle Sreta brought a barrel up from the cellar. Half the village is already drunk. The gypsies are playing on the roof. It's a madhouse. Should we go home, Ilija? *(Pevac shakes his head.)*

77.

(Nighttime in the roofless church. Many candles are burning. Father Jovan, four old women, and Ilija Pevac are present. Elderly sopranos and two male voices are singing a song about the nativity. They finish.)

FATHER JOVAN: Merry Christmas. *(The old women approach him to kiss his hand. Then they go out.)* Christ is born!
PEVAC: Verily. *(They kiss each other on the cheeks, then fall silent.)* I'll bring in the straw.
FATHER JOVAN: Radoja left. *(Snow is falling, extinguishing the lighted candles around the altar.)*

78.

(A party meeting. Golić, the Doctor, Ilija Ješanov, the Teacher, Nevena and others.)

GOLIĆ: Comrades, he was in church again this morning. Only him and four old women. Excuse me, Comrade Nevena, this has nothing to do with you, of course.
NEVENA: As far as I'm concerned, he's dead. For good.
TEACHER: Do you have something against Ilija, Golić? I mean personally.
GOLIĆ *(Loudly and assertively):* Nothing personal, Comrade Kovačević.
TEACHER: Then why don't you leave him in peace for once? And where did you get all this information? How do you find things out so quickly, for God's sake? Who tells you?
GOLIĆ: That's my business.
TEACHER: It's not your business. There is no my business, Comrade Golić. Everything is our business. There's no mine or yours any more, Comrade Golić.
GOLIĆ: We still haven't discussed your visit for Saint Nicholas, either.
TEACHER: And you won't, Golić. And it wasn't a visit for Saint Nicholas, it was a visit to Ilija Pevac on Saint Nicholas. You seem to be trying to make an enemy out of an honest man.
GOLIĆ: An honest man?!

TEACHER: Certainly. *(She turns to a villager.)* What are you cooking today?

VILLAGER: My wife is cooking beans.

TEACHER: Beans? On Christmas? Too bad, I would have liked to go somewhere for Christmas dinner.

GOLIĆ: You can't behave this way, Comerade Korčagin, no matter who you are, regardless of your revolutionary past and everything. *(He becomes angrier and angrier. At that moment, a man bursts in, agitated and completely out of breath.)*

MAN: Typhoid and dysentery at the camp, the Germans are dying like flies.

GOLIĆ: What . . . are you sure?

MAN: If there's one thing I learned to recognize during the war, it's those two things. *(There is some confusion among the party members. Golić is the first to collect himself.)*

GOLIĆ: Fence the camp in right away and post a guard. Don't let anyone in or out, on pain of death. What else, Doctor?

DOCTOR: Get drums for boiling water, quicklime, medicine, and some people. Nothing else.

GOLIĆ: Ilija, go to Mitrovica right away. First to the Committee, then to the hospital. How many people do you need, Doctor?

DOCTOR: They can't give us as many as we need to quarantine two hundred people. We'll need volunteers.

VILLAGER: To help fascists? That will be hard.

TEACHER: No, it won't. *(She raises her hand. Nevena and Velinka do the same without hesitation. The rest then follow suit.)*

79.

(The door of the church. The righted bell shines in the sun. Brana Radaković, also known as deaf Tujta, is setting a huge post in the ground. For a moment, it seems that the post will be too much for Radaković to handle, but he nevertheless succeeds in raising it and placing it in the hole. The post sways and then

stops moving. Radaković starts to fill in the hole with earth and stamp it down. Several children, picking their noses, watch from a distance.)

80.

(The house of Ilija Pevac. Old Miloš, young Miloš, and Pevac are present. Pevac refills his glass.)

OLD MILOŠ: You've been reaching for the bottle pretty often lately. *(Pevac does not answer.)* That never took care of any problems and it never got any work done. *(He nods towards the glass. Pevac refills his glass again.)* Do as you like, son, but brandy won't make you any stronger.
PEVAC: Cut out the proverbs, dad.
OLD MILOŠ: They're acting high and mighty but they'll come back down to earth. In the end, everything will be all right. It's like water, like a flood. Fools drown themselves, but wise men wait for the waters to go down and then they put up a mill. *(He goes to the window.)* You just have to be patient. What's suffocating me, for Christ's sake? *(He unbuttons his shirt.)* Every government is severe at the beginning. *(To Miloš)* Get me a glass of water. *(The boy goes for the water. Miloš grabs the knob of the window to close it. His legs give away beneath him and he falls. Pevac jumps up.)*
PEVAC: Dad! *(Miloš gasps for breath on the floor, struggling for air.)* Dad, what's wrong?! *(To Little Miloš.)* Run for the doctor.
LITTLE MILOŠ: It's no use, he's at the camp with the Germans. *(Pevac realizes that his father is dying.)*
PEVAC *(To Little Miloš):* Get me a candle, quick, a candle.
LITTLE MILOŠ: I won't.
PEVAC: Get a candle. He's dying!
LITTLE MILOŠ: I won't. *(The old man's legs jerk strangely*

once, then once more. Then he is still. Pevac gets up and crosses himself. Little Miloš runs up to Old Miloš.)

81.

(A party meeting. Korčagin is absent. Nevena is in mourning.)

GOLIĆ: Go ahead, Doc.
DOCTOR: I won't be long. First, without the help of the teacher, Nevena, and Velinka, it would have been difficult to do anything by myself. That's one thing. These three comrades spent thirty-six days with me there. I'm sure it is obvious to you what an effort that was, especially for women. We had eighty-four deaths, and without these women there would have been a lot more. Two. The teacher, Pavle Korčagin, is seriously ill. So sick that she should be in the hospital. She has refused to go, and I suggest that she be ordered to go to the hospital, as her duty to the party.
JEŠANOV: What's wrong with her?
DOCTOR: All kinds of things. The police beat her and tortured her, she was wounded in the war, she has a disease of the blood vessels as a result of her amputation, and her heart is weak, also a result of the amputation without anesthesia. Everything is wrong with her . . .
GOLIĆ: I'll take care of that.
DOCTOR: How?
GOLIĆ: I'll take care of it.
DOCTOR: As long as you take care of it quickly.
JEŠANOV *(In a whisper):* I still owe you that water.
VELINKA: You're taking your time about it.
GOLIĆ: And now, Comrades, I have to read you this material about the collectives. You all know that these farmer's collectives, called kolkhoses and sovhoses in the Soviet Union, have yielded exceptional results. Comrades, why not profit from

the experiences of the great, fraternal Soviet Union? We have received directives from higher up to prepare gradually for the establishment of our kolkhoses. To tell you the truth, it's high time.

82.

(The room of the teacher, Brana Kovačević, also known as Korčagin. The teacher is lying on the bed, obviously ill and exhausted. Someone knocks.)

TEACHER: Just a moment. I'll be right there. *(She gets up, adjusts her clothing, brushes her hair, and alters the expression on her face.)* Come in! *(Ilija Pevac enters.)* Oh! What are you doing here? Hello!
PEVAC: I heard you were sick, but you look like sunshine. I didn't need to bring these quinces. *(He takes five or six quinces out of his pockets and puts them on the table.)* Well, how are you?
TEACHER: Never better. And you?
PEVAC: Oh, I'm all right. *(They fall silent.)*
TEACHER: I can see you're fine.
PEVAC: How is the little one doing in school?
TEACHER: You know, I haven't been at school for thirty-six days. You're only saying that to make conversation. I heard that Grandpa Miloš died. *(Pevac nods.)* I was very sorry to hear about that. I would have come to the funeral. Was anyone there?
PEVAC: Two old women and the priest. No-one else. When he saw the priest, Little Miloš wouldn't carry a cross or walk behind the coffin. Oh, yes, and Radoja. But he met us at the cemetery.
TEACHER: Send Miloš to me this afternoon. *(Pevac nods.)* What can I offer you? There's no alcohol in my house.
PEVAC *(Laughing):* There's too much in my house. Everything happens to me.

TEACHER: It will all pass. Just be patient. Golić isn't a bad fellow, and he isn't stupid either. He's just too impulsive. Rash, you know? He doesn't think anything over. He just goes on his first impression. Do you see? He says what's on his mind. And his principles are inflexible. Last night young Đorđe Beleigški and Joviša Erak got into a fight, over that pretty little one, Radula's . . .
PEVAC: Cvijeta.
TEACHER: Right away he wanted the party to punish them, to bring them in front of the meeting, you see what I mean? He doesn't understand that we should be happy, you know what I mean? For eight months the Bosnians have lived in a ghetto, isolated. You don't accept them and they don't accept you. Both groups are good people. With that fight, it's started to get better, do you see? A boy from Srem fought with a Bosnian over a Bosnian girl. Well, that's fine, you see. You take them aside, scold them a little. Don't raise a big fuss. Sometimes you have to do things that way, do you see what I mean? He threw Čavka out of the party without batting an eye. On principle. All right, but now Čavka wanders around the village like an idiot. Boycott. The man has taken to drink and abandoned his home and children. You people from Srem are a strange lot anyway. As soon as you have some kind of troubles or a problem, you reach for the bottle. Whew, I haven't got carried away like that in a long time. How is Nevena?
PEVAC: To tell you the truth, I don't know.
TEACHER: You're still not speaking.
PEVAC: No.
TEACHER: She talked to me in the camp. Just be patient and don't press her. You've gone beyond your rights. That's called a double standard. But I'll explain that the next time you come.
PEVAC: How was it up there?
TEACHER: Horrible. There was every kind of shit you can imagine-those people with rifles all around, quicklime, typhoid.

They were dying on us two or three a day. Terrible.
PEVAC: Do you know that little Hans?
TEACHER: From a village not far from Jena?
PEVAC: That's the one.
TEACHER: He was our right-hand man until he got sick. One morning we found him in the latrine, already stiff. That's how we had to bury him. We couldn't even straighten him out. Poor guy. *(They fall silent. Pevac notices that the teacher is not well.)*
PEVAC: Don't you feel well?
TEACHER: You know, I think I will lie down awhile. I really don't feel too well. Look, be a pal and don't tell anyone. And send your son to me this afternoon, without fail. And that business with Golić. We'll take care of that. Just be patient and sensible. We'll set things right with both him and Nevena. He's not a bad guy at all.
PEVAC: Isn't your name Branislava Kovačevič? It's like a balm to me.

83.

(The house of Joviša Erak. Joviša and his mother are present. Joviša is just finishing packing a small knapsack.)

JOVIŠA: Here. *(He hands his pistol to his mother.)* Keep that for me. I hope I won't need it. Just so you won't worry.
MOTHER: You don't have to go back. It's not too late to stay.
JOVIŠA: I can't stand it here any longer, mother. You have to join the collective. Brother and sister will be there to help you. Tell them to write.
MOTHER: Think it over some more.
JOVIŠA: Mother, it's a lot to lose in one year—Bosnia and Cvijeta. *(He kisses his mother, turns, and goes out.)*

84.

(Velinka stands hidden behind a tree, leaning on a man's black bicycle. She is watching. From the building across the street comes an elegantly dressed man—Pavle. The woman on his arm laughs loudly and lays her head against his upper arm. They go off. Velinka gets on her bicycle and rides off in the opposite direction.)

85.

(The Youth League is at work, building a sidewalk. Golić calls out to them in passing.)

GOLIĆ: Hey, boys, when you come back from the girls, you won't be coming home dirty. *(Laughter. Song.)*
For the worker and the farmer
There's no going back, no stopping.
They are joined by a powerful force,
Stalin, Tito, work, and sweat. *(Velinka goes up to Ilija Ješanov.)*
VELINKA: Do you intend to return that water or not?
JEŠANOV: I do!

86.

(A large black limousine is parked in front of the school. The whole village is out in front, the children are crying. Pevac appears and goes up to Radula.)

PEVAC: What's all this?
RADULE: Her father came to take her away. She can't walk anymore, she's wasted away. A General. Jesus Christ. *(Lieutenant-General Kovačević comes out of the school carrying his daughter in his arms. Little Miloš throws a stone at the*

General.)
PEVAC *(Running forward)*: Excuse me, Comrade General, the boy . . .
GENERAL: That's all right. But would you bring me the stone and put it in my pocket. *(Pevac does as the general asks.)* If I can be proud of anything in this life, it's this stone. *(General Kovačević carefully lays his daughter in the car, gets in himself, and gives a sign to the driver. The black Čajka disappears in a cloud of dust.)*
PEVAC *(To himself)*: She's gone.

87.

(The blacksmith shop. The church door. Tujta is present, with his daughter beside him. He is putting another post in the ground. A crossbeam connects the two posts at their upper ends. This wooden structure forms a serviceable bell tower, strong enough to support a bell much heavier than Father Jovan's.)

88.

(The house of Big Radoja, or more precisely, the house of Đorđe Belegiški. Đorđe and Radoja are present.)

RADOJA: Watch out. Not so fast.
ĐORĐE: Watch out yourself. Don't shoot off your mouth. Don't make a fool of me.
RADOJA: I won't shoot off my mouth any more, but in this house we'll still cross ourselves and icons will hang on the walls, you know that.
ĐORĐE: That's what we agreed. And you'll look out for my girl. And join the collective, without fail, do you hear? *(Radoja nods his head. Father and son exchange a long, firm embrace. Đorđe picks up the wooden chest from next to the door and goes*

out.)
RADOJA *(In a voice that trembles slightly):* Goddamn snotnose little bastard.

89.

(Cvijeta and Đorđe are alone. Đorđe is holding the wooden chest.)

ĐORĐE: Just don't cry?
CVIJETA: Who's crying? *(They are silent.)*
ĐORĐE: It will go fast.
CVIJETA: Three years.
ĐORĐE: I'll have leave.
CVIJETA: Write.
ĐORĐE: And you behave yourself.
CVIJETA: Don't say things like that.
ĐORĐE: It's three years.
CVIJETA: Even if it were three hundred and three, I'd wait for you. *(They are silent again.)*
And be careful.
ĐORĐE: What's there to be careful of? I'm not going to war.
CVIJETA: You'll be on the border.
ĐORĐE: Some border. With Bulgaria. What do I have to fear from the Russians and the Bulgarians? They're our people. Just take care of yourself, so I can marry you when I get back. Will you? *(Cvijeta nods her head.)*
ĐORĐE: And go around and see Radoja once in a while. Take him some hot food. *(Cvijeta nods.)*
ĐORĐE: And, don't cry.
CVIJETA: Who's crying? *(A song reaches them from somewhere in the village, from another couple who are parting.)*
Oh thirty-six months is a long time. Comrade Tito, cut it in half.

90.

(The office of the new government. Ilija Ješanov, Golić, and Ilija Pevac are there.)

GOLIĆ: You've been called here about a very serious matter. You know that certain new taxes have been announced. Ilija is taking care of these for our village. When will they be ready, Ilija?
JEŠANOV: In two or three days.
GOLIĆ: This is only the first step. The second is the formation of village collectives. You've heard of those?
PEVAC: No.
GOLIĆ: That's real socialism, brother. Everybody in the collective, everything is communal, except for house and yard. Well, it's paradise. You'll see.
JEŠANOV: Joining the collective is voluntary, of course. Whoever wants to, joins, whoever doesn't want to, doesn't have to.
PEVAC: Wait a second. That means that no one has anything of his own?
JEŠANOV: You have your house and yard . . .
GOLIĆ: You know what kind of results this has got in Russia, brother. And it will here, too, I guarantee it. But that's enough farting around. What we called you in for is this. You're a prominent man in the village. If you were to join the collective . . . you understand?
PEVAC: No.
GOLIĆ: If you joined the collective, you'd pull others in behind you. People would say, "It's not only have-nots and Bosnians who join the collective, you see? Ilija Pevac joined too." Do you understand?
PEVAC: I do.
JEŠANOV: And?

PEVAC: I don't want to.
GOLIĆ: Pevac . . .
PEVAC (*Shaking his head*): I don't know about all this. I don't understand all this nobody's everybody's. As I understand it, a household needs one head and a lot of hands.
GOLIĆ: Pevac, you'll regret this . . .
JEŠANOV: Think it over a little more.
PEVAC: I won't give my land. You do what you like. You already took fifty-two hectares and I didn't say a word. I'm not giving the rest. It's my grandfather's land, and I have to leave something to my grandchildren . . .
GOLIĆ: You'll learn, you'll learn.
JEŠANOV: All right, namesake. You can go. *(Pevac goes out.)*
GOLIĆ: You know what you have to do.
JEŠANOV: I know.

91.

(Three people are carrying sacks from the barn of Ilija Pevac. Pevac is standing to one side. They carry out the last sack. Radule approaches Pevac.)

RADULE: You still owe us six cubic meters of grain.
PEVAC: From where? You've cleaned out my barn, there's not even a speck of mouseshit left. Where am I supposed to find six more meters?
RADULE: You'll manage. Look, Pevac, I don't have anything to do with this. I'm only following orders, understand?
PEVAC: Oh, I understand everything.
RADULE: Take care of this by tomorrow somehow. Don't make trouble for both of us. Please, as a friend. Well, I'm going. Aren't you going to the opening of the collective?
PEVAC: No.
RADULE: It might be better if you went.

PEVAC: Maybe.
RADULE: Get those six meters by tomorrow, OK, pal?
WORKER: Why ask him so nicely, the lousy kulak? He's got plenty stashed away. Let him get it out. What are you taking his side for? I've plucked plenty like him clean before.
RADULE: Okay, he'll get it. Let's go. See you tomorrow, Ilija. *(They leave. Ilija Pevac sits on the floor, his head and back against the wall. He remains sitting like that. Nevena comes into the barn. When she sees Pevac, she turns and starts for the door.)*
PEVAC: Nevena! *(Nevena goes out without looking at him.)*

92.

(The door of the church. Tujta is there with a team of oxen.)

TUJTA: Giddyup, giddyup. *(The oxen move, slowly raising the bell. The flag on top of the improvised bell tower sways a bit, then settles into its holder.)*

93.

(Ilija Pevac gets up, takes a rope from the wall and throws it over a beam. He turns a basket upside down and climbs onto it.)

94.

(Tujta gives a powerful tug on the rope. The bell starts to ring. Then Tujta stops. He doesn't hear. He begins to pull furiously on the rope. It doesn't do any good. There is still silence. He rages, jerks on the rope, and shouts.)

TUJTA: I don't hear! *(So all of his enormous efforts have been in vain.)*

95.

(Ilija Pevac puts the noose around his neck and kicks the basket out from under him. His legs jerk a few times and then are still.)

96.

(A meeting. The entire village is present. Ilija Ješanov and Golić are wearing new leather coats.)

GOLIĆ: Today will go down in the history of our village, and we can be especially proud that Manđelos has the honor of establishing the first workers' collective in the new Yugoslavia. *(The ringing of a bell resounds over Manđelos, more and more loudly and furiously. Only Tujta and Ilija Pevac cannot hear it.)*

Epilogue

The teacher, Pavle Korčagin, would die on April 7, 1949, at the Military Medical Academy in Belgrade. News of her death did not reach Manđelos for a long time. She was declared a national hero on November 29, 1953.

Velinka and Ilija Ješanov married soon after the death of Ilija Pevac, in a civil ceremony conducted by Golić. Ješanov later become head of the municipal administration in Manđelos. He remained there until his retirement. Both he and Velinka are still living, and have two children and four grandchildren.

When the decisive moment of 1948 arrived, Dušan Golić did not hesitate for an instant. He did not return from Goli Otok.[5]

---

[5] After he severed ties with Stalin, Tito (Josip Broz) built *Goli Otok* (Bald Island), a prison reserved for unrepentant Stalinists, most of whom had fought

Pavle Dobrenov went a long way. Today he is retired and lives in Novi Sad. He is a member of the Federal Council. On Sundays, he takes his grandson for walks along the Danube bank.

Đorđe Belegiški was killed on December 17, 1948, on the Bulgarian border, near the village of Batušno, while he was a soldier of the Yugoslav National Army. He was killed by a Bulgarian or Russian sniper, shot like a clay pigeon, in the temple. He thus became one of the seventeen hundred Yugoslav border guards who lost their lives on the border during those years. His father, Radoja, did not long survive his son. He died of grief less than a year after his son's death.

Brana Tujta died in 1967. His daughter married Miloš, the son of Ilija Pevac.

Nevena has survived to the present day. She lives with her son and daughter-in-law in Mitrovica.

The grandson of Ilija Pevac is the author of this play.

Belgrade, 1986

Translated by *Richard Williams*
Edited by *Dennis Barnett*

---

under him during WWII.

NEBOJŠA ROMČEVIĆ
(1962—)

Born in 1962 in Belgrade, Serbia, Romčević is a writer and an actor. He wrote some seventeen plays, some of which were performed in twenty countries. Romčević's play, *Caroline Neuber,* is a tragic story about a German actress and her striving to create a reputable theatre.

"The British Theatre Guide" (2005) describes Romčević's plays as highly relevant works presenting the life of intellectuals during the harsh years of rule of Serbia's President Slobodan Milošević, as in his comedy *Paradox*.

CAROLINE NEUBER

CHARACTERS:

CAROLINE NEUBER, born Weissenborn
JOHANN NEUBER
JOHANN
GOTTSCHED
MRS. GOTTSCHED
HANSWURST/ FATHER
SPIEGELBERG
MARGARETA HOFFMAN
A CORPORAL
A MERCHANT
I PROSTITUTE
II PROSTITUTE
A PEASANT

The play takes place in German lands in the 18th century.

1. HANSWURST

(A fair in a small town; clamor, the shouts of vendors, bargaining . . . the light falls on the stage set up at the fair. Hanswurst is on the stage. Hanswurst is a peasant from Salzburg and his costume is always the same: his hair tied into a pony tail, an enormous ribbon about his neck, a broad red jacket, on his chest a huge blue heart with the letters "H.W." red buttons and yellow trousers.)

HANSWURST: I was returning to my beautiful Salzburg from Bavaria. I had sold three little goats at the fair and I wanted to have a good time, to eat my food, and to get some woman in the sack – if I could. So I saw, a beautiful mother and her beautiful daughter. Oh, my dear Hanswurst, how could I pass them up? I looked at the mother – she had breasts soooo big. I looked at the daughter, she had breasts sooooooo big! How could I pass them up? I asked my head – it couldn't answer. I asked it *(He grabs at his fly)* and it said: "Hanswurst, you fool, why should you pass them up? Take them both!" Alright, I said, which one should I take first? I asked my head – it couldn't answer . . . I asked it, and it said "Hanswurst, you fool, take both of them, together!" How are we going to fuck both of them together? I asked him "Hanswurst, you fool, that's my problem, anyway!" Now I just stuff my head with food, but I listen to it. My grandfather thought with his dick, why should I do worse? *(Caroline climbs onto the stage. Hanswurst looks at her in surprise.)*
CAROLINE: You should be ashamed of yourself, sir! Is there no limit to your profanity? *(To the audience.)* Is it only because you're humble and backward that you let this man here drag you through the mud? You only need to be enlightened, all you need is the truth!

2. THE FATHER

(The Weissenborn home. The moonlight falls on the bed of Caroline Weissenborn (later Neuber). Caroline sits on the edge of the bed. The door opens with a thud. Her Father comes in. He is evidently drunk, but, even more evidently, he is beside himself with anger. He is in the costume of Hanswurst.)

FATHER: That you should do such a thing to me! In front of all those people! To insult me so! It is . . . It is . . . Now I'll . . . Who do you think you are?
CAROLINE: I don't feel well.
FATHER: Oh heavens, do you hear? She doesn't feel well! And we are stinking cattle! Hanswurst is the one who feeds you. Look: Twenty marks. She doesn't feel well! But the people come to see me and not those boring, revolting plays that you whippersnappers put on at people's homes. I don't care a rat's ass whose father killed whose father, so now their children can't get married! I don't care about what's Kairos and what's cairies! So what if we're repulsive to the fine Caroline! I happen to like that sort of thing. And, and, and . . . it's all healthy folk spirit; it's the vitalism of the simple folk and the honest peasants. You have contempt for the people. And who are you to feel contempt for the people? The people are our audience! And the audience is money! Oh, oh, that you should do that to me in front of all those people. Now I can forget about the ball at Tieschler's, the cabinetmaker's. That's for sure – after this. You are . . . Do you know what you are? You're . . . An artist! That's it and what I've watched you doing is the most ordinary artistry. I am an honest man, and I don't stick out of the duke's ass like you and your "poets" do, who sing his praises in the morning and pander their wives to him for a crust of bread at night. That you should do this to me! I was respected in this town. They would take their hats off to me and say: "We bow to you, master Weissenborn!" No,

"good day" – "we bow to you"! And now . . . that you should do such a thing to me . . . Ziegler, the builder, took ill, he was so offended. *(He sits down on the chair, breathless. He starts to get undressed.)*

CAROLINE: Please, cover yourself up!

FATHER: And why should I? Little Caroline finds her father hideous? The divine Caroline despises even her own father. Does she know how many nights this repulsive father carried the divine Caroline in his arms? Does she know how much he sacrificed himself for her sake, what the fine Caroline owes to her simple father?

CAROLINE: Get dressed.

FATHER: But your churchwarden doesn't repulse you? Does he? . . . *(He glares into her face.)* Come on, tell me? *(Caroline wants to leave the room.)*

FATHER: Where are you going? I'm your father! You must obey me. I have had enough of your disdain. Do you understand? Who are you to judge me? The future mistress of some married jackass, and who will bear a bunch of bastards to this monkey. Both he, and those children, and the children of your children will be just as vulgar as I am, vomiting in their beds and thinking how Hanswurst was . . . able to fuck both the mother and her daughter at the same time! Life is extremely simple: men fuck women; and I spit on all the rest. And I especially spit on the Last Judgment and Saint Peter and the raising of the dead. But you see that churchwarden of yours, so that together you can gorge on the body and guzzle the blood of Christ! I know what you and that devil's servant are doing. I've heard you panting in the altar, like puppies. Yes, yes, you mate like jackrabbits. First you work up a sweat, and then you gorge on the body and guzzle the blood of Christ! You cannibals! Hannibals! You've been eating the body of Christ for seventeen hundred years and you still haven't finished him. What is he? A lizard . . . so he can regenerate himself? . . . Ask that fellow of yours . . . And when you have gorged yourself full of Christ and guzzled yourself full of his blood, then he blesses what you have below your navel, but not with an incense burner. No, no, no not with an incense burner.

CAROLINE: Why are you talking to me like this?

FATHER: Because I enjoy shocking you . . . And to tell you that your father has just come from fornicating like an animal. The girls were your age, though perhaps not as skilled as you are! There were three of them. They were crazy drunk. The youngest one cried . . . probably from happiness. *(Pause.)* You hate me? *(Pause.)* No matter, go on and hate me. I don't care.

3. RUNNING AWAY FROM HOME

(Darkness. Johann is asleep. There is only a bed and a candle by the bedside. Caroline comes in.)

CAROLINE: Johann! Johann! Wake up!

JOHANN: What's happened?!

CAROLINE: I've run away from home. You are going to take me for your wife, leave your position, we'll leave this village and then start from the beginning. I'll bear you three children: Peter, Maria and Johann.

JOHANN: Fine.

CAROLINE: "Fine?" Is that all? Nothing more? You aren't interested in where, how, why?

JOHANN: You know why. That's enough for me.

CAROLINE: Johann, I've had enough . . . I've had enough of everything: of his crossed, drunken eyes, of the graying hairs on his chest . . . Let him be my father a thousand times over. I couldn't choose my father – right?

JOHANN: You have to decide for yourself. He'll find it hard without you.

CAROLINE: And so it should be . . . Let him suffer alone . . . Let him ask how I am. I simply can't stand him anymore. In this town, they're all like him: vulgar, drunk . . . and they call themselves "upstanding citizens." Let him enjoy being Hanswurst by himself. Johann, our people are terribly vulgar. Vulgarity is an illness of the heart without depth or strength. The heart needs to be enlightened . . . to be taught to love.

JOHANN: That would please God. Only, I think that the people will always be vulgar. Forever. And cursing the man who was crucified for their sake is what they like the most.

CAROLINE: You don't love the people?

JOHANN: I love God, and you. From today – you, then God.

CAROLINE: I know that the world is wide, that it doesn't end over there, behind the mill. I want to see it. To see people who know how to say "please" and "thank you". Especially "please." I want to forget these dull, peasant faces and my father . . . forever.

JOHANN: And go with me? But, I cannot . . .

CAROLINE: Yes you can! . . . Yes, we can! . . . To me – you are Atlas!

JOHANN: Me? Atlas?

CAROLINE: Don't make me angry, Johann. That's what you'll be – and that's the end of it! I say so.

JOHANN: All right. *(Pause.)*

CAROLINE: Get dressed. We're leaving this town. Forever!

JOHANN: Do you have the strength?

CAROLINE: Do you have the strength to follow me? *(Johann puts on his preacher's robe.)*

JOHANN: Just say where.

CAROLINE: Don't be afraid. Everything will be all right. Put your arms around me and swear that you'll never . . . never . . . Swear it. *(Johann embraces her.)*

JOHANN: I swear.

CAROLINE: Freedom. *(She stumbles on his robe. They fall to the ground.)*

4. SPIEGELBERG

(An inn. Spiegelberg is sitting at a table eating.)

CAROLINE: *(Fascinated.)* Johann . . . that is theatre! That is truth . . . "Let word of my death only remind you that I was." That is love . . . Poor Antioch. Poor Berenice. What an actor! Goodness, we're watching Spiegelberg eating. Think of it: this is also Horatio and Cato and Agrippa, Scippio . . .
JOHANN: And, to tell the truth, he is eating for four.
CAROLINE: He is the greatest actor. He was also Caesar and Cid . . .
JOHANN: Quite right, he's eating for six. The poor man.
CAROLINE: You don't like him?
JOHANN: I don't know. I don't believe him.
CAROLINE: You don't believe him? Even when he speaks Racine?!
JOHANN: I think real love is . . . less evident. Words serve to supplement, not express emotions. What is really felt is left unspoken. That's what I think.
CAROLINE: Then you must truly love me, since your love is certainly not evident? But what are feelings for, then? To wallow in them, like a pig? That's selfish! I love you, and I want you to know it! So here: I love you, Johann!!!
JOHANN: You don't have to shout it. I know you do.
CAROLINE: If you don't love the theatre, you don't love me either. Go back to your church.
JOHANN: You are my god, and where you are is my church. The portal is the altar. I think this is worthy of Racine. *(Pause. Johann approaches Spiegelberg. Johann is still in his priest's robe.)*

JOHANN: Sir, please let me introduce myself: I am Johann Neuber. I can find no words to express our delight that we can, so to say, breathe the same air as you do . . .

SPIEGELBERG: Thank you, thank you.

JOHANN: Master Spiegelberg, let me express my deepest respect for your divine talent and let me bow to your Ganymede form.

SPIEGELBERG: Sir . . . now you exaggerate . . .

JOHANN: How so? I don't know how I could exaggerate? How to praise the sun for the day that it gives us? The sun exists of itself, and it is ours to be grateful for that. You are like Phaeton whose father gave him the task of charioting the sun across the skies.

SPIEGELBERG: But, I hope, with a better ending. No, I'm not a god . . . still.

JOHANN: You are the closest thing to it.

CAROLINE: Johann, this is really impermissible. I apologize, sir. He's talking nonsense. You're talking nonsense.

JOHANN: Truly. I apologize. I got so carried away I exceeded all limits. Permit me, sir, to once again misuse your good nature and to present my wife to you. She is a worshipper of the cult of Thalia and with the greatest pleasure she offers her gifts to the altar of your theatre.

SPIEGELBERG: I don't understand anything you've said. She likes the theatre?

JOHANN: Modesty is her only fault. But her ideas about the theatre . . .

CAROLINE: Don't listen to anything he says. *(To Johann.)* I'll never forgive you for this!

JOHANN: She thinks that the theatre can improve people, if they're corrupt, and . . .

CAROLINE: *(In a whisper.)* Johann, don't you dare! Johann, I forbid you!

JOHANN: . . . and that good theatre, true theatre – educates people, teaches them beauty, and that a man who has come to know beauty cannot be evil.

SPIEGELBERG: Interesting.

CAROLINE: Johann, stop it . . .

JOHANN: And that the German people are unhappy because they are vulgar. The whole of Europe is laughing at their uncouthness! And why? Because of that damned Hanswurst, because of him the primitives are ruling the stage. Bad women, cunning servants, cuckolded husbands, all grimacing, slurring speech . . .

SPIEGELBERG: This is true! By God, madam, you're right!

JOHANN: What evil can a man do when he has seen how Cid solves the conflict between his heart and his duty?

SPIEGELBERG: None, madam!

JOHANN: Yet, the crowds rush to watch Hanswurst. And what kind of example does he make?

SPIEGELBERG: None. None at all! I'm always saying this! Right!

Only, you should know, it's difficult in life to be Cid and Horatio.

CAROLINE: But, when the German people transcend their vulgarity, when they come to know beauty . . . That's what they need, to be taught love, whether they like it or not. Corneille, Moliere, Racine! . . . They'll bring about the end of Hanswurst. People will become noble and there'll be no more murders, robberies, wars.

SPIEGELBERG: Yes! Yes . . .

CAROLINE: When our people learn to distinguish between Cairos and caries, they'll be on the paths of glory. Not military glory, not the glory of money, but the glory that comes from inner greatness. It's then that the German Voltaire, or the German Helvetius will be born, and Hanswurst will be gone

forever. When slurring, grimacing, blabbering will disappear from the stage, and the actor will preach the sermon of truth . . .
SPIEGELBERG: Madam is truly interested in acting?
CAROLINE: Oh, no. Not at all! I hate acting.
SPIEGELBERG: Interesting . . . Are you sure? *(Johann sneaks off the stage.)*

5. THE STAGE

(The stage is empty. Johann, Caroline. Caroline stands in the middle of the stage, as if in a trance.)

CAROLINE: *(Whispering in feverish excitement.)* Johann . . . a stage . . . a real stage. *(She touches the floor boards.)* This is where Cato, Mithridates were killed, this is where Phaedra poisoned herself, and this is where Medea murdered her own children . . .
JOHANN: A real slaughterhouse, that is true . . .
CAROLINE: Yet, a person could say . . . ordinary boards. They could have become a bed, a chair, a wine barrel . . .
JOHANN: The boards couldn't have become a barrel. For barrels we use hard wood, this is softwood. Though they could have been used to make a dozen coffins for all those deceased ...
CAROLINE: Think of it: a tree grows in the forest. The woodcutter chops it down, drags it to the lumber mill. In the mill they make these boards and a theatre buys them. They make a stage out of them. Do you know why all of this happens?
JOHANN: So that you can stand here.
CAROLINE: *(Screams with happiness.)* Look! My tray. At the end of the fifth act! I enter this way . . . I approach Margareta! This way! She takes a glass and drinks from it!
JOHANN: And?
CAROLINE: *(Exhilarated.)* And then I leave! Think of it! . . . "Oh! My misery has come to an end! Give it to me! Convey to

the king" . . . *(Enter Margareta Hoffman, the "divine Margareta". She is a beautiful woman, some thirty years old, aware of her feminine charm. She speaks slowly in a sonorous voice.)*

MARGARETA: *(Continues to speak her text.)* " . . . my words that his gifts have never been so dear and wanted by me." Only, my dear child . . . That is the way a village barmaid walks . . . The Roman court, my dear, has its own rules. Etiquette. That means the actress . . . This is the way it goes: carrying a moment of glory in her hands, the whole world is hers. The King becomes a burden to her, so she cheats on him, but then her lover leaves her. She remains alone, forgotten by all. The theatre is all that remains, but it doesn't belong to anyone. You walk, my dear, as if you have stolen the legs of a Swiss horseman and are finding it difficult to get used to them. An actress must walk the stage, just shuffling like that happens only in life. Do you see?

CAROLINE: But, no one walks like that . . .

MARGARETA: Of course not. Just as no one drinks deadly nightshade to cure heartsickness. You don't speak on stage as you do in real life, you don't walk as in real life, or feel as in real life – there is no real life here. Only its essence belongs on the stage. In real life, there's only the vulgar details . . . my dear child.

CAROLINE: I think . . .

JOHANN: Yes, I agree. Madame Hoffman's right. In real life, there's no essence, while in the theatre, it comes in bundles and sheaves. But I'm speaking awkwardly. Madame Hoffman has correctly determined the very sense and essence of a phenomenon, which I consider . . .

MARGARETA: Are you making fun of me?

JOHANN: I wouldn't think of such a thing, madam. *(Margareta goes over to him.)*

MARGARETA: Look into my eyes, you slave, not at my breasts or my legs.

JOHANN: I wasn't looking at your . . .
MARGARETA: Although you're only worthy of hatred, perhaps pity, although you are a speechless worm, who thinks he's a butterfly, ready to suck on a dung heap for his own satisfaction ...
CAROLINE: How dare you!
MARGARETA: *(Margareta declaims with great passion.)* "I cannot hide my heart, though my fear and reasoning spread before thee, turning the disgust I feel into dust. And it knows that, which I am loathe to know, that I and thee will become three." Act Three, Scene Two. That is the difference between essence and reality: in reality, he felt uncomfortable; in essence, he enjoyed it. *(He holds her gaze, frightened, and finally lowers his eyes. Margareta goes out.)*
MARGARETA: Please, applaud. I can't leave the stage without applause. *(Caroline and Johann applaud in surprise. Pause.) (Caroline goes to Johann.)*
CAROLINE: *(Places her hand on his chest.)* How your heart is beating . . .

6. MARGARETA

Spiegelberg and Margareta. Spiegelberg is half dressed for the role of Mithridates.

MARGARETA: Should God himself be in the audience, I'm not going out on the stage!
SPIEGELBERG: But, Gottsched is, at least, close to what I conceive of as God.
MARGARETA: And her dressing table has to go, or I'm not going on stage!
SPIEGELBERG: Come, Margareta, for the love of God . . . I can't put her in the courtyard.
MARGARETA: I'm not interested . . . The dressing tables of dilettantes can't be put in the dressing room of Margareta

Hoffman, no matter how clever they may be at fawning over you! Just two months ago she brought in the tray, and now she's playing my companion. What's next? Give her my part? Let her play Monima?
SPIEGELBERG: . . . Margareta . . . For the love of God! . . . What are you talking about? Listen, she simply adores you. It is almost a kind of religious adoration . . .
MARGARETA: I'm not interested! It's either her – or me!
SPEIGELBERG: Margareta . . .
MARGARETA: I'm leaving the company!
SPEIGELBERG: But, Margareta, you are the brightest jewel in the crown of our theatre . . .
MARGARETA: You know that I can't abide fawning . . .
SPIEGELBERG: Margareta . . . I must tell you . . .
MARGARETA: What?
SPIEGELBERG: I better not!
MARGARETA: Tell me.
SPIEGELBERG: It's too juicy. *(Whispers.)* Her husband is terribly in love with you. He's lost his head.
MARGARETA: Who are you talking about? Johann?
SPIEGELBERG: The little one is still naive, and she doesn't notice anything . . . Johann hides it cleverly . . .
MARGARETA: The priest . . .
SPIEGELBERG: Hides it . . . Last night he held me prisoner until dawn describing your charms.
MARGARETA: You exaggerate.
SPIEGELBERG: Oh, if my good manners would allow me to reveal the daydreams of a priest, you would be stunned and surprised.
MARGARETA: Quiet. I don't want to listen to you.
SPIEGELBERG: Is it too much to ask of you, whose heart is known far and wide for its kind nature, and which has not one, but two blind subjects, not counting myself who is notoriously crazy about you, to let her share your dressing room?

MARGARETA: Only for tonight!

SPIEGELBERG: Of course. You can rule your dressing room like the temple of Apollo is ruled by the blind Tiresias or, I mean, the beautiful Iphigenia at Aulis. *(Pause. Enter Caroline, who has witnessed this entire scene.)*

CAROLINE: *(To Spiegelberg.)* Why do you lie?

SPIEGELBERG: Ah, my dear child, this is the theatre, and Gottsched is coming to see . . .

CAROLINE: That a Spiegelberg should fall on his knees! And lie! Now, I'm leaving.

SPIEGELBERG: But, Caroline . . . My God, what's happening? Tonight Gottsched is coming to see us! . . . Children, Gottsched will be watching us! Gottsched!!! Be reasonable . . . I'm an old man! No! I'm the one who is leaving! I am! I have had enough!

CAROLINE: This isn't the theatre that you promised me, sir! How are people going to be improved by this? I'm leaving.

SPIEGELBERG: No, I'm leaving.

MARGARETA: *(To Caroline.)* Calm down, my dear . . . Only lead actresses have the right to be capricious.

CAROLINE: You mean I'm not a lead actress?

SPIEGELBERG: Caroline, Margareta . . . For goodness sake . . . Have pity on my gray hair! Gottsched's coming to see us . . . Do you know what that means? Oh, what kind of life is this?

CAROLINE: Gottsched, Gottsched, Gottsched!!! So who is he? God himself? Come down from Parnassus?

MARGARETA: Yes, and still wet from the waters of the Helicon, he's still dripping, so to speak . . . *(Caroline and Margareta suddenly start to laugh hysterically.)*

SPIEGELBERG: Does this mean that everything's alright? *(He shouts to someone behind the scenes.)* The performance will go on. God, you can forget us tomorrow, but please help us now!

7. AFTER THE PERFORMANCE

(Spiegelberg stands on a chair, in the costume of Mithridates, with a lifted glass. Present are Margareta, Caroline and Johann.)

JOHANN: What a success that was! What applause!
SPIEGELBERG: Let's wait and see what Gottsched says.
MARGARETA: I watched him all the time, and he seemed terribly bored. He yawned three times.
SPIEGELBERG: Three times??!
MARGARETA: At least.
SPIEGELBERG: Goodness! *(Pause.)* In any case, what do we care about Gottsched? *(Growing more subdued.)* What's important is that the audience liked it. And after all . . . we play for the audience, not for the critics. To your health! *(Pause.)*
CAROLINE: I knew it! I'm the one to blame . . . I am not good enough to play Monima's companion. *(To Johann.)* "You can do it! You're the best!" You're the one to blame!
JOHANN: I still think . . .
CAROLINE: I didn't know my lines, where to come in, where to go, what to do . . . and you keep telling me I'm the best. How can you say I'm the best!!!?
JOHANN: Caroline . . .
CAROLINE: I beg you, I plead with you, I don't want to talk about it anymore. I simply have no talent, and have to come to terms with it!
MARGARETA: Perhaps you're right.
SPIEGELBERG: What are you saying?! Are the two of you in your right minds?
CAROLINE: That's what he wants! . . . To have five children, to spend all day in church! But not me. I'll give up acting, but to spite you, I'll never have a child.

SPIEGELBERG: For the love of God! What is this foolishness? Johann has said nothing.
CAROLINE: Be quiet!!!
SPIEGELBERG: I'm quiet . . . *(He sits down.)* *(Enter Gottsched and Mrs. Gottsched. Gottsched is a handsome, large man, full of energy, red cheeked and of superior bearing. His wife's ugly, but because she's his wife, she is full of herself. Where and when Gottsched enters a room, there is a sense that life and positive energy shine.)*
GOTTSCHED: Good evening to all! Bravissimo! . . . Please let me express my delight with the performance.
SPIEGELBERG: Mr . . . Mr . . . Thank you . . . I . . . please sit down.
MRS. GOTTSCHED: A nice little performance . . .
GOTTSCHED: *(To Spiegelberg.)* You sir, truly have reasons to celebrate! You have such an actress in your company *(To Margareta.)*, and you in the role of Mithridates, you're not so bad.
SPIEGELBERG: Sir, you are very generous with your compliments.
MRS. GOTTSCHED: Yes, a nice little Mithridates.
GOTTSCHED: *(To Johann.)* But what this one's doing, that's what I call modern acting. This is the way they will act fifty years from now! Walking instead of parading, speaking instead of rhetoric. I cried, and my wife did, too.
CAROLINE: Are you speaking of me?
MRS. GOTTSCHED: *(To Johann.)* Quite a nice little role.
GOTTSCHED: What you have shown us tonight is equal, in my opinion, to the resurrection of Lazarus.
SPIEGELBERG: *(To Johann.)* Boy, bring some wine!
MARGARETA: I'll bring the wine for Mr. Gottsched.
GOTTSCHED: That would be a great honor.
JOHANN: No, no, you're tired, you just finished performing. I'll bring the wine.

CAROLINE: Yes, yes . . . That would be too great an honor for Mr. Gottsched.
SPIEGELBERG: In any case, what do we need wine for, when we are drunk with happiness?
CAROLINE: Sir, I've been told that you were yawning during the performance, and now you're congratulating us?
GOTTSCHED: Who told you I was yawning?
CAROLINE: She did. *(Pointing to Margareta.)*
GOTTSCHED: That's correct, madam is right. In her scenes, I found it hard to stay awake.
MARGARETA: I could tell you . . . I could tell you *(Leaves in tears.)*
JOHANN: Margareta . . . What sort of people are these? *(Goes after her.)*
MRS. GOTTSCHED: Yes, yes! Quite nice . . . Tres charmant . . .
SPIEGELBERG: I raise a glass in honor of the future's greatest German actress, Caroline Neuber and her husband Johann. Let God give you happiness, health and many children.
CAROLINE: Let him give us happiness and health!
MRS. GOTTSCHED: Ah, that is your husband? Love! Tres charmant!

8. JOHANN AND MARGARETA

(Continuation of the previous scene.)

JOHANN: Please don't drink any more.
MARGARETA: Why? So that I don't disgrace myself? My whole life has been a disgrace.
JOHANN: It's only theatre.
MARGARETA: You men really don't understand anything! You've been brought here by love, the rest of us have been brought here by a sickness. The theatre's been my life. And now life is all I have left. What am I going to do now?

JOHANN: You should live it.

MARGARETA: Poor Johann. In the name of love, you've given up on love. Don't expect anything other than endless and completely unnecessary sacrifice. We only can love after rehearsals are over, or when there's no performance.

JOHANN: I look at it this way: God's given each man a talent. My talent is to be with her. That's . . .

MARGARETA: You don't understand anything, my poor Johann. The theatre will sap all her energy, and the only remaining thing for you will be to comfort her after she fails. Her victories she will share with us. *(Caroline comes in and finds them sitting on the edge of the stage, with a bottle between them. Pause. Margareta spots her. Johann gets up.)*

MARGARETA: Have no fear, I won't take him from you, Caroline.

CAROLINE: I didn't know that we were on a first name basis, Mrs. Hoffman.

JOHANN: Caroline, don't go on like that, please.

CAROLINE: As usual, Johann, you understand nothing.

JOHANN: Margareta was feeling terrible, and it's only natural that I should be with her.

CAROLINE: Johann, I'm feeling wonderful, and it's only natural than that you should be with me. Let her find another shoulder to cry on. And while she is looking for a shoulder to cry on, let her also find another place for her dressing table, since I'm not sharing my dressing room with her anymore.

(Margareta begins to laugh.)

JOHANN: For heaven's sake, don't you see that she's not well!

MARGARETA: *(To Johann.)* With those same words, I sent Magdalena Kreger off, twelve years ago.

JOHANN: Who was Magdalena Kreger?

MARGARETA: That's it, poor Johann! Just that: Who was Magdalena Kreger?!

9. HANSWURST – THE SERGEANT

HANSWURST – THE SERGEANT: Long ago I was small. Then I grew. Then I grew some more. When I was full grown, my good father asked me: "Hanswurst, now that you've grown up, what are you going to be?" I thought and thought, and then I said: "Daddy I want to be a drunkard and for everyone to pay for my drinks." Then my good father put down his bottle, and he thought, and he thought and he thought, and he said: "Then Hanswurst, my son, you should be a soldier." Brothers! Join the army today. Six gold pieces a year! Six gold pieces! Free meals! First-class food! Field exercises only once a month, and those rare and far between. On Sunday afternoons a bottle of brandy for each man, and, often, on other days as well! Why shouldn't you live off of the government? Always a full belly, always warm, and your only job is to say "Yes, sir" and warm the feet of the captain's wife, when he's away. Once, I was warming them, and warming them, and warming them. And then, suddenly, the captain appeared: "Hanswurst, you swine! You'll kill my wife with so much warming! Join the army, all of you!"

10. THE REHEARSAL

(Caroline, Johann, Gottsched. Caroline is finishing her monologue. Her acting is in the style of the period: pompous, rhetorical and static.)

CAROLINE: ". . . And I feared that Nero had given me too much of a task to gain your liking . . . I feared the hidden flame of my own love, but in vain – I wished that I, alas, had never beheld you." *(Happily.)* I couldn't do it better! *(To Johann.)*
JOHANN: *(Applauding.)* Bravo! Bravo! I think she was exceptional. *(Pause.)*

GOTTSCHED: *(Ignoring Johann.)* Then we should stop doing theatre. This was poor, sad, trivial. You, young lady, have no talent. I'm sorry! I'm very sorry.

CAROLINE: *(Stuttering.)* If you could just tell me what was wrong, perhaps I could . . .

GOTTSCHED: Why waste words?! Why? It was terrible!!

JOHANN: I think good manners require some explanation . . .

GOTTSCHED: Good manners?! This is the theatre. Good manners!!! This is not a procession, a mass or a liturgy! This is the theatre! For the love of God!! Keep your preaching to the pulpit! I am the bishop here! I am!!

CAROLINE: You don't have to shout at him . . .

GOTTSCHED: I shout when I feel like shouting! I scream! I howl! I won't let untalented peasants silence me. Is that clear!! *(Caroline begins to cry.)*

JOHANN: Any art must first and foremost be humane. Even your theatre. But you, sir, are behaving in an inhumane manner. And more than anything, you're being impolite.

GOTTSCHED: Art is, my dear priest, both impolite and inhumane! Because it is the fruit of human truth, which is also impolite and inhumane!

CAROLINE: "Inhumanity and impoliteness!" These are phrases you use to charm young girls and cattle merchants at fairs! I demand you tell me this instant what I've done wrong! This instant! He sits here all day, and keeps his mouth shut, and then he finally shouts insults at me! I have had my fill of this esoteric. You're not leaving until you tell me!

GOTTSCHED: That's it! Fume! Break things! Cry! Passions, not diction! Truths! Truths! That's the way Iphigenia speaks to her father! Passions! Feelings! Psychological pauses. She doesn't stand in one place! She rushes around the stage, she pleads for support, understanding! She wrings her hands, she tears at her dress in despair! She doesn't know what she'll say, it comes out of her! That is the truth! No politeness, no delicacy! Passions are

what we need, not diction! This rehearsal is over! Forever. *(He leaves.)*
CAROLINE: The truth, Johann . . . the truth. He's right . . . I understand . . . *(Laughs.)* I didn't know such people existed! We're going to leave Spiegelberg and join Gottsched. That will be the end of Hanswurst – and the vulgarity of the Germans! God is our guide, Johann!
JOHANN: I hope that he is the one leading us.

11. SUCCESS

(Gottsched, Johann, Mrs. Gottsched. Gottsched is looking out of the window, he is in euphoria. Johann looks over his shoulder. Mrs. Gottsched counts the takings.)

MRS. GOTTSCHED: They're overdoing it! We're a serious theatre. It's impossible to understand audiences. Ten days haven't passed since they whistled at her in that role. One hundred and twenty-one, one hundred and twenty-two, one hundred and twenty-three, one hundred and twenty-four.
GOTTSCHED: They're carrying her across the square.
JOHANN: I hope that they don't drop her . . .
GOTTSCHED: Johann, my good fellow, she's a success. We've succeeded!
MRS. GOTTSCHED: One hundred and twenty-one, one hundred and twenty-one, one hundred and twenty-two . . .
GOTTSCHED: She really wasn't bad tonight . . .
JOHANN: *(Crossing himself.)* I didn't believe that I would be thanking God for this.
(Pause. Looks at the euphoric Gottsched.)
GOTTSCHED: Truly, she wasn't at all bad tonight . . .
MRS. GOTTSCHED: *(To Johann.)* It's been cold these last few days, hasn't it Mr. Neuber? One hundred and twenty-one, one hundred and twenty-two, one hundred and twenty three . . .

JOHANN: Yes, unusual this time of year. *(Caroline's father comes in.)* Mr. Weissenborn? Welcome *(Father doesn't react.)* This is Mr. Gottsched . . .

FATHER: Gottsched, you are a knave, a thief and a hypocrite! Where is she?

JOHANN: What's the matter with you?

FATHER: And you stay out of my way, you phony priest, stealing daughters from their fathers!

GOTTSCHED: What's wrong with this man?

MRS. GOTTSCHED: Sir, I must remind you of your language!

FATHER: Kiss my ass, madam! I've been playing Hanswurst for fifty years. I've offended no one, I've killed no one, yet she and this scoundrel here make me out to be the anti-Christ, a satyr, a highway robber!! Last week they burned an effigy in front of the audience! And who did the doll resemble? Me, madam! Next time they'll probably try to lynch me! I'm going to teach her a lesson. Where is she?

GOTTSCHED: Come, come, sir . . . you're being paranoid! The performance was not an attack on your saintly character. It was just an effort to improve the educational value of the theatre . . . Sit down, have a drink with us. Right from the stage coach, are you?

FATHER: I'll drink only at your funeral, sir. You, as you are, you want to educate the audience! Well, here's this to you! *(Caroline comes in, her hair is disheveled and she is happy. When she spots her father, her face turns grim.)*

CAROLINE: What's this creature doing here?

FATHER: Caroline, it's me . . .

CAROLINE: How do you dare to appear before me, sir? And are you brazen enough to set your foot in my theatre?!

GOTTSCHED: My, my . . . things are going bad for you.

FATHER: Caroline, my child . . .

CAROLINE: I have nothing to do with you, sir!

FATHER: You burnt an effigy resembling me in the street last week! That's how things are going!
CAROLINE: I don't know who you are.
FATHER: Don't behave like this, Caroline! It's me! Your father!
CAROLINE: Get away from me, sir! You've done more harm to my people than the Barbarians!
FATHER: Caroline . . . I'm an honest man, I have nothing to be ashamed of!
CAROLINE: With your grimacing you cater to the lowest, animal's passions, you stifle everything that is good and noble. You lie from the stage, sir, that women are whores, that husbands are cuckolds, that servants are thieves, that lawyers are villains, that killing is a nice invention, that gluttony and drink are the greatest of human achievements, that war is a showering of metal. The world is rotten. There is no God!
FATHER: Are you talking about of me?! If the people had asked for Seneca, I would have played Seneca. It's all the same to me.
CAROLINE: I'll grind you to dust! You and your vulgarity will disappear! That, that . . . damned cynicism about everything is going to disappear. You call it a vitalism in the people – maybe it is, but it's evil and conniving, and I've put an end to it today. Thank heavens, man is not such a miserable creature.
FATHER: But, Caroline, my dear, I still have to support our family! Your three younger sisters . . .
CAROLINE: *(Collecting herself.)* The destruction of your family is your own fault. There are consequences, you know. Your destruction was my dream as a child! *(She is enraged.)*
JOHANN: *(To Caroline's father.)* Sit down, please.
CAROLINE: Let him stand! There's no mercy for him! Man was created by God, and not by swine!
FATHER: I raised you with this grimacing. I carried you in my arms. How can you?!
CAROLINE: It's very easy, sir! And it gives me great satisfaction!

FATHER: Is it possible you can be so cruel! For a daughter to talk to her father like this, after so many years . . .
GOTTSCHED: Come now, sir, these are just words.
CAROLINE: They're are not just words. I've won over the audience. Truth has triumphed. Love has triumphed. This is the end for you, sir!
FATHER: Truth? Love? Oh, damn you! Damn all of you! I have spent my life on stage. Only death will get me off it. You believe your kind of theatre can make man good. Yet, you're the evil ones! Evil! And that's why you'll be destroyed. You hate me? Hate me then, for all I care. I curse you! With the curse of a father and an actor! *(He leaves. Johann heads after him.)*
CAROLINE: Johann, don't you dare move.
JOHANN: I won't stand for this! There's no goal that justifies this behavior. So many years have passed.
CAROLINE: Years have nothing to do with it!
GOTTSCHED: We're all a bit excited this evening . . .
CAROLINE: That man's a criminal and I'm sorry we didn't burn him instead of the effigy.
JOHANN: Caroline, what are you saying? What's the matter with all of you? This is only theatre! That's your father! *(To Gottsched.)* How can you watch this calmly?
GOTTSCHED: *(Spreads his arms out helplessly.)* What can I do? You see she is angry.
CAROLINE: In any case, I won't waste any more words on him. I am the queen this evening! Me!
JOHANN: *(Looking into her face.)* Caroline?
CAROLINE: *(Completely misshaped with anger.)* Why are you looking at me, priest?

12. THE WONDERFUL GOTTSCHED

(Johann is asleep. Caroline barges in, tipsy and euphoric.)

CAROLINE: *(Tottering.)* Johann . . . Are you sleeping? You're always sleeping. Go on, sleep.

JOHANN: I'm not sleeping. You looking for wine?

CAROLINE: Yes. And so what?

JOHANN: It's over there.

CAROLINE: You missed a lot by leaving early.

JOHANN: I was sleepy.

CAROLINE: Why do you withdraw from everyone?! Other people fight for their place, but you withdraw. You, if you wanted to, could be the equal of . . . Gottsched, even. But no, you love being on the sideline. As if you were misshapen or stupid. *(Pause.)* Why should I admire Mrs. Gottsched's husband, when my own husband can be equally witty, superior, educated and manly?

JOHANN: Perhaps I can't.

CAROLINE: You're withdrawing again! Why do you force me to be ashamed of you?! *(Pause.)* There, now I've said it. *(Pause.)* What is it now? *(Pause.)* I can't stand that anyone else should be better than you. *(Pause.)* You have to spoil it all for me! Everything! And now this jealousy of yours! But, you can't be all my world. I'm an actress. I have to keep these people company. You have to believe in me. You know how much I love you. You're my whole world . . . You're the most wonderful man in the world. Gottsched is no match for you! If only you'd show it . . . I want to bear you three children. Come let's make love. I want to give you Peter, Maria, Johann . . .

JOHANN: *(Holds her to his chest.)* My poor little girl . . .

13. THE LOVE SCENE

(Gottsched is on the edge of a bed, dressing himself. Caroline is lying in the bed.)

CAROLINE: My God, what have I done? What have we done? I'm going to tell Johann everything this very night!
GOTTSCHED: Don't speak about telling him! What kind of foolishness is that!? What are you going to achieve with that?
CAROLINE: I can't lie to him! He doesn't deserve it.
GOTTSCHED: He doesn't deserve to have you tell him that you've been unfaithful to him! This is life, and you are not Iphigenia. No one wants to know the truth!
CAROLINE: But, you're the one who talks about the truth all the time!
GOTTSCHED: About truth in the theatre!
CAROLINE: You're not going to tell your wife anything?
GOTTSCHED: Tell her about my escapades? Where would it lead me?
CAROLINE: You mean – I'm just an escapade?
GOTTSCHED: I didn't mean it that way . . .
CAROLINE: And what about our theatre! What about our plans?
GOTTSCHED: I smell of your perfume! Why did you have to put so much on? How am I going to get rid of it? I'm going to have to walk around for two hours in order to get rid of the scent.
CAROLINE: I don't care how you're going to get rid of it!
GOTTSCHED: And what do you want? That I should leave my family? That you should leave your husband – all for the sake of the theatre? That's simply not done! That's indecent.
CAROLINE: The theatre is indecent, is that what you mean to say?
GOTTSCHED: The theatre is the theatre, and life is life.
CAROLINE: But I love you, you swine!
GOTTSCHED: You love the theatre. *(He embraces her.)* It's too early for such radical measures. We have time. Slowly.
CAROLINE: *(Whimpering, with her head on his shoulder.)* And we're going to have our theatre? *(Buttoning his shirt scuffs behind her back.)*
GOTTSCHED: Of course.

CAROLINE: And we'll change . . .
GOTTSCHED: Of course. *(He has finished dressing.)* I am going to start immediately on an adaptation of Voltaire's Zaire. Oh, when I think of how you will look on the stage!
CAROLINE: Go! Go and finish the play and bring it to me, even if you finish at dawn! Write clearly! Don't forget about the Second Act! *(He kisses her and leaves. Pause. Johann comes in.)*
JOHANN: Aren't you feeling well? *(Pause.)*
CAROLINE: Johann, Johann . . .
JOHANN: Gottsched?
CAROLINE: Yes.
JOHANN: That's low! That's fitting of your Hanswurst.
CAROLINE: You don't understand. It's not a matter of physical pleasure . . .
JOHANN: The worse for it. I won't let you become his mistress. Has he told his wife?
CAROLINE: Of course. I think so. He has, he has.
JOHANN: And, what do you intend to do now?
CAROLINE: We're going to create a new theatre. We have enormous plans. He is at this moment translating Zaire for me. There's nothing dirty in it at all, Johann. We truly have a goal . . .
JOHANN: . . . which is unattainable for me! I know, I know!
CAROLINE: I am certain that as an honorable man and gentleman he'll come and explain everything to you. As an actress, I don't exist without him. As a person, I don't exist without your blessing.
JOHANN: And what about me? *(Pause. Caroline lowers her head.)* Alright, I . . . I'll leave in the morning.
CAROLINE: Johann *(She embraces him and kisses him.)* Thank you.
JOHANN: I have to pack now.
CAROLINE: Yes, yes! *(Then adds quickly.)* Can I help you? You should have these shirts washed as soon as possible. You can throw these away. They are torn, here, do you see? *(She*

packs.) This is a beautiful shirt. Why don't you wear it? When we go . . . *(Then she falls silent.)* Do you want to take something of mine? I'll give you the pendant . . . Hm . . . I need that for Iphigenia. I'll give you the fan . . . I need that for Mithridates. I'll give you a braid of my hair . . .
JOHANN: You need that for Salome. Caroline you have my blessing. I hope I'm not right about Gottsched.
CAROLINE: You aren't, I'm sure. I know it's all my fault. He's completely innocent, although he blames himself. Your opinion of him is completely wrong! Of course, you have every right to be angry, to challenge him to a duel, but – he's an honorable man. Johann, he's a genius. You have no idea what he knows how to do.
JOHANN: And I don't want to know.
CAROLINE: Yes. Yes.

14. JOHANN, MY FRIEND

GOTTSCHED: Caroline, my dear, good morning! Johann, my friend! As I promised, first thing in the morning! I solemnly declare that Mitzi has translated Zaire from the French like a master! Truly like a master! The role seems to have been written for you. Hasn't it, Mitzi?
MRS. GOTTSCHED: Good morning, my dear. *(Kissing her on the cheek.)*
GOTTSCHED: I know what you're going to say: what kind of manners is it to come calling on someone so early in the morning, and unannounced?! I agree, it isn't good manners. But, Caroline, my dear, Johann, my friend, this is truly a great and wonderful reason.
MRS. GOTTSCHED: Slowly, Johann. Let Caroline read it first.
GOTTSCHED: But, Mitzi, your translation is extraordinary. It is a model of good translation. The subtlety of the French original

has been retained and it's been enriched by the manly firmness of the German language.

MRS. GOTTSCHED: Perhaps Caroline will not like it.

GOTTSCHED: But, that's impossible. *(Turning around.)* Johann, you're not the only one who has a genius for a wife. *(Embraces Mitzi.)* I will be a triumph! *(Caroline begins to cry.)*

MRS. GOTTSCHED: Caroline, my little dear! Has Gottsched done something? *(To Gottsched.)* I told you that we should not barge in like this, like drunkards at a funeral . . . *(To Caroline.)* Nerves, nerves . . . The times, the times . . . *(To Johann.)* Isn't it so?

JOHANN: *(Seriously to Gottsched.)* Sit down, please, sir.

GOTTSCHED: Thank you, but I really . . . Here is the translation. It is exceptional. Some minor changes, perhaps . . . but you . . . when you have recovered . . . I will come back. I promise. A little later. The translation is . . . I will come back. *(He sits down. A pause. Caroline is crying. Mitzi consoles her. Gottsched tries to avoid Johann's eyes.)* Oh my god, it's all so unpleasant. I apologize. If I can help in any way . . . You know that you can always rely on . . . the two of us.

CAROLINE: Thank you very much, sir.

GOTTSCHED: I will come back . . . Let's go, Mitzi.

MRS GOTTSCHED: The best thing is mint tea. *(Pause. Gottsched looks at Caroline, Johann looks at Gottsched. Mrs. Gottsched begins to comprehend the situation.)*

MRS. GOTTSCHED: It isn't possible!

GOTTSCHED: Mitzi, you misunderstand . . .

MRS. GOTTSCHED: You swine, you freak! You, you . . . crocodile! Johann! *(She embraces Johann, weeping.)* My friend!

GOTTSCHED: She's been working all night. It's nervous tension. A cup of mint tea, perhaps . . .

MRS. GOTTSCHED: *(To Gottsched.)* We'll discuss this at home. Johann, my friend, good bye. *(She leaves.)*

GOTTSCHED: Mitzi! Caroline, I . . . Johann, my friend . . . Oh, my God . . . *(Leaves. Johann unpacks his suitcases.)*
CAROLINE: I want to persuade you that he had no choice . . .
JOHANN: We will never talk about this again.
CAROLINE: Fine.
JOHANN: You are Caroline Neuber and you can do without Gottsched. *(Pause.)*
CAROLINE: I'm going to have a good cry. *(She leaves.)*

15. FAILURE

(The dressing room. Gottsched is sitting on a chair, like on the deck of a ship. Caroline walks around him. She is absolutely furious. She tears at her dress, she throws her wig down.)

CAROLINE: I hate these people! These simple-minded masses. Is this an audience!? Those monkey faced, primitive, intoxicated masks! Why should I even try? All they want is swearing and vulgarity!
GOTTSCHED: The people need to be enlightened.
CAROLINE: What should I do? Tie those mongrels to the wheel and read Virgil to them until they breathe their last?! No, no . . . People are a cursed and wild horde.
GOTTSCHED: We knew it would be difficult.
CAROLINE: Sir, I am the famous Caroline Neuber, and tonight I played to fifteen oxen, who couldn't cram in to see that stinking Muller and all that grimacing! Someone should poison Muller for the future of the German people. This very night. Deadly nightshade, my dear sir? Mandragola!
GOTTSCHED: You're talking nonsense.
CAROLINE: And have I been unfaithful to my husband because of them? What kind of man is he? Because of you!
GOTTSCHED: Please, I beg you . . .

CAROLINE: Don't beg me! I'm fed up with your pleas. I'm fed up with your empty words about the power of art. We're nothing, and Muller is everything! It is Margareta – who has a speech impediment, who has two left feet. Margareta who doesn't know how to speak – she's the one the crowd lifts on their shoulders like a heroine! I can't stand it! And you beg me to calm down!

GOTTSCHED: I beg you, I didn't make you tell your husband about the two of us.

CAROLINE: Perhaps you can live your life with lies, I can't. And so, when your Mitzi appears, the moment that she crosses the doorstep of this dressing room, I'm going to . . . *(Mrs. Gottsched comes in. Caroline and Mrs. Gottsched clearly ignore each other.)*

GOTTSCHED: Mitzi, did you see the small audience.

MRS. GOTTSCHED: A small audience? Muller is doing an excellent business.

GOTTSCHED: Yes, they've all gone to see Hanswurst . . .

MRS. GOTTSCHED: There are only twenty-four marks here! What difference would it make if we performed something like he does, for at least one performance. You know that I need money for – *(Caroline turns around, breathless with anger.)* *(Defiantly.)* Yes, madam!

GOTTSCHED: Please! I beg of you! I am so tired . . . *(The door opens and Margareta enters, dressed in glamorous, bright clothes. Pause.)*

MARGARETA: Good evening to you all! Bravissimo! Allow me to express my delight with your performance! I didn't see it, truth to say, but I've been told it was enchanting. *(To Gottsched.)* You, sir, truly have reasons to be glad! To have an actress like this in your company. *(To Caroline.)* My dear! Finally someone powerful enough to re-educate this herd we call an audience! Corneille, Racine, and I hear Voltaire as well! That is it! What courage! They say that what Caroline is doing is modern acting. I'm so sorry I didn't see it. But, some other time. There will be another time, won't there? For there is no better actress in all of Germany. I really wonder at the people. Such a performance was being given here, while they were breaking down the gates at ours.

CAROLINE: Those people come to see your legs.

MARGARETA: That's what I'm saying. I am completely confused. I simply can't believe that given a choice between the divine Racine, your modern acting and my legs, they chose – my legs. True, my legs are worth seeing, but in comparison with modern acting and the divine Racine . . . I really don't know. Look here, they tore my dress while they were carrying me across the square. But, no matter, I'll buy five new ones. And the duke came to our performance. "My little bear," I said to him, "What is there in these legs?"

CAROLINE: We don't show our legs here, we don't show our thighs, we don't offer our cleavage.

MARGARETA: But what can you do that the people want? And the people are always right. To the people, the complete works of Racine are worth less than one, good, old authentic German swear word. A swear word that was perfected by hundreds of generations over centuries, the truth of the people.

CAROLINE: That's right. They thought for centuries and came up with – what? A swear word.

MARGARETA: Sometimes I think the people don't want to be enlightened. Perhaps they want lies, conniving . . .

CAROLINE: And legs.

MARGARETA: Quick-witted as ever. And legs of course, my dear . . .

CAROLINE: I am an artist, not a dancing bear at a village fair. We show the essence here!

MARGARETA: And what is the essence? Racine?

CAROLINE: Yes, Racine, Yes, my dear . . .

MARGARETA: And where do people like that live? Who is concerned with their problems?

CAROLINE: Racine creates the ideal man, better than we are, but that is something that you and your audience will never understand . . .

MARGARETA: Ha, ha . . . Racine . . . He was worse than we are. He was a flatterer, a cad and a hypocrite!

CAROLINE: Racine a cad!?

MRS. GOTTSCHED: There's no need for so much emotion . . .

CAROLINE AND MARGARETA: You, Mitzi, don't interfere!

CAROLINE: It's better to die of hunger for one's ideals than to live like a pig, in shame!

MARGARETA: I used to faint fourteen times playing Hecuba. I used to lose three kilos a night as Electra. And what for? Nothing? Now I play Colombine and the duke adores my legs. This dress brings more respect than all the real roles . . .

MRS. GOTTSCHED: *(To Margareta.)* That's what I was telling them.

CAROLINE: *(To Gottsched.)* Why are you silent? Say something.

GOTTSCHED: You have before you a long and difficult journey.

CAROLINE: Is that all?

MRS. GOTTSCHED: Theatre exists for the audience!

GOTTSCHED: Shut up!!! Be quiet this instant . . . Man must sacrifice something for his ideals, for the love of God!

MRS. GOTTSCHED: But not his family! Then he's just an egotistical swine!

CAROLINE: Who are you calling a swine?

GOTTSCHED: Caroline, she wasn't thinking of . . .

MRS. GOTTSCHED: I was, I was thinking! We've lost so many chances! Because of her we can't give the people what they want! So what if she sacrifices herself to art! What's that got to do with me! I'm not asking you to be a hero, but be rational. Let her husband be a hero for her.

CAROLINE: Then let your husband play Zaira in that miserable, tragic, sweet, idiotic translation of yours! I'm, not going to appear in that mess!
GOTTSCHED: Caroline, you're exaggerating. The translation is quite adequate.
CAROLINE: Excellent! Then we can also do Hanswurst, since your Mitzi wants to!
MRS. GOTTSCHED: And you will!
CAROLINE: Sir, I swear I will never, never, never speak any word translated by the creature you have the audacity to call your wife.
GOTTSCHED: Now, that's enough! It's in the repertory, and it will be played.
CAROLINE: *(To Gottsched.)* You miserable man! A lousy lover! And he is, madam! A lousy one! Good bye!
MARGARETA: Good heavens! I've come at the wrong moment. Has it come to this? God only knows how sorry I am for you.

16. A BAD DREAM

CAROLINE: *(In a night dress.)* Johann. This is terrible! Thank God it was only a dream. *(Embraces him.)* I dreamed that they forced me onto the stage and I didn't know what play it was, or who my character was, or what I was supposed to say. The actors around me were playing something quite different . . . Truthfully, energetically, I was slow, fake, boring. And then, in the middle of the performance, one actress said to me, out loud: "Mrs. Neuber, don't you see you're a nuisance? Don't you see that you're finished?" and I jumped on her, and we began to fight in front of the audience, but I knew she was right. Think of it, what a dream! *(Pause.)* What's the matter? *(Pause.)* What's the matter?!
JOHANN: Caroline . . . that's what happened last night. It wasn't a dream. *(Pause.)*

CAROLINE: It wasn't a dream . . . What do you mean it wasn't a dream?

17. SPIEGELBERG – THE SECOND TIME

(An inn. Spiegelberg is sitting at a table covered with food and eating shell fish, so that his slurping echoes in the quiet. Johann sits across from him and tries not to look at plateful of food. A long, noisy pause.)

SPIEGELBERG: It's all very awkward. I don't know, I don't know what to tell you.
JOHANN: Her father offered that she could act with him, but she would sooner die of hunger.
SPIEGELBERG: I heard. An unfortunate incident. Has she recovered?
JOHANN: She's not acted for a year. I would act. You would. Everybody would act. But not her. Sir, she is going to die!
SPIEGELBERG: My God . . . Calm down . . . *(Spiegelberg continues to eat systematically and noisily.)*
JOHANN: You say her acting is outdated, that she's been acting in the same way for years. Alright, but, she's the one who reformed acting. She is Caroline Neuber! The idol of German actors. The people owe it to her!
SPIEGELBERG: Do you know what could possibly happen to her? What are you going to do then?
JOHANN: I beg you . . . *(Pause.)*
SPIEGELBERG: What if they whistle at her? What if she fails? She is Caroline Neuber!
JOHANN: She won't. She can't.
SPIEGELBERG: "She won't. She can't . . ." Who does she think she is! You place me in an impossible position! You want me to pull the stool out from under her feet?! I am not an executioner! That's impossible! Besides, she was quite happy to leave my

company and join Gottsched. She destroyed my repertory and never looked back to see what she'd done.

JOHANN: At least you know how much she loved you. You introduced theatre to her. You put her on that stool to begin with.

SPIEGELBERG: I never put anyone up on a stool, sir. I made an actress of her, while Gottsched made her . . . what she is today. She left me, destroyed my repertory, and now you are asking me to . . . *(Continues to eat.)*

JOHANN: *(Bursting with anger.)* Will you stop gorging yourself!! You're humiliating me and enjoying it! But you're the one who's being humiliated, not me. I'm doing this for her sake, and all you care about is yourself. And your whole little, miserable world, which you praise to the stars, feeds on its own vanity, swims in malice and hypocrisy. Nothing gives you more pleasure than another's destruction. You hate each other and bite at each other like rabid dogs for the sake of the stage and the applause of the fickle audience, which you love only when it is praising you, and which you really despise from the depths of your heart, because you're afraid! Frightened and cruel children! I've been waiting all my life by her side to see, finally what will appear underneath it all, after all those tears and sweat! And what appears? Vanity, vanity and nothing but vanity! No one believed in those stories of yours about enlightening the people, except for one woman – Caroline Neuber. That's why she's the greatest, because she's willing to suffer for her faith. But I won't let her! I won't let her, because I know it's a lie!! *(Pause.)*

SPIEGELBERG: Oh my God . . . oh my God . . . We'll try one more time, and tomorrow, we'll see what happens!

JOHANN: Sir! *(Tries to kiss his hand.)*

SPIEGELBERG: Johann, don't humiliate yourself anymore! I'm not God . . . yet. Ha, ha . . . Come, take this for her . . .

(He wraps food in a napkin and hands it to Johann. Pause. Johann takes it. Darkness.)

18. HANSWURST – THE LAND OF COCKAIGNE

HANSWURST: Listen here, people, to a tale miraculous and wonderful. How Hanswurst the sailor sailed to faraway India. There was a terrible storm, the ship skipped like a donkey with a thistle under its tail. Our captain banged his head so hard against the wall that he ended up inside his own stomach. So he climbed to the bow, took his pants off and peered out of his ass hole to see where we were heading. They even stuffed a looking glass up his ass, to help him see better. Still, it was one shitty voyage! And when you look at the world through your own asshole, all you can see is shit, so we hit some rocks and all the hands were drowned. I, however, was saved by the good Lord who led me to this strange island I want to tell you about. What an island, oh my brothers! As soon as I set foot on it, pans full of food began barking at me, pots and baking dishes, frying pans and stewpots, trays and plates. In one of them a roll with peas, as big as that, from another a side of beef looked at me, in a third sauerkraut was giggling, and over there was mutton and potatoes. I shivered all over, my dear brothers, and scampered up a tree. But in the tree, instead of leaves, there were mince meat patties and cutlets. The pots and pans below were all barking at me and shouting, "Eat me! Eat me!" And then they threw hot cakes and pretzels at me, just to get me to come down. Some of them, seeing that I didn't want to eat them, ate themselves out of despair. What a land that was, my brothers! Spit roasted goats capered on the meadow, rivers of veal broth, others of hot fish soup. Like a nest of snakes, pancakes with fresh cheese, meats and greens hissing at me, and from the well you drew beer, while wine showered from the sky. Everything was hot, my brothers, golden brown, crispy, savory, crunchy, well baked, fat, it all slid down your throat, it called to you, it enticed you, it waved at you, it cursed you, it spied on you, it begged you. In the air, instead of flies, full spoons buzzed around and as soon as you opened your mouth

they'd head in. I was conversing with a carp in sour cream, when along comes a bowl full of dumplings and it said to me that I was being summoned by their priest, the Big Cookie. So then I mounted a salami and it took me to the Ementhaler Hills, where the Big Cookie proclaimed a Law for Men and I am going to pass it on to you here:
Never work! Just eat!
Never eat on an empty stomach. Don't do any work!
Never sweets before the savory. Don't do any work.
Don't mix wines; drink beer on the side. Never do any work!
When there's a roast don't forget the salad. Don't do any work!
Let your pork be fat and abundant. Don't do any work!
It's a sin to eat fish without wine. Don't do any work!
Don't crave meat that has no fat. Never do any work!
And never, not ever, whatever the weather. Don't do any work!
And shit regularly, for the love of God!
I spent wonderful years there. And when the time came for me to leave, I wanted to take some food for those actors who keep talking of great art, but are so hungry that they haven't got anything to shit. But the Big Cookie told me: Hanswurst, they eat air. "How is that?" That is why they fart so much, you can't breathe! They've eaten up all the air! I often remember my good friends: the Vegetable Stew, the stuffed cabbages, the leg roast with noodles (he was a real devil), and tears come to my mouth. *(He wipes away his "tears.")* Where are you, my unfaithful friends, in these hungry times? Think of me! Your loving Hanswurst!

19. THE INN

THE MERCHANT: Yes, the performance was sensational. I'm sorry . . .

CAROLINE: I'm not malicious. I'm glad that the performance was a success even though I wasn't in it. I'm really glad.

I PROSTITUTE: He's lying, the cad. He's saying it just to torment you. The performance was terrible. It was boring.

CAROLINE: Ha! Now they'll see who Caroline Neuber is! Let him perform in his wife's plays. Let him starve . . . *(She drinks while the others nudge each other.)* I didn't love Gottsched. No, I didn't. God knows I tried. If I had loved him, then everything would have been more proper.

I PROSTITUTE: Ah, yes, then it would have been quite different. Wouldn't it? *(To the others.)*

II PROSTITUTE: Absolutely. *(They all snicker.)*

CAROLINE: Say I'm lying, but I did it all for the theatre's sake.

I PROSTITUTE: Of course, sister, I also did it for the theatre's sake.

II PROSTITUTE: Me too!

CAROLINE: And for my father's sake. He's so vulgar, the poor man. And there are thousands like him . . .

I PROSTITUTE: I also did it for my father's sake.

THE MERCHANT: Please show some respect. This was once the celebrated Caroline Neuber.

CAROLINE: I haven't acted for a year. For a year!

I PROSTITUTE: Come, have a drink, sister.

CAROLINE: I won't. *(She drinks.)* The theatre . . . *(Pause.)* Oh, my poor Johann.

II PROSTITUTE: Come, let's drink.

CAROLINE: I won't. *(She drinks.)* My life is over. I've sacrificed my unborn child to the theatre, I've sacrificed my husband to the theatre, I've sacrificed my father to the theatre, and I've sacrificed my honor to the theatre. I've sacrificed everything.

I PROSTITUTE: Let's have a drink. Honor, children and the other odds and ends don't interest us.

CAROLINE: I won't. *(She drinks.)* They carried me in their hands! In their hands!

I PROSTITUTE: Of course, my dear sister. Of course they did.

II PROSTITUTE: We believe you.

THE MERCHANT: Yes we do, we believe each other completely. I am, in fact, a duke, but I've masked myself. This is princess Zoraida. She really is.

CAROLINE: They did carry me in their hands! I used to be a great actress.

THE MERCHANT: And I used to be a duke! *(General laughter.)*

CAROLINE: Iphigenia at Aulis! The mother discovers that her daughter will be sacrificed so that the ships can set sail. Look and see who the great Caroline Neuber is! *(She stumbles. They all laugh.)*

CAROLINE: "Defend your darling, the one they call yours though you are mistaken!

With a garland I took my daughter to you,

And now I follow her to slaughter!

By your heart, by your right arm, by your mother,

Your name has ruined me, let it be my salvation!

I have no sacrificial temple altar except for your knee!"

(Everyone else comments. The corporal sits motionless and looks at her in awe. The others are shouting and applauding. She stands on a chair as in a trance.)

CAROLINE: Applause . . . *(The Corporal is almost senseless with alcohol.)*

THE CORPORAL: *(Wiping his tears.)* Marry me! *(They all roar.)* How can you laugh at a woman who is going through such a tragedy! Are you human beings? She is sacrificing her daughter, and what are you doing? You're laughing! *(The*

Merchant falls under the table.) (To Caroline.) Where is your daughter Iphigenia? Perhaps it isn't too late . . . *(He belches.)* I beg your pardon . . . I'll save her!
(Caroline looks half crazed.)
I PROSTITUTE: Haven't you heard, you blockhead, that she sacrificed her to the theatre!?
II PROSTITUTE: Even before she was born!
THE MERCHANT: And even her father!
I PROSITITUTE: And even her husband!
THE CORPORAL: Not she! She would never do something like that! Isn't it so, Mrs. Clytemnestra?
CAROLINE: The theatre is my Aulis! These people are the Greek ships! Yes, I did all that . . .
II PROSTITUTE: The people are ships! Long live the ships with their masts!
THE MERCHANT: Long live trawlers with broad lower decks!
THE CORPORAL: *(Falls back onto his chair.)* Iphigenia . . .
(Johann comes in.)
JOHANN: Caroline, you're going to play in Hamburg! *(A pause. Johann's face grows dim.)* Caroline, let's go.
I PROSTITUTE: And who is this?
II PROSTITUTE: The poor Johann!
THE MERCHANT: Poor Johann, this lady is betrothed to this gentleman, the Corporal. In the meantime, the lady has sacrificed her daughter to the gods.
THE CORPORAL: Iphigenia . . . *(Johann ignores him.)*
CAROLINE: Let me go! I want to drink! I want to act! Leave me alone!
THE MERCHANT: Wait, my poor Johann, this lady is the corporal's betrothed! She is perhaps already carrying his child! *(Roar of laughter.)* And she will sacrifice him as well for the Greek ships!
JOHANN: *(Excited, but somewhat commanding.)* Caroline, I beg you. *(Caroline climbs down.)*

CAROLINE: Johann, catch me, I'm falling. *(The lights change. The inn disappears into darkness, Johann and Caroline are standing near the footlights.)*
CAROLINE: My God, Johann, what is happening to me? Tell me that I am still fourteen years old and that it's not too late.
JOHANN: It's not too late. The Hamburg theatre . . .
CAROLINE: Kiss me on the forehead before I go to bed. Say to me "Sleep, little angel" and . . . tiptoe out of the room and be careful . . . that the door does not squeak.
JOHANN: Don't cry. *(He kisses her on the forehead, on her cheeks, on her neck. Caroline looks absentmindedly at the dark sky with no stars, completely unaware of his kisses, even of Johann's presence. Johann gently lowers her to the floor. He lifts her skirt and unbuttons his trousers. Caroline seems to wake up.)*
CAROLINE: Johann? *(Johann, breathless and red in the face, stops what he is doing. Pause.)*
JOHANN: What? What! I'm a husband, a man. I love you. But, I have . . . I have the right for myself. In front of Spiegelberg I had to . . . I didn't vow celibacy to the theatre! When am I going to live!?
CAROLINE: Oh, Johann, I didn't know that you were suffering so much . . .

20. THE INN

(Enter the Father, Margareta, Spiegelberg, Gottsched, Mrs. Gottsched, a Peasant . . . Everyone except Johann. They resemble something like an audience. They sit down near the footlights, close to the audience and their faces toward it. During the scene they address the audience directly. Caroline comes in. Pause.)

PEASANT: The play was sensational, you'll see!
MARGARETA: He's lying, the cad! The play is terrible. Boring.

HANSWURST: Quiet!!! . . . Quiet please . . . And respect! The great Caroline Neuber! . . . Iphigenia in Aulis! The mother learns that her daughter will be sacrificed so that the ships can set sail . . .

CAROLINE: I haven't been acting for a year. For a year . . . I've given everything to the theatre . . . I've sacrificed my unborn child to the theatre, I've sacrificed my husband to the theatre, I've sacrificed my father to the theatre, and I've sacrificed my honor to the theatre. I've sacrificed everything.

MRS. GOTTSCHED: What's she saying? I can't hear . . .

GOTTSCHED: That she has sacrificed everything to the theatre.

MARGARETA: Of course, sister, so have I. Since I've been sacrificing everything to the duke, I'm much better off.

HANSWURST: Quiet! Shhhhhhhhh!

CAROLINE: My father. He was so vulgar, the poor man. There are thousands like him . . . *(Pause.)*

MRS. GOTTSCHED: What is she saying?

HANSWURST: She says she has thousands of fathers.

PEASANT: Her mother was an honest woman! She says she did it all because of her father!

MARGARETA: Of course . . . I also did it because of my father. Absolutely. I believe you.

HANSWURST: We generally believe each other completely. I am, in fact, a duke, but today I have masked myself. This is princess Zoraida. She really is. How are you Zoraida? How is your Kairos? Does it still hurt? *(Laughter from the "audience". Pause.)*

HANSWURST: Iphigenia at Aulis!

CAROLINE: *(Starts to recite softly.)* "Defend your darling, the one they call yours though you are mistaken!
With a garland I took my daughter to you,
And now I follow her to slaughter!
By your heart, by your right arm, by your mother,
Your name has ruined me, let it be my salvation!

I have no sacrificial temple altar except for your knee!"
(Applause, laughter.)
PEASANT: How can you laugh at a woman who is going through such a tragedy! Are you human beings? She's sacrificing her daughter, and what are you doing? You're laughing! *(To Caroline.)* Where is your daughter Iphigenia? Perhaps it's not too late . . . I'll save her! *(Caroline looks at him from the table like a madwoman.)*
MARGARETA: Haven't you heard, you blockhead, she sacrificed her to the theatre!?
MRS GOTTSCHED: Before she was born!
HANSWURST: Her father, too!
GOTTSCHED: And even her husband!
PEASANT: Not her! She'd never do something like that! Isn't it so, Mrs. Clytemnestra?
CAROLINE: The theatre is my Aulis. These people are the Greek ships! Yes, I did it . . .
MRS. GOTTSCHED: Come drink something . . . Some mint tea!
CAROLINE: I won't *(She drinks.)* the theatre . . . Oh, my poor Johann. *(Pause.)* They carried me in their hands. I was a great actress.
HANSWURST: And I used to be a duke. *(General laughter. Wiping his tears.)* Marry me! *(Like a clown, he wipes his nose on an enormous white handkerchief with red polka dots.)*
MARGARETA: The people are the ships . . . Long live the ships with stiff and large masts!
GOTTSCHED: Long live the fishing trawlers with large and wet lower decks! *(Johann comes in.)*
MARGARETA: Who is this?
GOTTSCHED: Poor Johann!
HANSWURST: Poor Johann, this lady is the betrothed of Mr. Muller. In the meantime, the lady was pleased to sacrifice her daughter to the gods.

PEASANT: Iphigenia, my child . . . *(Johann goes over to Caroline.)*
JOHANN: Let us go. You'll be acting in Hamburg. Spiegelberg wants you back. I've promised you'll come. Forgive me, we dined together. He sent you this . . . look . . . *(Shows her the food wrapped in a napkin.)*
CAROLINE: Let me go! I want to drink! I want to act! Leave me alone!
HANSWURST: Wait, poor Johann, this lady is another man's betrothed! Perhaps she's already carrying his child and will sacrifice it to the Greek ships as well! *(The "audience" approves.)*
CAROLINE: Johann, catch me, I'm falling!

21. THE HAMBURG THEATRE

(Johann and Spiegelberg are sitting in the dressing room. They are listening tensely, as if bombers were flying over their heads. Spiegelberg is biting his nails.)

SPIEGELBERG: Now comes the scene with the lover . . . *(Johann nods his head. They continue to listen. A long, long pause.)* I can't hear anything . . . *(A whistle breaks out. Johann and Spiegelberg jump up.)* I knew it! *(They rush off the stage. A spotlight goes on to reveal Caroline Neuber. The whistling continues. She stands motionless.)*
CAROLINE: Why are you like this? Why are you so cruel? What have I done to you? What are you getting back at me for? In order to please you, I have rehearsed a single gesture of the hand for seven days. And you? You hate me and look for my mistakes. You rejoice when I stumble. You're delighted when I forget my lines. You work hard trying to find where I've gone wrong. Each of you discusses the theatre, but when the theatre discusses you, you're offended. I'm not your enemy. I want to

help you. You are my children, you are my family and my ideal. Is your laughter, are your tears, more valuable than my life? And today you have come to bury me.

(Whistles.) You want lies, you want light entertainment? Well, Caroline Neuber won't give them to you! I won't pander to you! You vile, primitive crowd! I don't need your love! I couldn't care less about your applause. I spit on your false tears! I spit on a theatre in which you are the audience. Damn you! *(Darkness. Whistling.)*

SPIEGELBERG: My dear audience, I apologize! I ask your forgiveness a hundred times over. A million times. Today we'll be performing the hilarious comedy The Cuckolded Husband. You must come!

22. CAROLINE – JOHANN

(The inn disappears into the darkness. Johann and Caroline are near the footlights.)

CAROLINE: My God, Johann, what's happening to me? Tell me I'm still fourteen years old and that it's not too late.
JOHANN: It's not too late.
CAROLINE: Kiss me on the forehead before I go to bed. Say to me "Sleep, little angel" then . . . tiptoe out of the room and be careful . . . that the door doesn't squeak.
JOHANN: Don't cry. *(He kisses her on the forehead, on her cheeks, on her neck. Caroline looks absentmindedly at the dark sky with no stars, completely unaware of his kisses, even of Johann's presence. Johann gently lowers her to the floor. He lifts her skirt and unbuttons his trousers. Caroline seems to wake up.)*
CAROLINE: Johann? *(Johann, breathless, stops what he is doing. Pause.)*

JOHANN: What? What! I am a husband, a man. I love you. But, I have . . . I have a right . . . to you. I can't wait in vain any more. I want an ordinary life! Ordinary things!
CAROLINE: Oh, Johann, I didn't know that you were suffering so much . . .

23. HANSWURST (CIVILIAN AND SOLDIER)

HANSWURST: Then I became a sergeant and every fledgling soldier came to cry on my shoulder. I would stand like this and keep quiet. And he'd stand like this and keep quiet. And he would go: Sergeant, sir, my wife has just had a baby. I . . . can't go off to war. My mother is old . . . And I would say: Military shirt, sir. Military undershirt. Without looking at him. And he would take off his clothes, and slowly fold them on a chair. And I would say: The cap, and the one that goes under it, gloves, and helmet. And he would begin to whimper: my child is two months old. My wife has an infection. Oh God, what am I going to do now . . . All the while he's taking his clothes off. I would then say strictly: The water bottle, sir. Bayonet, sack, backpack. Then he would begin to wail: I'm shortsighted. No one will have any use of me. Trousers, boots, long underwear. Then he would go again: I've graduated from a conservatory. I am more useful to the state as a civilian. Someone has to entertain the people. He would take off his trousers. And then the sweetest part: your underwear, sir. And he would go: can't I keep my own? I have sensitive skin. No, sir. Then he'd begin to cry. He'd cover up his privates and put on the underwear. And he'd dress himself in the uniform. I'd give him a rifle: Here is your rifle. Congratulations, sir. He'd be in despair. Thank you . . . and then I'd be screaming: Attention! Down! Up! He'd look like this and his heart would be in his heels. What is the matter with you!? There's nothing for you to ask me!!! Is that clear!! Left turn! I am your God! Who is your God? But, sir . . . Who is your God, you monkey!? You are. That's right. I am God. And that's how Hanswurst became God.

24. SEVEN AGAINST THEBES

(Caroline, all out of breath, pulls the Peasant onto the stage.)

CAROLINE: Johann, Johann! We're beginning rehearsals. *(Johann comes in. In this scene it is evident that he is ill.)*
PEASANT: My son has been drafted into the army. I prayed to God for the war to stop, but it didn't help. The lady says that the . . . muses can stop the war.
CAROLINE: That's right! The people will see the tragedy of Polyneices and Eteocles . . .
PEASANT: And I'm going to be this . . . Eteocles.
CAROLINE: Johann, why are you standing there?! Give him a text! We have to start rehearsing!
PEASANT: Hurry, please. The winter will be upon us soon and my blockhead doesn't know how to look after himself.
CAROLINE: People will understand how senseless war is. They will throw down their arms and rush to embrace each other! They will become brothers, they will shed tears of joy!
PEASANT: *(Kissing Caroline's hands.)* Madam, God bless you! Ask of me what you will! Oh, just make it stop!
JOHANN: Friend, do you really think that the war can be stopped?
PEASANT: The lady says that it's the greatest magic in the world. She says that the . . . muses . . . with their wings . . . of truth . . . can bring my son back. *(He chokes.)* On the wings of truth! I believe that, sir, for God is silent, and the saints are silent! And my blockhead is alone out there! I'll even beg the devil, sir, the tailed Lucifer! *(Johann embraces him.)*

PEASANT: *(Pushing away his arm.)* I won't! Don't sir! I beg you! Give me that text, sir! I'll be Eteocles, I'll be anything you say! Give me that text! For my son's sake – I would kill!
CAROLINE: Quickly, quickly! It's still not too late! *(She takes the text.)* Do you know how to read? It doesn't matter. Say: And the beat of hoofs, the clanging of arms spreads over the field and draws near, the noise flies, echoes."
PEASANT: *(He stutters without comprehension.)* "And the beat of hoofs, the clanging of arms spreads over the field and draws near, the noise flies, echoes" . . .
CAROLINE: *(Continues.)* " . . . like raging waters when they split the rocks! Oh, gods, goddesses, defend us from evil!"
PEASANT: *(Repeats.)* "Oh, gods, goddesses defend us from evil!" *(They are both screaming. They are trying to overwhelm the sound of cannons heard in the distance. The cannons drown them out. Darkness.)*

25. ON THE DOORSTEP

(Caroline, Johann. Caroline is pulling Johann on some two-wheeled cart. They are both in tatters, dirty and disheveled. To the left is what is left of the wall of Caroline's house.)

JOHANN: This was where your house stood.
CAROLINE: The church stood here. No. The church wasn't red. Over there, where that pile of yellow bricks is.
JOHANN: The bakery used to stand over there.
CAROLINE: And over there, do you see that trench . . . that's where the rose garden was. And the park was behind it.
JOHANN: Do you remember?
CAROLINE: I remember.
JOHANN: And do you remember? . . .
CAROLINE: Of course. Do you remember?
JOHANN: Yes, yes . . . why shouldn't I?! You do remember?

CAROLINE: Do you remember?

JOHANN: I remember.

CAROLINE: I remember. *(Pause.)* As if it were yesterday. *(Pause.)* Is it possible that it's all over? Strange. I was angry at my father for some reason. You were lying on the bed . . . I said: let's go. And you said: let's go. Not asking where, not asking why.

JOHANN: Caroline, don't let me die.

CAROLINE: You've just caught a cold.

JOHANN: I'm ill. *(Pause.)*

CAROLINE: Oh, damn the people! They've destroyed everything! I've always said they were like animals! Animals! Bloodshed, killing and grimacing! They don't need theatre, they need the Great Flood! A fire up to the skies! *(Out of breath, she sits down.)* Let them all go to the devil! I've been lying to myself long enough! It's important to live.

JOHANN: I'm so ashamed, Caroline . . . for being afraid of death.

CAROLINE: What do you think, that I'm doing it for you?! I still need you. When I have taken all your goodness, all your strength, all your . . . then I'll let you die.

JOHANN: I'm no hero . . . Gottsched is.

CAROLINE: That was twenty years ago.

JOHANN: Has it been so long? Do you remember? *(Caroline is at the window, she nods her head.)*

JOHANN: You look . . . wonderful.

CAROLINE: Do you really think so?

26. THE END

CAROLINE: Listen, soldiers. What do you think happened to me once! I was returning to my beautiful Salzburg from Bavaria. I had sold three little goats at the fair and I wanted to have a good time, to eat my food, and to get some woman in the sack – if I could. So I saw, a beautiful mother and her beautiful daughter. Oh, my dear Hanswurst, how could I pass them up? I looked at the mother – she had breasts soooo big. I looked at the daughter, she had breasts sooooooo big!

Translated by *Dennis Barnett*
from the transcription by *Vladislava Felbabov*

BILJANA SRBLJANOVIĆ
(1970—)

Although born in Stockholm, Sweden, in 1970, Srbljanović now lives mostly in Belgrade, Serbia. She is an accomplished and award-winning playwright, whose plays have been staged in some fifty countries.

Srbljanović obtained her dramaturgy degree at the Faculty of Dramatic Arts in Belgrade. Her play, *The Belgrade Trilogy*, was performed in Belgrade in 1970 and was instantly acclaimed. Equally acclaimed is her play *Barbelo*, a contemplative work about Christianity and God.

BARBELO, ON DOGS AND CHILDREN

To my girlfriends: the suicides and the rest

CHARACTERS:

MILICA
MILA
MILENA
DRAGAN
DRAGO
ZORAN (SOMETIMES MARKO)
MARKO (ONLY MARKO)
DOG LADY
ONE DOCTOR, TWICE
TWO STRAYS, ONE A DRIFTER, ONE A DOG
ONE DOG,
ANOTHER DOG,
FOUR MORE DOGS
AT LEAST

The author insists on humane treatment of the animals in staging the play. The author does not insist on the same treatment of the people. The didascalia do not have to be respected either.

The action takes place today in transitional Serbia. Down with me, in a hole. And around it.

A young woman is sitting on a low wall, smoking and crying. (So what? I cry all the time, too.) I think she's smoking a joint. No one knows how sad she feels.

Another young woman is walking her dog. She's crying and doesn't know why. They have nothing to do with each other. Apparently.

Some people pass by, taking their children home from somewhere, taking their dogs home after their walk. No one is crying. But not because there isn't any reason.

Some facades are peeling while others are bright with the splendor of the newly rich. Dilapidated houses are set between two houses with security guards; there is dirt in the street, in and around the dumpster, around the parked cars, expensive with temporary plates. The garbage men have been on strike for a week, the dogs are wild but some are purebred; they all live together on the same street that has a house, a bench, and a cemetery.

What more do we need in life?

I. A Thousand Whys

A bench just like any other bench. Except that this one is in a cemetery.

A child, a little boy, all dressed up, too fat for his clothes, his hair combed by force, dragged to the funeral, close to tears, is sitting on the bench without understanding anything. Particularly not that he has just buried his mother.

The child sits there calmly, staring straight ahead, he's not even swinging his legs, he's just waiting for the circus to be over. He is sitting next to a youngish man who has had opportunities open up for some time in a continuous string, one after the other, each one better than the next, and who, just imagine, still wants—more. This is the child's father. Who doesn't know where to begin.

MARKO: Zoza . . .
ZORAN: I'm not Zoza. I hate that name. Mama says it doesn't suit me.
MARKO: All right, son. What would you prefer?
ZORAN: Marko.
MARKO: What do you mean, Marko? You can't, son. Because I'm Marko.
ZORAN: So what? Mama says that sometimes it's the same.
MARKO: Mama was just joking.
ZORAN: She wasn't joking.
MARKO: Yes, she was, I know.
ZORAN: And I know she wasn't. So why don't you go and ask her. Where is Mama, anyway? Why are we here? Who was that woman who dressed me? And who was that other one, the one who combed my hair? Why is everyone crying? Why are there so many candles?

Marko certainly can't answer a thousand questions. He can't answer even one. Or half of one. Marko can't even get the upper hand of half of one whole question.

His wife is dead, she killed herself and now he has to explain this to his son.

That's something no one can do.

MARKO: Zoran . . .

ZORAN: Marko.

MARKO: Please, be serious.

ZORAN: I am serious. Just look at me. I want my name to be Marko.

MARKO: But that's my name! You have your name and I have mine. You're not me!

ZORAN: How do you know I'm not? Who can say that? That woman, maybe?

Technically speaking, Marko is not a widower. He has been divorced for a year, even though neither he nor his ex—now late—wife had been able to find a way to explain this to their son. Zoran, not Marko.

The father is silent. So is the son.

MARKO: Are you hungry?

ZORAN: Yes, I'm hungry. We've been here since this morning. Mama didn't fix anything to eat. Mama never fixes anything. She just sits there all day long. Papa, what's wrong with her?

MARKO: You see—Son.

ZORAN: Is Mama sick?

MARKO: Yes, she's sick.

ZORAN: What does she have?

MARKO: It's her head. Mama gets headaches all the time.

ZORAN: I didn't notice it. Is it contagious? Is it inherited? Will my head start to ache too now? How much and when? When will it start?

MARKO: Zoza, son, where did you . . . ?

ZORAN: Marko. I said Marko.

MARKO: All right, Marko, where did you hear that? Where'd you get that "inherited," "contagious," they don't teach you that in school, do they?
ZORAN: In school? I don't think so.
MARKO: So where did it come from?
ZORAN: How do I know . . .
ZORAN *shrugs his shoulders. He doesn't know where he picked it up. Or won't say.*
MARKO: All right, if you know that, then you can understand that *Mama*'s not well. She fell and hurt herself.
ZORAN: How did she fall?
MARKO: On her head. From the window.
ZORAN: Did she hurt herself?
MARKO: A lot.
ZORAN: Is it painful?
MARKO: Not anymore.
ZORAN: Because she's in a coma? People who are in a coma don't feel anything. Except that they might feel something but can't say so. Then when they turn off the apparatus, they are actually killing them.
MARKO: Now it's coma and apparatus, where did that come from . . . ? Zoran, no one killed anyone!
ZORAN: Is Mama in a coma?
MARKO: Yes, Zoza, Mama's in a coma.
ZORAN: I'm not Zoza . . .
MARKO: Zoran, stop it now. That's enough. Now's not the time. Mama is very sick and might die. Die, do you understand? Do you know what that means?
ZORAN: What?
MARKO: She would go away. Leave us.
ZORAN: Like you left Mama?
MARKO: No, Zoran, not like that. Leave for good.
ZORAN: You left for good, too.
MARKO: That's right. But you still see me around.

ZORAN: Mama doesn't see you around. Mama says she doesn't see you at all anymore.
MARKO: This is different. Mama might leave, she might move to heaven.
ZORAN: With God?
MARKO: Yes, with God.
ZORAN: And with the angels?
MARKO: That's right. With the angels.
ZORAN: And with the devil?
MARKO: Where'd you pick up all that stuff?
ZORAN: In school. That's what they teach us.
MARKO: I don't know what they teach you, but Mama won't be with the devil. I can't believe that we're talking like this . . .
Nevertheless, Marko decides to play by the rules.
MARKO: Zoran, Mama was good and she's going to heaven.
Marko feels totally ridiculous mentioning God and the angels to a child who knows about comas and inherited diseases. But if that's what they learn in school . . .
MARKO: Mama's going to God and the angels.
ZORAN: What do you mean, "going." She's not dead yet.
MARKO: She's not. But she will be soon.
ZORAN: How soon? Do you know when that will happen?
MARKO: I don't know for sure. But very soon.
ZORAN: Are you sure?
Marko nods.
ZORAN: And I'll never see her again?
Marko shakes his head. Zoran ponders this, trying to understand.
ZORAN: She didn't even say good-bye.
MARKO: She didn't have time. She didn't know that she would fall. That she would hurt herself so much. She didn't know that she would fall on her head.
There is a long silence, heavy and sorrowful. It might be touching, if this weren't my play.

ZORAN: Why didn't she know when she jumped by herself? And left a letter where she wrote that she would jump. And how can she be alive when we just buried her? This is a cemetery, isn't it? We're at the cemetery now, because Mama died? Why don't you just say so? Why don't you just say: Marko, your Mama is dead. Because she is dead, isn't she?

Marko quickly reconsiders whether to continue the silly ruse he's started. Then, out of indolence and a strange helplessness before this fat eight-year-old child, he simply gives up.

MARKO: That's right, son. Mama is dead.

Zoran, as though hoping that at the last moment his father would convince him otherwise, as though thinking there would be a miracle, now seems to understand.

ZORAN: Really dead? Are you sure?

Marko nods. Zoza thinks it over.

ZORAN: Did you shake her? Hard, with your hand? Did you stick a needle in her? As hard as you could, so there was blood? Did you listen to her heart? Did her heart stop?

Marko is silent. Zoza hears something anyway.

ZORAN: Then say so.

Marko puts his arm around his son. Zoza, strangely enough, doesn't resist. They are silent. Some sort of mournful malice bursts out of the child.

ZORAN: Mama's with the devil now because she killed herself. Suicides don't go to heaven.

Zoran looks his father straight in the eye.

ZORAN: I know. We learned it in school.

Zoran, the fat, sad little child, stands up and heads home. To his new home.

Fade out.

II. The Child Is Fat and Has to Lose Weight

It's dinner time in Zoza's new home. Marko, a rapidly rising party official with future frustrations only in the formation stage, is sitting at the table, eating. This is his first serious meal in an extremely exhausting day full of irrepressible hierarchical groveling, he to his superiors, his inferiors to him. This, conversely, is Zoza's seventh. The child is eating his seventh serious meal with unbelievable enthusiasm, which keeps Milena away from the table.

MARKO: Where's the dog?
MILENA: I don't know. Somewhere.
MARKO: You didn't lose it, did you?
MILENA: Of course I didn't. I think.
MARKO: Then where is it?
MILENA: Here. Somewhere. I just saw it.
MARKO: Are you sure?
MILENA: Of course I am. I think.
MARKO *eats.*
MARKO: What'd you do today?
MILENA's *answers are always hesitant, as though she's having a hard time concentrating next to this greedy child and rather hungry husband.*
MILENA: I don't know. Nothing.
MARKO: What do you mean, nothing? You must have done something.
MILENA: Actually, I did. I read.
MARKO: There, you see. That's something. What did you read?
MILENA: I don't know. Actually, I do know. A book.
MARKO: Which one?
Milena ponders briefly, then is taken aback.
MILENA: Guess what. I forgot!

MARKO: How could you forget?
Milena is like a child. Or a dog.
MILENA: Just like that. I forgot. It wasn't interesting.
Marko continues to eat. Zoza takes a second helping.
MARKO: Why aren't you eating with us?
MILENA: I'm not hungry.
ZORAN: She already ate.
Milena takes on a motherly tone. Completely out of place.
MILENA: No, I didn't, honey.
MARKO: You never eat.
ZORAN: I'm telling you she ate.
MILENA: And I'm telling you I didn't.
ZORAN: Yes you did.
MILENA: No I didn't!
ZORAN: You don't say. So where's the bread? You ate the whole loaf; there's nothing left for me. That's why you're not eating now. Where would you put it?
Milena wants to show her authority. But there isn't any.
MILENA: That's not true. I don't eat bread.
ZORAN: The bread's gone.
MILENA: It's gone because I threw it out. I threw out the bread so you wouldn't eat it.
ZORAN: You devoured it all by yourself.
MILENA: Devoured? Me? What's that you're saying?
MARKO: Don't fight, Milena.
MILENA: I'm not fighting. He's fighting.
MARKO: Please stop it.
MILENA: He's the one who should stop it!
Marko looks at his wife, sincerely amazed.
MARKO: He's only a child. I should think you'd understand that much.
Milena would love to say, "I'm a child, too," but doesn't. She lies instead.
MILENA: I do understand.

MARKO: And I don't understand why you threw out the bread. You know Zoza loves it.
ZORAN: Marko.
MARKO: Stop it, Zoza.
ZORAN: My name is Marko.
MARKO: Zoran, that's enough!
Zoza sticks his fork into his father's hand. There isn't any blood, but the insolence is painful.
Marko cries out.
Encouraged, Milena *shouts.*
MILENA: The child is fat and has to lose weight!
This is really true. The child is fat and should lose weight. Marko stops eating and Zoran stops eating, but just for a moment, an instant. He doesn't look at his father or Milena. He lowers his head then looks up, listening and on the lookout. Like a dog.
Marko looks at his child. And then says what's the easiest for him to say.
MARKO: That's ridiculous. He just needs to get his growth.
Zoza, as though on cue, starts gobbling up everything that's left on the table. His father looks at him, almost terrified.
MARKO: He'll pull out of it. Upwards.
Marko puts his knife and fork down and pushes his plate away. Milena removes it immediately and then sits at the table, too. Right when she shouldn't. She avidly follows each one of *Zoza's mouthfuls.* Marko *watches, too, almost fascinated. It's truly rare to see such gluttony.*

    Milena *starts to talk, watching* Zoza *the whole time out of the corner of her eye.*
MILENA: Actually—it's good that we're all here together. I have something. To tell you.
But Marko isn't interested, Zoza certainly isn't interested, and even Milena isn't interested. She continues nonetheless.
MILENA: I'm not quite certain yet and should wait a little longer.

No one's listening. She's not even listening to herself.
MILENA: Even so, I have a feeling, it's not likely I'm mistaken. Marko, listen. We're going to have a baby.
Marko rouses halfway from the depths of his total indifference, his wish to be somewhere else and not here next to his wife and son. A place he would have gone to long ago without a second thought or reflection, if only he knew where it was. Where a man's "somewhere else" might be.
MARKO: Excuse me?
MILENA: I'm pregnant.
MARKO: That's just great.
And Marko really does think it's great, in spite of his indifferent tone, and would be happy if only he knew how to be.
MARKO: Isn't it, Zoza:? Wouldn't that be wonderful?
Zoza finally stops eating.
ZORAN: What?
MARKO: For you to have a sister or brother?
ZORAN: Oh, that. Well . . . Yes.
Milena cheers up. She almost becomes affectionate toward the fat creature.
MILENA: Do you really think so?
Zoza nods his head.
ZORAN: I'd really like that.
MARKO: But it's not sure yet?
MILENA: It's almost like it is.
MARKO: We have to wait?
MILENA: Just a very little bit.
MARKO: It won't be another—
Milena interrupts him.
MILENA: Not this time.
Zoza, of course, understands grown-up talk. And arguments and doubts. Particularly fear.
MARKO: Even so, you're not sure?
MILENA: I'm telling you I know.

Everyone goes silent for a moment.
MILENA: All right. We'll wait a little longer.
This is when Milena wants to take the last apple from the bowl on the table and take a bite out of it, thereby dispelling her doubts. But Zoza reaches for the apple, too. They grab it at the same time. Her hand and his fat paw. Neither one gives in.
MILENA: Hey, Zoza, I got there first . . .
ZORAN: No you didn't.
MILENA: Yes I did.
ZORAN: You certainly didn't.
Milena gives a forced laugh.
MILENA: I certainly did.
ZORAN: No you didn't.
Milena screams.
MILENA: I did!
Milena and Zoza tussle over the lousy apple. Like in fairy tales about stepmothers and a repulsive child.
ZORAN: Let go, let go! Leave it!
MILENA: I won't let go. You've eaten enough.
ZORAN: And I say let go!
MILENA: Marko!
ZORAN: Papa!
Marko should now arbitrate. But it's the furthest thing from his mind. He just gets up from the table.
MARKO: I have to go.
Zoza turns around, Milena takes advantage of the situation and grabs the apple away from the child. She quickly takes a bite out of it.
ZORAN: Papa, look at her!
Marko leaves so he doesn't have to see. He leaves without turning around.
MARKO: I've got work.
Milena and Zoran are alone. Milena gets up proudly, biting her apple.

Zoza just looks at her. Then he starts crying woefully. Everything pours out of him, all the sorrows of the world.
Milena doesn't know what to do.
MILENA: Zoza, Zoran, please don't cry! I didn't mean it, that's not what I wanted.
ZORAN: Yes you did. You meant it.
MILENA: I tell you I didn't. Here. Here's your apple.
Milena offers him the half-eaten fruit. As though it's the last, really, folks, like no other apple exists! Zoza keeps up his inconsolable crying.
ZORAN: Now it's too late.
Zoran kicks the apple. He goes out crying.
  Milena's not to blame. She didn't mean it. Or rather, she did, a little. Now she feels bad.
Fade out.

III. You Do Understand, Don't You, that I'm Talking About Dogs?

A bench like any other bench. This is a park. A middle-aged woman is sitting on a bench, covered with dew, uncombed, maybe even unwashed. Dog Lady. There are lots of dogs in the park. Four are hers. Maybe I shouldn't explain, but I'll say it anyway: dogs don't have to be used on stage. It's enough for us to know that they are there.

DOG LADY: Meals must always be at the same time. That's the most important thing. One in the morning, one in the evening and nothing in between. Only water. Take a seat, honey.
Milena, who has been standing until now, uncertain of how to avoid talking to an unwashed stranger, has to sit down. Dog Lady whistles.

MILENA: So, only water. I'll try . . . But I don't think it'll work. He loves to eat, he simply gobbles it up.

Dog Lady shouts to someone.

DOG LADY: Not that! No!

Then she continues explaining to Milena.

DOG LADY: They just love to get dirty, to roll in filth. They always find the worst place to play. No, Mathew, no! Mathew! What did Mama say?

Dog Lady shouts into the distance.

DOG LADY: Yesterday he found a carcass and rolled in it. He stank to high heaven of death.

MILENA: That's disgusting. What did you do?

DOG LADY: I took the carcass and pushed it under his nose. Then I got angry and said in a sharp voice, "Shame on you, Mathew, shame!" Then I washed him. I stank to high heaven. Of death.

MILENA: How awful. Do you think he understood?

DOG LADY: Oh, boy, did he, he sure did! When he gets two slaps on his backside, he understands everything, you know. He's really smart. That's the problem. He's the eldest, too. Top dog. Then his brothers look up to him.

Dog Lady stops talking, but just for a moment. Just long enough to sniff her hands and be disgusted.

DOG LADY: Such an awful carcass.

MILENA: So Mathew has brothers?

DOG LADY: Luke, Mark, and John.

Dog Lady explains her choice of names.

DOG LADY: I'm very devout, you know. How about you?

MILENA: Me? I don't know, actually. I mean, I'm not— anything. And I don't have anyone.

My husband has Zoran. That little fat boy. Playing with the dogs.

Dog Lady isn't listening very carefully. She keeps shouting somewhere in the distance.

DOG LADY: John! John, leave that alone. Don't make Mama get up! They won't listen to anything. They outnumber me. They join forces and give me a bad time.

MILENA: Zoran has no one to join forces with, but he still gives me a bad time.

DOG LADY: Actually, I just talk like that. 'Cause I don't know what I'd do without them.

Without my boys.

Without my four lads.

Without Mama's four sweethearts.

They mean everything to me.

MILENA: That's something else, after all. You gave birth to them.

DOG LADY: Well, in fact, I did.

Dog Lady sniffs her hands.

DOG LADY: I stink to high heaven. I smell like death.

MILENA: Where are they now?

DOG LADY: Who, honey?

MILENA: Where are your children?

DOG LADY: What do you mean. Over there. Fatty's pestering them.

    Marko, don't lick the boy! Marko!

Milena looks. She doesn't understand. Zoza, however, answers the call.

ZORAN: Yes? Who's calling me? What do you want from me? Why are you bugging me?

Dog Lady looks at the fat boy. Then at Milena. And asks.

DOG LADY: Honey, you do understand, don't you? I'm talking about dogs.

Fade out.

IV. Does Age Really Matter to You ?

Milena and Dragan are in Dragan's childhood bedroom. The dusty room holds many sad childhood memories for a man in his forties who has come back to live with his parents. It's as though he has had no life.

Milena and Dragan sit on the edge of the child's bed, their bodies sunk into the old mattress, knees touching their chins.

Except for memories of very early childhood, there is nothing in this man's room that indicates what happened afterward. Nothing to show that this man ever grew up.

There are no books, photographs, or other traces. There is nothing in this room to indicate that after age six, Dragan ever turned seven. Or eight. Or any other age.

Time has stopped in Dragan's room—before the alphabet, before his first lice, before his first real social life. And that's where it will stay.

Nevertheless, Milena feels completely comfortable. As though the surroundings aren't the least bit surprising.

DRAGAN: Sorry for the dog back there.
MILENA: It's not your fault. Our bitch is in heat. All the dogs jump on her. Particularly the big ones.
DRAGAN: Mine's got a short temper, I barely held him back. He won't obey me at all. He doesn't love me—I don't love him. He was my mother's dog. Now that Mama's dead, they're left to me. My father and the dog.
MILENA: So, that's it . . .
DRAGAN: That's it.
Milena and Dragan are silent for a moment. They're trying to think of what to say to each other.
DRAGAN: In any case, I'm sorry.
MILENA: It's all right, really.

DRAGAN: I feel rather foolish. I invited you to come over and don't have anything to offer.
MILENA: It doesn't matter. I don't want anything.
DRAGAN: I didn't expect . . . you would accept.
MILENA: Maybe I shouldn't have?
DRAGAN: Oh, no, it's really nice. We're neighbors after all. It's only fitting.
Milena looks at him a bit and suddenly shouts.
MILENA: I'm married!
DRAGAN: So what?
MILENA: Nothing. Just so you know.
DRAGAN: Your husband's puffed up.
MILENA: He is, you know.
DRAGAN: Conceited, full of himself.
MILENA: I'm telling you, I know.
DRAGAN: He never says hello. When I run into him in the stairwell.
MILENA: He'd say hello to me. But I never run into him.
DRAGAN: I know them all. But him the least.
MILENA: Who's that—all?
Dragan takes a bag of hashish, cigarette paper, and tobacco out of his pocket. Milena looks at him in amazement.
DRAGAN: Do you mind?
Milena just shrugs her shoulders.
DRAGAN: I know them all, from way back. Back when they were young. Back when they believed. Back when they were alive. I've worked with them for years. That's my job, understand.
Dragan holds a joint out to her. Milena hesitates a little.
MILENA: I haven't smoked since elementary school.
DRAGAN: Schoolchildren roll junk. Pure poison. Kids are stupid, they can't tell the difference. This is something else, try it. Go ahead.
Dragan insists. Milena takes the joint. She's not sure.

DRAGAN: This is for grownups.
Milena takes a drag. She doesn't cough or choke, none of those clichés. The shit's good. Milena looks around the room, interested. She looks at the old posters, the old soccer players.
MILENA: Do you work?
DRAGAN: I work.
MILENA: What do you do?
DRAGAN: Actually, I don't even know myself.
MILENA: I understand.
DRAGAN: I work a lot. But I don't know what I do or why.
MILENA: I know.
If anyone can understand Dragan right now, it's Milena. That's what she thinks.
MILENA: I understand that.
DRAGAN: Really? That's a rarity here. No one likes us.
MILENA: You?
DRAGAN: Us. Pigs. Dogs. Fuzz. People bark when they see us.
Dragan cheerfully explains.
DRAGAN: I work for the police. Understand?
MILENA: The police! *Now Milena coughs and chokes. She throws down the joint in reflex and it falls under the bed. Slapstick follows.*
DRAGAN: What's wrong?
MILENA: The police! The police!
DRAGAN: We'll catch fire!
Dragan crawls under the bed and takes out the still lighted joint.
MILENA: I have to go now. I'm really in a hurry to go somewhere.
DRAGAN: Calm down. Sit down. No one will see you here. No one ever comes in here. No one was ever in here.
Dragan finds a reason to be proud of what embarrasses normal people.
DRAGAN: Besides, that's not my job. It's not my level. I do other things. Big. Serious. Terrible. Dark. Dangerous.

Fool.
Dragan holds out the same joint to Milena. The smoke brings tears to her eyes.
Slapstick, I'm telling you.
MILENA: Even so. I don't want any more.
DRAGAN: One more drag?
Milena shakes her head.
DRAGAN: Just one more?
MILENA: No.
Dragan puts out the joint.
DRAGAN: His success really surprised me. He didn't stand out before. He wasn't promising.
MILENA: Who's that? What are you talking about? Who? I don't understand a thing.
DRAGAN: Why, your husband. He was never important. Back then, when it was important.
MILENA: My husband? Oh. Him.
Milena laughs a little. Not too much. Who told you to believe the cliché about blowing?
DRAGAN: What do they say, will he become minister?
Milena laughs again.
MILENA: He will. No, no he won't. *Then she gives it some thought.*
MILENA: Actually—I don't rightly know.
DRAGAN: He doesn't want to tell you?
MILENA: He does. He told me. He told me several times. It's just that I— always forget.
DRAGAN: It's better that way. Better for you not to know.
MILENA: Not to know—what?
Dragan doesn't reply. Or Milena is no longer listening to him. She looks around the room.
MILENA: It's really amazing here. Do you know that all these people are dead? Those soccer players in tight jerseys, in short pants, those men whose genitals are outlined through the

synthetic material, you do know don't you: they are all dead now.
It suddenly dawns on Milena.
MILENA: Ah . . . How old are you, really?
DRAGAN: Why do you ask? What do you mean by *really?* Why is that important? Why should I count?
Milena has already forgotten that she asked something.
MILENA: It's still amazing here. But you know what, I'm not at all amazed.
Dragan suddenly yells.
DRAGAN: Get lost, filthy mongrel! *He throws a shoe at the door. Milena recoils.*
DRAGAN: He's always on the prowl. Ear cocked. I don't have any peace.
MILENA: Do you think he understands you?
DRAGAN: Of course he understands. He's not feebleminded. He just doesn't hear very well.
MILENA: How old is he, anyway?
DRAGAN: Does age really matter to you?
MILENA: My bitch is a year old.
DRAGAN: Mine's almost seven.
MILENA: And he's already lost his hearing . . . ?
DRAGAN: Who?
MILENA: Your dog.
DRAGAN: His hearing is excellent. He's a hunter.
Dragan shouts at the top of his lungs.
DRAGAN: I can hear you there, nosy mongrel! If you don't watch out I'll come out and get you!
Milena hesitates. Dragan looks at her, bewildered. Then he explains.
DRAGAN: You do understand, don't you, that I'm talking about my father?
MILENA: doesn't react. At all.
Fade out.

V. The Fox Got Sick

Milena is going somewhere with the child and dog. She walks toward a bench next to a low wall. Milica is on the wall, teary-eyed until recently. Now she is smiling. Smiling and smoking. Milena can't see her, which is only normal. Milica is dead.

ZORAN: So?
MILENA: So what?
ZORAN: Are you still pregnant?
MILENA: Yes, I am.
ZORAN: You haven't changed your mind?
MILENA: What do you mean?
ZORAN: You don't have second thoughts?
MILENA: Of course not.
ZORAN: Regret it?
MILENA: No!
ZORAN: Given up on the idea?
MILENA: Marko, stop bugging me. I'm pregnant and that's that.
ZORAN: Fine, I'm just asking.
Milena and Zoza talk like two children with a problem. Just one, that they have in common.
ZORAN: Even so, you still have time. To jump into the sand. From that low wall. The blood will flow all by itself.
MILENA: Well, I won't, so there. I'm pregnant and I'm going to keep it. You can say whatever you want!
ZORAN: I'm not saying anything.
Milena's dog is in heat. "She's in high spirits," as the old women say. Milena and Zoza watch, interested and disgusted at the same time.
MILENA: That bitch has no shame. Just look at her raise her tail.
ZORAN: I see. Why does she do that? What does that mean? Why is she like that?

MILENA: How do I know?
Milena sits down. Zoran does something with the dog. He seems to be tormenting her, but the dog likes it nonetheless.
Milica, who has been sitting there grinning dumbly, starts to sing. Loudly. Milena pricks up her ears.
MILICA: The fox got sick, fell ill,
And shriveled up, I fear,
They treated her with pills,
For longer than two years.
Milena turns around. She sets her eyes on Milica and visibly jumps. Milica is her husband's first wife. Even if she wasn't dead, there would be reason to jump.
MILICA: They treated her with care, For many days on end,
Ay-yay-yay-yay-yay-yay!
Ay-yay-yay-yay-yay-yay.
Milena is rather in shock. Imagine if you were to look at a dead woman singing. And such a silly song. Zoza, however, doesn't hear a thing. That fat child has lard in his ears!
ZORAN: If you change your mind, I could push you off that wall. Just give me the word.
MILENA: Shut up! Listen! Listen to this!
Milica continues.
MILICA: But the damned old malady, Just got worse and worse,
And so the fox's body
Was put into a hearse.
MILENA: Do you hear that?
ZORAN: Hear what?
MILICA:
And so the fox's body
Was put into a hearse.
Ay-yay-yay-yay-yay-yay!
Ay-yay-yay-yay-yay-yay.
Milena gets up. A thin stream of blood starts to flow down her leg.

MILENA: Is that—you? But how . . . ?

MILICA: I think we can use first names. It would make more sense.

Milica finds it funny.

MILICA: You have my husband, you have my child. That makes us almost related. Doesn't it?

MILENA: *Zoza* . . .

Zoza doesn't react to that name. Milena corrects herself at once.

MILENA: *Marko, Marko!*

MILICA: Oh, no! Not that! That name is mine, not yours!

Milena pays no attention. As much as she can. She shouts.

MILENA: *Marko,* listen to me!

ZORAN: What's wrong? What do you want now? Why are you screaming like that?

MILENA: Look over there!

ZORAN: Where?

MILENA: Over there! There! You're not blind!

ZORAN: You're a pain. There's nothing over there.

MILENA: *Zoza,* look.

Zoran clenches his teeth and screams almost unintelligibly.

ZORAN: MAR-KOOOO!

MILICA: Marko, look at Mama.

ZORAN: Where should I look, dummy? You can see that I don't see a thing!

Milica goes up to her child. She wants to hug him. The child really doesn't see her or else is doing a terribly good and vicious job of pretending. He pushes his dead mother away from him, as though shrugging a coat off his back.

MILICA: It's me, son. Your Mama.

ZORAN: I don't see a thing. Understand, NOTHING!

MILICA: Here I am, son. I'm here.

Zoza pushes away the woman he can't see. He continues playing roughly with the dog.

MILICA: It's me, son. Your Mama. Mama was wrong. She wasn't thinking properly. She didn't know what to do. So she decided, without knowing, how much it would hurt.

Milica hugs her child. Zoran seems to give in and let her, as though letting everything be like it once was for a moment.

MILICA: I've missed you terribly. And really would like to make up for my mistake.

Milica hugs her child. Zoza pushes her away with all his strength, with all his brutality. He throws his dead mother off of him. He shouts at Milena.

ZORAN: What do you want from me, woman?

MILENA: But it wasn't me . . .

ZORAN: It's not my time yet.

MILENA: But it wasn't me! She turns to *Milica*.

MILENA: You tell him! You're his mother! Tell him, go ahead. Tell him now!

MILICA: How can I even tell him? Where should I start from?

MILENA: Just explain to him. Where you've been until now. What happened. But it really is amazing, you have to admit. Everyone thinks that you're . . .

MILICA: That's what I thought, too. But I'm not, you see. Or maybe I am. I don't know.

Milica thinks out loud, takes stock, does some soul-searching.

MILICA: I'm in want of nothing. There's nothing's that's missing. Life's not that important.

Death is neutral after all. It's not terrible. And doesn't hurt very much. When it happens. It's just that I miss my child so terribly.

Milena nods her head, repeating, or telling her own story.

MILENA: It's just that I miss my child so terribly.

Milica tries to hug her son one more time.

MILICA: It's me, son. I'm your Mama!

For the last time, Zoza energetically throws that old coat off his back.

Milica is left with her hands in the air. She waves them emptily. As though her child, heaven forbid, doesn't exist. As though her child, and not she, is a ghost.

Milica sits up. She accepts the blow, bears up. She might start to cry a little, but I'm not sure. I don't like to stare. In any case, I would cry. But maybe I wouldn't, I don't know.

MILICA: He's growing so quickly! Just look at him.

MILENA: He's getting fat quickly, too.

MILICA: Well, since he's greedy. You have to keep an eye on him.

MILENA: Like that's easy.

MILICA: Well, what else do you have to do?

MILENA: Lots of other things. I don't know exactly what. I could count them out for you. If you really want. But—some other time.

MILICA: Milena, wipe yourself off. You've got blood on your legs. You're bleeding.

Milena starts, stares at the bloody streaks on her legs and wipes herself.

MILENA: That's not me. That's my bitch. She's in heat, she leaves spots everywhere. My bitch bleeds so much that I'm really afraid for her.

MILICA: Your dog is fine. You're the one in need. You're missing something. Y'know?

Milica looks at her child in sorrow.

MILICA: He's really put on a lot of weight.

Fade out.

VI. You Do Know, Don't You, What it is That I Do?

Dinnertime in Zoza's new house, where he basically feels at home. In any case, his appetite isn't suffering. Zoza is bolting down his food. Marko and Milena are standing, watching in fascination.

Zoza eats and eats and eats.

Marko suddenly realizes that this greedy child strikes him with fear. He is afraid of him.

He is paralyzed by fear and a terrible lack of understanding for his own son.

MARKO: What if one day my son can't stop himself? What if he simply goes on eating when there's nothing left on his plate? What if he eats the plate, the knife and fork, the breadbasket and the napkins? And then moves on to the table, the chairs, all of this repulsively designed furniture, what if he chews the metal bookshelves, the silver teapot in the china cabinet, the windowpanes, the parquet floor, the curtains and plaster off the walls?

What if he then pounces on people, his father and stepmother who, faced by this monster already deformed by the metal, the polished wood, the plastic and porcelain he's swallowed, will simply be unable to defend themselves? What if this really happens?

When he looks at him like this, Marko thinks it isn't so impossible. Marko also thinks this child's stomach will kill him. And he even says so.

MARKO: This child's stomach will kill him.
MILENA: No it won't, don't worry.
MARKO: He'll swallow something that he won't be able to digest.
MILENA: No he won't, don't worry.
MARKO: Me, for example.
MILENA: How do you know?
MARKO: And how do you know that he won't? You have to keep an eye on him.
MILENA: Like that's easy.

MARKO: What else do you have to do?
MILENA: Well, actually, I don't know.
MARKO: I don't have time to do it. Or want to. That's not my job.
MILENA: I don't know where the time goes. It just flies. I turn around maybe two times and it's already night.
MARKO: Really, *Milena.* What do you do all day long?
MILENA: I tell you, I don't know.
ZORAN: I know.
MILENA: Take it easy, you'll choke.
ZORAN: Want me to tell you?
MILENA: Slow down, Marko, don't talk with your mouth full.
ZORAN: She doesn't do anything. She just sits there.
MARKO: You don't really call him Marko, do you?
MILENA: Well, that's what he wants. What can I do about it?
MARKO: But I am Marko. That's my name!
MILENA: Go ahead and be Marko, too. Who's stopping you?
MARKO: What's this "too"? What do you mean "you too"?!? I am the only Marko!
MILENA: Is it really so important to you? Why are you so mad? You're just like a child! Isn't it better when we get along nicely?
Milena hesitates, then strokes Zoza's hair. She watches the child as he enjoys his food. She doesn't know what to say.
MILENA: Chew your food a little. Don't swallow the chunks.
MARKO: Listen, Milena. We have to talk. Please, sit down.
Zoza stops swallowing his food without chewing. He stops for a moment without raising his eyes, on the lookout.
MILENA: All right. You sit down first.
MARKO: No, you first.
MILENA: No, you first.
MARKO: First you.
MILENA: First you.
MARKO: This is ridiculous. Childish.
MILENA: You're not afraid, are you?

MARKO: That's preposterous. And immature.
MILENA: Then sit down. You first.
MARKO: All right, that's enough! Here, I'll sit down first.
Marko doesn't sit down. He wouldn't think of it.
MILENA: You really are afraid of him.
MARKO: And you aren't? Not ever?
Marko, a dangerous politician who puts fear in the hearts of half the main board of his powerful party that holds all of society in the palm of its hand, nonetheless is afraid of his eight-year-old son. That he will eat him. Unusual, I admit.
Marko clears his throat.
MARKO: You see, son . . . Papa would like to say—something to* Milena.
Zoza gets up from the table.
ZORAN: Milena has something to tell you, too.
MILENA: You don't say, what's that?
ZORAN: Your decision. Or do you want me . . . ?
MILENA: I've got some bread for you. It's in my room. Under the blankets, wrapped in a dishtowel. In the back of the closet.
ZORAN: I'm really starving. I could eat the blankets.
Zoza leaves. Milena calls to him.
MILENA: Not the warm one!
Milena smiles. Marko takes it seriously.
MARKO: Does he really mean that?
MILENA: Don't be a numbskull. That's your child, not some monster.
Marko doesn't say anything, doesn't confirm this. He sits down.
MARKO: Clear this away, please.
Milena just pushes what's left of the butchered meal to one side of the table. She doesn't clean anything or take anything away.
Marko takes it all in without any comment. Milena looks at the greasy spots on the table. And comes to her own conclusion.
MILENA: I'm not much of a housewife.
MARKO: That's not important.

MILENA: Being pregnant tires me out.
MARKO: I understand completely.
MILENA: What was it that you wanted?
MARKO: Look, it's like this. You do know, don't you, what it is that I do?

Milena hasn't a clue. She nods her head.

MILENA: Of course I know.
MARKO: You haven't a clue, right?
MILENA: Well, I know that you're a minister.
MARKO: Not yet.
MILENA: But you will be. Or won't you?
MARKO: It's still not known yet.
MILENA: They know about you. Everyone tells me. They all say the same thing.
MARKO: What do they say?
MILENA: Well, that. That you're important. I don't know all the details.

Milena suddenly gets angry.

MILENA: I'm just not interested! What you do, what all of you do over there, I'm not interested. It brings nothing good to anyone, no one's interested in it. No one except you all!
MARKO: Don't be angry. Don't shout. You know I appreciate that, the fact that you don't interfere. It's not for women.
MILENA: Do you slug it out there?
MARKO: Where'd you get that idea?
MILENA: If it's not for women . . .
MARKO: Look, *Milena.* Let me be serious. Without any exaggeration. If they give me that post, if they put me there, there's something you have to know. What I do won't be fun and games. There are lots of dangerous people, lots of money at stake. What I do might cost someone dearly. And conversely, someone might get a bundle, understand? What I do might cost me dearly. And conversely, it could bring me a lot. Y'know?

You have to know that they're threatening me. They shadow me and eavesdrop. They offer things and pressure me. They dig through the garbage. They're looking for something, anything. They want to give me everything and take everything away all at once. Do you understand me? You have to understand, *Milena*.
MILENA: I will understand. I understand already. Just tell me— Who? Who is threatening you? Who is rummaging around and searching? And what is it that they might find?
MARKO: That's something you never know, Milena. That's them. Them or us. Them, them. Milena. Understand?
Milena doesn't understand. I, too, would really like to not understand.
MILENA: Even if I understood, there's one thing I don't understand: why do we need all that, Marko? Even if I understood everything, one thing I don't understand: what else do we need?
MARKO: I didn't even think you'd be able to comprehend. That you could ever understand anything.

I have to go. I've got a lot of work. Another place, Milena. *Fade out.*

VII. Foreign Body

Milena is sitting on the edge of a Doctor's bed wearing one of those humiliating gowns for a gynecological examination. If she even tries to stand up it won't hide her pubis.

Milena has to sit down. She sits doubled over. She is holding a metal dish in one hand with something metallic rattling around inside.

Milica is too disgusted to touch whatever it is, she bends over the dish left and right, staring at the bit of metal from all sides. A doctor is sitting on a chair next to her.

MILENA: I don't know.
DOCTOR: Do you know what it might be?
MILENA: No.
DOCTOR: You don't recognize this foreign body, found in your cavity?
MILENA: I don't wear a wedding ring.
DOCTOR: It looks like a ring.
MILENA: My husband didn't want it.
DOCTOR: You don't have a wedding ring?
MILENA: What's this?

Milena looks in true amazement at the wedding ring she never had in the dish that she waves left and right.

MILENA: In any case, it isn't mine.
DOCTOR: You don't know who it might belong to?
MILENA: What was that?
DOCTOR: Do you know what a foreign body like this might do to your organs? It might cause sterility. You might be barren forever. A sterile, barren woman. Do you understand?

Milena looks at him as though she doesn't understand. I don't understand that foul language either.

MILENA: How could it have been forgotten there?
DOCTOR: Did someone forget it?
MILENA: I thought I was pregnant.
DOCTOR: Did you feel any changes?
MILENA: My period was late. Until yesterday.
DOCTOR: Did you have any symptoms of pregnancy? In any case, I'd be surprised if you did.

Milena looks like she's lost her mind as she looks at the Doctor.

MILENA: I was nauseous. I got dizzy, threw up. I ate pickles, my breasts swelled. I bought two dresses and underwear for pregnant women. I gave considerable thought to the kind of mother I wanted to be and decided that I would breastfeed for a long time. One year at least. Maybe even longer, maybe even a lot longer. And that I would have a second child right away. And a third. I told everyone and everyone was happy. My husband loved me. And hit the child inside. And then I gave birth to a ring.

The Doctor writes some sort of prescription in the pompous style of physicians. He breathes on the stamp, places it at random, tears the paper off the pad and hands it to Milena.

DOCTOR: This is preventive, against any possible infection. It's all written there.

MILENA: I will be able to get pregnant one day, won't I?

DOCTOR: Is there anything else I can help you with?

Milena stares at the Doctor's hands. The fingers with long, pointed nails.

MILENA: Don't those disgusting nails . . . bother you while you work?

DOCTOR: What are you staring at?

Fade out.

VIII. Barbelo

A bench at the cemetery. It might be the same one. Stray (a drifter) is on the bench and his dog is with him. They've come out of some golden tunnel, beyond the golden doors, where the golden walls lead, where golden dust hovers in the air. They both have scruffy yellow hair, yellow eyes, yellowish skin, almost yellow nails, and totally yellow whites of the eye. Two wretched creatures, inseparable.

Stray is talking, as though going through pictures in a family photo album.

STRAY: This here is me. Next to me is my Mama.

Mama yawns and shows her yellow teeth.

STRAY: This is where we live. Right here next to you. We didn't know you'd drop by. Had we known we'd have guests, we might have prepared something. A show. And alcohol. Maybe a little food. We need a little, too. I don't eat anything, but Mama has to. She's old and sick—a lot. I, on the other hand, am perfectly healthy. Even if I don't look like it.

We live here because we like it here. When people come, they don't think about us. People cry an awful lot at the cemetery, did you know that? Some argue. They shout at the graves. They get mad and swear. As if that could change anything. We're peaceful here, my Mama and me. No one looks at us, no one pities us. We're not to be pitied! We are the same as you.
It's just that our life ran off somewhere. Well, if you are, then we are, too. To be pitied, I mean.

My Mama and I sneak around at night in between the graves. People are strange and think that corpses eat. Especially that they drink and smoke foreign cigarettes. People come to visit the dead, then they leave them: lots of food and even more drink, cigarettes, coffee, sugar, preserves, Turkish delight. Like the dead are expecting company. Like that makes up for not coming more often.

In the beginning the living come to the dead all the time. After seven days, fourteen days, six months, one year. Later they come much less often. Sometimes on a birthday, sometimes on an anniversary. Then less and less. And then not at all. It's better that way. The dead have the right to their solitude. The living leave the dead all kinds of things here: shoes, coats, hats, and books. Sometimes even the newspaper. Always yesterday's, never today's. They light candles, cry a little, wipe their eyes, blow their nose, spit and forget.

At night, when they all leave, my Mama: and I make the rounds of the plots and find all sorts of things. Cigarettes for me—some food for Mama. A bottle for me—something sweet for Mama. Even though I read in a kennel magazine that dogs shouldn't eat sugar. White sugar is a killer and it might make a dog go blind. Whatever.

Mama is seventeen years old already and has nothing left to live for. Or to see. I am rather ugly, life isn't any prettier. So I think: let her eat, since she likes it. Better to kick the bucket happy, than this way, like me. At night, when it's pouring rain, we sleep in the chapel. Mama doesn't like it, she gets scared and so she howls. Sometimes I get mad and threaten that I'll hit her. But how could I hit my mother?

In the summer when the weather's nice, we sleep under the stars. We look at the sky, like it's the Mother of God. And she puts her blue robe around us, and she looks at us with her shiny eyes, and she says—don't be afraid, children, don't be afraid! Then I put my head on Mama's stomach, I settle on her belly, sink into her old skin, among her withered nipples. I sink into the warmth and sleep peacefully. That's when I feel the best.

No one chased me away, no one did me any harm. I left of my own accord, left everything behind. And took Mama with me. I've got nothing in this terrible life, I never did have anything. No money, no ambitions, no desire to ever be anything. When the time came and it was a disgrace not to be successful, I left. And took Mama with me.

This is how we live now, waiting for it to pass. Don't pity us. We're not to be pitied. On the contrary, you might go ahead and pity yourself.

The two strays pet each other affectionately and go off somewhere. Or we leave. Whichever you want. But above all, folks, whatever's easiest for you.

Fade out.

IX. Dear Mama

A bench like any other. This one is somewhere, too. Milena is sitting, facing us. She is talking to us.

MILENA: Dear Mama,
I don't exactly know where you are. I hope you receive this letter. I'd like to ask you something, but I can't this way. Give me a call.
Yours, Milena
MILENA: Dear Mama,
If you've got a minute, I'd like to see you.
Your daughter, Milena
MILENA: Mama,
I'm your daughter, too. Please reply.
Milena
MILENA: Mother,
You said you'd call today. It's already evening, and there's no word from you.
Yours, Milena
MILENA: Mama, I'm not angry. Please give me a call.
Love, your Milena:
MILENA: Dear Mama,
Thanks for calling. I understand and know what you mean. I'm not at all angry. It's just that I miss you.
Yours, Milena
MILENA: Dear Mama,
Actually, I don't even know whether I really love you. How can I find out? Who can tell me, Mama? That's what I wanted. For us to talk about.
Love, Milena
MILENA: Because when you decide, dear Mama, to have a baby one day, how do you know, Mama, how that child will really repay you? For the tremendous effort and all the fears? Aren't you afraid, my dearest Mama, that a child will grow in your stomach, in your belly, in your flesh, that the child will stretch your skin, move your bones apart, suck out water and blood, and afterward milk and tears, that you will give the child everything you have: your body your blood, every breath and gulp. You'll

give him everything, and still not know what he's thinking? And does he love you? How do you know that, my dearest mother? Who will guarantee that? Who will give you their word? How can you let a child be born, when you know nothing about him? How, Mama?
Yours, Milena

MILENA: I know that you love me, Mama. And I know this conversation bothers you. I'm not accusing you, Mama. Just asking. I'm looking for advice.
Your daughter, Milena

MILENA: There are so many lonely children in the world, maybe it's better to just take one? Then at least you'll know it's not of your blood.

MILENA: I'm not talking nonsense, Mama. I'm not blaming you for anything and I'm not making a scene. I'm not talking about you at all.

MILENA: Where are you, Mama? Why don't you come? I think I'm pregnant. This time I know. And I have a ring, too.

MILENA: Your daughter loves you, Mama.

MILENA: Your daughter, Milena

Fade out.

X. Deluge

A bench and a low wall. Milica is on the wall. Dog Lady is next to her and it's raining cats and dogs.

DOG LADY: See the rain? The terrible downpour? Pouring out of the sky, like out of a gutter, pouring on people, streaming down Milica's face, down her body, down the wall she's sitting on, flowing somewhere, taking everything along with it—toys, children's shoes, pacifiers and rattles, strollers, cradles, walkers, baby pouches for young mothers, baby carriers, car seats,

orthopedic shoes, the ugly kind for flat feet; then braces to straighten crooked teeth, xylophones, mouth pianos and tin drums, torn books, scratched disks, notebooks with rabbit ears, spilled ink, rulers and compasses, grade books, sanitary napkins, acne cream, hydrogen peroxide, and razors.
Dog Lady stares at a puddle.
DOG LADY: Water's brought that terrible ring, too.
Dog Lady spits into the water. Milica is still sitting calmly, with a joint that keeps going out in her clenched teeth. Dog Lady shouts, calls, howls.
DOG LADY: Maaathew? Johhhn? Luuuke? Marko?
This is the only name Milica reacts to.
DOG LADY: Where are you hiding? Why are you tormenting me? Why are you tormenting your own mother?
Dog Lady looks for her boys.
DOG LADY: Didn't you promise you'd stay by me? Where are you now when I need you the most?
DOG LADY: Children, that's enough playing! Come on, let's go home!
Mama's going to die of sorrow and this awful rain!
DOG LADY: You mongrels! Spoiled mutts! Where'd you go? Where are you hiding? Why don't you tell me?
DOG LADY: Children, my sweet little boys. Is there any room for us over there?
Dog Lady goes off somewhere, taking her torments with her.
Milica looks at her as though she's a ghost. She sits there without moving. That's how she sings, as though from her belly.
MILICA:
Darling, so you find my cure,
Cross one hundred mountains,
Bravely swim across, endure
Two hundred blue oceans.

Darling, so I find your cure,

I'll cross a hundred mountains,
Bravely swim across, endure
Several blue oceans.

Ay-yay-yay-yay-yay-yay
Ay-yay-yay-yay-yay-yay
Milica is shivering from the cold. She manages to light the joint again. She takes a deep drag.
MILICA:
The fox's tears fell fast and loose.
She was so much sadder,
If she were to eat a goose,
She would feel much better!
Milica stands up and says to us calmly:
MILICA: If I were to eat a bitch, I would feel much better.
She looks at the sky, wipes herself off in vain. Then she speaks to us. Not to me, to you.
MILICA: What rain. Everyone's run off somewhere. And I have nowhere to go. What rain. A real deluge. Even so, it can't do anything to me. I won't get sick. And I'm not cold. You do know, don't you, that I'm not alive? The rain doesn't bother me. It can't do anything to me. It's just that I miss my child so terribly. It's just that this pitch dark is so utterly stark.
Fade out.

XI. My Child Writes a Lot

The bench again. This one is in a park. Mila and Drago are sitting on it, like old folks, but they aren't old at all.

MILA: My child writes a lot.
DRAGO: Mine doesn't ever.
MILA: Letters and cards, picture postcards.

DRAGO: My kid never does.
MILA: And asks questions, constantly asks questions.
DRAGO: What does she ask?
MILA: I don't know.
They are silent for a bit.
MILA: My daughter's always asking about things I know nothing about.
They are silent again. They're probably thinking about something.
DRAGO: My son doesn't ask anything. Because he doesn't know anything about anything. He knows so little that he doesn't even know what to ask.
MILA: My daughter asks things, lots of things.
DRAGO: What things?
Mila thinks it over. Actually, she doesn't know.
MILA: Actually, I don't know.
She gives it some more thought. It doesn't help much.
MILA: You know I simply have to hide. To avoid her. Remain silent. So she thinks I'm not here.
DRAGO: My son, you know, moved in with me. He didn't ask anyone, no one gave him permission. He just turned up one day, and he's been here since then.
MILA: Why, that's nice. I live in a home. With other old folks.
DRAGO: That's awful.
MILA: It's not so bad. I've got company. So do you. Your son is here.
DRAGO: I don't need company. I want to be alone.
MILA: Not me, I don't like solitude. But just imagine, I hide from my own daughter.
DRAGO: When my wife died, he came, like he was "helping" me. I didn't ask, didn't need it, didn't want it, I was totally against it.
MILA: I understand.

DRAGO: No, you don't understand. No one understands. When my wife died, when and how she wanted, the way she decided by herself, without asking anyone or thinking of anyone, without a second thought, without even stopping, and her hand didn't shake and her heart didn't tighten thinking of the consequences. That's when he came.
MILA: How do you know that she didn't? Think of you?
DRAGO: I just know.
MILA: Even so. How?
DRAGO: Because if she had, she wouldn't have done it. If she'd just thought it over, she wouldn't have done it like that.
MILA: She's the one who suffered the most, after all.
DRAGO: I hope she did.
They are silent again. After Mila's philosophical thought, we need a little rest. Refreshed, Mila remembers.
MILA: I collect stamps. I've got thousands of them. Mostly from my daughter, and some of them I trade. That's why it isn't so terrible that she writes that much. Wherever she travels. And she travels a lot. At least that's what she pretends.
Drago isn't really listening.
MILA: Sometimes she comes, though, and rings the bell and I go all quiet. I hide in a corner. I don't know what else to do in the face of countless questions.
MILA: My daughter says that life is strange. It puts a dilemma before you, and important decisions. And I don't know anything. Why would I even know?
Mila sniffs the air.
DRAGO: It's less than seven days that they haven't collected the garbage and life has already started to stink to high heaven.
He frowns.
MILA: Someone would say that pensioners have it easier now, have more choices. When, you know, they're digging through dumpsters. And actually, things are exactly the opposite.

In the middle of so much garbage, everything that is healthy—rots. *Mila thinks out loud.*

MILA: My daughter says that there are homeless people in the world. In foreign countries, under bridges, next to rivers. And that they used to be ordinary people, normal, just like you and me. But their pension isn't enough for them to live on. Well, my pension wouldn't be enough for me either if it wasn't for my daughter to help me. Even so, we don't live under a bridge.

DRAGO: I know what he wants. And why he came. He wants to push me out and take my apartment.

MILA: I don't know what's so great about that world, when people live so miserably.

DRAGO: He's lying low, biding his time. Waiting for me to go out. I'm sure he wants to change the lock!

MILA: What's wrong with you. Why are you so suspicious. In any case, you'll leave him everything.

DRAGO: And what if I won't?

MILA: Who else is there?

DRAGO: There is no one else.

Drago stands up suddenly, with the speed and elasticity that his osteoporotic bones allow him. Slowly and painfully.

DRAGO: I have to go. Good thing I thought of it!

Drago heads off somewhere. Angry. Mila doesn't like to be alone.

MILA: I think you're exaggerating. He's your child.

Drago turns around.

DRAGO: The fact that he's my child doesn't mean he loves me as his father. Do you understand that?

Mila thinks this over. It sounds silly, but that's the way it is. It's as though she somehow understands.

MILA: Actually, what's troubling my daughter is right. How can you know in advance what you'll give birth to? A man or a brute?

Fade out.

XII. Who Does this Man Work For?

Milena's apartment, which she nonetheless doesn't feel is hers. Dragan and Milena have been smoking an illegal substance. They are laughing. Music is playing. If you're interested, I'll tell you what it is.

MILENA: Good evening. Good evening. Oh, you're here, too. Good evening.
Dragan has been here a long time already.
MILENA: Shall we have something to drink?
DRAGAN: He won't be mad? Your husband?
MILENA: Why would he be mad? I've got my rights. This is my house, too. I think. In any case, he won't even notice. Just look at all the bottles. Who could drink all that. In any case, he won't count them. I think.
Milena hesitates. Dragan hesitates, too.
DRAGAN: Shall I open one?
MILENA: Go ahead. This is my house, too. I have my say.
DRAGAN: You think so?
MILENA: No. Well, now—does she or doesn't she think so? In any case, it's too late.
Dragan has already opened a bottle of expensive champagne.
DRAGAN: Yippee! Now it's too late. Now it's done. What shall we do now?
MILENA: What do you mean, "What shall we do"? Drink! We'll empty the bottle and then hide it. I don't suppose he'll count. And even if he does! We'll say we didn't do it. A very grown-up solution.
DRAGAN: Of course. Clever.
MILENA: Give me the glasses.
DRAGAN: Maybe it would be better out of the bottle?

Milena takes two glasses off the table where everything is ready for a reception.
MILENA: We're not children. Pour. Even if he does count. We'll say—we didn't do it. Clever. Brilliant take.
DRAGAN: Hey . . . do it again! What will you say to them?
Milena, as usual in my plays, toasts her imaginary rival.
MILENA: Good evening. Good evening. Oh, you're here, too! Good evening to you.
DRAGAN: What else? How? Do some more!
MILENA: Thank you. Thank you. Please help yourself. Thank you.
DRAGAN: It's actually very tiring.
MILENA: You know it really is.
DRAGAN: Do you get sick of it sometimes? Do you get sick of yourself, sometimes?
MILENA: Very often. I certainly do. Almost always. Always. Even before it starts. Even before all those people crowd into the house, I've had it up to here with them.
DRAGAN: So why do you do it?
MILENA: Why? Because that's my life. It's getting dark here. Shall we turn on the lights?
DRAGAN: It's still early. It's not night yet. Here.
What do you think Dragan is offering her?
MILENA: No more, thanks.
DRAGAN: Just a little?
MILENA: But not in the house. Marko smells everything. So what. Let him smell it.
Milena smokes the hashish that super cop Dragan is using to frame her. Little ninny.
MILENA: Is it already dark?
DRAGAN: Not yet. It just seems so.
MILENA: Shall I turn on the lights?
DRAGAN: It's still early. There's no need. Don't worry. I'll tell you when the time comes.

MILENA: I'm a real ninny to do this. In the house. You'd think it was on purpose.
Milena takes a deep drag.
MILENA: All I need now is a raid. Is that what it's called? Do you still do that? Burst into people's apartments, searching through their private things? Their private life?
DRAGAN: We do. But not very often.
MILENA: What do I care. Oh, good evening, good evening to you. Good evening, you're here, too!
Milena blows smoke in the direction of her invisible rival. Dragan pours some more champagne.
DRAGAN: You are actually having a celebration tonight, aren't you?
MILENA: I can't see you anymore.
DRAGAN: Minister, who would have thought. That's no small thing. Do you know it's dangerous?
MILENA: I can barely make you out.
DRAGAN: Believe me, no one expected that of him. We didn't know him. He didn't stand out. He wasn't anywhere. Earlier. Back then, when you had to be brave and have ideas.
MILENA: The moon's come out.
DRAGAN: Not yet. It just seems so.
MILENA: There it is. A full moon. The windows in this fancy apartment have double glazing so the moonlight has an unusual refraction. It falls in a curve. Do you know how much that costs?
DRAGAN: I know.
MILENA: Really? I have no idea. I really don't have a clue. I don't need that. That doesn't impress me. Even when light falls at a special angle, it's not worth everything they do. I can't see you. You see, all that money, risk, and dirty business isn't worth the terrible, awful guilty conscious it gives us.

Turn on the light.
DRAGAN: The lamp doesn't work. Take a little more.

MILENA: I don't want anymore. Maybe a little more. Just a little more.

Milena takes a lot of everything.

MILENA: Do you know everything he had to do in order to get that?

DRAGAN: I think I do know. Tell me and then I'll tell you.

MILENA: Terrible things. Awful secrets. Y'know? And one more thing, I've got a secret, too. I pay a heavy price, too. I run into that woman all the time. Y'know? I know she isn't real and it's just an illusion, but I see her, just like I see you now.

Please turn on the light.

DRAGAN: It's on.

MILENA: Really?

Milena looks around. She's amazed that she still can't see anything. Her nose in front of her face. Or that this man is a dangerous liar.

MILENA: Then I dream about her. She's pretty in my dreams, too. She tells me that she's not unhappy, just that she terribly misses her child.

DRAGAN: How about you? For that matter?

MILENA: Sometimes I dig through old photographs. Sometimes I look at albums with her pictures. And I dream about her sometimes, y'know? I dream that we're on our honeymoon (that we've never had). My dog, my husband, his wife, and me. We're lying next to a swimming pool, in a hotel, in the south of France. I think it's beautiful. I don't know, I've never been there. Suddenly there are rabbits all around. They're running in fear, fleeing before something that frightens my dog, too.

Marko appears, there, in front of us. And says—there are some wild bloodthirsty dogs here. We've got to watch out. We've really got to watch out for the rabbits and children. And I accept it all obediently, without a word. I run after the children and run after the rabbits. I hold them firmly by the scruff of their necks. And they aren't mine. Neither the rabbits nor the children.

And my dog runs away from me in fear and I can't find her anywhere. Where is she hiding?

Suddenly they lock me up in a shed. With a lot of other people who are panic-stricken by what is falling from the sky. Enormous dogs, like in a horror movie, rush at the door that is only protected by a latch. A simple, ordinary latch, like in an outhouse. And I am the only one to hold it closed. Only me and only with two fingers. But I'm steadfast! With all my strength. I save the children, someone else's children, some unknown people, even the rabbits, but my dog is nowhere to be found.

Then time somehow passes by and it's already one year later. I'm living alone in an outhouse, I don't have a child or husband or dog. Terribly sad, isn't it? Then my husband comes, riding in his expensive car. The one I know so well, the one I rode in so many times, sitting cowering in the back seat. My husband brings some papers to be signed.

Our dog's basket is still on the back seat. I know that those wild dogs have torn her apart. I even know where her grave is, I marked it myself.

Do you know what it's like when you're sure that someone who meant everything (absolutely everything) to you in this world—is dead for sure, and you still hope they aren't. You hope you're mistaken. You want to believe in a miracle. In wide-eyed stories. In fairy tales. You'd believe anything you were told. Any sort of lie. For children.

My dog's overturned basket is on the back seat of the expensive, overly expensive car of my husband who has certainly left me and gone somewhere, to another life.

I don't miss my husband, I don't miss my life, it's not at all hard for me to live alone, in that outhouse, in that toilet, alone among the shit, like everyone else, after all. I just wonder—when did all that actually happen? When did it start, now that it's over? How could time fly so quickly? Why didn't I notice anything? How is it possible that I didn't save what was dearest to me?

What's most important for a woman. How did it all happen so quickly?

In my dream, it's not easy for my husband either. He's not a criminal or a monster. It's not easy for him to tell me that he's met someone else, an ordinary, quite normal woman. And that the basket is now a child's seat. All you have to do is turn it over and it becomes a seat. For a child, the one I didn't have. Even if he didn't tell me, I would still know. When a man leaves like that, when life leaves like that, without even starting, it's not easy to stay behind. It's easy to leave everything. Y'know?

Dragan would like to reply. If only he knew what to say. All of a sudden Marko is standing next to the table. Honorable husband. No one saw him, like he sneaked in.

MARKO: What are you talking about, Milena?

Milena gives a start. Dragan not quite.

MARKO: And who are you talking to, Milena?

MILENA: When did you get here? I didn't hear you. I didn't notice.

MARKO: Who is this man? Who does he work for? What are you doing, Milena?

DRAGAN: We've started the celebration.

MARKO: What's there to celebrate, Milena? And you, in your condition, should you be drinking like that?

DRAGAN: What condition? Your wife isn't pregnant. Didn't she tell you?

MILENA: What? What are you talking about? And how do you know?!?

DRAGAN: Did you think I'd let it pass? Hey, I'm not a criminal or a monster. I have nothing against an unborn child. But there's no child. It won't be born.

MARKO: Who is this man?

MILENA: What are you saying? How do you know that?

DRAGAN: Excuse me, I didn't mean to interfere . . .

MARKO: Milena?

MILENA: This is our neighbor. His name is Dragan. He dropped by just for a minute. He's talking nonsense. How do you know that?
DRAGAN: I'm sorry, I didn't know you didn't know. He's your husband after all, I thought he knew everything.
MARKO: Who does this man work for, Milena?
Milena thinks it over. Then decides that—whatever she doesn't see, certainly doesn't exist.
MILENA: Out, get out!
DRAGAN: I tell you, I'm sorry. I'll leave if that will patch things up.
MARKO: What is it that he knows?
MILENA: He's talking through his hat, he's drunk. He won't spoil a thing.
Dragan puts his glass down as though insulted, but he isn't. He starts to go.
DRAGAN: That was not my intention. In any case, I didn't spoil anything. Everything fell through anyway. This morning, right?
MARKO: Get out.
DRAGAN: I'm surprised your husband didn't tell you. Here you are getting ready to celebrate, but things fell through hours ago. The main board met. And decided unanimously. The candidate's no good. He's liable to break under pressure in a delicate situation. They don't need someone like that and aren't afraid of him. With a small child and unstable wife who, it's said, is expecting another one. And who rattles off at the mouth. Talks too much.
Says everything. Even when no one asks. But if they'd known, if they'd only known that you will never have another one, they certainly would have felt sorry for you. In any case they would have given it more thought. Maybe.
MILENA: What are you talking about, Dragan? And how do you know that?

DRAGAN: And you say that's not true. Ask him. Ask your husband.
MARKO: Get out.
MILENA: Yes. Get out.
MARKO: Leave.
MILENA: Yes, leave.
DRAGAN: Can I at least try to explain it to you?
MILENA: OUT! Get out!
DRAGAN: Actually, I understand you, really I do. I would do the same thing. Shall I take this bottle? It would be a shame to waste it. Now that you no longer have any reason to celebrate.
Dragan leaves and takes the half-empty bottle of champagne. He's even going to finish it, the cur.
Milena is alone with her husband.
MARKO: I think it would be best for you to leave with him. To disappear, y'know?
Milena knows.
MILENA: I know.
Nevertheless, she doesn't go anywhere.
Fade out.

XIII. What Are Those Dogs Doing?

A bench or low wall, whichever you like. Zoza is sitting and Dragan is next to him. They've taken the dogs for a walk.

ZORAN: What's your name?
DRAGAN: Dragan, what's yours?
ZORAN: Well, I don't really know. They look at the dogs.
ZORAN: What are those dogs doing?
DRAGAN: Let them get to know each other.
ZORAN: Yours is big.
DRAGAN: No. Yours is small.

ZORAN: Does he obey you?
DRAGAN: Never.
ZORAN: Mine does. Sometimes. Look at how pretty she is.
DRAGAN: She really is.
ZORAN: The prettiest in the building.
DRAGAN: In the whole neighborhood.
ZORAN: Really? Dragan, was it?
DRAGAN: Uh-huh. And you?
ZORAN: I really don't know anymore. They watch the dogs sniff each other.
ZORAN: What are they doing there?
DRAGAN: You got me. How are . . . your parents?
ZORAN: They're still mad. They don't talk to each other. He won't even talk to me.
DRAGAN: That's so dumb.
ZORAN: What do I care. There's always food on the table. That's what's important.
DRAGAN: Sure is.
ZORAN: She told him a hundred times—that there's nothing between the two of you, that you're ugly, a freak, pitiful, she says. That she invited you out of pity. And loneliness. What does that word really mean? Loneliness?
DRAGAN: I don't know. I haven't a clue. Never heard of it. Look at your bitch.
ZORAN: I see. Should we separate them? What are they doing there?
DRAGAN: Your questions are getting on my nerves. I said I don't know.
ZORAN: Sorry. Don't go. I'm fed up with being alone all the time.
DRAGAN: All right. But don't bug me anymore.
ZORAN: I won't. I'll only say interesting things. I'll tell you where my father hides his money and papers.

DRAGAN: I know that even without you. Tell me something I don't know. She said I was ugly? A freak, she said?
ZORAN: Uh-huh. Do you have anything to eat?
DRAGAN: I do, but it's at home. You'll have to go there.
ZORAN: I can't do that. Milena won't let me. What's that they're doing? Sorry, sorry! It slipped out by accident. I didn't mean to bug you.

Zoza whistles to his dog. In vain.

ZORAN: Milena, here girl, Milena!
DRAGAN: Milena?
ZORAN: Malena. I said, malena [little one]. It just seemed like it.

Zoza calls to his dog.

ZORAN: Come here, I've got something to give you, hey! Come here, spoiled bitch! Why'd you go with the first one to come along?
DRAGAN: Leave them alone. You can see that they like it.
ZORAN: But what are they doing there . . . ? I thought I was the only one she loved. Sometimes, when we walk through the forest, my bitch and me, I decide to tie her to a tree, and leave. Then I hide behind a bush and listen and watch in secret. First she's quiet. Then she starts breathing heavily. She pants and looks all around. She's looking for me. Then she starts to whine. She cries at the top of her lungs, wails, howls, looking for me sadly. 'Cause, y'know. My bitch loves me. She wouldn't give up on me just like that. She wouldn't leave me unless she had to. So I let her wail, I let her cry and mourn, for about half an hour. Sometimes I fall asleep, her voice puts me to sleep. Her whimpering makes me close my eyes. And I wander off. Not really, just my thoughts.

Y'know? When I wake up, I go back. I untie her and let her go. I let her be happy to see me.
I let her almost die of happiness. Drop dead on the spot of a heart attack. That's when it's the best, that's when I feel the best.

When my dog is so happy to see me, when she's about to die of happiness that I'm alive.

DRAGAN: I sure know that one. That's nothing new. You didn't make it up. There's no sense in boasting. Sometimes I tie myself like that to a tree in the forest. And I wail dreadfully, from the top of my lungs, from the depths of my soul. I wait for her to come back. To come for me. To explain why I turned out this way. Ugly and monstrous. And why no one loves me. And where did she go, Mama? Why did she leave me? When will she come? If ever. I wail, tied to a tree like that, for more than half an hour. A lot more. Sometimes all night long. But no one ever comes so I'm happy to see them.

ZORAN: Not even your Mama?

DRAGAN: Not even her. She's dead.

ZORAN: Really? Mine, too. Imagine! What are they doing there? Your dog climbed up on mine.

DRAGAN: I'm telling you I don't know. And I don't really care.

ZORAN: All right. Don't get mad. I don't suppose he'll kill her.

DRAGAN: He won't for sure. She's a bitch. Both of them watch the dogs mate. The enormous male will certainly do fatal damage to the little female. Too bad no one understands. No one, except us.

Fade out.

XIV. Just Because I'm Fat, that Doesn't Mean I'm Deaf

A restaurant in the neighborhood. It's not important, I just got tired of the other place.
Milena, too: all she does is go from the house to the park and back; she needs a change. And she also wants to show off for her mother, take her out to lunch like an adult woman. She didn't

make a very good choice, the restaurant is empty, completely empty, no one is there, not even the waiter. The place is deserted.

MILENA: Are you sure this is where you want to go?
MILA: Yes, I am. There isn't anyone here.
MILENA: It's really deserted.
MILA: Where shall we sit?
MILENA: Anywhere. Just look at all the tables. We can take our pick. Or would you rather we went somewhere else?
MILA: No, no! That's out of the question. We've already come in.
MILENA: So what, Mama, even if we did come in. We can go out if we want. We're not prisoners of war.
MILA: No, no! It's out of the question! I don't want to cause problems.
MILENA: What problems, Mama? There isn't anyone here, no one has even seen us. And even if they had, we could still leave. No one's keeping us here.
MILA: I really like it here!
MILENA: Are you sure?
MILA: Sure. Word of honor, I'm telling you. I don't want to cause problems.
MILENA: Mama!
MILA: I just don't know where we should sit.
ZORAN: So? Are we staying or going? Well, I'm staying here. You can do whatever you want.
Zoran rushes up to a table and sits down.
ZORAN: Look, there's bread.
Zoza pours salt, pepper, and mustard from a bowl onto the plate in front of him and mixes it all together. Then he takes bread from the breadbasket and starts to eat.
MILA: Milena, *look at him.*
MILENA: I see. So what.
MILA: That's not right, we didn't ask if we could.

MILENA: Who are you afraid of, Mama? We're not in the forest, this isn't a witch's house.
We'll pay for whatever he eats.
Mila talks to Milena in a loud voice and thinks she can't be heard. That by some miracle the child can't hear.
MILA: Milena, just look. He's bolting his food.
MILENA: I see. What can I do about it?
MILA: The child is fat. Just look at him.
ZORAN: Excuse me, Milena, why is she insulting me? Your Mama?
Milena is fed up with her mother.
MILENA: There you go. Stop it, Mama.
MILA: I didn't say anything.
ZORAN: Yes, she did.
MILA: Tell him that I didn't.
MILENA: Stop it, Mama. Why are you talking like that? He can hear you, y'know?
MILA: All right, I'll stop. I won't say another word.
MILENA: What's with the "another word"? No one's forbidding you to speak, Mama. Just don't talk like that. Don't talk about the child.
ZORAN: About Marko. Tell her that my name is Marko.
MILENA: I'll tell her what I want to.
MILA: What's this about Marko, Milena? What's he talking about, Milena?
MILENA: I don't know, Mama. Let me be out of the know. You ask him if you want to. All by yourself.
MILA: All right, why do you have to get so mad? You're always about to explode.
MILENA: How do you know that, Mama?
ZORAN: How does she know how you "always" are when she never sees you?
MILA: He's so strange.

MILENA: Just because he's strange, that doesn't mean he's deaf. Mama.
MILA: All right, I understand. Now I really won't say another word. Tell him I'm sorry.
ZORAN: Tell her to tell me herself.
MILENA: I'll tell her what I want to.
MILA: I didn't want to cause any problems. The two women are silent, Zoza is, too. So he doesn't choke on the pepper and bread.
MILA: He'll choke like that. Bolting his food.
MILENA: No he won't. I've got my eye on him. They are both silent and so is Zoza.
MILA: Tell me, honey, why didn't you think of having a baby? It's not the same, y'know, when it's your own child.
MILENA: If you say so, Mama.
ZORAN: Papa won't be coming, y'know?
MILENA: I know.
ZORAN: There's no sense waiting for him.
MILENA: Even so. We'll wait a little longer.
ZORAN: I'll sit with you as long as you want. But he's not coming, y'know?
MILENA: I know, honey, I know.
MILA: You didn't think of it when there was time? Now the time has passed. Too bad.
MILENA: That's right, Mama. I didn't.
ZORAN: Why does she need another child when she has me?
MILA: Look at the little guy, he hears everything. And understands everything.
ZORAN: Of course I hear. The fact that I'm fat doesn't mean I'm deaf, Madam. Let's leave this place. There's no one here. No one will serve us, there's not even anyone to charge us for everything we've had in life up to now.
Zoran pulls Milena by the hand. She doesn't resist. Mila hesitates.

MILA: Maybe we should leave something? Shouldn't we pay? How much?
MILENA: Whatever you want, Mama. Pay, if you owe anything. We're leaving.
MILA: I don't know what to do. How to calculate. How much is all of this worth, everything up to now? Wait! Wait! I'm going with you!
Mila practically runs after her daughter and her daughter's stepchild.
Fade out.

XV. Nothing Will Ever Come Out of this Body, this Empty Cavity

Just imagine, the veterinarian's waiting room has the same bench. Dog Lady and Milena are sitting on the bench. Dog Lady hasn't washed since the last time. When was that? I don't remember anymore.

DOG LADY: How come you didn't notice?
MILENA: I just didn't. I thought she was nervous.
DOG LADY: Why weren't you on the alert?
MILENA: I just wasn't. But I thought I was.
DOG LADY: How come you didn't see the change in her behavior?
That she followed you everywhere?
That she looked at you without letup?
That she stared at you sadly?
That she was lonely.
That she was dragging herself around.
That she moped all the time.
And slept.

That she climbed onto your lap all the time?
That she had milk?
That her nipples were swelling.
That her stomach and her whole body were swelling?
MILENA: I did, I did see. But I didn't know, that it wasn't just, like, normal. What should I do now? I just thought it was, like, normal.
DOG LADY: I've got boys, but still I know. You've got to be on the alert, you've got to be terribly on the alert. Constantly keep close watch, listen, always be the first to know everything. Everything about everyone. That's what they do, you have to learn from them. They see everything and keep an eye on everything. They know everything. Since ever. They've always ruled here, in this country. Since ever. They join forces, and then torment us.

They can do us in. They think, "Better for us to do it to them than for them to do it to us." Like you here. Do you understand me?

Here, among us, they are the ones who rule. They know everything about everyone, they threaten or offer something important. Here, everyone has a price. Here, no one thinks about anyone else. And about what comes after us. Here, people sell everything and leave nothing for those to come later. Here, people think only of themselves and how to save their neck from them. In this country, on this street, right here, where you are sitting now, and maybe me, too. Everything is theirs. They've joined forces in order to torment us.

Understand? You do understand me, don't you, honey? You do understand, don't you, that I'm talking about dogs?
Milena doesn't understand anything anymore. I can barely keep things under control myself. Right then a door opens and the Doctor comes out. The same one.
Milena jumps up.
MILENA: So? Tell me? Where's my little girl?

DOCTOR: Where is that woman?
MILENA: Is the operation over?
DOCTOR: We operated on your dog.
MILENA: I didn't know she was pregnant.
DOCTOR: She was with young. Already four weeks along.
MILENA: I don't know when it happened.
DOCTOR: The puppies were too big.
MILENA: What's important is that she's all right.
DOCTOR: There was no way to save her.
MILENA: What's that?
DOCTOR: Don't be sad, it just happened. That's the way it was, no one's to blame. You'll have another one.
MILENA: What's that?
DOCTOR: There was nothing more we could do.
MILENA: Why didn't you do anything?
DOCTOR: You'll have another, you know.
MILENA: And you know, that I won't. I will not have another, I will never have another. Nothing will ever come out of this awful body, this empty cavity. Doctor.
DOCTOR: It's simple. All you have to do is want it and the matter's settled. After all, you know, it was only a dog. Do you have any other questions?
MILENA: Those horrendous nails? Don't they get in the way of your life?
DOCTOR: What are you staring at so hard?
Fade out.

XVI.

Milena's house, if that's what it's called. Milena, Marko and Zoran are sitting at the table. No one is eating, not even the child, just imagine! It's not the time.

MARKO: I'm leaving now.
MILENA: All right, go.
ZORAN: I know.
MARKO: I'm leaving you the kid, for a bit.
MILENA: It's all right.
ZORAN: I'm not complaining.
MILENA: There won't be any problems.
MARKO: I'll send for him, as soon as I decide what to do.
MILENA: As you like.
ZORAN: There's no need.
MILENA: We're all right like this.
MARKO: Can you understand me?
MILENA: I understand you.
ZORAN: Of course.
MARKO: I don't belong here anymore.
MILENA: If you say so.
ZORAN: You don't, y'know. Better leave as soon as possible. And keep in touch, so we know everything's all right. So we won't worry. I certainly won't, but that's how she is. Y'know.
MARKO: How grown up this child suddenly seems.
MILENA: Doesn't he, what do you say?
MARKO: He talks like a man.
MILENA: He talks the way he always does.
MARKO: I hadn't noticed. When it happened.
ZORAN: Now it's time to leave. Aren't they waiting for you? Isn't everything all set for your quiet departure?
Marko gets up.
MARKO: Yes, it's like you say. My time has really come. Are you sure you won't come with me?
MILENA: Sure.
ZORAN: Yes. Surer than ever before.
MILENA: The child leaves, goes off to school, I leave, go off somewhere, and, to be frank,

what do you need me for? If you can tell me that, if you can give me an answer, then let's get going.

How tender Milena is with Zoza. She asks his opinion.

MILENA: Isn't that so, honey?

ZORAN: Whatever you say.

Zoza is considerate, too. What's going on, folks?

MILENA: That's what I say. Just that. And what do you say, Marko?

MARKO: Is it me you're asking?

MILENA: Well, you are Marko.

ZORAN: That's your name, isn't it?

MARKO: All right, if you say so. Since you suddenly know everything so well. Tell me, since that's how it is, since that's how it is already, what did I do wrong? Where did I misjudge? What didn't I play out like I was supposed to?

MILENA: Nothing, Marko. Everything was fine. You were the same as all the others. You're not special, you're not different, you're just like all the others. That's why you have to leave. You'll all have to leave one day, y'know.

ZORAN: I think so, too.

MARKO: Now you're even thinking!

ZORAN: Of course, it's normal. I've got my say here. In any case, more than you.

Marko heads off somewhere.

MARKO: All right, then I'm off. But we didn't eat.

ZORAN: We don't eat.

MILENA: We eat, sometimes.

ZORAN: Where there's something to eat.

MARKO: You'll never want for anything.

MILENA: You either.

ZORAN: We don't need anything, anyway.

MARKO: I'll take care of you.

MILENA: You take care of yourself.

ZORAN: Leave us in peace. Y'know?

Marko really is leaving. He has a suitcase full of money. That's how I see it.
MARKO: I know, child, I know. Now I'm leaving this dreadful town and this stupid country that doesn't understand anything.
MILENA: Just go quietly.
ZORAN: And go as soon as possible.
MILENA: Don't worry about us. We'll make do. Without you and your suitcase full of gold plows, gold teeth, gold souls of the lost, the dead, the consumed, the killed—with a bullet in the back of the head. For something better. Something that's not you. Farewell, Marko, don't worry about us.
ZORAN: Yes, don't worry. Because we're all right. Aren't we, Milena?
MILENA: Aren't we, maleni [little one]?
ZORAN: Don't worry about us. In any case, we're certainly better off without you.
MARKO: This child has become awfully brutal, terrible, ever since he stopped eating.
ZORAN: I've only just begun. That's why you'd better go.
MILENA: Go, Marko. See you later. Somewhere.
Marko now really leaves. He knows where.
MARKO: I've always hated this town.
Fade out.

XVII. You Do Understand, Don't You, that We Are Dead?

Another low wall. What can I do, when that's the way it really is. Milica is on the wall and Drago is next to her. There is a bench there, too, and Dog Lady is on it. She's throwing bits of bread into the distance. That's all she knows how to do. She calls to her dead children.

MILICA: Do you believe in God?
DRAGO: What's got into your head?
MILICA: Where do you think we are here?
DRAGO: Leave me alone.
DOG LADY: Hey! That's enough!
MILICA: Where are we now? What do you think? Do you ever think about that?
DRAGO: What's got into your head?
DOG LADY: Children! Enough of that! Enough!
MILICA: They told me there's life afterward, life where we don't remember this.
DRAGO: They lied to you. But I'm not interested. Leave me alone.
MILICA: What's your name?
DRAGO: What do you care? Drago, so what?
MILICA: I'm Milica, it's nice to meet you.
DRAGO: So what?
MILICA: It's just that I don't know, is this really hell? Is this what it looks like?
DRAGO: Leave me. To rot in peace.
DOG LADY: I've had it with you! Children! Where are you?!? Where have you gone without me?
DRAGO: I was born in heaven. That's what they said. What you are living in is heaven. There's nothing better than that. And I really didn't need anything better.
MILICA: I wasn't born anywhere. And I kept on asking, Mama, where am I?
DRAGO: They told me, There's nothing better than this. And they weren't lying to me.
MILICA: They didn't tell me anything. So they wouldn't lie to me.
DRAGO: I loved him like a son.
MILICA: That's not all that much.
DRAGO: Even more!

MILICA: That's something else. Who?
DRAGO: Anyone. Everyone who ruled and promised heaven.
MILICA: Boy, you sure are naive.
DRAGO: Like you're not. Like, you think you can know everything by yourself?
MILICA: I actually don't know anything.
DRAGO: It shows.
MILICA: What shows on you is that you're a dried-up old man. Who died alone. And no one cried for him.
DRAGO: That's not true. Look!
MILICA: Why, it's true. That scarecrow's crying. What's she to you?
DRAGO: No one and nothing.
DOG LADY: Bastards! Bums! Stink bugs! Where are you hiding?
MILICA: They promised me life where I wouldn't remember this. Where nothing hurts anymore. They lied, y'know?
DRAGO: When you believe the priests. I don't believe anyone.
MILICA: It's not important, y'know. They roll the best shit in church.
DRAGO: I don't know. I didn't try it.
MILICA: You don't know what you're missing.
DRAGO: You don't understand either what a pity that is.
MILICA: What's a pity? The church or the shit?
DRAGO: God doesn't live in that house, y'know. God doesn't live here among greasy, dirty men, among those craving new blood. If God is alive, He doesn't live here. He lives somewhere where everything's nice. Where everything's as it should be.
MILICA: You sure are naive. Now I know why you're here. God doesn't live anywhere, y'know?
DRAGO: Of course I know. So what if I know. Why do you have to say it out loud?
DOG LADY: My children. My sons. Mama's going to die without you.

DRAGO: Who's going to tell that woman that her sons died. In the war, in the neighborhood next door. In the street up above. There, right next to the marketplace. All four died on the same day. So what? Why did she let them fight? A man told me, when stray shrapnel hit his bitch, she looked him straight in the eye. Then wagged her tail twice, as though saying, I'll be seeing you, y'know. Because this is waiting for you, too. Y'know. And it doesn't hurt at all. Have you seen my wife anywhere? My wife is burning now. She's burning somewhere else.
Who's going to tell this woman the truth? That there's nothing afterward? Just the darkness.
MILICA: I won't.
DOG LADY: Children! What shall I do now?
DRAGO: I won't either.
DOG LADY: What shall I do now? And where am I anyway? Why am I alone? What did I do in this life that was so terrible that I have to die all alone like this?
Dog Lady looks at us. Or at least at me.
DOG LADY: You do know, don't you, that we are all dead? Do you know that?
Fade out.

XVIII. You Do Understand, Don't You, That I'm Talking About Myself?

The same bench, the same cemetery. What importance I've given to an ordinary place. Right?
Milena is there, with Mama. Her own mother. Even though the cemetery and occasion are rather sad, she takes advantage of every moment. To enjoy the presence of her sweet Mama.

MILA: Pitiful service.
MILENA: Do you think so?

MILA: I sure do. No priest or candles. Just that terrible man who wouldn't stop crying.
MILENA: I had one. But there was no place to light it.
MILA: A shovel instead of a cross. That's unacceptable, after all.
MILENA: It's all the same to me.
MILA: Well, it's not to me. I want to leave the proper way. By the book.
MILENA: To leave, where?
MILA: That remains to be seen.
MILENA: Do you still believe? In those children's stories?
MILA: That remains to be seen.
MILENA: In any case, it's still too early. You're still so young, Mama.
MILA: You're not young anymore either, sweetheart. To say nothing of me.
MILENA: That's for sure.
MILA: Marko didn't come?
MILENA: Marko left. Forever. You know that perfectly well. Why do you pretend you don't know?
MILA: Well, if you think I'm pretending, let me pretend.
MILENA: All right, I'll let you. Believe whatever you want, even in the life after this one, that I won't give up, y'know?
MILA: I can see, I'm not blind. Just because I'm old, doesn't mean I don't understand things.
MILENA: You're not old, Mama. I'm older than you are.
MILA: That's for sure.
MILENA: Now will I see you more often? Can you come and live with us?
MILA: Do you really want that?
MILENA: That's all I need.
MILA: What about Marko?
MILENA: He's gone. He left us. He's gone to where he thinks he should be. And how do you find that out, Mama?
MILA: I don't know, honey.

MILENA: I don't know either, Mama. My little Mama. I know that it's foolish. That I'm too old for it. That I'm too big. Grown up. That it isn't done. Even so, little Mama, can I sit on your lap? Can I sink into your withered breasts, into your wilted stomach, push apart and stretch your hanging skin, plunge into that warm place, into your stomach. You created me, little Mama; I'd like to take a rest there.

MILA: Of course you can, honey. Even if you weren't mine, if you were a stray bitch, anyone would take you in, not just me.

Milena sits on her mother's lap.

Marko comes from somewhere, all dressed up, well-mannered, like at the beginning of this story. He's carrying a very tiny puppy. No bigger than the fat child's paw. And that's not small. He will grow into a hunter. At least.

ZORAN: Milena, look! Look what I found.

MILENA: What a pretty puppy. And so small. But look at its paws. It will grow into a hunter, won't it? Where did you find it?

ZORAN: Here, in the street. Right in front of the cemetery. A tramway ran over its Mama.

MILENA: You're lying.

ZORAN: I'm not lying. Honest to God.

MILENA: Don't swear.

ZORAN: Why not?

MILENA: Well, actually, I don't know. Tell me, really, where did you find it. What's its name?

ZORAN: I'm telling you, in the street. Ask your mother. She was there, weren't you?

MILA: Yes, I was there.

ZORAN: She'd just had her pups, they were still nursing. A tram passed by and boom.

There was nothing left. Just bowels and a bloody trail. Ask your Mama.

MILA: Yes. That's how it was.

MILENA: All right, so it was. What now?

ZORAN: Nothing? Can we keep him?
MILENA: How do you know it's a boy?
ZORAN: I know. His name is Marko.
MILENA: Nice name. Marko. Isn't that you?
ZORAN: Oh, no. I got tired of it. Marko is my father. And this dog here. My name is Zoran. They call me Zoza. Please, oh, please tell me,
Tell me, please, oh, please:
Can I keep him?
Can I adopt him?
Can Marko become mine?
Please, Milena, please. My dearest Milena?
MILENA: Why, of course you can. See how handsome he is. A real boy. There won't be any problems with him. He won't die because of some male.
Zoran rushes up to Milena. He is really happy, for the first time in a hundred pages. He kisses her.
ZORAN: Thank you. Things won't be bad for us, together?
MILENA: What's gotten into you? That's normal!
ZORAN: Even so. Even if it is. Thanks anyway. Can I ask you just one more question?
Will you keep me now, too?
MILENA: Of course I will. You mean everything to me. You're like my own. Like I gave birth to you.
ZORAN: It's better that you didn't.
MILA: That's for sure.
MILENA: You're mine all the same.
ZORAN: And you're mine, *Milena.* You, too, madam, though I don't know exactly what you are to me. Maybe I'll ask someone? And maybe I won't ask. Because it really doesn't matter to me. What's important is that it's like I'm dreaming. And like someone came and untied my leash. And let me alone. Y'know?
Mila takes Milena *on her lap. Milena takes* Zoran *on her lap. Zoran takes the sweet little puppy. On his small lap. Does it*

sound ridiculous? Almost grotesque? That's what life is like. Look at Leonardo if you don't believe me.
MILENA: With you, maleni [little one].
ZORAN: And with Marko.
MILENA: What an awful name he has.
ZORAN: We'll change it.
MILA: That's the easiest.
MILENA: Into something else.
ZORAN: Whatever you want.
ZORAN *turns toward us.*
ZORAN: Whatever she wants.
Milena also turns toward us.
MILENA: You do understand, don't you, that all this terribly long,
terribly long time, I'm talking about myself? They look at us. So funny, on one another's lap. And you look at them, too. I'm the only one going somewhere.
MILENA: But I really don't know where.
Fade out.

End.

Translated by *Alice Copple-Tošić*

BILJANA SRBLJANOVIĆ

MILENA MARKOVIĆ
(1974—)

Marković is an award-winning playwright born in Belgrade in 1974. She completed her studies at the Belgrade Academy of Arts where she now teaches. Her plays have been translated into many languages and performed in a number of European countries. Marković's *The Doll Ship* is a play about people and culture shaped by social conflicts and changes.

Milena's dramas often represent the panorama of Serbia through the eyes and experiences of fragile but enduring women.

A BOAT FOR DOLLS

An entire evening's drama
Belgrade 2004

CHARACTERS:

LITTLE SISTER
ALICE
SNOW WHITE
GOLDILOCKS
THUMBELINA
PRINCESS
WOMAN — All seven roles to be played by one actor

WITCH
MAMA (of WOMAN)
BIG SISTER (of WOMAN)

PAPA BEAR
MAMA BEAR
BABY BEAR, a nice kid and the father of the WOMAN'S child

EAGLE (of WOMAN)
BABY EAGLE — Both roles to be played by one actor

THE DWARVES
A Choir
DOC
SLEEPY
GRUMPY
A band of villains, orphans, drug addicts, sinners, proletarians.

FROG, Famous artist
HUNTER, Patron   Could be played by one actor.

HANSEL and
GRETEL, Young fans

Live music. Accordion and drums, guitar, flute.

SCENE ONE

A SMALL HUT
Mama, little sister and big sister.
Children's room, bunk beds.
Next to the bed there is a curtain separating the girls from their parents. Mama's head is turned, the girls can not be seen, only their voices are heard. Shadows of grown-ups dance on the curtain. They are holding bags, knives, pigs' heads, pitchforks, etc.

LITTLE SISTER: Why can't we come in?
MAMA: It's not time yet.
BIG SISTER: When's it going to be the right time?
MAMA: There are beasts in this room.
LITTLE SISTER: What beasts?
MAMA: One tells you now
the next one tells you no
the third stares at you grinning
the fourth one eats the wiggling meat
but its eyes are kind
the fifth one says do it do it
nothing will happen to you
the sixth has no eyes
the seventh no ears
the eighth no mouth
the ninth one is memory
the tenth one is death
BIG SISTER: I don't understand.
MAMA: You don't need to understand, you need to sleep.
LITTLE SISTER: Where are you going?
MAMA: I'm going to work.
LITTLE SISTER: What kind of work, mom?

MAMA: I've got homework to grade.
LITTLE SISTER: Do your students behave?
MAMA: Yes.
BIG SISTER: Who's better, boys or girls?
MAMA: The boys are better.
BIG SISTER: You like boys better?
MAMA: I do. They lie less.
LITTLE SISTER: But you've got two girls.
MAMA: But you are not like other girls.
BIG SISTER: How do you know?
MAMA: Come on, lights off.
LITTLE SISTER: Don't turn it off.
MAMA: I'll leave the hallway light on.
LITTLE SISTER : That one makes the shadows.
MAMA: It's just a shadow.
LITTLE SISTER: Daddy's friend is there.
BIG SISTER: I want to sleep.
MAMA: Your sister wants to sleep.
LITTLE SISTER: He really is there, threatening me with his finger.
MAMA: Nobody gets in here. I won't let them.
LITTLE SISTER: He shows up when you leave.
MAMA: Then I'll beat him up right now. Who's bothering my little girl?
I'll teach you to touch my girl.
I'll show you!
LITTLE SISTER: Did you –
MAMA: Yep.
LITTLE SISTER: Alright.
MAMA: Now go to sleep.
MAMA sings

MAMA'S SONG

Oochie, coochie, oochie coo, little children come along too
Kiddies, kiddies all so small, you have got no house at all,
They came and hauled off the lot, heading back to the same spot
I built up a little nest, my little hut was the best
A tiny God
Blew his wad
Sending that nest so far abroad
It hurts, it hurts, endure
It hurts, it hurts, endure.

SCENE TWO

TRIP

Alice and Big Sister are sitting in a room sharing a single cigarette. The curtain's gone. Alice's head is on her sister's lap, the sister is petting her. Alice straightens up. Fixes her hair. She has been crying.

BIG SISTER: So, what are you going to do now?
ALICE: I don't think I'll tell anyone. I'll just leave home.
BIG SISTER: What about mom and dad?
ALICE: They don't care.
BIG SISTER: That's not true.
ALICE: Dad grabbed my chin and gave me an ugly look.
BIG SISTER: That's nothing.
ALICE: Not to me.
BIG SISTER: Asshole.
ALICE: He never layed a finger on me before.
BIG SISTER: You should've just ignored it.
ALICE: I haven't done anything.
BIG SISTER: Right.

ALICE: I haven't.
BIG SISTER: You locked yourself in the basement with that idiot.
ALICE: Yeah.
BIG SISTER: You were naked.
ALICE: Yeah.
BIG SISTER: And?
ALICE: It was just a game. I took off my clothes and he had to look me in the eye.
BIG SISTER: He's our cousin.
ALICE: You've been with him, too.
BIG SISTER: I just jacked him off. A clean job.
ALICE: How –
BIG SISTER: I'm always fooling around, and then when they get really turned on, I jack'em off. It's a clean thing.
ALICE: Eccch!
BIG SISTER: It was real exciting. We went to where he keeps those horses and then to the meadow. I got pretty turned on. Then he did me, but I made him keep his eyes closed. Then I put the horse glove on and did him. Now, it's like nothing ever happened. It didn't even occur to me to look into his eyes. First of all, he's such a redneck, and then, well, he's also really strange.
ALICE: You think you're better than him?
BIG SISTER: You've always acted like you were so smart. You always had to have everything first. Whenever our aunt brought me candy, you would start howling. I'd bury it behind the house, and go out to eat it after you went to bed. And you'd refuse to have your hair cut. You'd run away.
ALICE: I remember.
BIG SISTER: You had lice and your hair was a big bundle of tangles and you had to have it all cut off.
ALICE: Grandpa used to put olive oil and lemon in my hair and then comb it for ages.

BIG SISTER: He used to pinch me in the butt when he got drunk.
ALICE: He never pinched my butt
BIG SISTER: You were too little.
ALICE: Did he do anything else to you?
BIG SISTER: No. He drowned a puppy once for barking too much.
ALICE: Liar.
BIG SISTER: You kept telling me me how much you hated me after that haircut, and I felt really guilty. But Mom had work and couldn't take you.
ALICE: I still hate you.
BIG SISTER: You hate me because I tell you the truth. I told you to be careful. Some things Mom and Dad don't need to see. They're sensitive people.
ALICE: So, tell me how it all started.
BIG SISTER: How what started?
ALICE: With boys.
BIG SISTER: No way, I am not telling *you* anything.
ALICE: Why not?
BIG SISTER: Because you wouldn't understand. You only pretend to understand and that always pisses me off. You are as thick as a brick.
ALICE: Fine, I'm not interested
BIG SISTER: Yes you are.
ALICE: Those guys you've been seeing are boring.
BIG SISTER: You're the boring one, the most boring little girl I've ever met in my life.
ALICE: I'm not a little girl.
BIG SISTER: Yes, you are, and you smell bad too. You touch your chin like you were stroking a beard. You are a disgusting little girl.
ALICE: You smell like a cookie.
BIG SISTER: Because I bathe.

ALICE: I bathe too.

BIG SISTER: You wash as fast as you can just so you won't stick to your pants, but I rub everywhere. You just wash behind your ears so they won't fall off. I enjoy my body.

ALICE: Is your boyfriend gonna take my photo?

BIG SISTER: No.

ALICE: It all bores me to death, anyway.

BIG SISTER: Why? What else you going to do?

ALICE: I want to do what no one's done before.

BIG SISTER: You don't know how to take care of yourself.

ALICE: Teach me.

BIG SISTER: Why would I ever teach you anything? Everything's too easy for you.

ALICE: I'm gonna leave.

BIG SISTER sings

THE LANDLADY SONG

You do what no one has done
I do what no one can see
I'll have a house with a pool
And a man to clean the pool
When leaves gather in my pool
He'll churn them round
Left right left right
The kids will wear nice things
The kids will be boys
And the boss will be rich
The boss will be rich
The boss will be mine
The boss will be stupid
Life will be pricey
Life will be mine
To watch

SCENE THREE

FOREST

Snowhite and the seven dwarfs. In their dining room. Crates with weapons and sacks of who-knows-what. Soiled placemats and broken cups. Damp.

DOC: Today, my daughter brought me some coffee and asked if I wanted sugar or milk. Kids are madness. Kids are from God. Kids are a direct way to defeat the aliens. I'll tell you that when she grows up, she'll be better than me, you, him, and better than her fucking mother who makes an issue about who's gonna go to the store. That's a problem. Who goes to the store. Who'll do the dishes. You get whole theories about fucking dishes, speeches from caveman times that normal people can't keep in their system longer than two minutes she keeps for weeks, fuck it, months. She's written it all down, she hasn't written it down, fuck, keeps it all in her head, what was I saying?
GRUMPY: How your wife got on your case about going to the store.
DOC: She didn't. She just nags. That's not the problem. You don't know a thing, boy. That's not the problem. The problem is not my vanity. When my wife talks, she is not my wife. She is my man, that's not the issue, the issue is this whole fucking thing about who does what.
GRUMPY: But you don't do anything.
DOC: What the fuck does she do?
GRUMPY: Well, the money comes from her side –
DOC: So, here we are.
GRUMPY: Yeah, here we are. So why weren't you *there* when we were *there*?
DOC: Always "there." What does it matter who's there, dickface, as long as we share it. She's adopted this whole way of thinking.

GRUMPY: I don't know.
DOC: What don't you know?
GRUMPY: I don't know how to answer such important questions so early in the morning.
DOC: Well, I do. You've no idea what I've already done.
GRUMPY: I know you got plastered, went to the store, and then you went to a beer joint after that and went to see the wife, wife said whatever about the dishes, and you came here to shoot up.
DOC: You piece of shit.
(They laugh.)
DWARVES: It smells here.
DOC: Of what?
DWARVES: It smells like young pussy.
GRUMPY: That's true.
DOC: Where?
GRUMPY: Better ask Sleepy.
DWARVES sing a song.

SONG OF LITTLE GIRLS

He did deliver them and there were three
One got sick and vomited
And then there were two
The second one then departed
So now we were down to one
One is the same as none
Nothing was left for us
No arms to take us in
Salvation
No arms to bake our cookies
Cause we don't have
Some little girls
No, we don't have
We want their arms to envelop us

We want their cookies
We want for them to blow us all
Once in awhile
We're not looking for so much
Cause everyone has to get it
Once in awhile
DOC: Didn't you get any?
GRUMPY: No, I didn't.
(He laughs.)
GRUMPY: It's not funny at all. She crashed here, she won't go home, had a fight with her folks.
DOC: So, we feed the chick.
GRUMPY: Meaning, I feed the chick

DWARVES sing

THE CHICKEN DANCE

Who feeds the little chick
Who feeds her little beak, her beak
With what
With what
Oh Oh the little chicken
Oh Oh the little chicken
GRUMPY: I feed the chick, 'cause I am the only one who works around here, no one else does shit, just me.
DOC: They work too.
GRUMPY: They work for a few minutes and then fuck around, I've been working here for as long as I can remember.
DOC: And today?
GRUMPY: Today I can't.
(They laugh. SLEEPY comes in, scratching himself everywhere.)
DOC: How do I know who her old man is? He wants to come over.

SLEEPY: She won't say anything. I popped her cherry, guys. I can't believe it. I popped her cherry, no joke. I'm worn out, really.
DOC: All I know is I don't care . . .I'm not interested in it. I'm interested in what comes next.
GRUMPY: Is she still sleeping?
SLEEPY: Yeah.
DWARVES sing

THE CHICKEN DANCE 2

Little chicken sleeps away
In our pretty little house
Our hearts are overflowing
In our pretty little house
Straight out of bed she climbed that day
Her mama made it
The chick is waiting
For life to begin
The chick is waiting
For dreams to emerge
Oh, lovely, lovely dreaming
We are ready for that
(They laugh.)

DOC: Sleepy's got to pay today.
SLEEPY: What for?
DOC: Call it tuition.
GRUMPY: No, he doesn't.
DOC: Then she should pay.
GRUMPY: No, she doesn't pay for anything.
DOC: How's she going to eat if she's not making money?
GRUMPY: Leave her alone. I'll take her home today, whatever happens.

SLEEPY: Why?
DOC: It's nice she's here, maybe her girlfriends from school will come too.
SLEEPY: Here's my joy boy.
(He finds the syringe.)
DOC: Wait a minute, shithead.
(He hits SLEEPY on the head).
GRUMPY: Why didn't you ask me about this kid?
SLEEPY: Since when do I ask you for anything?
GRUMPY: Since today.
SLEEPY: I'm asking.
GRUMPY: Ask.
SLEEPY: I am asking.
(They laugh.)
DOC: When people are at the beginning of a relationship, they look to know that they're moving towards a common goal, that they agree on things, that they're actually in it together. They do this by asking, you cunt. You bring a high school girl here, when the house is full of product. How come this man here, who struggles to feed us, to feed my wife, my daughter and several other honest streetwalkers, how come this man here is not asked anything when a girl who is a minor is brought to our house in the middle of the night, ok, cause now she just becomes more product, right?
SLEEPY : I didn't bring her, she came on her own.
DOC: On her own.
(SLEEPY injects himself.)
DOC: And when she wakes up and wants to cuddle, huh, pretty boy? Sad thing she came on her own, she wakes up on her own, now she'll have to cuddle on her own. Maybe one of us should be there.
SLEEPY : It would be nice for us to go away. I could draw portraits.
GRUMPY: Your hands are shaking, you can't hold a pencil.

SLEEPY: What do you know about holding a pencil?
GRUMPY: I know you can't do it.
SLEEPY: If only I had some fresh air, instead of this basement.
GRUMPY: I sent you for two months.
SLEEPY: Yeah, but where'd you send me?
DOC: Nice village, eggs, tits, some cows, a cottage.
SLEEPY: It was a shack.
GRUMPY: A castle for you.
SLEEPY: I spent all the time making fires.
DOC: You don't know how to make a fire.
SLEEPY: Yes, I do.
DOC: You can't keep a fire going. Let me show you.
(DOC starts piling up things to make a fire with in the middle of the room. SNOW WHITE comes out.)
SNOW WHITE: Hello.
(Silence.)
SNOW WHITE : Have I done something wrong?
(Silence.)
SNOW WHITE: Sometimes when I get drunk I talk nonsense. Should I do the dishes? I could.
DOC: Not a chance. Here – drink. I'll cut you some meat. Have breakfast, but you're not doing any work and that's final. Don't look at me like that, and don't take any drugs. You won't be able to cum very well after that.
(DOC leaves.)
SNOW WHITE: Any coffee?
GRUMPY: Nope.
SNOW WHITE: A pot?
GRUMPY: There's a small one.
SNOW WHITE: It's cracked.
GRUMPY: Go home.
SNOW WHITE: I can't go home.
GRUMPY: Why not?
SNOW WHITE: Because.

(DOC returns, he has cut his hand.)
DOC: Little chicken, I've got a roast.
GRUMPY: What's that?
DOC: It's a roast, red wine, white bread and cheese rich in calcium so your tits can grow.
SNOW WHITE: And your hand?
DOC: A hand is a part of the body you use to pick something up with, and when a foreign body appears between you and that something, i.e. glass, wood, and so on, the resistance that foreign body presents to your body creates –
SNOW WHITE: Let me help you with it.
DOC: Don't you try pulling that on me.
SNOW WHITE: I'm not.
DOC: I'm from an old family and the house, where the shop is now, used to be mine.
GRUMPY: Cut the crap and stop dripping on the floor.
SNOW WHITE: I'll clean it.
DOC: You're gonna sit and have breakfast.
SNOW WHITE: I'm not hungry.
DOC: Eat.
SNOW WHITE: Fine.
DOC: You're a doll. Maybe just a kid, but a doll all the same. Everything's gonna be just fine.
SNOW WHITE: What?
DOC: What I'd give –
SNOW WHITE: What?
DOC: What I'd give to feel you up.
SNOW WHITE: Why don't you?
DOC: No way. I got a wife. Don't piss me off. You got no idea where you are. You just woke up. Your cheeks are still swollen with sleep. You don't know where you are.
SLEEPY: I can't listen to this.
DOC: Then don't.
SLEEPY: I am so tired.

(SLEEPY leaves. They laugh.)
SNOW WHITE: Why did he leave?
DOC: I can't stand Sleepy fucking a piece of meat like you.
(He put her in his lap and strokes her back. She sits a bit and then gets up.)
SNOW WHITE: Where is he.?
GRUMPY: Listen kid, why don't you brush your teeth or whatever and go home.
DOC: I can't stand it.
GRUMPY: Don't bang your head, the shelf will fall.
DOC: Let the house fall, the whole world. I can't stand it. I can't stand the fact that there are people like that cunt, Sleepy. Do you really think he'd protect you, if I, you know, like wanted to abuse you? You know he can't even see straight. He's nothing but a little cunt. Has he asked you for money yet? You'll see, tomorrow he'll ask you for money.
GRUMPY: He's a handsome fellow.
DOC: You wouldn't mind giving him a blowjob, either, would you?
GRUMPY: Maybe, but there's no maybe about it in your case.
DOC: I wouldn't talk about such things.
GRUMPY: I think the girl should go, c'mon, before someone gets angry, before the others come, while the whole thing is still under control.
DOC: Who the hell are you to say anything? You're a slave. Every day you work for people who are even worse than you are and you think that makes you something, that you're somebody? You're just a slave. That's what you are. And this babe doesn't like you, she likes Sleepy. I can tell some stories, and you know it. You just sit around, and rest those obedient hands of yours and your legs with those ugly veins and you stink. You're nothing but a slave.
(GRUMPY gets up and angrily swings at everyone. Doc and the Dwarves run away. SNOW WHITE hides under the table.)

GRUMPY: Come here.
SNOW WHITE: I can't.
GRUMPY: Come now.
SNOW WHITE: I can't.
GRUMPY: Fine.
(She gets up and looks at him.)
GRUMPY: I know you haven't been thinking about me and you won't remember any of it. I know I don't smell good –
SNOW WHITE: No.
GRUMPY: But you like that I'm strong.
SNOW WHITE: I do.
GRUMPY: I'm not gonna be gentle.
SNOW WHITE: Alright.
GRUMPY: I am not forcing you.
SNOW WHITE: Good.
GRUMPY: Think about it. You can leave now, if you want. But you've had a good look and if you want to stay, then I . . . You understand? Or maybe all of us, you get me?
SNOW WHITE: Fine.
GRUMPY: Count to ten.
SNOW WHITE: 12345678910 . . .
GRUMPY: Now close your eyes and relax, it's gonna hurt a little, I have to . . .
(DWARVES clean the stage)

They sing.

DOWN HERE

> Every day we work real hard
> Down here under
> Such contrary folk arrive
> Down here under
> We're going to meet with death

Down here under
And those people will remember
Down here under
Never knowing
Who or what to call us
Who or what to call us
Down here under

SCENE FOUR

GOLDILOCKS and THREE BEARS

(Cave. The flat is neat.
GOLDILOCKS and BABY BEAR are under the covers.)

GOLDILOCKS: Once more?
BABY BEAR: Five more times . . .
GOLDILOCKS: Five is not a good number.
BABY BEAR: Why?
GOLDILOCKS: I don't know – but I like saying it.
BABY BEAR: Do you understand it?
GOLDILOCKS: No.
BABY BEAR: Why are you saying it then?
GOLDILOCKS: I'm just saying whatever I want to.
BABY BEAR: Oh, well then I'll just do whatever I want to you.
GOLDILOCKS: I'm sorry.
BABY BEAR: About what?
GOLDILOCKS: Not meeting you before.
BABY BEAR: What's that got to do with anything?
GOLDILOCKS: You're gonna be good.
BABY BEAR: I am good, that's just how I am.
GOLDILOCKS: You are a nice little teddy.
BABY BEAR: I am.
GOLDILOCKS: I've been with some bad people –

BABY BEAR: Don't talk about it. It doesn't matter. I'm here now. We'll be together.
GOLDILOCKS: We will, we will –
BABY BEAR: We can stay here or we can go somewhere else.
GOLDILOCKS: It's nice here –
BABY BEAR: You gotta be careful here, otherwise it's ok. I'm used to it.
GOLDILOCKS: What are your mom and dad like?
BABY BEAR: Well, they make their own water. I've never had normal water. And they say all sorts of things, but they'll do anything for me. For us.
(The light changes. Mama Bear and Papa Bear enter.)
MAMA B: What's going on?
PAPA B: Look, at the holes in the upholstery.
MAMA B: Horrible.
PAPA B: This upholstery's the only thing important to me about this chair.
MAMA B: We looked for it for forever.
PAPA B: We've waited for it to be repaired for so long.
MAMA B: I've only sat in it maybe three times.
PAPA B: It smells strange here.
MAMA B: Yeah, it does.
PAPA B: Ah –
MAMA B: What, love?
PAPA B: Someone's been drinking from my cup.
MAMA B: Terrible.
PAPA B: Someone's been eating from my plate.
MAMA B: Horror.
PAPA B: Someone's been using my razor.
MAMA B: She slept here!
PAPA B: What kind of girl is that?
PAPA B and MAMA B: What kind of girl stays overnight on her first date?

(Light changes again. Mama Bear, Papa Bear and Goldilocks are sitting at the table.)

GOLDILOCKS: I have to wake him up.

MAMA B: Why? It's not like he has to go tend to the sheep or something.

PAPA B: He's a student.

MAMA B: We worked hard so he'd become a gentleman.

PAPA B: He is a young gentleman.

MAMA B: Please, don't serve tea in the cups from yesterday, they're not tea cups.

PAPA B: Those are for café au lait. They were my mother's.

MAMA B: Baby Bear's grandmother was a very nice woman, taught me everything I know. I came here from a small village and supported Papa until he graduated.

PAPA B: There's no way my daughter-in-law is going to smoke with a baby in her stomach, like some gypsy! You're beautiful. You shouldn't be smoking.

MAMA B: Have you been baptized?

GOLDILOCKS: I'll get baptized, I will.

PAPA B: Baby Bear's grandmother was a teacher, She brought up Papa Bear and his brother, and they studied at the university. I love eating what Mama Bear prepares.

GOLDILOCKS: I have to wake him up.

MAMA B: Let him sleep. He needs his rest. He read last night.

GOLDILOCKS: He watched television.

MAMA B: We've provided for him, so let him sleep.

GOLDILOCKS: I can't sleep.

PAPA B: You should go for a walk.

MAMA B: Come walk with us.

PAPA B: We're going to Grandmother Bear's grave.

MAMA B: Let's go. You can plant a flower there.

PAPA B: Baby Bear used to be with a very nice girl. She went away. On a journey.

MAMA B: She never slept over.

PAPA B: Girls shouldn't sleep over.
MAMA B: It's alright. Baby Bear's heart is the most important consideration.
PAPA B: It's irrelevant whether we love you, it's more important Baby Bear loves you.
MAMA B: You'll try your best so we can love you too.
PAPA B: You'll plant a flower on Grandmother Bear's grave. My mother never brought anyone home.
MAMA B: She was an honest woman.
PAPA B: I've never seen a more proper woman.
MAMA B: You'll plant a flower for her.
GOLDILOCKS: I don't like to plant flowers.
MAMA B: Why not? Your not good with your hands? You'll learn.
GOLDILOCKS: All right, I'll learn. I want to get married in the church.
PAPA B: You make my heart sing, daughter, you'll do fine. *(The four of them sit. PAPA BEAR and MAMA BEAR sing.)*

IT'S NOT OURS

That thing you gave birth to
That's not a man
It's a plant
It's not a child of ours
It is a child of yours
That thing you gave birth to
You gave birth to your sin
That's what you've given birth to
Born from your womb
Your sin is from the womb
It is not ours
It is not ours
It's not a child, it is a thing

You're not a mother
You are ugly
Your own blood is ugly
That thing you gave birth to
Doesn't have a nose
It's just a hole of some sort
It's not ours
It's not ours

(Light change.)

MAMA B: She smoked, drank, how could she give birth to anything normal. She watched strange things. You've got weird things on your walls –
PAPA B: And what kind of name is Gelid anyway?
BABY BEAR: My sperm is good. Something wrong with her.
PAPA B: You're to blame.
MAMA B: When Baby Bear was in my belly, I played him some soothing music.
GOLDILOCKS: My milk is fine. Who wants some?
(She milks herself.)
MAMA B: Baby Bear is going to have healthy kids.
PAPA B: Baby Bear's sperm is good.
MAMA B: There's something wrong with you.
BABY BEAR: She doesn't do anything right.
MAMA B: I've heard her talking about me. What would she do if she had to cook and wash and change the the upholstery on the chairs?
PAPA B: And change the upholstery on the chairs?
MAMA B: And she keeps using Grandmother Bear's cups when her guests came.
PAPA B: You let her.
BABY BEAR: I though it was okay to let her, so she'd prove herself.

MAMA B: Haven't you seen her sister?
PAPA B: Haven't you seen how short her skirt is?
MAMA B: Her sister's –
BABY BEAR: I've seen her, yes –
MAMA B: And have you seen her mother and how yellow her –
PAPA B: Her fingers are yellow.
MAMA B: And have you seen her father?
PAPA B: I've seen him with younger women.
MAMA B: Really?
PAPA B: I've seen him around.
BABY BEAR: Why didn't you tell me?
GOLDILOCKS: You have no right to talk about my father.
PAPA B: Really? And who the hell does he think he is, never sitting down with me?
MAMA B: And never staying for lunch.
BABY BEAR: And telling me how to do things?
PAPA B: Who does he think he is?
MAMA B: Never even been baptized.
PAPA B: Baby Bear, make up your mind now.
BABY BEAR: I don't know –
MAMA B: She's never going to make a good wife.
PAPA B: She has no respect for you.
MAMA B: She has no respect for us.
BABY BEAR: The little boy is alone now.
MAMA B: He's not alone, there are doctors.
PAPA B: It makes no difference to him.
MAMA B: You'll have a proper wife and a proper child, yet.
(BABY BEAR sings)

FOR MY SON

He's not alone
The stars are there the moon is there
The dogs and cats are there

And those who sell their fruit at wholesale prices
There are those taxi drivers who stop to take a good look at you
The stars and the dogs and cats
And the light is on for him
Light in his room is on for him
And the light is on for him
Because he's afraid
Alone

<u>SCENE FIVE</u>

THE SWAMP

(The Frog's lair is filled with nice, expensive things.
There's a big sofa with many cushions.
There's a small one with fewer cushions.
There's a chair.
There a multicoloured air mattress with a big pillow where Frog usually rests his head after thinking a lot.
Next to the air mattress there's a low table with assorted delicacies on it.
When FROG and THUMBELINA enter, she doesn't know where to sit.
She drops into the chair, and he sits cross-legged, Turkish-style on the mattress. Feeling silly on the chair, she crosses and sits next to him.)

FROG: Great vintage. It's all drunk now. I rarely sit in this room. Really, I'm rarely here. I usually sit in the study when someone visits. To me, I'm looking rather monumental.
THUMBELINA: Why?
FROG: Because of the table. And the chair, I look huge, somehow.
THUMBELINA: It's a good table. Was it expensive?

FROG: Probably.
THUMBELINA: Did it belong to somebody?
FROG: Probably.
THUMBELINA: Imagine if something terrible happened to that family and you have their table now.
FROG: That's nothing – as long as you can handle ghosts.
THUMBELINA: I used to have this ring. I mean, I still have it. I bought it at an antique store. Nothing was going to keep me from getting this ring. It took me days to find the money for it. It was a lot for me back then. And then, I thought, the woman who'd had the ring before me, what if something terrible had happened to her?
FROG: Well, I'll tell you, nothing very terrible has ever happened to me.
THUMBELINA: Some day, maybe?
FROG: No, it's too late for that. Only thing I have to worry about's my children, that they do well. My son and daughter.
THUMBELINA: It's nice here. Let's not talk about children. I can't stand talking about children.
FROG: Let me tell you something. This is well conceived. It's really amazing. I'd almost think it was autobiographical.
THUMBELINA: I am glad you think there's something to it.
FROG: The whole situation feels as if you were really there in that place, it's so realistic, and yet all blurry.
THUMBELINA: I don't know, not really. But you actually like my work?
FROG: Just tell me, what is the paper boat all about?
THUMBELINA: Did you like it burning?
FROG: It must be about something to you?
THUMBELINA: That's banal.
FROG: I suppose, but I won't say anything. It'll stay between us. I'm not going to make it public. I don't like things that are banal, either, having explanations for everything. I think you are one of those rare irrational creatures who's conscious and not at the

same time, like you're subject to the greater will of a higher power. Sorry, you haven't come here to be questioned. I'll help you with the exhibition. I'll do anything. It's just that I have this sense, this vague feeling that that ship means something.

THUMBELINA: It does.

FROG: Did you lose your virginity on a ship? You grew up on the river. Pardon me for asking. Don't be ashamed. There can't be any shame between us.

THUMBELINA: I respect you –

FROG: None of this inferiority, though. I can't wait. I am an old man. I can't go through a bunch of crap to prove that you're my equal. I can't wait. We talk like two adults and if it works, it works. If not I'll just bullshit you the way I bullshit journalists. For Christ sake, why are you crossing your legs? Take a deep breath. Talk to me!

THUMBELINA: Fine.

FROG: Was that a first love?

THUMBELINA: My first love were the dwarves. That's what I call them.

FROG: Actual dwarves?

THUMBELINA: No, not actual dwarves. It was in this abandoned house. These friends lived there, so I went there every day instead of going to school.

FROG: Interesting. So it actually happened to you?

THUMBELINA: What?

FROG: The whole situation.

THUMBELINA: There's nothing particularly interesting in it. Nothing happened to me. It's all stories.

FROG: And your parents?

THUMBELINA: They didn't know. I was so proud they accepted me. I did everything they did. There were other girls around too, but I was so proud to be with them . . . as a part of their . . . they put up a tent for me in the middle of the house where I slept.

FROG: Was there any love?
THUMBELINA: I was in love with Sleepy. That's what I called him.
FROG: Sleepy.
THUMBELINA: I trusted them a lot.
FROG: So, who was your first?
THUMBELINA: It was with a couple of them.
FROG: Did you suffer?
THUMBELINA: No.
FROG: Why not?
THUMBELINA: Sleepy was there.
FROG: So, what's the ship?
THUMBELINA: My dad made it for me. He used to make one every year and put old toys in it. One time it was a stuffed bear without any eyes, another time it was a headless doll, then a pair of trousers so old you could see through them and so on. I couldn't bring myself to part with any of those things, but then he made a ship and put eveything on it and told me how the bear was going to his mama bear somewhere, or how this doll was going to meet the prince of dolls who'd give her another head and it was all so ceremonial.
FROG: So, your father was this figure you dreamt of?
THUMBELINA: Father was no figure, father was father. What are you saying?
FROG: Okay, let me be more direct. It doesn't matter, girls often project things on their fathers. So then you were married for a short time –
THUMBELINA: What do you mean project? You asked about the ship and I told you. And what marriage are you talking about? Where did that come from?
FROG: You're not like other people your age. They don't understand you. You've got a secret –
THUMBELINA: Can you do a forward roll?
FROG: I can.

THUMBELINA: Let me see.
FROG: Here you go.
THUMBELINA: Bravo.
FROG: I used to play football.
THUMBELINA: Really.
FROG: Yes. I was pretty skinny. I didn't look bad, but I was small.
THUMBELINA: I can't imagine fucking you.
FROG: Doesn't interest me.
THUMBELINA: And what are you interested in?
FROG: Getting close to you is enough. I'm not interested in the gymnastics. I've had plenty of that.
THUMBELINA: I doubt that.
FROG: What?
THUMBELINA: That you've had plenty.
FROG: I have.
THUMBELINA: Because you're famous.
FROG: That too.
THUMBELINA: What would you do to me now?
FROG: Nothing, why are you talking like that?
THUMBELINA: You have to tell me exactly.
FROG: Why are you being so crude?
THUMBELINA: That's what it's about, isn't it?
FROG: No.
THUMBELINA: You don't think my work is any good?
FROG: No, it's good. It just could be better.
THUMBELINA: I don't think so. I'm not worth anything.
(FROG starts kissing her. She gently pushes him away.)
THUMBELINA: This is a bit sickening.
FROG: I could just sit next to you. We don't have to kiss.
THUMBELINA: Okay.
FROG: Thanks.
THUMBELINA: That island that your house is on, what's it called?

FROG: It's called . . . I have no idea.
THUMBELINA: Have you got any water?
FROG: There's a tank of rain water for your hair.
THUMBELINA: Have I told you about when my hair fell out.
FROG: How did your hair fall out?
THUMBELINA: I was angry, everything was going wrong. And Gelid was not well, they wouldn't let me see him on weekends. I was upset. When he saw me he started hitting his head against the wall.

(FROG jacks off next to her.)

THUMBELINA: Nothing will ever be the same.

(Long applause, camera flashes. THUMBELINA drinks and dances. FROG and THUMBELINA sing.)

SONG OF SUCCESS

I've arrived at that beautiful place
And all of them were there
And then they looked at me
And yes I was there
And then I saw I was all alone and I went off
For a quick fuck with the bartender
The bartender was quick
Mama, can you see me now
Mama can you hear me now
Mama everything was all
'Cause of you
Mama
Why don't you talk to me
Mama

SCENE SIX

THE NEST

(The Hunter and the Princess observe the building across the road through binoculars. They share a bottle of wine and a joint.)

HUNTER: I'd love to have an empty room, a wall full of books, and then nothing but windows where I could see a crooked hill with a single tree, or a river with a single boat.
PRINCESS: I have a different dream. I can see roofs and a small aparrtment with a balcony looking towards other balconies and roofs, the roofs of another town and some people I can look at.
HUNTER: What people?
PRINCESS: A woman plucking her hair out in front of a mirror, then, she drinks a coffee on the balcony, and stares down all day long. It's always warm there, and below there's a shoemaker who looks up under her skirt.
HUNTER: The shoemaker has a secret passion. He loves collecting and coloring the eggs of exotic birds.
PRINCESS: And then one day he brings her some eggs.
HUNTER: And she makes scrambled eggs.
PRINCESS: And he gets terribly sad.
HUNTER: And they start living together.
PRINCESS: No, they don't.
HUNTER: They do.
PRINCESS: No, the shoemaker dies.
HUNTER: It's better if the woman with the big tits dies. Why aren't you saying anything?
PRINCESS: I think your son doesn't like me.
HUNTER: Why should he?
(They laugh.)
PRINCESS: I think he really can't stand me.

HUNTER: Give it time.
PRINCESS: He doesn't like talking to me.
HUNTER: He doesn't like talking period.
PRINCESS: And he never looks at me.
HUNTER: He's confused,. You're the same age.
PRINCESS: He looks younger.
HUNTER: No, you just look older.
(They laugh.)
PRINCESS: I think I'd be dead if it wasn't for you.
HUNTER: You think all these people know we're watching them, and what we are talking about?
PRINCESS: I think they'd be okay with that. I haven't done any work since I met you.
HUNTER: Why would you ever want to do such a thing?
(They laugh.)
PRINCESS: I think I'm feeling good.
HUNTER: Don't think so much. I've worked hard all my life. I haven't ever relaxed, not a single day. I love it when I see that you're safe. I love it when you succeed. We'll call your parents, go visit them. I really get your father, you know? We were sitting the other day, just talking about things, and I think he's pleased.
PRINCESS: About what?
HUNTER: That you've settled down.
PRINCESS: I don't think he thinks about it.
HUNTER: Everybody thinks about it.
PRINCESS: How long is this going to last?
HUNTER: Forever.
PRINCESS: Here he comes.
HUNTER: Put your clothes on.
PRINCESS: Why does it upset him so much?
HUNTER: It gets on his nerves.
PRINCESS: He is much too serious for his age.
HUNTER: Maybe it's my fault. I mean, I don't let him drink. Let's not talk about it.

(Son comes in.)
BABY EAGLE: You've got company.
HUNTER: I have.
PRINCESS: I can go for a walk.
BABY EAGLE: You are not dressed for a walk.
HUNTER: What does it mean to be dressed for a walk?
BABY EAGLE: I don't know, but all the same, she's not.
HUNTER: Are you hungry?
BABY EAGLE: Yes.
HUNTER: What should we eat?
BABY EAGLE: The same thing we ate the day before yesterday. It was pretty good.
HUNTER: I have to make it. I'll make you both some.
PRINCESS: I can't eat that stuff.
HUNTER: Try.
(The father leaves. Silence.)
PRINCESS: What am I supposed to wear?.
BABY EAGLE: Well, you could comb your hair, and take this thing off. You wear it all the time, try some other colour –
PRINCESS: I wear this shirt because I have to –
BABY EAGLE: Why?
PRINCESS: I just have to. What's that, that dirty rag you wear around your neck.
BABY EAGLE: It's my grandma's scarf. I grew up with her.
PRINCESS: Do you miss her?
BABY EAGLE: No, nor should you.
PRINCESS: Why, I don't even know her.
BABY EAGLE: You wouldn't pass muster with grandma. No way.
PRINCESS: Interesting. Why not?
BABY EAGLE: We simply need it quiet around here. That's not you.
PRINCESS: What are you? Some kind of expert on silence and noise? Silence, noise, silence, noise?

BABY EAGLE: Have you any idea how many women he's had? Unimaginable.
PRINCESS: He could still have them. I like women too.
BABY EAGLE: Have I shown you a picture of my girlfriend?
PRINCESS: I don't know, is this a trick question? You've never shown me anything.
BABY EAGLE: No really, let me show you.
PRINCESS: Why don't you just bring her over?
BABY EAGLE: Not on your life. Why should I do that? Maybe someday. I don't see why it is important.
PRINCESS: So I can meet her.
BABY EAGLE: Why would you want to?
PRINCESS: Why do you want to show me the picture?
BABY EAGLE: I feel strongly that you'd like to go somewhere else and be with me.
(HUNTER returns.)
HUNTER: You need to eat so you can get strong.
BABY EAGLE: You need to get stronger.
HUNTER: Let's have a drink now.
BABY EAGLE: I'm off.
(BABY EAGLE leaves.)
HUNTER: I've a strong feeling. That child is going to abandon me soon. He used to be sickly. Doesn't look all that healthy now, though, either. Look, night is falling. Look.
PRINCESS: Night is falling. Something both beautiful and horrible is waiting for me.
HUNTER: No, nothing's waiting for you. Let's be clear. You'll sit there naked, and I'll just watch and enjoy. Then I'll massage you from here to here. Then I'll get to work on your exhibition. It'll be the biggest ever. Then I'll take you to some deserted place.
PRINCESS: That's how it'll happen?
HUNTER: Of course.
PRINCESS: Do you think I'm any good?

HUNTER: That means nothing. What does it mean? I mean, I'm not . . . What does it mean to you? You've got a gift. One I wish I had, but I don't. But I enjoy you. My son's got something, too. I know that. And I enjoy both of you. But my only gift was the ability to steal thing. It's true – I was good at stealing things. But, here I'm at peace. I know everything. I do, yeah. But that's not something you need to know. Do something, have a drink, breathe, I don't want –

PRINCESS: How about I have a child?

HUNTER: I have a child.

PRINCESS: I could have a healthy child. I'm sure I'd have a healthy child.

HUNTER: This is no world for children. I don't want any children.

PRINCESS: I could live with a child and I could take care of you.

HUNTER: You should be doing other things.

PRINCESS: You think I can't.

HUNTER: I don't care. I'm not interested in being sixty with a ten-year old child. I don't like children. I didn't like this one, until we were able to sit and talk.

PRINCESS: I want to.

HUNTER: Who asked you?

PRINCESS: It could be good as long as nothing happened.

(HUNTER sings.)

THE WORLD IS YOURS SONG

Shhhhhhh . . .
It's all yours now
Just don't think about what used to be
You will have a balcony to wave from
You will have all the children of the world

They will look at what you've constructed here
All children and all people
They will see you waving
Seats for the balcony
You will charge for the children you will never have
You'll charge for your own hell
Take a piss on the world
From the balcony
The World is yours
And Hell is yours

SCENE SEVEN

DARK VILAYET

(Closed door. The WOMAN, in her underwear, is squatting in front of the door.)

WOMAN: Let me in. Let me in, love, please, I'm cold. Let me in. We'll talk tomorrow. Let me in! Let me in, you bastard. I'm sick. I'm in pain. I'm leaving tomorrow, you piece of shit. Let me. Why? Because I said something about the past. I talked about myself and a summer's day and the dress I wore. Let me in it's been raining. Why? You're afraid. I am leaving tomorrow. I can't take this. Let me in.
(He comes out and kneels.)
EAGLE: Forgive me, forgive me, forgive. Here, hit me . . .
WOMAN: No.
EAGLE: I just want to hold you. I can't let you go.
(They hold each other.)
WOMAN: Let's sleep. Tomorrow we can -
EAGLE: Does it hurt there?
WOMAN: Let me get warm and it'll pass.
EAGLE: I'll warm you up with my fire, I'll burn your –

WOMAN: I'm all burnt down there, already.
(The door disappears. Behind is a bed with a skeleton curtain. They are in the bed, making love.)
EAGLE: My father's cock and mine, they must be similar. A taste only you know. I bet our faces are similar too when we blow our wads. I never told him about you. I don't tell him much of anything. I'm just curious.
WOMAN: Don't ask me these things.
EAGLE: He's never stopped giving us money.
WOMAN: Don't talk about it.
EAGLE: He thinks I got talent.
WOMAN: You do.
EAGLE: No, I don't.
WOMAN: I love you.
EAGLE: I don't love you. I love fucking you, I do. But no, I guess I can't say I don't love you. I'm touched by the way you hang on.
(The WOMAN spits on him. They wrestle.)
WOMAN: You're squeezing my hand.
EAGLE: Fight.
(She spits on him. He pulls her hair.)
WOMAN: Why don't you kill me?
EAGLE: Because you're already dead. You were dead when I first laid eyes on you. You've been dying from the moment you were born. Because you're evil.
WOMAN: No.
EAGLE: You don't have any ovaries, your teeth are falling out, and when I look into your eyes, I see heads inside them and inside those heads I see more heads.
WOMAN: Forgive him for being better than you. He is better than you and always will be. Let me sleep. Let me sleep for once. If I leave now you'll just come after me again and again. Let me sleep. If I can't leave, then at least, let me sleep.
EAGLE: No.

WOMAN: Why not?
EAGLE: I won't let you sleep.
WOMAN: Let me.
EAGLE: No, you got to take care of me. Everything comes at me during the night. You got to protect me so I won't blow away.
WOMAN: Is there anything more important than you?
EAGLE: He's the same way.
WOMAN: He doesn't hate.
EAGLE: It's easy for a man like that not to hate.
WOMAN: Don't look at me.
EAGLE: When was the last time you saw your child?
WOMAN: They wouldn't let me go. I was late.
EAGLE: You were late on purpose.
WOMAN: No, I wasn't.
EAGLE: You were drunk. I wouldn't have let you go anywhere.
WOMAN: He can't see me.
EAGLE: He sees everything, he sits there and knows exactly what you're doing. *(He laughs.)* He's watching now. *(They start to make love.)*
WOMAN: Somebody has to leave.
EAGLE: You're not leaving.
(They dance, each on their own. At some point, he stops, puts the rope around his neck and picks up an accordion.)

SONG ABOUT DEVOURING

Every day I devour you
My beloved darling
I'm waiting for you to die
My beloved darling
I'm waiting to look straight at your naked heart
How it beats, tick tock tick tocking
My beloved darling
You are so dear to me

And I will be leaving
And I will be leaving
No one will ever eat you so slowly
No one will ever love you so dearly
As I
As I
My beloved
My darling one
(WOMAN screams.)

SCENE EIGHT

HANSEL AND GRETEL

(The trees are howling, as if someone's screaming, as if a child's crying, as if a woman's laughing. No one knows how, but it freezes the blood.)

GRETEL: She turned off the lights on purpose.
HANSEL: I am fed up with coming here.
GRETEL: I'm not. I love being here.
HANSEL: You admire her.
GRETEL: So what.
HANSEL: I don't at all.
GRETEL: It looks like a cookie.
HANSEL: She's disgusting.
GRETEL: Everything's disgusting to you.
HANSEL: I like simple houses.
GRETEL: There's a nice table for us, we can sit.
HANSEL: I can't sit when the wind is blowing.
GRETEL: Is there anything that doesn't bother you.
HANSEL: Of course. You. *(Hansel kisses her.)* Look, the light came on up there.
GRETEL: It's like a Christmas tree.

HANSEL: Stop cuddling.
GRETEL: Why should I?
HANSEL: Stop it.
GRETEL: I can stop being with you anytime. I can go out on that road, can you hear it, put my thumb out and hitch a ride to town.
HANSEL: Something could happen to you.
GRETEL: We could go inside the house.
HANSEL: Can't you see that she's got visitors? See the silhouettes.
GRETEL: So what? She'll welcome us even more because of it.
HANSEL: I don't know.
GRETEL: I wonder, how much would you do for me?
(They kiss. The door opens and lights up the kissing couple.)
WITCH: Who's there? Is it you?
HANSEL: Depends who you are looking for.
WITCH: How many of you are there?
GRETEL: Two.
WITCH: A boy and a girl.
HANSEL: She's completely drunk.
WITCH: How many of you are there, kids?
HANSEL: Two of us.
WITCH: Gelid, here is a boy and a girl, you won't be alone. Well, you are big kids.
HANSEL: I don't know what's so funny.
WITCH: You're a dangerous boy.
GRETEL: We'd like to sit for a while.
WITCH: Okay kids, remove the mud from your shoes, take them off. What are you looking at? Take this.
HANSEL: I don't want to wear this.
WITCH: It's warm, put it on.
GRETEL: Put it on, I like it.
WITCH: Take it home.
GRETEL: Really?
WITCH: Take it home.

GRETEL: Thank you.
WITCH: You're welcome, they're not mine anyway.
GRETEL: Whose are they?
WITCH: Who can remember? So many visitors. The one with the notebook. She forgot her notebook and her gloves. There's plenty to drink. Take it, son, drink.
(The house is around them.)
HANSEL: Son?
WITCH: Well, honey, you could be my son. My son is just like you. Well, fine, not exactly.
HANSEL: Where are the glasses?
WITCH: Glasses are everywhere.
(They look at each other.)
WITCH: Don't get upset with me. Look around. They're everywhere. What do you want, a cupboard?
(He looks around.)
WITCH: Shall I say hot or cold? *(He looks around.)* You want a cupboard lined with wrapping paper, don't you? *(He looks around.)* Well, I love it when you get dangerous. The glasses are in the piano.
GRETEL: It's hot in here.
WITCH: My dear, why don't you cut that hair off?
GRETEL: Why?
(Silence. HANSEL wants to sit next to GRETEL, but she sits on a chair by herself.)
WITCH: Well, what do you want to do?
(Silence.) Did you bring any of your work? *(Silence.)* C'mon, kids, tell me, it's going to be fun. Are you here to get warm, are you reporters or is there a worm eating at you to create something?
GRETEL: I brought something.
HANSEL: I've have something too.
GRETEL: Let's see what you've got. You go first.
WITCH: I have to piss, my dear, wait a sec.

(The WITCH leaves.)
GRETEL: You pretended you didn't want to come.
HANSEL: I don't know what I want or don't want.
GRETEL: We've come to this house five times. We've gotten lost and had to go back. We had that awful fight, and now you are ready to – Where are your works? Where did you put them. Show me.
HANSEL: No, just wait a bit. She's so disgusting. What can you learn from her? See how disgusting she is? I want to prove to you that she's nothing. Nothing.
GRETEL: No, I've got to learn.
HANSEL: Who are you? What has happened to you? I don't want to argue, not because of a drunken –
(The WITCH has been in the room listening for a while.)
WITCH: My brain works better when I drink and I piss a lot because giving birth tore me up so bad. I don't have ovaries, either. When they took them out, they found tiny bones in one of them. I'd probably eaten my twin. I was the stronger. In the other one they found a plastic bag.
GRETEL: A bag.
WITCH: Dear God, you're already drunk.
HANSEL: Shall we show you our work?
WITCH: Not now. Let me get to know you first. I can't do it now. Maybe not even tomorrow. Maybe we'll all be dead. Who gives a fuck about your works? I planted flowers there, but the wind . . . the wind . . . Who gives a fuck about the wind? Let's make cocktails, put on some music. That'll be nice.
GRETEL: What have you've been up to lately?
WITCH: Got into a fight with my neighbor. He has a cretin for a dog.
(HANSEL laughs.)
WITCH: There, now you're happy.
HANSEL: I don't know.

WITCH: I am telling you, pretty boy, you should be glad you don't know what you're capable of.

HANSEL: I know what I can do.

WITCH: You don't know your limits.

HANSEL: Neither do you.

WITCH: I am glad we've worked all that out.

(HANSEL leaves.)

GRETEL: He's a bit confused.

WITCH: Is he?

GRETEL: Yes.

WITCH: Why?

GRETEL: Actually, he appreciates your work more than I do. I don't know what he expected.

WITCH: Yes.

GRETEL: When you imagine famous artists, you always need to make it so –

WITCH: As if their shit doesn't stink.

GRETEL: I don't think it's that simple.

WITCH: I know, dear. I'm just a drunk in a messy house.

GRETEL: That's not what I meant.

WITCH: You're too polite to get what you want.

GRETEL: The effect doesn't interest me as much as the substance.

WITCH: Oh, really?

GRETEL: I think your work is outdated.

WITCH: You must think I'm just a big bitch.

GRETEL: What?

WITCH: I like that young girls are afraid of me. You've got no idea how much I hate young girls, and when I see they're afraid of me and grind their tiny teeth at me, I think, fuck it I'm not going to tell you. I am too big a bitch for you. Let me tell you something else. Forget art.

GRETEL: Suck my dick.

WITCH: Don't get pissed. I can help if you want. You just have to stay outside of it all. You have to. And no fighting. The fighting is inside you. Death is inside you. Listen, I'm telling you something, it's a bit like, well . . . I can't talk about it with men.
GRETEL: Tell me.
WITCH: I'll die soon, but I don't want it to hurt, and it's not important that –
(The wind howls.)
GRETEL: What's that?
WITCH: Gelid.
GRETEL: Is he real or is it just the house creaking?
WITCH: Gelid is real to me.
GRETEL: Are you serious?
WITCH: About what?
GRETEL: About dying.
WITCH: Yes.
GRETEL: I'm sorry.
WITCH: Me too.
GRETEL: Sorry I was rude.
WITCH: It's okay.
GRETEL: I'm really sorry.
WITCH: Why? You don't like my work. That doesn't mean you want to see me dead.
(The WITCH breaks a chair.)
GRETEL: No, I do like your work.
WITCH: I know. And I know you've been spinning around this house for months. You could do something for me.
GRETEL: Okay.
WITCH: You're free. I can tell.
GRETEL: What?
WITCH: I'd like to watch while you two –
(HANSEL comes in.)
HANSEL: I went through the house. There's lots of doors that won't open.

GRETEL: What are you looking so pleased about?
HANSEL: There's an incredible library. You have an incredible library.
GRETEL: Maybe you shouldn't be wandering through the house.
HANSEL: Well, someone who invites strangers into their house in the middle of the night should expect all sorts of things.
WITCH: Very well put. I would just love if all sorts of things would happen.
GRETEL: They will.
WITCH: My son. He's sleeping now. His girlfriend was over. He has a lovely girlfriend. When he was a little boy I used to imagine the kind of girl he should have. This one is really beautiful.
HANSEL: Why's the chair broken?
WITCH: What did you want to talk about?
GRETEL: How old are you?
WITCH: I was born in a year when my mother was more beautiful than ever. She got the first wrinkles around her eyes and I had a sister who was much prettier than me. I gotta take some milk to Gelid.

(The WITCH leaves. HANSEL and GRETEL make love. The WITCH returns to watch them.)

WITCH: Gelid, I'd really like you to come down and meet these young people. They're your age. I haven't drunk much at all, today. That's sweet of you, to worry about your mother like that. I mean, would you want another mother? I know I'm boring. You are such a serious boy. Who would have ever thought something so serious could come out of me? And your father. He wasn't very serious. He didn't even look serious, unlike me. I've always looked older. Until I turned thirty. Then I started to look like my father, and my face, which never could accept make-up, you know, just like those purebred cunts. Oops. Sorry. Suddenly my face started to look young. A little puffy. Ha, ha . . .

What do you think? How do you know? You were looking out the window? Yes, she is attractive. I'll bet she thinks she's a hot lover. She undresses so slowly. Who's gonna tell you about women if not your mother? I'm disgusting. Ha, ha. Really?

And the guy? Yes. He's interesting. There's a depth to him. Although he's uptight. She acts like she's free, but in fact, he's the one who's really free. To be free means to follow one's heart without looking back. I'm not free. But you are, Gelid. You are. You are the freest young man in the world.

(HANSEL and GRETEL sit in an embrace. GRETEL pulls away.)
GRETEL: I had no idea she had a son. Where is he?
HANSEL: What do you mean where is he?
GRETEL: Well, from what she's said, from what the woman has done, I wouldn't have thought she had any children.
HANSEL: Actually, I would think she did.
GRETEL: I don't think women like her should have children.
HANSEL: A moment ago, you were so excited you would have sucked the toe off her foot.
GRETEL: That's a different issue.
HANSEL: Why shouldn't she have children?
GRETEL: Well, when she went into his room. Her tit was hanging out.
HANSEL: So what, you've never seen your mother's tit?
GRETEL: Don't start on that.
HANSEL: No, you've really never seen your mother's tit, or your father's ball peeking out of his pants.
GRETEL: Don't start on that.
HANSEL: On what?
GRETEL: Well . . . well –
HANSEL: What?
GRETEL: We've been drinking . . .
HANSEL: What?
GRETEL: About my parents being common.

HANSEL: You are common. Your parents aren't common, they're just simple.
GRETEL: I am a thousand times better than you.
(The WITCH comes in.)
HANSEL: You think you should have children?
GRETEL: I don't want them now.
HANSEL: Ok, but if you did, do you think should?
GRETEL: Sure, I wouldn't be like her.
HANSEL: Like what?
GRETEL: She's been hitting on you.
(The WITCH talks.)
WITCH: What were you expecting, dear, a dignified woman who would sit in her study and impart wisdom to you.
GRETEL: No.
HANSEL: Tell me.
WITCH: I don't know why you kids are so nervous. I wasn't angry. Go upstairs and have a rest if you want. I can't –
GRETEL: Gelid's up there.
WITCH: Who?
GRETEL: Your son.
WITCH: Never mind, he's reading a book.
HANSEL: Why doesn't he come down here?
WITCH: I won't talk about it. He can't come down. I left him. I can't see him. Sometimes I see him through the window in that house. Then he can't see me. I am surprised he's survived this long. He's like a plant.
(HANSEL hugs her.)
WITCH: You are such a dear boy. If only . . . if only . . . such a dear boy. Next time. I won't be like this to you next time. Next time I'll take you to a place.
HANSEL: I am so sorry –
WITCH: No need to be. Don't.
(HANSEL hugs her, cuddles and rocks her.)
GRETEL: Let's all strip.

WITCH: Yes!
(They remove their clothes.)
GRETEL: And we'll just sit around here, naked.
HANSEL: I'll put some music on.
GRETEL: I'll dance.
WITCH: I am old.
(She cries.)
GRETEL: Hey, let's make those cocktails.
HANSEL: I'll make you one. There's not much here. The bottles are mostly empty.
WITCH: I'd like to be born now.
(The WITCH dances. HANSEL watches her.)
HANSEL: I am really happy we came. Such an exciting woman, she's incredible. Maybe I'll stick around tomorrow too.
GRETEL: Not me. I don't feel like it.
WITCH *(sits)*: Actually, I wouldn't like to be born now. Night is a lonely time. I want to be born in the morning. Now, I'll sleep and in the morning, I'll be born.
(HANSEL sits next to her and kisses her.)
GRETEL: How can you do that?
HANSEL: Come here.
GRETEL: I don't want to.
HANSEL: Come.
(The WITCH and HANSEL cuddle. The WITCH has her eyes closed. Then she opens them. She starts to scream.)
WITCH: No, don't. We'll only sleep. I'll make you something to eat tomorrow. She's not the one for you, Gelid. We'll drive her out. Oh! Go there, go there. No. I am your mother. Not to your mother.
GRETEL: Let's call an ambulance.
HANSEL: Don't.
WITCH: Stop holding me, Gelid, don't –
(The WITCH puts her arms around HANSEL's neck. She is strong.)

GRETEL: I am calling the police.
WITCH *(releasing HANSEL)*: I am so ugly.
HANSEL: No you're not.
(The WITCH starts hitting him.)
WITCH: I don't want to –
(GRETEL cries. The WITCH stops.)
WITCH: Go home, kids. Get dressed. Take whatever you like and go. I'll give you money.
HANSEL: I can't leave now.
WITCH: I'll put you in touch with the right people. I don't want to see you. I want to lie down, die and be born again.
HANSEL: Why?
WITCH: I want to lie in something clean.
(Darkness.)
GRETEL'S VOICE: We walked a long time that night, got lost several times, then I went to a club.
HANSEL: I don't know, should I write the scene the way it happened? Maybe, I can become a writer after that experience. But it's not at all clear to me how such things got in my mind. Afterwards, I was so embarrassed.
FROG *(dressed as a doctor)*: It's okay. All young people explore. Even me, when I was your age, you wouldn't believe it. Someday I'll tell you all about it. But our session is over for now. If you have trouble sleeping, take this.
SISTER: So many times, I wanted to see her. I've always loved her a lot. But that filthy mouth of hers, oh God. I wanted many times to see her but she always humiliated me. Oh God, how unpleasant. I can feel her hair in my fingers and she never properly combed it. Her hair was like a dog's tail. I started to braid it and then I woke up.
FROG: Women shouldn't meddle in the arts. It eats them up. They have no grounding. She was a complete idiot. She said some bad things about people who did nothing but good things for her. What should I say about the dead? Only good things?

That's hypocrisy. She was a complete shithead. I don't intend to say anything good about her. I don't want to say anything good about her. Leave me alone, all of you.

BABY BEAR: Nobody'll tell me how she died. If only I knew how she died. I can't sleep thinking about it. Our son doesn't know that she's dead. He doesn't even know she existed.

HUNTER: She fell asleep in the snow. Drunk and asleep in the snow. It's not a bad death. Sweet dreams, my beauty. Good night, my son.

WITCH: Daddy, I meant to ask you to make me a ship so I can get away
Daddy
Make me a ship so I can get away
Daddy
Sit with me on the ship
Daddy
I didn't drink. I wasn't there.
Watch over me on the ship
Daddy
That didn't happen to me
My darling Daddy
Let's go together to the ship
Daddy
We'll sail away and you'll tell me stories
Nice stories, Daddy
I want to be born again
My daddy

THE END

Translated by *Dennis Barnett* from original transcriptions by *Marija Stojanović, Goran Mimica* and *Therese Davies.*

AFTERWORD

Since the 1960s, theatre and drama have become increasingly recognized as useful lenses through which we can view the political and cultural realities within which the art is produced. My life as a theatre scholar and practitioner has been steeped in this recognition – and my interests in Serbian theatre have led me to look for this intersection of the socio-political and the artistic at every turn. In this short Afterword, I will outline an overview of how I see the works in this collection partaking of that phenomenon.

Branislav Nušić, the oldest Serbian playwright represented in this collection, died a few years before World War II broke out, at a time when the former Yugoslavia was still a kingdom. Earlier in his life, he spent two years in prison for a poem he wrote that was critical of the King, so he understood the political limits to which all writing had to adhere. The implicit censorship of writing within an autocracy, whether the ship was being steered by royalty or by a dictator, would be a constant reality throughout Eastern Europe for many years to come.

Yet, as writers in Poland, Czechoslovakia, Bulgaria and the other satellites of the Soviet Union, were closely watched and threatened with (and often punished by) imprisonment, in Yugoslavia, the writers had an easier time. Yugoslavia never succumbed to the pressures of Moscow, as their dictator, Josip Broz "Tito", cunningly outmaneuvered Stalin at the end of the war, and as the leader of the non-aligned movement, charted Yugoslavia's course following no one's map but his own. Oversight of what was written for public consumption in Yugoslavia enacted a much less severe type of censorship.

Three topics were off-limits. The most severe infraction was to openly criticize Tito or the Communist Party. One of the plays in this collection, *Hats Off!*, by Aleksander Popović, was prevented from being produced initially because in Serbian, the title, *Kape dole*, could also be translated as "Down with the Captain." Tito's other rules, implicit in his dictatorship, banned reference to ethnic differences, i.e., Serbs, Croats, Bosnians, etc., and to something called *Goli Otok*.

Goli Otok, meaning "bald island", was the largest of two islands where Tito maintained his postwar gulag, a prison for those men who still supported Stalin following the war, many of whom had been Partisans, his staunchest allies and fighters in his campaign against Hitler (these men were referred to as *ibeovci*. Aleksander Popović was one of them). One play dared to tackle this topic (*The Karamazovs* by Dušan Jovanović, also one of the *ibeovci*), but was swiftly shut down. It was not until *The Balkan Spy* by Dušan Kovačević in 1982, after Tito had died, that this censorship would loosen. Yet, even in that play, you'll notice the references are not explicit. Beyond these three topics, however, writers were given free reign.

This did not mean, however, that Tito's totalitarianism was any less abusive. He maintained three different organizations that were comprised of what we would call, in the West, secret police, the psychological effects of which we can see on the characters in *The Balkan Spy*. For thirty-five years, society was shaped and controlled by an ever-changing ideology, the main purpose of which was to keep Tito in power. His Machiavellian tactics were ruthless in pursuit of his goal and, ironically, when we look at the dissolution of Yugoslavia that occurred after he died, it is difficult not to credit his ruthlessness as the glue that held so many disparate factions together throughout Tito's rule.

Dušan Kovačević frames Tito's leniency towards the theatre as part of his brilliance. He explains Tito's strategy by paraphrasing Nietzsche: "The arts exist to help people keep from getting angry at their reality."[1] According to Kovačević, Tito understood that the tensions beneath the Yugoslav surface needed to be released, and that it was better to have them released in the theatre than in the streets.

Therefore, it's important to remember, that after Nušić, most of the writers in this collection (with the exception of Romčević, Srbljanović and Marković, who did not appear on the scene until the Milošević years) wrote from a liminal space and worked to express their frustrations about life under Tito without being able to speak directly, while, at the same time, working within a system that, on the surface, appeared to give them artistic freedom.

Whereas in Czechoslovakia, martyrs were being made and revolutionary fires were being lit, in Yugoslavia, an apparently unencumbered art scene had difficulty generating the slightest spark of open resistance. However, as you will see, this odd political tension, deeply at work within much of the literature of the time, made for some astonishing works.

Though all of the writers here created within the same circumstances, the one whose subversive mission was perhaps the most clearly perceived was Dušan Kovačević. Throughout the last decade of Tito's reign, Kovačević walked a thin line, managing to give an implicit voice, a veiled *samizdat* level of signification to the more subversive sentiments within the Belgrade society, while maintaining an explicit level of humor and good-natured love for his fellow countryman that made it possible to ignore the messages buried beneath the surface.

---

[1] Kovačević, Dušan. Interview with the author. September, 1997.

Such a balancing act can be seen in one of Kovačević's first plays, *Marathon Runners Run a Victory Lap of Honor* (*Maratonci trče počasni krug*). Written while he was still a student at the Dramatic Faculty of the University of Belgrade in 1973, it was an immediate success and ran for many years, also becoming a Yugoslavian film classic. It is about a family of undertakers, the Topalovićs, who are also crooks. Their practice is to bury a body in the afternoon and dig it back up at night in order to resell and reuse the coffin, which they have been doing for many years.

Kovačević nearly always pushes his concepts to the breaking point and the Topalovićs are no different. They are being run by male members from six generations of the family, the patriarch, Maximillian being 126 years old. The circumstances are ridiculous and deliciously extreme. On an explicit level, *Marathon Runners* is hilarious. Someone from outside of Yugoslavia, if they spoke the language, would have no trouble perceiving the cleverness of this absurd comedy. But for the Yugoslav in 1973, there was an entirely different level of meaning, absolutely clear in its subversive power.

Partly, this came from one of the rare moments under Tito of open dissent. In 1968, the economic inequality between the wealthier states (Croatia and Slovenia) and most of the rest of the country had become too obvious, and tensions had begun to mount. Most of the unrest was aimed at the Communist Party which had become top-heavy with older members, veterans of the earliest days. Many students and younger citizens felt disenfranchised and marched in protest, hoping that new and younger blood in the Party could be a step to solving the country's economic woes.

Tito and the government-controlled media characterized the demonstrations as "understandable," and "urged all the progressive forces to contribute to the resolute solution of problems in the economy and social development." In a televised speech that *Yugoslav Life* referred to as one that "will long be remembered," Tito read a list of student grievances, voicing his support for each of them.² He explained that they were really criticisms of the government's slowness in implementing the reforms which he had already set in motion. In *Review*, an English language magazine about Yugoslavia, the government's construction of these demonstrations is succinctly voiced:

> During the demonstrations last year at Belgrade, Zagreb and a number of other Yugoslav universities there were no reactionary slogans or calls for the destruction of the existing system. All that was demanded was the more consistent application of the principles which lie at the basis of our self-managing socialist society.³

According to one of the students who took part in the demonstrations, Vukica Đilas, any "calls for the destruction of the existing system" would have resulted in imprisonment.⁴ Clearly a sign of Tito's masterful manipulation of the media, the students' subversion of the dominant narrative was itself subverted by that narrative's subsuming of it. By these media accounts, the demonstrations led to quickening the pace of the reform that Tito himself had implemented, which was ostensibly convergent with the student's demands, giving the impression that the students had in fact been victorious, and that the country was in their debt. On June 20, 1968, the *New York Times*

---

² "Stress on Action," *Yugoslav Life*. July-August, 1968 (no author given and pages not numbered).

³ Misovic. It is interesting to imagine a similar quote in reference to the students on American campuses that same summer. If our society were able to reach the goals intrinsic to our Declaration of Independence, what would our dissidence look like then?

⁴ Vukica Đilas in an e-mail to the author. 5 January, 1998.

reported that "Yugoslav Students Feel That Their Protest Movement Reflects Confidence in Country's Way of Life."[5]

Kovačević, of course, framed the result in starkly different terms. For him and his fellow students, "the defeat of that student revolution was a big depression."[6] The romantic idea that had been proffered by their street protests had been squelched and very few things had changed.

When *Marathon Runners* opened, there was no doubt that the Topalović family represented the Communist Party, and that the patriarch, the oldest member was none other than Tito himself, often affectionately referred to as "Papa." For presenting them as crooks that needed to be overthrown, if there had been anything explicit about this criticism, Kovačević would have landed in prison. Throughout his career, his skill at finding the semiotic point at which the police were satisfied, while the audiences' subversive tendencies were supported made him an icon of the Yugoslavian theatre scene.

Though the other writers in the book who wrote during Tito's years in power had to negotiate the same pressures as Kovačević, signs of their dissent are more difficult to find. A consistent element in Tito's ever-changing ideology was his tendency (as was the case for most of the Communist leaders in other countries) to encourage the country's focus on the future, turning a blind eye as much as possible on their past. This was particularly important in Yugoslavia due to the multiple internecine rivalries that existed between the various factions. Whenever a playwright wrote a representation of the past, as in *Hallelujah* by Lebović, he had to be very careful. Though he had to be careful to never mention the contribution of a Serb without also mentioning a Croat and a Bosnian, the very act of looking into history could feel subversive during Tito's time. Perhaps it

---

[5] *New York Times*. 20 June, 1968, p.20.
[6] Interview with the author. 17 September, 1997.

wouldn't be as daring a choice as made by Kovačević, it nonetheless had to be carefully managed. When Siniša Kovačević wrote *The Times Have Changed* in 1986, this had begun to change, but not entirely.

After Tito died in 1980, the Yugoslavian government tried to pretend nothing had changed. Their motto was "After Tito – Tito". The rules may have become less strictly enforced, but their presence still hung in the air. Holding on to the days of Tito, of course, proved more aspirational than actual. Without him, the economic imbalance between different regions continued to grow more severe and the historical grudges between ethnic groups floated back to the surface, making the eventual dissolution of the country, in retrospect, seem like a foregone conclusion. Milošević, eventually, was a poor imitation of Tito – and, where Tito controlled political subversion with a nuanced cleverness, Milošević lost control of it through a brazen arrogance. This allowed for a short period of more explicitly political and defiant works. Nothing of that nature, however, is included in this collection.

The socio-political connections within the most contemporary works in the collection, *Barbelo* and *A Ship For Dolls*, are less local in their concerns – responding with a wider attack on the human condition within the 21st century. The theatrical imagination at work within these plays provokes and inspires simultaneously. They are both invested with similar visions that acknowledge and bemoan the corruption of our times – while also seducing audiences with recognition of humanity's insufferable and adamant refusal to succumb.

Though not about to compete yet on an international scale with the likes of New York or London, Belgrade has an astonishingly prolific theatre scene, and as Harold Clurman reminded us at every opportunity, great theatre can only exist where the efforts to make theatre are legion. Belgrade is such a place and as the reader who becomes familiar with the plays in this book will avouch, Belgrade has produced some of the greatest.

Dennis Barnett

ABOUT EDITORS

BRANKO MIKASINOVICH is a scholar of Yugoslav and Serbian literature as well as a noted Slavist. He has edited many anthologies of Yugoslav and Serbian literature, among whose are *Introduction to Yugoslav Literature, Five Modern Yugoslav Plays, Modern Yugoslav Satire, Yugoslav Fantastic Prose, Serbian Fantastic Prose,* and *Yugoslavia: Crisis and Disintegration.* He has appeared as a panelist on Yugoslav press on ABC's "Press International" in Chicago, PBS's "International Dateline" in New Orleans, Voice of America, and a Serbian Service television program, "Open Studio."

DEJAN STOJANOVIĆ is a poet, essayist, philosopher, and former journalist. His poetry books include *Circling, The Sun Watches the Sun, The Sign and Its Children, The Shape, The Creator,* and *Dance of Time.* In addition to poetry and prose, he has worked as a correspondent for the Serbian weekly magazine, *Viewpoints.* His book of interviews from 1990 to 1992 in Europe and America, entitled *Conversations,* included interviews with several major American writers, including Nobel Laureate Saul Bellow, Charles Simic, and Steve Tesich.

www.ingramcontent.com/pod-product-compliance
Lightning Source LLC
Chambersburg PA
CBHW020628230426
43665CB00008B/83